Israel's story continued when

JESUS CAME AS THE PROMISED KING.

He was

PUT TO DEATH, BUT GOD
RAISED HIM BACK TO LIFE.

Jesus won the

VICTORY OVER OUR
ENEMIES SIN AND DEATH.

God now invites

EVERYONE TO BE BROUGHT BACK TO HIM

and to share in the

NEW WORLD HE IS MAKING.

THIS IS THE STORY TOLD IN THE BOOKS OF THE NEW TESTAMENT

ZONDERVAN®

Published by Zondervan
Grand Rapids, Michigan 49546, U.S.A.

Printed in the United States of America

18 19 20 21 22 23 24 25 /DPM/ 20 19 18 17 16 15 14 13 12 11 10 9 8 7 6 5 4 3 2

You will be pleased to know that a portion of the purchase price of your new NIrV Bible has been provided to Biblica, Inc.® to help spread the gospel of Jesus Christ around the world!

LIVING THE SCRIPT

From the beginning God made it clear that he wants us to join him in his drama. The Bible is God's story first of all. But we can't sit back and just watch what happens. God invites humans to be active in the story with him.

Here are three key steps to finding how you can be a part of God's big story:

1. GO DEEP IN THE BIBLE

If we are not familiar with the stories and teachings of the Bible itself, there's no chance of living our parts well. Only when we read both deeply and widely in the Bible, will we be prepared to take up our roles. The more we read the Bible, the better readers we will become.

2. BECOME A FOLLOWER OF JESUS

Act 2 in the story of the Bible describes how death and wrongdoing came into the world. We all share in this. But the victory of Jesus in Act 4 gives us the chance to have our lives turned around. Our sins can be forgiven. We can become part of God's story of new creation.

Turn away from your wrongdoing and follow the way of life that God wants. Jesus has fought against evil. He won the battle when he died on the cross and rose again to new life. His death was a sacrifice for your sins. The power of a new life has come into our world.

3. LIVE YOUR PART IN THE STORY

Followers of Jesus come together to help each other be faithful to God's new way of life. We read the Bible so we understand what God has already done, especially through Jesus the Messiah. We also read the Bible so we know how to live this story today. It is not always easy to live for Jesus, but the Bible is our guide. God also promises to send his Holy Spirit to help us understand and obey the Bible.

THE TIMELINE OF THE DRAMA

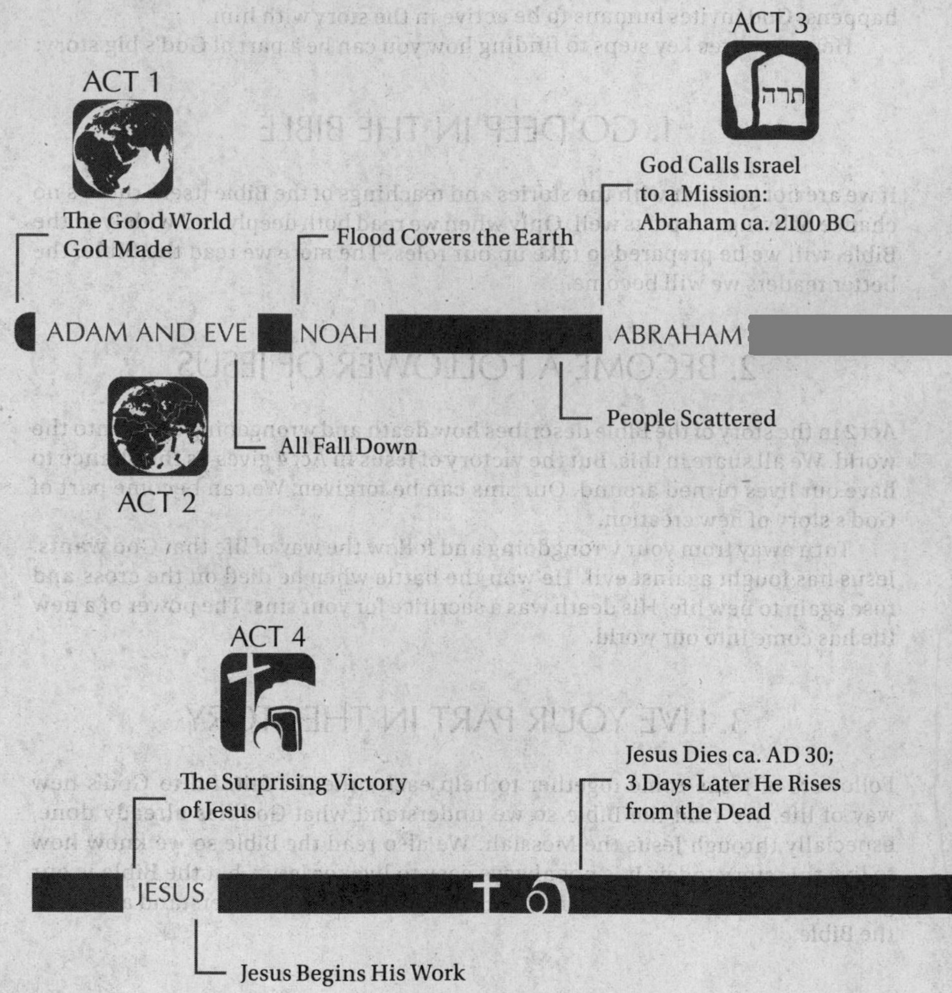

WORLD EVENTS

Pyramids built, 2500's BC
Hinduism gains influence in India, 1100's BC
Buddhism founded in India, 500's BC
Alexander the Great begins rule, 336 BC
China begins construction on The Great Wall, 214 BC
Rise of the Roman Empire, 27 BC

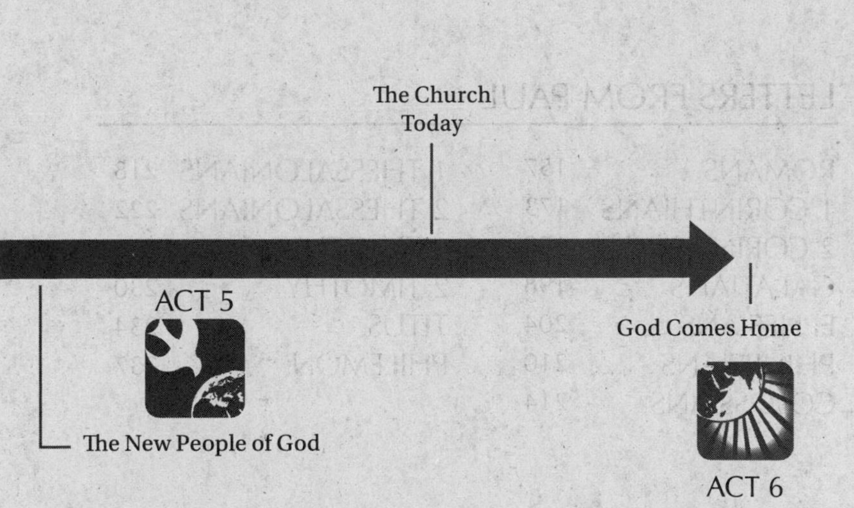

IN THE FRONT...

A GUIDE TO THE BOOKS OF THE NEW TESTAMENT

(pause and pray before you read the Scriptures)

STORIES ABOUT JESUS

LETTERS FROM PAUL

Messages on

STAYING FAITHFUL

WISDOM TEACHINGS

LETTERS from other leaders

AN APOCALYPSE

AT THE BACK...

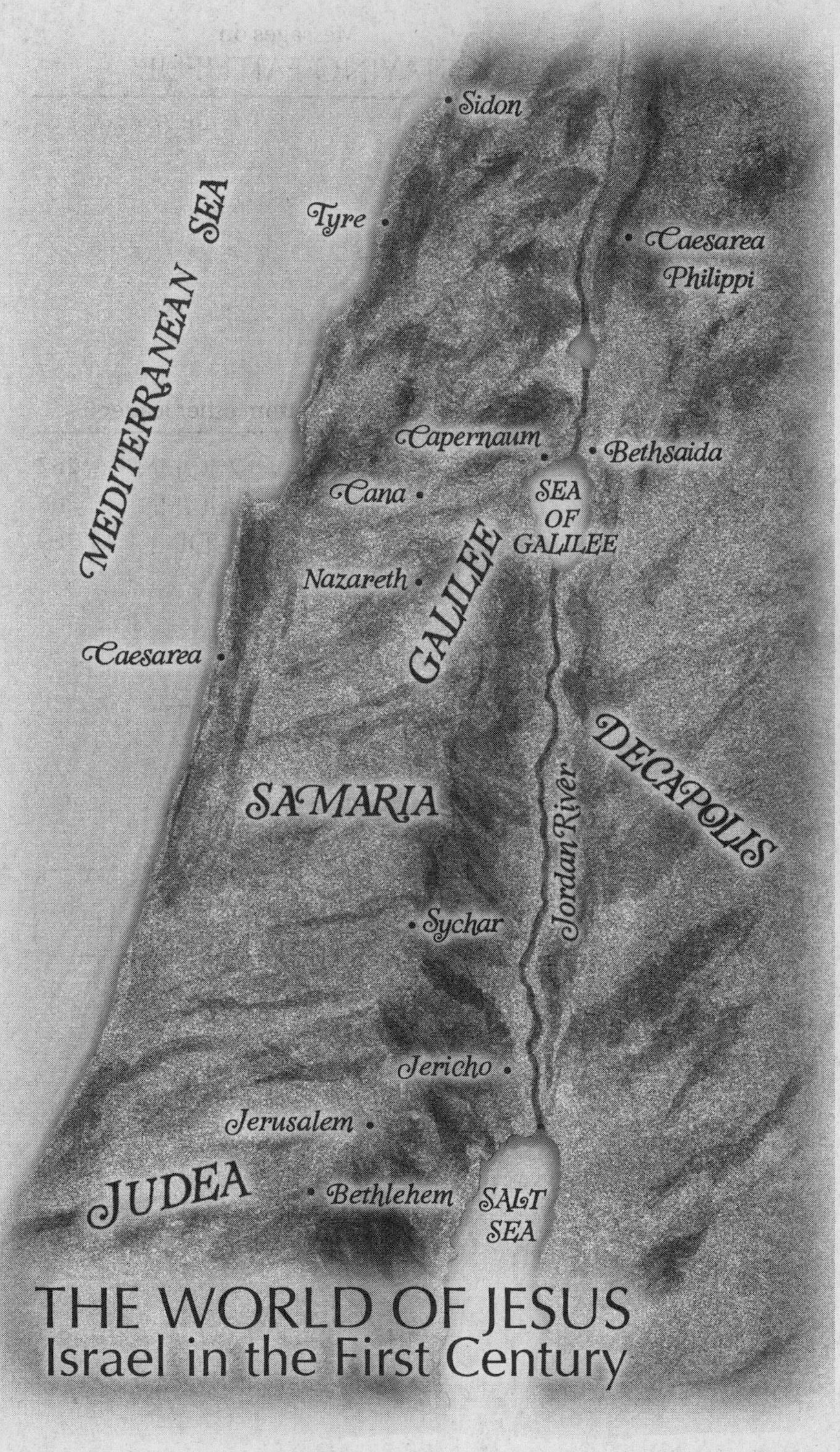

THE WORLD OF JESUS
Israel in the First Century

Sidon
MEDITERRANEAN SEA
Tyre
Caesarea Philippi
Capernaum
Bethsaida
Cana
SEA OF GALILEE
GALILEE
Nazareth
Caesarea
DECAPOLIS
SAMARIA
Jordan River
Sychar
Jericho
Jerusalem
JUDEA
Bethlehem
SALT SEA

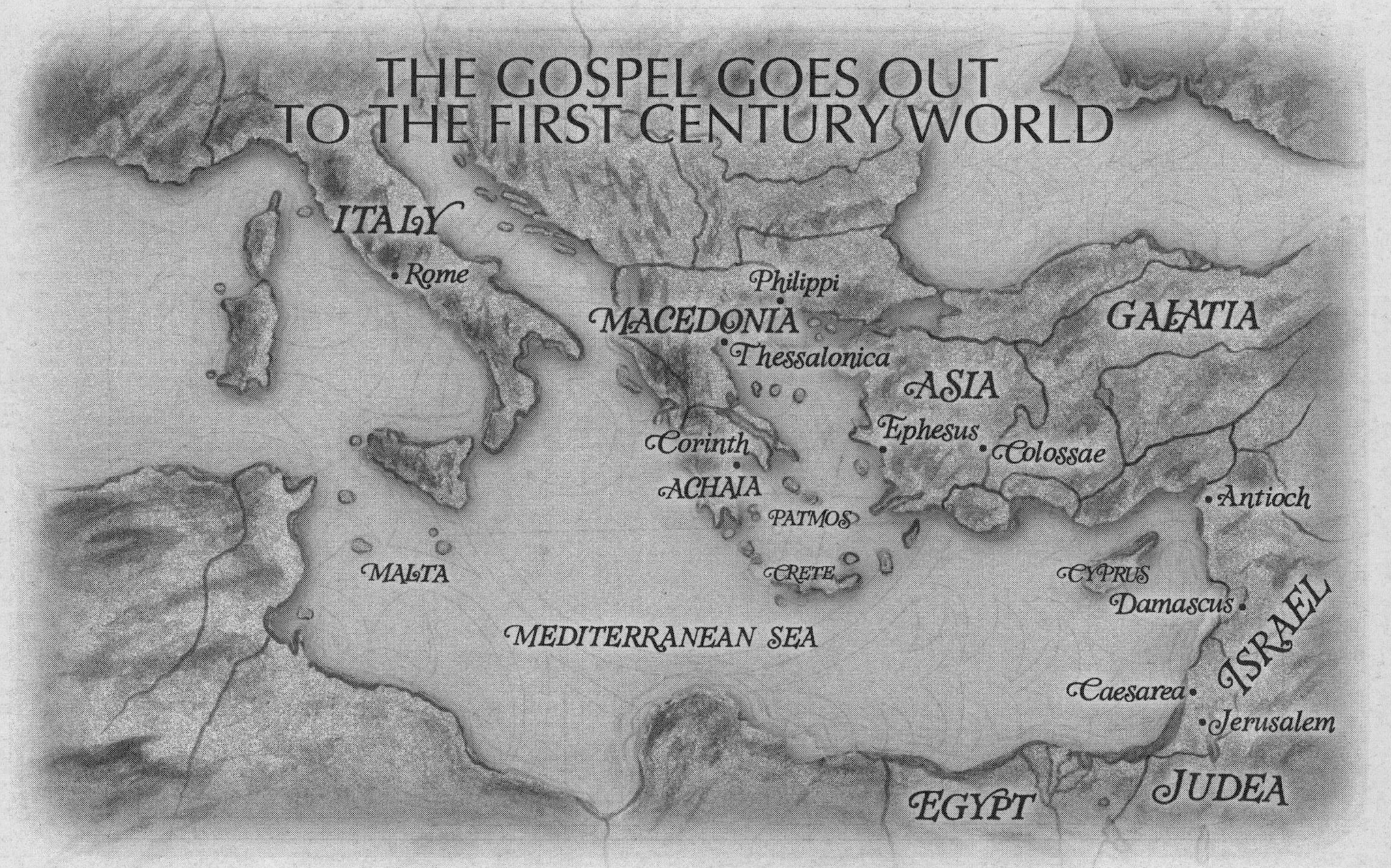
THE GOSPEL GOES OUT
TO THE FIRST CENTURY WORLD
ITALY
Rome
MACEDONIA
Philippi
Thessalonica
GALATIA
ASIA
Ephesus
Colossae
Corinth
ACHAIA
PATMOS
CRETE
MALTA
MEDITERRANEAN SEA
CYPRUS
Antioch
Damascus
ISRAEL
Caesarea
Jerusalem
JUDEA
EGYPT

David Thomason 2010

MATTHEW

The book of Matthew begins by showing that God has kept his promises to Israel. Jesus is the promised Messiah, or king. The rule of God has come to earth. This is what the story of Israel is about. Matthew lists the names of the people in the family line of Jesus. Jesus came from the family line of Abraham, the ancestor of all the tribes of Israel. That family line continued to the great King David. Then Matthew shows that Jesus came from David's family. God really had kept his ancient promises.

Matthew makes connections between Jesus' life and the story of Israel. Just as Israel crossed the Jordan River, Jesus went to the Jordan River. As Israel wandered in the desert, Jesus was tempted in the desert. In addition, Matthew presents Jesus as the new Moses. Matthew presents the story of Jesus' life and work in five parts. These five sections contain the five main speeches given by Jesus. Each speech ends with words similar to "After Jesus finished saying all these things." These five parts remind us of the five books of Moses in the Old Testament.

Jesus celebrates a Passover meal with his disciples. This is just like the time Israel celebrated the Passover meal before leaving Egypt. After the Passover Israel was freed and no longer in slavery in Egypt. Jesus died on the cross and rose again to make his people free. Those who believe in him will be free from sin and death.

At the beginning of the book, Jesus is given the name "Immanuel." That name means "God with us." At the end of the book, Jesus sends his followers into the world. He sends them out with a promise that he would always be with them.

The Family Line of Jesus the Messiah

1 This is the written story of the family line of Jesus the Messiah. He is the son of David. He is also the son of Abraham.

2 Abraham was the father of Isaac.
Isaac was the father of Jacob.
Jacob was the father of Judah and his brothers.
3 Judah was the father of Perez and Zerah. Tamar was their mother.
Perez was the father of Hezron.
Hezron was the father of Ram.
4 Ram was the father of Amminadab.
Amminadab was the father of Nahshon.
Nahshon was the father of Salmon.
5 Salmon was the father of Boaz. Rahab was Boaz's mother.
Boaz was the father of Obed. Ruth was Obed's mother.
Obed was the father of Jesse.
6 And Jesse was the father of King David.

David was the father of Solomon.
Solomon's mother had been Uriah's wife.
7 Solomon was the father of Rehoboam.
Rehoboam was the father of Abijah.
Abijah was the father of Asa.
8 Asa was the father of Jehoshaphat.
Jehoshaphat was the father of Jehoram.
Jehoram was the father of Uzziah.
9 Uzziah was the father of Jotham.
Jotham was the father of Ahaz.
Ahaz was the father of Hezekiah.
10 Hezekiah was the father of Manasseh.
Manasseh was the father of Amon.
Amon was the father of Josiah.
11 And Josiah was the father of Jeconiah and his brothers. At that time, the Jewish people were forced to go away to Babylon.

12 After this, the family line continued.
Jeconiah was the father of Shealtiel.
Shealtiel was the father of Zerubbabel.
13 Zerubbabel was the father of Abihud.
Abihud was the father of Eliakim.
Eliakim was the father of Azor.
14 Azor was the father of Zadok.
Zadok was the father of Akim.
Akim was the father of Elihud.
15 Elihud was the father of Eleazar.
Eleazar was the father of Matthan.
Matthan was the father of Jacob.
16 Jacob was the father of Joseph. Joseph was the husband of Mary.
And Mary was the mother of Jesus, who is called the Messiah.

17 So there were 14 generations from
Abraham to David. There were 14

from David until the Jewish people
were forced to go away to Babylon.
And there were 14 from that time to
the Messiah.

Joseph Accepts Jesus as His Son

18 This is how the birth of Jesus the Messiah came about. His mother Mary and
Joseph had promised to get married. But
before they started to live together, it became clear that she was going to have a
baby. She became pregnant by the power
of the Holy Spirit. 19 Her husband Joseph
was faithful to the law. But he did not
want to put her to shame in public. So he
planned to divorce her quietly.

20 But as Joseph was thinking about this,
an angel of the Lord appeared to him in
a dream. The angel said, "Joseph, son of
David, don't be afraid to take Mary home
as your wife. The baby inside her is from
the Holy Spirit. 21 She is going to have a
son. You must give him the name Jesus.
That's because he will save his people
from their sins."

22 All this took place to bring about what
the Lord had said would happen. He had
said through the prophet, 23 "The virgin is
going to have a baby. She will give birth to
a son. And he will be called Immanuel."
(Isaiah 7:14) The name Immanuel means
"God with us."

24 Joseph woke up. He did what the angel of the Lord commanded him to do. He
took Mary home as his wife. 25 But he did
not sleep with her until she gave birth to a
son. And Joseph gave him the name Jesus.

The Wise Men Visit Jesus

2 Jesus was born in Bethlehem in Judea. This happened while Herod was
king of Judea. After Jesus' birth, Wise Men
from the east came to Jerusalem. 2 They
asked, "Where is the child who has been
born to be king of the Jews? We saw his
star when it rose. Now we have come to
worship him."

3 When King Herod heard about it, he
was very upset. Everyone in Jerusalem
was troubled too. 4 So Herod called together all the chief priests of the people.
He also called the teachers of the law. He
asked them where the Messiah was going
to be born. 5 "In Bethlehem in Judea," they
replied. "This is what the prophet has
written. He said,

6 " 'But you, Bethlehem, in the land of
Judah,
are certainly not the least
important among the towns
of Judah.
A ruler will come out of you.
He will rule my people Israel like a
shepherd.' " (Micah 5:2)

7 Then Herod secretly called for the
Wise Men. He found out from them exactly when the star had appeared. 8 He
sent them to Bethlehem. He said, "Go and
search carefully for the child. As soon as
you find him, report it to me. Then I can
go and worship him too."

9 After the Wise Men had listened to
the king, they went on their way. The star
they had seen when it rose went ahead
of them. It finally stopped over the place
where the child was. 10 When they saw
the star, they were filled with joy. 11 The
Wise Men went to the house. There they
saw the child with his mother Mary. They
bowed down and worshiped him. Then
they opened their treasures. They gave
him gold, frankincense and myrrh. 12 But
God warned them in a dream not to go
back to Herod. So they returned to their
country on a different road.

Jesus' Family Escapes to Egypt

13 When the Wise Men had left, Joseph
had a dream. In the dream an angel of the
Lord appeared to Joseph. "Get up!" the
angel said. "Take the child and his mother and escape to Egypt. Stay there until I
tell you to come back. Herod is going to
search for the child. He wants to kill him."

14 So Joseph got up. During the night,
he left for Egypt with the child and his
mother Mary. 15 They stayed there until
King Herod died. So the words the Lord
had spoken through the prophet came
true. He had said, "I brought my son out
of Egypt." (Hosea 11:1)

16 Herod realized that the Wise Men
had tricked him. So he became very angry. He gave orders about Bethlehem and
the area around it. He ordered all the boys
two years old and under to be killed. This
agreed with the time when the Wise Men
had seen the star. 17 In this way, the words
Jeremiah the prophet spoke came true.
He had said,

18 "A voice is heard in Ramah.

It's the sound of crying and deep
sadness.
Rachel is crying over her children.
She refuses to be comforted,
because they are gone."
(Jeremiah 31:15)

Jesus' Family Returns to Nazareth

19 After Herod died, Joseph had a dream
while he was still in Egypt. In the dream
an angel of the Lord appeared to him.
20 The angel said, "Get up! Take the child
and his mother. Go to the land of Israel.
The people who were trying to kill the
child are dead."
21 So Joseph got up. He took the child
and his mother Mary back to the land of
Israel. 22 But then he heard that Archelaus
was king of Judea. Archelaus was ruling in
place of his father Herod. This made Joseph afraid to go there. Joseph had been
warned in a dream. So he went back to
the land of Galilee instead. 23 There he
lived in a town called Nazareth. So what
the prophets had said about Jesus came
true. They had said that he would be
called a Nazarene.

John the Baptist Prepares the Way

3 In those days John the Baptist came
and preached in the Desert of Judea.
2 He said, "Turn away from your sins! The
kingdom of heaven has come near." 3 John
is the one Isaiah the prophet had spoken
about. He had said,

"A messenger is calling out in the
desert,
'Prepare the way for the Lord.
Make straight paths for him.' "
(Isaiah 40:3)

4 John's clothes were made out of camel's hair. He had a leather belt around
his waist. His food was locusts and wild
honey. 5 People went out to him from Jerusalem and all Judea. They also came
from the whole area around the Jordan
River. 6 When they confessed their sins,
John baptized them in the Jordan.
7 John saw many Pharisees and Sadducees coming to where he was baptizing.
He said to them, "You are like a nest of
poisonous snakes! Who warned you to
escape the coming of God's anger? 8 Live
in a way that shows you have turned away
from your sins. 9 Don't think you can say
to yourselves, 'Abraham is our father.' I tell
you, God can raise up children for Abraham even from these stones. 10 The ax is
ready to cut the roots of the trees. All the
trees that don't produce good fruit will be
cut down. They will be thrown into the
fire.
11 "I baptize you with water, calling you
to turn away from your sins. But after me,
someone is coming who is more powerful than I am. I'm not worthy to carry his
sandals. He will baptize you with the Holy
Spirit and fire. 12 His pitchfork is in his
hand to clear the straw from his threshing floor. He will gather his wheat into the
storeroom. But he will burn up the husks
with fire that can't be put out."

Jesus Is Baptized

13 Jesus came from Galilee to the Jordan
River. He wanted to be baptized by John.
14 But John tried to stop him. So he told
Jesus, "I need to be baptized by you. So
why do you come to me?"
15 Jesus replied, "Let it be this way for
now. It is right for us to do this. It carries
out God's holy plan." Then John agreed.
16 As soon as Jesus was baptized, he
came up out of the water. At that moment
heaven was opened. Jesus saw the Spirit
of God coming down on him like a dove.
17 A voice from heaven said, "This is my
Son, and I love him. I am very pleased
with him."

Jesus Is Tempted in the Desert

4 The Holy Spirit led Jesus into the desert. There the devil tempted him. 2 After 40 days and 40 nights of going without
eating, Jesus was hungry. 3 The tempter
came to him. He said, "If you are the
Son of God, tell these stones to become
bread."
4 Jesus answered, "It is written, 'Man
must not live only on bread. He must also
live on every word that comes from the
mouth of God.' " (Deuteronomy 8:3)
5 Then the devil took Jesus to the holy
city. He had him stand on the highest
point of the temple. 6 "If you are the Son
of God," he said, "throw yourself down. It
is written,

" 'The Lord will command his angels
to take good care of you.

They will lift you up in their
hands.
Then you won't trip over a stone.' "
(Psalm 91:11,12)

7 Jesus answered him, "It is also written,
'Do not test the Lord your God.' " (Deuteronomy 6:16)
8 Finally, the devil took Jesus to a very
high mountain. He showed him all the
kingdoms of the world and their glory.
9 "If you bow down and worship me," he
said, "I will give you all this."
10 Jesus said to him, "Get away from
me, Satan! It is written, 'Worship the Lord
your God. He is the only one you should
serve.' " (Deuteronomy 6:13)
11 Then the devil left Jesus. Angels came
and took care of him.

Jesus Begins to Preach

12 John had been put in prison. When
Jesus heard about this, he returned to
Galilee. 13 Jesus left Nazareth and went to
live in the city of Capernaum. It was by the
lake in the area of Zebulun and Naphtali.
14 In that way, what the prophet Isaiah had
said came true. He had said,

15 "Land of Zebulun! Land of Naphtali!
Galilee, where Gentiles live!
Land along the Mediterranean
Sea! Territory east of the
Jordan River!
16 The people who are now living in
darkness
have seen a great light.
They are now living in a very dark
land.
But a light has shined on them."
(Isaiah 9:1,2)

17 From that time on Jesus began to
preach. "Turn away from your sins!" he
said. "The kingdom of heaven has come
near."

Jesus Chooses His First Disciples

18 One day Jesus was walking beside the
Sea of Galilee. There he saw two brothers, Simon Peter and his brother Andrew.
They were throwing a net into the lake,
because they were fishermen. 19 "Come
and follow me," Jesus said. "I will send
you out to fish for people." 20 At once they
left their nets and followed him.
21 Going on from there, he saw two other brothers. They were James, son of Zebedee, and his brother John. They were in
a boat with their father Zebedee. As they
were preparing their nets, Jesus called out
to them. 22 Right away they left the boat
and their father and followed Jesus.

Jesus Heals Sick People

23 Jesus went all over Galilee. There he
taught in the synagogues. He preached
the good news of God's kingdom. He
healed every illness and sickness the
people had. 24 News about him spread all
over Syria. People brought to him all who
were ill with different kinds of sicknesses.
Some were suffering great pain. Others
were controlled by demons. Some were
shaking wildly. Others couldn't move at
all. And Jesus healed all of them. 25 Large
crowds followed him. People came from
Galilee, from the area known as the Ten
Cities, and from Jerusalem and Judea.
Others came from the area across the Jordan River.

Jesus Teaches the Disciples and Crowds

5 Jesus saw the crowds. So he went up
on a mountainside and sat down. His
disciples came to him. 2 Then he began to
teach them.

Jesus Gives Blessings

He said,

3 "Blessed are those who are
spiritually needy.
The kingdom of heaven belongs to
them.
4 Blessed are those who are sad.
They will be comforted.
5 Blessed are those who are humble.
They will be given the earth.
6 Blessed are those who are hungry
and thirsty for what is right.
They will be filled.
7 Blessed are those who show mercy.
They will be shown mercy.
8 Blessed are those whose hearts are
pure.
They will see God.
9 Blessed are those who make peace.
They will be called children of
God.
10 Blessed are those who suffer for
doing what is right.
The kingdom of heaven belongs to
them.

11 "Blessed are you when people make
fun of you and hurt you because of me.
You are also blessed when they tell all
kinds of evil lies about you because of
me. 12 Be joyful and glad. Your reward in
heaven is great. In the same way, people
hurt the prophets who lived long ago.

Salt and Light

13 "You are the salt of the earth. But suppose the salt loses its saltiness. How can it
be made salty again? It is no longer good
for anything. It will be thrown out. People
will walk all over it.
14 "You are the light of the world. A town
built on a hill can't be hidden. 15 Also,
people do not light a lamp and put it
under a bowl. Instead, they put it on its
stand. Then it gives light to everyone in
the house. 16 In the same way, let your
light shine so others can see it. Then they
will see the good things you do. And they
will bring glory to your Father who is in
heaven.

Jesus Fulfills the Law

17 "Do not think I have come to get rid
of what is written in the Law or in the
Prophets. I have not come to do this. Instead, I have come to fulfill what is written. 18 What I'm about to tell you is true.
Heaven and earth will disappear before
the smallest letter disappears from the
Law. Not even the smallest mark of a pen
will disappear from the Law until everything is completed. 19 Do not ignore even
one of the least important commands.
And do not teach others to ignore them.
If you do, you will be called the least important person in the kingdom of heaven.
Instead, practice and teach these commands. Then you will be called important
in the kingdom of heaven. 20 Here is what I
tell you. You must be more godly than the
Pharisees and the teachers of the law. If
you are not, you will certainly not enter
the kingdom of heaven.

Murder

21 "You have heard what was said to
people who lived long ago. They were
told, 'Do not commit murder. (Exodus
20:13) Anyone who murders will be judged
for it.' 22 But here is what I tell you. Do not
be angry with a brother or sister. Anyone
who is angry with them will be judged.
Again, anyone who says to a brother or
sister, 'Raca,' must stand trial in court.
And anyone who says, 'You fool!' will be
in danger of the fire in hell.
23 "Suppose you are offering your gift
at the altar. And you remember that your
brother or sister has something against
you. 24 Leave your gift in front of the altar.
First go and make peace with them. Then
come back and offer your gift.
25 "Suppose someone has a claim
against you and is taking you to court. Settle the matter quickly. Do this while you
are still together on the way. If you don't,
you may be handed over to the judge. The
judge may hand you over to the officer to
be thrown into prison. 26 What I'm about
to tell you is true. You will not get out until
you have paid the very last penny!

Adultery

27 "You have heard that it was said, 'Do
not commit adultery.' (Exodus 20:14) 28 But
here is what I tell you. Do not even look at
a woman in the wrong way. Anyone who
does has already committed adultery
with her in his heart. 29 If your right eye
causes you to sin, poke it out and throw
it away. Your eye is only one part of your
body. It is better to lose an eye than for
your whole body to be thrown into hell.
30 If your right hand causes you to sin, cut
it off and throw it away. Your hand is only
one part of your body. It is better to lose a
hand than for your whole body to go into
hell.

Divorce

31 "It has been said, 'Suppose a man divorces his wife. If he does, he must give
her a letter of divorce.' (Deuteronomy 24:1)
32 But here is what I tell you. Anyone who
divorces his wife makes her a victim of
adultery. And anyone who gets married
to the divorced woman commits adultery. A man may divorce his wife only if
she has not been faithful to him.

Promises

33 "Again, you have heard what was said
to your people long ago. They were told,
'Do not break the promises you make to
the Lord. Keep your promises to the Lord
that you have made.' 34 But here is what I
tell you. Do not make any promises like
that at all. Do not make them in the name

of heaven. That is God's throne. 35 Do not
make them in the name of the earth. That
is the stool for God's feet. Do not make
them in the name of Jerusalem. That is
the city of the Great King. 36 And do not
make a promise in your own name. You
can't make even one hair of your head
white or black. 37 All you need to say is
simply 'Yes' or 'No.' Anything more than
this comes from the evil one.

Be Kind to Others

38 "You have heard that it was said, 'An
eye must be put out for an eye. A tooth
must be knocked out for a tooth.' (Exodus 21:24; Leviticus 24:20; Deuteronomy 19:21)
39 But here is what I tell you. Do not fight
against an evil person. Suppose someone slaps you on your right cheek. Turn
your other cheek to them also. 40 Suppose
someone takes you to court to get your
shirt. Let them have your coat also. 41 Suppose someone forces you to go one mile.
Go two miles with them. 42 Give to the one
who asks you for something. Don't turn
away from the one who wants to borrow
something from you.

Love Your Enemies

43 "You have heard that it was said, 'Love
your neighbor. (Leviticus 19:18) Hate your
enemy.' 44 But here is what I tell you. Love
your enemies. Pray for those who hurt
you. 45 Then you will be children of your
Father who is in heaven. He causes his
sun to shine on evil people and good people. He sends rain on those who do right
and those who don't. 46 If you love those
who love you, what reward will you get?
Even the tax collectors do that. 47 If you
greet only your own people, what more
are you doing than others? Even people
who are ungodly do that. 48 So be perfect,
just as your Father in heaven is perfect.

Giving to Needy People

6 "Be careful not to do good deeds in
front of other people. Don't do those
deeds to be seen by others. If you do, your
Father in heaven will not reward you.

2 "When you give to needy people,
do not announce it by having trumpets
blown. Do not be like those who only pretend to be holy. They announce what they
do in the synagogues and on the streets.
They want to be honored by other people.
What I'm about to tell you is true. They
have received their complete reward.
3 When you give to needy people, don't let
your left hand know what your right hand
is doing. 4 Then your giving will be done
secretly. Your Father will reward you, because he sees what you do secretly.

Prayer

5 "When you pray, do not be like those
who only pretend to be holy. They love
to stand and pray in the synagogues and
on the street corners. They want to be
seen by other people. What I'm about to
tell you is true. They have received their
complete reward. 6 When you pray, go
into your room. Close the door and pray
to your Father, who can't be seen. Your
Father will reward you, because he sees
what you do secretly. 7 When you pray, do
not keep talking on and on. That is what
ungodly people do. They think they will
be heard because they talk a lot. 8 Do not
be like them. Your Father knows what you
need even before you ask him.

9 "This is how you should pray.

"'Our Father in heaven,
may your name be honored.
10 May your kingdom come.
May what you want to happen be done
on earth as it is done in heaven.
11 Give us today our daily bread.
12 And forgive us our sins,
just as we also have forgiven those who sin against us.
13 Keep us from sinning when we are tempted.
Save us from the evil one.'

14 Forgive other people when they sin
against you. If you do, your Father who
is in heaven will also forgive you. 15 But if
you do not forgive the sins of other people, your Father will not forgive your sins.

Fasting

16 "When you go without eating, do not
look gloomy like those who only pretend
to be holy. They make their faces look
very sad. They want to show people they
are fasting. What I'm about to tell you is
true. They have received their complete
reward. 17 But when you go without eating, put olive oil on your head. Wash your
face. 18 Then others will not know that you

are fasting. Only your Father, who can't
be seen, will know it. Your Father will reward you, because he sees what you do
secretly.

Gather Riches in Heaven

19 "Do not gather for yourselves riches
on earth. Moths and rats can destroy
them. Thieves can break in and steal
them. 20 Instead, gather for yourselves
riches in heaven. There, moths and rats
do not destroy them. There, thieves do
not break in and steal them. 21 Your heart
will be where your riches are.
22 "The eye is like a lamp for the body.
Suppose your eyes are healthy. Then your
whole body will be full of light. 23 But suppose your eyes can't see well. Then your
whole body will be full of darkness. If the
light inside you is darkness, then it is very
dark!
24 "No one can serve two masters at the
same time. You will hate one of them and
love the other. Or you will be faithful to
one and dislike the other. You can't serve
God and money at the same time.

Do Not Worry

25 "I tell you, do not worry. Don't worry
about your life and what you will eat or
drink. And don't worry about your body
and what you will wear. Isn't there more
to life than eating? Aren't there more important things for the body than clothes?
26 Look at the birds of the air. They don't
plant or gather crops. They don't put away
crops in storerooms. But your Father who
is in heaven feeds them. Aren't you worth
much more than they are? 27 Can you add
even one hour to your life by worrying?
28 "And why do you worry about
clothes? See how the wild flowers grow.
They don't work or make clothing. 29 But
here is what I tell you. Not even Solomon
in all his royal robes was dressed like
one of these flowers. 30 If that is how God
dresses the wild grass, won't he dress you
even better? Your faith is so small! After
all, the grass is here only today. Tomorrow it is thrown into the fire. 31 So don't
worry. Don't say, 'What will we eat?' Or,
'What will we drink?' Or, 'What will we
wear?' 32 People who are ungodly run after all those things. Your Father who is
in heaven knows that you need them.
33 But put God's kingdom first. Do what
he wants you to do. Then all those things
will also be given to you. 34 So don't worry
about tomorrow. Tomorrow will worry
about itself. Each day has enough trouble
of its own.

Be Fair When You Judge Other People

7 "Do not judge other people. Then you
will not be judged. 2 You will be judged
in the same way you judge others. You
will be measured in the same way you
measure others.
3 "You look at the bit of sawdust in your
friend's eye. But you pay no attention to
the piece of wood in your own eye. 4 How
can you say to your friend, 'Let me take
the bit of sawdust out of your eye'? How
can you say this while there is a piece of
wood in your own eye? 5 You pretender!
First take the piece of wood out of your
own eye. Then you will be able to see
clearly to take the bit of sawdust out of
your friend's eye.
6 "Do not give holy things to dogs. Do
not throw your pearls to pigs. If you do,
they might walk all over them. They might
turn around and tear you to pieces.

Ask, Search, Knock

7 "Ask, and it will be given to you. Search,
and you will find. Knock, and the door
will be opened to you. 8 Everyone who
asks will receive. The one who searches
will find. The door will be opened to the
one who knocks.
9 "Suppose your son asks for bread.
Which of you will give him a stone? 10 Or
suppose he asks for a fish. Which of you
will give him a snake? 11 Even though you
are evil, you know how to give good gifts
to your children. How much more will
your Father who is in heaven give good
gifts to those who ask him! 12 In everything, do to others what you would want
them to do to you. This is what is written
in the Law and in the Prophets.

The Large and Small Gates

13 "Enter God's kingdom through the
narrow gate. The gate is large and the
road is wide that leads to ruin. Many people go that way. 14 But the gate is small and
the road is narrow that leads to life. Only a
few people find it.

True and False Prophets

15 “Watch out for false prophets. They
come to you pretending to be sheep. But
on the inside they are hungry wolves.
16 You can tell each tree by its fruit. Do
people pick grapes from bushes? Do they
pick figs from thorns? 17 In the same way,
every good tree bears good fruit. But a
bad tree bears bad fruit. 18 A good tree
can’t bear bad fruit. And a bad tree can’t
bear good fruit. 19 Every tree that does not
bear good fruit is cut down. It is thrown
into the fire. 20 You can tell each tree by its
fruit.

True and False Disciples

21 “Not everyone who says to me, ‘Lord,
Lord,’ will enter the kingdom of heaven.
Only those who do what my Father in
heaven wants will enter. 22 Many will say
to me on that day, ‘Lord! Lord! Didn’t we
prophesy in your name? Didn’t we drive
out demons in your name? Didn’t we do
many miracles in your name?’ 23 Then I
will tell them clearly, ‘I never knew you.
Get away from me, you who do evil!’

The Wise and Foolish Builders

24 “So then, everyone who hears my
words and puts them into practice is like
a wise man. He builds his house on the
rock. 25 The rain comes down. The water
rises. The winds blow and beat against
that house. But it does not fall. It is built
on the rock. 26 But everyone who hears my
words and does not put them into practice is like a foolish man. He builds his
house on sand. 27 The rain comes down.
The water rises. The winds blow and beat
against that house. And it falls with a loud
crash.”

28 Jesus finished saying all these things.
The crowds were amazed at his teaching.
29 That’s because he taught like one who
had authority. He did not speak like their
teachers of the law.

Jesus Heals a Man Who Had a Skin Disease

8 Jesus came down from the mountainside. Large crowds followed him. 2 A
man who had a skin disease came and got
down on his knees in front of Jesus. He
said, “Lord, if you are willing to make me
‘clean,’ you can do it.”

3 Jesus reached out his hand and
touched the man. “I am willing to do it,”
he said. “Be ‘clean’!” Right away the man
was healed of his skin disease. 4 Then
Jesus said to him, “Don’t tell anyone. Go
and show yourself to the priest, and offer
the gift Moses commanded. It will be a
witness to everyone.”

A Roman Commander Has Faith

5 When Jesus entered Capernaum, a
Roman commander came to him. He
asked Jesus for help. 6 “Lord,” he said, “my
servant lies at home and can’t move. He is
suffering terribly.”

7 Jesus said, “Shall I come and heal
him?”

8 The commander replied, “Lord, I am
not good enough to have you come into
my house. But just say the word, and my
servant will be healed. 9 I myself am a
man under authority. And I have soldiers
who obey my orders. I tell this one, ‘Go,’
and he goes. I tell that one, ‘Come,’ and he
comes. I say to my slave, ‘Do this,’ and he
does it.”

10 When Jesus heard this, he was
amazed. He said to those following him,
“What I’m about to tell you is true. In Israel
I have not found anyone whose faith is so
strong. 11 I say to you that many will come
from the east and the west. They will take
their places at the feast in the kingdom of
heaven. They will sit with Abraham, Isaac
and Jacob. 12 But those who think they belong in the kingdom will be thrown outside, into the darkness. There they will
weep and grind their teeth.”

13 Then Jesus said to the Roman commander, “Go! It will be done just as you
believed it would.” And his servant was
healed at that moment.

Jesus Heals Many People

14 When Jesus came into Peter’s house,
he saw Peter’s mother-in-law. She was
lying in bed. She had a fever. 15 Jesus
touched her hand, and the fever left her.
She got up and began to serve him.

16 When evening came, many people controlled by demons were brought
to Jesus. He drove out the spirits with a
word. He healed all who were sick. 17 This
happened so that what Isaiah the prophet
had said would come true. He had said,

"He suffered the things we should
have suffered.
He took on himself the sicknesses
that should have been ours."
(Isaiah 53:4)

The Cost of Following Jesus

18 Jesus saw the crowd around him. So
he gave his disciples orders to go to the
other side of the Sea of Galilee. 19 Then a
teacher of the law came to him. He said,
"Teacher, I will follow you no matter
where you go."
20 Jesus replied, "Foxes have dens. Birds
have nests. But the Son of Man has no
place to lay his head."
21 Another follower said to him, "Lord,
first let me go and bury my father."
22 But Jesus told him, "Follow me. Let
the dead bury their own dead."

Jesus Calms the Storm

23 Jesus got into a boat. His disciples followed him. 24 Suddenly a terrible storm
came up on the lake. The waves crashed
over the boat. But Jesus was sleeping.
25 The disciples went and woke him up.
They said, "Lord! Save us! We're going to
drown!"
26 He replied, "Your faith is so small!
Why are you so afraid?" Then Jesus got up
and ordered the winds and the waves to
stop. It became completely calm.
27 The disciples were amazed. They
asked, "What kind of man is this? Even
the winds and the waves obey him!"

Jesus Heals Two Men Controlled by Demons

28 Jesus arrived at the other side of the
lake in the area of the Gadarenes. Two
men controlled by demons met him.
They came from the tombs. The men
were so wild that no one could pass that
way. 29 "Son of God, what do you want
with us?" they shouted. "Have you come
here to punish us before the time for us to
be judged?"
30 Not very far away, a large herd of pigs
was feeding. 31 The demons begged Jesus,
"If you drive us out, send us into the herd
of pigs."
32 Jesus said to them, "Go!" So the demons came out of the men and went into
the pigs. The whole herd rushed down
the steep bank. They ran into the lake
and drowned in the water. 33 Those who
were tending the pigs ran off. They went
into the town and reported all this. They
told the people what had happened to
the men who had been controlled by demons. 34 Then the whole town went out
to meet Jesus. When they saw him, they
begged him to leave their area.

Jesus Forgives and Heals a Man Who Could Not Walk

9 Jesus stepped into a boat. He went over
to the other side of the lake and came
to his own town. 2 Some men brought to
him a man who could not walk. He was lying on a mat. Jesus saw that they had faith.
So he said to the man, "Don't lose hope,
son. Your sins are forgiven."
3 Then some teachers of the law said to
themselves, "This fellow is saying a very
evil thing!"
4 Jesus knew what they were thinking. So he said, "Why do you have evil
thoughts in your hearts? 5 Is it easier to
say, 'Your sins are forgiven'? Or to say,
'Get up and walk'? 6 But I want you to
know that the Son of Man has authority
on earth to forgive sins." So he spoke to
the man who could not walk. "Get up," he
said. "Take your mat and go home." 7 The
man got up and went home. 8 When the
crowd saw this, they were filled with wonder. They praised God for giving that kind
of authority to a human being.

Jesus Chooses Matthew and Eats With Sinners

9 As Jesus went on from there, he saw
a man named Matthew. He was sitting
at the tax collector's booth. "Follow me,"
Jesus told him. Matthew got up and followed him.
10 Later Jesus was having dinner at Matthew's house. Many tax collectors and
sinners came. They ate with Jesus and
his disciples. 11 The Pharisees saw this. So
they asked the disciples, "Why does your
teacher eat with tax collectors and sinners?"
12 Jesus heard this. So he said, "Those
who are healthy don't need a doctor.
Sick people do. 13 Go and learn what this
means, 'I want mercy and not sacrifice.'
(Hosea 6:6) I have not come to get those
who think they are right with God to fol-

low me. I have come to get sinners to follow me."

Jesus Is Asked About Fasting

14 One day John's disciples came. They said to Jesus, "We and the Pharisees often go without eating. Why don't your disciples go without eating?"

15 Jesus answered, "How can the guests of the groom be sad while he is with them? The time will come when the groom will be taken away from them. Then they will fast.

16 "People don't sew a patch of new cloth on old clothes. The new piece will pull away from the old. That will make the tear worse. 17 People don't pour new wine into old wineskins. If they do, the skins will burst. The wine will run out, and the wineskins will be destroyed. No, people pour new wine into new wineskins. Then both are saved."

Jesus Heals a Dead Girl and a Suffering Woman

18 While Jesus was saying this, a synagogue leader came. He got down on his knees in front of Jesus. He said, "My daughter has just died. But come and place your hand on her. Then she will live again." 19 Jesus got up and went with him. So did his disciples.

20 Just then a woman came up behind Jesus. She had a sickness that made her bleed. It had lasted for 12 years. She touched the edge of his clothes. 21 She thought, "I only need to touch his clothes. Then I will be healed."

22 Jesus turned and saw her. "Dear woman, don't give up hope," he said. "Your faith has healed you." The woman was healed at that moment.

23 When Jesus entered the synagogue leader's house, he saw the noisy crowd and people playing flutes. 24 He said, "Go away. The girl is not dead. She is sleeping." But they laughed at him. 25 After the crowd had been sent outside, Jesus went in. He took the girl by the hand, and she got up. 26 News about what Jesus had done spread all over that area.

Jesus Heals Two Blind Men

27 As Jesus went on from there, two blind men followed him. They called out, "Have mercy on us, Son of David!"

28 When Jesus went indoors, the blind men came to him. He asked them, "Do you believe that I can do this?"

"Yes, Lord," they replied.

29 Then he touched their eyes. He said, "It will happen to you just as you believed." 30 They could now see again. Jesus strongly warned them, "Be sure that no one knows about this." 31 But they went out and spread the news. They talked about him all over that area.

32 While they were going out, another man was brought to Jesus. A demon controlled him, and he could not speak. 33 When the demon was driven out, the man spoke. The crowd was amazed. They said, "Nothing like this has ever been seen in Israel."

34 But the Pharisees said, "He drives out demons by the power of the prince of demons."

There Are Only a Few Workers

35 Jesus went through all the towns and villages. He taught in their synagogues. He preached the good news of the kingdom. And he healed every illness and sickness. 36 When he saw the crowds, he felt deep concern for them. They were treated badly and were helpless, like sheep without a shepherd. 37 Then Jesus said to his disciples, "The harvest is huge. But there are only a few workers. 38 So ask the Lord of the harvest to send workers out into his harvest field."

Jesus Sends Out the Twelve Disciples

10 Jesus called for his 12 disciples to come to him. He gave them authority to drive out evil spirits and to heal every illness and sickness.

2 Here are the names of the 12 apostles. First there were Simon Peter and his brother Andrew. Then came James, son of Zebedee, and his brother John. 3 Next were Philip and Bartholomew, and also Thomas and Matthew the tax collector. Two more were James, son of Alphaeus, and Thaddaeus. 4 The last were Simon the Zealot and Judas Iscariot. Judas was the one who was later going to hand Jesus over to his enemies.

5 Jesus sent these 12 out with the following orders. "Do not go among the Gentiles," he said. "Do not enter any town of the Samaritans. 6 Instead, go to the people

of Israel. They are like sheep that have become lost. 7 As you go, preach this message, 'The kingdom of heaven has come
near.' 8 Heal those who are sick. Bring
those who are dead back to life. Make
those who have skin diseases 'clean'
again. Drive out demons. You have received freely, so give freely.

9 "Do not get any gold, silver or copper
to take with you in your belts. 10 Do not
take a bag for the journey. Do not take
extra clothes or sandals or walking sticks.
A worker should be given what he needs.
11 When you enter a town or village, look
for someone who is willing to welcome
you. Stay at their house until you leave.
12 As you enter the home, greet those who
live there. 13 If that home welcomes you,
give it your blessing of peace. If it does
not, don't bless it. 14 Some people may not
welcome you or listen to your words. If
they don't, leave that home or town, and
shake the dust off your feet. 15 What I'm
about to tell you is true. On judgment day
it will be easier for Sodom and Gomorrah
than for that town.

16 "I am sending you out like sheep
among wolves. So be as wise as snakes
and as harmless as doves. 17 Watch out!
You will be handed over to the local
courts. You will be whipped in the synagogues. 18 You will be brought to governors and kings because of me. You will
be witnesses to them and to the Gentiles.
19 But when they arrest you, don't worry
about what you will say or how you will
say it. At that time you will be given the
right words to say. 20 It will not be you
speaking. The Spirit of your Father will be
speaking through you.

21 "Brothers will hand over brothers
to be killed. Fathers will hand over their
children. Children will rise up against
their parents and have them put to death.
22 You will be hated by everyone because
of me. But anyone who remains strong in
the faith will be saved. 23 When people attack you in one place, escape to another.
What I'm about to tell you is true. You will
not finish going through the towns of Israel before the Son of Man comes.

24 "The student is not better than the
teacher. A slave is not better than his master. 25 It is enough for students to be like
their teachers. And it is enough for slaves
to be like their masters. If the head of the
house has been called Beelzebul, what
can the others who live there expect?

26 "So don't be afraid of your enemies.
Everything that is secret will be brought
out into the open. Everything that is hidden will be uncovered. 27 What I tell you
in the dark, speak in the daylight. What
is whispered in your ear, shout from the
rooftops. 28 Do not be afraid of those who
kill the body but can't kill the soul. Instead, be afraid of the one who can destroy both soul and body in hell. 29 Aren't
two sparrows sold for only a penny? But
not one of them falls to the ground outside your Father's care. 30 He even counts
every hair on your head! 31 So don't be
afraid. You are worth more than many
sparrows.

32 "What if someone says in front of others that they know me? I will also say in
front of my Father who is in heaven that I
know them. 33 But what if someone says in
front of others that they don't know me?
I will say in front of my Father who is in
heaven that I don't know them.

34 "Do not think that I came to bring
peace to the earth. I didn't come to bring
peace. I came to bring a sword. 35 I have
come to turn

" 'sons against their fathers.
Daughters will refuse to obey their
mothers.
Daughters-in-law will be against
their mothers-in-law.
36 A man's enemies will be the
members of his own family.'
(Micah 7:6)

37 "Anyone who loves their father or
mother more than me is not worthy of me.
Anyone who loves their son or daughter
more than me is not worthy of me. 38 Whoever does not pick up their cross and follow me is not worthy of me. 39 Whoever
finds their life will lose it. Whoever loses
their life because of me will find it.

40 "Anyone who welcomes you welcomes me. And anyone who welcomes
me welcomes the one who sent me.
41 Suppose someone welcomes a prophet
as a prophet. They will receive a prophet's reward. And suppose someone welcomes a godly person as a godly person.
They will receive a godly person's reward.
42 Suppose someone gives even a cup of
cold water to a little one who follows me.

What I'm about to tell you is true. That person will certainly be rewarded."

Jesus and John the Baptist

11 Jesus finished teaching his 12 disciples. Then he went on to teach and preach in the towns of Galilee.

2 John the Baptist was in prison. When he heard about the actions of the Messiah, he sent his disciples to him. 3 They asked Jesus, "Are you the one who is supposed to come? Or should we look for someone else?"

4 Jesus replied, "Go back to John. Report to him what you hear and see. 5 Blind people receive sight. Disabled people walk. Those who have skin diseases are made 'clean.' Deaf people hear. Those who are dead are raised to life. And the good news is preached to those who are poor. 6 Blessed is anyone who does not give up their faith because of me."

7 As John's disciples were leaving, Jesus began to speak to the crowd about John. He said, "What did you go out into the desert to see? Tall grass waving in the wind? 8 If not, what did you go out to see? A man dressed in fine clothes? No. People who wear fine clothes are in kings' palaces. 9 Then what did you go out to see? A prophet? Yes, I tell you, and more than a prophet. 10 He is the one written about in Scripture. It says,

> " 'I will send my messenger ahead of
> you.
> He will prepare your way for you.'
> (Malachi 3:1)

11 What I'm about to tell you is true. No one more important than John the Baptist has ever been born. But the least important person in the kingdom of heaven is more important than he is. 12 Since the days of John the Baptist, the kingdom of heaven has been under attack. And violent people are taking hold of it. 13 All the Prophets and the Law prophesied until John came. 14 If you are willing to accept it, John is the Elijah who was supposed to come. 15 Whoever has ears should listen.

16 "What can I compare today's people to? They are like children sitting in the markets and calling out to others. They say,

> 17 " 'We played the flute for you.
> But you didn't dance.
> We sang a funeral song.
> But you didn't become sad.'

18 When John came, he didn't eat or drink as you do. And people say, 'He has a demon.' 19 But when the Son of Man came, he ate and drank as you do. And people say, 'This fellow is always eating and drinking far too much. He's a friend of tax collectors and "sinners." ' By wise actions wisdom is shown to be right."

Towns That Do Not Turn Away From Sin

20 Jesus began to speak against the towns where he had done most of his miracles. The people there had not turned away from their sins. So he said, 21 "How terrible it will be for you, Chorazin! How terrible for you, Bethsaida! Suppose the miracles done in you had been done in Tyre and Sidon. They would have turned away from their sins long ago. They would have put on clothes for mourning. They would have sat down in ashes. 22 But I tell you this. On judgment day it will be easier for Tyre and Sidon than for you. 23 And what about you, Capernaum? Will you be lifted to the heavens? No! You will go down to the place of the dead. Suppose the miracles done in you had been done in Sodom. It would still be here today. 24 But I tell you this. On judgment day it will be easier for Sodom than for you."

Rest for All Who Are Tired

25 At that time Jesus said, "I praise you, Father. You are Lord of heaven and earth. You have hidden these things from wise and educated people. But you have shown them to little children. 26 Yes, Father. This is what you wanted to do.

27 "My Father has given all things to me. The Father is the only one who knows the Son. And the only ones who know the Father are the Son and those to whom the Son chooses to make him known.

28 "Come to me, all you who are tired and are carrying heavy loads. I will give you rest. 29 Become my servants and learn from me. I am gentle and free of pride. You will find rest for your souls. 30 Serving me is easy, and my load is light."

Jesus Is Lord of the Sabbath Day

12 One Sabbath day Jesus walked through the grainfields. His disciples were hungry. So they began to break

off some heads of grain and eat them.
2 The Pharisees saw this. They said to
Jesus, "Look! It is against the Law to do
this on the Sabbath day. But your disciples are doing it anyway!"
3 Jesus answered, "Haven't you read
about what David did? He and his men
were hungry. 4 So he entered the house
of God. He and his men ate the holy
bread. Only priests were allowed to eat
it. 5 Haven't you read the Law? It tells how
every Sabbath day the priests in the temple have to do their work on that day. But
they are not considered guilty. 6 I tell you
that something more important than the
temple is here. 7 Scripture says, 'I want
mercy and not sacrifice.' (Hosea 6:6) You
don't know what those words mean. If
you did, you would not bring charges
against those who are not guilty. 8 The Son
of Man is Lord of the Sabbath day."
9 Going on from that place, Jesus went
into their synagogue. 10 A man with a
weak and twisted hand was there. The
Pharisees were trying to accuse Jesus of a
crime. So they asked him, "Does the Law
allow us to heal on the Sabbath day?"
11 He said to them, "What if one of your
sheep falls into a pit on the Sabbath day?
Won't you take hold of it and lift it out? 12 A
person is worth more than sheep! So the
Law allows us to do good on the Sabbath
day."
13 Then Jesus said to the man, "Stretch
out your hand." So he stretched it out. It
had been made as good as new. It was
just as good as the other hand. 14 But the
Pharisees went out and planned how to
kill Jesus.

God's Chosen Servant

15 Jesus knew all about the Pharisees'
plans. So he left that place. A large crowd
followed him, and he healed all who were
sick. 16 But he warned them not to tell other people about him. 17 This was to make
what was spoken through the prophet
Isaiah come true. It says,

18 "Here is my servant. I have chosen
him.
He is the one I love. I am very
pleased with him.
I will put my Spirit on him.
He will announce to the nations
that everything will be made
right.
19 He will not argue or cry out.
No one will hear his voice in the
streets.
20 He will not break a bent twig.
He will not put out a dimly
burning flame.
He will make right win over wrong.
21 The nations will put their hope in
him." (Isaiah 42:1–4)

Jesus and Beelzebul

22 A man controlled by demons was
brought to Jesus. The man was blind and
could not speak. Jesus healed him. Then
the man could speak and see. 23 All the
people were amazed. They said, "Could
this be the Son of David?"
24 The Pharisees heard this. So they
said, "This fellow drives out demons by
the power of Beelzebul, the prince of demons."
25 Jesus knew what they were thinking.
So he said to them, "Every kingdom that
fights against itself will be destroyed. Every city or family that is divided against
itself will not stand. 26 If Satan drives out
Satan, he fights against himself. Then
how can his kingdom stand? 27 You say I
drive out demons by the power of Beelzebul. Then by whose power do your people
drive them out? So then, they will be your
judges. 28 But suppose I drive out demons
by the Spirit of God. Then the kingdom of
God has come to you.
29 "Or think about this. How can you
enter a strong man's house and just take
what the man owns? You must first tie
him up. Then you can rob his house.
30 "Anyone who is not with me is against
me. Anyone who does not gather sheep
with me scatters them. 31 So here is what
I tell you. Every kind of sin and every evil
word spoken against God will be forgiven.
But speaking evil things against the Holy
Spirit will not be forgiven. 32 Anyone who
speaks a word against the Son of Man
will be forgiven. But anyone who speaks
against the Holy Spirit will not be forgiven. A person like that won't be forgiven
either now or in days to come.
33 "If you make a tree good, its fruit will
be good. If you make a tree bad, its fruit
will be bad. You can tell a tree by its fruit.
34 You nest of poisonous snakes! How can
you who are evil say anything good? Your
mouths say everything that is in your

hearts. 35 A good man says good things. These come from the good that is stored up inside him. An evil man says evil things. These come from the evil that is stored up inside him. 36 But here is what I tell you. On judgment day, everyone will have to account for every empty word they have spoken. 37 By your words you will be found guilty or not guilty."

The Sign of Jonah

38 Some of the Pharisees and the teachers of the law came to Jesus. They said, "Teacher, we want to see a sign from you."

39 He answered, "Evil and unfaithful people ask for a sign! But none will be given except the sign of the prophet Jonah. 40 Jonah was in the belly of a huge fish for three days and three nights. Something like that will happen to the Son of Man. He will spend three days and three nights in the grave. 41 The men of Nineveh will stand up on judgment day with the people now living. And the Ninevites will prove that these people are guilty. The men of Nineveh turned away from their sins when Jonah preached to them. And now something more important than Jonah is here. 42 The Queen of the South will stand up on judgment day with the people now living. And she will prove that they are guilty. She came from very far away to listen to Solomon's wisdom. And now something more important than Solomon is here.

43 "What happens when an evil spirit comes out of a person? It goes through dry areas looking for a place to rest. But it doesn't find it. 44 Then it says, 'I will return to the house I left.' When it arrives there, it finds the house empty. The house has been swept clean and put in order. 45 Then the evil spirit goes and takes with it seven other spirits more evil than itself. They go in and live there. That person is worse off than before. That is how it will be with the evil people of today."

Jesus' Mother and Brothers

46 While Jesus was still talking to the crowd, his mother and brothers stood outside. They wanted to speak to him. 47 Someone told him, "Your mother and brothers are standing outside. They want to speak to you."

48 Jesus replied to him, "Who is my mother? And who are my brothers?" 49 Jesus pointed to his disciples. He said, "Here is my mother! Here are my brothers! 50 Anyone who does what my Father in heaven wants is my brother or sister or mother."

The Story of the Farmer

13 That same day Jesus left the house and sat by the Sea of Galilee. 2 Large crowds gathered around him. So he got into a boat and sat down. All the people stood on the shore. 3 Then he told them many things using stories. He said, "A farmer went out to plant his seed. 4 He scattered the seed on the ground. Some fell on a path. Birds came and ate it up. 5 Some seed fell on rocky places, where there wasn't much soil. The plants came up quickly, because the soil wasn't deep. 6 When the sun came up, it burned the plants. They dried up because they had no roots. 7 Other seed fell among thorns. The thorns grew up and crowded out the plants. 8 Still other seed fell on good soil. It produced a crop 100, 60 or 30 times more than what was planted. 9 Whoever has ears should listen."

10 The disciples came to him. They asked, "Why do you use stories when you speak to the people?"

11 He replied, "Because you have been given the knowledge of the secrets of the kingdom of heaven. It has not been given to outsiders. 12 Everyone who has this kind of knowledge will be given more knowledge. In fact, they will have very much. If anyone doesn't have this kind of knowledge, even what little they have will be taken away from them. 13 Here is why I use stories when I speak to the people. I say,

"They look, but they don't really see.
They listen, but they don't really
hear or understand.

14 In them the words of the prophet Isaiah come true. He said,

" 'You will hear but never
understand.
You will see but never know what
you are seeing.
15 The hearts of these people have
become stubborn.
They can barely hear with their
ears.
They have closed their eyes.

Otherwise they might see with their
eyes.
They might hear with their ears.
They might understand with their
hearts.
They might turn to the Lord, and
then he would heal them.'
(Isaiah 6:9,10)

16 But blessed are your eyes because they see. And blessed are your ears because they hear. 17 What I'm about to tell you is true. Many prophets and godly people wanted to see what you see. But they didn't see it. They wanted to hear what you hear. But they didn't hear it.

18 "Listen! Here is the meaning of the story of the farmer. 19 People hear the message about the kingdom but do not understand it. Then the evil one comes. He steals what was planted in their hearts. Those people are like the seed planted on a path. 20 The seed that fell on rocky places is like other people. They hear the message and at once receive it with joy. 21 But they have no roots. So they last only a short time. They quickly fall away from the faith when trouble or suffering comes because of the message. 22 The seed that fell among the thorns is like others who hear the message. But then the worries of this life and the false promises of wealth crowd it out. They keep the message from producing fruit. 23 But the seed that fell on good soil is like those who hear the message and understand it. They produce a crop 100, 60 or 30 times more than the farmer planted."

The Story of the Weeds

24 Jesus told the crowd another story. "Here is what the kingdom of heaven is like," he said. "A man planted good seed in his field. 25 But while everyone was sleeping, his enemy came. The enemy planted weeds among the wheat and then went away. 26 The wheat began to grow and form grain. At the same time, weeds appeared.

27 "The owner's slaves came to him. They said, 'Sir, didn't you plant good seed in your field? Then where did the weeds come from?'

28 " 'An enemy did this,' he replied.

"The slaves asked him, 'Do you want us to go and pull up the weeds?'

29 " 'No,' the owner answered. 'While you are pulling up the weeds, you might pull up the wheat with them. 30 Let both grow together until the harvest. At that time I will tell the workers what to do. Here is what I will say to them. First collect the weeds. Tie them in bundles to be burned. Then gather the wheat. Bring it into my storeroom.' "

The Stories of the Mustard Seed and the Yeast

31 Jesus told the crowd another story. He said, "The kingdom of heaven is like a mustard seed. Someone took the seed and planted it in a field. 32 It is the smallest of all seeds. But when it grows, it is the largest of all garden plants. It becomes a tree. Birds come and rest in its branches."

33 Jesus told them still another story. "The kingdom of heaven is like yeast," he said. "A woman mixed it into 60 pounds of flour. The yeast worked its way all through the dough."

34 Jesus spoke all these things to the crowd using stories. He did not say anything to them without telling a story. 35 So the words spoken by the prophet came true. He had said,

"I will open my mouth and tell
stories.
I will speak about things that were
hidden since the world was
made." (Psalm 78:2)

Jesus Explains the Story of the Weeds

36 Then Jesus left the crowd and went into the house. His disciples came to him. They said, "Explain to us the story of the weeds in the field."

37 He answered, "The one who planted the good seed is the Son of Man. 38 The field is the world. The good seed stands for the people who belong to the kingdom. The weeds are the people who belong to the evil one. 39 The enemy who plants them is the devil. The harvest is judgment day. And the workers are angels.

40 "The weeds are pulled up and burned in the fire. That is how it will be on judgment day. 41 The Son of Man will send out his angels. They will weed out of his kingdom everything that causes sin. They will also get rid of all who do evil. 42 They will throw them into the blazing furnace.

There people will weep and grind their teeth. [43]Then God's people will shine like the sun in their Father's kingdom. Whoever has ears should listen.

The Stories of the Hidden Treasure and the Pearl

[44]"The kingdom of heaven is like treasure that was hidden in a field. When a man found it, he hid it again. He was very happy. So he went and sold everything he had. And he bought that field.

[45]"Again, the kingdom of heaven is like a trader who was looking for fine pearls. [46]He found one that was very valuable. So he went away and sold everything he had. And he bought that pearl.

The Story of the Net

[47]"Again, the kingdom of heaven is like a net. It was let down into the lake. It caught all kinds of fish. [48]When it was full, the fishermen pulled it up on the shore. Then they sat down and gathered the good fish into baskets. But they threw the bad fish away. [49]This is how it will be on judgment day. The angels will come. They will separate the people who did what is wrong from those who did what is right. [50]They will throw the evil people into the blazing furnace. There the evil ones will weep and grind their teeth.

[51]"Do you understand all these things?" Jesus asked.

"Yes," they replied.

[52]He said to them, "Every teacher of the law who has become a disciple in the kingdom of heaven is like the owner of a house. He brings new treasures out of his storeroom as well as old ones."

A Prophet Without Honor

[53]Jesus finished telling these stories. Then he moved on from there. [54]He came to his hometown of Nazareth. There he began teaching the people in their synagogue. They were amazed. "Where did this man get this wisdom? Where did he get this power to do miracles?" they asked. [55]"Isn't this the carpenter's son? Isn't his mother's name Mary? Aren't his brothers James, Joseph, Simon and Judas? [56]Aren't all his sisters with us? Then where did this man get all these things?" [57]They were not pleased with him at all.

But Jesus said to them, "A prophet is honored everywhere except in his own town and in his own home."

[58]He did only a few miracles in Nazareth because the people there had no faith.

John the Baptist's Head Is Cut Off

14 At that time Herod, the ruler of Galilee and Perea, heard reports about Jesus. [2]He said to his attendants, "This is John the Baptist. He has risen from the dead! That is why he has the power to do miracles."

[3]Herod had arrested John. He had tied him up and put him in prison because of Herodias. She was the wife of Herod's brother Philip. [4]John had been saying to Herod, "It is against the Law for you to have her as your wife." [5]Herod wanted to kill John. But he was afraid of the people, because they thought John was a prophet.

[6]On Herod's birthday the daughter of Herodias danced for Herod and his guests. She pleased Herod very much. [7]So he promised to give her anything she asked for. [8]Her mother told her what to say. So the girl said to Herod, "Give me the head of John the Baptist on a big plate." [9]The king was very upset. But he thought of his promise and his dinner guests. So he told one of his men to give her what she asked for. [10]Herod had John's head cut off in the prison. [11]His head was brought in on a big plate and given to the girl. She then carried it to her mother. [12]John's disciples came and took his body and buried it. Then they went and told Jesus.

Jesus Feeds Five Thousand

[13]Jesus heard what had happened to John. He wanted to be alone. So he went in a boat to a quiet place. The crowds heard about this. They followed him on foot from the towns. [14]When Jesus came ashore, he saw a large crowd. He felt deep concern for them. He healed their sick people.

[15]When it was almost evening, the disciples came to him. "There is nothing here," they said. "It's already getting late. Send the crowds away. They can go and buy some food in the villages."

[16]Jesus replied, "They don't need to go away. You give them something to eat."

[17]"We have only five loaves of bread and two fish," they answered.

18 “Bring them here to me,” he said. 19 Then Jesus directed the people to sit down on the grass. He took the five loaves and the two fish. He looked up to heaven and gave thanks. He broke the loaves into pieces. Then he gave them to the disciples. And the disciples gave them to the people. 20 All of them ate and were satisfied. The disciples picked up 12 baskets of leftover pieces. 21 The number of men who ate was about 5,000. Women and children also ate.

Jesus Walks on the Water

22 Right away Jesus made the disciples get into the boat. He had them go on ahead of him to the other side of the Sea of Galilee. Then he sent the crowd away. 23 After he had sent them away, he went up on a mountainside by himself to pray. Later that night, he was there alone. 24 The boat was already a long way from land. It was being pounded by the waves because the wind was blowing against it.

25 Shortly before dawn, Jesus went out to the disciples. He walked on the lake. 26 They saw him walking on the lake and were terrified. “It’s a ghost!” they said. And they cried out in fear.

27 Right away Jesus called out to them, “Be brave! It is I. Don’t be afraid.”

28 “Lord, is it you?” Peter asked. “If it is, tell me to come to you on the water.”

29 “Come,” Jesus said.

So Peter got out of the boat. He walked on the water toward Jesus. 30 But when Peter saw the wind, he was afraid. He began to sink. He cried out, “Lord! Save me!”

31 Right away Jesus reached out his hand and caught him. “Your faith is so small!” he said. “Why did you doubt me?”

32 When they climbed into the boat, the wind died down. 33 Then those in the boat worshiped Jesus. They said, “You really are the Son of God!”

34 They crossed over the lake and landed at Gennesaret. 35 The men who lived there recognized Jesus. So they sent a message all over the nearby countryside. People brought all those who were sick to Jesus. 36 They begged him to let those who were sick just touch the edge of his clothes. And all who touched his clothes were healed.

What Makes People “Unclean”?

15 Some Pharisees and some teachers of the law came from Jerusalem to see Jesus. They asked, 2 “Why don’t your disciples obey what the elders teach? Your disciples don’t wash their hands before they eat!”

3 Jesus replied, “And why don’t you obey God’s command? You would rather follow your own teachings! 4 God said, ‘Honor your father and mother.’ (Exodus 20:12; Deuteronomy 5:16) He also said, ‘Anyone who asks for bad things to happen to their father or mother must be put to death.’ (Exodus 21:17; Leviticus 20:9) 5 But suppose people have something that might be used to help their parents. You allow them to say it is instead ‘a gift set apart for God.’ 6 So they do not need to honor their father or mother with their gift. You make the word of God useless in order to follow your own teachings. 7 You pretenders! Isaiah was right when he prophesied about you. He said,

8 “ ‘These people honor me by what
they say.
But their hearts are far away from
me.
9 Their worship doesn’t mean
anything to me.
They teach nothing but human
rules.’ ” (Isaiah 29:13)

10 Jesus called the crowd to him. He said, “Listen and understand. 11 What goes into someone’s mouth does not make them ‘unclean.’ It’s what comes out of their mouth that makes them ‘unclean.’ ”

12 Then the disciples came to him. They asked, “Do you know that the Pharisees were angry when they heard this?”

13 Jesus replied, “They are plants that my Father in heaven has not planted. They will be pulled up by the roots. 14 Leave the Pharisees. They are blind guides. If one blind person leads another blind person, both of them will fall into a pit.”

15 Peter said, “Explain this to us.”

16 “Don’t you understand yet?” Jesus asked them. 17 “Don’t you see? Everything that enters the mouth goes into the stomach. Then it goes out of the body. 18 But the things that come out of a person’s mouth come from the heart. Those are the things that make someone ‘unclean.’ 19 Evil thoughts come out of a person’s heart.

So do murder, adultery, and other sexual sins. And so do stealing, false witness, and telling lies about others. 20 Those are the things that make you 'unclean.' But eating without washing your hands does not make you 'unclean.' "

The Faith of a Woman From Canaan

21 Jesus left Galilee and went to the area of Tyre and Sidon. 22 A woman from Canaan lived near Tyre and Sidon. She came to him and cried out, "Lord! Son of David! Have mercy on me! A demon controls my daughter. She is suffering terribly."

23 Jesus did not say a word. So his disciples came to him. They begged him, "Send her away. She keeps crying out after us."

24 Jesus answered, "I was sent only to the people of Israel. They are like lost sheep."

25 Then the woman fell to her knees in front of him. "Lord! Help me!" she said.

26 He replied, "It is not right to take the children's bread and throw it to the dogs."

27 "Yes it is, Lord," she said. "Even the dogs eat the crumbs that fall from their owner's table."

28 Then Jesus said to her, "Woman, you have great faith! You will be given what you are asking for." And her daughter was healed at that moment.

Jesus Feeds Four Thousand

29 Jesus left there. He walked along the Sea of Galilee. Then he went up on a mountainside and sat down. 30 Large crowds came to him. They brought blind people and those who could not walk. They also brought disabled people, those who could not speak, and many others. They laid them at his feet, and he healed them. 31 The people were amazed. Those who could not speak were speaking. The disabled were made well. Those not able to walk were walking. Those who were blind could see. So the people praised the God of Israel.

32 Then Jesus called for his disciples to come to him. He said, "I feel deep concern for these people. They have already been with me three days. They don't have anything to eat. I don't want to send them away hungry. If I do, they will become too weak on their way home."

33 His disciples answered him. "There is nothing here," they said. "Where could we get enough bread to feed this large crowd?"

34 "How many loaves do you have?" Jesus asked.

"Seven," they replied, "and a few small fish."

35 Jesus told the crowd to sit down on the ground. 36 He took the seven loaves and the fish and gave thanks. Then he broke them and gave them to the disciples. And the disciples passed them out to the people. 37 All of them ate and were satisfied. After that, the disciples picked up seven baskets of leftover pieces. 38 The number of men who ate was 4,000. Women and children also ate. 39 After Jesus had sent the crowd away, he got into the boat. He went to the area near Magadan.

Jesus Is Asked for a Sign

16 The Pharisees and Sadducees came to test Jesus. They asked him to show them a sign from heaven.

2 He replied, "In the evening you look at the sky. You say, 'It will be good weather. The sky is red.' 3 And in the morning you say, 'Today it will be stormy. The sky is red and cloudy.' You know the meaning of what you see in the sky. But you can't understand the signs of what is happening right now. 4 An evil and unfaithful people look for a sign. But none will be given to them except the sign of Jonah." Then Jesus left them and went away.

The Yeast of the Pharisees and Sadducees

5 The disciples crossed over to the other side of the lake. They had forgotten to take bread. 6 "Be careful," Jesus said to them. "Watch out for the yeast of the Pharisees and Sadducees."

7 The disciples talked about this among themselves. They said, "He must be saying this because we didn't bring any bread."

8 Jesus knew what they were saying. So he said, "Your faith is so small! Why are you talking to each other about having no bread? 9 Don't you understand yet? Don't you remember the five loaves for the 5,000? Don't you remember how many baskets of pieces you gathered? 10 Don't you remember the seven loaves for the 4,000? Don't you remember how many baskets of pieces you gathered? 11 How

can you possibly not understand? I wasn't talking to you about bread. But watch out for the yeast of the Pharisees and Sadducees." 12 Then the disciples understood that Jesus was not telling them to watch out for the yeast used in bread. He was warning them against what the Pharisees and Sadducees taught.

Peter Says That Jesus Is the Messiah

13 Jesus went to the area of Caesarea Philippi. There he asked his disciples, "Who do people say the Son of Man is?"

14 They replied, "Some say John the Baptist. Others say Elijah. Still others say Jeremiah, or one of the prophets."

15 "But what about you?" he asked. "Who do you say I am?"

16 Simon Peter answered, "You are the Messiah. You are the Son of the living God."

17 Jesus replied, "Blessed are you, Simon, son of Jonah! No mere human showed this to you. My Father in heaven showed it to you. 18 Here is what I tell you. You are Peter. On this rock I will build my church. The gates of hell will not be strong enough to destroy it. 19 I will give you the keys to the kingdom of heaven. What you lock on earth will be locked in heaven. What you unlock on earth will be unlocked in heaven." 20 Then Jesus ordered his disciples not to tell anyone that he was the Messiah.

Jesus Speaks About His Coming Death

21 From that time on Jesus began to explain to his disciples what would happen to him. He told them he must go to Jerusalem. There he must suffer many things from the elders, the chief priests and the teachers of the law. He must be killed and on the third day rise to life again.

22 Peter took Jesus to one side and began to scold him. "Never, Lord!" he said. "This will never happen to you!"

23 Jesus turned and said to Peter, "Get behind me, Satan! You are standing in my way. You do not have in mind the things God cares about. Instead, you only have in mind the things humans care about."

24 Then Jesus spoke to his disciples. He said, "Whoever wants to be my disciple must say no to themselves. They must pick up their cross and follow me. 25 Whoever wants to save their life will lose it. But whoever loses their life for me will find it. 26 What good is it if someone gains the whole world but loses their soul? Or what can anyone trade for their soul? 27 The Son of Man is going to come in his Father's glory. His angels will come with him. And he will reward everyone in keeping with what they have done.

28 "What I'm about to tell you is true. Some who are standing here will not die before they see the Son of Man coming in his kingdom."

Jesus' Appearance Is Changed

17 After six days Jesus took Peter, James, and John the brother of James with him. He led them up a high mountain. They were all alone. 2 There in front of them his appearance was changed. His face shone like the sun. His clothes became as white as the light. 3 Just then Moses and Elijah appeared in front of them. Moses and Elijah were talking with Jesus.

4 Peter said to Jesus, "Lord, it is good for us to be here. If you wish, I will put up three shelters. One will be for you, one for Moses, and one for Elijah."

5 While Peter was still speaking, a bright cloud covered them. A voice from the cloud said, "This is my Son, and I love him. I am very pleased with him. Listen to him!"

6 When the disciples heard this, they were terrified. They fell with their faces to the ground. 7 But Jesus came and touched them. "Get up," he said. "Don't be afraid." 8 When they looked up, they saw no one except Jesus.

9 They came down the mountain. On the way down, Jesus told them what to do. "Don't tell anyone what you have seen," he said. "Wait until the Son of Man has been raised from the dead."

10 The disciples asked him, "Why do the teachers of the law say that Elijah has to come first?"

11 Jesus replied, "That's right. Elijah is supposed to come and make all things new again. 12 But I tell you, Elijah has already come. People didn't recognize him. They have done to him everything they wanted to do. In the same way, they are going to make the Son of Man suffer." 13 Then the disciples understood that Jesus was talking to them about John the Baptist.

Jesus Heals a Boy Who Is Controlled by a Demon

14 When they came near the crowd, a
man approached Jesus. He got on his
knees in front of him. 15 "Lord," he said,
"have mercy on my son. He shakes wildly
and suffers a great deal. He often falls into
the fire or into the water. 16 I brought him
to your disciples. But they couldn't heal
him."

17 "You unbelieving and evil people!" Jesus replied. "How long do I have
to stay with you? How long do I have to
put up with you? Bring the boy here to
me." 18 Jesus ordered the demon to leave
the boy, and it came out of him. He was
healed at that moment.

19 Then the disciples came to Jesus in
private. They asked, "Why couldn't we
drive out the demon?"

20-21 He replied, "Because your faith is much too small. What I'm about to tell you is true. If you have faith as small as a mustard seed, it is enough. You can say to this mountain, 'Move from here to there.' And it will move. Nothing will be impossible for you."

Jesus Speaks a Second Time About His Coming Death

22 They came together in Galilee. Then
Jesus said to them, "The Son of Man is going to be handed over to men. 23 They will
kill him. On the third day he will rise from the dead." Then the disciples were filled with deep sadness.

Jesus Pays the Temple Tax

24 Jesus and his disciples arrived in Capernaum. There the people who collect the temple tax came to Peter. They asked him, "Doesn't your teacher pay the temple tax?"

25 "Yes, he does," he replied.

When Peter came into the house, Jesus spoke first. "What do you think, Simon?" he asked. "Who do the kings of the earth collect taxes and fees from? Do they collect them from their own children or from others?"

26 "From others," Peter answered.

"Then the children don't have to pay,"
Jesus said to him. 27 "But we don't want to
make them angry. So go to the lake and throw out your fishing line. Take the first fish you catch. Open its mouth. There you will find the exact coin you need. Take it and give it to them for my tax and yours."

Who Is the Most Important Person in the Kingdom?

18 At that time the disciples came to Jesus. They asked him, "Then who is the most important person in the kingdom of heaven?"

2 Jesus called a little child over to him.
He had the child stand among them.
3 Jesus said, "What I'm about to tell you
is true. You need to change and become
like little children. If you don't, you will
never enter the kingdom of heaven. 4 Anyone who takes the humble position of this
child is the most important in the kingdom of heaven. 5 Anyone who welcomes
a little child like this one in my name welcomes me.

Do Not Cause People to Sin

6 "What if someone causes one of these
little ones who believe in me to sin? If they
do, it would be better for them to have a
large millstone hung around their neck
and be drowned at the bottom of the sea.
7 How terrible it will be for the world because of the things that cause people to
sin! Things like that must come. But how
terrible for the person who causes them!
8 If your hand or foot causes you to sin, cut
it off and throw it away. It would be better to enter the kingdom of heaven with
only one hand than go into hell with two
hands. It would be better to enter the
kingdom of heaven with only one foot
than go into hell with two feet. In hell
the fire burns forever. 9 If your eye causes
you to sin, poke it out and throw it away.
It would be better to enter the kingdom of heaven with one eye than to have two eyes and be thrown into the fire of hell.

The Story of the Wandering Sheep

10-11 "See that you don't look down on one of these little ones. Here is what I tell you. Their angels in heaven are always with my Father who is in heaven.

12 "What do you think? Suppose a man
owns 100 sheep and one of them wanders
away. Won't he leave the 99 sheep on the
hills? Won't he go and look for the one
that wandered off? 13 What I'm about to
tell you is true. If he finds that sheep, he
is happier about the one than about the

99 that didn't wander off. 14 It is the same
with your Father in heaven. He does not
want any of these little ones to die.

When Someone Sins Against You

15 "If your brother or sister sins against
you, go to them. Tell them what they did
wrong. Keep it between the two of you.
If they listen to you, you have won them
back. 16 But what if they won't listen to
you? Then take one or two others with
you. Scripture says, 'Every matter must be
proved by the words of two or three witnesses.' (Deuteronomy 19:15) 17 But what if
they also refuse to listen to the witnesses?
Then tell it to the church. And what if they
refuse to listen even to the church? Then
don't treat them as a brother or sister.
Treat them as you would treat an ungodly
person or a tax collector.

18 "What I'm about to tell you is true.
What you lock on earth will be locked in
heaven. What you unlock on earth will be
unlocked in heaven.

19 "Again, here is what I tell you. Suppose two of you on earth agree about anything you ask for. My Father in heaven will
do it for you. 20 Where two or three people
gather in my name, I am there with them."

The Servant Who Had No Mercy

21 Peter came to Jesus. He asked, "Lord,
how many times should I forgive my
brother or sister who sins against me? Up
to seven times?"

22 Jesus answered, "I tell you, not seven
times, but 77 times.

23 "The kingdom of heaven is like a king
who wanted to collect all the money his
servants owed him. 24 As the king began to
do it, a man who owed him 10,000 bags of
gold was brought to him. 25 The man was
not able to pay. So his master gave an order. The man, his wife, his children, and
all he owned had to be sold to pay back
what he owed.

26 "Then the servant fell on his knees in
front of him. 'Give me time,' he begged.
'I'll pay everything back.' 27 His master
felt sorry for him. He forgave him what he
owed and let him go.

28 "But then that servant went out and
found one of the other servants who owed
him 100 silver coins. He grabbed him and
began to choke him. 'Pay back what you
owe me!' he said.

29 "The other servant fell on his knees.
'Give me time,' he begged him. 'I'll pay it
back.'

30 "But the first servant refused. Instead,
he went and had the man thrown into
prison. The man would be held there until he could pay back what he owed. 31 The
other servants saw what had happened
and were very angry. They went and told
their master everything that had happened.

32 "Then the master called the first servant in. 'You evil servant,' he said. 'I forgave all that you owed me because you
begged me to. 33 Shouldn't you have had
mercy on the other servant just as I had
mercy on you?' 34 In anger his master
handed him over to the jailers. He would
be punished until he paid back everything he owed.

35 "This is how my Father in heaven will
treat each of you unless you forgive your
brother or sister from your heart."

Jesus Teaches About Divorce

19 When Jesus finished saying these
things, he left Galilee. He went into
the area of Judea on the other side of the
Jordan River. 2 Large crowds followed
him. He healed them there.

3 Some Pharisees came to test Jesus.
They asked, "Does the Law allow a man
to divorce his wife for any reason at all?"

4 Jesus replied, "Haven't you read that
in the beginning the Creator 'made them
male and female'? (Genesis 1:27) 5 He said,
'That's why a man will leave his father and
mother and be joined to his wife. The two
will become one.' (Genesis 2:24) 6 They are
no longer two, but one. So no one should
separate what God has joined together."

7 They asked, "Then why did Moses
command that a man can give his wife a
letter of divorce and send her away?"

8 Jesus replied, "Moses let you divorce
your wives because you were stubborn.
But it was not this way from the beginning. 9 Here is what I tell you. Anyone who
divorces his wife and marries another
woman commits adultery. A man may
divorce his wife only if she has not been
faithful to him."

10 Here is what the disciples said to him.
"If that's the way it is between a husband
and wife, it is better not to get married."

11 Jesus replied, "Not everyone can ac-

cept the idea of staying single. Only those who have been helped to live without getting married can accept it. 12 Some men are not able to have children because they were born that way. Some have been made that way by other people. Others have chosen to live that way in order to serve the kingdom of heaven. The one who can accept this should accept it."

Little Children Are Brought to Jesus

13 Some people brought little children to Jesus. They wanted him to place his hands on the children and pray for them. But the disciples told them not to do it.

14 Jesus said, "Let the little children come to me. Don't keep them away. The kingdom of heaven belongs to people like them." 15 Jesus placed his hands on them to bless them. Then he went on from there.

Rich People and the Kingdom of God

16 Just then, a man came up to Jesus. He asked, "Teacher, what good thing must I do to receive eternal life?"

17 "Why do you ask me about what is good?" Jesus replied. "There is only one who is good. If you want to enter the kingdom, obey the commandments."

18 "Which ones?" the man asked.

Jesus said, " 'Do not murder. Do not commit adultery. Do not steal. Do not be a false witness. 19 Honor your father and mother.' (Exodus 20:12–16; Deuteronomy 5:16–20) And 'love your neighbor as you love yourself.' " (Leviticus 19:18)

20 "I have obeyed all those commandments," the young man said. "What else do I need to do?"

21 Jesus answered, "If you want to be perfect, go and sell everything you have. Give the money to those who are poor. You will have treasure in heaven. Then come and follow me."

22 When the young man heard this, he went away sad. He was very rich.

23 Then Jesus said to his disciples, "What I'm about to tell you is true. It is hard for someone who is rich to enter the kingdom of heaven. 24 Again I tell you, it is hard for a camel to go through the eye of a needle. But it is even harder for someone who is rich to enter the kingdom of God."

25 When the disciples heard this, they were really amazed. They asked, "Then who can be saved?"

26 Jesus looked at them and said, "With people, this is impossible. But with God, all things are possible."

27 Peter answered him, "We have left everything to follow you! What reward will be given to us?"

28 "What I'm about to tell you is true," Jesus said to them. "When all things are made new, the Son of Man will sit on his glorious throne. Then you who have followed me will also sit on 12 thrones. You will judge the 12 tribes of Israel. 29 Suppose anyone has left houses, brothers or sisters, father or mother, husband or wife, children or fields because of me. Anyone who has done that will receive 100 times as much. They will also receive eternal life. 30 But many who are first will be last. And many who are last will be first.

The Story of the Workers in the Vineyard

20 "The kingdom of heaven is like a man who owned land. He went out early in the morning to hire workers for his vineyard. 2 He agreed to give them the usual pay for a day's work. Then he sent them into his vineyard.

3 "About nine o'clock in the morning he went out again. He saw others standing in the market doing nothing. 4 He told them, 'You also go and work in my vineyard. I'll pay you what is right.' 5 So they went.

"He went out again about noon and at three o'clock and did the same thing. 6 About five o'clock he went out and found still others standing around. He asked them, 'Why have you been standing here all day long doing nothing?'

7 " 'Because no one has hired us,' they answered.

"He said to them, 'You also go and work in my vineyard.'

8 "When evening came, the owner of the vineyard spoke to the person who was in charge of the workers. He said, 'Call the workers and give them their pay. Begin with the last ones I hired. Then go on to the first ones.'

9 "The workers who were hired about five o'clock came. Each received the usual day's pay. 10 So when those who were hired first came, they expected to receive more. But each of them also received the usual day's pay. 11 When they received it,

they began to complain about the owner.
12 ‘These people who were hired last
worked only one hour,’ they said. ‘You
have paid them the same as us. We have
done most of the work and have been in
the hot sun all day.’
13 “The owner answered one of them.
‘Friend,’ he said, ‘I’m being fair to you.
Didn’t you agree to work for the usual
day’s pay? 14 Take your money and go. I
want to give the one I hired last the same
pay I gave you. 15 Don’t I have the right to
do what I want with my own money? Do
you feel cheated because I gave so freely
to the others?’
16 “So those who are last will be first.
And those who are first will be last.”

Jesus Speaks a Third Time About His Coming Death

17 Jesus was going up to Jerusalem. On
the way, he took his 12 disciples to one
side to talk to them. 18 “We are going up
to Jerusalem,” he said. “The Son of Man
will be handed over to the chief priests
and the teachers of the law. They will sentence him to death. 19 Then they will hand
him over to the Gentiles. The people will
make fun of him and whip him. They will
nail him to a cross. On the third day, he
will rise from the dead!”

A Mother Asks a Favor of Jesus

20 The mother of Zebedee’s sons came
to Jesus. Her sons came with her. Getting
on her knees, she asked a favor of him.
21 “What do you want?” Jesus asked.
She said, “Promise me that one of my
two sons may sit at your right hand in
your kingdom. Promise that the other one
may sit at your left hand.”
22 “You don’t know what you’re asking
for,” Jesus said to them. “Can you drink
the cup of suffering I am going to drink?”
“We can,” they answered.
23 Jesus said to them, “You will certainly
drink from my cup. But it is not for me to
say who will sit at my right or left hand.
These places belong to those my Father
has prepared them for.”
24 The other ten disciples heard about
this. They became angry at the two brothers. 25 Jesus called them together. He said,
“You know about the rulers of the Gentiles. They hold power over their people.
Their high officials order them around.
26 Don’t be like that. Instead, anyone who
wants to be important among you must
be your servant. 27 And anyone who wants
to be first must be your slave. 28 Be like
the Son of Man. He did not come to be
served. Instead, he came to serve others.
He came to give his life as the price for
setting many people free.”

Two Blind Men Receive Their Sight

29 Jesus and his disciples were leaving Jericho. A large crowd followed him.
30 Two blind men were sitting by the side
of the road. They heard that Jesus was going by. So they shouted, “Lord! Son of David! Have mercy on us!”
31 The crowd commanded them to stop.
They told them to be quiet. But the two
men shouted even louder, “Lord! Son of
David! Have mercy on us!”
32 Jesus stopped and called out to them.
“What do you want me to do for you?” he
asked.
33 “Lord,” they answered, “we want to be
able to see.”
34 Jesus felt deep concern for them. He
touched their eyes. Right away they could
see. And they followed him.

Jesus Comes to Jerusalem as King

21 As they all approached Jerusalem,
they came to Bethphage. It was on
the Mount of Olives. Jesus sent out two
disciples. 2 He said to them, “Go to the
village ahead of you. As soon as you get
there, you will find a donkey tied up. Her
colt will be with her. Untie them and bring
them to me. 3 If anyone says anything to
you, say that the Lord needs them. The
owner will send them right away.”
4 This took place so that what was spoken through the prophet would come
true. It says,

5 “Say to the city of Zion,
‘See, your king comes to you.
He is gentle and riding on a donkey.
He is riding on a donkey’s colt.’ ”
(Zechariah 9:9)

6 The disciples went and did what Jesus
told them to do. 7 They brought the donkey and the colt. They placed their coats
on them for Jesus to sit on. 8 A very large
crowd spread their coats on the road.
Others cut branches from the trees and
spread them on the road. 9 Some of the

people went ahead of him, and some followed. They all shouted,

"Hosanna to the Son of David!"

"Blessed is the one who comes
in the name of the Lord!"
(Psalm 118:26)

"Hosanna in the highest heaven!"

10 When Jesus entered Jerusalem, the
whole city was stirred up. The people
asked, "Who is this?"
11 The crowds answered, "This is Jesus.
He is the prophet from Nazareth in Galilee."

Jesus Clears Out the Temple

12 Jesus entered the temple courtyard.
He began to drive out all those who were
buying and selling there. He turned over
the tables of the people who were exchanging money. He also turned over the
benches of those who were selling doves.
13 He said to them, "It is written that the
Lord said, 'My house will be called a
house where people can pray.' (Isaiah 56:7)
But you are making it 'a den for robbers.'"
(Jeremiah 7:11)
14 Blind people and those who were disabled came to Jesus at the temple. There
he healed them. 15 The chief priests and
the teachers of the law saw the wonderful
things he did. They also saw the children
in the temple courtyard shouting, "Hosanna to the Son of David!" But when they
saw all this, they became angry.
16 "Do you hear what these children are
saying?" they asked him.
"Yes," replied Jesus. "Haven't you ever
read about it in Scripture? It says,

"'Lord, you have made sure that
children and infants
praise you.'" (Psalm 8:2)

17 Then Jesus left the people and went
out of the city to Bethany. He spent the
night there.

Jesus Makes a Fig Tree Dry Up

18 Early in the morning, Jesus was on his
way back to Jerusalem. He was hungry.
19 He saw a fig tree by the road. He went up
to it but found nothing on it except leaves.
Then he said to it, "May you never bear
fruit again!" Right away the tree dried up.
20 When the disciples saw this, they
were amazed. "How did the fig tree dry up
so quickly?" they asked.
21 Jesus replied, "What I'm about to tell
you is true. You must have faith and not
doubt. Then you can do what was done to
the fig tree. And you can say to this mountain, 'Go and throw yourself into the sea.'
It will be done. 22 If you believe, you will
receive what you ask for when you pray."

The Authority of Jesus Is Questioned

23 Jesus entered the temple courtyard.
While he was teaching there, the chief
priests and the elders of the people came
to him. "By what authority are you doing
these things?" they asked. "Who gave you
this authority?"
24 Jesus replied, "I will also ask you one
question. If you answer me, I will tell you
by what authority I am doing these things.
25 Where did John's baptism come from?
Was it from heaven? Or did it come from
human authority?"
They talked to one another about it.
They said, "If we say, 'From heaven,' he
will ask, 'Then why didn't you believe
him?' 26 But what if we say, 'From human authority'? We are afraid of the people. Everyone believes that John was a
prophet."
27 So they answered Jesus, "We don't
know."
Jesus said, "Then I won't tell you by
what authority I am doing these things
either.

The Story of the Two Sons

28 "What do you think about this? A
man had two sons. He went to the first
and said, 'Son, go and work today in the
vineyard.'
29 "'I will not,' the son answered. But
later he changed his mind and went.
30 "Then the father went to the other
son. He said the same thing. The son answered, 'I will, sir.' But he did not go.
31 "Which of the two sons did what his
father wanted?"
"The first," they answered.
Jesus said to them, "What I'm about to
tell you is true. Tax collectors and prostitutes will enter the kingdom of God ahead
of you. 32 John came to show you the right
way to live. And you did not believe him.
But the tax collectors and the prostitutes
did. You saw this. But even then you did

not turn away from your sins and believe
him.

The Story of the Renters

33 “Listen to another story. A man who
owned some land planted a vineyard.
He put a wall around it. He dug a pit for
a winepress in it. He also built a lookout
tower. He rented the vineyard out to some
farmers. Then he moved to another place.
34 When harvest time approached, he sent
his slaves to the renters. He told the slaves
to collect his share of the fruit.

35 “But the renters grabbed his slaves.
They beat one of them. They killed another. They threw stones at the third to kill
him. 36 Then the man sent other slaves to
the renters. He sent more than he did the
first time. The renters treated them the
same way. 37 Last of all, he sent his son to
them. ‘They will respect my son,’ he said.

38 “But the renters saw the son coming.
They said to one another, ‘This is the one
who will receive all the owner’s property
someday. Come, let’s kill him. Then everything will be ours.’ 39 So they took him
and threw him out of the vineyard. Then
they killed him.

40 “When the owner of the vineyard
comes back, what will he do to those renters?”

41 “He will destroy those evil people,”
they replied. “Then he will rent the vineyard out to other renters. They will give
him his share of the crop at harvest time.”

42 Jesus said to them, “Haven’t you ever
read what the Scriptures say,

“ ‘The stone the builders didn’t
accept
has become the most important
stone of all.
The Lord has done it.
It is wonderful in our eyes’?
(Psalm 118:22,23)

43 “So here is what I tell you. The kingdom of God will be taken away from you.
It will be given to people who will produce
its fruit. 44 Anyone who falls on that stone
will be broken to pieces. But the stone will
crush anyone it falls on.”

45 The chief priests and the Pharisees
heard Jesus’ stories. They knew he was
talking about them. 46 So they looked for a
way to arrest him. But they were afraid of
the crowd. The people believed that Jesus
was a prophet.

The Story of the Wedding Dinner

22 Jesus told them more stories. He
said, 2 “Here is what the kingdom of
heaven is like. A king prepared a wedding
dinner for his son. 3 He sent his slaves to
those who had been invited to the dinner.
The slaves told them to come. But they refused.

4 “Then he sent some more slaves. He
said, ‘Tell those who were invited that I
have prepared my dinner. I have killed my
oxen and my fattest cattle. Everything is
ready. Come to the wedding dinner.’

5 “But the people paid no attention.
One went away to his field. Another went
away to his business. 6 The rest grabbed
his slaves. They treated them badly and
then killed them. 7 The king became very
angry. He sent his army to destroy them.
They killed those murderers and burned
their city.

8 “Then the king said to his slaves, ‘The
wedding dinner is ready. But those I invited were not fit to come. 9 So go to the
street corners. Invite to the dinner anyone
you can find.’ 10 So the slaves went out into
the streets. They gathered all the people
they could find, the bad as well as the
good. Soon the wedding hall was filled
with guests.

11 “The king came in to see the guests.
He noticed a man there who was not
wearing wedding clothes. 12 ‘Friend,’ he
asked, ‘how did you get in here without wedding clothes?’ The man couldn’t
think of anything to say.

13 “Then the king told his slaves, ‘Tie up
his hands and feet. Throw him outside
into the darkness. Out there people will
weep and grind their teeth.’

14 “Many are invited, but few are chosen.”

Is It Right to Pay the Royal Tax to Caesar?

15 The Pharisees went out. They made
plans to trap Jesus with his own words.
16 They sent their followers to him. They
sent the Herodians with them. “Teacher,”
they said, “we know that you are a man of
honor. You teach the way of God truthfully. You don’t let others tell you what
to do or say. You don’t care how important they are. 17 Tell us then, what do you

think? Is it right to pay the royal tax to Caesar or not?"

18 But Jesus knew their evil plans. He said, "You pretenders! Why are you trying to trap me? 19 Show me the coin people use for paying the tax." They brought him a silver coin. 20 He asked them, "Whose picture is this? And whose words?"

21 "Caesar's," they replied.

Then he said to them, "So give back to Caesar what belongs to Caesar. And give back to God what belongs to God."

22 When they heard this, they were amazed. So they left him and went away.

Marriage When the Dead Rise

23 That same day the Sadducees came to Jesus with a question. They do not believe that people rise from the dead. 24 "Teacher," they said, "here is what Moses told us. If a man dies without having children, his brother must get married to the widow. He must provide children to carry on his brother's name. 25 There were seven brothers among us. The first one got married and died. Since he had no children, he left his wife to his brother. 26 The same thing happened to the second and third brothers. It happened right on down to the seventh brother. 27 Finally, the woman died. 28 Now then, when the dead rise, whose wife will she be? All seven of them were married to her."

29 Jesus replied, "You are mistaken, because you do not know the Scriptures. And you do not know the power of God. 30 When the dead rise, they won't get married. And their parents won't give them to be married. They will be like the angels in heaven. 31 What about the dead rising? Haven't you read what God said to you? 32 He said, 'I am the God of Abraham. I am the God of Isaac. And I am the God of Jacob.' (Exodus 3:6) He is not the God of the dead. He is the God of the living."

33 When the crowds heard this, they were amazed by what he taught.

The Most Important Commandment

34 The Pharisees heard that the Sadducees weren't able to answer Jesus. So the Pharisees got together. 35 One of them was an authority on the law. So he tested Jesus with a question. 36 "Teacher," he asked, "which is the most important commandment in the Law?"

37 Jesus replied, " 'Love the Lord your God with all your heart and with all your soul. Love him with all your mind.' (Deuteronomy 6:5) 38 This is the first and most important commandment. 39 And the second is like it. 'Love your neighbor as you love yourself.' (Leviticus 19:18) 40 Everything that is written in the Law and the Prophets is based on these two commandments."

Whose Son Is the Messiah?

41 The Pharisees were gathered together. Jesus asked them, 42 "What do you think about the Messiah? Whose son is he?"

"The son of David," they replied.

43 He said to them, "Then why does David call him 'Lord'? The Holy Spirit spoke through David himself. David said,

44 " 'The Lord said to my Lord,
"Sit at my right hand
until I put your enemies
under your control." ' (Psalm 110:1)

45 So if David calls him 'Lord,' how can he be David's son?" 46 No one could give any answer to him. From that day on, no one dared to ask him any more questions.

A Warning Against Doing Things for the Wrong Reasons

23 Jesus spoke to the crowds and to his disciples. 2 "The teachers of the law and the Pharisees sit in Moses' seat," he said. 3 "So you must be careful to do everything they say. But don't do what they do. They don't practice what they preach. 4 They tie up heavy loads that are hard to carry. Then they put them on other people's shoulders. But they themselves aren't willing to lift a finger to move them.

5 "Everything they do is done for others to see. On their foreheads and arms they wear little boxes that hold Scripture verses. They make the boxes very wide. And they make the tassels on their coats very long. 6 They love to sit down in the place of honor at dinners. They also love to have the most important seats in the synagogues. 7 They love to be greeted with respect in the markets. They love it when people call them 'Rabbi.'

8 "But you shouldn't be called 'Rabbi.' You have only one Teacher, and you are all brothers. 9 Do not call anyone on earth 'father.' You have one Father, and he is

in heaven. [10]You shouldn't be called 'teacher.' You have one Teacher, and he is the Messiah. [11]The most important person among you will be your servant. [12]People who lift themselves up will be made humble. And people who make themselves humble will be lifted up.

How Terrible for the Teachers of the Law and the Pharisees

[13-14]"How terrible it will be for you, teachers of the law and Pharisees! You pretenders! You shut the door of the kingdom of heaven in people's faces. You yourselves do not enter. And you will not let those enter who are trying to.

[15]"How terrible for you, teachers of the law and Pharisees! You pretenders! You travel everywhere to win one person to your faith. Then you make them twice as much a child of hell as you are.

[16]"How terrible for you, blind guides! You say, 'If anyone makes a promise in the name of the temple, it means nothing. But anyone who makes a promise in the name of the gold of the temple must keep that promise.' [17]You are blind and foolish! Which is more important? Is it the gold? Or is it the temple that makes the gold holy? [18]You also say, 'If anyone makes a promise in the name of the altar, it means nothing. But anyone who makes a promise in the name of the gift on the altar must keep that promise.' [19]You are blind! Which is more important? Is it the gift? Or is it the altar that makes the gift holy? [20]So anyone making a promise in the name of the altar makes a promise in the name of it and everything on it. [21]And anyone making a promise in the name of the temple makes a promise in the name of it and the one who lives in it. [22]And anyone making a promise in the name of heaven makes a promise in the name of God's throne and the one who sits on it.

[23]"How terrible for you, teachers of the law and Pharisees! You pretenders! You give God a tenth of your spices, like mint, dill and cumin. But you have not practiced the more important things of the law, which are fairness, mercy and faithfulness. You should have practiced the last things without failing to do the first. [24]You blind guides! You remove the smallest insect from your food. But you swallow a whole camel!

[25]"How terrible for you, teachers of the law and Pharisees! You pretenders! You clean the outside of a cup and dish. But on the inside you are full of greed. You only want to satisfy yourselves. [26]Blind Pharisee! First clean the inside of the cup and dish. Then the outside will also be clean.

[27]"How terrible for you, teachers of the law and Pharisees! You pretenders! You are like tombs that are painted white. They look beautiful on the outside. But on the inside they are full of the bones of the dead. They are also full of other things that are not pure and 'clean.' [28]It is the same with you. On the outside you seem to be doing what is right. But on the inside you are full of what is wrong. You pretend to be what you are not.

[29]"How terrible for you, teachers of the law and Pharisees! You pretenders! You build tombs for the prophets. You decorate the graves of the godly. [30]And you say, 'If we had lived in the days of those who lived before us, we wouldn't have done what they did. We wouldn't have helped to kill the prophets.' [31]So you are witnesses against yourselves. You admit that you are the children of those who murdered the prophets. [32]So go ahead and finish the sins that those who lived before you started!

[33]"You nest of poisonous snakes! How will you escape from being sentenced to hell? [34]So I am sending you prophets, wise people, and teachers. You will kill some of them. You will nail some to a cross. Others you will whip in your synagogues. You will chase them from town to town. [35]So you will pay for all the godly people's blood spilled on earth. I mean from the blood of godly Abel to the blood of Zechariah, the son of Berekiah. Zechariah was the one you murdered between the temple and the altar. [36]What I'm about to tell you is true. All this will happen to those who are now living.

[37]"Jerusalem! Jerusalem! You kill the prophets and throw stones in order to kill those who are sent to you. Many times I have wanted to gather your people together. I have wanted to be like a hen who gathers her chicks under her wings. And you would not let me! [38]Look, your house is left empty. [39]I tell you, you will not see me again until you say, 'Blessed is the one

who comes in the name of the Lord.'"
(Psalm 118:26)

When the Temple Will Be Destroyed and the Signs of the End

24 Jesus left the temple. He was walking away when his disciples came
up to him. They wanted to call his attention to the temple buildings. 2 "Do you see
all these things?" Jesus asked. "What I'm
about to tell you is true. Not one stone
here will be left on top of another. Every
stone will be thrown down."
3 Jesus was sitting on the Mount of Olives. There the disciples came to him in
private. "Tell us," they said. "When will
this happen? And what will be the sign of
your coming? What will be the sign of the
end?"
4 Jesus answered, "Keep watch! Be
careful that no one fools you. 5 Many will
come in my name. They will claim, 'I am
the Messiah!' They will fool many people.
6 You will hear about wars. You will also
hear people talking about future wars.
Don't be alarmed. Those things must
happen. But the end still isn't here. 7 Nation will fight against nation. Kingdom
will fight against kingdom. People will
go hungry. There will be earthquakes in
many places. 8 All these are the beginning
of birth pains.
9 "Then people will hand you over to be
treated badly and killed. All nations will
hate you because of me. 10 At that time,
many will turn away from their faith. They
will hate each other. They will hand each
other over to their enemies. 11 Many false
prophets will appear. They will fool many
people. 12 Because evil will grow, most
people's love will grow cold. 13 But the one
who remains strong in the faith will be
saved. 14 This good news of the kingdom
will be preached in the whole world. It
will be a witness to all nations. Then the
end will come.
15 "The prophet Daniel spoke about
'the hated thing that destroys.' (Daniel 9:27;
11:31; 12:11) Someday you will see it standing in the holy place. The reader should
understand this. 16 Then those who are in
Judea should escape to the mountains.
17 No one on the housetop should go down
into the house to take anything out. 18 No
one in the field should go back to get their
coat. 19 How awful it will be in those days
for pregnant women! How awful for nursing mothers! 20 Pray that you will not have
to escape in winter or on the Sabbath day.
21 There will be terrible suffering in those
days. It will be worse than any other from
the beginning of the world until now. And
there will never be anything like it again.
22 "If the time had not been cut short,
no one would live. But because of God's
chosen people, it will be shortened. 23 At
that time someone may say to you, 'Look!
Here is the Messiah!' Or, 'There he is!' Do
not believe it. 24 False messiahs and false
prophets will appear. They will do great
signs and miracles. They will try to fool
God's chosen people if possible. 25 See, I
have told you ahead of time.
26 "So if anyone tells you, 'He is a long
way out in the desert,' do not go out there.
Or if anyone says, 'He is deep inside the
house,' do not believe it. 27 Lightning that
comes from the east can be seen in the
west. It will be the same when the Son
of Man comes. 28 The vultures will gather
wherever there is a dead body.
29 "Right after the terrible suffering of
those days,

"'The sun will be darkened.
  The moon will not shine.
The stars will fall from the sky.
  The heavenly bodies will be
    shaken.' (Isaiah 13:10; 34:4)

30 "Then the sign of the Son of Man will
appear in heaven. At that time, all the
peoples of the earth will mourn. They
will mourn when they see the Son of Man
coming on the clouds of heaven. He will
come with power and great glory. 31 He
will send his angels with a loud trumpet
call. They will gather his chosen people
from all four directions. They will bring
them from one end of the heavens to the
other.
32 "Learn a lesson from the fig tree. As
soon as its twigs get tender and its leaves
come out, you know that summer is near.
33 In the same way, when you see all these
things happening, you know that the end
is near. It is right at the door. 34 What I'm
about to tell you is true. The people living
now will certainly not pass away until all
these things have happened. 35 Heaven
and earth will pass away. But my words
will never pass away.

The Day and Hour Are Not Known

36 “But no one knows about that day
or hour. Not even the angels in heaven
know. The Son does not know. Only the
Father knows. 37 Remember how it was
in the days of Noah. It will be the same
when the Son of Man comes. 38 In the
days before the flood, people were eating and drinking. They were getting married. They were giving their daughters
to be married. They did all those things
right up to the day Noah entered the ark.
39 They knew nothing about what would
happen until the flood came and took
them all away. That is how it will be when
the Son of Man comes. 40 Two men will
be in the field. One will be taken and the
other left. 41 Two women will be grinding
with a hand mill. One will be taken and
the other left.

42 “So keep watch. You do not know
on what day your Lord will come. 43 You
must understand something. Suppose
the owner of the house knew what time
of night the robber was coming. Then
he would have kept watch. He would not
have let his house be broken into. 44 So
you also must be ready. The Son of Man
will come at an hour when you don’t expect him.

45 “Suppose a master puts one of his
slaves in charge of the other slaves in his
house. The slave’s job is to give them their
food at the right time. The master wants
a faithful and wise slave for this. 46 It will
be good for the slave if the master finds
him doing his job when the master returns. 47 What I’m about to tell you is true.
The master will put that slave in charge of
everything he owns. 48 But suppose that
slave is evil. Suppose he says to himself,
‘My master is staying away a long time.’
49 Suppose he begins to beat the other
slaves. And suppose he eats and drinks
with those who drink too much. 50 The
master of that slave will come back on a
day the slave doesn’t expect him. He will
return at an hour the slave does not know.
51 Then the master will cut him to pieces.
He will send him to the place where pretenders go. There people will weep and
grind their teeth.

The Story of Ten Bridesmaids

25 “Here is what the kingdom of
heaven will be like at that time. Ten
bridesmaids took their lamps and went
out to meet the groom. 2 Five of them were
foolish. Five were wise. 3 The foolish ones
took their lamps but didn’t take any olive
oil with them. 4 The wise ones took oil in
jars along with their lamps. 5 The groom
did not come for a long time. So the
bridesmaids all grew tired and fell asleep.

6 “At midnight someone cried out,
‘Here’s the groom! Come out to meet
him!’

7 “Then all the bridesmaids woke up
and got their lamps ready. 8 The foolish
ones said to the wise ones, ‘Give us some
of your oil. Our lamps are going out.’

9 “ ‘No,’ they replied. ‘There may not be
enough for all of us. Instead, go to those
who sell oil. Buy some for yourselves.’

10 “So they went to buy the oil. But while
they were on their way, the groom arrived. The bridesmaids who were ready
went in with him to the wedding dinner.
Then the door was shut.

11 “Later, the other bridesmaids also
came. ‘Sir! Sir!’ they said. ‘Open the door
for us!’

12 “But he replied, ‘What I’m about to
tell you is true. I don’t know you.’

13 “So keep watch. You do not know the
day or the hour that the groom will come.

The Story of Three Slaves

14 “Again, here is what the kingdom of
heaven will be like. A man was going on
a journey. He sent for his slaves and put
them in charge of his money. 15 He gave
five bags of gold to one. He gave two
bags to another. And he gave one bag
to the third. The man gave each slave
the amount of money he knew the slave
could take care of. Then he went on his
journey. 16 The slave who had received
five bags of gold went at once and put
his money to work. He earned five bags
more. 17 The one with the two bags of gold
earned two more. 18 But the man who had
received one bag went and dug a hole in
the ground. He hid his master’s money
in it.

19 “After a long time the master of those
slaves returned. He wanted to collect
all the money they had earned. 20 The
man who had received five bags of gold
brought the other five. ‘Master,’ he said,
‘you trusted me with five bags of gold.
See, I have earned five more.’

21 "His master replied, 'You have done well, good and faithful slave! You have been faithful with a few things. I will put you in charge of many things. Come and share your master's happiness!'

22 "The man with two bags of gold also came. 'Master,' he said, 'you trusted me with two bags of gold. See, I have earned two more.'

23 "His master replied, 'You have done well, good and faithful slave! You have been faithful with a few things. I will put you in charge of many things. Come and share your master's happiness!'

24 "Then the man who had received one bag of gold came. 'Master,' he said, 'I knew that you are a hard man. You harvest where you have not planted. You gather crops where you have not scattered seed. 25 So I was afraid. I went out and hid your gold in the ground. See, here is what belongs to you.'

26 "His master replied, 'You evil, lazy slave! So you knew that I harvest where I have not planted? You knew that I gather crops where I have not scattered seed? 27 Well then, you should have put my money in the bank. When I returned, I would have received it back with interest.'

28 "Then his master commanded the other slaves, 'Take the bag of gold from him. Give it to the one who has ten bags. 29 Everyone who has will be given more. They will have more than enough. And what about anyone who doesn't have? Even what they have will be taken away from them. 30 Throw that worthless slave outside. There in the darkness, people will weep and grind their teeth.'

The Sheep and the Goats

31 "The Son of Man will come in all his glory. All the angels will come with him. Then he will sit in glory on his throne. 32 All the nations will be gathered in front of him. He will separate the people into two groups. He will be like a shepherd who separates the sheep from the goats. 33 He will put the sheep to his right and the goats to his left.

34 "Then the King will speak to those on his right. He will say, 'My Father has blessed you. Come and take what is yours. It is the kingdom prepared for you since the world was created. 35 I was hungry. And you gave me something to eat. I was thirsty. And you gave me something to drink. I was a stranger. And you invited me in. 36 I needed clothes. And you gave them to me. I was sick. And you took care of me. I was in prison. And you came to visit me.'

37 "Then the people who have done what is right will answer him. 'Lord,' they will ask, 'when did we see you hungry and feed you? When did we see you thirsty and give you something to drink? 38 When did we see you as a stranger and invite you in? When did we see you needing clothes and give them to you? 39 When did we see you sick or in prison and go to visit you?'

40 "The King will reply, 'What I'm about to tell you is true. Anything you did for one of the least important of these brothers and sisters of mine, you did for me.'

41 "Then he will say to those on his left, 'You are cursed! Go away from me into the fire that burns forever. It has been prepared for the devil and his angels. 42 I was hungry. But you gave me nothing to eat. I was thirsty. But you gave me nothing to drink. 43 I was a stranger. But you did not invite me in. I needed clothes. But you did not give me any. I was sick and in prison. But you did not take care of me.'

44 "They also will answer, 'Lord, when did we see you hungry or thirsty and not help you? When did we see you as a stranger or needing clothes or sick or in prison and not help you?'

45 "He will reply, 'What I'm about to tell you is true. Anything you didn't do for one of the least important of these, you didn't do for me.'

46 "Then they will go away to be punished forever. But those who have done what is right will receive eternal life."

The Plan to Kill Jesus

26 Jesus finished saying all these things. Then he said to his disciples, 2 "As you know, the Passover Feast is two days away. The Son of Man will be handed over to be nailed to a cross."

3 Then the chief priests met with the elders of the people. They met in the palace of Caiaphas, the high priest. 4 They made plans to arrest Jesus secretly. They wanted to kill him. 5 "But not during the feast," they said. "The people may stir up trouble."

A Woman Pours Perfume on Jesus

6 Jesus was in Bethany. He was in the
home of Simon, who had a skin disease.
7 A woman came to Jesus with a special
sealed jar of very expensive perfume. She
poured the perfume on his head while he
was at the table.

8 When the disciples saw this, they
became angry. "Why this waste?" they
asked. 9 "The perfume could have been
sold at a high price. The money could
have been given to poor people."

10 Jesus was aware of this. So he said to
them, "Why are you bothering this woman? She has done a beautiful thing to me.
11 You will always have poor people with
you. But you will not always have me.
12 She poured the perfume on my body
to prepare me to be buried. 13 What I'm
about to tell you is true. What she has
done will be told anywhere this good
news is preached all over the world. It will
be told in memory of her."

Judas Agrees to Hand Jesus Over

14 One of the 12 disciples went to the
chief priests. His name was Judas Iscariot. 15 He asked, "What will you give me if I
hand Jesus over to you?" So they counted
out 30 silver coins for him. 16 From then
on, Judas watched for the right time to
hand Jesus over to them.

The Lord's Supper

17 It was the first day of the Feast of Unleavened Bread. The disciples came to
Jesus. They asked, "Where do you want
us to prepare for you to eat the Passover
meal?"

18 He replied, "Go into the city to a certain man. Tell him, 'The Teacher says,
"My time is near. I am going to celebrate
the Passover at your house with my disciples." ' " 19 So the disciples did what Jesus
had told them to do. They prepared the
Passover meal.

20 When evening came, Jesus was at the
table with his 12 disciples. 21 While they
were eating, he said, "What I'm about to
tell you is true. One of you will hand me
over to my enemies."

22 The disciples became very sad. One
after the other, they began to say to him,
"Surely you don't mean me, Lord, do
you?"

23 Jesus replied, "The one who has
dipped his hand into the bowl with me
will hand me over. 24 The Son of Man will
go just as it is written about him. But how
terrible it will be for the one who hands
over the Son of Man! It would be better for
him if he had not been born."

25 Judas was the one who was going to
hand him over. He said, "Surely you don't
mean me, Teacher, do you?"

Jesus answered, "You have said so."

26 While they were eating, Jesus took
bread. He gave thanks and broke it. He
handed it to his disciples and said, "Take
this and eat it. This is my body."

27 Then he took a cup. He gave thanks
and handed it to them. He said, "All of
you drink from it. 28 This is my blood of
the covenant. It is poured out to forgive
the sins of many people. 29 Here is what I
tell you. From now on, I won't drink wine
with you again until the day I drink it with
you in my Father's kingdom."

30 Then they sang a hymn and went out
to the Mount of Olives.

Jesus Says That the Disciples Will Turn Away

31 Jesus told them, "This very night you
will all turn away because of me. It is written that the Lord said,

" 'I will strike the shepherd down.
Then the sheep of the flock will be
scattered.' (Zechariah 13:7)

32 But after I rise from the dead, I will go
ahead of you into Galilee."

33 Peter replied, "All the others may turn
away because of you. But I never will."

34 "What I'm about to tell you is true,"
Jesus answered. "It will happen tonight.
Before the rooster crows, you will say
three times that you don't know me."

35 But Peter said, "I may have to die with
you. But I will never say I don't know you."
And all the other disciples said the same
thing.

Jesus Prays in Gethsemane

36 Then Jesus went with his disciples
to a place called Gethsemane. He said to
them, "Sit here while I go over there and
pray." 37 He took Peter and the two sons of
Zebedee along with him. He began to be
sad and troubled. 38 Then he said to them,
"My soul is very sad. I feel close to death.
Stay here. Keep watch with me."

39 He went a little farther. Then he fell
with his face to the ground. He prayed,
"My Father, if it is possible, take this cup of
suffering away from me. But let what you
want be done, not what I want."
40 Then he returned to his disciples and
found them sleeping. "Couldn't you men
keep watch with me for one hour?" he
asked Peter. 41 "Watch and pray. Then you
won't fall into sin when you are tempted.
The spirit is willing, but the body is weak."
42 Jesus went away a second time. He
prayed, "My Father, is it possible for this
cup to be taken away? But if I must drink
it, may what you want be done."
43 Then he came back. Again he found
them sleeping. They couldn't keep their
eyes open. 44 So he left them and went
away once more. For the third time he
prayed the same thing.
45 Then he returned to the disciples. He
said to them, "Are you still sleeping and
resting? Look! The hour has come. The
Son of Man is about to be handed over to
sinners. 46 Get up! Let us go! Here comes
the one who is handing me over to them!"

Jesus Is Arrested

47 While Jesus was still speaking, Judas
arrived. He was one of the 12 disciples. A
large crowd was with him. They were carrying swords and clubs. The chief priests
and the elders of the people had sent
them. 48 Judas, who was going to hand
Jesus over, had arranged a signal with
them. "The one I kiss is the man," he said.
"Arrest him." 49 So Judas went to Jesus at
once. He said, "Greetings, Rabbi!" And he
kissed him.
50 Jesus replied, "Friend, do what you
came to do."
Then the men stepped forward. They
grabbed Jesus and arrested him. 51 At
that moment, one of Jesus' companions
reached for his sword. He pulled it out
and struck the slave of the high priest with
it. He cut off the slave's ear.
52 "Put your sword back in its place,"
Jesus said to him. "All who use the sword
will die by the sword. 53 Do you think I
can't ask my Father for help? He would
send an army of more than 70,000 angels right away. 54 But then how would the
Scriptures come true? They say it must
happen in this way."
55 At that time Jesus spoke to the crowd.
"Am I leading a band of armed men
against you?" he asked. "Do you have to
come out with swords and clubs to capture me? Every day I sat in the temple
courtyard teaching. And you didn't arrest
me. 56 But all this has happened so that
the words of the prophets would come
true." Then all the disciples left him and
ran away.

Jesus Is Taken to the Sanhedrin

57 Those who had arrested Jesus took
him to Caiaphas, the high priest. The
teachers of the law and the elders had
come together there. 58 Not too far away,
Peter followed Jesus. He went right up to
the courtyard of the high priest. He entered and sat down with the guards to see
what would happen.
59 The chief priests and the whole Sanhedrin were looking for something to use
against Jesus. They wanted to put him to
death. 60 But they did not find any proof,
even though many false witnesses came
forward.
Finally, two other witnesses came forward. 61 They said, "This fellow claimed,
'I am able to destroy the temple of God. I
can build it again in three days.' "
62 Then the high priest stood up. He
asked Jesus, "Aren't you going to answer?
What are these charges that these men
are bringing against you?" 63 But Jesus remained silent.
The high priest said to him, "I am commanding you in the name of the living
God. May he judge you if you don't tell
the truth. Tell us if you are the Messiah,
the Son of God."
64 "You have said so," Jesus replied. "But
here is what I say to all of you. From now
on, you will see the Son of Man sitting at
the right hand of the Mighty One. You will
see the Son of Man coming on the clouds
of heaven."
65 Then the high priest tore his clothes.
He said, "He has spoken a very evil thing
against God! Why do we need any more
witnesses? You have heard him say this
evil thing. 66 What do you think?"
"He must die!" they answered.
67 Then they spit in his face. They hit
him with their fists. Others slapped him.
68 They said, "Prophesy to us, Messiah!
Who hit you?"

Peter Says He Does Not Know Jesus

69 Peter was sitting out in the courtyard.
A female servant came to him. "You also
were with Jesus of Galilee," she said.
70 But in front of all of them, Peter said
he was not. "I don't know what you're
talking about," he said.
71 Then he went out to the gate leading
into the courtyard. There another servant
saw him. She said to the people, "This fellow was with Jesus of Nazareth."
72 Again he said he was not. With a curse
he said, "I don't know the man!"
73 After a little while, those standing
there went up to Peter. "You must be one
of them," they said. "The way you talk
gives you away."
74 Then Peter began to curse and said to
them, "I don't know the man!"
Right away a rooster crowed. 75 Then
Peter remembered what Jesus had said.
"The rooster will crow," Jesus had told
him. "Before it does, you will say three
times that you don't know me." Peter
went outside. He broke down and cried.

Judas Hangs Himself

27 It was early in the morning. All the
chief priests and the elders of the
people planned how to put Jesus to death.
2 So they tied him up and led him away.
Then they handed him over to Pilate, who
was the governor.
3 Judas, who had handed him over, saw
that Jesus had been sentenced to die. He
felt deep shame and sadness for what he
had done. So he returned the 30 silver
coins to the chief priests and the elders.
4 "I have sinned," he said. "I handed over a
man who is not guilty."
"What do we care?" they replied. "That's
your problem."
5 So Judas threw the money into the
temple and left. Then he went away and
hanged himself.
6 The chief priests picked up the coins.
They said, "It's against the law to put this
money into the temple fund. It is blood
money. It has paid for a man's death." 7 So
they decided to use the money to buy a
potter's field. People from other countries
would be buried there. 8 That is why it has
been called the Field of Blood to this day.
9 Then the words spoken by Jeremiah the
prophet came true. He had said, "They
took the 30 silver coins. That price was
set for him by the people of Israel. 10 They
used the coins to buy a potter's field, just
as the Lord commanded me." (Zechariah
11:12,13; Jeremiah 19:1–13; 32:6–9)

Jesus Is Brought to Pilate

11 Jesus was standing in front of the governor. The governor asked him, "Are you
the king of the Jews?"
"Yes. You have said so," Jesus replied.
12 But when the chief priests and the
elders brought charges against him, he
did not answer. 13 Then Pilate asked him,
"Don't you hear the charges they are
bringing against you?" 14 But Jesus made
no reply, not even to a single charge. The
governor was really amazed.
15 It was the governor's practice at the
Passover Feast to let one prisoner go free.
The people could choose the one they
wanted. 16 At that time they had a well-
known prisoner named Jesus Barabbas.
17 So when the crowd gathered, Pilate
asked them, "Which one do you want me
to set free? Jesus Barabbas? Or Jesus who
is called the Messiah?" 18 Pilate knew that
the leaders wanted to get their own way.
He knew this was why they had handed
Jesus over to him.
19 While Pilate was sitting on the judge's
seat, his wife sent him a message. It said,
"Don't have anything to do with that man.
He is not guilty. I have suffered a great
deal in a dream today because of him."
20 But the chief priests and the elders
talked the crowd into asking for Barabbas
and having Jesus put to death.
21 "Which of the two do you want me to
set free?" asked the governor.
"Barabbas," they answered.
22 "Then what should I do with Jesus
who is called the Messiah?" Pilate asked.
They all answered, "Crucify him!"
23 "Why? What wrong has he done?"
asked Pilate.
But they shouted even louder, "Crucify
him!"
24 Pilate saw that he wasn't getting anywhere. Instead, the crowd was starting to
get angry. So he took water and washed
his hands in front of them. "I am not
guilty of this man's death," he said. "You
are accountable for that!"
25 All the people answered, "Put the
blame for his death on us and our children!"

26 Pilate let Barabbas go free. But he had Jesus whipped. Then he handed him over to be nailed to a cross.

The Soldiers Make Fun of Jesus

27 The governor's soldiers took Jesus into the palace, which was called the Praetorium. All the rest of the soldiers gathered around him. 28 They took off his clothes and put a purple robe on him. 29 Then they twisted thorns together to make a crown. They placed it on his head. They put a stick in his right hand. Then they fell on their knees in front of him and made fun of him. "We honor you, king of the Jews!" they said. 30 They spit on him. They hit him on the head with the stick again and again. 31 After they had made fun of him, they took off the robe. They put his own clothes back on him. Then they led him away to nail him to a cross.

Jesus Is Nailed to a Cross

32 On their way out of the city, they met a man from Cyrene. His name was Simon. They forced him to carry the cross. 33 They came to a place called Golgotha. The word Golgotha means the Place of the Skull. 34 There they mixed wine with bitter spices and gave it to Jesus to drink. After tasting it, he refused to drink it. 35 When they had nailed him to the cross, they divided up his clothes by casting lots. 36 They sat down and kept watch over him there. 37 Above his head they placed the written charge against him. It read, THIS IS JESUS, THE KING OF THE JEWS.

38 Two rebels against Rome were crucified with him. One was on his right and one was on his left. 39 Those who passed by shouted at Jesus and made fun of him. They shook their heads 40 and said, "So you are going to destroy the temple and build it again in three days? Then save yourself! Come down from the cross, if you are the Son of God!" 41 In the same way the chief priests, the teachers of the law and the elders made fun of him. 42 "He saved others," they said. "But he can't save himself! He's the king of Israel! Let him come down now from the cross! Then we will believe in him. 43 He trusts in God. Let God rescue him now if he wants him. He's the one who said, 'I am the Son of God.' " 44 In the same way the rebels who were being crucified with Jesus also made fun of him.

Jesus Dies

45 From noon until three o'clock, the whole land was covered with darkness. 46 About three o'clock, Jesus cried out in a loud voice. He said, "*Eli, Eli, lema sabachthani?*" This means "My God, my God, why have you deserted me?" (Psalm 22:1)

47 Some of those standing there heard Jesus cry out. They said, "He's calling for Elijah."

48 Right away one of them ran and got a sponge. He filled it with wine vinegar and put it on a stick. He offered it to Jesus to drink. 49 The rest said, "Leave him alone. Let's see if Elijah comes to save him."

50 After Jesus cried out again in a loud voice, he died.

51 At that moment the temple curtain was torn in two from top to bottom. The earth shook. The rocks split. 52 Tombs broke open. The bodies of many holy people who had died were raised to life. 53 They came out of the tombs. After Jesus was raised from the dead, they went into the holy city. There they appeared to many people.

54 The Roman commander and those guarding Jesus saw the earthquake and all that had happened. They were terrified. They exclaimed, "He was surely the Son of God!"

55 Not very far away, many women were watching. They had followed Jesus from Galilee to take care of his needs. 56 Mary Magdalene was among them. Mary, the mother of James and Joseph, was also there. So was the mother of Zebedee's sons.

Jesus Is Buried

57 As evening approached, a rich man came from the town of Arimathea. His name was Joseph. He had become a follower of Jesus. 58 He went to Pilate and asked for Jesus' body. Pilate ordered that it be given to him. 59 Joseph took the body and wrapped it in a clean linen cloth. 60 He placed it in his own new tomb that he had cut out of the rock. He rolled a big stone in front of the entrance to the tomb. Then he went away. 61 Mary Magdalene and the other Mary were sitting there across from the tomb.

The Guards at the Tomb

[62]The next day was the day after Preparation Day. The chief priests and the Pharisees went to Pilate. [63]"Sir," they said, "we remember something that liar said while he was still alive. He claimed, 'After three days I will rise again.' [64]So give the order to make the tomb secure until the third day. If you don't, his disciples might come and steal the body. Then they will tell the people that Jesus has been raised from the dead. This last lie will be worse than the first."

[65]"Take some guards with you," Pilate answered. "Go. Make the tomb as secure as you can." [66]So they went and made the tomb secure. They put a royal seal on the stone and placed some guards on duty.

Jesus Rises From the Dead

28 The Sabbath day was now over. It was dawn on the first day of the week. Mary Magdalene and the other Mary went to look at the tomb.

[2]There was a powerful earthquake. An angel of the Lord came down from heaven. The angel went to the tomb. He rolled back the stone and sat on it. [3]His body shone like lightning. His clothes were as white as snow. [4]The guards were so afraid of him that they shook and became like dead men.

[5]The angel said to the women, "Don't be afraid. I know that you are looking for Jesus, who was crucified. [6]He is not here! He has risen, just as he said he would! Come and see the place where he was lying. [7]Go quickly! Tell his disciples, 'He has risen from the dead. He is going ahead of you into Galilee. There you will see him.' Now I have told you."

[8]So the women hurried away from the tomb. They were afraid, but they were filled with joy. They ran to tell the disciples. [9]Suddenly Jesus met them. "Greetings!" he said. They came to him, took hold of his feet and worshiped him. [10]Then Jesus said to them, "Don't be afraid. Go and tell my brothers to go to Galilee. There they will see me."

The Guards Report to the Chief Priests

[11]While the women were on their way, some of the guards went into the city. They reported to the chief priests all that had happened. [12]When the chief priests met with the elders, they came up with a plan. They gave the soldiers a large amount of money. [13]They told the soldiers, "We want you to say, 'His disciples came during the night. They stole his body while we were sleeping.' [14]If the governor hears this report, we will pay him off. That will keep you out of trouble." [15]So the soldiers took the money and did as they were told. This story has spread all around among the Jews to this day.

Jesus' Final Orders to His Disciples

[16]Then the 11 disciples went to Galilee. They went to the mountain where Jesus had told them to go. [17]When they saw him, they worshiped him. But some still had their doubts. [18]Then Jesus came to them. He said, "All authority in heaven and on earth has been given to me. [19]So you must go and make disciples of all nations. Baptize them in the name of the Father and of the Son and of the Holy Spirit. [20]Teach them to obey everything I have commanded you. And you can be sure that I am always with you, to the very end."

MARK

The Gospel of Mark was written by John Mark. He worked very closely with Peter, one of Jesus' disciples. Mark tells the story of Jesus for people living in Rome. Near the end of the story Mark tells about a Roman soldier. This soldier says that Jesus is the Son of God.

The Gospel of Mark moves quickly from one event to the next. The first half deals with the key question: Who do people say Jesus is? An event at the end of this section shows Jesus healing a blind man. The blind man slowly comes to see. In the same way the disciples slowly come to understand who Jesus is. Finally Peter states clearly that Jesus is the Messiah.

In the second half of the book there is a struggle between the religious leaders and Jesus. Jesus has come to introduce a very different way of life. That way of life will change things. It will change the existing power relationships among the leaders and the people. This second half of the story is presented in three parts.

First, Jesus and his disciples travel to Jerusalem. Jesus enters Jerusalem being called a king.

Second, Jesus teaches in the temple. There he challenges the leaders of the temple.

Third, those leaders put into action their plan against Jesus. They have Jesus arrested and crucify him. They believe they have undone the work of Jesus. But God overturns their evil deed and raises Jesus from the dead.

Those who read the book of Mark are called to be faithful to Jesus, even when they suffer. Jesus had to suffer in order for God's saving plan to be completed. It is through suffering that God's plan of new life is established.

John the Baptist Prepares the Way

1 This is the beginning of the good news about Jesus the Messiah, the Son of God. 2 Long ago Isaiah the prophet wrote,

"I will send my messenger ahead of you.
He will prepare your way."
(Malachi 3:1)

3 "A messenger is calling out in the desert,
'Prepare the way for the Lord.
Make straight paths for him.' "
(Isaiah 40:3)

4 And so John the Baptist appeared in the desert. He preached that people should be baptized and turn away from their sins. Then God would forgive them. 5 All the people from the countryside of Judea went out to him. All the people from Jerusalem went too. When they admitted they had sinned, John baptized them in the Jordan River. 6 John wore clothes made out of camel's hair. He had a leather belt around his waist. And he ate locusts and wild honey. 7 Here is what John was preaching. "After me, there is someone coming who is more powerful than I am. I'm not good enough to bend down and untie his sandals. 8 I baptize you with water. But he will baptize you with the Holy Spirit."

Jesus Is Baptized and Tempted

9 At that time Jesus came from Nazareth in Galilee. John baptized Jesus in the Jordan River. 10 Jesus was coming up out of the water. Just then he saw heaven being torn open. Jesus saw the Holy Spirit coming down on him like a dove. 11 A voice spoke to him from heaven. It said, "You are my Son, and I love you. I am very pleased with you."

12 At once the Holy Spirit sent Jesus out into the desert. 13 He was in the desert 40 days. There Satan tempted him. The wild animals didn't harm Jesus. Angels took care of him.

Jesus Preaches the Good News

14 After John was put in prison, Jesus went into Galilee. He preached the good news of God. 15 "The time has come," he said. "The kingdom of God has come near. Turn away from your sins and believe the good news!"

Jesus Chooses His First Disciples

16 One day Jesus was walking beside the Sea of Galilee. There he saw Simon and his brother Andrew. They were throwing a net into the lake. They were fishermen. 17 "Come and follow me," Jesus said. "I will send you out to fish for people." 18 At once they left their nets and followed him.

19 Then Jesus walked a little farther. As he did, he saw James, the son of Zebedee, and his brother John. They were in a boat preparing their nets. 20 Right away he

called out to them. They left their father Zebedee in the boat with the hired men. Then they followed Jesus.

Jesus Drives Out an Evil Spirit

21 Jesus and those with him went to Capernaum. When the Sabbath day came, he went into the synagogue. There he began to teach. 22 The people were amazed at his teaching. That's because he taught them like one who had authority. He did not talk like the teachers of the law. 23 Just then a man in their synagogue cried out. He was controlled by an evil spirit. He said, 24 "What do you want with us, Jesus of Nazareth? Have you come to destroy us? I know who you are. You are the Holy One of God!"

25 "Be quiet!" said Jesus firmly. "Come out of him!" 26 The evil spirit shook the man wildly. Then it came out of him with a scream.

27 All the people were amazed. So they asked each other, "What is this? A new teaching! And with so much authority! He even gives orders to evil spirits, and they obey him." 28 News about Jesus spread quickly all over Galilee.

Jesus Heals Many People

29 Jesus and those with him left the synagogue. Right away they went with James and John to the home of Simon and Andrew. 30 Simon's mother-in-law was lying in bed with a fever. They told Jesus about her right away. 31 So he went to her. He took her hand and helped her up. The fever left her. Then she began to serve them.

32 That evening after sunset, the people brought to Jesus all who were sick. They also brought all who were controlled by demons. 33 All the people in town gathered at the door. 34 Jesus healed many of them. They had all kinds of sicknesses. He also drove out many demons. But he would not let the demons speak, because they knew who he was.

Jesus Prays in a Quiet Place

35 It was very early in the morning and still dark. Jesus got up and left the house. He went to a place where he could be alone. There he prayed. 36 Simon and his friends went to look for Jesus. 37 When they found him, they called out, "Everyone is looking for you!"

38 Jesus replied, "Let's go somewhere else. I want to go to the nearby towns. I must preach there also. That is why I have come." 39 So he traveled all around Galilee. He preached in their synagogues. He also drove out demons.

Jesus Heals a Man Who Had a Skin Disease

40 A man who had a skin disease came to Jesus. On his knees he begged Jesus. He said, "If you are willing to make me 'clean,' you can do it."

41 Jesus became angry. He reached out his hand and touched the man. "I am willing to do it," Jesus said. "Be 'clean'!" 42 Right away the disease left the man, and he was "clean."

43 Jesus sent him away at once. He gave the man a strong warning. 44 "Don't tell this to anyone," he said. "Go and show yourself to the priest. Offer the sacrifices that Moses commanded. It will be a witness to the priest and the people that you are 'clean.' " 45 But the man went out and started talking right away. He spread the news to everyone. So Jesus could no longer enter a town openly. He stayed outside in lonely places. But people still came to him from everywhere.

Jesus Forgives and Heals a Man Who Could Not Walk

2 A few days later, Jesus entered Capernaum again. The people heard that he had come home. 2 So many people gathered that there was no room left. There was not even room outside the door. And Jesus preached the word to them. 3 Four of those who came were carrying a man who could not walk. 4 But they could not get him close to Jesus because of the crowd. So they made a hole by digging through the roof above Jesus. Then they lowered the man through it on a mat. 5 Jesus saw their faith. So he said to the man, "Son, your sins are forgiven."

6 Some teachers of the law were sitting there. They were thinking, 7 "Why is this fellow talking like that? He's saying a very evil thing! Only God can forgive sins!"

8 Right away Jesus knew what they were thinking. So he said to them, "Why are you thinking these things? 9 Is it easier to say to this man, 'Your sins are forgiven'? Or to say, 'Get up, take your mat and walk'? 10 But I want you to know that

the Son of Man has authority on earth to
forgive sins." So Jesus spoke to the man
who could not walk. 11 "I tell you," he said,
"get up. Take your mat and go home."
12 The man got up and took his mat. Then
he walked away while everyone watched.
All the people were amazed. They praised
God and said, "We have never seen anything like this!"

Jesus Chooses Levi and Eats With Sinners

13 Once again Jesus went out beside the
Sea of Galilee. A large crowd came to him.
He began to teach them. 14 As he walked
along he saw Levi, the son of Alphaeus.
Levi was sitting at the tax collector's
booth. "Follow me," Jesus told him. Levi
got up and followed him.

15 Later Jesus was having dinner at
Levi's house. Many tax collectors and
sinners were eating with him and his disciples. They were part of the large crowd
following Jesus. 16 Some teachers of the
law who were Pharisees were there. They
saw Jesus eating with sinners and tax collectors. So they asked his disciples, "Why
does he eat with tax collectors and sinners?"

17 Jesus heard that. So he said to them,
"Those who are healthy don't need a doctor. Sick people do. I have not come to get
those who think they are right with God
to follow me. I have come to get sinners
to follow me."

Jesus Is Asked About Fasting

18 John's disciples and the Pharisees
were going without eating. Some people
came to Jesus. They said to him, "John's
disciples are fasting. The disciples of the
Pharisees are also fasting. But your disciples are not. Why aren't they?"

19 Jesus answered, "How can the guests
of the groom go without eating while he
is with them? They will not fast as long as
he is with them. 20 But the time will come
when the groom will be taken away from
them. On that day they will go without
eating.

21 "No one sews a patch of new cloth on
old clothes. Otherwise, the new piece will
pull away from the old. That will make
the tear worse. 22 No one pours new wine
into old wineskins. Otherwise, the wine
will burst the skins. Then the wine and
the wineskins will both be destroyed. No,
people pour new wine into new wineskins."

Jesus Is Lord of the Sabbath Day

23 One Sabbath day Jesus was walking
with his disciples through the grainfields.
The disciples began to break off some
heads of grain. 24 The Pharisees said to
Jesus, "Look! It is against the Law to do
this on the Sabbath day. Why are your disciples doing it?"

25 He answered, "Haven't you ever read
about what David did? He and his men
were hungry. They needed food. 26 It was
when Abiathar was high priest. David entered the house of God and ate the holy
bread. Only priests were allowed to eat it.
David also gave some to his men."

27 Then Jesus said to them, "The Sabbath day was made for man. Man was not
made for the Sabbath day. 28 So the Son of
Man is Lord even of the Sabbath day."

Jesus Heals on the Sabbath Day

3 Another time Jesus went into the
synagogue. A man with a weak and
twisted hand was there. 2 Some Pharisees
were trying to find fault with Jesus. They
watched him closely. They wanted to see
if he would heal the man on the Sabbath
day. 3 Jesus spoke to the man with the
weak and twisted hand. "Stand up in front
of everyone," he said.

4 Then Jesus asked them, "What does
the Law say we should do on the Sabbath
day? Should we do good? Or should we
do evil? Should we save life? Or should we
kill?" But no one answered.

5 Jesus looked around at them in anger.
He was very upset because their hearts
were stubborn. Then he said to the man,
"Stretch out your hand." He stretched it
out, and his hand had become as good as
new. 6 Then the Pharisees went out and
began to make plans with the Herodians.
They wanted to kill Jesus.

Crowds Follow Jesus

7 Jesus went off to the Sea of Galilee with
his disciples. A large crowd from Galilee
followed. 8 People heard about all that
Jesus was doing. And many came to him.
They came from Judea, Jerusalem and Id-
umea. They came from the lands east of
the Jordan River. And they came from the
area around Tyre and Sidon. 9 Because of

the crowd, Jesus told his disciples to get a
small boat ready for him. This would keep
the people from crowding him. 10 Jesus
had healed many people. So those who
were sick were pushing forward to touch
him. 11 When people controlled by evil
spirits saw him, they fell down in front of
him. The spirits shouted, "You are the Son
of God!" 12 But Jesus ordered them not to
tell people about him.

Jesus Appoints the Twelve Disciples

13 Jesus went up on a mountainside.
He called for certain people to come to
him, and they came. 14 He appointed 12
of them so that they would be with him.
He would also send them out to preach.
15 And he gave them authority to drive out
demons. 16 So Jesus appointed the 12 disciples. Simon was one of them. Jesus gave
him the name Peter. 17 There were James,
son of Zebedee, and his brother John.
Jesus gave them the name Boanerges. Boanerges means Sons of Thunder. 18 There
were also Andrew, Philip, Bartholomew,
Matthew, Thomas, and James, son of Alphaeus. And there were Thaddaeus and
Simon the Zealot. 19 Judas Iscariot was
one of them too. He was the one who was
later going to hand Jesus over to his enemies.

Jesus Is Accused by Teachers of the Law

20 Jesus entered a house. Again a crowd
gathered. It was so large that Jesus and his
disciples were not even able to eat. 21 His
family heard about this. So they went to
take charge of him. They said, "He is out
of his mind."

22 Some teachers of the law were there.
They had come down from Jerusalem.
They said, "He is controlled by Beelzebul!
He is driving out demons by the power of
the prince of demons."

23 So Jesus called them over to him.
He began to speak to them using stories.
He said, "How can Satan drive out Satan? 24 If a kingdom fights against itself,
it can't stand. 25 If a family is divided, it
can't stand. 26 And if Satan fights against
himself, and his helpers are divided,
he can't stand. That is the end of him.
27 In fact, none of you can enter a strong
man's house unless you tie him up first.
Then you can steal things from his house.
28 What I'm about to tell you is true. Everyone's sins and evil words against God will
be forgiven. 29 But whoever speaks evil
things against the Holy Spirit will never
be forgiven. Their guilt will last forever."

30 Jesus said this because the teachers
of the law were saying, "He has an evil
spirit."

Jesus' Mother and Brothers

31 Jesus' mother and brothers came
and stood outside. They sent someone in
to get him. 32 A crowd was sitting around
Jesus. They told him, "Your mother and
your brothers are outside. They are looking for you."

33 "Who is my mother? Who are my
brothers?" he asked.

34 Then Jesus looked at the people sitting in a circle around him. He said, "Here
is my mother! Here are my brothers!
35 Anyone who does what God wants is my
brother or sister or mother."

The Story of the Farmer

4 Again Jesus began to teach by the Sea
of Galilee. The crowd that gathered
around him was very large. So he got into
a boat. He sat down in it out on the lake.
All the people were along the shore at
the water's edge. 2 He taught them many
things using stories. In his teaching he
said, 3 "Listen! A farmer went out to plant
his seed. 4 He scattered the seed on the
ground. Some fell on a path. Birds came
and ate it up. 5 Some seed fell on rocky
places, where there wasn't much soil. The
plants came up quickly, because the soil
wasn't deep. 6 When the sun came up, it
burned the plants. They dried up because
they had no roots. 7 Other seed fell among
thorns. The thorns grew up and crowded
out the plants. So the plants did not bear
grain. 8 Still other seed fell on good soil.
It grew up and produced a crop 30, 60,
or even 100 times more than the farmer
planted."

9 Then Jesus said, "Whoever has ears
should listen."

10 Later Jesus was alone. The 12 disciples asked him about the stories. So did
the others around him. 11 He told them,
"The secret of God's kingdom has been
given to you. But to outsiders everything
is told using stories. 12 In that way,

"'They will see but never know what
they are seeing.
They will hear but never
understand.
Otherwise they might turn and be
forgiven!'" (Isaiah 6:9,10)

13 Then Jesus said to them, "Don't you understand this story? Then how will you understand any stories of this kind? 14 The seed the farmer plants is God's message. 15 What is seed scattered on a path like? The message is planted. The people hear the message. Then Satan comes. He takes away the message that was planted in them. 16 And what is seed scattered on rocky places like? The people hear the message. At once they receive it with joy. 17 But they have no roots. So they last only a short time. They quickly fall away from the faith when trouble or suffering comes because of the message. 18 And what is seed scattered among thorns like? The people hear the message. 19 But then the worries of this life come to them. Wealth comes with its false promises. The people also long for other things. All of these are the kinds of things that crowd out the message. They keep it from producing fruit. 20 And what is seed scattered on good soil like? The people hear the message. They accept it. They produce a good crop 30, 60, or even 100 times more than the farmer planted."

A Lamp on a Stand

21 Jesus said to them, "Do you bring in a lamp to put it under a large bowl or a bed? Don't you put it on its stand? 22 What is hidden is meant to be seen. And what is put out of sight is meant to be brought out into the open. 23 Whoever has ears should listen."

24 "Think carefully about what you hear," he said. "As you give, so you will receive. In fact, you will receive even more. 25 Whoever has something will be given more. Whoever has nothing, even what they have will be taken away from them."

The Story of the Growing Seed

26 Jesus also said, "Here is what God's kingdom is like. A farmer scatters seed on the ground. 27 Night and day the seed comes up and grows. It happens whether the farmer sleeps or gets up. He doesn't know how it happens. 28 All by itself the soil produces grain. First the stalk comes up. Then the head appears. Finally, the full grain appears in the head. 29 Before long the grain ripens. So the farmer cuts it down, because the harvest is ready."

The Story of the Mustard Seed

30 Again Jesus said, "What can we say God's kingdom is like? What story can we use to explain it? 31 It is like a mustard seed, which is the smallest of all seeds on earth. 32 But when you plant the seed, it grows. It becomes the largest of all garden plants. Its branches are so big that birds can rest in its shade."

33 Using many stories like these, Jesus spoke the word to them. He told them as much as they could understand. 34 He did not say anything to them without using a story. But when he was alone with his disciples, he explained everything.

Jesus Calms the Storm

35 When evening came, Jesus said to his disciples, "Let's go over to the other side of the lake." 36 They left the crowd behind. And they took him along in a boat, just as he was. There were also other boats with him. 37 A wild storm came up. Waves crashed over the boat. It was about to sink. 38 Jesus was in the back, sleeping on a cushion. The disciples woke him up. They said, "Teacher! Don't you care if we drown?"

39 He got up and ordered the wind to stop. He said to the waves, "Quiet! Be still!" Then the wind died down. And it was completely calm.

40 He said to his disciples, "Why are you so afraid? Don't you have any faith at all yet?"

41 They were terrified. They asked each other, "Who is this? Even the wind and the waves obey him!"

Jesus Heals a Man Controlled by Demons

5 They went across the Sea of Galilee to the area of the Gerasenes. 2 Jesus got out of the boat. A man controlled by an evil spirit came from the tombs to meet him. 3 The man lived in the tombs. No one could keep him tied up anymore. Not even a chain could hold him. 4 His hands and feet had often been chained. But he tore the chains apart. And he broke

the iron cuffs on his ankles. No one was strong enough to control him. 5 Night and day he screamed among the tombs and in the hills. He cut himself with stones.

6 When he saw Jesus a long way off, he ran to him. He fell on his knees in front of him. 7 He shouted at the top of his voice, "Jesus, Son of the Most High God, what do you want with me? Swear to God that you won't hurt me!" 8 This was because Jesus had said to him, "Come out of this man, you evil spirit!"

9 Then Jesus asked the demon, "What is your name?"

"My name is Legion," he replied. "There are many of us." 10 And he begged Jesus again and again not to send them out of the area.

11 A large herd of pigs was feeding on the nearby hillside. 12 The demons begged Jesus, "Send us among the pigs. Let us go into them." 13 Jesus allowed it. The evil spirits came out of the man and went into the pigs. There were about 2,000 pigs in the herd. The whole herd rushed down the steep bank. They ran into the lake and drowned.

14 Those who were tending the pigs ran off. They told the people in the town and countryside what had happened. The people went out to see for themselves. 15 Then they came to Jesus. They saw the man who had been controlled by many demons. He was sitting there. He was now dressed and thinking clearly. All this made the people afraid. 16 Those who had seen it told them what had happened to the man. They told about the pigs as well. 17 Then the people began to beg Jesus to leave their area.

18 Jesus was getting into the boat. The man who had been controlled by demons begged to go with him. 19 Jesus did not let him. He said, "Go home to your own people. Tell them how much the Lord has done for you. Tell them how kind he has been to you." 20 So the man went away. In the area known as the Ten Cities, he began to tell how much Jesus had done for him. And all the people were amazed.

Jesus Heals a Dead Girl and a Suffering Woman

21 Jesus went across the Sea of Galilee in a boat. It landed at the other side. There a large crowd gathered around him. 22 Then a man named Jairus came. He was a synagogue leader. When he saw Jesus, he fell at his feet. 23 He begged Jesus, "Please come. My little daughter is dying. Place your hands on her to heal her. Then she will live." 24 So Jesus went with him.

A large group of people followed. They crowded around him. 25 A woman was there who had a sickness that made her bleed. It had lasted for 12 years. 26 She had suffered a great deal, even though she had gone to many doctors. She had spent all the money she had. But she was getting worse, not better. 27 Then she heard about Jesus. She came up behind him in the crowd and touched his clothes. 28 She thought, "I just need to touch his clothes. Then I will be healed." 29 Right away her bleeding stopped. She felt in her body that her suffering was over.

30 At once Jesus knew that power had gone out from him. He turned around in the crowd. He asked, "Who touched my clothes?"

31 "You see the people," his disciples answered. "They are crowding against you. And you still ask, 'Who touched me?' "

32 But Jesus kept looking around. He wanted to see who had touched him. 33 Then the woman came and fell at his feet. She knew what had happened to her. She was shaking with fear. But she told him the whole truth. 34 He said to her, "Dear woman, your faith has healed you. Go in peace. You are free from your suffering."

35 While Jesus was still speaking, some people came from the house of Jairus. He was the synagogue leader. "Your daughter is dead," they said. "Why bother the teacher anymore?"

36 Jesus heard what they were saying. He told the synagogue leader, "Don't be afraid. Just believe."

37 He let only Peter, James, and John, the brother of James, follow him. 38 They came to the home of the synagogue leader. There Jesus saw a lot of confusion. People were crying and sobbing loudly. 39 He went inside. Then he said to them, "Why all this confusion and sobbing? The child is not dead. She is only sleeping." 40 But they laughed at him.

He made them all go outside. He took only the child's father and mother and the disciples who were with him. And he went in where the child was. 41 He took her by the hand. Then he said to her, "*Talitha koum!*" This means, "Little girl, I say to you, get up!" 42 The girl was 12 years old. Right away she stood up and began to walk around. They were totally amazed at this. 43 Jesus gave strict orders not to let anyone know what had happened. And he told them to give her something to eat.

A Prophet Without Honor

6 Jesus left there and went to his hometown of Nazareth. His disciples went with him. 2 When the Sabbath day came, he began to teach in the synagogue. Many who heard him were amazed.

"Where did this man get these things?" they asked. "What's this wisdom that has been given to him? What are these remarkable miracles he is doing? 3 Isn't this the carpenter? Isn't this Mary's son? Isn't this the brother of James, Joseph, Judas and Simon? Aren't his sisters here with us?" They were not pleased with him at all.

4 Jesus said to them, "A prophet is honored everywhere except in his own town. He doesn't receive any honor among his relatives or in his own home." 5 Jesus placed his hands on a few sick people and healed them. But he could not do any other miracles there. 6 He was amazed because they had no faith.

Jesus Sends Out the Twelve Disciples

Jesus went around teaching from village to village. 7 He called the 12 disciples to him. Then he began to send them out two by two. He gave them authority to drive out evil spirits.

8 Here is what he told them to do. "Take only a walking stick for your trip. Do not take bread or a bag. Take no money in your belts. 9 Wear sandals. But do not take extra clothes. 10 When you are invited into a house, stay there until you leave town. 11 Some places may not welcome you or listen to you. If they don't, leave that place and shake the dust off your feet. That will be a witness against the people living there."

12 They went out. And they preached that people should turn away from their sins. 13 They drove out many demons. They poured olive oil on many sick people and healed them.

John the Baptist's Head Is Cut Off

14 King Herod heard about this. Jesus' name had become well known. Some were saying, "John the Baptist has been raised from the dead! That is why he has the power to do miracles."

15 Others said, "He is Elijah."

Still others claimed, "He is a prophet. He is like one of the prophets of long ago."

16 But when Herod heard this, he said, "I had John's head cut off. And now he has been raised from the dead!"

17 In fact, it was Herod himself who had given orders to arrest John. He had him tied up and put in prison. He did this because of Herodias. She was the wife of Herod's brother Philip. But now Herod was married to her. 18 John had been saying to Herod, "It is against the Law for you to be married to your brother's wife." 19 Herodias couldn't forgive John for saying that. She wanted to kill him. But she could not, 20 because Herod was afraid of John. So he kept John safe. Herod knew John was a holy man who did what was right. When Herod heard him, he was very puzzled. But he liked to listen to John.

21 Finally the right time came. Herod gave a banquet on his birthday. He invited his high officials and military leaders. He also invited the most important men in Galilee. 22 Then the daughter of Herodias came in and danced. She pleased Herod and his dinner guests.

The king said to the girl, "Ask me for anything you want. I'll give it to you." 23 And he gave her his promise. He said to her, "Anything you ask for I will give you. I'll give you up to half my kingdom."

24 She went out and said to her mother, "What should I ask for?"

"The head of John the Baptist," she answered.

25 At once the girl hurried to ask the king. She said, "I want you to give me the head of John the Baptist on a big plate right now."

26 The king was very upset. But he thought about his promise and his dinner guests. So he did not want to say no to the girl. 27 He sent a man right away to bring John's head. The man went to the prison and cut off John's head. 28 He brought it back on a big plate. He gave it to the girl, and she gave it to her mother. 29 John's disciples heard about this. So they came

and took his body. Then they placed it in
a tomb.

Jesus Feeds Five Thousand

30 The apostles gathered around Jesus.
They told him all they had done and
taught. 31 But many people were coming
and going. So they did not even have a
chance to eat. Then Jesus said to his apostles, "Come with me by yourselves to a
quiet place. You need to get some rest."

32 So they went away by themselves in
a boat to a quiet place. 33 But many people who saw them leaving recognized
them. They ran from all the towns and got
there ahead of them. 34 When Jesus came
ashore, he saw a large crowd. He felt deep
concern for them. They were like sheep
without a shepherd. So he began teaching them many things.

35 By that time it was late in the day. His
disciples came to him. "There is nothing
here," they said. "It's already very late.
36 Send the people away. Then they can go
to the nearby countryside and villages to
buy something to eat."

37 But Jesus answered, "You give them
something to eat."

They said to him, "That would take
more than half a year's pay! Should we go
and spend that much on bread? Are we
supposed to feed them?"

38 "How many loaves do you have?"
Jesus asked. "Go and see."

When they found out, they said, "Five
loaves and two fish."

39 Then Jesus directed them to have
all the people sit down in groups on the
green grass. 40 So they sat down in groups
of 100s and 50s. 41 Jesus took the five
loaves and the two fish. He looked up to
heaven and gave thanks. He broke the
loaves into pieces. Then he gave them to
his disciples to pass around to the people. He also divided the two fish among
them all. 42 All of them ate and were satisfied. 43 The disciples picked up 12 baskets
of broken pieces of bread and fish. 44 The
number of men who had eaten was 5,000.

Jesus Walks on the Water

45 Right away Jesus made his disciples
get into the boat. He had them go on
ahead of him to Bethsaida. Then he sent
the crowd away. 46 After leaving them, he
went up on a mountainside to pray.

47 Later that night, the boat was in the
middle of the Sea of Galilee. Jesus was
alone on land. 48 He saw the disciples pulling hard on the oars. The wind was blowing against them. Shortly before dawn,
he went out to them. He walked on the
lake. When he was about to pass by them,
49 they saw him walking on the lake. They
thought he was a ghost, so they cried out.
50 They all saw him and were terrified.

Right away Jesus said to them, "Be
brave! It is I. Don't be afraid." 51 Then he
climbed into the boat with them. The
wind died down. And they were completely amazed. 52 They had not understood about the loaves. They were
stubborn.

53 They went across the lake and landed
at Gennesaret. There they tied up the
boat. 54 As soon as Jesus and his disciples
got out, people recognized him. 55 They
ran through that whole area to bring to
him those who were sick. They carried
them on mats to where they heard he was.
56 He went into the villages, the towns and
the countryside. Everywhere he went, the
people brought the sick to the market areas. Those who were sick begged him to
let them touch just the edge of his clothes.
And all who touched his clothes were
healed.

What Makes People "Unclean"?

7 The Pharisees gathered around Jesus.
So did some of the teachers of the law.
All of them had come from Jerusalem.
2 They saw some of his disciples eating
food with "unclean" hands. That means
they were not washed. 3 The Pharisees
and all the Jews do not eat unless they
wash their hands to make them "clean."
That's what the elders teach. 4 When they
come from the market, they do not eat
unless they wash. And they follow many
other teachings. For example, they wash
cups, pitchers, and kettles in a special
way.

5 So the Pharisees and the teachers of
the law questioned Jesus. "Why don't
your disciples live by what the elders
teach?" they asked. "Why do they eat their
food with 'unclean' hands?"

6 He replied, "Isaiah was right. He
prophesied about you people who pretend to be good. He said,

"'These people honor me by what
they say.
But their hearts are far away from
me.
7 Their worship doesn't mean
anything to me.
They teach nothing but human
rules.' (Isaiah 29:13)

8 You have let go of God's commands. And you are holding on to teachings that people have made up."

9 Jesus continued speaking, "You have a fine way of setting aside God's commands! You do this so you can follow your own teachings. 10 Moses said, 'Honor your father and mother.' (Exodus 20:12; Deuteronomy 5:16) He also said, 'Anyone who asks for bad things to happen to their father or mother must be put to death.' (Exodus 21:17; Leviticus 20:9) 11 But you allow people to say that what might have been used to help their parents is Corban. Corban means A Gift Set Apart for God. 12 So you no longer let them do anything for their parents. 13 You make the word of God useless by putting your own teachings in its place. And you do many things like this."

14 Again Jesus called the crowd to him. He said, "Listen to me, everyone. Understand this. 15-16 Nothing outside of a person can make them 'unclean' by going into them. It is what comes out of them that makes them 'unclean.'"

17 Then he left the crowd and entered the house. His disciples asked him about this teaching. 18 "Don't you understand?" Jesus asked. "Don't you see? Nothing that enters a person from the outside can make them 'unclean.' 19 It doesn't go into their heart. It goes into their stomach. Then it goes out of the body." In saying this, Jesus was calling all foods "clean."

20 He went on to say, "What comes out of a person is what makes them 'unclean.' 21 Evil thoughts come from the inside, from a person's heart. So do sexual sins, stealing and murder. 22 Adultery, greed, hate and cheating come from a person's heart too. So do desires that are not pure, and wanting what belongs to others. And so do telling lies about others and being proud and being foolish. 23 All these evil things come from inside a person and make them 'unclean.'"

Jesus Honors a Greek Woman's Faith

24 Jesus went from there to a place near Tyre. He entered a house. He did not want anyone to know where he was. But he could not keep it a secret. 25 Soon a woman heard about him. An evil spirit controlled her little daughter. The woman came to Jesus and fell at his feet. 26 She was a Greek, born in Syrian Phoenicia. She begged Jesus to drive the demon out of her daughter.

27 "First let the children eat all they want," he told her. "It is not right to take the children's bread and throw it to the dogs."

28 "Lord," she replied, "even the dogs under the table eat the children's crumbs."

29 Then he told her, "That was a good reply. You may go. The demon has left your daughter."

30 So she went home and found her child lying on the bed. And the demon was gone.

Jesus Heals a Man Who Could Not Hear or Speak

31 Then Jesus left the area of Tyre and went through Sidon. He went down to the Sea of Galilee and into the area known as the Ten Cities. 32 There some people brought a man to Jesus. The man was deaf and could hardly speak. They begged Jesus to place his hand on the man.

33 Jesus took the man to one side, away from the crowd. He put his fingers into the man's ears. Then he spit and touched the man's tongue. 34 Jesus looked up to heaven. With a deep sigh, he said to the man, "*Ephphatha!*" That means "Be opened!" 35 The man's ears were opened. His tongue was freed up, and he began to speak clearly.

36 Jesus ordered the people not to tell anyone. But the more he did so, the more they kept talking about it. 37 People were really amazed. "He has done everything well," they said. "He even makes deaf people able to hear. And he makes those who can't speak able to talk."

Jesus Feeds the Four Thousand

8 During those days another large crowd gathered. They had nothing to eat. So Jesus called for his disciples to come to him. He said, 2 "I feel deep concern for these people. They have already

been with me three days. They don't have
anything to eat. 3 If I send them away hungry, they will become too weak on their
way home. Some of them have come from
far away."
4 His disciples answered him. "There is
nothing here," they said. "Where can anyone get enough bread to feed them?"
5 "How many loaves do you have?"
Jesus asked.
"Seven," they replied.
6 He told the crowd to sit down on the
ground. He took the seven loaves and gave
thanks to God. Then he broke them and
gave them to his disciples. They passed
the pieces of bread around to the people.
7 The disciples also had a few small fish.
Jesus gave thanks for them too. He told
the disciples to pass them around. 8 The
people ate and were satisfied. After that,
the disciples picked up seven baskets of
leftover pieces. 9 About 4,000 people were
there. After Jesus sent them away, 10 he got
into a boat with his disciples. He went to
the area of Dalmanutha.
11 The Pharisees came and began to ask
Jesus questions. They wanted to test him.
So they asked him for a sign from heaven.
12 He sighed deeply. He said, "Why do you
people ask for a sign? What I'm about to
tell you is true. No sign will be given to
you." 13 Then he left them. He got back
into the boat and crossed to the other side
of the lake.

The Yeast of the Pharisees and Herod

14 The disciples had forgotten to bring
bread. They had only one loaf with them
in the boat. 15 "Be careful," Jesus warned
them. "Watch out for the yeast of the
Pharisees. And watch out for the yeast of
Herod."
16 They talked about this with each other. They said, "He must be saying this because we don't have any bread."
17 Jesus knew what they were saying.
So he asked them, "Why are you talking
about having no bread? Why can't you see
or understand? Are you stubborn? 18 Do
you have eyes and still don't see? Do you
have ears and still don't hear? And don't
you remember? 19 Earlier I broke five
loaves for the 5,000. How many baskets of
pieces did you pick up?"
"Twelve," they replied.
20 "Later I broke seven loaves for the
4,000. How many baskets of pieces did
you pick up?"
"Seven," they answered.
21 He said to them, "Can't you understand yet?"

Jesus Heals a Blind Man at Bethsaida

22 Jesus and his disciples came to Bethsaida. Some people brought a blind man
to him. They begged Jesus to touch him.
23 He took the blind man by the hand.
Then he led him outside the village. He
spit on the man's eyes and placed his
hands on him. "Do you see anything?"
Jesus asked.
24 The man looked up. He said, "I see
people. They look like trees walking
around."
25 Once more Jesus put his hands on the
man's eyes. Then his eyes were opened
so that he could see again. He saw everything clearly. 26 Jesus sent him home. He
told him, "Don't even go into the village."

Peter Says That Jesus Is the Messiah

27 Jesus and his disciples went on to the
villages around Caesarea Philippi. On the
way he asked them, "Who do people say
I am?"
28 They replied, "Some say John the
Baptist. Others say Elijah. Still others say
one of the prophets."
29 "But what about you?" he asked.
"Who do you say I am?"
Peter answered, "You are the Messiah."
30 Jesus warned them not to tell anyone
about him.

Jesus Tells About His Coming Death

31 Jesus then began to teach his disciples. He taught them that the Son of Man
must suffer many things. He taught them
that the elders would not accept him. The
chief priests and the teachers of the law
would not accept him either. He must be
killed and after three days rise again. 32 He
spoke clearly about this. Peter took Jesus
to one side and began to scold him.
33 Jesus turned and looked at his disciples. He scolded Peter. "Get behind me,
Satan!" he said. "You are not thinking
about the things God cares about. Instead, you are thinking only about the
things humans care about."

You Must Pick Up Your Cross

34 Jesus called the crowd to him along
with his disciples. He said, "Whoever
wants to be my disciple must say no to
themselves. They must pick up their cross
and follow me. 35 Whoever wants to save
their life will lose it. But whoever loses
their life for me and for the good news will
save it. 36 What good is it if someone gains
the whole world but loses their soul? 37 Or
what can anyone trade for their soul?
38 Suppose anyone is ashamed of me and
my words among these adulterous and
sinful people. Then the Son of Man will be
ashamed of them when he comes in his
Father's glory with the holy angels."

9 Jesus said to them, "What I'm about to
tell you is true. Some who are standing here will not die before they see that
God's kingdom has come with power."

Jesus' Appearance Is Changed

2 After six days Jesus took Peter, James
and John with him. He led them up a high
mountain. They were all alone. There
in front of them his appearance was
changed. 3 His clothes became so white
they shone. They were whiter than anyone in the world could bleach them. 4 Elijah and Moses appeared in front of Jesus
and his disciples. The two of them were
talking with Jesus.

5 Peter said to Jesus, "Rabbi, it is good
for us to be here. Let us put up three shelters. One will be for you, one for Moses,
and one for Elijah." 6 Peter didn't really
know what to say, because they were so
afraid.

7 Then a cloud appeared and covered
them. A voice came from the cloud. It
said, "This is my Son, and I love him. Listen to him!"

8 They looked around. Suddenly they
no longer saw anyone with them except
Jesus.

9 They came down the mountain. On
the way down, Jesus ordered them not to
tell anyone what they had seen. He told
them to wait until the Son of Man had
risen from the dead. 10 So they kept the
matter to themselves. But they asked each
other what "rising from the dead" meant.

11 Then they asked Jesus, "Why do the
teachers of the law say that Elijah has to
come first?"

12 Jesus replied, "That's right. Elijah does
come first. He makes all things new again.
So why is it written that the Son of Man
must suffer much and not be accepted? 13 I
tell you, Elijah has come. They have done
to him everything they wanted to do. They
did it just as it is written about him."

Jesus Heals a Boy Who Is Controlled by an Evil Spirit

14 When Jesus and those who were with
him came to the other disciples, they saw
a large crowd around them. The teachers of the law were arguing with them.
15 When all the people saw Jesus, they
were filled with wonder. And they ran to
greet him.

16 "What are you arguing with them
about?" Jesus asked.

17 A man in the crowd answered.
"Teacher," he said, "I brought you my
son. He is controlled by an evil spirit.
Because of this, my son can't speak anymore. 18 When the spirit takes hold of him,
it throws him to the ground. He foams at
the mouth. He grinds his teeth. And his
body becomes stiff. I asked your disciples
to drive out the spirit. But they couldn't
do it."

19 "You unbelieving people!" Jesus replied. "How long do I have to stay with
you? How long do I have to put up with
you? Bring the boy to me."

20 So they brought him. As soon as the
spirit saw Jesus, it threw the boy into a fit.
He fell to the ground. He rolled around
and foamed at the mouth.

21 Jesus asked the boy's father, "How
long has he been like this?"

"Since he was a child," he answered.
22 "The spirit has often thrown him into
fire or water to kill him. But if you can do
anything, take pity on us. Please help us."

23 " 'If you can'?" said Jesus. "Everything
is possible for the one who believes."

24 Right away the boy's father cried out,
"I do believe! Help me overcome my unbelief!"

25 Jesus saw that a crowd was running
over to see what was happening. Then
he ordered the evil spirit to leave the boy.
"You spirit that makes him unable to hear
and speak!" he said. "I command you,
come out of him. Never enter him again."

26 The spirit screamed. It shook the boy
wildly. Then it came out of him. The boy
looked so lifeless that many people said,

"He's dead." 27 But Jesus took him by the
hand. He lifted the boy to his feet, and the
boy stood up.
28 Jesus went indoors. Then his disciples asked him in private, "Why couldn't
we drive out the evil spirit?"
29 He replied, "This kind can come out
only by prayer."

Jesus Speaks a Second Time About His Coming Death

30 They left that place and passed
through Galilee. Jesus did not want anyone to know where they were. 31 That was
because he was teaching his disciples. He
said to them, "The Son of Man is going
to be handed over to men. They will kill
him. After three days he will rise from the
dead." 32 But they didn't understand what
he meant. And they were afraid to ask him
about it.

Who Is the Most Important Person?

33 Jesus and his disciples came to a
house in Capernaum. There he asked
them, "What were you arguing about on
the road?" 34 But they kept quiet. On the
way, they had argued about which one of
them was the most important person.
35 Jesus sat down and called for the 12
disciples to come to him. Then he said,
"Anyone who wants to be first must be the
very last. They must be the servant of everyone."
36 Jesus took a little child and had the
child stand among them. Then he took
the child in his arms. He said to them,
37 "Anyone who welcomes one of these
little children in my name welcomes me.
And anyone who welcomes me also welcomes the one who sent me."

Anyone Who Is Not Against Us Is for Us

38 "Teacher," said John, "we saw someone driving out demons in your name. We
told him to stop, because he was not one
of us."
39 "Do not stop him," Jesus said. "For
no one who does a miracle in my name
can in the next moment say anything bad
about me. 40 Anyone who is not against
us is for us. 41 What I'm about to tell you
is true. Suppose someone gives you a cup
of water in my name because you belong
to the Messiah. That person will certainly
not go without a reward.

Leading People to Sin

42 "What if someone leads one of these
little ones who believe in me to sin? If
they do, it would be better if a large millstone were hung around their neck and
they were thrown into the sea. 43-44 If your
hand causes you to sin, cut it off. It would
be better for you to enter God's kingdom
with only one hand than to go into hell
with two hands. In hell the fire never goes
out. 45-46 If your foot causes you to sin, cut
it off. It would be better to enter God's
kingdom with only one foot than to have
two feet and be thrown into hell. 47 If your
eye causes you to sin, poke it out. It would
be better for you to enter God's kingdom
with only one eye than to have two eyes
and be thrown into hell. 48 In hell,

> " 'The worms that eat them do not
> die.
> The fire is not put out.' (Isaiah 66:24)

49 Everyone will be salted with fire.
50 "Salt is good. But suppose it loses
its saltiness. How can you make it salty
again? Have salt among yourselves. And
be at peace with each other."

Jesus Teaches About Divorce

10 Jesus left that place and went into
the area of Judea and across the Jordan River. Again crowds of people came
to him. As usual, he taught them.
2 Some Pharisees came to test Jesus.
They asked, "Does the Law allow a man
to divorce his wife?"
3 "What did Moses command you?" he
replied.
4 They said, "Moses allowed a man
to write a letter of divorce and send her
away."
5 "You were stubborn. That's why Moses wrote you this law," Jesus replied.
6 "But at the beginning of creation, God
'made them male and female.' (Genesis
1:27) 7 'That's why a man will leave his father and mother and be joined to his wife.
8 The two of them will become one.' (Genesis 2:24) They are no longer two, but one.
9 So no one should separate what God has
joined together."
10 When they were in the house again,
the disciples asked Jesus about this. 11 He
answered, "What if a man divorces his
wife and gets married to another woman?
He commits adultery against her. 12 And

what if she divorces her husband and gets married to another man? She commits adultery."

Little Children Are Brought to Jesus

13 People were bringing little children to Jesus. They wanted him to place his hands on them to bless them. But the disciples told them to stop. 14 When Jesus saw this, he was angry. He said to his disciples, "Let the little children come to me. Don't keep them away. God's kingdom belongs to people like them. 15 What I'm about to tell you is true. Anyone who will not receive God's kingdom like a little child will never enter it." 16 Then he took the children in his arms. He placed his hands on them to bless them.

Rich People and the Kingdom of God

17 As Jesus started on his way, a man ran up to him. He fell on his knees before Jesus. "Good teacher," he said, "what must I do to receive eternal life?"

18 "Why do you call me good?" Jesus answered. "No one is good except God. 19 You know what the commandments say. 'Do not murder. Do not commit adultery. Do not steal. Do not be a false witness. Do not cheat. Honor your father and mother.' " (Exodus 20:12–16; Deuteronomy 5:16–20)

20 "Teacher," he said, "I have obeyed all those commandments since I was a boy."

21 Jesus looked at him and loved him. "You are missing one thing," he said. "Go and sell everything you have. Give the money to those who are poor. You will have treasure in heaven. Then come and follow me."

22 The man's face fell. He went away sad, because he was very rich.

23 Jesus looked around. He said to his disciples, "How hard it is for rich people to enter God's kingdom!"

24 The disciples were amazed at his words. But Jesus said again, "Children, how hard it is to enter God's kingdom! 25 Is it hard for a camel to go through the eye of a needle? It is even harder for someone who is rich to enter God's kingdom!"

26 The disciples were even more amazed. They said to each other, "Then who can be saved?"

27 Jesus looked at them and said, "With people, this is impossible. But not with God. All things are possible with God."

28 Then Peter spoke up, "We have left everything to follow you!"

29 "What I'm about to tell you is true," Jesus replied. "Has anyone left home or family or fields for me and the good news? 30 They will receive 100 times as much in this world. They will have homes and families and fields. But they will also be treated badly by others. In the world to come they will live forever. 31 But many who are first will be last. And the last will be first."

Jesus Speaks a Third Time About His Coming Death

32 They were on their way up to Jerusalem. Jesus was leading the way. The disciples were amazed. Those who followed were afraid. Again Jesus took the 12 disciples to one side. He told them what was going to happen to him. 33 "We are going up to Jerusalem," he said. "The Son of Man will be handed over to the chief priests and the teachers of the law. They will sentence him to death. Then they will hand him over to the Gentiles. 34 They will make fun of him and spit on him. They will whip him and kill him. Three days later he will rise from the dead!"

James and John Ask Jesus for a Favor

35 James and John came to Jesus. They were the sons of Zebedee. "Teacher," they said, "we would like to ask you for a favor."

36 "What do you want me to do for you?" he asked.

37 They replied, "Let one of us sit at your right hand in your glorious kingdom. Let the other one sit at your left hand."

38 "You don't know what you're asking for," Jesus said. "Can you drink the cup of suffering I drink? Or can you go through the baptism of suffering I must go through?"

39 "We can," they answered.

Jesus said to them, "You will drink the cup I drink. And you will go through the baptism I go through. 40 But it is not for me to say who will sit at my right or left hand. These places belong to those they are prepared for."

41 The other ten disciples heard about it. They became angry at James and John. 42 Jesus called them together. He said,

"You know about those who are rulers of the Gentiles. They hold power over their people. Their high officials order them around. 43 Don't be like that. Instead, anyone who wants to be important among you must be your servant. 44 And anyone who wants to be first must be the slave of everyone. 45 Even the Son of Man did not come to be served. Instead, he came to serve others. He came to give his life as the price for setting many people free."

Blind Bartimaeus Receives His Sight

46 Jesus and his disciples came to Jericho. They were leaving the city. A large crowd was with them. A blind man was sitting by the side of the road begging. His name was Bartimaeus. Bartimaeus means Son of Timaeus. 47 He heard that Jesus of Nazareth was passing by. So he began to shout, "Jesus! Son of David! Have mercy on me!"

48 Many people commanded him to stop. They told him to be quiet. But he shouted even louder, "Son of David! Have mercy on me!"

49 Jesus stopped and said, "Call for him."

So they called out to the blind man, "Cheer up! Get up on your feet! Jesus is calling for you." 50 He threw his coat to one side. Then he jumped to his feet and came to Jesus.

51 "What do you want me to do for you?" Jesus asked him.

The blind man said, "Rabbi, I want to be able to see."

52 "Go," said Jesus. "Your faith has healed you." Right away he could see. And he followed Jesus along the road.

Jesus Comes to Jerusalem as King

11 As they all approached Jerusalem, they came to Bethphage and Bethany at the Mount of Olives. Jesus sent out two of his disciples. 2 He said to them, "Go to the village ahead of you. Just as you enter it, you will find a donkey's colt tied there. No one has ever ridden it. Untie it and bring it here. 3 Someone may ask you, 'Why are you doing this?' If so, say, 'The Lord needs it. But he will send it back here soon.'"

4 So they left. They found a colt out in the street. It was tied at a doorway. They untied it. 5 Some people standing there asked, "What are you doing? Why are you untying that colt?" 6 They answered as Jesus had told them to. So the people let them go. 7 They brought the colt to Jesus. They threw their coats over it. Then he sat on it. 8 Many people spread their coats on the road. Others spread branches they had cut in the fields. 9 Those in front and those in back shouted,

"Hosanna!"

"Blessed is the one who comes
in the name of the Lord!"
(Psalm 118:25,26)

10 "Blessed is the coming kingdom of
our father David!"

"Hosanna in the highest heaven!"

11 Jesus entered Jerusalem and went into the temple courtyard. He looked around at everything. But it was already late. So he went out to Bethany with the 12 disciples.

Jesus Curses a Fig Tree and Clears Out the Temple Courtyard

12 The next day as Jesus and his disciples were leaving Bethany, they were hungry. 13 Not too far away, he saw a fig tree. It was covered with leaves. He went to find out if it had any fruit. When he reached it, he found nothing but leaves. It was not the season for figs. 14 Then Jesus said to the tree, "May no one ever eat fruit from you again!" And his disciples heard him say it.

15 When Jesus reached Jerusalem, he entered the temple courtyard. He began to drive out those who were buying and selling there. He turned over the tables of the people who were exchanging money. He also turned over the benches of those who were selling doves. 16 He would not allow anyone to carry items for sale through the temple courtyard. 17 Then he taught them. He told them, "It is written that the Lord said, 'My house will be called a house where people from all nations can pray.' (Isaiah 56:7) But you have made it a 'den for robbers.'" (Jeremiah 7:11)

18 The chief priests and the teachers of the law heard about this. They began looking for a way to kill Jesus. They were afraid of him, because the whole crowd was amazed at his teaching.

19 When evening came, Jesus and his disciples left the city.

The Dried-Up Fig Tree

20 In the morning as Jesus and his disciples walked along, they saw the fig tree.
It was dried up all the way down to the
roots. 21 Peter remembered. He said to
Jesus, "Rabbi, look! The fig tree you put a
curse on has dried up!"
22 "Have faith in God," Jesus said.
23 "What I'm about to tell you is true.
Suppose someone says to this mountain, 'Go and throw yourself into the sea.'
They must not doubt in their heart. They
must believe that what they say will happen. Then it will be done for them. 24 So
I tell you, when you pray for something,
believe that you have already received it.
Then it will be yours. 25-26 And when you
stand praying, forgive anyone you have
anything against. Then your Father in
heaven will forgive your sins."

The Authority of Jesus Is Questioned

27 Jesus and his disciples arrived again
in Jerusalem. He was walking in the temple courtyard. Then the chief priests
came to him. The teachers of the law and
the elders came too. 28 "By what authority
are you doing these things?" they asked.
"Who gave you authority to do this?"
29 Jesus replied, "I will ask you one
question. Answer me, and I will tell you
by what authority I am doing these things.
30 Was John's baptism from heaven? Or
did it come from human authority? Tell
me!"
31 They talked to each other about it.
They said, "If we say, 'From heaven,' he
will ask, 'Then why didn't you believe
him?' 32 But what if we say, 'From human
authority'?" They were afraid of the people. Everyone believed that John really
was a prophet.
33 So they answered Jesus, "We don't
know."

Jesus said, "Then I won't tell you by
what authority I am doing these things
either."

The Story of the Renters

12 Jesus began to speak to the people using stories. He said, "A man
planted a vineyard. He put a wall around
it. He dug a pit for a winepress. He also
built a lookout tower. He rented the vineyard out to some farmers. Then he went to
another place. 2 At harvest time he sent a
servant to the renters. He told the servant
to collect from them some of the fruit of
the vineyard. 3 But they grabbed the servant and beat him up. Then they sent him
away with nothing. 4 So the man sent another servant to the renters. They hit this
one on the head and treated him badly.
5 The man sent still another servant. The
renters killed him. The man sent many
others. The renters beat up some of them.
They killed the others.
6 "The man had one person left to send.
It was his son, and he loved him. He sent
him last of all. He said, 'They will respect
my son.'
7 "But the renters said to each other,
'This is the one who will receive all the
owner's property someday. Come, let's
kill him. Then everything will be ours.' 8 So
they took him and killed him. They threw
him out of the vineyard.
9 "What will the owner of the vineyard
do then? He will come and kill those renters. He will give the vineyard to others.
10 Haven't you read what this part of Scripture says,

" 'The stone the builders didn't
accept
has become the most important
stone of all.
11 The Lord has done it.
It is wonderful in our eyes'?"
(Psalm 118:22,23)

12 Then the chief priests, the teachers
of the law and the elders looked for a way
to arrest Jesus. They knew he had told the
story against them. But they were afraid
of the crowd. So they left him and went
away.

Is It Right to Pay the Royal Tax to Caesar?

13 Later the religious leaders sent some
of the Pharisees and Herodians to Jesus.
They wanted to trap him with his own
words. 14 They came to him and said,
"Teacher, we know that you are a man of
honor. You don't let other people tell you
what to do or say. You don't care how important they are. But you teach the way of
God truthfully. Is it right to pay the royal
tax to Caesar or not? 15 Should we pay or
shouldn't we?"

But Jesus knew what they were trying
to do. So he asked, "Why are you trying
to trap me? Bring me a silver coin. Let me

look at it." 16 They brought the coin. He
asked them, "Whose picture is this? And
whose words?"
"Caesar's," they replied.
17 Then Jesus said to them, "Give back
to Caesar what belongs to Caesar. And
give back to God what belongs to God."
They were amazed at him.

Marriage When the Dead Rise

18 The Sadducees came to Jesus with a
question. They do not believe that people
rise from the dead. 19 "Teacher," they said,
"Moses wrote for us about a man who
died and didn't have any children. But
he did leave a wife behind. That man's
brother must get married to the widow.
He must provide children to carry on his
dead brother's name. 20 There were seven
brothers. The first one got married. He
died without leaving any children. 21 The
second one got married to the widow.
He also died and left no child. It was the
same with the third one. 22 In fact, none of
the seven left any children. Last of all, the
woman died too. 23 When the dead rise,
whose wife will she be? All seven of them
were married to her."
24 Jesus replied, "You are mistaken because you do not know the Scriptures.
And you do not know the power of God.
25 When the dead rise, they won't get married. And their parents won't give them to
be married. They will be like the angels
in heaven. 26 What about the dead rising?
Haven't you read in the Book of Moses
the story of the burning bush? God said
to Moses, 'I am the God of Abraham. I am
the God of Isaac. And I am the God of Jacob.' (Exodus 3:6) 27 He is not the God of the
dead. He is the God of the living. You have
made a big mistake!"

The Most Important Commandment

28 One of the teachers of the law came
and heard the Sadducees arguing. He noticed that Jesus had given the Sadducees a
good answer. So he asked him, "Which is
the most important of all the commandments?"
29 Jesus answered, "Here is the most
important one. Moses said, 'Israel, listen
to me. The Lord is our God. The Lord is
one. 30 Love the Lord your God with all
your heart and with all your soul. Love
him with all your mind and with all your
strength.' (Deuteronomy 6:4,5) 31 And here is
the second one. 'Love your neighbor as
you love yourself.' (Leviticus 19:18) There is
no commandment more important than
these."
32 "You have spoken well, teacher," the
man replied. "You are right in saying that
God is one. There is no other God but
him. 33 To love God with all your heart and
mind and strength is very important. So is
loving your neighbor as you love yourself.
These things are more important than all
burnt offerings and sacrifices."
34 Jesus saw that the man had answered
wisely. He said to him, "You are not far
from God's kingdom." From then on, no
one dared to ask Jesus any more questions.

Whose Son Is the Messiah?

35 Jesus was teaching in the temple
courtyard. He asked, "Why do the teachers of the law say that the Messiah is the
son of David? 36 The Holy Spirit spoke
through David himself. David said,

" 'The Lord said to my Lord,
"Sit at my right hand
until I put your enemies
under your control." ' (Psalm 110:1)

37 David himself calls him 'Lord.' So how
can he be David's son?"
The large crowd listened to Jesus with
delight.

Warning Against the Teachers of the Law

38 As he taught, he said, "Watch out for
the teachers of the law. They like to walk
around in long robes. They like to be
greeted with respect in the market. 39 They
love to have the most important seats in
the synagogues. They also love to have
the places of honor at dinners. 40 They
take over the houses of widows. They say
long prayers to show off. God will punish
these men very much."

The Widow's Offering

41 Jesus sat down across from the place
where people put their temple offerings. He watched the crowd putting their
money into the offering boxes. Many rich
people threw large amounts into them.
42 But a poor widow came and put in two
very small copper coins. They were worth
only a few pennies.

43 Jesus asked his disciples to come to him. He said, "What I'm about to tell you is true. That poor widow has put more into the offering box than all the others. 44 They all gave a lot because they are rich. But she gave even though she is poor. She put in everything she had. That was all she had to live on."

When the Temple Will Be Destroyed and the Signs of the End

13 Jesus was leaving the temple. One of his disciples said to him, "Look, Teacher! What huge stones! What wonderful buildings!"

2 "Do you see these huge buildings?" Jesus asked. "Not one stone here will be left on top of another. Every stone will be thrown down."

3 Jesus was sitting on the Mount of Olives, across from the temple. Peter, James, John and Andrew asked him a question in private. 4 "Tell us," they said. "When will these things happen? And what will be the sign that they are all about to come true?"

5 Jesus said to them, "Keep watch! Be careful that no one fools you. 6 Many will come in my name. They will claim, 'I am he.' They will fool many people. 7 You will hear about wars. You will also hear people talking about future wars. Don't be alarmed. These things must happen. But the end still isn't here. 8 Nation will fight against nation. Kingdom will fight against kingdom. There will be earthquakes in many places. People will go hungry. All these things are the beginning of birth pains.

9 "Watch out! You will be handed over to the local courts. You will be whipped in the synagogues. You will stand in front of governors and kings because of me. In that way you will be witnesses to them. 10 The good news has to be preached to all nations before the end comes. 11 You will be arrested and brought to trial. But don't worry ahead of time about what you will say. Just say what God brings to your mind at the time. It is not you speaking, but the Holy Spirit.

12 "Brothers will hand over brothers to be killed. Fathers will hand over their children. Children will rise up against their parents and have them put to death. 13 Everyone will hate you because of me. But the one who remains strong in the faith will be saved.

14 "You will see 'the hated thing that destroys.' (Daniel 9:27; 11:31; 12:11) It will stand where it does not belong. The reader should understand this. Then those who are in Judea should escape to the mountains. 15 No one on the roof should go down into the house to take anything out. 16 No one in the field should go back to get their coat. 17 How awful it will be in those days for pregnant women! How awful for nursing mothers! 18 Pray that this will not happen in winter. 19 Those days will be worse than any others from the time God created the world until now. And there will never be any like them again.

20 "If the Lord had not cut the time short, no one would live. But because of God's chosen people, he has shortened it. 21 At that time someone may say to you, 'Look! Here is the Messiah!' Or, 'Look! There he is!' Do not believe it. 22 False messiahs and false prophets will appear. They will do signs and miracles. They will try to fool God's chosen people if possible. 23 Keep watch! I have told you everything ahead of time.

24 "So in those days there will be terrible suffering. After that, Scripture says,

" 'The sun will be darkened.
  The moon will not shine.
25 The stars will fall from the sky.
  The heavenly bodies will be
    shaken.' (Isaiah 13:10; 34:4)

26 "At that time people will see the Son of Man coming in clouds. He will come with great power and glory. 27 He will send his angels. He will gather his chosen people from all four directions. He will bring them from the ends of the earth to the ends of the heavens.

28 "Learn a lesson from the fig tree. As soon as its twigs get tender and its leaves come out, you know that summer is near. 29 In the same way, when you see these things happening, you know that the end is near. It is right at the door. 30 What I'm about to tell you is true. The people living now will certainly not pass away until all those things have happened. 31 Heaven and earth will pass away. But my words will never pass away.

The Day and Hour Are Not Known

32 “But no one knows about that day or hour. Not even the angels in heaven know. The Son does not know. Only the Father knows. 33 Keep watch! Stay awake! You do not know when that time will come. 34 It’s like a man going away. He leaves his house and puts his servants in charge. Each one is given a task to do. He tells the one at the door to keep watch.

35 “So keep watch! You do not know when the owner of the house will come back. It may be in the evening or at midnight. It may be when the rooster crows or at dawn. 36 He may come suddenly. So do not let him find you sleeping. 37 What I say to you, I say to everyone. ‘Watch!’ ”

A Woman Pours Perfume on Jesus at Bethany

14 The Passover and the Feast of Unleavened Bread were only two days away. The chief priests and the teachers of the law were plotting to arrest Jesus secretly. They wanted to kill him. 2 “But not during the feast,” they said. “The people may stir up trouble.”

3 Jesus was in Bethany. He was at the table in the home of Simon, who had a skin disease. A woman came with a special sealed jar. It contained very expensive perfume made out of pure nard. She broke the jar open and poured the perfume on Jesus’ head.

4 Some of the people there became angry. They said to one another, “Why waste this perfume? 5 It could have been sold for more than a year’s pay. The money could have been given to poor people.” So they found fault with the woman.

6 “Leave her alone,” Jesus said. “Why are you bothering her? She has done a beautiful thing to me. 7 You will always have poor people with you. You can help them any time you want to. But you will not always have me. 8 She did what she could. She poured perfume on my body to prepare me to be buried. 9 What I’m about to tell you is true. What she has done will be told anywhere the good news is preached all over the world. It will be told in memory of her.”

10 Judas Iscariot was one of the 12 disciples. He went to the chief priests to hand Jesus over to them. 11 They were delighted to hear that he would do this. They promised to give Judas money. So he watched for the right time to hand Jesus over to them.

The Last Supper

12 It was the first day of the Feast of Unleavened Bread. That was the time to sacrifice the Passover lamb. Jesus’ disciples asked him, “Where do you want us to go and prepare for you to eat the Passover meal?”

13 So he sent out two of his disciples. He told them, “Go into the city. A man carrying a jar of water will meet you. Follow him. 14 He will enter a house. Say to its owner, ‘The Teacher asks, “Where is my guest room? Where can I eat the Passover meal with my disciples?” ’ 15 He will show you a large upstairs room. It will have furniture and will be ready. Prepare for us to eat there.”

16 The disciples left and went into the city. They found things just as Jesus had told them. So they prepared the Passover meal.

17 When evening came, Jesus arrived with the 12 disciples. 18 While they were at the table eating, Jesus said, “What I’m about to tell you is true. One of you who is eating with me will hand me over to my enemies.”

19 The disciples became sad. One by one they said to him, “Surely you don’t mean me?”

20 “It is one of you,” Jesus replied. “It is the one who dips bread into the bowl with me. 21 The Son of Man will go just as it is written about him. But how terrible it will be for the one who hands over the Son of Man! It would be better for him if he had not been born.”

22 While they were eating, Jesus took bread. He gave thanks and broke it. He handed it to his disciples and said, “Take it. This is my body.”

23 Then he took a cup. He gave thanks and handed it to them. All of them drank from it.

24 “This is my blood of the covenant,” he said to them. “It is poured out for many. 25 What I’m about to tell you is true. I won’t drink wine with you again until the day I drink it in God’s kingdom.”

26 Then they sang a hymn and went out to the Mount of Olives.

Jesus Says That the Disciples Will Turn Away

27 "You will all turn away," Jesus told the
disciples. "It is written,

" 'I will strike the shepherd down.
Then the sheep will be scattered.'
(Zechariah 13:7)

28 But after I rise from the dead, I will go
ahead of you into Galilee."

29 Peter said, "All the others may turn
away. But I will not."

30 "What I'm about to tell you is true,"
Jesus answered. "It will happen today,
in fact tonight. Before the rooster crows
twice, you yourself will say three times
that you don't know me."

31 But Peter would not give in. He said,
"I may have to die with you. But I will
never say I don't know you." And all the
others said the same thing.

Jesus Prays in Gethsemane

32 Jesus and his disciples went to a place
called Gethsemane. Jesus said to them,
"Sit here while I pray." 33 He took Peter,
James and John along with him. He began
to be very upset and troubled. 34 "My soul
is very sad. I feel close to death," he said to
them. "Stay here. Keep watch."

35 He went a little farther. Then he fell
to the ground. He prayed that, if possible,
the hour might pass by him. 36 "*Abba*, Father" he said, "everything is possible for
you. Take this cup of suffering away from
me. But let what you want be done, not
what I want."

37 Then he returned to his disciples and
found them sleeping. "Simon," he said to
Peter, "are you asleep? Couldn't you keep
watch for one hour? 38 Watch and pray.
Then you won't fall into sin when you
are tempted. The spirit is willing, but the
body is weak."

39 Once more Jesus went away and
prayed the same thing. 40 Then he came
back. Again he found them sleeping. They
couldn't keep their eyes open. They did
not know what to say to him.

41 Jesus returned the third time. He said
to them, "Are you still sleeping and resting? Enough! The hour has come. Look!
The Son of Man is about to be handed
over to sinners. 42 Get up! Let us go! Here
comes the one who is handing me over to
them!"

Jesus Is Arrested

43 Just as Jesus was speaking, Judas appeared. He was one of the 12 disciples. A
crowd was with him. They were carrying
swords and clubs. The chief priests, the
teachers of the law, and the elders had
sent them.

44 Judas, who was going to hand Jesus
over, had arranged a signal with them.
"The one I kiss is the man," he said. "Arrest him and have the guards lead him
away." 45 So Judas went to Jesus at once.
Judas said, "Rabbi!" And he kissed Jesus.
46 The men grabbed Jesus and arrested
him. 47 Then one of those standing nearby
pulled his sword out. He struck the servant of the high priest and cut off his ear.

48 "Am I leading a band of armed men
against you?" asked Jesus. "Do you have
to come out with swords and clubs to
capture me? 49 Every day I was with you.
I taught in the temple courtyard, and you
didn't arrest me. But the Scriptures must
come true." 50 Then everyone left him and
ran away.

51 A young man was following Jesus.
The man was wearing nothing but a piece
of linen cloth. When the crowd grabbed
him, 52 he ran away naked. He left his
clothing behind.

Jesus Is Taken to the Sanhedrin

53 The crowd took Jesus to the high
priest. All the chief priests, the elders, and
the teachers of the law came together.
54 Not too far away, Peter followed Jesus.
He went right into the courtyard of the
high priest. There he sat with the guards.
He warmed himself at the fire.

55 The chief priests and the whole Sanhedrin were looking for something to use
against Jesus. They wanted to put him to
death. But they did not find any proof.
56 Many witnesses lied about him. But
their stories did not agree.

57 Then some of them stood up. Here
is what those false witnesses said about
him. 58 "We heard him say, 'I will destroy
this temple made by human hands. In
three days I will build another temple, not
made by human hands.' " 59 But what they
said did not agree.

60 Then the high priest stood up in front
of them. He asked Jesus, "Aren't you going
to answer? What are these charges these

men are bringing against you?" 61 But
Jesus remained silent. He gave no answer.
Again the high priest asked him, "Are
you the Messiah? Are you the Son of the
Blessed One?"
62 "I am," said Jesus. "And you will see
the Son of Man sitting at the right hand
of the Mighty One. You will see the Son of
Man coming on the clouds of heaven."
63 The high priest tore his clothes.
"Why do we need any more witnesses?"
he asked. 64 "You have heard him say a
very evil thing against God. What do you
think?"
They all found him guilty and said he
must die. 65 Then some began to spit at
him. They blindfolded him. They hit him
with their fists. They said, "Prophesy!"
And the guards took him and beat him.

Peter Says He Does Not Know Jesus

66 Peter was below in the courtyard.
One of the high priest's female servants
came by. 67 When she saw Peter warming
himself, she looked closely at him.
"You also were with Jesus, that Nazarene," she said.
68 But Peter said he had not been with
him. "I don't know or understand what
you're talking about," he said. He went
out to the entrance to the courtyard.
69 The servant saw him there. She said
again to those standing around, "This fellow is one of them." 70 Again he said he
was not.
After a little while, those standing
nearby said to Peter, "You must be one of
them. You are from Galilee."
71 Then Peter began to curse. He said to
them, "I don't know this man you're talking about!"
72 Right away the rooster crowed the
second time. Then Peter remembered
what Jesus had spoken to him. "The
rooster will crow twice," he had said. "Before it does, you will say three times that
you don't know me." Peter broke down
and cried.

Jesus Is Brought to Pilate

15 It was very early in the morning. The
chief priests, with the elders, the
teachers of the law, and the whole Sanhedrin, made their plans. So they tied Jesus
up and led him away. Then they handed
him over to Pilate.
2 "Are you the king of the Jews?" asked
Pilate.
"You have said so," Jesus replied.
3 The chief priests brought many
charges against him. 4 So Pilate asked him
again, "Aren't you going to answer? See
how many things they charge you with."
5 But Jesus still did not reply. Pilate was
amazed.
6 It was the usual practice at the Passover Feast to let one prisoner go free.
The people could choose the one they
wanted. 7 A man named Barabbas was
in prison. He was there with some other
people who had fought against the country's rulers. They had committed murder
while they were fighting against the rulers. 8 The crowd came up and asked Pilate
to do for them what he usually did.
9 "Do you want me to let the king of the
Jews go free?" asked Pilate. 10 He knew that
the chief priests had handed Jesus over to
him because they wanted to get their own
way. 11 But the chief priests stirred up the
crowd. So the crowd asked Pilate to let
Barabbas go free instead.
12 "Then what should I do with the one
you call the king of the Jews?" Pilate asked
them.
13 "Crucify him!" the crowd shouted.
14 "Why? What wrong has he done?"
asked Pilate.
But they shouted even louder, "Crucify
him!"
15 Pilate wanted to satisfy the crowd. So
he let Barabbas go free. He ordered that
Jesus be whipped. Then he handed him
over to be nailed to a cross.

The Soldiers Make Fun of Jesus

16 The soldiers led Jesus away into the
palace. It was called the Praetorium. They
called together the whole company of soldiers. 17 The soldiers put a purple robe on
Jesus. Then they twisted thorns together
to make a crown. They placed it on his
head. 18 They began to call out to him,
"We honor you, king of the Jews!" 19 Again
and again they hit him on the head with a
stick. They spit on him. They fell on their
knees and pretended to honor him. 20 After they had made fun of him, they took
off the purple robe. They put his own
clothes back on him. Then they led him
out to nail him to a cross.

Jesus Is Nailed to a Cross

21 A man named Simon was passing
by. He was from Cyrene. He was the father of Alexander and Rufus. Simon was
on his way in from the country. The soldiers forced him to carry the cross. 22 They
brought Jesus to the place called Golgotha. The word Golgotha means the Place
of the Skull. 23 Then they gave him wine
mixed with spices. But he did not take it.
24 They nailed him to the cross. Then they
divided up his clothes. They cast lots to
see what each of them would get.

25 It was nine o'clock in the morning
when they crucified him. 26 They wrote
out the charge against him. It read, THE
KING OF THE JEWS.

27-28 They crucified with him two rebels
against Rome. One was on his right and
one was on his left. 29 Those who passed
by shouted at Jesus and made fun of him.
They shook their heads and said, "So you
are going to destroy the temple and build
it again in three days? 30 Then come down
from the cross! Save yourself!" 31 In the
same way the chief priests and the teachers of the law made fun of him among
themselves. "He saved others," they said.
"But he can't save himself! 32 Let this Messiah, this king of Israel, come down now
from the cross! When we see that, we will
believe." Those who were being crucified
with Jesus also made fun of him.

Jesus Dies

33 At noon, darkness covered the whole
land. It lasted three hours. 34 At three
o'clock in the afternoon Jesus cried out
in a loud voice, "*Eloi, Eloi, lema sabachthani?*" This means "My God, my God,
why have you deserted me?" (Psalm 22:1)

35 Some of those standing nearby heard
Jesus cry out. They said, "Listen! He's calling for Elijah."

36 Someone ran and filled a sponge
with wine vinegar. He put it on a stick.
He offered it to Jesus to drink. "Leave him
alone," he said. "Let's see if Elijah comes
to take him down."

37 With a loud cry, Jesus took his last
breath.

38 The temple curtain was torn in two
from top to bottom. 39 A Roman commander was standing there in front of
Jesus. He saw how Jesus died. Then he
said, "This man was surely the Son of
God!"

40 Not very far away, some women were
watching. Mary Magdalene was among
them. Mary, the mother of the younger
James and of Joseph, was also there. So
was Salome. 41 In Galilee these women
had followed Jesus. They had taken care
of his needs. Many other women were
also there. They had come up with him to
Jerusalem.

Jesus Is Buried

42 It was the day before the Sabbath. That
day was called Preparation Day. As evening approached, 43 Joseph went boldly to
Pilate and asked for Jesus' body. Joseph
was from the town of Arimathea. He was
a leading member of the Jewish Council.
He was waiting for God's kingdom. 44 Pilate was surprised to hear that Jesus was
already dead. So he called for the Roman
commander. He asked him if Jesus had already died. 45 The commander said it was
true. So Pilate gave the body to Joseph.
46 Then Joseph bought some linen cloth.
He took down the body and wrapped it
in the linen. He put it in a tomb cut out
of rock. Then he rolled a stone against the
entrance to the tomb. 47 Mary Magdalene
and Mary the mother of Joseph saw where
Jesus' body had been placed.

Jesus Rises From the Dead

16 The Sabbath day ended. Mary Magdalene, Mary the mother of James,
and Salome bought spices. They were
going to use them for Jesus' body. 2 Very
early on the first day of the week, they
were on their way to the tomb. It was just
after sunrise. 3 They asked each other,
"Who will roll the stone away from the entrance to the tomb?"

4 Then they looked up and saw that
the stone had been rolled away. The
stone was very large. 5 They entered the
tomb. As they did, they saw a young man
dressed in a white robe. He was sitting on
the right side. They were alarmed.

6 "Don't be alarmed," he said. "You are
looking for Jesus the Nazarene, who was
crucified. But he has risen! He is not here!
See the place where they had put him.
7 Go! Tell his disciples and Peter, 'He is going ahead of you into Galilee. There you
will see him. It will be just as he told you.'"

8 The women were shaking and con-
fused. They went out and ran away from
the tomb. They said nothing to anyone,
because they were afraid.

9 Jesus rose from the dead early on the
first day of the week. He appeared first to
Mary Magdalene. He had driven seven
demons out of her. 10 She went and told
those who had been with him. She found
them crying. They were very sad. 11 They
heard that Jesus was alive and that she
had seen him. But they did not believe it.

12 After that, Jesus appeared in a different form to two of them. This happened
while they were walking out in the country. 13 The two returned and told the others about it. But the others did not believe
them either.

14 Later Jesus appeared to the 11 disciples as they were eating. He spoke firmly
to them because they had no faith. They
would not believe those who had seen
him after he rose from the dead.

15 He said to them, "Go into all the
world. Preach the good news to everyone.
16 Anyone who believes and is baptized
will be saved. But anyone who does not
believe will be punished. 17 Here are the
miraculous signs that those who believe
will do. In my name they will drive out demons. They will speak in languages they
had not known before. 18 They will pick up
snakes with their hands. And when they
drink deadly poison, it will not hurt them
at all. They will place their hands on sick
people. And the people will get well."

19 When the Lord Jesus finished
speaking to them, he was taken up into
heaven. He sat down at the right hand of
God. 20 Then the disciples went out and
preached everywhere. The Lord worked
with them. And he backed up his word by
the signs that went with it.

LUKE

Luke wrote a two-part story of Jesus and the early Christians. These two parts are called Luke and Acts. They tell how God first invited the people of Israel to follow Jesus. And then later people from all nations are invited to follow him. In the book of Luke the story moves to Jerusalem. Jerusalem is the center of Israel's national life. In the book of Acts the story moves from Jerusalem to other nations. In the end a man named Paul preaches about the kingdom of God to the people living in Rome. Rome is the capital of the Roman Empire.

Luke writes his books for a Roman official named Theophilus. Luke wants Theophilus and others who are not Jews to know the story of Jesus. Luke wants everyone to know that God's saving plan is being fulfilled. Through his chosen people Israel, a light was brought into the world. Jesus the Messiah has come to all people. He has conquered sin and death. And now his followers are bringing this message about Jesus to all the nations.

The Gospel of Luke has three main parts:

First, Jesus does his work in Galilee, the northern area in the land of Israel.

Second, Jesus takes a long journey to Jerusalem. Along the way he tells people about the kingdom of God. And he shows what life is like when God rules the world.

Third, Luke tells how Jesus gave his life for others in Jerusalem. Then Jesus rises from the dead and sends his followers to tell the world about him.

Luke Writes an Orderly Report

1 Many people have attempted to write
about the things that have taken place
among us. 2 Reports of these things were
handed down to us. There were people
who saw these things for themselves from
the beginning. They saw them and then
passed the word on. 3 With this in mind,
I myself have carefully looked into everything from the beginning. So I also decided to write down an orderly report of
exactly what happened. I am doing this
for you, most excellent Theophilus. 4 I
want you to know that the things you have
been taught are true.

The Coming Birth of John the Baptist

5 Herod was king of Judea. During the
time he was ruling, there was a priest
named Zechariah. He belonged to a
group of priests named after Abijah. His
wife Elizabeth also came from the family
line of Aaron. 6 Both of them did what was
right in the sight of God. They obeyed all
the Lord's commands and rules faithfully.
7 But they had no children, because Elizabeth was not able to have any. And they
were both very old.
8 One day Zechariah's group was on
duty. He was serving as a priest in God's
temple. 9 He happened to be chosen, in
the usual way, to go into the temple of
the Lord. There he was supposed to burn
incense. 10 The time came for this to be
done. All who had gathered to worship
were praying outside.
11 Then an angel of the Lord appeared
to Zechariah. The angel was standing at
the right side of the incense altar. 12 When
Zechariah saw him, he was amazed and
terrified. 13 But the angel said to him, "Do
not be afraid, Zechariah. Your prayer has
been heard. Your wife Elizabeth will have
a child. It will be a boy, and you must call
him John. 14 He will be a joy and delight to
you. His birth will make many people very
glad. 15 He will be important in the sight of
the Lord. He must never drink wine or
other such drinks. He will be filled with
the Holy Spirit even before he is born.
16 He will bring back many of the people of
Israel to the Lord their God. 17 And he will
prepare the way for the Lord. He will have
the same spirit and power that Elijah had.
He will bring peace between parents and
their children. He will teach people who
don't obey to be wise and do what is right.
In this way, he will prepare a people who
are ready for the Lord."
18 Zechariah asked the angel, "How can
I be sure of this? I am an old man, and my
wife is old too."
19 The angel said to him, "I am Gabriel.
I serve God. I have been sent to speak to
you and to tell you this good news. 20 And
now you will have to be silent. You will not
be able to speak until after John is born.
That's because you did not believe my

words. They will come true at the time
God has chosen."
21 During that time, the people were
waiting for Zechariah to come out of the
temple. They wondered why he stayed
there so long. 22 When he came out, he
could not speak to them. They realized
he had seen a vision in the temple. They
knew this because he kept gesturing to
them. He still could not speak.
23 When his time of service was over,
he returned home. 24 After that, his wife
Elizabeth became pregnant. She stayed
at home for five months. 25 "The Lord has
done this for me," she said. "In these days,
he has been kind to me. He has taken
away my shame among the people."

The Coming Birth of Jesus

26 In the sixth month after Elizabeth
had become pregnant, God sent the angel Gabriel to Nazareth, a town in Galilee.
27 He was sent to a virgin. The girl was engaged to a man named Joseph. He came
from the family line of David. The virgin's
name was Mary. 28 The angel greeted her
and said, "The Lord has blessed you in a
special way. He is with you."
29 Mary was very upset because of his
words. She wondered what kind of greeting this could be. 30 But the angel said to
her, "Do not be afraid, Mary. God is very
pleased with you. 31 You will become pregnant and give birth to a son. You must call
him Jesus. 32 He will be great and will be
called the Son of the Most High God. The
Lord God will make him a king like his father David of long ago. 33 The Son of the
Most High God will rule forever over his
people. They are from the family line of
Jacob. That kingdom will never end."
34 "How can this happen?" Mary asked
the angel. "I am a virgin."
35 The angel answered, "The Holy Spirit
will come to you. The power of the Most
High God will cover you. So the holy one
that is born will be called the Son of God.
36 Your relative Elizabeth will have a child
even though she is old. People thought
she could not have children. But she
has been pregnant for six months now.
37 That's because what God says will always come true."
38 "I serve the Lord," Mary answered.
"May it happen to me just as you said it
would." Then the angel left her.

Mary Visits Elizabeth

39 At that time Mary got ready and hurried to a town in Judea's hill country.
40 There she entered Zechariah's home
and greeted Elizabeth. 41 When Elizabeth
heard Mary's greeting, the baby inside her
jumped. And Elizabeth was filled with the
Holy Spirit. 42 In a loud voice she called
out, "God has blessed you more than other women. And blessed is the child you
will have! 43 But why is God so kind to me?
Why has the mother of my Lord come to
me? 44 As soon as I heard the sound of
your voice, the baby inside me jumped for
joy. 45 You are a woman God has blessed.
You have believed that the Lord would
keep his promises to you!"

Mary's Song

46 Mary said,

"My soul gives glory to the Lord.
47 My spirit delights in God my
Savior.
48 He has taken note of me
even though I am not considered
important.
From now on all people will call me
blessed.
49 The Mighty One has done great
things for me.
His name is holy.
50 He shows his mercy to those who
have respect for him,
from parent to child down
through the years.
51 He has done mighty things with his
powerful arm.
He has scattered those who
are proud in their deepest
thoughts.
52 He has brought down rulers from
their thrones.
But he has lifted up people
who are not considered
important.
53 He has filled with good things those
who are hungry.
But he has sent away empty those
who are rich.
54 He has helped the people of Israel,
who serve him.
He has always remembered to be
kind
55 to Abraham and his children down
through the years.

He has done it just as he promised
to our people of long ago."

56 Mary stayed with Elizabeth about
three months. Then she returned home.

John the Baptist Is Born

57 The time came for Elizabeth to have
her baby. She gave birth to a son. 58 Her
neighbors and relatives heard that the
Lord had been very kind to her. They
shared her joy.

59 On the eighth day, they came to have
the child circumcised. They were going to
name him Zechariah, like his father. 60 But
his mother spoke up. "No!" she said. "He
must be called John."

61 They said to her, "No one among your
relatives has that name."

62 Then they motioned to his father.
They wanted to find out what he would
like to name the child. 63 He asked for
something to write on. Then he wrote,
"His name is John." Everyone was
amazed. 64 Right away Zechariah could
speak again. Right away he praised God.
65 All his neighbors were filled with fear
and wonder. Throughout Judea's hill
country, people were talking about all
these things. 66 Everyone who heard this
wondered about it. And because the Lord
was with John, they asked, "What is this
child going to be?"

Zechariah's Song

67 John's father Zechariah was filled
with the Holy Spirit. He prophesied,

68 "Give praise to the Lord, the God of
Israel!
He has come to his people and
purchased their freedom.
69 He has acted with great power and
has saved us.
He did it for those who are from
the family line of his servant
David.
70 Long ago holy prophets said he
would do it.
71 He has saved us from our enemies.
We are rescued from all who hate
us.
72 He has been kind to our people of
long ago.
He has remembered his holy
covenant.
73 He made a promise to our father
Abraham.
74 He promised to save us from our
enemies.
Then we could serve him without
fear.
75 He wants us to be holy and godly
as long as we live.

76 "And you, my child, will be called
a prophet of the Most High
God.
You will go ahead of the Lord to
prepare the way for him.
77 You will tell his people how they can
be saved.
You will tell them that their sins
can be forgiven.
78 All of that will happen because our
God is tender and caring.
His kindness will bring the rising
sun to us from heaven.
79 It will shine on those living in
darkness
and in the shadow of death.
It will guide our feet on the path of
peace."

80 The child grew up, and his spirit became strong. He lived in the desert until
he appeared openly to Israel.

Jesus Is Born

2 In those days, Caesar Augustus made
a law. It required that a list be made of
everyone in the whole Roman world. 2 It
was the first time a list was made of the
people while Quirinius was governor of
Syria. 3 Everyone went to their own town
to be listed.

4 So Joseph went also. He went from
the town of Nazareth in Galilee to Judea.
That is where Bethlehem, the town of David, was. Joseph went there because he
belonged to the family line of David. 5 He
went there with Mary to be listed. Mary
was engaged to him. She was expecting a
baby. 6 While Joseph and Mary were there,
the time came for the child to be born.
7 She gave birth to her first baby. It was a
boy. She wrapped him in large strips of
cloth. Then she placed him in a manger.
That's because there was no guest room
where they could stay.

8 There were shepherds living out in the
fields nearby. It was night, and they were
taking care of their sheep. 9 An angel of the

Lord appeared to them. And the glory of
the Lord shone around them. They were
terrified. 10 But the angel said to them,
"Do not be afraid. I bring you good news.
It will bring great joy for all the people.
11 Today in the town of David a Savior has
been born to you. He is the Messiah, the
Lord. 12 Here is how you will know I am
telling you the truth. You will find a baby
wrapped in strips of cloth and lying in a
manger."

13 Suddenly a large group of angels from
heaven also appeared. They were praising God. They said,

14 "May glory be given to God in the
highest heaven!
And may peace be given to those
he is pleased with on earth!"

15 The angels left and went into heaven.
Then the shepherds said to one another,
"Let's go to Bethlehem. Let's see this thing
that has happened, which the Lord has
told us about."

16 So they hurried off and found Mary
and Joseph and the baby. The baby was
lying in the manger. 17 After the shepherds
had seen him, they told everyone. They
reported what the angel had said about
this child. 18 All who heard it were amazed
at what the shepherds said to them. 19 But
Mary kept all these things like a secret
treasure in her heart. She thought about
them over and over. 20 The shepherds returned. They gave glory and praise to
God. Everything they had seen and heard
was just as they had been told.

21 When the child was eight days old, he
was circumcised. At the same time he was
named Jesus. This was the name the angel had given him before his mother became pregnant.

Joseph and Mary Take Jesus to the Temple

22 The time came for making Mary
"clean" as required by the Law of Moses.
So Joseph and Mary took Jesus to Jerusalem. There they presented him to the
Lord. 23 In the Law of the Lord it says,
"The first boy born in every family must
be set apart for the Lord." (Exodus 13:2,12)
24 They also offered a sacrifice. They did
it in keeping with the Law, which says, "a
pair of doves or two young pigeons." (Leviticus 12:8)

25 In Jerusalem there was a man named
Simeon. He was a good and godly man.
He was waiting for God's promise to Israel
to come true. The Holy Spirit was with
him. 26 The Spirit had told Simeon that
he would not die before he had seen the
Lord's Messiah. 27 The Spirit led him into
the temple courtyard. Then Jesus' parents
brought the child in. They came to do for
him what the Law required. 28 Simeon
took Jesus in his arms and praised God.
He said,

29 "Lord, you are the King over all.
Now let me, your servant, go in
peace.
That is what you promised.
30 My eyes have seen your salvation.
31 You have prepared it in the sight
of all nations.
32 It is a light to be given to the
Gentiles.
It will be the glory of your people
Israel."

33 The child's father and mother were
amazed at what was said about him.
34 Then Simeon blessed them. He said to
Mary, Jesus' mother, "This child is going to cause many people in Israel to fall
and to rise. God has sent him. But many
will speak against him. 35 The thoughts of
many hearts will be known. A sword will
wound your own soul too."

36 There was also a prophet named
Anna. She was the daughter of Penuel
from the tribe of Asher. Anna was very
old. After getting married, she lived with
her husband seven years. 37 Then she was
a widow until she was 84. She never left
the temple. She worshiped night and day,
praying and going without food. 38 Anna
came up to Jesus' family at that moment.
She gave thanks to God. And she spoke
about the child to all who were looking forward to the time when Jerusalem
would be set free.

39 Joseph and Mary did everything the
Law of the Lord required. Then they returned to Galilee. They went to their own
town of Nazareth. 40 And the child grew
and became strong. He was very wise. He
was blessed by God's grace.

The Boy Jesus at the Temple

41 Every year Jesus' parents went to Jerusalem for the Passover Feast. 42 When
Jesus was 12 years old, they went up to

the feast as usual. [43]After the feast was over, his parents left to go back home. The boy Jesus stayed behind in Jerusalem. But they were not aware of it. [44]They thought he was somewhere in their group. So they traveled on for a day. Then they began to look for him among their relatives and friends. [45]They did not find him. So they went back to Jerusalem to look for him. [46]After three days they found him in the temple courtyard. He was sitting with the teachers. He was listening to them and asking them questions. [47]Everyone who heard him was amazed at how much he understood. They also were amazed at his answers. [48]When his parents saw him, they were amazed. His mother said to him, "Son, why have you treated us like this? Your father and I have been worried about you. We have been looking for you everywhere."

[49]"Why were you looking for me?" he asked. "Didn't you know I had to be in my Father's house?" [50]But they did not understand what he meant by that.

[51]Then he went back to Nazareth with them, and he obeyed them. But his mother kept all these things like a secret treasure in her heart. [52]Jesus became wiser and stronger. He also became more and more pleasing to God and to people.

John the Baptist Prepares the Way

3 Tiberius Caesar had been ruling for 15 years. Pontius Pilate was governor of Judea. Herod was the ruler of Galilee. His brother Philip was the ruler of Iturea and Traconitis. Lysanias was ruler of Abilene. [2]Annas and Caiaphas were high priests. At that time God's word came to John, son of Zechariah, in the desert. [3]He went into all the countryside around the Jordan River. There he preached that people should be baptized and turn away from their sins. Then God would forgive them. [4]Here is what is written in the book of Isaiah the prophet. It says,

"A messenger is calling out in the
desert,
'Prepare the way for the Lord.
Make straight paths for him.
[5]Every valley will be filled in.
Every mountain and hill will be
made level.
The crooked roads will become
straight.
The rough ways will become
smooth.
[6]And all people will see God's
salvation.' " (Isaiah 40:3–5)

[7]John spoke to the crowds coming to be baptized by him. He said, "You are like a nest of poisonous snakes! Who warned you to escape the coming of God's anger? [8]Live in a way that shows you have turned away from your sins. And don't start saying to yourselves, 'Abraham is our father.' I tell you, God can raise up children for Abraham even from these stones. [9]The ax is already lying at the roots of the trees. All the trees that don't produce good fruit will be cut down. They will be thrown into the fire."

[10]"Then what should we do?" the crowd asked.

[11]John answered, "Anyone who has extra clothes should share with the one who has none. And anyone who has extra food should do the same."

[12]Even tax collectors came to be baptized. "Teacher," they asked, "what should we do?"

[13]"Don't collect any more than you are required to," John told them.

[14]Then some soldiers asked him, "And what should we do?"

John replied, "Don't force people to give you money. Don't bring false charges against people. Be happy with your pay."

[15]The people were waiting. They were expecting something. They were all wondering in their hearts if John might be the Messiah. [16]John answered them all, "I baptize you with water. But one who is more powerful than I am will come. I'm not good enough to untie the straps of his sandals. He will baptize you with the Holy Spirit and fire. [17]His pitchfork is in his hand to toss the straw away from his threshing floor. He will gather the wheat into his barn. But he will burn up the husks with fire that can't be put out." [18]John said many other things to warn the people. He also announced the good news to them.

[19]But John found fault with Herod, the ruler of Galilee, because of his marriage to Herodias. She was the wife of Herod's brother. John also spoke strongly to Herod about all the other evil things he had done. [20]So Herod locked John up in prison. Herod added this sin to all his others.

The Baptism and Family Line of Jesus

[21] When all the people were being baptized, Jesus was baptized too. And as he
was praying, heaven was opened. [22] The
Holy Spirit came to rest on him in the
form of a dove. A voice came from heaven.
It said, "You are my Son, and I love you. I
am very pleased with you."

[23] Jesus was about 30 years old when he
began his special work for God and others. It was thought that he was the son of
Joseph.

Joseph was the son of Heli.
[24] Heli was the son of Matthat.
Matthat was the son of Levi.
Levi was the son of Melki.
Melki was the son of Jannai.
Jannai was the son of Joseph.
[25] Joseph was the son of Mattathias.
Mattathias was the son of Amos.
Amos was the son of Nahum.
Nahum was the son of Esli.
Esli was the son of Naggai.
[26] Naggai was the son of Maath.
Maath was the son of Mattathias.
Mattathias was the son of Semein.
Semein was the son of Josek.
Josek was the son of Joda.
[27] Joda was the son of Joanan.
Joanan was the son of Rhesa.
Rhesa was the son of Zerubbabel.
Zerubbabel was the son of Shealtiel.
Shealtiel was the son of Neri.
[28] Neri was the son of Melki.
Melki was the son of Addi.
Addi was the son of Cosam.
Cosam was the son of Elmadam.
Elmadam was the son of Er.
[29] Er was the son of Joshua.
Joshua was the son of Eliezer.
Eliezer was the son of Jorim.
Jorim was the son of Matthat.
Matthat was the son of Levi.
[30] Levi was the son of Simeon.
Simeon was the son of Judah.
Judah was the son of Joseph.
Joseph was the son of Jonam.
Jonam was the son of Eliakim.
[31] Eliakim was the son of Melea.
Melea was the son of Menna.
Menna was the son of Mattatha.
Mattatha was the son of Nathan.
Nathan was the son of David.
[32] David was the son of Jesse.
Jesse was the son of Obed.
Obed was the son of Boaz.
Boaz was the son of Salmon.
Salmon was the son of Nahshon.
[33] Nahshon was the son of Ammina-
dab.
Amminadab was the son of Ram.
Ram was the son of Hezron.
Hezron was the son of Perez.
Perez was the son of Judah.
[34] Judah was the son of Jacob.
Jacob was the son of Isaac.
Isaac was the son of Abraham.
Abraham was the son of Terah.
Terah was the son of Nahor.
[35] Nahor was the son of Serug.
Serug was the son of Reu.
Reu was the son of Peleg.
Peleg was the son of Eber.
Eber was the son of Shelah.
[36] Shelah was the son of Cainan.
Cainan was the son of Arphaxad.
Arphaxad was the son of Shem.
Shem was the son of Noah.
Noah was the son of Lamech.
[37] Lamech was the son of Methuselah.
Methuselah was the son of Enoch.
Enoch was the son of Jared.
Jared was the son of Mahalalel.
Mahalalel was the son of Kenan.
[38] Kenan was the son of Enosh.
Enosh was the son of Seth.
Seth was the son of Adam.
Adam was the son of God.

Jesus Is Tempted in the Desert

4 Jesus, full of the Holy Spirit, left the
Jordan River. The Spirit led him into
the desert. [2] There the devil tempted him
for 40 days. Jesus ate nothing during that
time. At the end of the 40 days, he was
hungry.

[3] The devil said to him, "If you are the
Son of God, tell this stone to become
bread."

[4] Jesus answered, "It is written, 'Man
must not live only on bread.'" (Deuteronomy 8:3)

[5] Then the devil led Jesus up to a high
place. In an instant, he showed Jesus all
the kingdoms of the world. [6] He said to
Jesus, "I will give you all their authority
and glory. It has been given to me, and
I can give it to anyone I want to. [7] If you
worship me, it will all be yours."

[8] Jesus answered, "It is written, 'Wor-

ship the Lord your God. He is the only one
you should serve.' " (Deuteronomy 6:13)
9 Then the devil led Jesus to Jerusalem.
He had Jesus stand on the highest point
of the temple. "If you are the Son of God,"
he said, "throw yourself down from here.
10 It is written,

" 'The Lord will command his angels
to take good care of you.
11 They will lift you up in their hands.
Then you won't trip over a stone.' "
(Psalm 91:11,12)

12 Jesus answered, "Scripture says, 'Do
not test the Lord your God.' " (Deuteronomy
6:16)
13 When the devil finished all this
tempting, he left Jesus until a better time.

Jesus Is Not Accepted in Nazareth

14 Jesus returned to Galilee in the power
of the Holy Spirit. News about him spread
through the whole countryside. 15 He was
teaching in their synagogues, and everyone praised him.
16 Jesus went to Nazareth, where he had
been brought up. On the Sabbath day
he went into the synagogue as he usually did. He stood up to read. 17 And the
scroll of Isaiah the prophet was handed to
him. Jesus unrolled it and found the right
place. There it is written,

18 "The Spirit of the Lord is on me.
He has anointed me
to announce the good news to
poor people.
He has sent me to announce
freedom for prisoners.
He has sent me so that the blind
will see again.
He wants me to set free those who
are treated badly.
19 And he has sent me to announce
the year when he will set his
people free." (Isaiah 61:1,2)

20 Then Jesus rolled up the scroll. He
gave it back to the attendant and sat
down. The eyes of everyone in the synagogue were staring at him. 21 He began
by saying to them, "Today this passage of
Scripture is coming true as you listen."
22 Everyone said good things about him.
They were amazed at the gracious words
they heard from his lips. "Isn't this Joseph's son?" they asked.
23 Jesus said, "Here is a saying you will
certainly apply to me. 'Doctor, heal yourself!' And you will tell me this. 'Do the
things here in your hometown that we
heard you did in Capernaum.' "
24 "What I'm about to tell you is true,"
he continued. "A prophet is not accepted
in his hometown. 25 I tell you for sure that
there were many widows in Israel in the
days of Elijah. And there had been no rain
for three and a half years. There wasn't
enough food to eat anywhere in the land.
26 But Elijah was not sent to any of those
widows. Instead, he was sent to a widow
in Zarephath near Sidon. 27 And there
were many in Israel who had skin diseases in the days of Elisha the prophet.
But not one of them was healed except
Naaman the Syrian."
28 All the people in the synagogue were
very angry when they heard that. 29 They
got up and ran Jesus out of town. They
took him to the edge of the hill on which
the town was built. They planned to throw
him off the cliff. 30 But Jesus walked right
through the crowd and went on his way.

Jesus Drives Out an Evil Spirit

31 Then Jesus went to Capernaum, a
town in Galilee. On the Sabbath day he
taught the people. 32 They were amazed at
his teaching, because his words had authority.
33 In the synagogue there was a man
controlled by a demon, an evil spirit. He
cried out at the top of his voice. 34 "Go
away!" he said. "What do you want with
us, Jesus of Nazareth? Have you come to
destroy us? I know who you are. You are
the Holy One of God!"
35 "Be quiet!" Jesus said firmly. "Come
out of him!" Then the demon threw the
man down in front of everybody. And it
came out without hurting him.
36 All the people were amazed. They
said to each other, "What he says is amazing! With authority and power he gives
orders to evil spirits. And they come out!"
37 The news about Jesus spread throughout the whole area.

Jesus Heals Many People

38 Jesus left the synagogue and went to
the home of Simon. At that time, Simon's
mother-in-law was suffering from a high
fever. So they asked Jesus to help her. 39 He

bent over her and commanded the fever
to leave, and it left her. She got up right
away and began to serve them.
40 At sunset, people brought to Jesus all
who were sick. He placed his hands on
each one and healed them. 41 Also, demons came out of many people. The demons shouted, "You are the Son of God!"
But he commanded them to be quiet. He
would not allow them to speak, because
they knew he was the Messiah.
42 At dawn, Jesus went out to a place
where he could be by himself. The people
went to look for him. When they found
him, they tried to keep him from leaving
them. 43 But he said, "I must announce the
good news of God's kingdom to the other
towns also. That is why I was sent." 44 And
he kept on preaching in the synagogues of
Judea.

Jesus Chooses His First Disciples

5 One day Jesus was standing by the
Sea of Galilee. The people crowded
around him and listened to the word of
God. 2 Jesus saw two boats at the edge of
the water. They had been left there by the
fishermen, who were washing their nets.
3 He got into the boat that belonged to Simon. Jesus asked him to go out a little way
from shore. Then he sat down in the boat
and taught the people.
4 When he finished speaking, he turned
to Simon. Jesus said, "Go out into deep
water. Let down the nets so you can catch
some fish."
5 Simon answered, "Master, we've
worked hard all night and haven't caught
anything. But because you say so, I will let
down the nets."
6 When they had done so, they caught a
large number of fish. There were so many
that their nets began to break. 7 So they
motioned to their partners in the other
boat to come and help them. They came
and filled both boats so full that they began to sink.
8 When Simon Peter saw this, he fell at
Jesus' knees. "Go away from me, Lord!" he
said. "I am a sinful man!" 9 He and everyone with him were amazed at the number
of fish they had caught. 10 So were James
and John, the sons of Zebedee, who
worked with Simon.
Then Jesus said to Simon, "Don't be
afraid. From now on you will fish for people." 11 So they pulled their boats up on
shore. Then they left everything and followed him.

Jesus Heals a Man Who Had a Skin Disease

12 While Jesus was in one of the towns,
a man came along. He had a skin disease
all over his body. When he saw Jesus, the
man fell with his face to the ground. He
begged him, "Lord, if you are willing to
make me 'clean,' you can do it."
13 Jesus reached out his hand and
touched the man. "I am willing to do it,"
he said. "Be 'clean'!" Right away the disease left him.
14 Then Jesus ordered him, "Don't tell
anyone. Go and show yourself to the
priest. Offer the sacrifices that Moses
commanded. It will be a witness to the
priest and the people that you are 'clean.' "
15 But the news about Jesus spread even
more. So crowds of people came to hear
him. They also came to be healed of their
sicknesses. 16 But Jesus often went away to
be by himself and pray.

Jesus Forgives and Heals a Man Who Could Not Walk

17 One day Jesus was teaching. Pharisees and teachers of the law were sitting
there. They had come from every village
of Galilee and from Judea and Jerusalem.
They heard that the Lord had given Jesus
the power to heal the sick. 18 So some men
came carrying a man who could not walk.
He was lying on a mat. They tried to take
him into the house to place him in front
of Jesus. 19 They could not find a way to
do this because of the crowd. So they
went up on the roof. Then they lowered
the man on his mat through the opening
in the roof tiles. They lowered him into
the middle of the crowd, right in front of
Jesus.
20 When Jesus saw that they had faith,
he spoke to the man. He said, "Friend,
your sins are forgiven."
21 The Pharisees and the teachers of the
law began to think, "Who is this fellow
who says such an evil thing? Who can forgive sins but God alone?"
22 Jesus knew what they were thinking.
So he asked, "Why are you thinking these
things in your hearts? 23 Is it easier to say,
'Your sins are forgiven'? Or to say, 'Get up

and walk'? 24 But I want you to know that
the Son of Man has authority on earth to
forgive sins." So he spoke to the man who
could not walk. "I tell you," he said, "get
up. Take your mat and go home." 25 Right
away, the man stood up in front of them.
He took his mat and went home praising
God. 26 Everyone was amazed and gave
praise to God. They were filled with wonder. They said, "We have seen unusual
things today."

Jesus Chooses Levi and Eats With Sinners

27 After this, Jesus left the house. He saw
a tax collector sitting at the tax booth. The
man's name was Levi. "Follow me," Jesus
said to him. 28 Levi got up, left everything
and followed him.

29 Then Levi gave a huge banquet for
Jesus at his house. A large crowd of tax
collectors and others were eating with
them. 30 But the Pharisees and their teachers of the law complained to Jesus' disciples. They said, "Why do you eat and
drink with tax collectors and sinners?"

31 Jesus answered them, "Healthy people don't need a doctor. Sick people do.
32 I have not come to get those who think
they are right with God to follow me. I
have come to get sinners to turn away
from their sins."

Jesus Is Asked About Fasting

33 Some of the people who were there
said to Jesus, "John's disciples often pray
and go without eating. So do the disciples
of the Pharisees. But yours go on eating
and drinking."

34 Jesus answered, "Can you make the
friends of the groom fast while he is with
them? 35 But the time will come when the
groom will be taken away from them. In
those days they will go without eating."

36 Then Jesus gave them an example.
He said, "No one tears a piece out of new
clothes to patch old clothes. Otherwise,
they will tear the new clothes. Also, the
patch from the new clothes will not match
the old clothes. 37 No one pours new wine
into old wineskins. Otherwise, the new
wine will burst the skins. The wine will
run out, and the wineskins will be destroyed. 38 No, new wine must be poured
into new wineskins. 39 After drinking old
wine, no one wants the new. They say,
'The old wine is better.' "

Jesus Is Lord of the Sabbath Day

6 One Sabbath day Jesus was walking
through the grainfields. His disciples
began to break off some heads of grain.
They rubbed them in their hands and ate
them. 2 Some of the Pharisees said, "It is
against the Law to do this on the Sabbath
day. Why are you doing it?"

3 Jesus answered them, "Haven't you
ever read about what David did? He and
his men were hungry. 4 He entered the
house of God and took the holy bread.
He ate the bread that only priests were allowed to eat. David also gave some to his
men." 5 Then Jesus said to them, "The Son
of Man is Lord of the Sabbath day."

6 On another Sabbath day, Jesus went
into the synagogue and was teaching.
A man whose right hand was weak and
twisted was there. 7 The Pharisees and
the teachers of the law were trying to find
fault with Jesus. So they watched him
closely. They wanted to see if he would
heal on the Sabbath day. 8 But Jesus knew
what they were thinking. He spoke to the
man who had the weak and twisted hand.
"Get up and stand in front of everyone,"
he said. So the man got up and stood
there.

9 Then Jesus said to them, "What does
the Law say we should do on the Sabbath
day? Should we do good? Or should we
do evil? Should we save life? Or should we
destroy it?"

10 He looked around at all of them. Then
he said to the man, "Stretch out your
hand." He did, and his hand had been
made as good as new. 11 But the Pharisees and the teachers of the law were very
angry. They began to talk to one another
about what they might do to Jesus.

Jesus Chooses the Twelve Apostles

12 On one of those days, Jesus went out
to a mountainside to pray. He spent the
night praying to God. 13 When morning
came, he called for his disciples to come to
him. He chose 12 of them and made them
apostles. 14 Simon was one of them. Jesus
gave him the name Peter. There were also
Simon's brother Andrew, James, John,
Philip and Bartholomew. 15 And there
were Matthew, Thomas, and James, son
of Alphaeus. There were also Simon who
was called the Zealot 16 and Judas, son
of James. Judas Iscariot was one of them

too. He was the one who would later hand Jesus over to his enemies.

Jesus Gives Blessings and Warnings

17 Jesus went down the mountain with them and stood on a level place. A large crowd of his disciples was there. A large number of other people were there too. They came from all over Judea, including Jerusalem. They also came from the coastland around Tyre and Sidon. 18 They had all come to hear Jesus and to be healed of their sicknesses. People who were troubled by evil spirits were made well. 19 Everyone tried to touch Jesus. Power was coming from him and healing them all.

20 Jesus looked at his disciples. He said to them,

"Blessed are you who are needy.
  God's kingdom belongs to you.
21 Blessed are you who are hungry
    now.
  You will be satisfied.
Blessed are you who are sad now.
  You will laugh.
22 Blessed are you when people hate
    you,
  when they have nothing to do
    with you
  and say bad things about you,
  and when they treat your name as
    something evil.
 They do all this because you are
    followers of the Son of Man.

23 "The prophets of long ago were treated the same way. When these things happen to you, be glad and jump for joy. You will receive many blessings in heaven.

24 "But how terrible it will be for you
    who are rich!
  You have already had your easy
    life.
25 How terrible for you who are well
    fed now!
  You will go hungry.
How terrible for you who laugh now!
  You will cry and be sad.
26 How terrible for you when everyone
    says good things about you!
  Their people treated the false
    prophets the same way long
    ago.

Love Your Enemies

27 "But here is what I tell you who are listening. Love your enemies. Do good to those who hate you. 28 Bless those who call down curses on you. And pray for those who treat you badly. 29 Suppose someone slaps you on one cheek. Let them slap you on the other cheek as well. Suppose someone takes your coat. Don't stop them from taking your shirt as well. 30 Give to everyone who asks you. And if anyone takes what belongs to you, don't ask to get it back. 31 Do to others as you want them to do to you.

32 "Suppose you love those who love you. Should anyone praise you for that? Even sinners love those who love them. 33 And suppose you do good to those who are good to you. Should anyone praise you for that? Even sinners do that. 34 And suppose you lend money to those who can pay you back. Should anyone praise you for that? Even a sinner lends to sinners, expecting them to pay everything back. 35 But love your enemies. Do good to them. Lend to them without expecting to get anything back. Then you will receive a lot in return. And you will be children of the Most High God. He is kind to people who are evil and are not thankful. 36 So have mercy, just as your Father has mercy.

Be Fair When You Judge Other People

37 "If you do not judge other people, then you will not be judged. If you do not find others guilty, then you will not be found guilty. Forgive, and you will be forgiven. 38 Give, and it will be given to you. A good amount will be poured into your lap. It will be pressed down, shaken together, and running over. The same amount you give will be measured out to you."

39 Jesus also gave them another example. He asked, "Can a blind person lead another blind person? Won't they both fall into a pit? 40 The student is not better than the teacher. But everyone who is completely trained will be like their teacher.

41 "You look at the bit of sawdust in your friend's eye. But you pay no attention to the piece of wood in your own eye. 42 How can you say to your friend, 'Let me take the bit of sawdust out of your eye'? How can you say this while there is a piece of

wood in your own eye? You pretender! First take the piece of wood out of your own eye. Then you will be able to see clearly to take the bit of sawdust out of your friend's eye.

A Tree and Its Fruit

43 "A good tree doesn't bear bad fruit. And a bad tree doesn't bear good fruit. 44 You can tell each tree by the kind of fruit it bears. People do not pick figs from thorns. And they don't pick grapes from bushes. 45 A good man says good things. These come from the good that is stored up in his heart. An evil man says evil things. These come from the evil that is stored up in his heart. A person's mouth says everything that is in their heart.

The Wise and Foolish Builders

46 "Why do you call me, 'Lord, Lord,' and still don't do what I say? 47 Some people come and listen to me and do what I say. I will show you what they are like. 48 They are like a man who builds a house. He digs down deep and sets it on solid rock. When a flood comes, the river rushes against the house. But the water can't shake it. The house is well built. 49 But here is what happens when people listen to my words and do not obey them. They are like a man who builds a house on soft ground instead of solid rock. The moment the river rushes against that house, it falls down. It is completely destroyed."

A Roman Commander Has Faith

7 Jesus finished saying all these things to the people who were listening. Then he entered Capernaum. 2 There the servant of a Roman commander was sick and about to die. His master thought highly of him. 3 The commander heard about Jesus. So he sent some elders of the Jews to him. He told them to ask Jesus to come and heal his servant. 4 They came to Jesus and begged him, "This man deserves to have you do this. 5 He loves our nation and has built our synagogue." 6 So Jesus went with them.

When Jesus came near the house, the Roman commander sent friends to him. He told them to say, "Lord, don't trouble yourself. I am not good enough to have you come into my house. 7 That is why I did not even think I was fit to come to you. But just say the word, and my servant will be healed. 8 I myself am a man who is under authority. And I have soldiers who obey my orders. I tell this one, 'Go,' and he goes. I tell that one, 'Come,' and he comes. I say to my servant, 'Do this,' and he does it."

9 When Jesus heard this, he was amazed at the commander. Jesus turned to the crowd that was following him. He said, "I tell you, even in Israel I have not found anyone whose faith is so strong." 10 Then the men who had been sent to Jesus returned to the house. They found that the servant was healed.

Jesus Raises a Widow's Son From the Dead

11 Some time later, Jesus went to a town called Nain. His disciples and a large crowd went along with him. 12 He approached the town gate. Just then, a dead person was being carried out. He was the only son of his mother. She was a widow. A large crowd from the town was with her. 13 When the Lord saw her, he felt sorry for her. So he said, "Don't cry."

14 Then he went up and touched the coffin. Those carrying it stood still. Jesus said, "Young man, I say to you, get up!" 15 The dead man sat up and began to talk. Then Jesus gave him back to his mother.

16 The people were all filled with wonder and praised God. "A great prophet has appeared among us," they said. "God has come to help his people." 17 This news about Jesus spread all through Judea and the whole country.

Jesus and John the Baptist

18 John's disciples told him about all these things. So he chose two of them. 19 He sent them to the Lord. John told them to ask him, "Are you the one who is supposed to come? Or should we look for someone else?"

20 The men came to Jesus. They said, "John the Baptist sent us to ask you, 'Are you the one who is supposed to come? Or should we look for someone else?' "

21 At that time Jesus healed many people. They had illnesses, sicknesses and evil spirits. He also gave sight to many who were blind. 22 So Jesus replied to the messengers, "Go back to John. Tell him what you have seen and heard. Blind peo-

ple receive sight. Disabled people walk. Those who have skin diseases are made 'clean.' Deaf people hear. Those who are dead are raised to life. And the good news is announced to those who are poor. 23 Blessed is anyone who does not give up their faith because of me."

24 So John's messengers left. Then Jesus began to speak to the crowd about John. He said, "What did you go out into the desert to see? Tall grass waving in the wind? 25 If not, what did you go out to see? A man dressed in fine clothes? No. Those who wear fine clothes and have many expensive things are in palaces. 26 Then what did you go out to see? A prophet? Yes, I tell you, and more than a prophet. 27 He is the one written about in Scripture. It says,

"'I will send my messenger ahead of
you.
He will prepare your way for you.'
(Malachi 3:1)

28 I tell you, no one more important than John has ever been born. But the least important person in God's kingdom is more important than John is."

29 All the people who heard Jesus' words agreed that God's way was right. Even the tax collectors agreed. These people had all been baptized by John. 30 But the Pharisees and the authorities on the law did not accept for themselves God's purpose. So they had not been baptized by John.

31 Jesus went on to say, "What can I compare today's people to? What are they like? 32 They are like children sitting in the market and calling out to each other. They say,

"'We played the flute for you.
But you didn't dance.
We sang a funeral song.
But you didn't cry.'

33 That is how it has been with John the Baptist. When he came to you, he didn't eat bread or drink wine. And you say, 'He has a demon.' 34 But when the Son of Man came, he ate and drank as you do. And you say, 'This fellow is always eating and drinking far too much. He's a friend of tax collectors and sinners.' 35 All who follow wisdom prove that wisdom is right."

A Sinful Woman Pours Perfume on Jesus

36 One of the Pharisees invited Jesus to have dinner with him. So he went to the Pharisee's house. He took his place at the table. 37 There was a woman in that town who had lived a sinful life. She learned that Jesus was eating at the Pharisee's house. So she came there with a special jar of perfume. 38 She stood behind Jesus and cried at his feet. And she began to wet his feet with her tears. Then she wiped them with her hair. She kissed them and poured perfume on them.

39 The Pharisee who had invited Jesus saw this. He said to himself, "If this man were a prophet, he would know who is touching him. He would know what kind of woman she is. She is a sinner!"

40 Jesus answered him, "Simon, I have something to tell you."

"Tell me, teacher," he said.

41 "Two people owed money to a certain lender. One owed him 500 silver coins. The other owed him 50 silver coins. 42 Neither of them had the money to pay him back. So he let them go without paying. Which of them will love him more?"

43 Simon replied, "I suppose the one who owed the most money."

"You are right," Jesus said.

44 Then he turned toward the woman. He said to Simon, "Do you see this woman? I came into your house. You did not give me any water to wash my feet. But she wet my feet with her tears and wiped them with her hair. 45 You did not give me a kiss. But this woman has not stopped kissing my feet since I came in. 46 You did not put any olive oil on my head. But she has poured this perfume on my feet. 47 So I tell you this. Her many sins have been forgiven. She has shown that she understands this by her great acts of love. But whoever has been forgiven only a little loves only a little."

48 Then Jesus said to her, "Your sins are forgiven."

49 The other guests began to talk about this among themselves. They said, "Who is this who even forgives sins?"

50 Jesus said to the woman, "Your faith has saved you. Go in peace."

The Story of the Farmer

8 After this, Jesus traveled around from one town and village to another. He announced the good news of God's kingdom. His 12 disciples were with him. 2 So

were some women who had been healed
of evil spirits and sicknesses. One was
Mary Magdalene. Seven demons had
come out of her. 3Another was Joanna,
the wife of Chuza. He was the manager of
Herod's household. Susanna and many
others were there also. These women
were helping to support Jesus and the 12
disciples with their own money.

4A large crowd gathered together. People came to Jesus from town after town.
As they did, he told a story. He said, 5"A
farmer went out to plant his seed. He
scattered the seed on the ground. Some
fell on a path. People walked on it, and the
birds ate it up. 6Some seed fell on rocky
ground. When it grew, the plants dried up
because they had no water. 7Other seed
fell among thorns. The thorns grew up
with it and crowded out the plants. 8Still
other seed fell on good soil. It grew up
and produced a crop 100 times more than
the farmer planted."

When Jesus said this, he called out,
"Whoever has ears should listen."

9His disciples asked him what the story
meant. 10He said, "You have been given
the chance to understand the secrets of
God's kingdom. But to outsiders I speak
by using stories. In that way,

" 'They see, but they will not know
what they are seeing.
They hear, but they will not
understand what they are
hearing.' (Isaiah 6:9)

11"Here is what the story means. The
seed is God's message. 12The seed on
the path stands for God's message in the
hearts of those who hear. But then the
devil comes. He takes away the message
from their hearts. He does it so they won't
believe. Then they can't be saved. 13The
seed on rocky ground stands for those
who hear the message and receive it with
joy. But they have no roots. They believe
for a while. But when they are tested,
they fall away from the faith. 14The seed
that fell among thorns stands for those
who hear the message. But as they go on
their way, they are choked by life's worries, riches and pleasures. So they do not
reach full growth. 15But the seed on good
soil stands for those with an honest and
good heart. Those people hear the message. They keep it in their hearts. They
remain faithful and produce a good crop.

A Lamp on a Stand

16"No one lights a lamp and then hides
it in a clay jar or puts it under a bed. Instead, they put it on a stand. Then those
who come in can see its light. 17What is
hidden will be seen. And what is out of
sight will be brought into the open and
made known. 18So be careful how you listen. Whoever has something will be given
more. Whoever has nothing, even what
they think they have will be taken away
from them."

Jesus' Mother and Brothers

19Jesus' mother and brothers came
to see him. But they could not get near
him because of the crowd. 20Someone
told him, "Your mother and brothers are
standing outside. They want to see you."

21He replied, "My mother and brothers
are those who hear God's word and do
what it says."

Jesus Calms the Storm

22One day Jesus said to his disciples,
"Let's go over to the other side of the lake."
So they got into a boat and left. 23As they
sailed, Jesus fell asleep. A storm came
down on the lake. It was so bad that the
boat was about to sink. They were in great
danger.

24The disciples went and woke Jesus
up. They said, "Master! Master! We're going to drown!"

He got up and ordered the wind and
the huge waves to stop. The storm quieted
down. It was completely calm. 25"Where
is your faith?" he asked his disciples.

They were amazed and full of fear. They
asked one another, "Who is this? He commands even the winds and the waves, and
they obey him."

Jesus Heals a Man Controlled by Demons

26Jesus and his disciples sailed to the
area of the Gerasenes across the lake from
Galilee. 27When Jesus stepped on shore,
he was met by a man from the town.
The man was controlled by demons. For
a long time he had not worn clothes or
lived in a house. He lived in the tombs.
28When he saw Jesus, he cried out and
fell at his feet. He shouted at the top of his

voice, "Jesus, Son of the Most High God,
what do you want with me? I beg you,
don't hurt me!" 29 This was because Jesus
had commanded the evil spirit to come
out of the man. Many times the spirit had
taken hold of him. The man's hands and
feet were chained, and he was kept under
guard. But he had broken his chains. And
then the demon had forced him to go out
into lonely places in the countryside.

30 Jesus asked him, "What is your
name?"

"Legion," he replied, because many
demons had gone into him. 31 And they
begged Jesus again and again not to order
them to go into the Abyss.

32 A large herd of pigs was feeding there
on the hillside. The demons begged Jesus
to let them go into the pigs. And he allowed it. 33 When the demons came out of
the man, they went into the pigs. Then the
herd rushed down the steep bank. They
ran into the lake and drowned.

34 Those who were tending the pigs saw
what had happened. They ran off and reported it in the town and countryside.
35 The people went out to see what had
happened. Then they came to Jesus. They
found the man who was now free of the
demons. He was sitting at Jesus' feet. He
was dressed and thinking clearly. All this
made the people afraid. 36 Those who had
seen it told the others how the man who
had been controlled by demons was now
healed. 37 Then all the people who lived in
the area of the Gerasenes asked Jesus to
leave them. They were filled with fear. So
he got into the boat and left.

38 The man who was now free of the demons begged to go with him. But Jesus
sent him away. He said to him, 39 "Return
home and tell how much God has done
for you." So the man went away. He told
people all over town how much Jesus had
done for him.

Jesus Heals a Dead Girl and a Suffering Woman

40 When Jesus returned, a crowd welcomed him. They were all expecting him.
41 Then a man named Jairus came. He was
a synagogue leader. He fell at Jesus' feet
and begged Jesus to come to his house.
42 His only daughter was dying. She was
about 12 years old. As Jesus was on his
way, the crowds almost crushed him.

43 A woman was there who had a sickness that made her bleed. Her sickness
had lasted for 12 years. No one could
heal her. 44 She came up behind Jesus and
touched the edge of his clothes. Right
away her bleeding stopped.

45 "Who touched me?" Jesus asked.

Everyone said they didn't do it. Then
Peter said, "Master, the people are crowding and pushing against you."

46 But Jesus said, "Someone touched
me. I know that power has gone out from
me."

47 The woman realized that people
would notice her. Shaking with fear, she
came and fell at his feet. In front of everyone, she told why she had touched him.
She also told how she had been healed in
an instant. 48 Then he said to her, "Dear
woman, your faith has healed you. Go in
peace."

49 While Jesus was still speaking, someone came from the house of Jairus. Jairus
was the synagogue leader. "Your daughter
is dead," the messenger said. "Don't bother the teacher anymore."

50 Hearing this, Jesus said to Jairus,
"Don't be afraid. Just believe. She will be
healed."

51 When he arrived at the house of Jairus, he did not let everyone go in with
him. He took only Peter, John and James,
and the child's father and mother. 52 During this time, all the people were crying
and sobbing loudly over the child. "Stop
crying!" Jesus said. "She is not dead. She
is sleeping."

53 They laughed at him. They knew she
was dead. 54 But he took her by the hand
and said, "My child, get up!" 55 Her spirit
returned, and right away she stood up.
Then Jesus told them to give her something to eat. 56 Her parents were amazed.
But Jesus ordered them not to tell anyone
what had happened.

Jesus Sends Out the Twelve Disciples

9 Jesus called together the 12 disciples.
He gave them power and authority
to drive out all demons and to heal sicknesses. 2 Then he sent them out to announce God's kingdom and to heal those
who were sick. 3 He told them, "Don't take
anything for the journey. Do not take a
walking stick or a bag. Do not take any
bread, money or extra clothes. 4 When

you are invited into a house, stay there until you leave town. 5 Some people may not welcome you. If they don't, leave their town and shake the dust off your feet. This will be a witness against the people living there." 6 So the 12 disciples left. They went from village to village. They announced the good news and healed people everywhere.

7 Now Herod, the ruler of Galilee, heard about everything that was going on. He was bewildered, because some were saying that John the Baptist had been raised from the dead. 8 Others were saying that Elijah had appeared. Still others were saying that a prophet of long ago had come back to life. 9 But Herod said, "I had John's head cut off. So who is it that I hear such things about?" And he tried to see Jesus.

Jesus Feeds the Five Thousand

10 The disciples returned. They told Jesus what they had done. Then he took them with him. They went off by themselves to a town called Bethsaida. 11 But the crowds learned about it and followed Jesus. He welcomed them and spoke to them about God's kingdom. He also healed those who needed to be healed.

12 Late in the afternoon the 12 disciples came to him. They said, "Send the crowd away. They can go to the nearby villages and countryside. There they can find food and a place to stay. There is nothing here."

13 Jesus replied, "You give them something to eat."

The disciples answered, "We have only five loaves of bread and two fish. We would have to go and buy food for all this crowd." 14 About 5,000 men were there.

But Jesus said to his disciples, "Have them sit down in groups of about 50 each." 15 The disciples did so, and everyone sat down. 16 Jesus took the five loaves and the two fish. He looked up to heaven and gave thanks. He broke them into pieces. Then he gave them to the disciples to give to the people. 17 All of them ate and were satisfied. The disciples picked up 12 baskets of leftover pieces.

Peter Says That Jesus Is the Messiah

18 One day Jesus was praying alone. Only his disciples were with him. He asked them, "Who do the crowds say I am?"

19 They replied, "Some say John the Baptist. Others say Elijah. Still others say that one of the prophets of long ago has come back to life."

20 "But what about you?" he asked. "Who do you say I am?"

Peter answered, "God's Messiah."

Jesus Speaks About His Coming Death

21 Jesus strongly warned them not to tell this to anyone. 22 He said, "The Son of Man must suffer many things. The elders will not accept him. The chief priests and the teachers of the law will not accept him either. He must be killed and on the third day rise from the dead."

23 Then he said to all of them, "Whoever wants to follow me must say no to themselves. They must pick up their cross every day and follow me. 24 Whoever wants to save their life will lose it. But whoever loses their life for me will save it. 25 What good is it if someone gains the whole world but loses or gives up their very self? 26 Suppose someone is ashamed of me and my words. The Son of Man will come in his glory and in the glory of the Father and the holy angels. Then he will be ashamed of that person.

27 "What I'm about to tell you is true. Some who are standing here will not die before they see God's kingdom."

Jesus' Appearance Is Changed

28 About eight days after Jesus said this, he went up on a mountain to pray. He took Peter, John and James with him. 29 As he was praying, the appearance of his face changed. His clothes became as bright as a flash of lightning. 30 Two men, Moses and Elijah, appeared in shining glory. Jesus and the two of them talked together. 31 They talked about how he would be leaving them soon. This was going to happen in Jerusalem. 32 Peter and his companions had been very sleepy. But then they became completely awake. They saw Jesus' glory and the two men standing with him. 33 As the men were leaving Jesus, Peter spoke up. "Master," he said to him, "it is good for us to be here. Let us put up three shelters. One will be for you, one for Moses, and one for Elijah." Peter didn't really know what he was saying.

34 While he was speaking, a cloud appeared and covered them. The disciples were afraid as they entered the cloud. 35 A

voice came from the cloud. It said, "This is my Son, and I have chosen him. Listen to him." 36 When the voice had spoken, they found that Jesus was alone. The disciples kept quiet about this. They didn't tell anyone at that time what they had seen.

Jesus Heals a Boy Who Is Controlled by an Evil Spirit

37 The next day Jesus and those who were with him came down from the mountain. A large crowd met Jesus. 38 A man in the crowd called out. "Teacher," he said, "I beg you to look at my son. He is my only child. 39 A spirit takes hold of him, and he suddenly screams. It throws him into fits so that he foams at the mouth. It hardly ever leaves him. It is destroying him. 40 I begged your disciples to drive it out. But they couldn't do it."

41 "You unbelieving and evil people!" Jesus replied. "How long do I have to stay with you? How long do I have to put up with you?" Then he said to the man, "Bring your son here."

42 Even while the boy was coming, the demon threw him into a fit. The boy fell to the ground. But Jesus ordered the evil spirit to leave the boy. Then Jesus healed him and gave him back to his father. 43 They were all amazed at God's greatness.

Jesus Speaks a Second Time About His Coming Death

Everyone was wondering about all that Jesus did. Then Jesus said to his disciples, 44 "Listen carefully to what I am about to tell you. The Son of Man is going to be handed over to men." 45 But they didn't understand what this meant. That was because it was hidden from them. And they were afraid to ask Jesus about it.

Who Is the Most Important Person?

46 The disciples began to argue about which one of them would be the most important person. 47 Jesus knew what they were thinking. So he took a little child and had the child stand beside him. 48 Then he spoke to them. "Anyone who welcomes this little child in my name welcomes me," he said. "And anyone who welcomes me welcomes the one who sent me. The one considered least important among all of you is really the most important."

49 "Master," said John, "we saw someone driving out demons in your name. We tried to stop him, because he is not one of us."

50 "Do not stop him," Jesus said. "Anyone who is not against you is for you."

The Samaritans Do Not Welcome Jesus

51 The time grew near for Jesus to be taken up to heaven. So he made up his mind to go to Jerusalem. 52 He sent messengers on ahead. They went into a Samaritan village to get things ready for him. 53 But the people there did not welcome Jesus. That was because he was heading for Jerusalem. 54 The disciples James and John saw this. They asked, "Lord, do you want us to call down fire from heaven to destroy them?" 55 But Jesus turned and commanded them not to do it. 56 Then Jesus and his disciples went on to another village.

The Cost of Following Jesus

57 Once Jesus and those who were with him were walking along the road. A man said to Jesus, "I will follow you no matter where you go."

58 Jesus replied, "Foxes have dens. Birds have nests. But the Son of Man has no place to lay his head."

59 He said to another man, "Follow me."

But the man replied, "Lord, first let me go and bury my father."

60 Jesus said to him, "Let dead people bury their own dead. You go and tell others about God's kingdom."

61 Still another person said, "I will follow you, Lord. But first let me go back and say goodbye to my family."

62 Jesus replied, "Suppose someone starts to plow and then looks back. That person is not fit for service in God's kingdom."

Jesus Sends Out the Seventy-Two

10 After this the Lord appointed 72 others. He sent them out two by two ahead of him. They went to every town and place where he was about to go. 2 He told them, "The harvest is huge, but the workers are few. So ask the Lord of the harvest to send out workers into his harvest field. 3 Go! I am sending you out like lambs among wolves. 4 Do not take a purse

or bag or sandals. And don't greet anyone
on the road.
5 “When you enter a house, first say,
‘May this house be blessed with peace.’ 6 If
someone there works to bring peace, your
blessing of peace will rest on them. If not,
it will return to you. 7 Stay there, and eat
and drink anything they give you. Workers are worthy of their pay. Do not move
around from house to house.
8 “When you enter a town and are welcomed, eat what is given to you. 9 Heal
the sick people who are there. Tell them,
‘God's kingdom has come near to you.’
10 But what if you enter a town and are
not welcomed? Then go into its streets
and say, 11 ‘We wipe from our feet even
the dust of your town. We do it to warn
you. But here is what you can be sure of.
God's kingdom has come near.’ 12 I tell you
this. On judgment day it will be easier for
Sodom than for that town.
13 “How terrible it will be for you, Chorazin! How terrible for you, Bethsaida!
Suppose the miracles done in you had
been done in Tyre and Sidon. They would
have turned away from their sins long
ago. They would have put on the rough
clothing people wear when they're sad.
They would have sat down in ashes. 14 On
judgment day it will be easier for Tyre
and Sidon than for you. 15 And what about
you, Capernaum? Will you be lifted up to
the heavens? No! You will go down to the
place of the dead.
16 “Whoever listens to you listens to me.
Whoever does not accept you does not
accept me. But whoever does not accept
me does not accept the one who sent me.”
17 The 72 returned with joy. They said,
“Lord, even the demons obey us when we
speak in your name.”
18 Jesus replied, “I saw Satan fall like
lightning from heaven. 19 I have given you
authority to walk all over snakes and scorpions. You will be able to destroy all the
power of the enemy. Nothing will harm
you. 20 But do not be glad when the evil
spirits obey you. Instead, be glad that
your names are written in heaven.”
21 At that time Jesus was full of joy
through the Holy Spirit. He said, “I praise
you, Father. You are Lord of heaven and
earth. You have hidden these things from
wise and educated people. But you have
shown them to little children. Yes, Father.
This is what you wanted to do.
22 “My Father has given all things to me.
The Father is the only one who knows
who the Son is. And the only ones who
know the Father are the Son and those to
whom the Son chooses to make the Father known.”
23 Then Jesus turned to his disciples. He
said to them in private, “Blessed are the
eyes that see what you see. 24 I tell you,
many prophets and kings wanted to see
what you see. But they didn't see it. They
wanted to hear what you hear. But they
didn't hear it.”

The Story of the Good Samaritan

25 One day an authority on the law
stood up to test Jesus. “Teacher,” he asked,
“what must I do to receive eternal life?”
26 “What is written in the Law?” Jesus replied. “How do you understand it?”
27 He answered, “ ‘Love the Lord your
God with all your heart and with all your
soul. Love him with all your strength and
with all your mind.’ (Deuteronomy 6:5) And,
‘Love your neighbor as you love yourself.’ ” (Leviticus 19:18)
28 “You have answered correctly,” Jesus
replied. “Do that, and you will live.”
29 But the man wanted to make himself
look good. So he asked Jesus, “And who is
my neighbor?”
30 Jesus replied, “A man was going down
from Jerusalem to Jericho. Robbers attacked him. They stripped off his clothes
and beat him. Then they went away, leaving him almost dead. 31 A priest happened
to be going down that same road. When
he saw the man, he passed by on the other side. 32 A Levite also came by. When he
saw the man, he passed by on the other
side too. 33 But a Samaritan came to the
place where the man was. When he saw
the man, he felt sorry for him. 34 He went
to him, poured olive oil and wine on his
wounds and bandaged them. Then he put
the man on his own donkey. He brought
him to an inn and took care of him. 35 The
next day he took out two silver coins. He
gave them to the owner of the inn. ‘Take
care of him,’ he said. ‘When I return, I will
pay you back for any extra expense you
may have.’
36 “Which of the three do you think was

a neighbor to the man who was attacked
by robbers?"

37 The authority on the law replied,
"The one who felt sorry for him."

Jesus told him, "Go and do as he did."

Jesus at the Home of Martha and Mary

38 Jesus and his disciples went on their
way. Jesus came to a village where a
woman named Martha lived. She welcomed him into her home. 39 She had a
sister named Mary. Mary sat at the Lord's
feet listening to what he said. 40 But Martha was busy with all the things that had
to be done. She came to Jesus and said,
"Lord, my sister has left me to do the work
by myself. Don't you care? Tell her to help
me!"

41 "Martha, Martha," the Lord answered.
"You are worried and upset about many
things. 42 But few things are needed. Really,
only one thing is needed. Mary has chosen
what is better. And it will not be taken away
from her."

Jesus Teaches About Prayer

11 One day Jesus was praying in a certain place. When he finished, one of
his disciples spoke to him. "Lord," he said,
"teach us to pray, just as John taught his
disciples."

2 Jesus said to them, "When you pray,
this is what you should say.

" 'Father,
may your name be honored.
May your kingdom come.
3 Give us each day our daily bread.
4 Forgive us our sins,
as we also forgive everyone who
sins against us.
Keep us from falling into sin when
we are tempted.' "

5 Then Jesus said to them, "Suppose you
have a friend. You go to him at midnight
and say, 'Friend, lend me three loaves of
bread. 6 A friend of mine on a journey has
come to stay with me. I have no food to
give him.' 7 And suppose the one inside
answers, 'Don't bother me. The door is
already locked. My children and I are in
bed. I can't get up and give you anything.'
8 I tell you, that person will not get up. And
he won't give you bread just because he is
your friend. But because you keep bothering him, he will surely get up. He will
give you as much as you need.

9 "So here is what I say to you. Ask, and
it will be given to you. Search, and you
will find. Knock, and the door will be
opened to you. 10 Everyone who asks will
receive. The one who searches will find.
And the door will be opened to the one
who knocks.

11 "Fathers, suppose your son asks for a
fish. Which of you will give him a snake
instead? 12 Or suppose he asks for an egg.
Which of you will give him a scorpion?
13 Even though you are evil, you know how
to give good gifts to your children. How
much more will your Father who is in
heaven give the Holy Spirit to those who
ask him!"

Jesus and Beelzebul

14 Jesus was driving out a demon. The
man who had the demon could not speak.
When the demon left, the man began
to speak. The crowd was amazed. 15 But
some of them said, "Jesus is driving out
demons by the power of Beelzebul, the
prince of demons." 16 Others tested Jesus
by asking for a sign from heaven.

17 Jesus knew what they were thinking.
So he said to them, "Any kingdom that
fights against itself will be destroyed. A
family that is divided against itself will
fall. 18 If Satan fights against himself, how
can his kingdom stand? I say this because of what you claim. You say I drive
out demons by the power of Beelzebul.
19 Suppose I do drive out demons with Beelzebul's help. With whose help do your
followers drive them out? So then, they
will be your judges. 20 But suppose I drive
out demons with the help of God's powerful finger. Then God's kingdom has come
upon you.

21 "When a strong man is completely
armed and guards his house, what he
owns is safe. 22 But when someone stronger attacks, he is overpowered. The at-
tacker takes away the armor the man had
trusted in. Then he divides up what he
has stolen.

23 "Whoever is not with me is against
me. And whoever does not gather with
me scatters.

24 "What happens when an evil spirit
comes out of a person? It goes through
dry areas looking for a place to rest. But it

doesn't find it. Then it says, 'I will return to the house I left.' 25 When it arrives there, it finds the house swept clean and put in order. 26 Then the evil spirit goes and takes seven other spirits more evil than itself. They go in and live there. That person is worse off than before."

27 As Jesus was saying these things, a woman in the crowd called out. She shouted, "Blessed is the mother who gave you birth and nursed you."

28 He replied, "Instead, blessed are those who hear God's word and obey it."

The Sign of Jonah

29 As the crowds grew larger, Jesus spoke to them. "The people of today are evil," he said. "They ask for a sign from God. But none will be given except the sign of Jonah. 30 He was a sign from God to the people of Nineveh. In the same way, the Son of Man will be a sign from God to the people of today. 31 The Queen of the South will stand up on judgment day with the people now living. And she will prove that they are guilty. She came from very far away to listen to Solomon's wisdom. And now something more important than Solomon is here. 32 The men of Nineveh will stand up on judgment day with the people now living. And the Ninevites will prove that those people are guilty. The men of Nineveh turned away from their sins when Jonah preached to them. And now something more important than Jonah is here.

The Eye Is the Lamp of the Body

33 "No one lights a lamp and hides it. No one puts it under a bowl. Instead, they put a lamp on its stand. Then those who come in can see the light. 34 Your eye is like a lamp for your body. Suppose your eyes are healthy. Then your whole body also is full of light. But suppose your eyes can't see well. Then your body also is full of darkness. 35 So make sure that the light inside you is not darkness. 36 Suppose your whole body is full of light. And suppose no part of it is dark. Then your body will be full of light. It will be just as when a lamp shines its light on you."

Six Warnings

37 Jesus finished speaking. Then a Pharisee invited him to eat with him. So Jesus went in and took his place at the table. 38 But the Pharisee was surprised. He noticed that Jesus did not wash before the meal.

39 Then the Lord spoke to him. "You Pharisees clean the outside of the cup and dish," he said. "But inside you are full of greed and evil. 40 You foolish people! Didn't the one who made the outside make the inside also? 41 Give freely to poor people to show what is inside you. Then everything will be clean for you.

42 "How terrible it will be for you Pharisees! You give God a tenth of your garden plants, such as mint and rue. But you have forgotten to be fair and to love God. You should have practiced the last things without failing to do the first.

43 "How terrible for you Pharisees! You love the most important seats in the synagogues. You love having people greet you with respect in the market.

44 "How terrible for you! You are like graves that are not marked. People walk over them without knowing it."

45 An authority on the law spoke to Jesus. He said, "Teacher, when you say things like that, you say bad things about us too."

46 Jesus replied, "How terrible for you authorities on the law! You put such heavy loads on people that they can hardly carry them. But you yourselves will not lift one finger to help them.

47 "How terrible for you! You build tombs for the prophets. It was your people of long ago who killed them. 48 So you show that you agree with what your people did long ago. They killed the prophets, and now you build the prophets' tombs. 49 So God in his wisdom said, 'I will send prophets and apostles to them. They will kill some. And they will try to hurt others.' 50 So the people of today will be punished. They will pay for all the prophets' blood spilled since the world began. 51 I mean from the blood of Abel to the blood of Zechariah. He was killed between the altar and the temple. Yes, I tell you, the people of today will be punished for all these things.

52 "How terrible for you authorities on the law! You have taken away the key to the door of knowledge. You yourselves have not entered. And you have stood in the way of those who were entering."

53 When Jesus went outside, the Pharisees and the teachers of the law strongly opposed him. They threw a lot of questions at him. 54 They set traps for him. They wanted to catch him in something he might say.

Jesus Gives Words of Warning and Hope

12 During that time a crowd of many thousands had gathered. There were so many people that they were stepping on one another. Jesus spoke first to his disciples. "Be on your guard against the yeast of the Pharisees," he said. "They just pretend to be godly. 2 Everything that is secret will be brought out into the open. Everything that is hidden will be uncovered. 3 What you have said in the dark will be heard in the daylight. What you have whispered to someone behind closed doors will be shouted from the rooftops.

4 "My friends, listen to me. Don't be afraid of those who kill the body but can't do any more than that. 5 I will show you whom you should be afraid of. Be afraid of the one who has the authority to throw you into hell after you have been killed. Yes, I tell you, be afraid of him. 6 Aren't five sparrows sold for two pennies? But God does not forget even one of them. 7 In fact, he even counts every hair on your head! So don't be afraid. You are worth more than many sparrows.

8 "What about someone who says in front of others that he knows me? I tell you, the Son of Man will say in front of God's angels that he knows that person. 9 But what about someone who says in front of others that he doesn't know me? I, the Son of Man, will say in front of God's angels that I don't know him. 10 Everyone who speaks a word against the Son of Man will be forgiven. But anyone who speaks evil things against the Holy Spirit will not be forgiven.

11 "You will be brought before synagogues, rulers and authorities. But do not worry about how to stand up for yourselves or what to say. 12 The Holy Spirit will teach you at that time what you should say."

The Story of the Rich Fool

13 Someone in the crowd spoke to Jesus. "Teacher," he said, "tell my brother to divide the family property with me."

14 Jesus replied, "Friend, who made me a judge or umpire between you?" 15 Then he said to them, "Watch out! Be on your guard against wanting to have more and more things. Life is not made up of how much a person has."

16 Then Jesus told them a story. He said, "A certain rich man's land produced a very large crop. 17 He thought to himself, 'What should I do? I don't have any place to store my crops.'

18 "Then he said, 'This is what I'll do. I will tear down my barns and build bigger ones. I will store my extra grain in them. 19 I'll say to myself, "You have plenty of grain stored away for many years. Take life easy. Eat, drink and have a good time." '

20 "But God said to him, 'You foolish man! Tonight I will take your life away from you. Then who will get what you have prepared for yourself?'

21 "That is how it will be for whoever stores things away for themselves but is not rich in the sight of God."

Do Not Worry

22 Then Jesus spoke to his disciples. He said, "I tell you, do not worry. Don't worry about your life and what you will eat. And don't worry about your body and what you will wear. 23 There is more to life than eating. There are more important things for the body than clothes. 24 Think about the ravens. They don't plant or gather crops. They don't have any barns at all. But God feeds them. You are worth much more than birds! 25 Can you add even one hour to your life by worrying? 26 You can't do that very little thing. So why worry about the rest?

27 "Think about how the wild flowers grow. They don't work or make clothing. But here is what I tell you. Not even Solomon in his royal robes was dressed like one of those flowers. 28 If that is how God dresses the wild grass, how much better will he dress you! After all, the grass is here only today. Tomorrow it is thrown into the fire. Your faith is so small! 29 Don't spend time thinking about what you will eat or drink. Don't worry about it. 30 People who are ungodly run after all those things. Your Father knows that you need them. 31 But put God's kingdom first. Then those other things will also be given to you.

32 "Little flock, do not be afraid. Your

Father has been pleased to give you the kingdom. 33 Sell what you own. Give to those who are poor. Provide purses for yourselves that will not wear out. Store up riches in heaven that will never be used up. There, no thief can come near it. There, no moth can destroy it. 34 Your heart will be where your riches are.

Be Ready

35 "Be dressed and ready to serve. Keep your lamps burning. 36 Be like servants waiting for their master to return from a wedding dinner. When he comes and knocks, they can open the door for him at once. 37 It will be good for those servants whose master finds them ready when he comes. What I'm about to tell you is true. The master will then dress himself so he can serve them. He will have them take their places at the table. And he will come and wait on them. 38 It will be good for those servants whose master finds them ready. It will even be good if he comes in the middle of the night or toward morning. 39 But here is what you must understand. Suppose the owner of the house knew at what hour the robber was coming. He would not have let his house be broken into. 40 You also must be ready. The Son of Man will come at an hour when you don't expect him."

41 Peter asked, "Lord, are you telling this story to us, or to everyone?"

42 The Lord answered, "Suppose a master puts one of his servants in charge of his other servants. The servant's job is to give them the food they are to receive at the right time. The master wants a faithful and wise manager for this. 43 It will be good for the servant if the master finds him doing his job when the master returns. 44 What I'm about to tell you is true. The master will put that servant in charge of everything he owns. 45 But suppose the servant says to himself, 'My master is taking a long time to come back.' Suppose that servant begins to beat the other servants, both men and women. Suppose he feeds himself. And suppose he drinks until he gets drunk. 46 The master of that servant will come back on a day the servant doesn't expect him. The master will return at an hour the servant doesn't know. Then the master will cut him to pieces. He will send the servant to the place where unbelievers go.

47 "Suppose a servant knows the master's wishes. But the servant doesn't get ready and doesn't do what the master wants. Then that servant will receive a heavy beating. 48 But suppose the servant does not know his master's wishes. And suppose the servant does things for which he should be punished. He will receive a lighter beating. Much will be required of everyone who has been given much. Even more will be asked of the person who is supposed to take care of much.

Jesus Will Separate People From One Another

49 "I have come to bring fire on the earth. How I wish the fire had already started! 50 But I have a baptism of suffering to go through. And I must go through it. 51 Do you think I came to bring peace on earth? No, I tell you. I have come to separate people. 52 From now on there will be five members in a family, each one against the other. There will be three against two and two against three. 53 They will be separated. Father will turn against son and son against father. Mother will turn against daughter and daughter against mother. Mother-in-law will turn against daughter-in-law and daughter-in-law against mother-in-law."

Understanding the Meaning of What Is Happening

54 Jesus spoke to the crowd. He said, "You see a cloud rising in the west. Right away you say, 'It's going to rain.' And it does. 55 The south wind blows. So you say, 'It's going to be hot.' And it is. 56 You pretenders! You know how to understand the appearance of the earth and the sky. Why can't you understand the meaning of what is happening right now?

57 "Why don't you judge for yourselves what is right? 58 Suppose someone has a claim against you, and you are on your way to court. Try hard to settle the matter on the way. If you don't, that person may drag you off to the judge. The judge may turn you over to the officer. And the officer may throw you into prison. 59 I tell you, you will not get out until you have paid the very last penny!"

Turn Away From Sin or Die

13 Some people who were there at that
time told Jesus about certain Galileans. Pilate had mixed their blood with
their sacrifices. 2 Jesus said, "These people from Galilee suffered greatly. Do you
think they were worse sinners than all the
other Galileans? 3 I tell you, no! But unless
you turn away from your sins, you will all
die too. 4 Or what about the 18 people in
Siloam? They died when the tower fell on
them. Do you think they were more guilty
than all the others living in Jerusalem?
5 I tell you, no! But unless you turn away
from your sins, you will all die too."
6 Then Jesus told a story. "A man had
a fig tree," he said. "It was growing in his
vineyard. When he went to look for fruit
on it, he didn't find any. 7 So he went to
the man who took care of the vineyard.
He said, 'For three years now I've been
coming to look for fruit on this fig tree.
But I haven't found any. Cut it down! Why
should it use up the soil?'
8 " 'Sir,' the man replied, 'leave it alone
for one more year. I'll dig around it and
feed it. 9 If it bears fruit next year, fine! If
not, then cut it down.' "

Jesus Heals a Disabled Woman on the Sabbath Day

10 Jesus was teaching in one of the synagogues on a Sabbath day. 11 A woman
there had been disabled by an evil spirit
for 18 years. She was bent over and could
not stand up straight. 12 Jesus saw her. He
asked her to come to him. He said to her,
"Woman, you will no longer be disabled.
I am about to set you free." 13 Then he put
his hands on her. Right away she stood up
straight and praised God.
14 Jesus had healed the woman on the
Sabbath day. This made the synagogue
leader angry. He told the people, "There
are six days for work. So come and be
healed on those days. But do not come on
the Sabbath day."
15 The Lord answered him, "You pretenders! Doesn't each of you go to the
barn and untie your ox or donkey on the
Sabbath day? Then don't you lead it out
to give it water? 16 This woman is a member of Abraham's family line. But Satan
has kept her disabled for 18 long years.
Shouldn't she be set free on the Sabbath
day from what was keeping her disabled?"
17 When Jesus said this, all those who
opposed him were put to shame. But the
people were delighted. They loved all the
wonderful things he was doing.

The Stories of the Mustard Seed and the Yeast

18 Then Jesus asked, "What is God's
kingdom like? What can I compare it to?
19 It is like a mustard seed. Someone took
the seed and planted it in a garden. It
grew and became a tree. The birds sat in
its branches."
20 Again he asked, "What can I compare God's kingdom to? 21 It is like yeast
that a woman used. She mixed it into 60
pounds of flour. The yeast worked its way
all through the dough."

The Narrow Door

22 Then Jesus went through the towns
and villages, teaching the people. He
was on his way to Jerusalem. 23 Someone
asked him, "Lord, are only a few people
going to be saved?"
He said to them, 24 "Try very hard to
enter through the narrow door. I tell you,
many will try to enter and will not be able
to. 25 The owner of the house will get up
and close the door. Then you will stand
outside knocking and begging. You will
say, 'Sir, open the door for us.'
"But he will answer, 'I don't know you.
And I don't know where you come from.'
26 "Then you will say, 'We ate and drank
with you. You taught in our streets.'
27 "But he will reply, 'I don't know you.
And I don't know where you come from.
Get away from me, all you who do evil!'
28 "You will weep and grind your teeth
together when you see those who are in
God's kingdom. You will see Abraham,
Isaac and Jacob and all the prophets
there. But you yourselves will be thrown
out. 29 People will come from east and
west and north and south. They will take
their places at the feast in God's kingdom.
30 Then the last will be first. And the first
will be last."

Jesus' Sadness Over Jerusalem

31 At that time some Pharisees came to
Jesus. They said to him, "Leave this place.
Go somewhere else. Herod wants to kill
you."
32 He replied, "Go and tell that fox, 'I will

keep on driving out demons. I will keep
on healing people today and tomorrow.
And on the third day I will reach my goal.'
33 In any case, I must keep going today and
tomorrow and the next day. Certainly no
prophet can die outside Jerusalem!

34 "Jerusalem! Jerusalem! You kill the
prophets and throw stones in order to kill
those who are sent to you. Many times I
have wanted to gather your people together. I have wanted to be like a hen
who gathers her chicks under her wings.
And you would not let me. 35 Look, your
house is left empty. I tell you, you will not
see me again until you say, 'Blessed is the
one who comes in the name of the Lord.' "
(Psalm 118:26)

Jesus Eats at a Pharisee's House

14 One Sabbath day, Jesus went to eat
in the house of a well-known Pharisee. While he was there, he was being
carefully watched. 2 In front of him was
a man whose body was badly swollen.
3 Jesus turned to the Pharisees and the authorities on the law. He asked them, "Is it
breaking the Law to heal on the Sabbath
day?" 4 But they remained silent. So Jesus
took hold of the man and healed him.
Then he sent him away.

5 He asked them another question. He
said, "Suppose one of you has a child or
an ox that falls into a well on the Sabbath
day. Wouldn't you pull it out right away?"
6 And they had nothing to say.

7 Jesus noticed how the guests picked
the places of honor at the table. So he
told them a story. 8 He said, "Suppose
someone invites you to a wedding feast.
Do not take the place of honor. A person
more important than you may have been
invited. 9 If so, the host who invited both
of you will come to you. He will say, 'Give
this person your seat.' Then you will be
filled with shame. You will have to take
the least important place. 10 But when
you are invited, take the lowest place.
Then your host will come over to you.
He will say, 'Friend, move up to a better
place.' Then you will be honored in front
of all the other guests. 11 All those who lift
themselves up will be made humble. And
those who make themselves humble will
be lifted up."

12 Then Jesus spoke to his host. "Suppose you give a lunch or a dinner," he said.
"Do not invite your friends, your brothers or sisters, or your relatives, or your
rich neighbors. If you do, they may invite
you to eat with them. So you will be paid
back. 13 But when you give a banquet, invite those who are poor. Also invite those
who can't see or walk. 14 Then you will be
blessed. Your guests can't pay you back.
But you will be paid back when those who
are right with God rise from the dead."

The Story of the Great Banquet

15 One of the people at the table with
Jesus heard him say those things. So he
said to Jesus, "Blessed is the one who will
eat at the feast in God's kingdom."

16 Jesus replied, "A certain man was preparing a great banquet. He invited many
guests. 17 Then the day of the banquet arrived. He sent his servant to those who
had been invited. The servant told them,
'Come. Everything is ready now.'

18 "But they all had the same idea. They
began to make excuses. The first one said,
'I have just bought a field. I have to go and
see it. Please excuse me.'

19 "Another said, 'I have just bought five
pairs of oxen. I'm on my way to try them
out. Please excuse me.'

20 "Still another said, 'I just got married,
so I can't come.'

21 "The servant came back and reported
this to his master. Then the owner of the
house became angry. He ordered his servant, 'Go out quickly into the streets and
lanes of the town. Bring in those who are
poor. Also bring those who can't see or
walk.'

22 " 'Sir,' the servant said, 'what you ordered has been done. But there is still
room.'

23 "Then the master told his servant,
'Go out to the roads. Go out to the country lanes. Make the people come in. I want
my house to be full. 24 I tell you, not one of
those people who were invited will get a
taste of my banquet.' "

The Cost of Being a Disciple

25 Large crowds were traveling with
Jesus. He turned and spoke to them.
He said, 26 "Anyone who comes to
me must hate their father and mother. They must hate their wife and children. They must hate their brothers and
sisters. And they must hate even their own

life. Unless they do this, they can't be my disciple. [27]Whoever doesn't carry their cross and follow me can't be my disciple.

[28]"Suppose one of you wants to build a tower. Won't you sit down first and figure out how much it will cost? Then you will see whether you have enough money to finish it. [29]Suppose you start building and are not able to finish. Then everyone who sees what you have done will laugh at you. [30]They will say, 'This person started to build but wasn't able to finish.'

[31]"Or suppose a king is about to go to war against another king. And suppose he has 10,000 men, while the other has 20,000 coming against him. Won't he first sit down and think about whether he can win? [32]And suppose he decides he can't win. Then he will send some men to ask how peace can be made. He will do this while the other king is still far away. [33]In the same way, you must give up everything you have. Those of you who don't cannot be my disciple.

[34]"Salt is good. But suppose it loses its saltiness. How can it be made salty again? [35]It is not good for the soil. And it is not good for the trash pile. It will be thrown out.

"Whoever has ears should listen."

The Story of the Lost Sheep

15 The tax collectors and sinners were all gathering around to hear Jesus. [2]But the Pharisees and the teachers of the law were whispering among themselves. They said, "This man welcomes sinners and eats with them."

[3]Then Jesus told them a story. [4]He said, "Suppose one of you has 100 sheep and loses one of them. Won't he leave the 99 in the open country? Won't he go and look for the one lost sheep until he finds it? [5]When he finds it, he will joyfully put it on his shoulders [6]and go home. Then he will call his friends and neighbors together. He will say, 'Be joyful with me. I have found my lost sheep.' [7]I tell you, it will be the same in heaven. There will be great joy when one sinner turns away from sin. Yes, there will be more joy than for 99 godly people who do not need to turn away from their sins.

The Story of the Lost Coin

[8]"Or suppose a woman has ten silver coins and loses one. Won't she light a lamp and sweep the house? Won't she search carefully until she finds the coin? [9]And when she finds it, she will call her friends and neighbors together. She will say, 'Be joyful with me. I have found my lost coin.' [10]I tell you, it is the same in heaven. There is joy in heaven over one sinner who turns away from sin."

The Story of the Lost Son

[11]Jesus continued, "There was a man who had two sons. [12]The younger son spoke to his father. He said, 'Father, give me my share of the family property.' So the father divided his property between his two sons.

[13]"Not long after that, the younger son packed up all he had. Then he left for a country far away. There he wasted his money on wild living. [14]He spent everything he had. Then the whole country ran low on food. So the son didn't have what he needed. [15]He went to work for someone who lived in that country. That person sent the son to the fields to feed the pigs. [16]The son wanted to fill his stomach with the food the pigs were eating. But no one gave him anything.

[17]"Then he began to think clearly again. He said, 'How many of my father's hired servants have more than enough food! But here I am dying from hunger! [18]I will get up and go back to my father. I will say to him, "Father, I have sinned against heaven. And I have sinned against you. [19]I am no longer fit to be called your son. Make me like one of your hired servants." ' [20]So he got up and went to his father.

"While the son was still a long way off, his father saw him. He was filled with tender love for his son. He ran to him. He threw his arms around him and kissed him.

[21]"The son said to him, 'Father, I have sinned against heaven and against you. I am no longer fit to be called your son.'

[22]"But the father said to his servants, 'Quick! Bring the best robe and put it on him. Put a ring on his finger and sandals on his feet. [23]Bring the fattest calf and kill it. Let's have a feast and celebrate. [24]This son of mine was dead. And now he is alive again. He was lost. And now he is found.' So they began to celebrate.

[25]"The older son was in the field. When

he came near the house, he heard music
and dancing. 26 So he called one of the
servants. He asked him what was going
on. 27 'Your brother has come home,' the
servant replied. 'Your father has killed the
fattest calf. He has done this because your
brother is back safe and sound.'
28 "The older brother became angry. He
refused to go in. So his father went out
and begged him. 29 But he answered his
father, 'Look! All these years I've worked
like a slave for you. I have always obeyed
your orders. You never gave me even a
young goat so I could celebrate with my
friends. 30 But this son of yours wasted
your money with some prostitutes. Now
he comes home. And for him you kill the
fattest calf!'
31 " 'My son,' the father said, 'you are always with me. Everything I have is yours.
32 But we had to celebrate and be glad.
This brother of yours was dead. And now
he is alive again. He was lost. And now he
is found.' "

The Story of the Clever Manager

16 Jesus told his disciples another
story. He said, "There was a rich
man who had a manager. Some said that
the manager was wasting what the rich
man owned. 2 So the rich man told him
to come in. He asked him, 'What is this I
hear about you? Tell me exactly how you
have handled what I own. You can't be my
manager any longer.'
3 "The manager said to himself, 'What
will I do now? My master is taking away
my job. I'm not strong enough to dig. And
I'm too ashamed to beg. 4 I know what
I'm going to do. I'll do something so that
when I lose my job here, people will welcome me into their houses.'
5 "So he called in each person who
owed his master something. He asked the
first one, 'How much do you owe my master?'
6 " 'I owe 900 gallons of olive oil,' he replied.
"The manager told him, 'Take your bill.
Sit down quickly and change it to 450 gallons.'
7 "Then he asked the second one, 'And
how much do you owe?'
" 'I owe 1,000 bushels of wheat,' he replied.
"The manager told him, 'Take your bill
and change it to 800 bushels.'
8 "The manager had not been honest. But the master praised him for being
clever. The people of this world are clever
in dealing with those who are like themselves. They are more clever than God's
people. 9 I tell you, use the riches of this
world to help others. In that way, you will
make friends for yourselves. Then when
your riches are gone, you will be welcomed into your eternal home in heaven.
10 "Suppose you can be trusted with
something very little. Then you can also
be trusted with something very large. But
suppose you are not honest with something very little. Then you will also not be
honest with something very large. 11 Suppose you have not been worthy of trust in
handling worldly wealth. Then who will
trust you with true riches? 12 Suppose you
have not been worthy of trust in handling
someone else's property. Then who will
give you property of your own?
13 "No one can serve two masters at the
same time. Either you will hate one of
them and love the other. Or you will be
faithful to one and dislike the other. You
can't serve God and money at the same
time."
14 The Pharisees loved money. They
heard all that Jesus said and made fun
of him. 15 Jesus said to them, "You try to
make yourselves look good in the eyes of
other people. But God knows your hearts.
What people think is worth a lot is hated
by God.

More Teachings

16 "The teachings of the Law and the
Prophets were preached until John the
Baptist came. Since then, the good news
of God's kingdom is being preached. And
everyone is trying very hard to enter it. 17 It
is easier for heaven and earth to disappear than for the smallest part of a letter
to drop out of the Law.
18 "Anyone who divorces his wife and
marries another woman commits adultery. Also, the man who marries a divorced woman commits adultery.

The Rich Man and Lazarus

19 "Once there was a rich man. He was
dressed in purple cloth and fine linen.
He lived an easy life every day. 20 A man

named Lazarus was placed at his gate.
Lazarus was a beggar. His body was covered with sores. 21 Even dogs came and
licked his sores. All he wanted was to eat
what fell from the rich man's table.

22 "The time came when the beggar
died. The angels carried him to Abraham's side. The rich man also died and
was buried. 23 In the place of the dead, the
rich man was suffering terribly. He looked
up and saw Abraham far away. Lazarus
was by his side. 24 So the rich man called
out, 'Father Abraham! Have pity on me!
Send Lazarus to dip the tip of his finger in
water. Then he can cool my tongue with
it. I am in terrible pain in this fire.'

25 "But Abraham replied, 'Son, remember what happened in your lifetime. You
received your good things. Lazarus received bad things. Now he is comforted
here, and you are in terrible pain. 26 Besides, a wide space has been placed between us and you. So those who want to
go from here to you can't go. And no one
can cross over from there to us.'

27 "The rich man answered, 'Then I beg
you, father Abraham. Send Lazarus to my
family. 28 I have five brothers. Let Lazarus
warn them. Then they will not come to
this place of terrible suffering.'

29 "Abraham replied, 'They have the
teachings of Moses and the Prophets. Let
your brothers listen to them.'

30 " 'No, father Abraham,' he said. 'But
if someone from the dead goes to them,
they will turn away from their sins.'

31 "Abraham said to him, 'They do not
listen to Moses and the Prophets. So they
will not be convinced even if someone
rises from the dead.' "

Sin, Faith and Duty

17 Jesus spoke to his disciples. "Things
that make people sin are sure to
come," he said. "But how terrible it will
be for anyone who causes those things
to come! 2 Suppose people lead one of
these little ones to sin. It would be better
for those people to be thrown into the sea
with a millstone tied around their neck.
3 So watch what you do.

"If your brother or sister sins against
you, tell them they are wrong. Then if they
turn away from their sins, forgive them.
4 Suppose they sin against you seven
times in one day. And suppose they come
back to you each time and say, 'I'm sorry.'
You must forgive them."

5 The apostles said to the Lord, "Give us
more faith!"

6 He replied, "Suppose you have faith as
small as a mustard seed. Then you can say
to this mulberry tree, 'Be pulled up. Be
planted in the sea.' And it will obey you.

7 "Suppose one of you has a servant
plowing or looking after the sheep. And
suppose the servant came in from the
field. Will you say to him, 'Come along
now and sit down to eat'? 8 No. Instead,
you will say, 'Prepare my supper. Get
yourself ready. Wait on me while I eat
and drink. Then after that you can eat
and drink.' 9 Will you thank the servant
because he did what he was told to do?
10 It's the same with you. Suppose you
have done everything you were told to
do. Then you should say, 'We are not worthy to serve you. We have only done our
duty.' "

Jesus Heals Ten Men Who Have a Skin Disease

11 Jesus was on his way to Jerusalem.
He traveled along the border between
Samaria and Galilee. 12 As he was going
into a village, ten men met him. They had
a skin disease. They were standing close
by. 13 And they called out in a loud voice,
"Jesus! Master! Have pity on us!"

14 Jesus saw them and said, "Go. Show
yourselves to the priests." While they were
on the way, they were healed.

15 When one of them saw that he was
healed, he came back. He praised God in
a loud voice. 16 He threw himself at Jesus'
feet and thanked him. The man was a Samaritan.

17 Jesus asked, "Weren't all ten healed?
Where are the other nine? 18 Didn't anyone else return and give praise to God except this outsider?" 19 Then Jesus said to
him, "Get up and go. Your faith has healed
you."

The Coming of God's Kingdom

20 Once the Pharisees asked Jesus when
God's kingdom would come. He replied,
"The coming of God's kingdom is not
something you can see. 21 People will not
say, 'Here it is.' Or, 'There it is.' That's because God's kingdom is among you."

22 Then Jesus spoke to his disciples.

"The time is coming," he said, "when you will long to see one of the days of the Son of Man. But you won't see it. [23]People will tell you, 'There he is!' Or, 'Here he is!' Don't go running off after them. [24]When the Son of Man comes, he will be like the lightning. It flashes and lights up the sky from one end to the other. [25]But first the Son of Man must suffer many things. He will not be accepted by the people of today.

[26]"Remember how it was in the days of Noah. It will be the same when the Son of Man comes. [27]People were eating and drinking. They were getting married. They were giving their daughters to be married. They did all those things right up to the day Noah entered the ark. Then the flood came and destroyed them all.

[28]"It was the same in the days of Lot. People were eating and drinking. They were buying and selling. They were planting and building. [29]But on the day Lot left Sodom, fire and sulfur rained down from heaven. And all the people were destroyed.

[30]"It will be just like that on the day the Son of Man is shown to the world. [31]Suppose someone is on the housetop on that day. And suppose what they own is inside the house. They should not go down to get what they own. No one in the field should go back for anything either. [32]Remember Lot's wife! [33]Whoever tries to keep their life will lose it. Whoever loses their life will keep it. [34]I tell you, on that night two people will be in one bed. One person will be taken and the other left. [35-36]Two women will be grinding grain together. One will be taken and the other left."

[37]"Where, Lord?" his disciples asked.

He replied, "The vultures will gather where there is a dead body."

The Story of the Widow Who Would Not Give Up

18 Jesus told his disciples a story. He wanted to show them that they should always pray and not give up. [2]He said, "In a certain town there was a judge. He didn't have any respect for God or care about what people thought. [3]A widow lived in that town. She came to the judge again and again. She kept begging him, 'Make things right for me. Someone is treating me badly.'

[4]"For some time the judge refused. But finally he said to himself, 'I don't have any respect for God. I don't care about what people think. [5]But this widow keeps bothering me. So I will see that things are made right for her. If I don't, she will someday come and attack me!' "

[6]The Lord said, "Listen to what the unfair judge says. [7]God's chosen people cry out to him day and night. Won't he make things right for them? Will he keep putting them off? [8]I tell you, God will see that things are made right for them. He will make sure it happens quickly. But when the Son of Man comes, will he find people on earth who have faith?"

The Story of the Pharisee and the Tax Collector

[9]Jesus told a story to some people who were sure they were right with God. They looked down on everyone else. [10]He said to them, "Two men went up to the temple to pray. One was a Pharisee. The other was a tax collector. [11]The Pharisee stood by himself and prayed. 'God, I thank you that I am not like other people,' he said. 'I am not like robbers or those who do other evil things. I am not like those who commit adultery. I am not even like this tax collector. [12]I fast twice a week. And I give a tenth of all I get.'

[13]"But the tax collector stood farther away than the Pharisee. He would not even look up to heaven. He brought his hand to his heart and prayed. He said, 'God, have mercy on me. I am a sinner.'

[14]"I tell you, the tax collector went home accepted by God. But not the Pharisee. All those who lift themselves up will be made humble. And those who make themselves humble will be lifted up."

Little Children Are Brought to Jesus

[15]People were also bringing babies to Jesus. They wanted him to place his hands on the babies. When the disciples saw this, they told the people to stop. [16]But Jesus asked the children to come to him. "Let the little children come to me," he said. "Don't keep them away. God's kingdom belongs to people like them. [17]What I'm about to tell you is true. Anyone who will not receive God's kingdom like a little child will never enter it."

Rich People and the Kingdom of God

18 A certain ruler asked Jesus a question.
"Good teacher," he said, "what must I do
to receive eternal life?"
19 "Why do you call me good?" Jesus
answered. "No one is good except God.
20 You know what the commandments say.
'Do not commit adultery. Do not commit
murder. Do not steal. Do not be a false
witness. Honor your father and mother.' "
(Exodus 20:12–16; Deuteronomy 5:16–20)
21 "I have obeyed all those commandments since I was a boy," the ruler said.
22 When Jesus heard this, he said to
him, "You are still missing one thing. Sell
everything you have. Give the money to
those who are poor. You will have treasure
in heaven. Then come and follow me."
23 When the ruler heard this, he became
very sad. He was very rich. 24 Jesus looked
at him. Then he said, "How hard it is for
rich people to enter God's kingdom! 25 Is
it hard for a camel to go through the eye
of a needle? It is even harder for someone
who is rich to enter God's kingdom!"
26 Those who heard this asked, "Then
who can be saved?"
27 Jesus replied, "Things that are impossible with people are possible with God."
28 Peter said to him, "We have left everything we had in order to follow you!"
29 "What I'm about to tell you is true,"
Jesus said to them. "Has anyone left home
or wife or husband or brothers or sisters
or parents or children for God's kingdom?
30 They will receive many times as much
in this world. In the world to come they
will receive eternal life."

Jesus Speaks a Third Time About His Coming Death

31 Jesus took the 12 disciples to one side.
He told them, "We are going up to Jerusalem. Everything that the prophets wrote
about the Son of Man will come true. 32 He
will be handed over to the Gentiles. They
will make fun of him. They will laugh at
him and spit on him. 33 They will whip
him and kill him. On the third day, he will
rise from the dead!"
34 The disciples did not understand
any of this. Its meaning was hidden from
them. So they didn't know what Jesus was
talking about.

A Blind Beggar Receives His Sight

35 Jesus was approaching Jericho. A
blind man was sitting by the side of the
road begging. 36 The blind man heard the
crowd going by. He asked what was happening. 37 They told him, "Jesus of Nazareth is passing by."
38 So the blind man called out, "Jesus!
Son of David! Have mercy on me!"
39 Those who led the way commanded
him to stop. They told him to be quiet. But
he shouted even louder, "Son of David!
Have mercy on me!"
40 Jesus stopped and ordered the man to
be brought to him. When the man came
near, Jesus spoke to him. 41 "What do you
want me to do for you?" Jesus asked.
"Lord, I want to be able to see," the
blind man replied.
42 Jesus said to him, "Receive your sight.
Your faith has healed you." 43 Right away
he could see. He followed Jesus, praising
God. When all the people saw it, they also
praised God.

Zacchaeus the Tax Collector

19 Jesus entered Jericho and was passing through. 2 A man named Zacchaeus lived there. He was a chief tax
collector and was very rich. 3 Zacchaeus
wanted to see who Jesus was. But he was
a short man. He could not see Jesus because of the crowd. 4 So he ran ahead and
climbed a sycamore-fig tree. He wanted
to see Jesus, who was coming that way.
5 Jesus reached the spot where Zacchaeus was. He looked up and said, "Zacchaeus, come down at once. I must stay at
your house today." 6 So Zacchaeus came
down at once and welcomed him gladly.
7 All the people saw this. They began to
whisper among themselves. They said,
"Jesus has gone to be the guest of a sinner."
8 But Zacchaeus stood up. He said,
"Look, Lord! Here and now I give half of
what I own to those who are poor. And if
I have cheated anybody out of anything, I
will pay it back. I will pay back four times
the amount I took."
9 Jesus said to Zacchaeus, "Today salvation has come to your house. You are a
member of Abraham's family line. 10 The
Son of Man came to look for the lost and
save them."

The Story of Three Slaves

11 While the people were listening to these things, Jesus told them a story. He was near Jerusalem. The people thought that God's kingdom was going to appear right away. 12 Jesus said, "A man from an important family went to a country far away. He went there to be made king and then return home. 13 So he sent for ten of his slaves. He gave them each about three months' pay. 'Put this money to work until I come back,' he said.

14 "But those he ruled over hated him. They sent some messengers after him. They were sent to say, 'We don't want this man to be our king.'

15 "But he was made king and returned home. Then he sent for the slaves he had given the money to. He wanted to find out what they had earned with it.

16 "The first one came to him. He said, 'Sir, your money has earned ten times as much.'

17 " 'You have done well, my good slave!' his master replied. 'You have been faithful in a very small matter. So I will put you in charge of ten towns.'

18 "The second slave came to his master. He said, 'Sir, your money has earned five times as much.'

19 "His master answered, 'I will put you in charge of five towns.'

20 "Then another slave came. He said, 'Sir, here is your money. I have kept it hidden in a piece of cloth. 21 I was afraid of you. You are a hard man. You take out what you did not put in. You harvest what you did not plant.'

22 "His master replied, 'I will judge you by your own words, you evil slave! So you knew that I am a hard man? You knew that I take out what I did not put in? You knew that I harvest what I did not plant? 23 Then why didn't you put my money in the bank? When I came back, I could have collected it with interest.'

24 "Then he said to those standing by, 'Take his money away from him. Give it to the one who has ten times as much.'

25 " 'Sir,' they said, 'he already has ten times as much!'

26 "He replied, 'I tell you that everyone who has will be given more. But here is what will happen to anyone who has nothing. Even what they have will be taken away from them. 27 And what about my enemies who did not want me to be king over them? Bring them here! Kill them in front of me!' "

Jesus Comes to Jerusalem as King

28 After Jesus had said this, he went on ahead. He was going up to Jerusalem. 29 He approached Bethphage and Bethany. The hill there was called the Mount of Olives. Jesus sent out two of his disciples. He said to them, 30 "Go to the village ahead of you. As soon as you get there, you will find a donkey's colt tied up. No one has ever ridden it. Untie it and bring it here. 31 Someone may ask you, 'Why are you untying it?' If so, say, 'The Lord needs it.' "

32 Those who were sent ahead went and found the young donkey. It was there just as Jesus had told them. 33 They were untying the colt when its owners came. The owners asked them, "Why are you untying the colt?"

34 They replied, "The Lord needs it."

35 Then the disciples brought the colt to Jesus. They threw their coats on the young donkey and put Jesus on it. 36 As he went along, people spread their coats on the road.

37 Jesus came near the place where the road goes down the Mount of Olives. There the whole crowd of disciples began to praise God with joy. In loud voices they praised him for all the miracles they had seen. They shouted,

38 "Blessed is the king who comes
in the name of the Lord!"
(Psalm 118:26)

"May there be peace and glory in the
highest heaven!"

39 Some of the Pharisees in the crowd spoke to Jesus. "Teacher," they said, "tell your disciples to stop!"

40 "I tell you," he replied, "if they keep quiet, the stones will cry out."

41 He approached Jerusalem. When he saw the city, he began to weep. 42 He said, "I wish you had known today what would bring you peace! But now it is hidden from your eyes. 43 The days will come when your enemies will arrive. They will build a wall of dirt up against your city. They will surround you and close you in on every side. 44 You didn't recognize the time when God came to you. So your en-

emies will smash you to the ground. They will destroy you and all the people inside your walls. They will not leave one stone on top of another."

Jesus Clears Out the Temple

[45]Then Jesus entered the temple courtyard. He began to drive out those who were selling there. [46]He told them, "It is written that the Lord said, 'My house will be a house where people can pray.' (Isaiah 56:7) But you have made it a 'den for robbers.' " (Jeremiah 7:11)

[47]Every day Jesus was teaching at the temple. But the chief priests and the teachers of the law were trying to kill him. So were the leaders among the people. [48]But they couldn't find any way to do it. All the people were paying close attention to his words.

The Authority of Jesus Is Questioned

20 One day Jesus was teaching the people in the temple courtyard. He was announcing the good news to them. The chief priests and the teachers of the law came up to him. The elders came with them. [2]"Tell us by what authority you are doing these things," they all said. "Who gave you this authority?"

[3]Jesus replied, "I will also ask you a question. Tell me, [4]was John's baptism from heaven? Or did it come from people?"

[5]They talked to one another about it. They said, "If we say, 'From heaven,' he will ask, 'Why didn't you believe him?' [6]But if we say, 'From people,' all the people will throw stones at us and kill us. They believe that John was a prophet."

[7]So they answered Jesus, "We don't know where John's baptism came from."

[8]Jesus said, "Then I won't tell you by what authority I am doing these things either."

The Story of the Renters

[9]Jesus went on to tell the people a story. "A man planted a vineyard," he said. "He rented it out to some farmers. Then he went away for a long time. [10]At harvest time he sent a slave to the renters. They were supposed to give him some of the fruit of the vineyard. But the renters beat the slave. Then they sent him away with nothing. [11]So the man sent another slave. They beat that one and treated him badly. They also sent him away with nothing. [12]The man sent a third slave. The renters wounded him and threw him out.

[13]"Then the owner of the vineyard said, 'What should I do? I have a son, and I love him. I will send him. Maybe they will respect him.'

[14]"But when the renters saw the son, they talked the matter over. 'This is the one who will receive all the owner's property someday,' they said. 'Let's kill him. Then everything will be ours.' [15]So they threw him out of the vineyard. And they killed him.

"What will the owner of the vineyard do to the renters? [16]He will come and kill them. He will give the vineyard to others."

When the people heard this, they said, "We hope this never happens!"

[17]Jesus looked right at them and said, "Here is something I want you to explain the meaning of. It is written,

" 'The stone the builders didn't
accept
has become the most important
stone of all.' (Psalm 118:22)

[18]Everyone who falls on that stone will be broken to pieces. But the stone will crush anyone it falls on."

[19]The teachers of the law and the chief priests looked for a way to arrest Jesus at once. They knew he had told that story against them. But they were afraid of the people.

Is It Right to Pay the Royal Tax to Caesar?

[20]The religious leaders sent spies to keep a close watch on Jesus. The spies pretended to be sincere. They hoped they could trap Jesus with something he would say. Then they could hand him over to the power and authority of the governor. [21]So the spies questioned Jesus. "Teacher," they said, "we know that you speak and teach what is right. We know you don't favor one person over another. You teach the way of God truthfully. [22]Is it right for us to pay taxes to Caesar or not?"

[23]Jesus saw they were trying to trick him. So he said to them, [24]"Show me a silver coin. Whose picture and words are on it?"

"Caesar's," they replied.

[25]He said to them, "Then give back to

Caesar what belongs to Caesar. And give back to God what belongs to God."

[26]They were not able to trap him with what he had said there in front of all the people. Amazed by his answer, they became silent.

Marriage When the Dead Rise

[27]The Sadducees do not believe that people rise from the dead. Some of them came to Jesus with a question. [28]"Teacher," they said, "Moses wrote for us about a man's brother who dies. Suppose the brother leaves a wife but has no children. Then the man must marry the widow. He must provide children to carry on his dead brother's name. [29]There were seven brothers. The first one married a woman. He died without leaving any children. [30]The second one married her. [31]And then the third one married her. One after another, the seven brothers married her. They all died. None left any children. [32]Finally, the woman died too. [33]Now then, when the dead rise, whose wife will she be? All seven brothers were married to her."

[34]Jesus replied, "People in this world get married. And their parents give them to be married. [35]But it will not be like that when the dead rise. Those who are considered worthy to take part in the world to come won't get married. And their parents won't give them to be married. [36]They can't die anymore. They are like the angels. They are God's children. They will be given a new form of life when the dead rise. [37]Remember the story of Moses and the burning bush. Even Moses showed that the dead rise. The Lord said to him, 'I am the God of Abraham. I am the God of Isaac. And I am the God of Jacob.' (Exodus 3:6) [38]He is not the God of the dead. He is the God of the living. In his eyes, everyone is alive."

[39]Some of the teachers of the law replied, "You have spoken well, teacher!" [40]And no one dared to ask him any more questions.

Whose Son Is the Messiah?

[41]Jesus said to them, "Why do people say that the Messiah is the son of David? [42]David himself says in the Book of Psalms,

"'The Lord said to my Lord,
"Sit at my right hand
[43]until I put your enemies
under your control."' (Psalm 110:1)

[44]David calls him 'Lord.' So how can he be David's son?"

Warning Against the Teachers of the Law

[45]All the people were listening. Jesus said to his disciples, [46]"Watch out for the teachers of the law. They like to walk around in long robes. They love to be greeted with respect in the market. They love to have the most important seats in the synagogues. They also love to have the places of honor at banquets. [47]They take over the houses of widows. They say long prayers to show off. God will punish these men very much."

The Widow's Offering

21 As Jesus looked up, he saw rich people putting their gifts into the temple offering boxes. [2]He also saw a poor widow put in two very small copper coins. [3]"What I'm about to tell you is true," Jesus said. "That poor widow has put in more than all the others. [4]All these other people gave a lot because they are rich. But even though she is poor, she put in everything. She had nothing left to live on."

When the Temple Will Be Destroyed and the Signs of the End

[5]Some of Jesus' disciples were talking about the temple. They spoke about how it was decorated with beautiful stones and with gifts that honored God. But Jesus asked, [6]"Do you see all this? The time will come when not one stone will be left on top of another. Every stone will be thrown down."

[7]"Teacher," they asked, "when will these things happen? And what will be the sign that they are about to take place?"

[8]Jesus replied, "Keep watch! Be careful that you are not fooled. Many will come in my name. They will claim, 'I am he!' And they will say, 'The time is near!' Do not follow them. [9]Do not be afraid when you hear about wars and about fighting against rulers. Those things must happen first. But the end will not come right away."

[10]Then Jesus said to them, "Nation will

fight against nation. Kingdom will fight against kingdom. 11 In many places there will be powerful earthquakes. People will go hungry. There will be terrible sicknesses. Things will happen that will make people afraid. There will be great and miraculous signs from heaven.

12 "But before all this, people will arrest you and treat you badly. They will hand you over to synagogues and put you in prison. You will be brought to kings and governors. All this will happen to you because of my name. 13 And so you will be witnesses about me. 14 But make up your mind not to worry ahead of time about how to stand up for yourselves. 15 I will give you words of wisdom. None of your enemies will be able to withstand them or prove them wrong. 16 Even your parents, brothers, sisters, relatives and friends will hand you over to the authorities. The authorities will put some of you to death. 17 Everyone will hate you because of me. 18 But not a hair on your head will be harmed. 19 Remain strong in the faith, and you will receive eternal life.

20 "A time is coming when you will see armies surround Jerusalem. Then you will know that it will soon be destroyed. 21 Those who are in Judea should then escape to the mountains. Those in the city should get out. Those in the country should not enter the city. 22 This is the time when God will punish Jerusalem. Everything will come true, just as it has been written. 23 How awful it will be in those days for pregnant women! How awful for nursing mothers! There will be terrible suffering in the land. There will be great anger against those people. 24 Some will be killed by the sword. Others will be taken as prisoners to all the nations. Jerusalem will be taken over by Gentiles until the times of the Gentiles come to an end.

25 "There will be signs in the sun, moon and stars. The nations of the earth will be in terrible pain. They will be puzzled by the roaring and tossing of the sea. 26 Terror will make people faint. They will be worried about what is happening in the world. The sun, moon and stars will be shaken from their places. 27 At that time people will see the Son of Man coming in a cloud. He will come with power and great glory. 28 When these things begin to take place, stand up. Hold your head up with joy and hope. The time when you will be set free will be very close."

29 Jesus told them a story. "Look at the fig tree and all the trees," he said. 30 "When you see leaves appear on the branches, you know that summer is near. 31 In the same way, when you see these things happening, you will know that God's kingdom is near.

32 "What I'm about to tell you is true. The people living now will certainly not pass away until all these things have happened. 33 Heaven and earth will pass away. But my words will never pass away.

34 "Be careful. If you aren't, your hearts will be loaded down with wasteful living, drunkenness and the worries of life. Then the day the Son of Man returns will close on you like a trap. It will happen suddenly. 35 That day will come on every person who lives on the whole earth. 36 Always keep watching. Pray that you will be able to escape all that is about to happen. Also, pray that you will not be judged guilty when the Son of Man comes."

37 Each day Jesus taught at the temple. And each evening he went to spend the night on the hill called the Mount of Olives. 38 All the people came to the temple early in the morning. They wanted to hear Jesus speak.

Judas Agrees to Hand Jesus Over

22 The Feast of Unleavened Bread, called the Passover, was near. 2 The chief priests and the teachers of the law were looking for a way to get rid of Jesus. They were afraid of the people. 3 Then Satan entered Judas, who was called Iscariot. Judas was one of the 12 disciples. 4 He went to the chief priests and the officers of the temple guard. He talked with them about how he could hand Jesus over to them. 5 They were delighted and agreed to give him money. 6 Judas accepted their offer. He watched for the right time to hand Jesus over to them. He wanted to do it when no crowd was around.

The Last Supper

7 Then the day of Unleavened Bread came. That was the time the Passover lamb had to be sacrificed. 8 Jesus sent Peter and John on ahead. "Go," he told them. "Prepare for us to eat the Passover meal."

9 "Where do you want us to prepare for
it?" they asked.
10 Jesus replied, "When you enter the
city, a man carrying a jar of water will
meet you. Follow him to the house he enters. 11 Then say to the owner of the house,
'The Teacher asks, "Where is the guest
room? Where can I eat the Passover meal
with my disciples?" ' 12 He will show you a
large upstairs room with furniture already
in it. Prepare for us to eat there."
13 Peter and John left. They found things
just as Jesus had told them. So they prepared the Passover meal.
14 When the hour came, Jesus and his
apostles took their places at the table.
15 He said to them, "I have really looked
forward to eating this Passover meal with
you. I wanted to do this before I suffer. 16 I
tell you, I will not eat the Passover meal
again until it is celebrated in God's kingdom."
17 After Jesus took the cup, he gave
thanks. He said, "Take this cup and share
it among yourselves. 18 I tell you, I will not
drink wine with you again until God's
kingdom comes."
19 Then Jesus took bread. He gave
thanks and broke it. He handed it to them
and said, "This is my body. It is given for
you. Every time you eat it, do this in memory of me."
20 In the same way, after the supper he
took the cup. He said, "This cup is the new
covenant in my blood. It is poured out for
you. 21 But someone here is going to hand
me over to my enemies. His hand is with
mine on the table. 22 The Son of Man will
go to his death, just as God has already
decided. But how terrible it will be for the
one who hands him over!" 23 The apostles
began to ask one another about this. They
wondered which one of them would do it.
24 They also started to argue. They disagreed about which of them was thought
to be the most important person. 25 Jesus
said to them, "The kings of the Gentiles
hold power over their people. And those
who order them around call themselves
Protectors. 26 But you must not be like
that. Instead, the most important among
you should be like the youngest. The one
who rules should be like the one who
serves. 27 Who is more important? Is it the
one at the table, or the one who serves?
Isn't it the one who is at the table? But I
am among you as one who serves. 28 You
have stood by me during my troubles.
29 And I give you a kingdom, just as my Father gave me a kingdom. 30 Then you will
eat and drink at my table in my kingdom.
And you will sit on thrones, judging the 12
tribes of Israel.
31 "Simon, Simon! Satan has asked to
sift all of you disciples like wheat. 32 But I
have prayed for you, Simon. I have prayed
that your faith will not fail. When you
have turned back, help your brothers to
be strong."
33 But Simon replied, "Lord, I am ready
to go with you to prison and to death."
34 Jesus answered, "I tell you, Peter, you
will say three times that you don't know
me. And you will do it before the rooster
crows today."
35 Then Jesus asked the disciples, "Did
you need anything when I sent you without a purse, bag or sandals?"
"Nothing," they answered.
36 He said to them, "But now if you have
a purse, take it. And also take a bag. If you
don't have a sword, sell your coat and
buy one. 37 It is written, 'He was counted
among those who had committed crimes.'
(Isaiah 53:12) I tell you that what is written
about me must come true. Yes, it is already coming true."
38 The disciples said, "See, Lord, here
are two swords."
"Two swords are enough!" he replied.

Jesus Prays on the Mount of Olives

39 Jesus went out as usual to the Mount
of Olives. His disciples followed him.
40 When they reached the place, Jesus
spoke. "Pray that you won't fall into sin
when you are tempted," he said to them.
41 Then he went a short distance away
from them. There he got down on his
knees and prayed. 42 He said, "Father, if
you are willing, take this cup of suffering
away from me. But do what you want, not
what I want." 43 An angel from heaven appeared to Jesus and gave him strength.
44 Because he was very sad and troubled,
he prayed even harder. His sweat was like
drops of blood falling to the ground.
45 After that, he got up from prayer and
went back to the disciples. He found
them sleeping. They were worn out because they were very sad. 46 "Why are you
sleeping?" he asked them. "Get up! Pray

that you won't fall into sin when you are tempted."

Jesus Is Arrested

47 While Jesus was still speaking, a crowd came up. The man named Judas was leading them. He was one of the 12 disciples. Judas approached Jesus to kiss him. 48 But Jesus asked him, "Judas, are you handing over the Son of Man with a kiss?"

49 Jesus' followers saw what was going to happen. So they said, "Lord, should we use our swords against them?" 50 One of them struck the slave of the high priest and cut off his right ear.

51 But Jesus answered, "Stop this!" And he touched the man's ear and healed him.

52 Then Jesus spoke to the chief priests, the officers of the temple guard, and the elders. They had all come for him. "Am I leading a band of armed men against you?" he asked. "Do you have to come with swords and clubs? 53 Every day I was with you in the temple courtyard. And you didn't lay a hand on me. But this is your hour. This is when darkness rules."

Peter Says He Does Not Know Jesus

54 Then the men arrested Jesus and led him away. They took him into the high priest's house. Peter followed from far away. 55 Some people there started a fire in the middle of the courtyard. Then they sat down together. Peter sat down with them. 56 A female servant saw him sitting there in the firelight. She looked closely at him. Then she said, "This man was with Jesus."

57 But Peter said he had not been with him. "Woman, I don't know him," he said.

58 A little later someone else saw Peter. "You also are one of them," he said.

"No," Peter replied. "I'm not!"

59 About an hour later, another person spoke up. "This fellow must have been with Jesus," he said. "He is from Galilee."

60 Peter replied, "Man, I don't know what you're talking about!" Just as he was speaking, the rooster crowed. 61 The Lord turned and looked right at Peter. Then Peter remembered what the Lord had spoken to him. "The rooster will crow today," Jesus had said. "Before it does, you will say three times that you don't know me." 62 Peter went outside. He broke down and cried.

The Guards Make Fun of Jesus

63 There were men guarding Jesus. They began laughing at him and beating him. 64 They blindfolded him. They said, "Prophesy! Who hit you?" 65 They also said many other things to make fun of him.

Jesus Is Brought to Pilate and Herod

66 At dawn the elders of the people met together. These included the chief priests and the teachers of the law. Jesus was led to them. 67 "If you are the Messiah," they said, "tell us."

Jesus answered, "If I tell you, you will not believe me. 68 And if I asked you, you would not answer. 69 But from now on, the Son of Man will be seated at the right hand of the mighty God."

70 They all asked, "Are you the Son of God then?"

He replied, "You say that I am."

71 Then they said, "Why do we need any more witnesses? We have heard it from his own lips."

23 Then the whole group got up and led Jesus off to Pilate. 2 They began to bring charges against Jesus. They said, "We have found this man misleading our people. He is against paying taxes to Caesar. And he claims to be Messiah, a king."

3 So Pilate asked Jesus, "Are you the king of the Jews?"

"You have said so," Jesus replied.

4 Then Pilate spoke to the chief priests and the crowd. He announced, "I find no basis for a charge against this man."

5 But they kept it up. They said, "His teaching stirs up the people all over Judea. He started in Galilee and has come all the way here."

6 When Pilate heard this, he asked if the man was from Galilee. 7 He learned that Jesus was from Herod's area of authority. So Pilate sent Jesus to Herod. At that time Herod was also in Jerusalem.

8 When Herod saw Jesus, he was very pleased. He had been wanting to see Jesus for a long time. He had heard much about him. He hoped to see Jesus perform a sign of some kind. 9 Herod asked him many questions, but Jesus gave him no answer. 10 The chief priests and the teachers of the law were standing there. With loud

shouts they brought charges against him.
11 Herod and his soldiers laughed at him
and made fun of him. They dressed him in
a beautiful robe. Then they sent him back
to Pilate. 12 That day Herod and Pilate became friends. Before this time they had
been enemies.

13 Pilate called together the chief priests,
the rulers and the people. 14 He said to
them, "You brought me this man. You
said he was turning the people against
the authorities. I have questioned him
in front of you. I have found no basis for
your charges against him. 15 Herod hasn't
either. So he sent Jesus back to us. As you
can see, Jesus has done nothing that is
worthy of death. 16-17 So I will just have
him whipped and let him go."

18 But the whole crowd shouted, "Kill
this man! But let Barabbas go!" 19 Barabbas had been thrown into prison. He had
taken part in a struggle in the city against
the authorities. He had also committed
murder.

20 Pilate wanted to let Jesus go. So he
made an appeal to the crowd again. 21 But
they kept shouting, "Crucify him! Crucify
him!"

22 Pilate spoke to them for the third
time. "Why?" he asked. "What wrong has
this man done? I have found no reason to
have him put to death. So I will just have
him whipped and let him go."

23 But with loud shouts they kept calling for Jesus to be crucified. The people's shouts won out. 24 So Pilate decided
to give them what they wanted. 25 He set
free the man they asked for. The man had
been thrown in prison for murder and
for fighting against the authorities. Pilate
handed Jesus over to them so they could
carry out their plans.

Jesus Is Nailed to a Cross

26 As the soldiers led Jesus away, they
took hold of Simon. Simon was from
Cyrene. He was on his way in from the
country. They put a wooden cross on his
shoulders. Then they made him carry it
behind Jesus. 27 A large number of people
followed Jesus. Some were women whose
hearts were filled with sorrow. They cried
loudly because of him. 28 Jesus turned and
said to them, "Daughters of Jerusalem, do
not weep for me. Weep for yourselves and
for your children. 29 The time will come
when you will say, 'Blessed are the wom-
en who can't have children! Blessed are
those who never gave birth or nursed babies!' 30 It is written,

" 'The people will say to the
mountains, "Fall on us!"
They'll say to the hills, "Cover
us!" ' (Hosea 10:8)

31 People do these things when trees are
green. So what will happen when trees
are dry?"

32 Two other men were also led out with
Jesus to be killed. Both of them had broken the law. 33 The soldiers brought them
to the place called the Skull. There they
nailed Jesus to the cross. He hung between the two criminals. One was on his
right and one was on his left. 34 Jesus said,
"Father, forgive them. They don't know
what they are doing." The soldiers divided
up his clothes by casting lots.

35 The people stood there watching. The
rulers even made fun of Jesus. They said,
"He saved others. Let him save himself if
he is God's Messiah, the Chosen One."

36 The soldiers also came up and poked
fun at him. They offered him wine vinegar. 37 They said, "If you are the king of
the Jews, save yourself."

38 A written sign had been placed above
him. It read, THIS IS THE KING OF THE JEWS.

39 One of the criminals hanging there
made fun of Jesus. He said, "Aren't you
the Messiah? Save yourself! Save us!"

40 But the other criminal scolded him.
"Don't you have any respect for God?" he
said. "Remember, you are under the same
sentence of death. 41 We are being punished fairly. We are getting just what our
actions call for. But this man hasn't done
anything wrong."

42 Then he said, "Jesus, remember me
when you come into your kingdom."

43 Jesus answered him, "What I'm about
to tell you is true. Today you will be with
me in paradise."

Jesus Dies

44 It was now about noon. Then darkness covered the whole land until three
o'clock. 45 The sun had stopped shining. The temple curtain was torn in two.
46 Jesus called out in a loud voice, "Father,
into your hands I commit my life." After
he said this, he took his last breath.

[47]The Roman commander saw what had happened. He praised God and said, "Jesus was surely a man who did what was right." [48]The people had gathered to watch this sight. When they saw what happened, they felt very sad. Then they went away. [49]But all those who knew Jesus stood not very far away, watching these things. They included the women who had followed him from Galilee.

Jesus Is Buried

[50]A man named Joseph was a member of the Jewish Council. He was a good and honest man. [51]Joseph had not agreed with what the leaders had decided and done. He was from Arimathea, a town in Judea. He himself was waiting for God's kingdom. [52]Joseph went to Pilate and asked for Jesus' body. [53]Joseph took it down and wrapped it in linen cloth. Then he placed it in a tomb cut in the rock. No one had ever been buried there. [54]It was Preparation Day. The Sabbath day was about to begin.

[55]The women who had come with Jesus from Galilee followed Joseph. They saw the tomb and how Jesus' body was placed in it. [56]Then they went home. There they prepared spices and perfumes. But they rested on the Sabbath day in order to obey the Law.

Jesus Rises From the Dead

24 It was very early in the morning on the first day of the week. The women took the spices they had prepared. Then they went to the tomb. [2]They found the stone rolled away from it. [3]When they entered the tomb, they did not find the body of the Lord Jesus. [4]They were wondering about this. Suddenly two men in clothes as bright as lightning stood beside them. [5]The women were terrified. They bowed down with their faces to the ground. Then the men said to them, "Why do you look for the living among the dead? [6]Jesus is not here! He has risen! Remember how he told you he would rise. It was while he was still with you in Galilee. [7]He said, 'The Son of Man must be handed over to sinful people. He must be nailed to a cross. On the third day he will rise from the dead.' " [8]Then the women remembered Jesus' words.

[9]They came back from the tomb. They told all these things to the 11 apostles and to all the others. [10]Mary Magdalene, Joanna, Mary the mother of James, and the others with them were the ones who told the apostles. [11]But the apostles did not believe the women. Their words didn't make any sense to them. [12]But Peter got up and ran to the tomb. He bent over and saw the strips of linen lying by themselves. Then he went away, wondering what had happened.

On the Road to Emmaus

[13]That same day two of Jesus' followers were going to a village called Emmaus. It was about seven miles from Jerusalem. [14]They were talking with each other about everything that had happened. [15]As they talked about those things, Jesus himself came up and walked along with them. [16]But God kept them from recognizing him.

[17]Jesus asked them, "What are you talking about as you walk along?"

They stood still, and their faces were sad. [18]One of them was named Cleopas. He said to Jesus, "Are you the only person visiting Jerusalem who doesn't know? Don't you know about the things that have happened there in the last few days?"

[19]"What things?" Jesus asked.

"About Jesus of Nazareth," they replied. "He was a prophet. He was powerful in what he said and did in the sight of God and all the people. [20]The chief priests and our rulers handed Jesus over to be sentenced to death. They nailed him to a cross. [21]But we had hoped that he was the one who was going to set Israel free. Also, it is the third day since all this happened. [22]Some of our women amazed us too. Early this morning they went to the tomb. [23]But they didn't find his body. So they came and told us what they had seen. They saw angels, who said Jesus was alive. [24]Then some of our friends went to the tomb. They saw it was empty, just as the women had said. They didn't see Jesus' body there."

[25]Jesus said to them, "How foolish you are! How long it takes you to believe all that the prophets said! [26]Didn't the Messiah have to suffer these things and then receive his glory?" [27]Jesus explained to them what was said about himself in all

the Scriptures. He began with Moses and
all the Prophets.
28 They approached the village where
they were going. Jesus kept walking as
if he were going farther. 29 But they tried
hard to keep him from leaving. They said,
"Stay with us. It is nearly evening. The day
is almost over." So he went in to stay with
them.
30 He joined them at the table. Then he
took bread and gave thanks. He broke it
and began to give it to them. 31 Their eyes
were opened, and they recognized him.
But then he disappeared from their sight.
32 They said to each other, "He explained
to us what the Scriptures meant. Weren't
we excited as he talked with us on the
road?"
33 They got up and returned at once to
Jerusalem. There they found the 11 disciples and those with them. They were all
gathered together. 34 They were saying,
"It's true! The Lord has risen! He has appeared to Simon!" 35 Then the two of them
told what had happened to them on the
way. They told how they had recognized
Jesus when he broke the bread.

Jesus Appears to the Disciples

36 The disciples were still talking about
this when Jesus himself suddenly stood
among them. He said, "May you have
peace!"
37 They were surprised and terrified.
They thought they were seeing a ghost.
38 Jesus said to them, "Why are you troubled? Why do you have doubts in your
minds? 39 Look at my hands and my feet.
It's really me! Touch me and see. A ghost
does not have a body or bones. But you
can see that I do."
40 After he said that, he showed them
his hands and feet. 41 But they still did not
believe it. They were amazed and filled
with joy. So Jesus asked them, "Do you
have anything here to eat?" 42 They gave
him a piece of cooked fish. 43 He took it
and ate it in front of them.
44 Jesus said to them, "This is what I told
you while I was still with you. Everything
written about me in the Law of Moses,
the Prophets and the Psalms must come
true."
45 Then he opened their minds so they
could understand the Scriptures. 46 He
told them, "This is what is written. The
Messiah will suffer. He will rise from the
dead on the third day. 47 His followers will
preach in his name. They will tell others
to turn away from their sins and be forgiven. People from every nation will hear
it, beginning at Jerusalem. 48 You have
seen these things with your own eyes. 49 I
am going to send you what my Father has
promised. But for now, stay in the city.
Stay there until you have received power
from heaven."

Jesus Is Taken Up Into Heaven

50 Jesus led his disciples out to the area
near Bethany. Then he lifted up his hands
and blessed them. 51 While he was blessing them, he left them. He was taken up
into heaven. 52 Then they worshiped him.
With great joy, they returned to Jerusalem. 53 Every day they went to the temple,
praising God.

JOHN

John was a disciple of Jesus. At the end of his book John tells why he wrote the story of Jesus. "But these are written so that you may believe that Jesus is the Messiah, the Son of God. If you believe this, you will have life because you belong to him."

John begins the book by using the words from the Bible's story of creation. These words are "In the beginning." By using these words John shows us that Jesus' story is about a new creation. The first story of creation takes place in seven days. So John uses the number seven in his new creation story too. In the Bible the number seven means that God has finished his work. Then we can see what God wants.

Seven times John shows Jesus using the words "I am" for himself. In the Old Testament God used those words to say who he was. John also shows Jesus performing seven mighty signs. All of this was to help people believe in Jesus.

John tells the story of Jesus' life in two parts. The first part tells about Jesus' teachings and mighty acts. John does this to make clear that Jesus really is the promised king of Israel. The second part tells about Jesus' teaching during the last week of his life. And it tells about Jesus' death and resurrection. When Jesus was raised from the dead, John uses the words "On the first day of the week." This shows that it was the first day of the new creation.

The Word Became a Human Being

1 In the beginning, the Word was already there. The Word was with God, and the Word was God. 2 He was with God in the beginning. 3 All things were made through him. Nothing that has been made was made without him. 4 Life was in him, and that life was the light for all people. 5 The light shines in the darkness. But the darkness has not overcome the light.

6 There was a man sent from God. His name was John. 7 He came to be a witness about that light. He was a witness so that all people might believe. 8 John himself was not the light. He came only as a witness to the light.

9 The true light that gives light to everyone was coming into the world. 10 The Word was in the world. And the world was made through him. But the world did not recognize him. 11 He came to what was his own. But his own people did not accept him. 12 Some people did accept him and did believe in his name. He gave them the right to become children of God. 13 To be a child of God has nothing to do with human parents. Children of God are not born because of human choice or because a husband wants them to be born. They are born because of what God does.

14 The Word became a human being. He made his home with us. We have seen his glory. It is the glory of the One and Only, who came from the Father. And the Word was full of grace and truth.

15 John was a witness about the Word. John cried out and said, "This was the one I was talking about. I said, 'He who comes after me is more important than I am. He is more important because he existed before I was born.' " 16 God is full of grace. From him we have all received grace in place of the grace already given. 17 In the past, God gave us grace through the law of Moses. Now, grace and truth come to us through Jesus Christ. 18 No one has ever seen God. But the One and Only is God and is at the Father's side. The one at the Father's side has shown us what God is like.

John the Baptist Says That He Is Not the Messiah

19 The Jewish leaders in Jerusalem sent priests and Levites to ask John who he was. John spoke the truth to them. 20 He did not try to hide the truth. He spoke to them openly. He said, "I am not the Messiah."

21 They asked him, "Then who are you? Are you Elijah?"

He said, "I am not."

"Are you the Prophet we've been expecting?" they asked.

"No," he answered.

22 They asked one last time, "Who are you? Give us an answer to take back to those who sent us. What do you say about yourself?"

23 John replied, using the words of Isaiah the prophet. John said, "I'm the messenger who is calling out in the desert,

'Make the way for the Lord straight.' " (Isaiah 40:3)
24 The Pharisees who had been sent
25 asked him, "If you are not the Messiah,
why are you baptizing people? Why are
you doing that if you aren't Elijah or the
Prophet we've been expecting?"
26 "I baptize people with water," John replied. "But someone is standing among
you whom you do not know. 27 He is the
one who comes after me. I am not good
enough to untie his sandals."
28 This all happened at Bethany on the
other side of the Jordan River. That was
where John was baptizing.

What John Says About Jesus

29 The next day John saw Jesus coming toward him. John said, "Look! The
Lamb of God! He takes away the sin of
the world! 30 This is the one I was talking
about. I said, 'A man who comes after me
is more important than I am. That's because he existed before I was born.' 31 I did
not know him. But God wants to make it
clear to Israel who this person is. That's
the reason I came baptizing with water."
32 Then John told them, "I saw the Holy
Spirit come down from heaven like a
dove. The Spirit remained on Jesus. 33 I
myself did not know him. But the one
who sent me to baptize with water told
me, 'You will see the Spirit come down
and remain on someone. He is the one
who will baptize with the Holy Spirit.' 34 I
have seen it happen. I am a witness that
this is God's Chosen One."

John's Disciples Follow Jesus

35 The next day John was there again
with two of his disciples. 36 He saw Jesus
walking by. John said, "Look! The Lamb
of God!"
37 The two disciples heard him say
this. So they followed Jesus. 38 Then Jesus
turned around and saw them following.
He asked, "What do you want?"
They said, "Rabbi, where are you staying?"Rabbi means Teacher.
39 "Come," he replied. "You will see."
So they went and saw where he was
staying. They spent the rest of the day
with him. It was about four o'clock in the
afternoon.
40 Andrew was Simon Peter's brother.
Andrew was one of the two disciples who
heard what John had said. He had also
followed Jesus. 41 The first thing Andrew
did was to find his brother Simon. He told
him, "We have found the Messiah." Messiah means Christ. 42 And he brought Simon to Jesus.
Jesus looked at him and said, "You are
Simon, son of John. You will be called Cephas." Cephas means Peter, or Rock.

Jesus Chooses Philip and Nathanael

43 The next day Jesus decided to leave
for Galilee. He found Philip and said to
him, "Follow me."
44 Philip was from the town of Bethsaida. So were Andrew and Peter. 45 Philip
found Nathanael and told him, "We have
found the one whom Moses wrote about
in the Law. The prophets also wrote about
him. He is Jesus of Nazareth, the son of Joseph."
46 "Nazareth! Can anything good come
from there?" Nathanael asked.
"Come and see," said Philip.
47 Jesus saw Nathanael approaching.
Here is what Jesus said about him. "He
is a true Israelite. Nothing about him is
false."
48 "How do you know me?" Nathanael
asked.
Jesus answered, "I saw you while you
were still under the fig tree. I saw you
there before Philip called you."
49 Nathanael replied, "Rabbi, you are
the Son of God. You are the king of Israel."
50 Jesus said, "You believe because I told
you I saw you under the fig tree. You will
see greater things than that." 51 Then he
said to the disciples, "What I'm about to
tell you is true. You will see heaven open.
You will see the angels of God going up
and coming down on the Son of Man."

Jesus Changes Water Into Wine

2 On the third day there was a wedding.
It took place at Cana in Galilee. Jesus'
mother was there. 2 Jesus and his disciples had also been invited to the wedding.
3 When the wine was gone, Jesus' mother
said to him, "They have no more wine."
4 "Dear woman, why are you telling me
about this?" Jesus replied. "The time for
me to show who I really am isn't here yet."
5 His mother said to the servants, "Do
what he tells you."
6 Six stone water jars stood nearby. The

Jews used water from that kind of jar for special washings. They did that to make themselves pure and "clean." Each jar could hold 20 to 30 gallons.

[7]Jesus said to the servants, "Fill the jars with water." So they filled them to the top. [8]Then he told them, "Now dip some out. Take it to the person in charge of the dinner."

They did what he said. [9]The person in charge tasted the water that had been turned into wine. He didn't realize where it had come from. But the servants who had brought the water knew. Then the person in charge called the groom to one side. [10]He said to him, "Everyone brings out the best wine first. They bring out the cheaper wine after the guests have had too much to drink. But you have saved the best until now."

[11]What Jesus did here in Cana in Galilee was the first of his signs. Jesus showed his glory by doing this sign. And his disciples believed in him.

[12]After this, Jesus went down to Capernaum. His mother and brothers and disciples went with him. They all stayed there for a few days.

Jesus Clears Out the Temple Courtyard

[13]It was almost time for the Jewish Passover Feast. So Jesus went up to Jerusalem. [14]In the temple courtyard he found people selling cattle, sheep and doves. Others were sitting at tables exchanging money. [15]So Jesus made a whip out of ropes. He chased all the sheep and cattle from the temple courtyard. He scattered the coins of the people exchanging money. And he turned over their tables. [16]He told those who were selling doves, "Get these out of here! Stop turning my Father's house into a market!" [17]His disciples remembered what had been written. It says, "My great love for your house will destroy me." (Psalm 69:9)

[18]Then the Jewish leaders asked him, "What sign can you show us to prove your authority to do this?"

[19]Jesus answered them, "When you destroy this temple, I will raise it up again in three days."

[20]They replied, "It has taken 46 years to build this temple. Are you going to raise it up in three days?" [21]But the temple Jesus had spoken about was his body. [22]His disciples later remembered what he had said. That was after he had been raised from the dead. Then they believed the Scripture. They also believed the words that Jesus had spoken.

[23]Meanwhile, he was in Jerusalem at the Passover Feast. Many people saw the signs he was doing. And they believed in his name. [24]But Jesus did not fully trust them. He knew what people are like. [25]He didn't need anyone to tell him what people are like. He already knew why people do what they do.

Jesus Teaches Nicodemus

3 There was a Pharisee named Nicodemus. He was one of the Jewish rulers. [2]He came to Jesus at night and said, "Rabbi, we know that you are a teacher who has come from God. We know that God is with you. If he weren't, you couldn't do the signs you are doing."

[3]Jesus replied, "What I'm about to tell you is true. No one can see God's kingdom unless they are born again."

[4]"How can someone be born when they are old?" Nicodemus asked. "They can't go back inside their mother! They can't be born a second time!"

[5]Jesus answered, "What I'm about to tell you is true. No one can enter God's kingdom unless they are born with water and the Holy Spirit. [6]People give birth to people. But the Spirit gives birth to spirit. [7]You should not be surprised when I say, 'You must all be born again.' [8]The wind blows where it wants to. You hear the sound it makes. But you can't tell where it comes from or where it is going. It is the same with everyone who is born with the Spirit."

[9]"How can this be?" Nicodemus asked.

[10]"You are Israel's teacher," said Jesus. "Don't you understand these things? [11]What I'm about to tell you is true. We speak about what we know. We are witnesses about what we have seen. But still you people do not accept what we say. [12]I have spoken to you about earthly things, and you do not believe. So how will you believe if I speak about heavenly things? [13]No one has ever gone into heaven except the one who came from heaven. He is the Son of Man. [14]Moses lifted up the snake in the desert. In the same way, the Son of Man must also be lifted up. [15]Then

everyone who believes may have eternal life in him."

16 God so loved the world that he gave his one and only Son. Anyone who believes in him will not die but will have eternal life. 17 God did not send his Son into the world to judge the world. He sent his Son to save the world through him. 18 Anyone who believes in him is not judged. But anyone who does not believe is judged already. They have not believed in the name of God's one and only Son. 19 Here is the judgment. Light has come into the world, but people loved darkness instead of light. They loved darkness because what they did was evil. 20 Everyone who does evil deeds hates the light. They will not come into the light. They are afraid that what they do will be seen. 21 But anyone who lives by the truth comes into the light. They live by the truth with God's help. They come into the light so that it will be easy to see their good deeds.

John the Baptist Is a Witness About Jesus

22 After this, Jesus and his disciples went out into the countryside of Judea. There he spent some time with them. And he baptized people there. 23 John was also baptizing. He was at Aenon near Salim, where there was plenty of water. People were coming and being baptized. 24 This was before John was put in prison. 25 Some of John's disciples and a certain Jew began to argue. They argued about special washings to make people "clean." 26 They came to John and here is what they said to him. "Rabbi, that man who was with you on the other side of the Jordan River is baptizing people. He is the one you told us about. Everyone is going to him."

27 John replied, "A person can receive only what God gives them from heaven. 28 You yourselves are witnesses that I said, 'I am not the Messiah. I was sent ahead of him.' 29 The bride belongs to the groom. The friend who helps the groom waits and listens for him. He is full of joy when he hears the groom's voice. That joy is mine, and it is now complete. 30 He must become more important. I must become less important.

31 "The one who comes from above is above everything. The one who is from the earth belongs to the earth and speaks like someone from the earth. The one who comes from heaven is above everything. 32 He is a witness to what he has seen and heard. But no one accepts what he says. 33 Anyone who has accepted it has said, 'Yes. God is truthful.' 34 The one whom God has sent speaks God's words. That's because God gives the Holy Spirit without limit. 35 The Father loves the Son and has put everything into his hands. 36 Anyone who believes in the Son has eternal life. Anyone who does not believe in the Son will not have life. God's anger remains on them."

Jesus Talks With a Woman From Samaria

4 Now Jesus learned that the Pharisees had heard about him. They had heard that he was gaining and baptizing more disciples than John. 2 But in fact Jesus was not baptizing. His disciples were. 3 So Jesus left Judea and went back again to Galilee.

4 Jesus had to go through Samaria. 5 He came to a town in Samaria called Sychar. It was near the piece of land Jacob had given his son Joseph. 6 Jacob's well was there. Jesus was tired from the journey. So he sat down by the well. It was about noon.

7 A woman from Samaria came to get some water. Jesus said to her, "Will you give me a drink?" 8 His disciples had gone into the town to buy food.

9 The Samaritan woman said to him, "You are a Jew. I am a Samaritan woman. How can you ask me for a drink?" She said this because Jews don't have anything to do with Samaritans.

10 Jesus answered her, "You do not know what God's gift is. And you do not know who is asking you for a drink. If you did, you would have asked him. He would have given you living water."

11 "Sir," the woman said, "you don't have anything to get water with. The well is deep. Where can you get this living water? 12 Our father Jacob gave us the well. He drank from it himself. So did his sons and his livestock. Are you more important than he is?"

13 Jesus answered, "Everyone who drinks this water will be thirsty again. 14 But anyone who drinks the water I give them will never be thirsty. In fact, the water I give them will become a spring of

water in them. It will flow up into eternal
life."
15 The woman said to him, "Sir, give me
this water. Then I will never be thirsty.
And I won't have to keep coming here to
get water."
16 He told her, "Go. Get your husband
and come back."
17 "I have no husband," she replied.
Jesus said to her, "You are right when
you say you have no husband. 18 The fact
is, you have had five husbands. And the
man you live with now is not your husband. What you have just said is very
true."
19 "Sir," the woman said, "I can see that
you are a prophet. 20 Our people have always worshiped on this mountain. But
you Jews claim that the place where we
must worship is in Jerusalem."
21 Jesus said, "Woman, believe me. A
time is coming when you will not worship the Father on this mountain or in Jerusalem. 22 You Samaritans worship what
you do not know. We worship what we
do know. Salvation comes from the Jews.
23 But a new time is coming. In fact, it is already here. True worshipers will worship
the Father in the Spirit and in truth. They
are the kind of worshipers the Father is
looking for. 24 God is spirit. His worshipers must worship him in the Spirit and in
truth."
25 The woman said, "I know that Messiah is coming." Messiah means Christ.
"When he comes, he will explain everything to us."
26 Then Jesus said, "The one you're talking about is the one speaking to you. I am
he."

The Disciples Join Jesus Again

27 Just then Jesus' disciples returned.
They were surprised to find him talking
with a woman. But no one asked, "What
do you want from her?" No one asked,
"Why are you talking with her?"
28 The woman left her water jar and
went back to the town. She said to the
people, 29 "Come. See a man who told
me everything I've ever done. Could this
be the Messiah?" 30 The people came out
of the town and made their way toward
Jesus.
31 His disciples were saying to him,
"Rabbi, eat something!"
32 But he said to them, "I have food to
eat that you know nothing about."
33 Then his disciples asked each other,
"Did someone bring him food?"
34 Jesus said, "My food is to do what my
Father sent me to do. My food is to finish
his work. 35 Don't you have a saying? You
say, 'It's still four months until harvest
time.' But I tell you, open your eyes! Look
at the fields! They are ripe for harvest right
now. 36 Even now the one who gathers the
crop is getting paid. They are already har-
vesting the crop for eternal life. So the
one who plants and the one who gathers
can now be glad together. 37 Here is a true
saying. 'One plants and another gathers.'
38 I sent you to gather what you have not
worked for. Others have done the hard
work. You have gathered the benefits of
their work."

Many Samaritans Believe in Jesus

39 Many of the Samaritans from the
town of Sychar believed in Jesus. They
believed because of what the woman had
said about him. She said, "He told me everything I've ever done." 40 Then the Samaritans came to him and tried to get
him to stay with them. So he stayed two
days. 41 Because of what he said, many
more people became believers.
42 They said to the woman, "We no longer believe just because of what you said.
We have now heard for ourselves. We
know that this man really is the Savior of
the world."

Jesus Heals an Official's Son

43 After the two days, Jesus left for Galilee. 44 He himself had pointed out that a
prophet is not respected in his own country. 45 When he arrived in Galilee, the people living there welcomed him. They had
seen everything he had done in Jerusalem
at the Passover Feast. That was because
they had also been there.
46 Once more, Jesus visited Cana in Galilee. Cana is where he had turned the water into wine. A royal official was there.
His son was sick in bed at Capernaum.
47 The official heard that Jesus had arrived
in Galilee from Judea. So he went to Jesus
and begged him to come and heal his son.
The boy was close to death.
48 Jesus told him, "You people will never

believe unless you see signs and wonders."

49 The royal official said, "Sir, come down before my child dies."

50 "Go," Jesus replied. "Your son will live."

The man believed what Jesus said, and so he left. 51 While he was still on his way home, his slaves met him. They gave him the news that his boy was living. 52 He asked what time his son got better. They said to him, "Yesterday, at one o'clock in the afternoon, the fever left him."

53 Then the father realized what had happened. That was the exact time Jesus had said to him, "Your son will live." So he and his whole family became believers.

54 This was the second sign that Jesus did after coming from Judea to Galilee.

Jesus Heals a Man at the Pool

5 Some time later, Jesus went up to Jerusalem for one of the Jewish feasts. 2 In Jerusalem near the Sheep Gate is a pool. In the Aramaic language it is called Bethesda. It is surrounded by five rows of columns with a roof over them. 3-4 Here a great number of disabled people used to lie down. Among them were those who were blind, those who could not walk, and those who could hardly move. 5 One person was there who had not been able to walk for 38 years. 6 Jesus saw him lying there. He knew that the man had been in that condition for a long time. So he asked him, "Do you want to get well?"

7 "Sir," the disabled man replied, "I have no one to help me into the pool when an angel stirs up the water. I try to get in, but someone else always goes down ahead of me."

8 Then Jesus said to him, "Get up! Pick up your mat and walk." 9 The man was healed right away. He picked up his mat and walked.

This happened on a Sabbath day. 10 So the Jewish leaders said to the man who had been healed, "It is the Sabbath day. The law does not allow you to carry your mat."

11 But he replied, "The one who made me well said to me, 'Pick up your mat and walk.'"

12 They asked him, "Who is this fellow? Who told you to pick it up and walk?"

13 The one who was healed had no idea who it was. Jesus had slipped away into the crowd that was there.

14 Later Jesus found him at the temple. Jesus said to him, "See, you are well again. Stop sinning, or something worse may happen to you." 15 The man went away. He told the Jewish leaders it was Jesus who had made him well.

The Authority of the Son

16 Jesus was doing these things on the Sabbath day. So the Jewish leaders began to oppose him. 17 Jesus defended himself. He said to them, "My Father is always doing his work. He is working right up to this day. I am working too." 18 For this reason the Jewish leaders tried even harder to kill him. According to them, Jesus was not only breaking the law of the Sabbath day. He was even calling God his own Father. He was making himself equal with God.

19 Jesus answered, "What I'm about to tell you is true. The Son can do nothing by himself. He can do only what he sees his Father doing. What the Father does, the Son also does. 20 This is because the Father loves the Son. The Father shows him everything he does. Yes, and the Father will show the Son even greater works than these. And you will be amazed. 21 The Father raises the dead and gives them life. In the same way, the Son gives life to anyone he wants to. 22 Also, the Father does not judge anyone. He has given the Son the task of judging. 23 Then all people will honor the Son just as they honor the Father. Whoever does not honor the Son does not honor the Father, who sent him.

24 "What I'm about to tell you is true. Anyone who hears my word and believes him who sent me has eternal life. They will not be judged. They have crossed over from death to life. 25 What I'm about to tell you is true. A time is coming for me to give life. In fact, it has already begun. The dead will hear the voice of the Son of God. Those who hear it will live. 26 The Father has life in himself. He has allowed the Son also to have life in himself. 27 And the Father has given him the authority to judge. This is because he is the Son of Man.

28 "Do not be amazed at this. A time is coming when all who are in their graves will hear his voice. 29 They will all come out of their graves. People who have done

what is good will rise and live again. People who have done what is evil will rise and be found guilty. 30 I can do nothing by myself. I judge only as I hear. And my judging is fair. I do not try to please myself. I try to please the one who sent me.

Being a Witness About Jesus

31 "If I am a witness about myself, what I say is not true. 32 There is someone else who is a witness in my favor. And I know that what he says about me is true.

33 "You have sent people to John the Baptist. He has been a witness to the truth. 34 I do not accept what a person says. I only talk about what John says so that you can be saved. 35 John was like a lamp that burned and gave light. For a while you chose to enjoy his light.

36 "What I say about myself is more important than what John says about me. I am doing the works the Father gave me to finish. These works are a witness that the Father has sent me. 37 The Father who sent me is himself a witness about me. You have never heard his voice. You have never seen what he really looks like. 38 And his word does not live in you. That's because you do not believe the one he sent. 39 You study the Scriptures carefully. You study them because you think they will give you eternal life. The Scriptures you study are a witness about me. 40 But you refuse to come to me and receive life.

41 "I do not accept praise from human beings. 42 But I know you. I know that you do not have love for God in your hearts. 43 I have come in my Father's name, and you do not accept me. But if someone else comes in his own name, you will accept him. 44 You accept praise from one another. But you do not seek the praise that comes from the only God. So how can you believe?

45 "Do not think I will bring charges against you in front of the Father. Moses is the one who does that. And he is the one you build your hopes on. 46 Do you believe Moses? Then you should believe me. He wrote about me. 47 But you do not believe what he wrote. So how are you going to believe what I say?"

Jesus Feeds the Five Thousand

6 Some time after this, Jesus crossed over to the other side of the Sea of Galilee. It is also called the Sea of Tiberias. 2 A large crowd of people followed him. They had seen the signs he had done by healing sick people. 3 Then Jesus went up on a mountainside. There he sat down with his disciples. 4 The Jewish Passover Feast was near.

5 Jesus looked up and saw a large crowd coming toward him. So he said to Philip, "Where can we buy bread for these people to eat?" 6 He asked this only to test Philip. He already knew what he was going to do.

7 Philip answered him, "Suppose we were able to buy enough bread for each person to have just a bite. That would take more than half a year's pay!"

8 Another of his disciples spoke up. It was Andrew, Simon Peter's brother. He said, 9 "Here is a boy with five small loaves of barley bread. He also has two small fish. But how far will that go in such a large crowd?"

10 Jesus said, "Have the people sit down." There was plenty of grass in that place, and they sat down. About 5,000 men were there. 11 Then Jesus took the loaves and gave thanks. He handed out the bread to those who were seated. He gave them as much as they wanted. And he did the same with the fish.

12 When all of them had enough to eat, Jesus spoke to his disciples. "Gather the leftover pieces," he said. "Don't waste anything." 13 So they gathered what was left over from the five barley loaves. They filled 12 baskets with the pieces left by those who had eaten.

14 The people saw the sign that Jesus did. Then they began to say, "This must be the Prophet who is supposed to come into the world." 15 But Jesus knew that they planned to come and force him to be their king. So he went away again to a mountain by himself.

Jesus Walks on the Water

16 When evening came, Jesus' disciples went down to the Sea of Galilee. 17 There they got into a boat and headed across the lake toward Capernaum. By now it was dark. Jesus had not yet joined them. 18 A strong wind was blowing, and the water became rough. 19 They rowed about three or four miles. Then they saw Jesus coming toward the boat. He was walking

on the water. They were frightened. 20 But he said to them, "It is I. Don't be afraid." 21 Then they agreed to take him into the boat. Right away the boat reached the shore where they were heading.

22 The next day the crowd that had stayed on the other side of the lake realized something. They saw that only one boat had been there. They knew that Jesus had not gotten into it with his disciples. And they knew that the disciples had gone away alone. 23 Then some boats arrived from Tiberias. It was near the place where the people had eaten the bread after the Lord gave thanks. 24 The crowd realized that Jesus and his disciples were not there. So they got into boats and went to Capernaum to look for Jesus.

Jesus Is the Bread of Life

25 They found him on the other side of the lake. They asked him, "Rabbi, when did you get here?"

26 Jesus answered, "What I'm about to tell you is true. You are not looking for me because you saw the signs I did. You are looking for me because you ate the loaves until you were full. 27 Do not work for food that spoils. Work for food that lasts forever. That is the food the Son of Man will give you. For God the Father has put his seal of approval on him."

28 Then they asked him, "What does God want from us? What works does he want us to do?"

29 Jesus answered, "God's work is to believe in the one he has sent."

30 So they asked him, "What sign will you give us? What will you do so we can see it and believe you? 31 Long ago our people ate the manna in the desert. It is written in Scripture, 'The Lord gave them bread from heaven to eat.'" (Exodus 16:4; Nehemiah 9:15; Psalm 78:24,25)

32 Jesus said to them, "What I'm about to tell you is true. It is not Moses who has given you the bread from heaven. It is my Father who gives you the true bread from heaven. 33 The bread of God is the bread that comes down from heaven. He gives life to the world."

34 "Sir," they said, "always give us this bread."

35 Then Jesus said, "I am the bread of life. Whoever comes to me will never go hungry. And whoever believes in me will never be thirsty. 36 But it is just as I told you. You have seen me, and you still do not believe. 37 Everyone the Father gives me will come to me. I will never send away anyone who comes to me. 38 I have not come down from heaven to do what I want to do. I have come to do what the one who sent me wants me to do. 39 The one who sent me doesn't want me to lose anyone he has given me. He wants me to raise them up on the last day. 40 My Father wants all who look to the Son and believe in him to have eternal life. I will raise them up on the last day."

41 Then the Jews there began to complain about Jesus. That was because he said, "I am the bread that came down from heaven." 42 They said, "Isn't this Jesus, the son of Joseph? Don't we know his father and mother? How can he now say, 'I came down from heaven'?"

43 "Stop complaining among yourselves," Jesus answered. 44 "No one can come to me unless the Father who sent me brings them. Then I will raise them up on the last day. 45 It is written in the Prophets, 'God will teach all of them.' (Isaiah 54:13) Everyone who has heard the Father and learned from him comes to me. 46 No one has seen the Father except the one who has come from God. Only he has seen the Father. 47 What I'm about to tell you is true. Everyone who believes has life forever. 48 I am the bread of life. 49 Long ago your people ate the manna in the desert, and they still died. 50 But here is the bread that comes down from heaven. A person can eat it and not die. 51 I am the living bread that came down from heaven. Everyone who eats some of this bread will live forever. This bread is my body. I will give it for the life of the world."

52 Then the Jews began to argue sharply among themselves. They said, "How can this man give us his body to eat?"

53 Jesus said to them, "What I'm about to tell you is true. You must eat the Son of Man's body and drink his blood. If you don't, you have no life in you. 54 Anyone who eats my body and drinks my blood has eternal life. I will raise them up on the last day. 55 My body is real food. My blood is real drink. 56 Anyone who eats my body and drinks my blood remains in me. And I remain in them. 57 The living Father sent me, and I live because of him. In the same

way, those who feed on me will live because of me. 58 This is the bread that came down from heaven. Long ago your people ate manna and died. But whoever eats this bread will live forever." 59 He said this while he was teaching in the synagogue in Capernaum.

Many Disciples Leave Jesus

60 Jesus' disciples heard this. Many of them said, "This is a hard teaching. Who can accept it?"

61 Jesus was aware that his disciples were complaining about his teaching. So he said to them, "Does this upset you? 62 Then what if you see the Son of Man go up to where he was before? 63 The Holy Spirit gives life. The body means nothing at all. The words I have spoken to you are full of the Spirit. They give life. 64 But there are some of you who do not believe." Jesus had known from the beginning which of them did not believe. And he had known who was going to hand him over to his enemies. 65 So he continued speaking. He said, "This is why I told you that no one can come to me unless the Father helps them."

66 From this time on, many of his disciples turned back. They no longer followed him.

67 "You don't want to leave also, do you?" Jesus asked the 12 disciples.

68 Simon Peter answered him, "Lord, who can we go to? You have the words of eternal life. 69 We have come to believe and to know that you are the Holy One of God."

70 Then Jesus replied, "Didn't I choose you, the 12 disciples? But one of you is a devil!" 71 He meant Judas, the son of Simon Iscariot. Judas was one of the 12 disciples. But later he was going to hand Jesus over to his enemies.

Jesus Goes to the Feast of Booths

7 After this, Jesus went around in Galilee. He didn't want to travel around in Judea. That was because the Jewish leaders there were looking for a way to kill him. 2 The Jewish Feast of Booths was near. 3 Jesus' brothers said to him, "Leave Galilee and go to Judea. Then your disciples there will see the works that you do. 4 No one who wants to be well known does things in secret. Since you are doing these things, show yourself to the world." 5 Even Jesus' own brothers did not believe in him.

6 So Jesus told them, "The time for me to show who I really am is not here yet. For you, any time would be the right time. 7 The people of the world can't hate you. But they hate me. This is because I am a witness that their works are evil. 8 You go to the feast. I am not going up to this feast. This is because my time has not yet fully come." 9 After he said this, he stayed in Galilee.

10 But when his brothers had left for the feast, he went also. But he went secretly, not openly. 11 At the feast the Jewish leaders were watching for Jesus. They were asking, "Where is he?"

12 Many people in the crowd were whispering about him. Some said, "He is a good man."

Others replied, "No. He fools the people." 13 But no one would say anything about him openly. They were afraid of the leaders.

Jesus Teaches at the Feast

14 Jesus did nothing until halfway through the feast. Then he went up to the temple courtyard and began to teach. 15 The Jews there were amazed. They asked, "How did this man learn so much without being taught?"

16 Jesus answered, "What I teach is not my own. It comes from the one who sent me. 17 Here is how someone can find out whether my teaching comes from God or from me. That person must choose to do what God wants them to do. 18 Whoever speaks on their own does it to get personal honor. But someone who works for the honor of the one who sent him is truthful. Nothing about him is false. 19 Didn't Moses give you the law? But not one of you obeys the law. Why are you trying to kill me?"

20 "You are controlled by demons," the crowd answered. "Who is trying to kill you?"

21 Jesus said to them, "I did one miracle, and you are all amazed. 22 Moses gave you circumcision, and so you circumcise a child on the Sabbath day. But circumcision did not really come from Moses. It came from Abraham. 23 You circumcise a boy on the Sabbath day. You think that if

you do, you won't break the law of Moses. Then why are you angry with me? I
healed a man's entire body on the Sabbath day! 24 Stop judging only by what you
see. Judge in the right way."

People Don't Agree About Who Jesus Is

25 Then some of the people of Jerusalem
began asking questions. They said, "Isn't
this the man some people are trying to
kill? 26 Here he is! He is speaking openly.
They aren't saying a word to him. Have
the authorities really decided that he is
the Messiah? 27 But we know where this
man is from. When the Messiah comes,
no one will know where he is from."

28 Jesus was still teaching in the temple
courtyard. He cried out, "Yes, you know
me. And you know where I am from. I am
not here on my own authority. The one
who sent me is true. You do not know
him. 29 But I know him. I am from him,
and he sent me."

30 When he said this, they tried to arrest
him. But no one laid a hand on him. The
time for him to show who he really was
had not yet come. 31 Still, many people
in the crowd believed in him. They said,
"How will it be when the Messiah comes?
Will he do more signs than this man?"

32 The Pharisees heard the crowd whispering things like this about him. Then
the chief priests and the Pharisees sent
temple guards to arrest him.

33 Jesus said, "I am with you for only a
short time. Then I will go to the one who
sent me. 34 You will look for me, but you
won't find me. You can't come where I am
going."

35 The Jews said to one another, "Where
does this man plan to go? Does he think
we can't find him? Will he go where our
people live scattered among the Greeks?
Will he go there to teach the Greeks?
36 What did he mean when he said, 'You
will look for me, but you won't find me'?
And what did he mean when he said, 'You
can't come where I am going'?"

37 It was the last and most important
day of the feast. Jesus stood up and spoke
in a loud voice. He said, "Let anyone who
is thirsty come to me and drink. 38 Does
anyone believe in me? Then, just as Scripture says, rivers of living water will flow
from inside them." 39 When he said this,
he meant the Holy Spirit. Those who believed in Jesus would receive the Spirit
later. Up to that time, the Spirit had not
been given. This was because Jesus had
not yet received glory.

40 The people heard his words. Some of
them said, "This man must be the Prophet
we've been expecting."

41 Others said, "He is the Messiah."

Still others asked, "How can the Messiah come from Galilee? 42 Doesn't Scripture say that the Messiah will come from
the family line of David? Doesn't it say
that he will come from Bethlehem, the
town where David lived?" 43 So the people did not agree about who Jesus was.
44 Some wanted to arrest him. But no one
laid a hand on him.

The Jewish Leaders Do Not Believe

45 Finally the temple guards went back
to the chief priests and the Pharisees.
They asked the guards, "Why didn't you
bring him in?"

46 "No one ever spoke the way this man
does," the guards replied.

47 "You mean he has fooled you also?"
the Pharisees asked. 48 "Have any of the
rulers or Pharisees believed in him? 49 No!
But this mob knows nothing about the
law. There is a curse on them."

50 Then Nicodemus, a Pharisee, spoke.
He was the one who had gone to Jesus
earlier. He asked, 51 "Does our law find
a man guilty without hearing him first?
Doesn't it want to find out what he is doing?"

52 They replied, "Are you from Galilee too? Look into it. You will find that a
prophet does not come out of Galilee."

8 53 Then they all went home. 1 But Jesus
went to the Mount of Olives.

2 At sunrise he arrived again in the temple courtyard. All the people gathered
around him there. He sat down to teach
them. 3 The teachers of the law and the
Pharisees brought in a woman. She had
been caught committing adultery. They
made her stand in front of the group.
4 They said to Jesus, "Teacher, this woman was caught sleeping with a man who
was not her husband. 5 In the Law, Moses commanded us to kill such women
by throwing stones at them. Now what do
you say?" 6 They were trying to trap Jesus

with that question. They wanted to have a reason to bring charges against him.

But Jesus bent down and started to write on the ground with his finger. [7]They kept asking him questions. So he stood up and said to them, "Has any one of you not sinned? Then you be the first to throw a stone at her." [8]He bent down again and wrote on the ground.

[9]Those who heard what he had said began to go away. They left one at a time, the older ones first. Soon only Jesus was left. The woman was still standing there. [10]Jesus stood up and asked her, "Woman, where are they? Hasn't anyone found you guilty?"

[11]"No one, sir," she said.

"Then I don't find you guilty either," Jesus said. "Go now and leave your life of sin."

Challenge to What Jesus Says About Himself

[12]Jesus spoke to the people again. He said, "I am the light of the world. Anyone who follows me will never walk in darkness. They will have that light. They will have life."

[13]The Pharisees argued with him. "Here you are," they said, "appearing as your own witness. But your witness does not count."

[14]Jesus answered, "Even if I am a witness about myself, what I say does count. I know where I came from. And I know where I am going. But you have no idea where I come from or where I am going. [15]You judge by human standards. I don't judge anyone. [16]But if I do judge, what I decide is true. This is because I am not alone. I stand with the Father, who sent me. [17]Your own Law says that the witness of two people proves the truth about something. [18]I am a witness about myself. The other witness about me is the Father, who sent me."

[19]Then they asked him, "Where is your father?"

"You do not know me or my Father," Jesus replied. "If you knew me, you would know my Father also." [20]He spoke these words while he was teaching in the temple courtyard. He was near the place where the offerings were put. But no one arrested him. That's because the time for him to die had not yet come.

Challenge to Who Jesus Claims to Be

[21]Once more Jesus said to them, "I am going away. You will look for me, and you will die in your sin. You can't come where I am going."

[22]This made the Jews ask, "Will he kill himself? Is that why he says, 'You can't come where I am going'?"

[23]But Jesus said, "You are from below. I am from heaven. You are from this world. I am not from this world. [24]I told you that you would die in your sins. This will happen if you don't believe that I am he. If you don't believe, you will certainly die in your sins."

[25]"Who are you?" they asked.

"Just what I have been telling you from the beginning," Jesus replied. [26]"I have a lot to say that will judge you. But the one who sent me can be trusted. And I tell the world what I have heard from him."

[27]They did not understand that Jesus was telling them about his Father. [28]So Jesus said, "You will lift up the Son of Man. Then you will know that I am he. You will also know that I do nothing on my own. I speak just what the Father has taught me. [29]The one who sent me is with me. He has not left me alone, because I always do what pleases him." [30]Even while Jesus was speaking, many people believed in him.

Challenge to the Claim to Be Children of Abraham

[31]Jesus spoke to the Jews who had believed him. "If you obey my teaching," he said, "you are really my disciples. [32]Then you will know the truth. And the truth will set you free."

[33]They answered him, "We are Abraham's children. We have never been slaves of anyone. So how can you say that we will be set free?"

[34]Jesus replied, "What I'm about to tell you is true. Everyone who sins is a slave of sin. [35]A slave has no lasting place in the family. But a son belongs to the family forever. [36]So if the Son of Man sets you free, you will really be free. [37]I know that you are Abraham's children. But you are looking for a way to kill me. You have no room for my word. [38]I am telling you what I saw when I was with my Father. You are doing what you have heard from your father."

39 “Abraham is our father,” they answered.

Jesus said, “Are you really Abraham’s children? If you are, you will do what Abraham did. 40 But you are looking for a way to kill me. I am a man who has told you the truth I heard from God. Abraham didn’t do the things you want to do. 41 You are doing what your own father does.”

“We have the right to claim to be God’s children,” they objected. “The only Father we have is God himself.”

42 Jesus said to them, “If God were your Father, you would love me. I have come here from God. I have not come on my own. God sent me. 43 Why aren’t my words clear to you? Because you can’t really hear what I say. 44 You belong to your father, the devil. You want to obey your father’s wishes. From the beginning, the devil was a murderer. He has never obeyed the truth. There is no truth in him. When he lies, he speaks his natural language. He does this because he is a liar. He is the father of lies. 45 But because I tell the truth, you don’t believe me! 46 Can any of you prove I am guilty of sinning? Am I not telling the truth? Then why don’t you believe me? 47 Whoever belongs to God hears what God says. The reason you don’t hear is that you don’t belong to God.”

Jesus Makes Claims About Himself

48 The Jews answered Jesus, “Aren’t we right when we say you are a Samaritan? Aren’t you controlled by a demon?”

49 “I am not controlled by a demon,” said Jesus. “I honor my Father. You do not honor me. 50 I am not seeking glory for myself. But there is one who brings glory to me. He is the judge. 51 What I’m about to tell you is true. Whoever obeys my word will never die.”

52 Then they cried out, “Now we know you are controlled by a demon! Abraham died. So did the prophets. But you say that whoever obeys your word will never die. 53 Are you greater than our father Abraham? He died. So did the prophets. Who do you think you are?”

54 Jesus replied, “If I bring glory to myself, my glory means nothing. You claim that my Father is your God. He is the one who brings glory to me. 55 You do not know him. But I know him. If I said I did not, I would be a liar like you. But I do know him. And I obey his word. 56 Your father Abraham was filled with joy at the thought of seeing my day. He saw it and was glad.”

57 “You are not even 50 years old,” they said to Jesus. “And you have seen Abraham?”

58 “What I’m about to tell you is true,” Jesus answered. “Before Abraham was born, I am!” 59 When he said this, they picked up stones to kill him. But Jesus hid himself. He slipped away from the temple area.

Jesus Makes Claims About Himself

9 As Jesus went along, he saw a man who was blind. He had been blind since he was born. 2 Jesus’ disciples asked him, “Rabbi, who sinned? Was this man born blind because he sinned? Or did his parents sin?”

3 “It isn’t because this man sinned,” said Jesus. “It isn’t because his parents sinned. He was born blind so that God’s power could be shown by what’s going to happen. 4 While it is still day, we must do the works of the one who sent me. Night is coming. Then no one can work. 5 While I am in the world, I am the light of the world.”

6 After he said this, he spit on the ground. He made some mud with the spit. Then he put the mud on the man’s eyes. 7 “Go,” he told him. “Wash in the Pool of Siloam.” Siloam means Sent. So the man went and washed. And he came home able to see.

8 His neighbors and people who had seen him earlier begging asked questions. “Isn’t this the same man who used to sit and beg?” they asked. 9 Some claimed that he was.

Others said, “No. He only looks like him.”

But the man who had been blind kept saying, “I am the man.”

10 “Then how were your eyes opened?” they asked.

11 He replied, “The man they call Jesus made some mud and put it on my eyes. He told me to go to Siloam and wash. So I went and washed. Then I could see.”

12 “Where is this man?” they asked him.

“I don’t know,” he said.

The Pharisees Want to Know How the
Blind Man Was Healed

13 They brought to the Pharisees the
man who had been blind. 14 The day Jesus
made the mud and opened the man's
eyes was a Sabbath day. 15 So the Pharisees also asked him how he was able to
see. "He put mud on my eyes," the man
replied. "Then I washed. And now I can
see."

16 Some of the Pharisees said, "Jesus has
not come from God. He does not keep the
Sabbath day."

But others asked, "How can a sinner
do such signs?" So the Pharisees did not
agree with one another.

17 Then they turned again to the blind
man. "What do you have to say about
him?" they asked. "It was your eyes he
opened."

The man replied, "He is a prophet."

18 They still did not believe that the man
had been blind and now could see. So
they sent for his parents. 19 "Is this your
son?" they asked. "Is this the one you say
was born blind? How is it that now he can
see?"

20 "We know he is our son," the parents
answered. "And we know he was born
blind. 21 But we don't know how he can
now see. And we don't know who opened
his eyes. Ask him. He is an adult. He can
speak for himself." 22 His parents said this
because they were afraid of the Jewish
leaders. The leaders had already made
this decision about Jesus. Anyone who
said Jesus was the Messiah would be put
out of the synagogue. 23 That was why the
man's parents said, "He is an adult. Ask
him."

24 Again the Pharisees called the man
who had been blind to come to them.
"Give glory to God by telling the truth!"
they said. "We know that the man who
healed you is a sinner."

25 He replied, "I don't know if he is a
sinner or not. I do know one thing. I was
blind, but now I can see!"

26 Then they asked him, "What did he
do to you? How did he open your eyes?"

27 He answered, "I have already told
you. But you didn't listen. Why do you
want to hear it again? Do you want to become his disciples too?"

28 Then they began to attack him with
their words. "You are this fellow's disciple!" they said. "We are disciples of Moses! 29 We know that God spoke to Moses.
But we don't even know where this fellow
comes from."

30 The man answered, "That is really
surprising! You don't know where he
comes from, and yet he opened my eyes.
31 We know that God does not listen to sinners. He listens to the godly person who
does what he wants them to do. 32 Nobody has ever heard of anyone opening
the eyes of a person born blind. 33 If this
man had not come from God, he could do
nothing."

34 Then the Pharisees replied, "When
you were born, you were already deep in
sin. How dare you talk like that to us!" And
they threw him out of the synagogue.

People Who Can't See the Truth

35 Jesus heard that the Pharisees had
thrown the man out of the synagogue.
When Jesus found him, he said, "Do you
believe in the Son of Man?"

36 "Who is he, sir?" the man asked. "Tell
me, so I can believe in him."

37 Jesus said, "You have now seen him.
In fact, he is the one speaking with you."

38 Then the man said, "Lord, I believe."
And he worshiped him.

39 Jesus said, "I have come into this
world to judge it. I have come so that people who are blind will see. I have come
so that people who can see will become
blind."

40 Some Pharisees who were with him
heard him say this. They asked, "What?
Are we blind too?"

41 Jesus said, "If you were blind, you
would not be guilty of sin. But since you
claim you can see, you remain guilty.

The Good Shepherd and His Sheep

10 "What I'm about to tell you Pharisees is true. What if someone does
not enter the sheep pen through the gate
but climbs in another way? That person is
a thief and a robber. 2 The one who enters
through the gate is the shepherd of the
sheep. 3 The gatekeeper opens the gate
for him. The sheep listen to his voice. He
calls his own sheep by name and leads
them out. 4 When he has brought out all
his own sheep, he goes on ahead of them.
His sheep follow him because they know
his voice. 5 But they will never follow a

stranger. In fact, they will run away from him. They don't recognize a stranger's voice." 6 Jesus told this story. But the Pharisees didn't understand what he was telling them.

7 So Jesus said again, "What I'm about to tell you is true. I am like a gate for the sheep. 8 All who have come before me are thieves and robbers. But the sheep have not listened to them. 9 I'm like a gate. Anyone who enters through me will be saved. They will come in and go out. And they will find plenty of food. 10 A thief comes only to steal and kill and destroy. I have come so they may have life. I want them to have it in the fullest possible way.

11 "I am the good shepherd. The good shepherd gives his life for the sheep. 12 The hired man is not the shepherd and does not own the sheep. So when the hired man sees the wolf coming, he leaves the sheep and runs away. Then the wolf attacks the flock and scatters it. 13 The man runs away because he is a hired man. He does not care about the sheep.

14 "I am the good shepherd. I know my sheep, and my sheep know me. 15 They know me just as the Father knows me and I know the Father. And I give my life for the sheep. 16 I have other sheep that do not belong to this sheep pen. I must bring them in too. They also will listen to my voice. Then there will be one flock and one shepherd. 17 The reason my Father loves me is that I give up my life. But I will take it back again. 18 No one takes it from me. I give it up myself. I have the authority to give it up. And I have the authority to take it back again. I received this command from my Father."

19 The Jews who heard these words could not agree with one another. 20 Many of them said, "He is controlled by a demon. He has gone crazy! Why should we listen to him?"

21 But others said, "A person controlled by a demon does not say things like this. Can a demon open the eyes of someone who is blind?"

Another Challenge to Jesus' Claims

22 Then came the Feast of Hanukkah at Jerusalem. It was winter. 23 Jesus was in the temple courtyard walking in Solomon's Porch. 24 The Jews who were gathered there around Jesus spoke to him. They said, "How long will you keep us waiting? If you are the Messiah, tell us plainly."

25 Jesus answered, "I did tell you. But you do not believe. The works that I do in my Father's name are a witness for me. 26 But you do not believe, because you are not my sheep. 27 My sheep listen to my voice. I know them, and they follow me. 28 I give them eternal life, and they will never die. No one will steal them out of my hand. 29 My Father, who has given them to me, is greater than anyone. No one can steal them out of my Father's hand. 30 I and the Father are one."

31 Again the Jews who had challenged him picked up stones to kill him. 32 But Jesus said to them, "I have shown you many good works from the Father. Which good work are you throwing stones at me for?"

33 "We are not throwing stones at you for any good work," they replied. "We are stoning you for saying a very evil thing. You are only a man. But you claim to be God."

34 Jesus answered them, "Didn't God say in your Law, 'I have said you are "gods" '? (Psalm 82:6) 35 We know that Scripture is always true. God spoke to some people and called them 'gods.' 36 If that is true, what about the one the Father set apart as his very own? What about this one the Father sent into the world? Why do you charge me with saying a very evil thing? Is it because I said, 'I am God's Son'? 37 Don't believe me unless I do the works of my Father. 38 But what if I do them? Even if you don't believe me, believe these works. Then you will know and understand that the Father is in me and I am in the Father." 39 Again they tried to arrest him. But he escaped from them.

40 Then Jesus went back across the Jordan River. He went to the place where John had been baptizing in the early days. There he stayed. 41 Many people came to him. They said, "John never performed a sign. But everything he said about this man was true." 42 And in that place many believed in Jesus.

Lazarus Dies

11 A man named Lazarus was sick. He was from Bethany, the village where Mary and her sister Martha lived. 2 Mary

would later pour perfume on the Lord. She would also wipe Jesus' feet with her hair. It was her brother Lazarus who was sick in bed. 3 So the sisters sent a message to Jesus. "Lord," they told him, "the one you love is sick."

4 When Jesus heard this, he said, "This sickness will not end in death. No, it is for God's glory. God's Son will receive glory because of it." 5 Jesus loved Martha and her sister and Lazarus. 6 So after he heard Lazarus was sick, he stayed where he was for two more days. 7 And then he said to his disciples, "Let us go back to Judea."

8 "But Rabbi," they said, "a short time ago the Jews there tried to kill you with stones. Are you still going back?"

9 Jesus answered, "Aren't there 12 hours of daylight? Anyone who walks during the day won't trip and fall. They can see because of this world's light. 10 But when they walk at night, they'll trip and fall. They have no light."

11 After he said this, Jesus went on speaking to them. "Our friend Lazarus has fallen asleep," he said. "But I am going there to wake him up."

12 His disciples replied, "Lord, if he's sleeping, he will get better." 13 Jesus had been speaking about the death of Lazarus. But his disciples thought he meant natural sleep.

14 So then he told them plainly, "Lazarus is dead. 15 For your benefit, I am glad I was not there. Now you will believe. But let us go to him."

16 Then Thomas, who was also called Didymus, spoke to the rest of the disciples. "Let us go also," he said. "Then we can die with Jesus."

Jesus Comforts the Sisters of Lazarus

17 When Jesus arrived, he found out that Lazarus had already been in the tomb for four days. 18 Bethany was less than two miles from Jerusalem. 19 Many Jews had come to Martha and Mary. They had come to comfort them because their brother was dead. 20 When Martha heard that Jesus was coming, she went out to meet him. But Mary stayed at home.

21 "Lord," Martha said to Jesus, "I wish you had been here! Then my brother would not have died. 22 But I know that even now God will give you anything you ask for."

23 Jesus said to her, "Your brother will rise again."

24 Martha answered, "I know he will rise again. This will happen when people are raised from the dead on the last day."

25 Jesus said to her, "I am the resurrection and the life. Anyone who believes in me will live, even if they die. 26 And whoever lives by believing in me will never die. Do you believe this?"

27 "Yes, Lord," she replied. "I believe that you are the Messiah, the Son of God. I believe that you are the one who is supposed to come into the world."

28 After she said this, she went back home. She called her sister Mary to one side to talk to her. "The Teacher is here," Martha said. "He is asking for you." 29 When Mary heard this, she got up quickly and went to him. 30 Jesus had not yet entered the village. He was still at the place where Martha had met him. 31 Some Jews had been comforting Mary in the house. They noticed how quickly she got up and went out. So they followed her. They thought she was going to the tomb to mourn there.

32 Mary reached the place where Jesus was. When she saw him, she fell at his feet. She said, "Lord, I wish you had been here! Then my brother would not have died."

33 Jesus saw her crying. He saw that the Jews who had come along with her were crying also. His spirit became very sad, and he was troubled. 34 "Where have you put him?" he asked.

"Come and see, Lord," they replied.

35 Jesus wept.

36 Then the Jews said, "See how much he loved him!"

37 But some of them said, "He opened the eyes of the blind man. Couldn't he have kept this man from dying?"

Jesus Raises Lazarus From the Dead

38 Once more Jesus felt very sad. He came to the tomb. It was a cave with a stone in front of the entrance. 39 "Take away the stone," he said.

"But, Lord," said Martha, the sister of the dead man, "by this time there is a bad smell. Lazarus has been in the tomb for four days."

40 Then Jesus said, "Didn't I tell you that if you believe, you will see God's glory?"

41 So they took away the stone. Then
Jesus looked up. He said, "Father, I thank
you for hearing me. 42 I know that you always hear me. But I said this for the benefit of the people standing here. I said it so
they will believe that you sent me."
43 Then Jesus called in a loud voice. He
said, "Lazarus, come out!" 44 The dead
man came out. His hands and feet were
wrapped with strips of linen. A cloth was
around his face.
Jesus said to them, "Take off the clothes
he was buried in and let him go."

The Plan to Kill Jesus

45 Many of the Jews who had come to
visit Mary saw what Jesus did. So they believed in him. 46 But some of them went
to the Pharisees. They told the Pharisees
what Jesus had done. 47 Then the chief
priests and the Pharisees called a meeting of the Sanhedrin.
"What can we do?" they asked. "This
man is performing many signs. 48 If we let
him keep on doing this, everyone will believe in him. Then the Romans will come.
They will take away our temple and our
nation."
49 One of the Jewish leaders spoke up.
His name was Caiaphas. He was high
priest at that time. He said, "You don't
know anything at all! 50 You don't realize what is good for you. It is better if one
man dies for the people than if the whole
nation is destroyed."
51 He did not say this on his own because he was high priest at that time.
He prophesied that Jesus would die for
the Jewish nation. 52 He also prophesied
that Jesus would die for God's children
scattered everywhere. He would die to
bring them together and make them one.
53 So from that day on, the Jewish rulers
planned to kill Jesus.
54 Jesus no longer moved around openly
among the people of Judea. Instead, he
went away to an area near the desert. He
went to a village called Ephraim. There he
stayed with his disciples.
55 It was almost time for the Jewish
Passover Feast. Many people went up
from the country to Jerusalem. They
went there for the special washing that
would make them pure before the Passover Feast. 56 They kept looking for Jesus
as they stood in the temple courtyard.
They asked one another, "What do you
think? Isn't he coming to the feast at all?"
57 But the chief priests and the Pharisees
had given orders. They had commanded
anyone who found out where Jesus was
staying to report it. Then they could arrest
him.

Mary Pours Perfume on Jesus at Bethany

12 It was six days before the Passover
Feast. Jesus came to Bethany, where
Lazarus lived. Lazarus was the one Jesus
had raised from the dead. 2 A dinner was
given at Bethany to honor Jesus. Martha served the food. Lazarus was among
the people at the table with Jesus. 3 Then
Mary took about a pint of pure nard. It
was an expensive perfume. She poured
it on Jesus' feet and wiped them with her
hair. The house was filled with the sweet
smell of the perfume.
4 But Judas Iscariot didn't like what
Mary did. He was one of Jesus' disciples.
Later he was going to hand Jesus over to
his enemies. Judas said, 5 "Why wasn't
this perfume sold? Why wasn't the money
given to poor people? It was worth a year's
pay." 6 He didn't say this because he cared
about the poor. He said it because he was
a thief. Judas was in charge of the money
bag. He used to help himself to what was
in it.
7 "Leave her alone," Jesus replied. "The
perfume was meant for the day I am buried. 8 You will always have the poor among
you. But you won't always have me."
9 Meanwhile a large crowd of Jews found
out that Jesus was there, so they came. But
they did not come only because of Jesus.
They also came to see Lazarus. After all,
Jesus had raised him from the dead. 10 So
the chief priests made plans to kill Lazarus too. 11 Because of Lazarus, many of the
Jews were starting to follow Jesus. They
were believing in him.

Jesus Comes to Jerusalem as King

12 The next day the large crowd that had
come for the feast heard that Jesus was
on his way to Jerusalem. 13 So they took
branches from palm trees and went out to
meet him. They shouted,

"Hosanna!"

"Blessed is the one who comes
in the name of the Lord!"
(Psalm 118:25,26)

"Blessed is the king of Israel!"

14 Jesus found a young donkey and sat on
it. This is just as it is written in Scripture.
It says,

15 "City of Zion, do not be afraid.
See, your king is coming.
He is sitting on a donkey's colt."
(Zechariah 9:9)

16 At first, Jesus' disciples did not understand all this. They realized it only after
he had received glory. Then they realized
that these things had been written about
him. They realized that these things had
been done to him.
17 A crowd had been with Jesus when he
called Lazarus from the tomb and raised
him from the dead. So they continued to
tell everyone about what had happened.
18 Many people went out to meet him.
They had heard that he had done this sign.
19 So the Pharisees said to one another,
"This isn't getting us anywhere. Look how
the whole world is following him!"

Jesus Tells About His Coming Death

20 There were some Greeks among the
people who went up to worship during
the feast. 21 They came to ask Philip for a
favor. Philip was from Bethsaida in Galilee. "Sir," they said, "we would like to see
Jesus." 22 Philip went to tell Andrew. Then
Andrew and Philip told Jesus.
23 Jesus replied, "The time has come for
the Son of Man to receive glory. 24 What
I'm about to tell you is true. Unless a grain
of wheat falls to the ground and dies, it remains only one seed. But if it dies, it produces many seeds. 25 Anyone who loves
their life will lose it. But anyone who hates
their life in this world will keep it and
have eternal life. 26 Anyone who serves me
must follow me. And where I am, my servant will also be. My Father will honor the
one who serves me.
27 "My soul is troubled. What should I
say? 'Father, keep me from having to go
through with this'? No. This is the very
reason I have come to this point in my life.
28 Father, bring glory to your name!"
Then a voice came from heaven. It said,
"I have brought glory to my name. I will
bring glory to it again." 29 The crowd there
heard the voice. Some said it was thunder.
Others said an angel had spoken to Jesus.
30 Jesus said, "This voice was for your
benefit, not mine. 31 Now it is time for the
world to be judged. Now the prince of this
world will be thrown out. 32 And I am going to be lifted up from the earth. When I
am, I will bring all people to myself." 33 He
said this to show them how he was going
to die.
34 The crowd spoke up. "The Law tells
us that the Messiah will remain forever,"
they said. "So how can you say, 'The Son
of Man must be lifted up'? Who is this
'Son of Man'?"
35 Then Jesus told them, "You are going
to have the light just a little while longer.
Walk while you have the light. Do this before darkness catches up with you. Whoever walks in the dark does not know
where they are going. 36 While you have
the light, believe in it. Then you can become children of light." When Jesus had
finished speaking, he left and hid from
them.

Some Jews Believe and Some Don't

37 Jesus had performed so many signs
in front of them. But they still would not
believe in him. 38 This happened as Isaiah the prophet had said it would. He had
said,

"Lord, who has believed what we've
been saying?
Who has seen the Lord's saving
power?" (Isaiah 53:1)

39 For this reason, they could not believe. As Isaiah says in another place,

40 "The Lord has blinded their eyes.
He has closed their minds.
So they can't see with their eyes.
They can't understand with their
minds.
They can't turn to the Lord. If they
could, he would heal them."
(Isaiah 6:10)

41 Isaiah said this because he saw Jesus'
glory and spoke about him.
42 At the same time that Jesus did those
signs, many of the Jewish leaders believed
in him. But because of the Pharisees, they
would not openly admit they believed.
They were afraid they would be thrown

out of the synagogue. 43 They loved praise
from people more than praise from God.
44 Then Jesus cried out, "Whoever believes in me does not believe in me only.
They also believe in the one who sent me.
45 The one who looks at me sees the one
who sent me. 46 I have come into the world
to be its light. So no one who believes in
me will stay in darkness.
47 "I don't judge a person who hears my
words but does not obey them. I didn't
come to judge the world. I came to save
the world. 48 But there is a judge for anyone who does not accept me and my
words. These words I have spoken will
judge them on the last day. 49 I did not
speak on my own. The Father who sent
me commanded me to say all that I have
said. 50 I know that his command leads to
eternal life. So everything I say is just what
the Father has told me to say."

Jesus Washes His Disciples' Feet

13 It was just before the Passover Feast.
Jesus knew that the time had come
for him to leave this world. It was time for
him to go to the Father. Jesus loved his
disciples who were in the world. So he
now loved them to the very end.
2 They were having their evening meal.
The devil had already tempted Judas,
son of Simon Iscariot. He had urged Judas to hand Jesus over to his enemies.
3 Jesus knew that the Father had put everything under his power. He also knew
he had come from God and was returning
to God. 4 So he got up from the meal and
took off his outer clothes. He wrapped a
towel around his waist. 5 After that, he
poured water into a large bowl. Then he
began to wash his disciples' feet. He dried
them with the towel that was wrapped
around him.
6 He came to Simon Peter. "Lord," Peter said to him, "are you going to wash my
feet?"
7 Jesus replied, "You don't realize now
what I am doing. But later you will understand."
8 "No," said Peter. "You will never wash
my feet."
Jesus answered, "Unless I wash you,
you can't share life with me."
9 "Lord," Simon Peter replied, "not just
my feet! Wash my hands and my head
too!"
10 Jesus answered, "People who have
had a bath need to wash only their feet.
The rest of their body is clean. And you
are clean. But not all of you are." 11 Jesus
knew who was going to hand him over to
his enemies. That was why he said not every one was clean.
12 When Jesus finished washing their
feet, he put on his clothes. Then he returned to his place. "Do you understand
what I have done for you?" he asked
them. 13 "You call me 'Teacher' and 'Lord.'
You are right. That is what I am. 14 I, your
Lord and Teacher, have washed your feet.
So you also should wash one another's
feet. 15 I have given you an example. You
should do as I have done for you. 16 What
I'm about to tell you is true. A slave is not
more important than his master. And a
messenger is not more important than
the one who sends him. 17 Now you know
these things. So you will be blessed if you
do them.

Jesus Tells What Judas Will Do

18 "I am not talking about all of you. I
know the ones I have chosen. But this
will happen so that this passage of Scripture will come true. It says, 'The one who
shared my bread has turned against me.'
(Psalm 41:9)
19 "I am telling you now, before it happens. When it does happen, you will
believe that I am who I am. 20 What I'm
about to tell you is true. Anyone who accepts someone I send accepts me. And
anyone who accepts me accepts the one
who sent me."
21 After he had said this, Jesus' spirit was
troubled. He said, "What I'm about to tell
you is true. One of you is going to hand
me over to my enemies."
22 His disciples stared at one another.
They had no idea which one of them he
meant. 23 The disciple Jesus loved was
next to him at the table. 24 Simon Peter
motioned to that disciple. He said, "Ask
Jesus which one he means."
25 The disciple was leaning back against
Jesus. He asked him, "Lord, who is it?"
26 Jesus answered, "It is the one I will
give this piece of bread to. I will give it to
him after I have dipped it in the dish." He
dipped the piece of bread. Then he gave it
to Judas, son of Simon Iscariot. 27 As soon

as Judas took the bread, Satan entered
into him.
So Jesus told him, "Do quickly what
you are going to do." [28]But no one at the
meal understood why Jesus said this to
him. [29]Judas was in charge of the money.
So some of the disciples thought Jesus
was telling him to buy what was needed
for the feast. Others thought Jesus was
talking about giving something to poor
people. [30]As soon as Judas had taken the
bread, he went out. And it was night.

Peter Says He Does Not Know Jesus

[31]After Judas was gone, Jesus spoke.
He said, "Now the Son of Man receives
glory. And he brings glory to God. [32]If the
Son brings glory to God, God himself will
bring glory to the Son. God will do it at
once.
[33]"My children, I will be with you only a
little longer. You will look for me. Just as I
told the Jews, so I am telling you now. You
can't come where I am going.
[34]"I give you a new command. Love
one another. You must love one another,
just as I have loved you. [35]If you love one
another, everyone will know you are my
disciples."
[36]Simon Peter asked him, "Lord, where
are you going?"
Jesus replied, "Where I am going you
can't follow now. But you will follow me
later."
[37]"Lord," Peter asked, "why can't I follow you now? I will give my life for you."
[38]Then Jesus answered, "Will you really
give your life for me? What I'm about to
tell you is true. Before the rooster crows,
you will say three times that you don't
know me!

Jesus Comforts His Disciples

14 "Do not let your hearts be troubled.
You believe in God. Believe in me
also. [2]There are many rooms in my Father's house. If this were not true, would
I have told you that I am going there?
Would I have told you that I would prepare a place for you there? [3]If I go and
do that, I will come back. And I will take
you to be with me. Then you will also be
where I am. [4]You know the way to the
place where I am going."

Jesus Is the Way to the Father

[5]Thomas said to him, "Lord, we don't
know where you are going. So how can we
know the way?"
[6]Jesus answered, "I am the way and the
truth and the life. No one comes to the
Father except through me. [7]If you really
know me, you will know my Father also.
From now on, you do know him. And you
have seen him."
[8]Philip said, "Lord, show us the Father.
That will be enough for us."
[9]Jesus answered, "Don't you know me,
Philip? I have been among you such a long
time! Anyone who has seen me has seen
the Father. So how can you say, 'Show us
the Father'? [10]Don't you believe that I am
in the Father? Don't you believe that the
Father is in me? The words I say to you I
do not speak on my own authority. The
Father lives in me. He is the one who is
doing his work. [11]Believe me when I say I
am in the Father. Also believe that the Father is in me. Or at least believe what the
works I have been doing say about me.
[12]What I'm about to tell you is true. Anyone who believes in me will do the works I
have been doing. In fact, they will do even
greater things. That's because I am going
to the Father. [13]And I will do anything you
ask in my name. Then the Father will receive glory from the Son. [14]You may ask
me for anything in my name. I will do it.

Jesus Promises That the Holy Spirit Will Come

[15]"If you love me, obey my commands.
[16]I will ask the Father. And he will give you
another friend to help you and to be with
you forever. [17]That friend is the Spirit of
truth. The world can't accept him. That's
because the world does not see him or
know him. But you know him. He lives
with you, and he will be in you. [18]I will not
leave you like children who don't have
parents. I will come to you. [19]Before long,
the world will not see me anymore. But
you will see me. Because I live, you will
live also. [20]On that day you will realize
that I am in my Father. You will know that
you are in me, and I am in you. [21]Anyone
who has my commands and obeys them
loves me. My Father will love the one who
loves me. I too will love them. And I will
show myself to them."
[22]Then Judas spoke. "Lord," he said,

"why do you plan to show yourself only to us? Why not also to the world?" The Judas who spoke those words was not Judas Iscariot.

23 Jesus replied, "Anyone who loves me will obey my teaching. My Father will love them. We will come to them and make our home with them. 24 Anyone who does not love me will not obey my teaching. The words you hear me say are not my own. They belong to the Father who sent me.

25 "I have spoken all these things while I am still with you. 26 But the Father will send the Friend in my name to help you. The Friend is the Holy Spirit. He will teach you all things. He will remind you of everything I have said to you. 27 I leave my peace with you. I give my peace to you. I do not give it to you as the world does. Do not let your hearts be troubled. And do not be afraid.

28 "You heard me say, 'I am going away. And I am coming back to you.' If you loved me, you would be glad I am going to the Father. The Father is greater than I am. 29 I have told you now before it happens. Then when it does happen, you will believe. 30 I will not say much more to you. The prince of this world is coming. He has no power over me. 31 But he comes so that the world may learn that I love the Father. They must also learn that I do exactly what my Father has commanded me to do.

"Come now. Let us leave.

The Vine and the Branches

15 "I am the true vine. My Father is the gardener. 2 He cuts off every branch joined to me that does not bear fruit. He trims every branch that does bear fruit. Then it will bear even more fruit. 3 You are already clean because of the word I have spoken to you. 4 Remain joined to me, just as I also remain joined to you. No branch can bear fruit by itself. It must remain joined to the vine. In the same way, you can't bear fruit unless you remain joined to me.

5 "I am the vine. You are the branches. If you remain joined to me, and I to you, you will bear a lot of fruit. You can't do anything without me. 6 If you don't remain joined to me, you are like a branch that is thrown away and dries up. Branches like those are picked up. They are thrown into the fire and burned. 7 If you remain joined to me and my words remain in you, ask for anything you wish. And it will be done for you. 8 When you bear a lot of fruit, it brings glory to my Father. It shows that you are my disciples.

9 "Just as the Father has loved me, I have loved you. Now remain in my love. 10 If you obey my commands, you will remain in my love. In the same way, I have obeyed my Father's commands and remain in his love. 11 I have told you this so that you will have the same joy that I have. I also want your joy to be complete. 12 Here is my command. Love one another, just as I have loved you. 13 No one has greater love than the one who gives their life for their friends. 14 You are my friends if you do what I command. 15 I do not call you slaves anymore. Slaves do not know their master's business. Instead, I have called you friends. I have told you everything I learned from my Father. 16 You did not choose me. Instead, I chose you. I appointed you so that you might go and bear fruit that will last. I also appointed you so that the Father will give you what you ask for. He will give you whatever you ask for in my name. 17 Here is my command. Love one another.

The World Hates the Disciples

18 "My disciples, does the world hate you? Remember that it hated me first. 19 If you belonged to the world, it would love you like one of its own. But you do not belong to the world. I have chosen you out of the world. That is why the world hates you. 20 Remember what I told you. I said, 'A slave is not more important than his master.' (John 13:16) If people hated me and tried to hurt me, they will do the same to you. If they obeyed my teaching, they will obey yours also. 21 They will treat you like that because of my name. They do not know the one who sent me. 22 If I had not come and spoken to them, they would not be guilty of sin. But now they have no excuse for their sin. 23 Whoever hates me hates my Father also. 24 I did works among them that no one else did. If I hadn't, they would not be guilty of sin. But now they have seen those works. And still they have hated both me and my Father. 25 This has happened so that what is written in their

Law would come true. It says, ‘They hated me without any reason.’ (Psalms 35:19; 69:4)

The Work of the Holy Spirit

26 “I will send the Friend to you from the Father. He is the Spirit of truth, who comes out from the Father. When the Friend comes to help you, he will be a witness about me. 27 You must also be witnesses about me. That’s because you have been with me from the beginning.

16 “I have told you all this so that you will not turn away from the truth. 2 You will be thrown out of the synagogue. In fact, the time is coming when someone may kill you. And they will think they are doing God a favor. 3 They will do things like that because they do not know the Father or me. 4 Why have I told you this? So that when their time comes, you will remember that I warned you about them. I didn’t tell you this from the beginning because I was with you. 5 But now I am going to the one who sent me. None of you asks me, ‘Where are you going?’ 6 Instead, you are filled with sadness because I have said these things. 7 But what I’m about to tell you is true. It is for your good that I am going away. Unless I go away, the Friend will not come to help you. But if I go, I will send him to you. 8 When he comes, he will prove that the world’s people are guilty. He will prove their guilt concerning sin and godliness and judgment. 9 The world is guilty as far as sin is concerned. That’s because people do not believe in me. 10 The world is guilty as far as godliness is concerned. That’s because I am going to the Father, where you can’t see me anymore. 11 The world is guilty as far as judgment is concerned. That’s because the devil, the prince of this world, has already been judged.

12 “I have much more to say to you. It is more than you can handle right now. 13 But when the Spirit of truth comes, he will guide you into all the truth. He will not speak on his own. He will speak only what he hears. And he will tell you what is still going to happen. 14 He will bring me glory. That’s because what he receives from me he will show to you. 15 Everything that belongs to the Father is mine. That is why I said what the Holy Spirit receives from me he will show to you.

The Disciples’ Sadness Will Turn Into Joy

16 Jesus continued, “In a little while, you will no longer see me. Then after a little while, you will see me.”

17 After they heard this, some of his disciples spoke to one another. They said, “What does he mean by saying, ‘In a little while, you will no longer see me. Then after a little while, you will see me’? And what does he mean by saying, ‘I am going to the Father’?” 18 They kept asking, “What does he mean by ‘a little while’? We don’t understand what he is saying.”

19 Jesus saw that they wanted to ask him about these things. So he said to them, “Are you asking one another what I meant? Didn’t you understand when I said, ‘In a little while, you will no longer see me. Then after a little while, you will see me’? 20 What I’m about to tell you is true. You will weep and mourn while the world is full of joy. You will be sad, but your sadness will turn into joy. 21 A woman giving birth to a baby has pain. That’s because her time to give birth has come. But when her baby is born, she forgets the pain. She forgets because she is so happy that a baby has been born into the world. 22 That’s the way it is with you. Now it’s your time to be sad. But I will see you again. Then you will be full of joy. And no one will take away your joy. 23 When that day comes, you will no longer ask me for anything. What I’m about to tell you is true. My Father will give you anything you ask for in my name. 24 Until now you have not asked for anything in my name. Ask, and you will receive what you ask for. Then your joy will be complete.

25 “I have not been speaking to you plainly. But a time is coming when I will speak clearly. Then I will tell you plainly about my Father. 26 When that day comes, you will ask for things in my name. I am not saying I will ask the Father instead of you asking him. 27 No, the Father himself loves you because you have loved me. He also loves you because you have believed that I came from God. 28 I came from the Father and entered the world. Now I am leaving the world and going back to the Father.”

29 Then Jesus’ disciples said, “Now you are speaking plainly. You are using examples that are clear. 30 Now we can see that you know everything. You don’t even

need anyone to ask you questions. This
makes us believe that you came from
God."
31 "Do you believe now?" Jesus replied.
32 "A time is coming when you will be scattered and go to your own homes. In fact,
that time is already here. You will leave
me all alone. But I am not really alone. My
Father is with me.
33 "I have told you these things, so that
you can have peace because of me. In this
world you will have trouble. But be encouraged! I have won the battle over the
world."

Jesus Prays for Himself

17 After Jesus said this, he looked toward heaven and prayed. He said,
"Father, the time has come. Bring
glory to your Son. Then your Son will
bring glory to you. 2 You gave him authority over all people. He gives eternal life to all those you have given
him. 3 And what is eternal life? It is
knowing you, the only true God, and
Jesus Christ, whom you have sent. 4 I
have brought you glory on earth. I
have finished the work you gave me
to do. 5 So now, Father, give glory to
me in heaven where your throne is.
Give me the glory I had with you before the world began.

Jesus Prays for His Disciples

6 "I have shown you to the disciples you gave me out of the world.
They were yours. You gave them
to me. And they have obeyed your
word. 7 Now they know that everything you have given me comes from
you. 8 I gave them the words you gave
me. And they accepted them. They
knew for certain that I came from
you. They believed that you sent
me. 9 I pray for them. I am not praying for the world. I am praying for
those you have given me, because
they are yours. 10 All I have is yours,
and all you have is mine. Glory has
come to me because of my disciples.
11 I will not remain in the world any
longer. But they are still in the world,
and I am coming to you. Holy Father,
keep them safe by the power of your
name. It is the name you gave me.
Keep them safe so they can be one,
just as you and I are one. 12 While I
was with them, I guarded them. I
kept them safe through the name you
gave me. None of them has been lost,
except the one who was headed for
ruin. It happened so that Scripture
would come true.
13 "I am coming to you now. But
I say these things while I am still in
the world. I say them so that those
you gave me can have the same joy
that I have. 14 I have given them your
word. The world has hated them.
That's because they are not part of
the world any more than I am. 15 I do
not pray that you will take them out
of the world. I pray that you will keep
them safe from the evil one. 16 They
do not belong to the world, just as I
do not belong to it. 17 Use the truth to
make them holy. Your word is truth.
18 You sent me into the world. In the
same way, I have sent them into the
world. 19 I make myself holy for them
so that they too can be made holy by
the truth.

Jesus Prays for All Believers

20 "I do not pray only for them. I
pray also for everyone who will believe in me because of their message.
21 Father, I pray they will be one, just
as you are in me and I am in you. I
want them also to be in us. Then the
world will believe that you have sent
me. 22 I have given them the glory you
gave me. I did this so they would be
one, just as we are one. 23 I will be in
them, just as you are in me. This is so
that they may be brought together
perfectly as one. Then the world will
know that you sent me. It will also
show the world that you have loved
those you gave me, just as you have
loved me.
24 "Father, I want those you have
given me to be with me where I am. I
want them to see my glory, the glory
you have given me. You gave it to me
because you loved me before the
world was created.
25 "Father, you are holy. The world
does not know you, but I know you.
Those you have given me know you
have sent me. 26 I have shown you to

them. And I will continue to show
you to them. Then the love you have
for me will be in them. I myself will
be in them."

Jesus Is Arrested

18 When Jesus had finished praying, he
left with his disciples. They crossed
the Kidron Valley. On the other side there
was a garden. Jesus and his disciples went
into it.
2 Judas knew the place. He was going
to hand Jesus over to his enemies. Jesus
had often met in that place with his disciples. 3 So Judas came to the garden. He
was guiding a group of soldiers and some
officials. The chief priests and the Pharisees had sent them. They were carrying
torches, lanterns and weapons.
4 Jesus knew everything that was going to happen to him. So he went out and
asked them, "Who do you want?"
5 "Jesus of Nazareth," they replied.
"I am he," Jesus said. Judas, who was
going to hand Jesus over, was standing
there with them. 6 When Jesus said, "I am
he," they moved back. Then they fell to
the ground.
7 He asked them again, "Who do you
want?"
"Jesus of Nazareth," they said.
8 Jesus answered, "I told you I am he. If
you are looking for me, then let these men
go." 9 This happened so that the words
Jesus had spoken would come true. He
had said, "I have not lost anyone God has
given me." (John 6:39)
10 Simon Peter had a sword and pulled
it out. He struck the high priest's slave and
cut off his right ear. The slave's name was
Malchus.
11 Jesus commanded Peter, "Put your
sword away! Shouldn't I drink the cup of
suffering the Father has given me?"
12 Then the group of soldiers, their commander and the Jewish officials arrested
Jesus. They tied him up 13 and brought
him first to Annas. He was the father-in-
law of Caiaphas, the high priest at that
time. 14 Caiaphas had advised the Jewish
leaders that it would be good if one man
died for the people.

Peter Says He Is Not Jesus' Disciple

15 Simon Peter and another disciple
were following Jesus. The high priest
knew the other disciple. So that disciple went with Jesus into the high priest's
courtyard. 16 But Peter had to wait outside
by the door. The other disciple came back.
He was the one the high priest knew. He
spoke to the servant woman who was on
duty there. Then he brought Peter in.
17 She asked Peter, "You aren't one of
Jesus' disciples too, are you?"
"I am not," he replied.
18 It was cold. The slaves and officials
stood around a fire. They had made it to
keep warm. Peter was also standing with
them. He was warming himself.

The High Priest Questions Jesus

19 Meanwhile, the high priest questioned Jesus. He asked him about his disciples and his teaching.
20 "I have spoken openly to the world,"
Jesus replied. "I always taught in synagogues or at the temple, where all the
Jews come together. I didn't say anything in secret. 21 Why question me? Ask
the people who heard me. They certainly
know what I said."
22 When Jesus said that, one of the officials nearby slapped him in the face. "Is
this any way to answer the high priest?"
he asked.
23 "Have I said something wrong?" Jesus
replied. "If I have, then tell everyone what
it was. But if I spoke the truth, why did you
hit me?" 24 Annas sent him, tied up, to Caiaphas, the high priest.

Peter Again Says He Is Not Jesus' Disciple

25 Meanwhile, Simon Peter was still
standing there warming himself by the
fire. So they asked him, "You aren't one of
Jesus' disciples too, are you?"
He said, "I am not."
26 One of the high priest's slaves was a
relative of the man whose ear Peter had
cut off. He said to Peter, "Didn't I see you
with Jesus in the garden?" 27 Again Peter
said no. At that exact moment a rooster
began to crow.

Jesus Is Brought to Pilate

28 Then the Jewish leaders took Jesus
from Caiaphas to the palace of the Roman governor. By now it was early morning. The Jewish leaders did not want to
be made "unclean." They wanted to be
able to eat the Passover meal. So they did

not enter the palace. 29 Pilate came out to
them. He asked, "What charges are you
bringing against this man?"
30 "He has committed crimes," they replied. "If he hadn't, we would not have
handed him over to you."
31 Pilate said, "Take him yourselves.
Judge him by your own law."
"But we don't have the right to put anyone to death," they complained. 32 This
happened so that what Jesus said about
how he was going to die would come true.
33 Then Pilate went back inside the palace. He ordered Jesus to be brought to
him. Pilate asked him, "Are you the king
of the Jews?"
34 "Is that your own idea?" Jesus asked.
"Or did others talk to you about me?"
35 "Am I a Jew?" Pilate replied. "Your
own people and chief priests handed you
over to me. What have you done?"
36 Jesus said, "My kingdom is not from
this world. If it were, those who serve me
would fight. They would try to keep the
Jewish leaders from arresting me. My
kingdom is from another place."
37 "So you are a king, then!" said Pilate.
Jesus answered, "You say that I am a
king. In fact, that's the reason I was born.
I was born and came into the world to be
a witness to the truth. Everyone who is on
the side of truth listens to me."
38 "What is truth?" Pilate replied. Then
Pilate went out again to the Jews gathered there. He said, "I find no basis for
any charge against him. 39 But you have
a practice at Passover time. At that time,
you ask me to set one prisoner free for
you. Do you want me to set 'the king of
the Jews' free?"
40 They shouted back, "No! Not him!
Give us Barabbas!" Barabbas had taken
part in an armed struggle against the
country's rulers.

Jesus Is Sentenced to Be Crucified

19 Then Pilate took Jesus and had him
whipped. 2 The soldiers twisted
thorns together to make a crown. They
put it on Jesus' head. Then they put a purple robe on him. 3 They went up to him
again and again. They kept saying, "We
honor you, king of the Jews!" And they
slapped him in the face.
4 Once more Pilate came out. He said
to the Jews gathered there, "Look, I am
bringing Jesus out to you. I want to let
you know that I find no basis for a charge
against him." 5 Jesus came out wearing
the crown of thorns and the purple robe.
Then Pilate said to them, "Here is the
man!"
6 As soon as the chief priests and their
officials saw him, they shouted, "Crucify
him! Crucify him!"
But Pilate answered, "You take him and
crucify him. I myself find no basis for a
charge against him."
7 The Jewish leaders replied, "We have
a law. That law says he must die. He
claimed to be the Son of God."
8 When Pilate heard that, he was even
more afraid. 9 He went back inside the
palace. "Where do you come from?" he
asked Jesus. But Jesus did not answer
him. 10 "Do you refuse to speak to me?" Pilate said. "Don't you understand? I have
the power to set you free or to nail you to
a cross."
11 Jesus answered, "You were given
power from heaven. If you weren't, you
would have no power over me. So the one
who handed me over to you is guilty of a
greater sin."
12 From then on, Pilate tried to set Jesus
free. But the Jewish leaders kept shouting,
"If you let this man go, you are not Caesar's friend! Anyone who claims to be a
king is against Caesar!"
13 When Pilate heard that, he brought
Jesus out. Pilate sat down on the judge's
seat. It was at a place called the Stone
Walkway. In the Aramaic language it was
called Gabbatha. 14 It was about noon on
Preparation Day in Passover Week.
"Here is your king," Pilate said to the
Jews.
15 But they shouted, "Take him away!
Take him away! Crucify him!"
"Should I crucify your king?" Pilate
asked.
"We have no king but Caesar," the chief
priests answered.
16 Finally, Pilate handed Jesus over to
them to be nailed to a cross.

Jesus Is Nailed to a Cross

So the soldiers took charge of Jesus.
17 He had to carry his own cross. He went
out to a place called the Skull. In the Aramaic language it was called Golgotha.
18 There they nailed Jesus to the cross.

Two other men were crucified with him.
One was on each side of him. Jesus was in
the middle.
[19] Pilate had a notice prepared. It was
fastened to the cross. It read, JESUS OF
NAZARETH, THE KING OF THE JEWS. [20] Many
of the Jews read the sign. That's because
the place where Jesus was crucified was
near the city. And the sign was written in
the Aramaic, Latin and Greek languages.
[21] The chief priests of the Jews argued with
Pilate. They said, "Do not write 'The King
of the Jews.' Write that this man claimed
to be king of the Jews."
[22] Pilate answered, "I have written what
I have written."
[23] When the soldiers crucified Jesus,
they took his clothes. They divided them
into four parts. Each soldier got one part.
All that was left was Jesus' long, inner
robe. It did not have any seams. It was
made out of one piece of cloth from top
to bottom.
[24] "Let's not tear it," they said to one another. "Let's cast lots to see who will get
it."

This happened so that Scripture would come true. It says,

"They divided up my clothes among
them.
They cast lots for what I was
wearing." (Psalm 22:18)

So that is what the soldiers did.
[25] Jesus' mother stood near his cross. So
did his mother's sister, Mary the wife of
Clopas, and Mary Magdalene. [26] Jesus saw
his mother there. He also saw the disciple
he loved standing nearby. Jesus said to his
mother, "Dear woman, here is your son."
[27] He said to the disciple, "Here is your
mother." From that time on, the disciple
took her into his home.

Jesus Dies

[28] Later, Jesus knew that everything had
now been finished. He also knew that
what Scripture said must come true. So
he said, "I am thirsty." [29] A jar of wine vinegar was there. So they soaked a sponge
in it. They put the sponge on the stem of
a hyssop plant. Then they lifted it up to
Jesus' lips. [30] After Jesus drank he said, "It
is finished." Then he bowed his head and
died.
[31] It was Preparation Day. The next day
would be a special Sabbath day. The Jewish leaders did not want the bodies left on
the crosses during the Sabbath day. So
they asked Pilate to have the legs broken
and the bodies taken down. [32] The soldiers came and broke the legs of the first
man who had been crucified with Jesus.
Then they broke the legs of the other man.
[33] But when they came to Jesus, they saw
that he was already dead. So they did not
break his legs. [34] Instead, one of the soldiers stuck his spear into Jesus' side. Right
away, blood and water flowed out. [35] The
man who saw it has been a witness about
it. And what he has said is true. He knows
that he tells the truth. He is a witness so
that you also may believe. [36] These things
happened in order that Scripture would
come true. It says, "Not one of his bones
will be broken." (Exodus 12:46; Numbers 9:12;
Psalm 34:20) [37] Scripture also says, "They
will look to the one they have pierced."
(Zechariah 12:10)

Jesus Is Buried

[38] Later Joseph asked Pilate for Jesus'
body. Joseph was from the town of Arimathea. He was a follower of Jesus. But
he followed Jesus secretly because he was
afraid of the Jewish leaders. After Pilate
gave him permission, Joseph came and
took the body away. [39] Nicodemus went
with Joseph. He was the man who had
earlier visited Jesus at night. Nicodemus
brought some mixed spices that weighed
about 75 pounds. [40] The two men took
Jesus' body. They wrapped it in strips of
linen cloth, along with the spices. That
was the way the Jews buried people. [41] At
the place where Jesus was crucified, there
was a garden. A new tomb was there. No
one had ever been put in it before. [42] That
day was the Jewish Preparation Day, and
the tomb was nearby. So they placed
Jesus there.

The Tomb Is Empty

20 Early on the first day of the week,
Mary Magdalene went to the tomb.
It was still dark. She saw that the stone had
been moved away from the entrance. [2] So
she ran to Simon Peter and another disciple, the one Jesus loved. She said, "They
have taken the Lord out of the tomb! We
don't know where they have put him!"
[3] So Peter and the other disciple started

out for the tomb. 4 Both of them were running. The other disciple ran faster than Peter. He reached the tomb first. 5 He bent over and looked in at the strips of linen lying there. But he did not go in. 6 Then Simon Peter came along behind him. He went straight into the tomb. He saw the strips of linen lying there. 7 He also saw the funeral cloth that had been wrapped around Jesus' head. The cloth was still lying in its place. It was separate from the linen. 8 The disciple who had reached the tomb first also went inside. He saw and believed. 9 They still did not understand from Scripture that Jesus had to rise from the dead. 10 Then the disciples went back to where they were staying.

Jesus Appears to Mary Magdalene

11 But Mary stood outside the tomb crying. As she cried, she bent over to look into the tomb. 12 She saw two angels dressed in white. They were seated where Jesus' body had been. One of them was where Jesus' head had been laid. The other sat where his feet had been placed.

13 They asked her, "Woman, why are you crying?"

"They have taken my Lord away," she said. "I don't know where they have put him." 14 Then she turned around and saw Jesus standing there. But she didn't realize that it was Jesus.

15 He asked her, "Woman, why are you crying? Who are you looking for?"

She thought he was the gardener. So she said, "Sir, did you carry him away? Tell me where you put him. Then I will go and get him."

16 Jesus said to her, "Mary."

She turned toward him. Then she cried out in the Aramaic language, "Rabboni!" Rabboni means Teacher.

17 Jesus said, "Do not hold on to me. I have not yet ascended to the Father. Instead, go to those who believe in me. Tell them, 'I am ascending to my Father and your Father, to my God and your God.' "

18 Mary Magdalene went to the disciples with the news. She said, "I have seen the Lord!" And she told them that he had said these things to her.

Jesus Appears to His Disciples

19 On the evening of that first day of the week, the disciples were together. They had locked the doors because they were afraid of the Jewish leaders. Jesus came in and stood among them. He said, "May peace be with you!" 20 Then he showed them his hands and his side. The disciples were very happy when they saw the Lord.

21 Again Jesus said, "May peace be with you! The Father has sent me. So now I am sending you." 22 He then breathed on them. He said, "Receive the Holy Spirit. 23 If you forgive anyone's sins, their sins are forgiven. If you do not forgive them, they are not forgiven."

Jesus Appears to Thomas

24 Thomas was one of the 12 disciples. He was also called Didymus. He was not with the other disciples when Jesus came. 25 So they told him, "We have seen the Lord!"

But he said to them, "First I must see the nail marks in his hands. I must put my finger where the nails were. I must put my hand into his side. Only then will I believe."

26 A week later, Jesus' disciples were in the house again. Thomas was with them. Even though the doors were locked, Jesus came in and stood among them. He said, "May peace be with you!" 27 Then he said to Thomas, "Put your finger here. See my hands. Reach out your hand and put it into my side. Stop doubting and believe."

28 Thomas said to him, "My Lord and my God!"

29 Then Jesus told him, "Because you have seen me, you have believed. Blessed are those who have not seen me but still have believed."

The Purpose of John's Gospel

30 Jesus performed many other signs in front of his disciples. They are not written down in this book. 31 But these are written so that you may believe that Jesus is the Messiah, the Son of God. If you believe this, you will have life because you belong to him.

Jesus and the Miracle of Many Fish

21 After this, Jesus appeared to his disciples again. It was by the Sea of Galilee. Here is what happened. 2 Simon Peter and Thomas, who was also called Didymus, were there together. Nathanael

from Cana in Galilee and the sons of Zebedee were with them. So were two other disciples. 3 “I’m going out to fish,” Simon Peter told them. They said, “We’ll go with you.” So they went out and got into the boat. That night they didn’t catch anything.

4 Early in the morning, Jesus stood on the shore. But the disciples did not realize that it was Jesus.

5 He called out to them, “Friends, don’t you have any fish?”

“No,” they answered.

6 He said, “Throw your net on the right side of the boat. There you will find some fish.” When they did, they could not pull the net into the boat. There were too many fish in it.

7 Then the disciple Jesus loved said to Simon Peter, “It is the Lord!” As soon as Peter heard that, he put his coat on. He had taken it off earlier. Then he jumped into the water. 8 The other disciples followed in the boat. They were towing the net full of fish. The shore was only about 100 yards away. 9 When they landed, they saw a fire of burning coals. There were fish on it. There was also some bread.

10 Jesus said to them, “Bring some of the fish you have just caught.” 11 So Simon Peter climbed back into the boat. He dragged the net to shore. It was full of large fish. There were 153 of them. But even with that many fish the net was not torn. 12 Jesus said to them, “Come and have breakfast.” None of the disciples dared to ask him, “Who are you?” They knew it was the Lord. 13 Jesus came, took the bread and gave it to them. He did the same thing with the fish. 14 This was the third time Jesus appeared to his disciples after he was raised from the dead.

Jesus Gives Peter His Task

15 When Jesus and the disciples had finished eating, Jesus spoke to Simon Peter. He asked, “Simon, son of John, do you love me more than these others do?”

“Yes, Lord,” he answered. “You know that I love you.”

Jesus said, “Feed my lambs.”

16 Again Jesus asked, “Simon, son of John, do you love me?”

He answered, “Yes, Lord. You know that I love you.”

Jesus said, “Take care of my sheep.”

17 Jesus spoke to him a third time. He asked, “Simon, son of John, do you love me?”

Peter felt bad because Jesus asked him the third time, “Do you love me?” He answered, “Lord, you know all things. You know that I love you.”

Jesus said, “Feed my sheep. 18 What I’m about to tell you is true. When you were younger, you dressed yourself. You went wherever you wanted to go. But when you are old, you will stretch out your hands. Someone else will dress you. Someone else will lead you where you do not want to go.” 19 Jesus said this to point out how Peter would die. His death would bring glory to God. Then Jesus said to him, “Follow me!”

20 Peter turned around. He saw that the disciple Jesus loved was following them. He was the one who had leaned back against Jesus at the supper. He had said, “Lord, who is going to hand you over to your enemies?” 21 When Peter saw that disciple, he asked, “Lord, what will happen to him?”

22 Jesus answered, “Suppose I want him to remain alive until I return. What does that matter to you? You must follow me.” 23 Because of what Jesus said, a false report spread among the believers. The story was told that the disciple Jesus loved wouldn’t die. But Jesus did not say he would not die. He only said, “Suppose I want him to remain alive until I return. What does that matter to you?”

24 This is the disciple who is a witness about these things. He also wrote them down. We know that what he says is true.

25 Jesus also did many other things. What if every one of them were written down? I suppose that even the whole world would not have room for the books that would be written.

ACTS

Luke wrote the book of Acts as well as the book of Luke. Acts continues the story of the good news of life in Jesus Christ. In the book of Acts the story moves from Jerusalem to other nations. It tells about the Holy Spirit coming to the believers in Jerusalem. And it tells about the teaching and work of Peter and Paul. They were followers of Jesus and leaders of the new church. People from many nations became believers.

The book of Acts has six main parts. Each part tells about a new step in the spread of the good news about Jesus. Each part is marked by words similar to "God's word spread and grew."

First, the church is established in Jerusalem. For the first time the Greek language is used in the church. This allowed for the message of the good news to spread throughout the Roman Empire.

Second, the message of the good news spread to Galilee and Samaria.

Third, it became clear that the message about Jesus was also for people who were not Jews.

Fourth, messengers of the good news went west into the Roman part of Asia.

Fifth, the message went from Asia into Europe.

Sixth, the last part of the book tells how the message of good news spread to Rome. Rome was the capital city of the Empire. The good news of God's kingdom is reaching all nations.

Jesus Is Taken Up Into Heaven

1 Theophilus, I wrote about Jesus in my earlier book. I wrote about all he did and taught 2 until the day he was taken up to heaven. Before Jesus left, he gave orders to the apostles he had chosen. He did this through the Holy Spirit. 3 After his suffering and death, he appeared to them. In many ways he proved that he was alive. He appeared to them over a period of 40 days. During that time he spoke about God's kingdom. 4 One day Jesus was eating with them. He gave them a command. "Do not leave Jerusalem," he said. "Wait for the gift my Father promised. You have heard me talk about it. 5 John baptized with water. But in a few days you will be baptized with the Holy Spirit."

6 Then the apostles gathered around Jesus and asked him a question. "Lord," they said, "are you going to give the kingdom back to Israel now?"

7 He said to them, "You should not be concerned about times or dates. The Father has set them by his own authority. 8 But you will receive power when the Holy Spirit comes on you. Then you will tell people about me in Jerusalem, and in all Judea and Samaria. And you will even tell other people about me from one end of the earth to the other."

9 After Jesus said this, he was taken up to heaven. The apostles watched until a cloud hid him from their sight.

10 While he was going up, they kept on looking at the sky. Suddenly two men dressed in white clothing stood beside them. 11 "Men of Galilee," they said, "why do you stand here looking at the sky? Jesus has been taken away from you into heaven. But he will come back in the same way you saw him go."

Matthias Is Chosen to Take the Place of Judas Iscariot

12 The apostles returned to Jerusalem from the hill called the Mount of Olives. It is just over half a mile from the city. 13 When they arrived, they went upstairs to the room where they were staying. Peter, John, James and Andrew were there. Philip, Thomas, Bartholomew and Matthew were there too. So were James son of Alphaeus, Simon the Zealot, and Judas son of James. 14 They all came together regularly to pray. The women joined them too. So did Jesus' mother Mary and his brothers.

15 In those days Peter stood up among the believers. About 120 of them were there. 16 Peter said, "Brothers and sisters, a long time ago the Holy Spirit spoke through David. He spoke about Judas Iscariot. What the Scripture said would happen had to come true. Judas was the guide for the men who arrested Jesus. 17 But Judas was one of us. He shared with us in our work for God."

18 Judas bought a field with the payment he received for the evil thing he had done. He fell down headfirst in the field. His body burst open. All his insides spilled out. 19 Everyone in Jerusalem heard about

this. So they called that field Akeldama. In their language, Akeldama means the Field of Blood.

20 Peter said, "Here is what is written in the Book of Psalms. It says,

> " 'May his home be deserted.
> May no one live in it.' (Psalm 69:25)

The Psalms also say,

> " 'Let someone else take his place as
> leader.' (Psalm 109:8)

21 So we need to choose someone to take his place. It will have to be a man who was with us the whole time the Lord Jesus was living among us. 22 That time began when John was baptizing. It ended when Jesus was taken up from us. The one we choose must join us in telling people that Jesus rose from the dead."

23 So they suggested the names of two men. One was Joseph, who was called Barsabbas. He was also called Justus. The other man was Matthias. 24 Then the believers prayed. They said, "Lord, you know everyone's heart. Show us which of these two you have chosen. 25 Show us who should take the place of Judas as an apostle. He gave up being an apostle to go where he belongs." 26 Then they cast lots. Matthias was chosen. So he was added to the 11 apostles.

The Holy Spirit Comes at Pentecost

2 When the day of Pentecost came, all the believers gathered in one place. 2 Suddenly a sound came from heaven. It was like a strong wind blowing. It filled the whole house where they were sitting. 3 They saw something that looked like fire in the shape of tongues. The flames separated and came to rest on each of them. 4 All of them were filled with the Holy Spirit. They began to speak in languages they had not known before. The Spirit gave them the ability to do this.

5 Godly Jews from every country in the world were staying in Jerusalem. 6 A crowd came together when they heard the sound. They were bewildered because each of them heard their own language being spoken. 7 The crowd was really amazed. They asked, "Aren't all these people who are speaking Galileans? 8 Then why do we each hear them speaking in our own native language? 9 We are Parthians, Medes and Elamites. We live in Mesopotamia, Judea and Cappadocia. We are from Pontus, Asia, 10 Phrygia and Pamphylia. Others of us are from Egypt and the parts of Libya near Cyrene. Still others are visitors from Rome. 11 Some of the visitors are Jews. Others have accepted the Jewish faith. Also, Cretans and Arabs are here. We hear all these people speaking about God's wonders in our own languages!" 12 They were amazed and bewildered. They asked one another, "What does this mean?"

13 But some people in the crowd made fun of the believers. "They've had too much wine!" they said.

Peter Speaks to the Crowd

14 Then Peter stood up with the 11 apostles. In a loud voice he spoke to the crowd. "My fellow Jews," he said, "let me explain this to you. All of you who live in Jerusalem, listen carefully to what I say. 15 You think these people are drunk. But they aren't. It's only nine o'clock in the morning! 16 No, here is what the prophet Joel meant. 17 He said,

> " 'In the last days, God says,
> I will pour out my Holy Spirit on
> all people.
> Your sons and daughters will
> prophesy.
> Your young men will see visions.
> Your old men will have dreams.
> 18 In those days, I will pour out my
> Spirit on my servants.
> I will pour out my Spirit on both
> men and women.
> When I do, they will prophesy.
> 19 I will show wonders in the heavens
> above.
> I will show signs on the earth below.
> There will be blood and fire and
> clouds of smoke.
> 20 The sun will become dark.
> The moon will turn red like blood.
> This will happen before the
> coming of the great and
> glorious day of the Lord.
> 21 Everyone who calls
> on the name of the Lord will be
> saved.' (Joel 2:28–32)

22 "Fellow Israelites, listen to this! Jesus of Nazareth was a man who had God's approval. God did miracles, wonders and signs among you through Jesus. You yourselves know this. 23 Long ago God planned that Jesus would be handed over to you.

With the help of evil people, you put Jesus to death. You nailed him to the cross. 24 But God raised him from the dead. He set him free from the suffering of death. It wasn't possible for death to keep its hold on Jesus. 25 David spoke about him. He said,

"'I know that the Lord is always with
me.
Because he is at my right hand,
I will always be secure.
26 So my heart is glad and joy is on my
tongue.
My whole body will be full of hope.
27 You will not leave me in the place of
the dead.
You will not let your holy one rot
away.
28 You always show me the path that
leads to life.
You will fill me with joy when I am
with you.' (Psalm 16:8–11)

29 "Fellow Israelites, you can be sure that King David died. He was buried. His tomb is still here today. 30 But David was a prophet. He knew that God had made a promise to him. God had promised that he would make someone in David's family line king after him. 31 David saw what was coming. So he spoke about the Messiah rising from the dead. He said that the Messiah would not be left in the place of the dead. His body wouldn't rot in the ground. 32 God has raised this same Jesus back to life. We are all witnesses of this. 33 Jesus has been given a place of honor at the right hand of God. He has received the Holy Spirit from the Father. This is what God had promised. It is Jesus who has poured out what you now see and hear. 34 David did not go up to heaven. But he said,

"'The Lord said to my Lord,
"Sit at my right hand.
35 I will put your enemies
under your control."' (Psalm 110:1)

36 "So be sure of this, all you people of Israel. You nailed Jesus to the cross. But God has made him both Lord and Messiah."

37 When the people heard this, it had a deep effect on them. They said to Peter and the other apostles, "Brothers, what should we do?"

38 Peter replied, "All of you must turn away from your sins and be baptized in the name of Jesus Christ. Then your sins will be forgiven. You will receive the gift of the Holy Spirit. 39 The promise is for you and your children. It is also for all who are far away. It is for all whom the Lord our God will choose."

40 Peter said many other things to warn them. He begged them, "Save yourselves from these evil people." 41 Those who accepted his message were baptized. About 3,000 people joined the believers that day.

The Believers Share Their Lives Together

42 The believers studied what the apostles taught. They shared their lives together. They ate and prayed together. 43 Everyone was amazed at what God was doing. They were amazed when the apostles performed many wonders and signs. 44 All the believers were together. They shared everything they had. 45 They sold property and other things they owned. They gave to anyone who needed something. 46 Every day they met together in the temple courtyard. They ate meals together in their homes. Their hearts were glad and sincere. 47 They praised God. They were respected by all the people. Every day the Lord added to their group those who were being saved.

Peter Heals a Beggar Who Can't Walk

3 One day Peter and John were going up to the temple. It was three o'clock in the afternoon. It was the time for prayer. 2 A man unable to walk was being carried to the temple gate called Beautiful. He had been that way since he was born. Every day someone put him near the gate. There he would beg from people going into the temple courtyards. 3 He saw that Peter and John were about to enter. So he asked them for money. 4 Peter looked straight at him, and so did John. Then Peter said, "Look at us!" 5 So the man watched them closely. He expected to get something from them.

6 Peter said, "I don't have any silver or gold. But I'll give you what I do have. In the name of Jesus Christ of Nazareth, get up and walk." 7 Then Peter took him by the right hand and helped him up. At once the man's feet and ankles became strong. 8 He jumped to his feet and began to walk. He went with Peter and John into the temple courtyards. He walked and jumped and praised God. 9 All the people saw him

walking and praising God. 10They recognized him as the same man who used to sit
and beg at the temple gate called Beautiful.
They were filled with wonder. They were
amazed at what had happened to him.

Peter Speaks to the People at the Temple

11The man was holding on to Peter and
John. All the people were amazed. They
came running to them at the place called
Solomon's Porch. 12When Peter saw this,
he said, "Fellow Israelites, why does this
surprise you? Why do you stare at us? It's
not as if we've made this man walk by
our own power or godliness. 13The God
of our fathers, Abraham, Isaac and Jacob,
has done this. God has brought glory to
Jesus, who serves him. But you handed
Jesus over to be killed. Pilate had decided
to let him go. But you spoke against Jesus
when he was in Pilate's court. 14You spoke
against the Holy and Blameless One. You
asked for a murderer to be set free instead. 15You killed the one who gives life.
But God raised him from the dead. We are
witnesses of this. 16This man whom you
see and know was made strong because
of faith in Jesus' name. Faith in Jesus has
healed him completely. You can see it
with your own eyes.

17"My fellow Israelites, I know you
didn't realize what you were doing. Neither did your leaders. 18But God had given
a promise through all the prophets. And
this is how he has made his promise come
true. He said that his Messiah would suffer. 19So turn away from your sins. Turn to
God. Then your sins will be wiped away.
The time will come when the Lord will
make everything new. 20He will send the
Messiah. Jesus has been appointed as the
Messiah for you. 21Heaven must receive
him until the time when God makes everything new. He promised this long ago
through his holy prophets. 22Moses said,
'The Lord your God will raise up for you
a prophet like me. He will be one of your
own people. You must listen to everything
he tells you. 23Anyone who does not listen to him will be completely cut off from
their people.' (Deuteronomy 18:15,18,19)

24"Beginning with Samuel, all the prophets spoke about this. They said these days
would come. 25What the prophets said was
meant for you. The covenant God made
with your people long ago is yours also. He
said to Abraham, 'All nations on earth will
be blessed through your children.' (Genesis 22:18; 26:4) 26God raised up Jesus, who
serves him. God sent him first to you. He
did it to bless you. He wanted to turn each
of you from your evil ways."

Peter and John Are Taken to the Sanhedrin

4 Peter and John were speaking to the
people. The priests, the captain of the
temple guard, and the Sadducees came
up to the apostles. 2They were very upset by what the apostles were teaching
the people. The apostles were saying that
people can be raised from the dead. They
said this can happen because Jesus rose
from the dead. 3So the temple authorities
arrested Peter and John. It was already
evening, so they put them in prison until the next day. 4But many who heard the
message believed. The number of men
who believed grew to about 5,000.

5The next day the rulers, the elders
and the teachers of the law met in Jerusalem. 6Annas, the high priest, was there.
So were Caiaphas, John, Alexander and
other people in the high priest's family. 7They had Peter and John brought to
them. They wanted to question them. "By
what power did you do this?" they asked.
"And through whose name?"

8Peter was filled with the Holy Spirit.
He said to them, "Rulers and elders of
the people! 9Are you asking us to explain
our actions today? Do you want to know
why we were kind to a man who couldn't
walk? Are you asking how he was healed?
10Then listen to this, you and all the people of Israel! You nailed Jesus Christ of
Nazareth to the cross. But God raised him
from the dead. It is through Jesus' name
that this man stands healed in front of
you. 11Scripture says that Jesus is

" 'the stone you builders did not
accept.
But it has become the most
important stone of all.'
(Psalm 118:22)

12You can't be saved by believing in anyone else. God has given people no other
name under heaven that will save them."

13The leaders saw how bold Peter and
John were. They also realized that Peter and John were ordinary men with no

training. This surprised the leaders. They
realized that these men had been with
Jesus. 14 The leaders could see the man
who had been healed. He was standing there with them. So there was nothing they could say. 15 They ordered Peter
and John to leave the Sanhedrin. Then
they talked things over. 16 "What can we
do with these men?" they asked. "Everyone living in Jerusalem knows they have
performed an unusual miracle. We can't
say it didn't happen. 17 We have to stop
this thing. It must not spread any further
among the people. We have to warn these
men. They must never speak to anyone in
Jesus' name again."

18 Once again the leaders called in Peter
and John. They commanded them not to
speak or teach at all in Jesus' name. 19 But
Peter and John replied, "Which is right
from God's point of view? Should we listen to you? Or should we listen to God?
You be the judges! 20 There's nothing else
we can do. We have to speak about the
things we've seen and heard."

21 The leaders warned them again.
Then they let them go. They couldn't decide how to punish Peter and John. They
knew that all the people were praising
God for what had happened. 22 The man
who had been healed by the miracle was
over 40 years old.

The Believers Pray

23 Peter and John were allowed to leave.
They went back to their own people. They
reported everything the chief priests and
the elders had said to them. 24 The believers heard this. Then they raised their
voices together in prayer to God. "Lord
and King," they said, "you made the heavens, the earth and the sea. You made everything in them. 25 Long ago you spoke
by the Holy Spirit. You spoke through the
mouth of our father David, who served
you. You said,

" 'Why are the nations angry?
Why do the people make useless
plans?
26 The kings of the earth rise up.
The rulers of the earth gather
together
against the Lord
and against his anointed king.'
(Psalm 2:1,2)

27 In fact, Herod and Pontius Pilate met
with the Gentiles in this city. They also
met with the people of Israel. All of them
made plans against your holy servant
Jesus. He is the one you anointed. 28 They
did what your power and purpose had
already decided should happen. 29 Now,
Lord, consider the bad things they say
they are going to do. Help us to be very
bold when we speak your word. 30 Stretch
out your hand to heal. Do signs and wonders through the name of your holy servant Jesus."

31 After they prayed, the place where
they were meeting was shaken. They were
all filled with the Holy Spirit. They were
bold when they spoke God's word.

The Believers Share What They Own

32 All the believers were agreed in heart
and mind. They didn't claim that anything they had was their own. Instead,
they shared everything they owned.
33 With great power the apostles continued their teaching. They were telling people that the Lord Jesus had risen from the
dead. And God's grace was working powerfully in all of them. 34 So there were no
needy persons among them. From time
to time, those who owned land or houses
sold them. They brought the money from
the sales. 35 They put it down at the apostles' feet. It was then given out to anyone
who needed it.

36 Joseph was a Levite from Cyprus. The
apostles called him Barnabas. The name
Barnabas means Son of Help. 37 Barnabas sold a field he owned. He brought the
money from the sale. He put it down at
the apostles' feet.

Ananias and Sapphira

5 A man named Ananias and his wife,
Sapphira, also sold some land. 2 He
kept part of the money for himself. Sapphira knew he had kept it. He brought the
rest of it and put it down at the apostles'
feet.

3 Then Peter said, "Ananias, why did
you let Satan fill your heart? He made you
lie to the Holy Spirit. You have kept some
of the money you received for the land.
4 Didn't the land belong to you before it
was sold? After it was sold, you could have
used the money as you wished. What
made you think of doing such a thing?

You haven't lied just to people. You've also lied to God."

5 When Ananias heard this, he fell down and died. All who heard what had happened were filled with fear. 6 Some young men came and wrapped up his body. They carried him out and buried him.

7 About three hours later, the wife of Ananias came in. She didn't know what had happened. 8 Peter asked her, "Tell me. Is this the price you and Ananias sold the land for?"

"Yes," she said. "That's the price."

9 Peter asked her, "How could you agree to test the Spirit of the Lord? Listen! You can hear the steps of the men who buried your husband. They are at the door. They will carry you out also."

10 At that moment she fell down at Peter's feet and died. Then the young men came in. They saw that Sapphira was dead. So they carried her out and buried her beside her husband. 11 The whole church and all who heard about these things were filled with fear.

The Apostles Heal Many People

12 The apostles did many signs and wonders among the people. All the believers used to meet together at Solomon's Porch. 13 No outsider dared to join them. But the people thought highly of them. 14 More and more men and women believed in the Lord. They joined the other believers. 15 So people brought those who were sick into the streets. They placed them on beds and mats. They hoped that at least Peter's shadow might fall on some of them as he walked by. 16 Crowds even gathered from the towns around Jerusalem. They brought their sick people. They also brought those who were suffering because of evil spirits. All of them were healed.

The Apostles Are Treated Badly

17 The high priest and all his companions were Sadducees. They were very jealous of the apostles. 18 So they arrested them and put them in the public jail. 19 But during the night an angel of the Lord came. He opened the doors of the jail and brought the apostles out. 20 "Go! Stand in the temple courtyard," the angel said. "Tell the people all about this new life."

21 Early the next day they did as they had been told. They entered the temple courtyard. There they began to teach the people.

The high priest and his companions arrived. They called the Sanhedrin together. The Sanhedrin was a gathering of all the elders of Israel. They sent for the apostles who were in jail. 22 The officers arrived at the jail. But they didn't find the apostles there. So they went back and reported it. 23 "We found the jail locked up tight," they said. "The guards were standing at the doors. But when we opened the doors, we didn't find anyone inside." 24 When the captain of the temple guard and the chief priests heard this report, they were bewildered. They wondered what would happen next.

25 Then someone came and said, "Look! The men you put in jail are standing in the temple courtyard. They are teaching the people." 26 So the captain went with his officers and brought the apostles back. But they didn't use force. They were afraid the people would kill them by throwing stones at them.

27 They brought the apostles to the Sanhedrin. The high priest questioned them. 28 "We gave you clear orders not to teach in Jesus' name," he said. "But you have filled Jerusalem with your teaching. You want to make us guilty of this man's death."

29 Peter and the other apostles replied, "We must obey God instead of people! 30 You had Jesus killed by nailing him to a cross. But the God of our people raised Jesus from the dead. 31 Now Jesus is Prince and Savior. God has proved this by giving Jesus a place of honor with him. He did it to turn Israel away from their sins and forgive them. 32 We are telling people about these things. And so is the Holy Spirit. God has given the Spirit to those who obey him."

33 When the leaders heard this, they became very angry. They wanted to put the apostles to death. 34 But a Pharisee named Gamaliel stood up in the Sanhedrin. He was a teacher of the law. He was honored by all the people. He ordered the apostles to be taken outside for a little while. 35 Then Gamaliel spoke to the Sanhedrin. "Men of Israel," he said, "think carefully about what you plan to do to these men. 36 Some time ago Theudas appeared. He

claimed he was really somebody. About
400 people followed him. But he was
killed. All his followers were scattered. So
they accomplished nothing. 37 After this,
Judas from Galilee came along. This was
in the days when the Romans made a list
of all the people. Judas led a gang of men
against the Romans. He too was killed. All
his followers were scattered. 38 So let me
give you some advice. Leave these men
alone! Let them go! If their plans and actions only come from people, they will
fail. 39 But if their plans come from God,
you won't be able to stop these men. You
will only find yourselves fighting against
God."

40 His speech won the leaders over.
They called the apostles in and had them
whipped. The leaders ordered them not
to speak in Jesus' name. Then they let the
apostles go.

41 The apostles were full of joy as they
left the Sanhedrin. They considered it
an honor to suffer shame for the name of
Jesus. 42 Every day they taught in the temple courtyards and from house to house.
They never stopped telling people the
good news that Jesus is the Messiah.

Seven Leaders Are Chosen

6 In those days the number of believers was growing. The Greek Jews
complained about the non-Greek Jews.
They said that the widows of the Greek
Jews were not being taken care of. They
weren't getting their fair share of food
each day. 2 So the 12 apostles gathered
all the believers together. They said, "It
wouldn't be right for us to give up teaching God's word. And we'd have to stop
teaching to wait on tables. 3 Brothers and
sisters, choose seven of your men. They
must be known as men who are wise and
full of the Holy Spirit. We will turn this important work over to them. 4 Then we can
give our attention to prayer and to teaching God's word."

5 This plan pleased the whole group.
They chose Stephen. He was full of faith
and of the Holy Spirit. Philip, Procorus,
Nicanor, Timon and Parmenas were chosen too. The group also chose Nicolas
from Antioch. He had accepted the Jewish faith. 6 The group brought them to the
apostles. Then the apostles prayed and
placed their hands on them.

7 So God's word spread. The number of
believers in Jerusalem grew quickly. Also,
a large number of priests began to obey
Jesus' teachings.

Stephen Is Arrested

8 Stephen was full of God's grace and
power. He did great wonders and signs
among the people. 9 But members of the
group called the Synagogue of the Freed-
men began to oppose him. Some of them
were Jews from Cyrene and Alexandria.
Others were Jews from Cilicia and Asia
Minor. They all began to argue with Stephen. 10 But he was too wise for them.
That's because the Holy Spirit gave Stephen wisdom whenever he spoke.

11 Then in secret they talked some men
into lying about Stephen. They said, "We
heard Stephen speak evil things against
Moses and against God."

12 So the people were stirred up. The
elders and the teachers of the law were
stirred up too. They arrested Stephen and
brought him to the Sanhedrin. 13 They
found witnesses who were willing to tell
lies. These liars said, "This fellow never
stops speaking against this holy place.
He also speaks against the law. 14 We have
heard him say that this Jesus of Nazareth
will destroy this place. He says Jesus will
change the practices that Moses handed
down to us."

15 All who were sitting in the Sanhedrin
looked right at Stephen. They saw that his
face was like the face of an angel.

Stephen Speaks to the Sanhedrin

7 Then the high priest questioned Stephen. "Is what these people are saying
true?" he asked.

2 "Brothers and fathers, listen to me!"
Stephen replied. "The God of glory ap-
peared to our father Abraham. At that
time Abraham was still in Mesopotamia.
He had not yet begun living in Harran.
3 'Leave your country and your people,'
God said. 'Go to the land I will show you.'
(Genesis 12:1)

4 "So Abraham left the land of Babylo-
nia. He settled in Harran. After his father died, God sent Abraham to this land
where you are now living. 5 God didn't give
him any property here. He didn't even
give him enough land to set his foot on.
But God made a promise to him and to all

his family after him. He said they would possess the land. The promise was made even though at that time Abraham had no child. [6]Here is what God said to him. 'For 400 years your family after you will be strangers in a country not their own. They will be slaves and will be treated badly. [7]But I will punish the nation that makes them slaves,' God said. 'After that, they will leave that country and worship me here.' (Genesis 15:13,14) [8]Then God made a covenant with Abraham. God told him that circumcision would show who the members of the covenant were. Abraham became Isaac's father. He circumcised Isaac eight days after he was born. Later, Isaac became Jacob's father. Jacob had 12 sons. They became the founders of the 12 tribes of Israel.

[9]"Jacob's sons were jealous of their brother Joseph. So they sold him as a slave. He was taken to Egypt. But God was with him. [10]He saved Joseph from all his troubles. God made Joseph wise. He helped him to become the friend of Pharaoh, the king of Egypt. So Pharaoh made Joseph ruler over Egypt and his whole palace.

[11]"There was not enough food for all Egypt and Canaan. This brought great suffering. Jacob and his sons couldn't find food. [12]But Jacob heard that there was grain in Egypt. So he sent his sons on their first visit. [13]On their second visit, Joseph told his brothers who he was. Pharaoh learned about Joseph's family. [14]After this, Joseph sent for his father Jacob and his whole family. The total number of people was 75. [15]Then Jacob went down to Egypt. There he and his family died. [16]Some of their bodies were brought back to Shechem. They were placed in a tomb Abraham had bought. He had purchased it from Hamor's sons at Shechem. He had purchased it for a certain amount of money.

[17]"In Egypt the number of our people grew and grew. It was nearly time for God to make his promise to Abraham come true. [18]Then 'a new king came to power in Egypt. Joseph didn't mean anything to him.' (Exodus 1:8) [19]The king was very evil and dishonest with our people. He treated them badly. He forced them to throw out their newborn babies to die.

[20]"At that time Moses was born. He was not an ordinary child. For three months he was taken care of by his family. [21]Then he was placed outside. But Pharaoh's daughter took him home. She brought him up as her own son. [22]Moses was taught all the knowledge of the people of Egypt. He became a powerful speaker and a man of action.

[23]"When Moses was 40 years old, he decided to visit the people of Israel. They were his own people. [24]He saw one of them being treated badly by an Egyptian. So he went to help him. He got even by killing the man. [25]Moses thought his own people would realize that God was using him to save them. But they didn't. [26]The next day Moses saw two Israelites fighting. He tried to make peace between them. 'Men, you are both Israelites,' he said. 'Why do you want to hurt each other?'

[27]"But the man who was treating the other one badly pushed Moses to one side. He said, 'Who made you ruler and judge over us? [28]Are you thinking of killing me as you killed the Egyptian yesterday?' (Exodus 2:14) [29]When Moses heard this, he escaped to Midian. He lived there as an outsider. He became the father of two sons there.

[30]"Forty years passed. Then an angel appeared to Moses in the flames of a burning bush. This happened in the desert near Mount Sinai. [31]When Moses saw the bush, he was amazed. He went over for a closer look. There he heard the Lord say, [32]'I am the God of your fathers. I am the God of Abraham, Isaac and Jacob.' (Exodus 3:6) Moses shook with fear. He didn't dare to look.

[33]"Then the Lord said to him, 'Take off your sandals. You must do this because the place where you are standing is holy ground. [34]I have seen my people beaten down in Egypt. I have heard their groans. I have come down to set them free. Now come. I will send you back to Egypt.' (Exodus 3:5,7,8,10)

[35]"This is the same Moses the two men of Israel would not accept. They had said, 'Who made you ruler and judge?' But God himself sent Moses to rule the people of Israel and set them free. He spoke to Moses through an angel. The angel had appeared to him in the bush. [36]So Moses led them out of Egypt. He did wonders and

signs in Egypt, at the Red Sea, and for 40 years in the desert.

37 "This is the same Moses who spoke to the Israelites. 'God will send you a prophet,' he said. 'He will be like me. He will come from your own people.' (Deuteronomy 18:15) 38 Moses was with the Israelites in the desert. He was with the angel who spoke to him on Mount Sinai. Moses was with our people of long ago. He received living words to pass on to us.

39 "But our people refused to obey Moses. They would not accept him. In their hearts, they wished they were back in Egypt. 40 They told Aaron, 'Make us a god who will lead us. This fellow Moses brought us up out of Egypt. But we don't know what has happened to him!' (Exodus 32:1) 41 That was the time they made a statue to be their god. It was shaped like a calf. They brought sacrifices to it. They even enjoyed what they had made with their own hands. 42 But God turned away from them. He let them go on worshiping the sun, moon and stars. This agrees with what is written in the book of the prophets. There it says,

"'People of Israel, did you bring me
sacrifices and offerings
for 40 years in the desert?
43 You have taken with you the shrine
of your false god Molek.
You have taken with you the star
of your false god Rephan.
You made statues of those gods to
worship.
So I will send you away from your
country.' (Amos 5:25–27)
God sent them to Babylon and
even farther.

44 "Long ago our people were in the desert. They had with them the holy tent. The tent was where the tablets of the covenant law were kept. Moses had made the holy tent as God had commanded him. Moses made it like the pattern he had seen. 45 Our people received the tent from God. Then they brought it with them when they took the land of Canaan. God drove out the nations that were in their way. At that time Joshua was Israel's leader. The tent remained in the land until David's time. 46 David was blessed by God. So David asked if he could build a house for the God of Jacob. 47 But it was Solomon who built the temple for God.

48 "But the Most High God does not live in houses made by human hands. As God says through the prophet,

49 "'Heaven is my throne.
The earth is under my control.
What kind of house will you build
for me?
says the Lord.
Where will my resting place be?
50 Didn't my hand make all these
things?' (Isaiah 66:1,2)

51 "You stubborn people! You won't obey! You won't listen! You are just like your people of long ago! You always oppose the Holy Spirit! 52 Was there ever a prophet your people didn't try to hurt? They even killed those who told about the coming of the Blameless One. And now you have handed him over to his enemies. You have murdered him. 53 The law you received was given by angels. But you haven't obeyed it."

Stephen Is Killed

54 When the members of the Sanhedrin heard this, they became very angry. They were so angry they ground their teeth at Stephen. 55 But he was full of the Holy Spirit. He looked up to heaven and saw God's glory. He saw Jesus standing at God's right hand. 56 "Look!" he said. "I see heaven open. The Son of Man is standing at God's right hand."

57 When the Sanhedrin heard this, they covered their ears. They yelled at the top of their voices. They all rushed at him. 58 They dragged him out of the city. They began to throw stones at him to kill him. The people who had brought false charges against Stephen took off their coats. They placed them at the feet of a young man named Saul.

59 While the members of the Sanhedrin were throwing stones at Stephen, he prayed. "Lord Jesus, receive my spirit," he said. 60 Then he fell on his knees. He cried out, "Lord! Don't hold this sin against them!" When he had said this, he died.

8 And Saul had agreed with the Sanhedrin that Stephen should die.

The Church Is Treated Badly and Scattered

On that day the church in Jerusalem
began to be attacked and treated badly.
All except the apostles were scattered
throughout Judea and Samaria. 2 Godly
Jews buried Stephen. They mourned
deeply for him. 3 But Saul began to destroy
the church. He went from house to house.
He dragged away men and women and
put them in prison.

Philip Goes to Samaria

4 The believers who had been scattered
preached the word everywhere they went.
5 Philip went down to a city in Samaria.
There he preached about the Messiah.
6 The crowds listened to Philip and saw
the signs he did. All of them paid close
attention to what he said. 7 Evil spirits
screamed and came out of many people.
Many people who were disabled or who
couldn't walk were healed. 8 So there was
great joy in that city.

Simon the Evil Magician

9 A man named Simon lived in the city.
For quite a while he had practiced evil
magic there. He amazed all the people
of Samaria. He claimed to be someone
great. 10 And all the people listened to
him, from the least important of them to
the most important. They exclaimed, "It
is right to call this man the Great Power
of God!" 11 He had amazed them for a long
time with his evil magic. So they followed
him. 12 But Philip announced the good
news of God's kingdom and the name of
Jesus Christ. So men and women believed
and were baptized. 13 Simon himself believed and was baptized. He followed
Philip everywhere. He was amazed by the
great signs and miracles he saw.

14 The apostles in Jerusalem heard that
people in Samaria had accepted God's
word. So they sent Peter and John to Samaria. 15 When they arrived there, they
prayed for the new believers. They prayed
that they would receive the Holy Spirit.
16 The Holy Spirit had not yet come on any
of them. They had only been baptized in
the name of the Lord Jesus. 17 Then Peter
and John placed their hands on them.
And they received the Holy Spirit.

18 Simon watched as the apostles
placed their hands on them. He saw that
the Spirit was given to them. So he offered
money to Peter and John. 19 He said, "Give
me this power too. Then everyone I place
my hands on will receive the Holy Spirit."

20 Peter answered, "May your money be
destroyed with you! Do you think you can
buy God's gift with money? 21 You have no
part or share in this holy work. Your heart
is not right with God. 22 Turn away from
this evil sin of yours. Pray to the Lord. Perhaps he will forgive you for having such a
thought in your heart. 23 I see that you are
very bitter. You are a prisoner of sin."

24 Then Simon answered, "Pray to the
Lord for me. Pray that nothing you have
said will happen to me."

25 Peter and John continued to preach
the word of the Lord and tell people about
Jesus. Then they returned to Jerusalem.
On the way they preached the good news
in many villages in Samaria.

Philip and the Man From Ethiopia

26 An angel of the Lord spoke to Philip.
"Go south to the desert road," he said.
"It's the road that goes down from Jerusalem to Gaza." 27 So Philip started out. On
his way he met an Ethiopian official. The
man had an important position in charge
of all the wealth of the Kandake. Kandake
means Queen of Ethiopia. This official
had gone to Jerusalem to worship. 28 On
his way home he was sitting in his chariot. He was reading the Book of Isaiah the
prophet. 29 The Holy Spirit told Philip, "Go
to that chariot. Stay near it."

30 So Philip ran up to the chariot.
He heard the man reading Isaiah the
prophet. "Do you understand what you're
reading?" Philip asked.

31 "How can I?" he said. "I need someone to explain it to me." So he invited
Philip to come up and sit with him.

32 Here is the part of Scripture the official was reading. It says,

"He was led like a sheep to be killed.
Just as lambs are silent while their
wool is being cut off,
he did not open his mouth.
33 When he was treated badly, he was
refused a fair trial.
Who can say anything about his
children?
His life was cut off from the earth."
(Isaiah 53:7,8)

34 The official said to Philip, "Tell me,
please. Who is the prophet talking about?
Himself, or someone else?" 35 Then Philip
began with that same part of Scripture.
He told him the good news about Jesus.
36-37 As they traveled along the road,
they came to some water. The official
said, "Look! Here is water! What can stop
me from being baptized?" 38 He gave orders to stop the chariot. Then both Philip
and the official went down into the water.
Philip baptized him. 39 When they came
up out of the water, the Spirit of the Lord
suddenly took Philip away. The official
did not see him again. He went on his way
full of joy. 40 Philip was seen next at Azo-
tus. From there he traveled all around. He
preached the good news in all the towns.
Finally he arrived in Caesarea.

Saul Becomes a Believer

9 Meanwhile, Saul continued to oppose the Lord's followers. He said
they would be put to death. He went to
the high priest. 2 He asked the priest for
letters to the synagogues in Damascus.
He wanted to find men and women who
belonged to the Way of Jesus. The letters
would allow him to take them as prisoners to Jerusalem. 3 On his journey, Saul
approached Damascus. Suddenly a light
from heaven flashed around him. 4 He fell
to the ground. He heard a voice speak to
him, "Saul! Saul! Why are you opposing
me?"
5 "Who are you, Lord?" Saul asked.
"I am Jesus," he replied. "I am the one
you are opposing. 6 Now get up and go
into the city. There you will be told what
you must do."
7 The men traveling with Saul stood
there. They weren't able to speak. They
had heard the sound. But they didn't see
anyone. 8 Saul got up from the ground. He
opened his eyes, but he couldn't see. So
they led him by the hand into Damascus.
9 For three days he was blind. He didn't
eat or drink anything.
10 In Damascus there was a believer
named Ananias. The Lord called out to
him in a vision. "Ananias!" he said.
"Yes, Lord," he answered.
11 The Lord told him, "Go to the house
of Judas on Straight Street. Ask for a man
from Tarsus named Saul. He is praying.
12 In a vision Saul has seen a man come
and place his hands on him. That man's
name is Ananias. In the vision, Ananias
placed his hands on Saul so he could see
again."
13 "Lord," Ananias answered, "I've
heard many reports about this man. They
say he has done great harm to your holy
people in Jerusalem. 14 Now he has come
here to arrest all those who worship you.
The chief priests have given him authority
to do this."
15 But the Lord said to Ananias, "Go! I
have chosen this man to work for me. He
will announce my name to the Gentiles
and to their kings. He will also announce
my name to the people of Israel. 16 I will
show him how much he must suffer for
me."
17 Then Ananias went to the house and
entered it. He placed his hands on Saul.
"Brother Saul," he said, "you saw the Lord
Jesus. He appeared to you on the road as
you were coming here. He has sent me so
that you will be able to see again. You will
be filled with the Holy Spirit." 18 Right away
something like scales fell from Saul's eyes.
And he could see again. He got up and
was baptized. 19 After eating some food,
he got his strength back.

Saul in Damascus and Jerusalem

Saul spent several days with the believers in Damascus. 20 Right away he began
to preach in the synagogues. He taught
that Jesus is the Son of God. 21 All who
heard him were amazed. They asked,
"Isn't he the man who caused great trouble in Jerusalem? Didn't he make trouble
for those who worship Jesus? Hasn't he
come here to take them as prisoners to
the chief priests?" 22 But Saul grew more
and more powerful. The Jews living in Damascus couldn't believe what was happening. Saul proved to them that Jesus is
the Messiah.
23 After many days, the Jews had a meeting. They planned to kill Saul. 24 But he
learned about their plan. Day and night
they watched the city gates closely in order to kill him. 25 But his followers helped
him escape by night. They lowered him in
a basket through an opening in the wall.
26 When Saul came to Jerusalem, he
tried to join the believers. But they were
all afraid of him. They didn't believe he
was really one of Jesus' followers. 27 But

Barnabas took him to the apostles. He
told them about Saul's journey. He said
that Saul had seen the Lord. He told how
the Lord had spoken to Saul. Barnabas
also said that Saul had preached without fear in Jesus' name in Damascus. 28 So
Saul stayed with the believers. He moved
about freely in Jerusalem. He spoke
boldly in the Lord's name. 29 He talked
and argued with the Greek Jews. But they
tried to kill him. 30 The other believers
heard about this. They took Saul down to
Caesarea. From there they sent him off to
Tarsus.
31 Then the church throughout Judea,
Galilee and Samaria enjoyed a time of
peace. The church was strengthened
and grew larger. That's because they
worshiped the Lord and the Holy Spirit
helped them.

Peter Heals Aeneas and Dorcas

32 Peter traveled around the country. He
went to visit the Lord's people who lived
in Lydda. 33 There he found a disabled
man named Aeneas. For eight years the
man had spent most of his time in bed.
34 "Aeneas," Peter said to him, "Jesus Christ
heals you. Get up! Roll up your mat!" So
Aeneas got up right away. 35 Everyone who
lived in Lydda and Sharon saw him. They
turned to the Lord.
36 In Joppa there was a believer named
Tabitha. Her name in the Greek language
is Dorcas. She was always doing good and
helping poor people. 37 About that time
she became sick and died. Her body was
washed and placed in a room upstairs.
38 Lydda was near Joppa. The believers
heard that Peter was in Lydda. So they
sent two men to him. They begged him,
"Please come at once!"
39 Peter went with them. When he arrived, he was taken upstairs to the room.
All the widows stood around him crying.
They showed him the robes and other
clothes Dorcas had made before she died.
40 Peter sent them all out of the room.
Then he got down on his knees and
prayed. He turned toward the dead woman. He said, "Tabitha, get up." She opened
her eyes. When she saw Peter, she sat up.
41 He took her by the hand and helped
her to her feet. Then he called the believers and especially the widows. He
brought her to them. They saw that she
was alive. 42 This became known all over
Joppa. Many people believed in the Lord.
43 Peter stayed in Joppa for some time. He
stayed with Simon, a man who worked
with leather.

Cornelius Calls for Peter

10 A man named Cornelius lived in
Caesarea. He was a Roman commander in the Italian Regiment. 2 Cornelius and all his family were faithful and
worshiped God. He gave freely to people
who were in need. He prayed to God regularly. 3 One day about three o'clock in the
afternoon he had a vision. He saw clearly
an angel of God. The angel came to him
and said, "Cornelius!"
4 Cornelius was afraid. He stared at the
angel. "What is it, Lord?" he asked.
The angel answered, "Your prayers and
gifts to poor people are like an offering to
God. So he has remembered you. 5 Now
send men to Joppa. Have them bring back
a man named Simon. He is also called Peter. 6 He is staying with another Simon, a
man who works with leather. His house is
by the sea."
7 The angel who spoke to him left. Then
Cornelius called two of his servants. He
also called a godly soldier who was one of
his attendants. 8 He told them everything
that had happened. Then he sent them to
Joppa.

Peter Has a Vision

9 It was about noon the next day. The
men were on their journey and were approaching the city. Peter went up on the
roof to pray. 10 He became hungry. He
wanted something to eat. While the meal
was being prepared, Peter had a vision.
11 He saw heaven open up. There he saw
something that looked like a large sheet.
It was being let down to earth by its four
corners. 12 It had all kinds of four-footed
animals in it. It also had reptiles and birds
in it. 13 Then a voice told him, "Get up, Peter. Kill and eat."
14 "No, Lord! I will not!" Peter replied. "I
have never eaten anything that is not pure
and 'clean.'"
15 The voice spoke to him a second
time. It said, "Do not say anything is not
pure that God has made 'clean.'"
16 This happened three times. Right

away the sheet was taken back up to
heaven.
[17] Peter was wondering what the vision
meant. At that very moment the men sent
by Cornelius found Simon's house. They
stopped at the gate [18] and called out. They
asked if Simon Peter was staying there.
[19] Peter was still thinking about the vision. The Holy Spirit spoke to him. "Simon," he said, "three men are looking for
you. [20] Get up and go downstairs. Don't let
anything keep you from going with them.
I have sent them."
[21] Peter went down and spoke to the
men. "I'm the one you're looking for," he
said. "Why have you come?"
[22] The men replied, "We have come
from Cornelius, the Roman commander.
He is a good man who worships God. All
the Jewish people respect him. A holy angel told him to invite you to his house.
Then Cornelius can hear what you have
to say." [23] Then Peter invited the men into
the house to be his guests.

Peter Goes to the House of Cornelius

The next day Peter went with the three
men. Some of the believers from Joppa
went along. [24] The following day he arrived in Caesarea. Cornelius was expecting them. He had called together his
relatives and close friends. [25] When Peter
entered the house, Cornelius met him.
As a sign of respect, he fell at Peter's feet.
[26] But Peter made him get up. "Stand up,"
he said. "I am only a man myself."
[27] As he was talking with Cornelius, Peter went inside. There he found a large
group of people. [28] He said to them, "You
know that it is against our law for a Jew
to enter a Gentile home. A Jew shouldn't
have any close contact with a Gentile. But
God has shown me that I should not say
anyone is not pure and 'clean.' [29] So when
you sent for me, I came without asking
any questions. May I ask why you sent for
me?"
[30] Cornelius answered, "Three days ago
at this very hour I was in my house praying. It was three o'clock in the afternoon.
Suddenly a man in shining clothes stood
in front of me. [31] He said, 'Cornelius, God
has heard your prayer. He has remembered your gifts to poor people. [32] Send
someone to Joppa to get Simon Peter. He
is a guest in the home of another Simon,
who works with leather. He lives by the
sea.' [33] So I sent for you right away. It was
good of you to come. Now we are all here.
And God is here with us. We are ready to
listen to everything the Lord has commanded you to tell us."
[34] Then Peter began to speak. "I now
realize how true it is that God treats everyone the same," he said. [35] "He accepts
people from every nation. He accepts
anyone who has respect for him and does
what is right. [36] You know the message
God sent to the people of Israel. It is the
good news of peace through Jesus Christ.
He is Lord of all. [37] You know what has
happened all through the area of Judea.
It started in Galilee after John preached
about baptism. [38] You know how God
anointed Jesus of Nazareth with the Holy
Spirit and with power. Jesus went around
doing good. He healed all who were under the devil's power. God was with him.
[39] "We are witnesses of everything he
did in the land of the Jews and in Jerusalem. They killed him by nailing him to a
cross. [40] But on the third day God raised
him from the dead. God allowed Jesus to
be seen. [41] But he wasn't seen by all the
people. He was seen only by us. We are
witnesses whom God had already chosen. We ate and drank with him after he
rose from the dead. [42] He commanded us
to preach to the people. He told us to tell
people that he is the one appointed by
God to judge the living and the dead. [43] All
the prophets tell about him. They say that
all who believe in him have their sins forgiven through his name."
[44] While Peter was still speaking, the
Holy Spirit came on all who heard the
message. [45] Some Jewish believers had
come with Peter. They were amazed because the gift of the Holy Spirit had been
poured out even on the Gentiles. [46] They
heard them speaking in languages they
had not known before. They also heard
them praising God.

Then Peter said, [47] "Surely no one can
keep these people from being baptized
with water. They have received the Holy
Spirit just as we have." [48] So he ordered
that they be baptized in the name of Jesus
Christ. Then they asked Peter to stay with
them for a few days.

Peter Explains His Actions

11 The apostles and the believers all
through Judea heard that Gentiles
had also received God's word. 2 Peter went
up to Jerusalem. There the Jewish believers found fault with him. 3 They said, "You
went into the house of Gentiles. You ate
with them."

4 Starting from the beginning, Peter told
them the whole story. 5 "I was in the city
of Joppa praying," he said. "There I had a
vision. I saw something that looked like
a large sheet. It was being let down from
heaven by its four corners. It came down
to where I was. 6 I looked into it and saw
four-footed animals of the earth. There
were also wild animals, reptiles and birds.
7 Then I heard a voice speaking to me. 'Get
up, Peter,' the voice said. 'Kill and eat.'

8 "I replied, 'No, Lord! I will not! Nothing that is not pure and "clean" has ever
entered my mouth.'

9 "A second time the voice spoke from
heaven. The voice said, 'Do not say anything is not pure that God has made
"clean."' 10 This happened three times.
Then the sheet was pulled up into heaven.

11 "Just then three men stopped at the
house where I was staying. They had been
sent to me from Caesarea. 12 The Holy
Spirit told me not to let anything keep me
from going with them. These six brothers
here went with me. We entered the man's
house. 13 He told us how he had seen an
angel appear in his house. The angel said,
'Send to Joppa for Simon Peter. 14 He has
a message to bring to you. You and your
whole family will be saved through it.'

15 "As I began to speak, the Holy Spirit
came on them. He came just as he had
come on us at the beginning. 16 Then I remembered the Lord's words. 'John baptized with water,' he had said. 'But you will
be baptized with the Holy Spirit.' 17 God
gave them the same gift he gave those of
us who believed in the Lord Jesus Christ.
So who was I to think that I could stand in
God's way?"

18 When they heard this, they didn't ob-
ject anymore. They praised God. They
said, "So then, God has allowed even
Gentiles to turn away from their sins. He
did this so that they could live."

The Believers in Antioch

19 Some believers had been scattered by
the suffering that unbelievers had caused
them. They were scattered after Stephen
was killed. Those believers traveled as far
as Phoenicia, Cyprus and Antioch. But
they spread the word only among Jews.
20 Some believers from Cyprus and Cyrene went to Antioch. There they began to
speak to Greeks also. They told them the
good news about the Lord Jesus. 21 The
Lord's power was with them. Large numbers of people believed and turned to the
Lord.

22 The church in Jerusalem heard about
this. So they sent Barnabas to Antioch.
23 When he arrived and saw what the
grace of God had done, he was glad. He
told them all to remain true to the Lord
with all their hearts. 24 Barnabas was a
good man. He was full of the Holy Spirit
and of faith. Large numbers of people
came to know the Lord.

25 Then Barnabas went to Tarsus to look
for Saul. 26 He found him there. Then he
brought him to Antioch. For a whole year
Barnabas and Saul met with the church.
They taught large numbers of people. At
Antioch the believers were called Christians for the first time.

27 In those days some prophets came
down from Jerusalem to Antioch. 28 One
of them was named Agabus. He stood
up and spoke through the Spirit. He said
there would not be nearly enough food
anywhere in the Roman world. This happened while Claudius was the emperor.
29 The believers decided to provide help
for the brothers and sisters living in Judea.
All of them helped as much as they could.
30 They sent their gift to the elders through
Barnabas and Saul.

An Angel Helps Peter Escape From Prison

12 About this time, King Herod arrested some people who belonged
to the church. He planned to make them
suffer greatly. 2 He had James killed with a
sword. James was John's brother. 3 Herod
saw that the death of James pleased some
Jews. So he arrested Peter also. This happened during the Feast of Unleavened
Bread. 4 After Herod arrested Peter, he put
him in prison. Peter was placed under
guard. He was watched by four groups of
four soldiers each. Herod planned to put
Peter on public trial. It would take place
after the Passover Feast.

5 So Peter was kept in prison. But the
church prayed hard to God for him.
6 It was the night before Herod was going to bring him to trial. Peter was sleeping between two soldiers. Two chains
held him there. Lookouts stood guard
at the entrance. 7 Suddenly an angel of
the Lord appeared. A light shone in the
prison cell. The angel struck Peter on his
side. Peter woke up. "Quick!" the angel
said. "Get up!" The chains fell off Peter's
wrists.
8 Then the angel said to him, "Put on
your clothes and sandals." Peter did so.
"Put on your coat," the angel told him.
"Follow me." 9 Peter followed him out
of the prison. But he had no idea that
what the angel was doing was really happening. He thought he was seeing a vision. 10 They passed the first and second
guards. Then they came to the iron gate
leading to the city. It opened for them by
itself. They went through it. They walked
the length of one street. Suddenly the angel left Peter.
11 Then Peter realized what had happened. He said, "Now I know for sure that
the Lord has sent his angel. He set me free
from Herod's power. He saved me from
everything the Jewish people were hoping would happen."
12 When Peter understood what had
happened, he went to Mary's house. Mary
was the mother of John Mark. Many people had gathered in her home. They were
praying there. 13 Peter knocked at the outer
entrance. A servant named Rhoda came
to answer the door. 14 She recognized Peter's voice. She was so excited that she ran
back without opening the door. "Peter is
at the door!" she exclaimed.
15 "You're out of your mind," they said to
her. But she kept telling them it was true.
So they said, "It must be his angel."
16 Peter kept on knocking. When they
opened the door and saw him, they were
amazed. 17 Peter motioned with his hand
for them to be quiet. He explained how
the Lord had brought him out of prison.
"Tell James and the other brothers and
sisters about this," he said. Then he went
to another place.
18 In the morning the soldiers were bewildered. They couldn't figure out what
had happened to Peter. 19 So Herod had
them look everywhere for Peter. But they
didn't find him. Then Herod questioned
the guards closely. He ordered that they
be put to death.

Herod Dies

Then Herod went from Judea to Caesarea and stayed there. 20 He had been
quarreling with the people of Tyre and Sidon. So they got together and asked for a
meeting with him. This was because they
depended on the king's country to supply
them with food. They gained the support
of Blastus and then asked for peace. Blastus was a trusted personal servant of the
king.
21 The appointed day came. Herod was
seated on his throne. He was wearing
his royal robes. He made a speech to the
people. 22 Then they shouted, "This is the
voice of a god. It's not the voice of a man."
23 Right away an angel of the Lord struck
Herod down. Herod had not given praise
to God. So he was eaten by worms and
died.
24 But God's word continued to spread
and many people believed the message.

Barnabas and Saul Are Sent Off

25 Barnabas and Saul finished their task.
Then they returned from Jerusalem. They
13 took John Mark with them. 1 In the
church at Antioch there were prophets and teachers. Among them were Barnabas, Simeon, and Lucius from Cyrene.
Simeon was also called Niger. Another
was Manaen. He had been brought up
with Herod, the ruler of Galilee. Saul was
among them too. 2 While they were worshiping the Lord and fasting, the Holy
Spirit spoke. "Set apart Barnabas and Saul
for me," he said. "I have appointed them
to do special work." 3 The prophets and
teachers fasted and prayed. They placed
their hands on Barnabas and Saul. Then
they sent them off.

Events on Cyprus

4 Barnabas and Saul were sent on their
way by the Holy Spirit. They went down
to Seleucia. From there they sailed to
Cyprus. 5 They arrived at Salamis. There
they preached God's word in the Jewish
synagogues. John was with them as their
helper.
6 They traveled all across the island until they came to Paphos. There they met

a Jew named Bar-Jesus. He was an evil
magician and a false prophet. [7]He was an
attendant of Sergius Paulus, the governor.
Paulus was a man of understanding. He
sent for Barnabas and Saul. He wanted
to hear God's word. [8]But the evil magician named Elymas opposed them. The
name Elymas means Magician. He tried
to keep the governor from becoming a believer. [9]Saul was also known as Paul. He
was filled with the Holy Spirit. He looked
straight at Elymas. He said to him, [10]"You
are a child of the devil! You are an enemy
of everything that is right! You cheat people. You use all kinds of tricks. Won't you
ever stop twisting the right ways of the
Lord? [11]Now the Lord's hand is against
you. You are going to go blind. For a while
you won't even be able to see the light of
the sun."

Right away mist and darkness came
over him. He tried to feel his way around.
He wanted to find someone to lead him
by the hand. [12]When the governor saw
what had happened, he believed. He was
amazed at what Paul was teaching about
the Lord.

Paul Preaches in Pisidian Antioch

[13]From Paphos, Paul and his companions sailed to Perga in Pamphylia. There
John Mark left them and returned to Jerusalem. [14]From Perga they went on to Pisidian Antioch. On the Sabbath day they
entered the synagogue and sat down.
[15]The Law and the Prophets were read
aloud. Then the leaders of the synagogue
sent word to Paul and his companions.
They said, "Brothers, do you have any
words of instruction for the people? If you
do, please speak."

[16]Paul stood up and motioned with his
hand. Then he said, "Fellow Israelites,
and you Gentiles who worship God, listen
to me! [17]The God of Israel chose our people who lived long ago. He blessed them
greatly while they were in Egypt. With
his mighty power he led them out of that
country. [18]He put up with their behavior
for about 40 years in the desert. [19]And he
destroyed seven nations in Canaan. Then
he gave the land to his people as their
rightful share. [20]All this took about 450
years.

"After this, God gave them judges until
the time of Samuel the prophet. [21]Then
the people asked for a king. He gave them
Saul, son of Kish. Saul was from the tribe
of Benjamin. He ruled for 40 years. [22]God
removed him and made David their king.
Here is God's witness about him. 'David,
son of Jesse, is a man dear to my heart,' he
said. 'David will do everything I want him
to do.'

[23]"From this man's family line God has
brought to Israel the Savior Jesus. This
is what he had promised. [24]Before Jesus
came, John preached that we should turn
away from our sins and be baptized. He
preached this to all Israel. [25]John was
coming to the end of his work. 'Who do
you suppose I am?' he said. 'I am not
the one you are looking for. But there is
someone coming after me. I am not good
enough to untie his sandals.'

[26]"Listen, fellow children of Abraham!
Listen, you Gentiles who worship God!
This message of salvation has been sent
to us. [27]The people of Jerusalem and their
rulers did not recognize Jesus. By finding him guilty, they made the prophets'
words come true. These are read every
Sabbath day. [28]The people and their rulers had no reason at all for sentencing
Jesus to death. But they asked Pilate to
have him killed. [29]They did everything
that had been written about Jesus. Then
they took him down from the cross. They
laid him in a tomb. [30]But God raised him
from the dead. [31]For many days he was
seen by those who had traveled with him
from Galilee to Jerusalem. Now they are
telling our people about Jesus.

[32]"We are telling you the good news.
What God promised our people long ago
[33]he has done for us, their children. He
has raised up Jesus. This is what is written
in the second Psalm. It says,

" 'You are my son.
Today I have become your father.'
(Psalm 2:7)

[34]God raised Jesus from the dead. He will
never rot in the grave. As God has said,

" 'Holy and sure blessings were
promised to David.
I will give them to you.' (Isaiah 55:3)

[35]In another place it also says,

" 'You will not let your holy one rot
away.' (Psalm 16:10)

36 "David carried out God's purpose
while he lived. Then he died. He was buried with his people. His body rotted away.
37 But the one whom God raised from the
dead did not rot away.

38 "My friends, here is what I want you
to know. I announce to you that your sins
can be forgiven because of what Jesus has
done. 39 Through him everyone who believes is set free from every sin. Moses' law
could not make you right in God's eyes.
40 Be careful! Don't let what the prophets
spoke about happen to you. They said,

41 " 'Look, you who make fun of the
truth!
Wonder and die!
I am going to do something in your
days
that you would never believe.
You wouldn't believe it even
if someone told you.' "
(Habakkuk 1:5)

42 Paul and Barnabas started to leave
the synagogue. The people invited them
to say more about these things on the
next Sabbath day. 43 The people were told
they could leave the service. Many Jews
followed Paul and Barnabas. Many Gentiles who faithfully worshiped the God of
the Jews did the same. Paul and Barnabas
talked with them. They tried to get them
to keep living in God's grace.

44 On the next Sabbath day, almost the
whole city gathered. They gathered to
hear the word of the Lord. 45 When the
Jews saw the crowds, they became very
jealous. They began to disagree with what
Paul was saying. They said evil things
against him.

46 Then Paul and Barnabas answered
them boldly. "We had to speak God's
word to you first," they said. "But you
don't accept it. You don't think you are
good enough for eternal life. So now we
are turning to the Gentiles. 47 This is what
the Lord has commanded us to do. He
said,

" 'I have made you a light for the
Gentiles.
You will bring salvation to the
whole earth.' " (Isaiah 49:6)

48 When the Gentiles heard this, they
were glad. They honored the word of the
Lord. All who were appointed for eternal
life believed.

49 The word of the Lord spread through
the whole area. 50 But the Jewish leaders stirred up the important women who
worshiped God. They also stirred up the
men who were leaders in the city. The
Jewish leaders tried to get the women and
men to attack Paul and Barnabas. They
threw Paul and Barnabas out of that area.
51 Paul and Barnabas shook the dust off
their feet. This was a warning to the people who had opposed them. Then Paul
and Barnabas went on to Iconium. 52 The
believers were filled with joy and with the
Holy Spirit.

Paul and Barnabas Preach in Iconium

14 At Iconium, Paul and Barnabas went
into the Jewish synagogue as usual.
They spoke there with great power. Large
numbers of Jews and Greeks became believers. 2 But the Jews who refused to believe stirred up some of the Gentiles who
were there. They turned them against the
two men and the new believers. 3 So Paul
and Barnabas spent a lot of time there.
They spoke boldly for the Lord. He gave
them the ability to do signs and wonders.
In this way the Lord showed that they
were telling the truth about his grace.
4 The people of the city did not agree with
one another. Some were on the side of the
Jews. Others were on the side of the apostles. 5 Jews and Gentiles alike planned
to treat Paul and Barnabas badly. Their
leaders agreed. They planned to kill them
by throwing stones at them. 6 But Paul and
Barnabas found out about the plan. They
escaped to the Lycaonian cities of Lystra
and Derbe and to the surrounding area.
7 There they continued to preach the good
news.

Paul Preaches in Lystra

8 In Lystra there sat a man who couldn't
walk. He hadn't been able to use his feet
since the day he was born. 9 He listened as
Paul spoke. Paul looked right at him. He
saw that the man had faith to be healed.
10 So he called out, "Stand up on your
feet!" Then the man jumped up and began to walk.

11 The crowd saw what Paul had done.
They shouted in the Lycaonian language. "The gods have come down to us

in human form!" they exclaimed. 12 They
called Barnabas Zeus. Paul was the main
speaker. So they called him Hermes.
13 Just outside the city was the temple of
the god Zeus. The priest of Zeus brought
bulls and wreaths to the city gates. He and
the crowd wanted to offer sacrifices to
Paul and Barnabas.

14 But the apostles Barnabas and Paul
heard about this. So they tore their
clothes. They rushed out into the crowd.
They shouted, 15 "Friends, why are you
doing this? We are only human, just like
you. We are bringing you good news. Turn
away from these worthless things. Turn to
the living God. He is the one who made
the heavens and the earth and the sea. He
made everything in them. 16 In the past,
he let all nations go their own way. 17 But
he has given proof of what he is like. He
has shown kindness by giving you rain
from heaven. He gives you crops in their
seasons. He provides you with plenty of
food. He fills your hearts with joy." 18 Paul
and Barnabas told them all these things.
But they had trouble keeping the crowd
from offering sacrifices to them.

19 Then some Jews came from Antioch
and Iconium. They won the crowd over to
their side. They threw stones at Paul. They
thought he was dead, so they dragged
him out of the city. 20 The believers gathered around Paul. Then he got up and
went back into the city. The next day he
and Barnabas left for Derbe.

Paul and Barnabas Return to Antioch

21 Paul and Barnabas preached the
good news in the city of Derbe. They won
large numbers of followers. Then they
returned to Lystra, Iconium and Antioch. 22 There they helped the believers
gain strength. They told them to remain
faithful to what they had been taught.
"We must go through many hard times to
enter God's kingdom," they said. 23 Paul
and Barnabas appointed elders for them
in each church. The elders had trusted
in the Lord. Paul and Barnabas prayed
and fasted. They placed the elders in the
Lord's care. 24 After going through Pisidia,
Paul and Barnabas came into Pamphylia.
25 They preached the good news in Perga.
Then they went down to Attalia.

26 From Attalia they sailed back to Antioch. In Antioch they had been put in
God's care to preach the good news. They
had now completed the work God had
given them to do. 27 When they arrived
at Antioch, they gathered the church together. They reported all that God had
done through them. They told how he
had opened a way for the Gentiles to believe. 28 And they stayed there a long time
with the believers.

Church Leaders Meet in Jerusalem

15 Certain people came down from
Judea to Antioch. Here is what they
were teaching the believers. "Moses commanded you to be circumcised," they
said. "If you aren't, you can't be saved."
2 But Paul and Barnabas didn't agree with
this. They argued strongly with them. So
Paul and Barnabas were appointed to go
up to Jerusalem. Some other believers
were chosen to go with them. They were
told to ask the apostles and elders about
this question. 3 The church sent them on
their way. They traveled through Phoenicia and Samaria. There they told how
the Gentiles had turned to God. This news
made all the believers very glad. 4 When
they arrived in Jerusalem, the church
welcomed them. The apostles and elders
welcomed them too. Then Paul and Barnabas reported everything God had done
through them.

5 Some of the believers were Pharisees.
They stood up and said, "The Gentiles
must be circumcised. They must obey the
law of Moses."

6 The apostles and elders met to consider this question. 7 After they had talked
it over, Peter got up and spoke to them.
"Brothers," he said, "you know that some
time ago God chose me. He appointed me
to take the good news to the Gentiles. He
wanted them to hear the good news and
believe. 8 God knows the human heart.
By giving the Holy Spirit to the Gentiles,
he showed that he accepted them. He did
the same for them as he had done for us.
9 God showed that there is no difference
between us and them. That's because he
made their hearts pure because of their
faith. 10 Now then, why are you trying to
test God? You test him when you put a
heavy load on the shoulders of Gentiles.
Our people of long ago couldn't carry that
load. We can't either. 11 No! We believe we
are saved through the grace of our Lord

Jesus. The Gentiles are saved in the same
way."
12 Everyone became quiet as they listened to Barnabas and Paul. They were
telling about the signs and wonders God
had done through them among the Gentiles. 13 When they finished, James spoke
up. "Brothers," he said, "listen to me. 14 Simon Peter has explained to us what God
has now done. He has chosen some of the
Gentiles to be among his very own people. 15 The prophets' words agree with
that. They say,

16 " 'After this I will return
and set up again David's fallen
tent.
I will rebuild what was destroyed.
I will make it what it used to be.
17 Then everyone else can look to the
Lord.
This includes all the Gentiles who
belong to me, says the Lord.
The Lord is the one who does these
things.' (Amos 9:11,12)
18 The Lord does things that have
been known from long ago.

19 "Now here is my decision. We should
not make it hard for the Gentiles who are
turning to God. 20 Here is what we should
write to them. They must not eat food that
has been made impure by being offered
to statues of gods. They must not commit
sexual sins. They must not eat the meat of
animals that have been choked to death.
And they must not drink blood. 21 These
laws of Moses have been preached in every city from the earliest times. They are
read out loud in the synagogues every
Sabbath day."

A Letter Is Written to Gentile Believers

22 Then the apostles, the elders and the
whole church decided what to do. They
would choose some of their own men
who were leaders among the believers.
They would send them to Antioch with
Paul and Barnabas. So they chose Judas
Barsabbas and Silas. They were leaders
among the believers. 23 Here is the letter
they sent with them.

The apostles and elders, your brothers, are writing this letter.

We are sending it to the Gentile believers in Antioch, Syria and Cilicia.

Greetings.

24 We have heard that some of our
people came to you and caused trouble. You were upset by what they
said. But we had given them no authority to go. 25 So we all agreed to
send our dear friends Barnabas and
Paul to you. We chose some other
men to go with them. 26 Barnabas
and Paul have put their lives in danger. They did it for the name of our
Lord Jesus Christ. 27 So we are sending Judas and Silas with them. What
they say will agree with this letter.
28 Here is what seemed good to the
Holy Spirit and to us. We will not
give you a load that is too heavy. So
here are a few basic rules. 29 Don't eat
food that has been offered to statues
of gods. Don't drink blood. Don't eat
the meat of animals that have been
choked to death. And don't commit
sexual sins. You will do well to keep
away from these things.

Farewell.

30 So the men were sent down to Antioch. There they gathered the church
together. They gave the letter to them.
31 The people read it. They were glad for
its message of hope. 32 Judas and Silas
were prophets. They said many things to
give strength and hope to the believers.
33-34 Judas and Silas stayed there for some
time. Then the believers sent them away
with the blessing of peace. They sent
them back to those who had sent them
out. 35 Paul and Barnabas remained in Antioch. There they and many others taught
and preached the word of the Lord.

Paul and Barnabas Do Not Agree

36 Some time later Paul spoke to Barnabas. "Let's go back to all the towns where
we preached the word of the Lord," he
said. "Let's visit the believers and see
how they are doing." 37 Barnabas wanted
to take John Mark with them. 38 But Paul
didn't think it was wise to take him. Mark
had deserted them in Pamphylia. He
hadn't continued with them in their work.
39 Barnabas and Paul strongly disagreed
with each other. So they went their separate ways. Barnabas took Mark and sailed
for Cyprus. 40 But Paul chose Silas. The
believers asked the Lord to give his grace

to Paul and Silas as they went. 41 Paul traveled through Syria and Cilicia. He gave strength to the churches there.

Timothy Joins Paul and Silas

16 Paul came to Derbe. Then he went on to Lystra. A believer named Timothy lived there. His mother was Jewish and a believer. His father was a Greek. 2 The believers at Lystra and Iconium said good things about Timothy. 3 Paul wanted to take him along on the journey. So he circumcised Timothy because of the Jews who lived in that area. They all knew that Timothy's father was a Greek. 4 Paul and his companions traveled from town to town. They reported what the apostles and elders in Jerusalem had decided. The people were supposed to obey what was in the report. 5 So the churches were made strong in the faith. The number of believers grew every day.

Paul's Vision of the Man From Macedonia

6 Paul and his companions traveled all through the area of Phrygia and Galatia. The Holy Spirit had kept them from preaching the word in Asia Minor. 7 They came to the border of Mysia. From there they tried to enter Bithynia. But the Spirit of Jesus would not let them. 8 So they passed by Mysia. Then they went down to Troas. 9 During the night Paul had a vision. He saw a man from Macedonia standing and begging him. "Come over to Macedonia!" the man said. "Help us!" 10 After Paul had seen the vision, we got ready at once to leave for Macedonia. We decided that God had called us to preach the good news there.

Lydia Becomes a Believer in Philippi

11 At Troas we got into a boat. We sailed straight for Samothrace. The next day we went on to Neapolis. 12 From there we traveled to Philippi, a Roman colony. It is an important city in that part of Macedonia. We stayed there several days.

13 On the Sabbath day we went outside the city gate. We walked down to the river. There we expected to find a place of prayer. We sat down and began to speak to the women who had gathered together. 14 One of the women listening was from the city of Thyatira. Her name was Lydia, and her business was selling purple cloth. She was a worshiper of God. The Lord opened her heart to accept Paul's message. 15 She and her family were baptized. Then she invited us to her home. "Do you consider me a believer in the Lord?" she asked. "If you do, come and stay at my house." She succeeded in getting us to go home with her.

Paul and Silas Are Thrown Into Prison

16 One day we were going to the place of prayer. On the way we were met by a female slave. She had a spirit that helped her tell people what was going to happen. She earned a lot of money for her owners by doing this. 17 She followed Paul and the rest of us around. She shouted, "These men serve the Most High God. They are telling you how to be saved." 18 She kept this up for many days. Finally Paul became upset. Turning around, he spoke to the spirit that was in her. "In the name of Jesus Christ," he said, "I command you to come out of her!" At that very moment the spirit left the woman.

19 Her owners realized that their hope of making money was gone. So they grabbed Paul and Silas. They dragged them into the market place to face the authorities. 20 They brought them to the judges. "These men are Jews," her owners said. "They are making trouble in our city. 21 They are suggesting practices that are against Roman law. These are practices we can't accept or take part in."

22 The crowd joined the attack against Paul and Silas. The judges ordered that Paul and Silas be stripped and beaten with rods. 23 They were whipped without mercy. Then they were thrown into prison. The jailer was commanded to guard them carefully. 24 When he received these orders, he put Paul and Silas deep inside the prison. He fastened their feet so they couldn't get away.

25 About midnight Paul and Silas were praying. They were also singing hymns to God. The other prisoners were listening to them. 26 Suddenly there was a powerful earthquake. It shook the prison from top to bottom. All at once the prison doors flew open. Everyone's chains came loose. 27 The jailer woke up. He saw that the prison doors were open. He pulled out his sword and was going to kill himself. He thought the prisoners had escaped.

28 “Don’t harm yourself!” Paul shouted.
“We are all here!”
29 The jailer called out for some lights.
He rushed in, shaking with fear. He fell
down in front of Paul and Silas. 30 Then he
brought them out. He asked, “Sirs, what
must I do to be saved?”
31 They replied, “Believe in the Lord
Jesus. Then you and everyone living in
your house will be saved.” 32 They spoke
the word of the Lord to him. They also
spoke to all the others in his house. 33 At
that hour of the night, the jailer took Paul
and Silas and washed their wounds. Right
away he and everyone who lived with him
were baptized. 34 The jailer brought them
into his house. He set a meal in front of
them. He and everyone who lived with
him were filled with joy. They had become believers in God.
35 Early in the morning the judges sent
their officers to the jailer. They ordered
him, “Let those men go.” 36 The jailer told
Paul, “The judges have ordered me to set
you and Silas free. You can leave now. Go
in peace.”
37 But Paul replied to the officers. “They
beat us in public,” he said. “We weren’t
given a trial. And we are Roman citizens!
They threw us into prison. And now do
they want to get rid of us quietly? No! Let
them come themselves and personally
lead us out.”
38 The officers reported this to the
judges. When the judges heard that Paul
and Silas were Roman citizens, they became afraid. 39 So they came and said
they were sorry. They led them out of the
prison. Then they asked them to leave the
city. 40 After Paul and Silas came out of the
prison, they went to Lydia’s house. There
they met with the brothers and sisters.
They told them to be brave. Then they left.

Paul and Silas Arrive in Thessalonica

17 Paul and those traveling with him
passed through Amphipolis and
Apollonia. They came to Thessalonica. A
Jewish synagogue was there. 2 Paul went
into the synagogue as he usually did. For
three Sabbath days in a row he talked
with the Jews about the Scriptures. 3 He
explained and proved that the Messiah
had to suffer and rise from the dead. “This
Jesus I am telling you about is the Messiah!” he said. 4 His words won over some
of the Jews. They joined Paul and Silas. A
large number of Greeks who worshiped
God joined them too. So did quite a few
important women.
5 But other Jews were jealous. So they
rounded up some evil people from the
market place. Forming a crowd, they
started all kinds of trouble in the city. The
Jews rushed to Jason’s house. They were
looking for Paul and Silas. They wanted
to bring them out to the crowd. 6 But they
couldn’t find them. So they dragged Jason
and some other believers to the city officials. “These men have caused trouble all
over the world,” they shouted. “Now they
have come here. 7 Jason has welcomed
them into his house. They are all disobeying Caesar’s commands. They say there is
another king. He is called Jesus.” 8 When
the crowd and the city officials heard this,
they became very upset. 9 They made Jason and the others give them money. The
officials did this to make sure they would
return to the court. Then they let Jason
and the others go.

Paul and Silas Are Sent to Berea

10 As soon as it was night, the believers
sent Paul and Silas away to Berea. When
they arrived, they went to the Jewish synagogue. 11 The Berean Jews were very glad
to receive Paul’s message. They studied
the Scriptures carefully every day. They
wanted to see if what Paul said was true.
So they were more noble than the Thessalonian Jews. 12 Because of this, many of
the Berean Jews believed. A number of
important Greek women also became believers. And so did many Greek men.
13 But the Jews in Thessalonica found
out that Paul was preaching God’s word
in Berea. So some of them went there too.
They stirred up the crowds and got them
all worked up. 14 Right away the believers
sent Paul to the coast. But Silas and Timothy stayed in Berea. 15 The believers who
went with Paul took him to Athens. Then
they returned with orders that Silas and
Timothy were supposed to join him as
soon as they could.

Paul Preaches in Athens

16 Paul was waiting for Silas and Timothy in Athens. He was very upset to see
that the city was full of statues of gods.
17 So he went to the synagogue. There he

talked both with Jews and with Greeks who worshiped God. Each day he spoke with anyone who happened to be in the market place. 18 A group of Epicurean and Stoic thinkers began to argue with him. Some of them asked, "What is this fellow chattering about?" Others said, "He seems to be telling us about gods we've never heard of." They said this because Paul was preaching the good news about Jesus. He was telling them that Jesus had risen from the dead. 19 They took him to a meeting of the Areopagus. There they said to him, "What is this new teaching you're giving us? 20 You have some strange ideas we've never heard before. We would like to know what they mean." 21 All the people of Athens spent their time talking about and listening to the latest ideas. People from other lands who lived there did the same.

22 Then Paul stood up in the meeting of the Areopagus. He said, "People of Athens! I see that you are very religious in every way. 23 As I walked around, I looked carefully at the things you worship. I even found an altar with TO AN UNKNOWN GOD written on it. So you don't know what you are worshiping. Now I am going to tell you about this 'unknown god.'

24 "He is the God who made the world. He also made everything in it. He is the Lord of heaven and earth. He doesn't live in temples built by human hands. 25 He is not served by human hands. He doesn't need anything. Instead, he himself gives life and breath to all people. He also gives them everything else they have. 26 From one man he made all the people of the world. Now they live all over the earth. He decided exactly when they should live. And he decided exactly where they should live. 27 God did this so that people would seek him. And perhaps they would reach out for him and find him. They would find him even though he is not far from any of us. 28 'In him we live and move and exist.' As some of your own poets have also said, 'We are his children.'

29 "Yes, we are God's children. So we shouldn't think that God is made out of gold or silver or stone. He isn't a statue planned and made by clever people. 30 In the past, God didn't judge people for what they didn't know. But now he commands all people everywhere to turn away from their sins. 31 He has set a day when he will judge the world fairly. He has appointed a man to be its judge. God has proved this to everyone by raising that man from the dead."

32 They heard Paul talk about the dead being raised. Some of them made fun of this idea. But others said, "We want to hear you speak about this again." 33 So Paul left the meeting of the Areopagus. 34 Some of the people became followers of Paul and believed in Jesus. Dionysius was one of them. He was a member of the Areopagus. A woman named Damaris also became a believer. And so did some others.

Paul Goes to Corinth

18 After this, Paul left Athens and went to Corinth. 2 There he met a Jew named Aquila, who was a native of Pontus. Aquila had recently come from Italy with his wife Priscilla. The emperor Claudius had ordered all Jews to leave Rome. Paul went to see Aquila and Priscilla. 3 They were tentmakers, just as he was. So he stayed and worked with them. 4 Every Sabbath day he went to the synagogue. He was trying to get both Jews and Greeks to believe in the Lord.

5 Silas and Timothy came from Macedonia. Then Paul spent all his time preaching. He was a witness to the Jews that Jesus was the Messiah. 6 But they opposed Paul. They treated him badly. So he shook out his clothes in protest. Then he said to them, "God's judgment against you will be your own fault! Don't blame me for it! From now on I will go to the Gentiles."

7 Then Paul left the synagogue and went to the house next door. It was the house of Titius Justus, a man who worshiped God. 8 Crispus was the synagogue leader. He and everyone living in his house came to believe in the Lord. Many others who lived in Corinth heard Paul. They too believed and were baptized.

9 One night the Lord spoke to Paul in a vision. "Don't be afraid," he said. "Keep on speaking. Don't be silent. 10 I am with you. No one will attack you and harm you. I have many people in this city." 11 So Paul stayed in Corinth for a year and a half. He taught them God's word.

12 At that time Gallio was governor of

Achaia. The Jews of Corinth got together and attacked Paul. They brought him into court. [13]They made a charge against Paul. They said, "This man is talking people into worshiping God in wrong ways. Those ways are against the law."

[14]Paul was about to give reasons for his actions. But just then Gallio spoke to them. He said, "You Jews don't claim that Paul has committed a great or small crime. If you did, it would make sense for me to listen to you. [15]But this is about your own law. It is a question of words and names. Settle the matter yourselves. I will not be a judge of such things." [16]So he made them leave. [17]Then the crowd there turned against Sosthenes, the synagogue leader. They beat him up in front of the governor. But Gallio didn't care at all.

Priscilla and Aquila Teach Apollos

[18]Paul stayed in Corinth for some time. Then he left the brothers and sisters and sailed for Syria. Priscilla and Aquila went with him. Before he sailed, he had his hair cut off at Cenchreae. He did this because he had made a promise to God. [19]They arrived at Ephesus. There Paul said goodbye to Priscilla and Aquila. He himself went into the synagogue and talked with the Jews. [20]The Jews asked him to spend more time with them. But he said no. [21]As he left, he made them a promise. "If God wants me to," he said, "I will come back." Then he sailed from Ephesus. [22]When he landed at Caesarea, he went up to Jerusalem. There he greeted the church. He then went down to Antioch.

[23]Paul spent some time in Antioch. Then he left and traveled all over Galatia and Phrygia. He gave strength to all the believers there.

[24]At that time a Jew named Apollos came to Ephesus. He was an educated man from Alexandria. He knew the Scriptures very well. [25]Apollos had been taught the way of the Lord. He spoke with great power. He taught the truth about Jesus. But he only knew about John's baptism. [26]He began to speak boldly in the synagogue. Priscilla and Aquila heard him. So they invited him to their home. There they gave him a better understanding of the way of God.

[27]Apollos wanted to go to Achaia. The brothers and sisters agreed with him. They wrote to the believers there. They asked them to welcome him. When he arrived, he was a great help to those who had become believers by God's grace. [28]In public meetings, he argued strongly against Jews who disagreed with him. He proved from the Scriptures that Jesus was the Messiah.

Paul Goes to Ephesus

19 While Apollos was at Corinth, Paul took the road to Ephesus. When he arrived, he found some believers there. [2]He asked them, "Did you receive the Holy Spirit when you became believers?"

"No," they answered. "We haven't even heard that there is a Holy Spirit."

[3]So Paul asked, "Then what baptism did you receive?"

"John's baptism," they replied.

[4]Paul said, "John baptized people, calling them to turn away from their sins. He told them to believe in the one who was coming after him. Jesus is that one." [5]After hearing this, they were baptized in the name of the Lord Jesus. [6]Paul placed his hands on them. Then the Holy Spirit came on them. They spoke in languages they had not known before. They also prophesied. [7]There were about 12 men in all.

[8]Paul entered the synagogue. There he spoke boldly for three months. He gave good reasons for believing the truth about God's kingdom. [9]But some of them wouldn't listen. They refused to believe. In public they said evil things about the Way of Jesus. So Paul left them. He took the believers with him. Each day he talked with people in the lecture hall of Tyrannus. [10]This went on for two years. So all the Jews and Greeks who lived in Asia Minor heard the word of the Lord.

[11]God did amazing miracles through Paul. [12]Even handkerchiefs and aprons that had touched him were taken to those who were sick. When this happened, their sicknesses were healed and evil spirits left them.

[13]Some Jews went around driving out evil spirits. They tried to use the name of the Lord Jesus to set free those who were controlled by demons. They said, "In Jesus' name I command you to come out. He is the Jesus that Paul is preaching about." [14]Seven sons of Sceva were do-

ing this. Sceva was a Jewish chief priest.
15 One day the evil spirit answered them,
"I know Jesus. And I know about Paul. But
who are you?" 16 Then the man who had
the evil spirit jumped on Sceva's sons. He
overpowered them all. He gave them a
terrible beating. They ran out of the house
naked and bleeding.

17 The Jews and Greeks living in Ephesus heard about this. They were all overcome with fear. They held the name of
the Lord Jesus in high honor. 18 Many who
believed now came and openly admitted
what they had done. 19 A number of those
who had practiced evil magic brought
their scrolls together. They set them
on fire out in the open. They added up
the value of the scrolls. The scrolls were
worth more than someone could earn
in two lifetimes. 20 The word of the Lord
spread everywhere. It became more and
more powerful.

21 After all this had happened, Paul decided to go to Jerusalem. He went through
Macedonia and Achaia. "After I have been
to Jerusalem," he said, "I must visit Rome
also." 22 He sent Timothy and Erastus,
two of his helpers, to Macedonia. But he
stayed a little longer in Asia Minor.

Trouble in Ephesus

23 At that time many people became
very upset about the Way of Jesus. 24 There
was a man named Demetrius who made
things out of silver. He made silver models
of the temple of the goddess Artemis. He
brought in a lot of business for the other
skilled workers there. 25 One day he called
them together. He also called others who
were in the same kind of business. "My
friends," he said, "you know that we make
good money from our work. 26 You have
seen and heard what this fellow Paul is
doing. He has talked to large numbers of
people here in Ephesus. Almost everywhere in Asia Minor he has led people
away from our gods. He says that the gods
made by human hands are not gods at all.
27 Our work is in danger of losing its good
name. People's faith in the temple of the
great goddess Artemis will be weakened.
Now she is worshiped all over Asia Minor
and the whole world. But soon she will be
robbed of her greatness."

28 When they heard this, they became
very angry. They began shouting, "Great
is Artemis of the Ephesians!" 29 Soon people were making trouble in the whole city.
They all rushed into the theater. They
dragged Gaius and Aristarchus along with
them. These two men had come with Paul
from Macedonia. 30 Paul wanted to appear
in front of the crowd. But the believers
wouldn't let him. 31 Some of the officials
in Asia Minor were friends of Paul. They
sent him a message, begging him not to
go into the theater.

32 The crowd didn't know what was going on. Some were shouting one thing and
some another. Most of the people didn't
even know why they were there. 33 The
Jews in the crowd pushed Alexander to
the front. They tried to tell him what to
say. But he motioned for them to be quiet.
He was about to give the people reasons
for his actions. 34 But then they realized
that he was a Jew. So they all shouted the
same thing for about two hours. "Great is
Artemis of the Ephesians!" they yelled.

35 The city clerk quieted the crowd
down. "People of Ephesus!" he said. "The
city of Ephesus guards the temple of the
great Artemis. The whole world knows
this. They know that Ephesus guards her
statue, which fell from heaven. 36 These
facts can't be questioned. So calm down.
Don't do anything foolish. 37 These men
haven't robbed any temples. They haven't
said evil things against our female god.
But you have brought them here anyhow.
38 Demetrius and the other skilled workers may feel they have been wronged by
someone. Let them bring charges. The
courts are open. We have our governors.
39 Is there anything else you want to bring
up? Settle it in a court of law. 40 As it is,
we are in danger of being charged with a
crime. We could be charged with causing
all this trouble today. There is no reason
for it. So we wouldn't be able to explain
what has happened." 41 After he said this,
he sent the people away.

Paul Travels Through Macedonia and Greece

20 All the trouble came to an end.
Then Paul sent for the believers.
After encouraging them, he said goodbye. He then left for Macedonia. 2 He traveled through that area, speaking many
words of hope to the people. Finally he
arrived in Greece. 3 There he stayed for

three months. He was just about to sail for
Syria. But some Jews were making plans
against him. So he decided to go back
through Macedonia. 4 Sopater, son of Pyr-
rhus, from Berea went with him. Aristarchus and Secundus from Thessalonica,
Gaius from Derbe, and Timothy went too.
Tychicus and Trophimus from Asia Minor
also went with him. 5 These men went on
ahead. They waited for us at Troas. 6 But
we sailed from Philippi after the Feast
of Unleavened Bread. Five days later we
joined the others at Troas. We stayed
there for seven days.

Eutychus Is Raised From the Dead at Troas

7 On the first day of the week we met to
break bread and eat together. Paul spoke
to the people. He kept on talking until
midnight because he planned to leave the
next day. 8 There were many lamps in the
room upstairs where we were meeting. 9 A
young man named Eutychus was sitting
in a window. He sank into a deep sleep as
Paul talked on and on. Sound asleep, Eutychus fell from the third floor. When they
picked him up from the ground, he was
dead. 10 Paul went down and threw himself on the young man. He put his arms
around him. "Don't be alarmed," he told
them. "He's alive!" 11 Then Paul went upstairs again. He broke bread and ate with
them. He kept on talking until daylight.
Then he left. 12 The people took the young
man home. They were greatly comforted
because he was alive.

Paul Says Goodbye to the Ephesian Elders

13 We went on ahead to the ship. We
sailed for Assos. There we were going to
take Paul on board. He had planned it this
way because he wanted to go to Assos by
land. 14 So he met us there. We took him
on board and went on to Mitylene. 15 The
next day we sailed from there. We arrived
near Chios. The day after that we crossed
over to Samos. We arrived at Miletus the
next day. 16 Paul had decided to sail past
Ephesus. He didn't want to spend time
in Asia Minor. He was in a hurry to get to
Jerusalem. If he could, he wanted to be
there by the day of Pentecost.

17 From Miletus, Paul sent for the elders
of the church at Ephesus. 18 When they arrived, he spoke to them. "You know how
I lived the whole time I was with you,"
he said. "From the first day I came into
Asia Minor, 19 I served the Lord with tears
and without pride. I served him when
I was greatly tested. I was tested by the
evil plans of the Jews who disagreed with
me. 20 You know that nothing has kept
me from preaching whatever would help
you. I have taught you in public and from
house to house. 21 I have told both Jews
and Greeks that they must turn away from
their sins to God. They must have faith in
our Lord Jesus.

22 "Now I am going to Jerusalem. The
Holy Spirit compels me. I don't know
what will happen to me there. 23 I only
know that in every city the Spirit warns
me. He tells me that I will face prison and
suffering. 24 But my life means nothing to
me. My only goal is to finish the race. I
want to complete the work the Lord Jesus
has given me. He wants me to tell others
about the good news of God's grace.

25 "I have spent time with you preaching about the kingdom. I know that none
of you will ever see me again. 26 So I tell
you today that I am not guilty if any of
you don't believe. 27 I haven't let anyone
keep me from telling you everything God
wants you to do. 28 Keep watch over yourselves. Keep watch over all the believers.
The Holy Spirit has made you leaders
over them. Be shepherds of God's church.
He bought it with his own blood. 29 I know
that after I leave, wild wolves will come in
among you. They won't spare any of the
sheep. 30 Even men from your own people
will rise up and twist the truth. They want
to get the believers to follow them. 31 So be
on your guard! Remember that for three
years I never stopped warning you. Night
and day I warned each of you with tears.

32 "Now I trust God to take care of you.
I commit you to the message about his
grace. It can build you up. Then you will
share in what God plans to give all his
people. 33 I haven't longed for anyone's
silver or gold or clothing. 34 You yourselves
know that I have used my own hands to
meet my needs. I have also met the needs
of my companions. 35 In everything I did,
I showed you that we must work hard
and help the weak. We must remember
the words of the Lord Jesus. He said, 'It is
more blessed to give than to receive.' "

36 Paul finished speaking. Then he got

down on his knees with all of them and
prayed. 37 They all wept as they hugged
and kissed him. 38 Paul had said that they
would never see him again. That's what
hurt them the most. Then they went with
him to the ship.

Paul Continues His Journey to Jerusalem

21 After we had torn ourselves away
from the Ephesian elders, we
headed out to sea. We sailed straight to
Kos. The next day we went to Rhodes.
From there we continued on to Patara.
2 We found a ship crossing over to Phoenicia. So we went on board and headed
out to sea. 3 We came near Cyprus and
passed to the south of it. Then we sailed
on to Syria. We landed at Tyre. There our
ship was supposed to unload. 4 We looked
for the believers there and stayed with
them for seven days. The believers tried
to keep Paul from going on to Jerusalem.
They were led by the Holy Spirit to do this.
5 When it was time to leave, we continued
on our way. All the believers, including
their whole families, went with us out of
the city. There on the beach we got down
on our knees to pray. 6 We said goodbye
to each other. Then we went on board the
ship. And they returned home.

7 Continuing on from Tyre, we landed
at Ptolemais. There we greeted the brothers and sisters. We stayed with them for a
day. 8 The next day we left and arrived at
Caesarea. We stayed at the house of Philip
the evangelist. He was one of the seven
deacons. 9 He had four unmarried daughters who prophesied.

10 We stayed there several days. Then a
prophet named Agabus came down from
Judea. 11 He came over to us. Then he took
Paul's belt and tied his own hands and
feet with it. He said, "The Holy Spirit says,
'This is how the Jewish leaders in Jerusalem will tie up the owner of this belt. They
will hand him over to the Gentiles.' "

12 When we heard this, we all begged
Paul not to go up to Jerusalem. 13 He
asked, "Why are you crying? Why are you
breaking my heart? I'm ready to be put
in prison. In fact, I'm ready to die in Jerusalem for the Lord Jesus." 14 We couldn't
change his mind. So we gave up. We said,
"May what the Lord wants to happen be
done."

15 After this, we started on our way to
Jerusalem. 16 Some of the believers from
Caesarea went with us. They brought us
to Mnason's home. We were supposed to
stay there. Mnason was from Cyprus. He
was one of the first believers.

Paul Arrives in Jerusalem

17 When we arrived in Jerusalem, the
brothers and sisters gave us a warm welcome. 18 The next day Paul and the rest of
us went to see James. All the elders were
there. 19 Paul greeted them. Then he reported everything God had done among
the Gentiles through his work.

20 When they heard this, they praised
God. Then they spoke to Paul. "Brother," they said, "you see that thousands of
Jews have become believers. All of them
try very hard to obey the law. 21 They have
been told that you teach Jews to turn away
from the Law of Moses. You teach this to
the Jews who live among the Gentiles.
They think that you teach those Jews not
to circumcise their children. They think
that you teach them to give up our Jewish ways. 22 What should we do? They will
certainly hear that you have come. 23 So
do what we tell you. There are four men
with us who have made a promise to God.
24 Take them with you. Join them in the
Jewish practice that makes people pure
and 'clean.' Pay their expenses so they can
have their heads shaved. Then everyone
will know that these reports about you are
not true in any way. They will know that
you yourself obey the law. 25 We have already given written directions to the believers who are not Jews. They must not
eat food that has been offered to statues
of gods. They must not drink blood. They
must not eat the meat of animals that have
been choked to death. And they must not
commit sexual sins."

26 The next day Paul took the men with
him. They all made themselves pure and
"clean" in the usual way. Then Paul went
to the temple. There he reported the date
when the days of cleansing would end.
At that time the proper offering would be
made for each of them.

Paul Is Arrested

27 The seven days of cleansing were almost over. Some Jews from Asia Minor
saw Paul at the temple. They stirred up the
whole crowd and grabbed Paul. 28 "Fellow

Israelites, help us!" they shouted. "This
is the man who teaches everyone in all
places against our people. He speaks
against our law and against this holy
place. Besides, he has brought Greeks
into the temple. He has made this holy
place 'unclean.'" 29 They said this because
they had seen Trophimus the Ephesian in
the city with Paul. They thought Paul had
brought him into the temple.

30 The whole city was stirred up. People
came running from all directions. They
grabbed Paul and dragged him out of the
temple. Right away the temple gates were
shut. 31 The people were trying to kill Paul.
But news reached the commander of the
Roman troops. He heard that people were
making trouble in the whole city of Jerusalem. 32 Right away he took some officers
and soldiers with him. They ran down to
the crowd. The people causing the trouble saw the commander and his soldiers.
So they stopped beating Paul.

33 The commander came up and arrested Paul. He ordered him to be held
with two chains. Then he asked who Paul
was and what he had done. 34 Some in the
crowd shouted one thing, some another.
But the commander couldn't get the facts
because of all the noise. So he ordered
that Paul be taken into the fort. 35 Paul
reached the steps. But then the mob became so wild that he had to be carried by
the soldiers. 36 The crowd that followed
kept shouting, "Get rid of him!"

Paul Speaks to the Crowd

37 The soldiers were about to take Paul
into the fort. Then he asked the commander, "May I say something to you?"

"Do you speak Greek?" he replied.
38 "Aren't you the Egyptian who turned
some of our people against their leaders?
Didn't you lead 4,000 terrorists out into
the desert some time ago?"

39 Paul answered, "I am a Jew from
Tarsus in Cilicia. I am a citizen of an important city. Please let me speak to the
people."

40 The commander told him he could.
So Paul stood on the steps and motioned
to the crowd. When all of them were
quiet, he spoke to them in the Aramaic
22 language. 1 "Brothers and fathers,"
Paul began, "listen to me now. I
want to give you reasons for my actions."

2 When they heard that he was speaking to them in Aramaic, they became very
quiet.

Then Paul said, 3 "I am a Jew. I was born
in Tarsus in Cilicia, but I grew up here in
Jerusalem. I studied with Gamaliel. I was
well trained by him in the law given to our
people long ago. I wanted to serve God as
much as any of you do today. 4 I hurt the
followers of the Way of Jesus. I sent many
of them to their death. I arrested men and
women. I threw them into prison. 5 The
high priest and the whole Council can be
witnesses of this themselves. I even had
some official letters they had written to
their friends in Damascus. So I went there
to bring these people as prisoners to Jerusalem to be punished.

6 "I had almost reached Damascus.
About noon a bright light from heaven
suddenly flashed around me. 7 I fell to the
ground and heard a voice speak to me.
'Saul! Saul!' it said. 'Why are you opposing me?'

8 "'Who are you, Lord?' I asked.

"'I am Jesus of Nazareth,' he replied. 'I
am the one you are opposing.' 9 The light
was seen by my companions. But they
didn't understand the voice of the one
speaking to me.

10 "'What should I do, Lord?' I asked.

"'Get up,' the Lord said. 'Go into Damascus. There you will be told everything
you have been given to do.' 11 The brightness of the light had blinded me. So my
companions led me by the hand into Damascus.

12 "A man named Ananias came to see
me. He was a godly Jew who obeyed the
law. All the Jews living there respected
him very much. 13 He stood beside me and
said, 'Brother Saul, receive your sight!' At
that very moment I was able to see him.

14 "Then he said, 'The God of our people has chosen you. He wanted to tell
you his plans for you. You have seen the
Blameless One. You have heard words
from his mouth. 15 Now you will tell everyone about what you have seen and heard.
16 So what are you waiting for? Get up and
call on his name. Be baptized. Have your
sins washed away.'

17 "I returned to Jerusalem and was
praying at the temple. Then it seemed to
me that I was dreaming. 18 I saw the Lord
speaking to me. 'Quick!' he said. 'Leave

Jerusalem at once. The people here will
not accept what you tell them about me.'
19 " 'Lord,' I replied, 'these people know
what I used to do. I went from one synagogue to another and put believers in
prison. I also beat them. 20 Stephen was
a man who told other people about you.
I stood there when he was killed. I had
agreed that he should die. I even guarded
the coats of those who were killing him.'
21 "Then the Lord said to me, 'Go. I will
send you far away to people who are not
Jews.' "

Paul the Roman Citizen

22 The crowd listened to Paul until he
said this. Then they shouted, "Kill him!
He isn't fit to live!"
23 They shouted and threw off their
coats. They threw dust into the air. 24 So
the commanding officer ordered that
Paul be taken into the fort. He gave orders for Paul to be whipped and questioned. He wanted to find out why the
people were shouting at him like this. 25 A
commander was standing there as they
stretched Paul out to be whipped. Paul
said to him, "Does the law allow you to
whip a Roman citizen who hasn't even
been found guilty?"
26 When the commander heard this, he
went to the commanding officer and reported it. "What are you going to do?" the
commander asked. "This man is a Roman
citizen."
27 So the commanding officer went to
Paul. "Tell me," he asked. "Are you a Roman citizen?"
"Yes, I am," Paul answered.
28 Then the officer said, "I had to pay a
lot of money to become a citizen."
"But I was born a citizen," Paul replied.
29 Right away those who were about to
question him left. Even the officer was
alarmed. He realized that he had put
Paul, a Roman citizen, in chains.

Paul Is Taken to the Sanhedrin

30 The commanding officer wanted to
find out exactly what the Jews had against
Paul. So the next day he let Paul out of
prison. He ordered a meeting of the chief
priests and all the members of the Sanhedrin. Then he brought Paul and had him
stand in front of them.

23 Paul looked straight at the Sanhedrin. "My brothers," he said, "I have
always done my duty to God. To this day
I feel that I have done nothing wrong."
2 Ananias the high priest heard this. So
he ordered the men standing near Paul
to hit him on the mouth. 3 Then Paul said
to him, "You pretender! God will hit you!
You sit there and judge me by the law.
But you yourself broke the law when you
commanded them to hit me!"
4 Those who were standing near Paul
spoke to him. They said, "How dare you
talk like that to God's high priest!"
5 Paul replied, "Brothers, I didn't realize
he was the high priest. It is written, 'Do
not speak evil about the ruler of your people.' " (Exodus 22:28)
6 Paul knew that some of them were
Sadducees and the others were Pharisees.
So he called out to the members of the
Sanhedrin. "My brothers," he said, "I am
a Pharisee. I come from a family of Pharisees. I believe that people will rise from
the dead. That's why I am on trial." 7 When
he said this, the Pharisees and the Sadducees started to argue. They began to take
sides. 8 The Sadducees say that people will
not rise from the dead. They don't believe
there are angels or spirits either. But the
Pharisees believe all these things.
9 People were causing trouble and making a lot of noise. Some of the teachers
of the law who were Pharisees stood up.
They argued strongly. "We find nothing
wrong with this man," they said. "What if
a spirit or an angel has spoken to him?"
10 The people arguing were getting out
of control. The commanding officer was
afraid that Paul would be torn to pieces
by them. So he ordered the soldiers to go
down and take him away from them by
force. The officer had told them to bring
Paul into the fort.
11 The next night the Lord stood near
Paul. He said, "Be brave! You have told
people about me in Jerusalem. You must
do the same in Rome."

The Plan to Kill Paul

12 The next morning some Jews gathered secretly to make plans against Paul.
They made a promise to themselves. They
promised that they would not eat or drink
anything until they killed him. 13 More
than 40 men took part in this plan. 14 They

went to the chief priests and the elders. They said, "We have made a special promise to God. We will not eat anything until we have killed Paul. 15 Now then, you and the Sanhedrin must make an appeal to the commanding officer. Ask him to bring Paul to you. Pretend you want more facts about his case. We are ready to kill him before he gets here."

16 But Paul's nephew heard about this plan. So he went into the fort and told Paul.

17 Then Paul called one of the commanders. He said to him, "Take this young man to the commanding officer. He has something to tell him." 18 So the commander took Paul's nephew to the officer.

The commander said, "Paul, the prisoner, sent for me. He asked me to bring this young man to you. The young man has something to tell you."

19 The commanding officer took the young man by the hand. He spoke to him in private. "What do you want to tell me?" the officer asked.

20 He said, "Some Jews have agreed to ask you to bring Paul to the Sanhedrin tomorrow. They will pretend they want more facts about him. 21 Don't give in to them. More than 40 of them are waiting in hiding to attack him. They have promised that they will not eat or drink anything until they have killed him. They are ready now. All they need is for you to bring Paul to the Sanhedrin."

22 The commanding officer let the young man go. But he gave him a warning. "Don't tell anyone you have reported this to me," he said.

Paul Is Taken to Caesarea

23 Then the commanding officer called for two of his commanders. He ordered them, "Gather a company of 200 soldiers, 70 horsemen and 200 men armed with spears. Get them ready to go to Caesarea at nine o'clock tonight. 24 Provide horses for Paul so that he may be taken safely to Governor Felix."

25 Here is the letter the officer wrote.

> 26 I, Claudius Lysias, am writing this letter.
>
> I am sending it to His Excellency, Governor Felix.
>
> Greetings.
>
> 27 The Jews grabbed Paul. They were about to kill him. But I came with my soldiers and saved him. I had learned that he is a Roman citizen. 28 I wanted to know why they were bringing charges against him. So I brought him to their Sanhedrin. 29 I found out that the charge against him was based on questions about their law. But there was no charge against him worthy of death or prison. 30 Then I was told about a plan against the man. So I sent him to you at once. I also ordered those bringing charges against him to present their case to you.

31 The soldiers followed their orders. During the night they took Paul with them. They brought him as far as Antipatris. 32 The next day they let the horsemen go on with him. The soldiers returned to the fort. 33 The horsemen arrived in Caesarea. They gave the letter to the governor. Then they handed Paul over to him. 34 The governor read the letter. He asked Paul where he was from. He learned that Paul was from Cilicia. 35 So he said, "I will hear your case when those bringing charges against you get here." Then he ordered that Paul be kept under guard in Herod's palace.

Paul's Trial in Front of Felix

24 Five days later Ananias the high priest went down to Caesarea. Some elders and a lawyer named Tertullus went with him. They brought their charges against Paul to the governor. 2 So Paul was called in. Tertullus began to bring the charges against Paul. He said to Felix, "We have enjoyed a long time of peace while you have been ruling. You are a wise leader. You have made this a better nation. 3 Most excellent Felix, we gladly admit this everywhere and in every way. And we are very thankful. 4 I don't want to bother you. But would you be kind enough to listen to us for a short time?

5 "We have found that Paul is a troublemaker. This man stirs up trouble among Jews all over the world. He is a leader of those who follow Jesus of Nazareth. 6-7 He even tried to make our temple impure. So we arrested him. 8 Question him your-

self. Then you will learn the truth about
all these charges we are bringing against
him."
9 The other Jews said the same thing.
They agreed that the charges were true.
10 The governor motioned for Paul to
speak. Paul said, "I know that you have
been a judge over this nation for quite a
few years. So I am glad to explain my actions to you. 11 About 12 days ago I went
up to Jerusalem to worship. You can easily
check on this. 12 Those bringing charges
against me did not find me arguing with
anyone at the temple. I wasn't stirring up
a crowd in the synagogues or anywhere
else in the city. 13 They can't prove to you
any of the charges they are making against
me. 14 It is true that I worship the God of
our people. I am a follower of the Way
of Jesus. Those bringing charges against
me call it a cult. I believe everything that
is in keeping with the Law. I believe everything that is in keeping with what is
written in the Prophets. 15 I have the same
hope in God that these men themselves
have. I believe that both the godly and the
ungodly will rise from the dead. 16 So I always try not to do anything wrong in the
eyes of God or in the eyes of people.
17 "I was away for several years. Then
I came to Jerusalem to bring my people
gifts for those who were poor. I also came
to offer sacrifices. 18 They found me doing
this in the temple courtyard. I had already
been made pure and 'clean' in the usual
way. There was no crowd with me. I didn't
stir up any trouble. 19 But there are some
other Jews who should be here in front
of you. They are from Asia Minor. They
should bring charges if they have anything against me. 20 Let the Jews who are
here tell you what crime I am guilty of. After all, I was put on trial by the Sanhedrin.
21 Perhaps they blame me for what I said
when I was on trial. I shouted, 'I believe
that people will rise from the dead. That
is why I am on trial here today.' "
22 Felix knew all about the Way of Jesus.
So he put off the trial for the time being. "Lysias the commanding officer will
come," he said. "Then I will decide your
case." 23 He ordered the commander to
keep Paul under guard. He told him to
give Paul some freedom. He also told him
to allow Paul's friends to take care of his
needs.
24 Several days later Felix came with his
wife Drusilla. She was a Jew. Felix sent
for Paul and listened to him speak about
faith in Christ Jesus. 25 Paul talked about
how to live a godly life. He talked about
how people should control themselves.
He also talked about the time when God
will judge everyone. Then Felix became
afraid. "That's enough for now!" he said.
"You may leave. When I find the time, I
will send for you." 26 He was hoping that
Paul would offer him some money to
let him go. So he often sent for Paul and
talked with him.
27 Two years passed. Porcius Festus took
the place of Felix. But Felix wanted to do
the Jews a favor. So he left Paul in prison.

Paul's Trial in Front of Festus

25 Three days after Festus arrived, he
went up from Caesarea to Jerusa-
lem. 2 There the chief priests and the Jewish leaders came to Festus. They brought
their charges against Paul. 3 They tried
very hard to get Festus to have Paul taken
to Jerusalem. They asked for this as a favor. They were planning to hide and attack Paul along the way. They wanted to
kill him. 4 Festus answered, "Paul is being
held at Caesarea. Soon I'll be going there
myself. 5 Let some of your leaders come
with me. If the man has done anything
wrong, they can bring charges against
him there."
6 Festus spent eight or ten days in Jerusalem with them. Then he went down to
Caesarea. The next day he called the court
together. He ordered Paul to be brought
to him. 7 When Paul arrived, the Jews who
had come down from Jerusalem stood
around him. They brought many strong
charges against him. But they couldn't
prove that these charges were true.
8 Then Paul spoke up for himself. He
said, "I've done nothing wrong against
the law of the Jews or against the temple.
I've done nothing wrong against Caesar."
9 But Festus wanted to do the Jews a favor. So he said to Paul, "Are you willing
to go up to Jerusalem? Are you willing to
go on trial there? Are you willing to face
these charges in my court?"
10 Paul answered, "I'm already standing
in Caesar's court. This is where I should
go on trial. I haven't done anything wrong
to the Jews. You yourself know that very

well. [11]If I am guilty of anything worthy of death, I'm willing to die. But the charges brought against me by these Jews are not true. No one has the right to hand me over to them. I make my appeal to Caesar!"

[12]Festus talked it over with the members of his court. Then he said, "You have made an appeal to Caesar. To Caesar you will go!"

Festus Talks With King Agrippa

[13]A few days later King Agrippa and Bernice arrived in Caesarea. They came to pay a visit to Festus. [14]They were spending many days there. So Festus talked with the king about Paul's case. He said, "There's a man here that Felix left as a prisoner. [15]When I went to Jerusalem, the Jewish chief priests and the elders brought charges against the man. They wanted him to be found guilty.

[16]"I told them that this is not the way Romans do things. We don't judge people before they have faced those bringing charges against them. They must have a chance to argue against the charges for themselves. [17]When the Jewish leaders came back with me, I didn't waste any time. I called the court together the next day. I ordered the man to be brought in. [18]Those bringing charges against him got up to speak. But they didn't charge him with any of the crimes I had expected. [19]Instead, they argued with him about their own beliefs. They didn't agree about a man named Jesus. They said Jesus was dead, but Paul claimed Jesus was alive. [20]I had no idea how to look into such matters. So I asked Paul if he would be willing to go to Jerusalem. There he could be tried on these charges. [21]But Paul made an appeal to have the Emperor decide his case. So I ordered him to be held until I could send him to Caesar."

[22]Then Agrippa said to Festus, "I would like to hear this man myself."

Festus replied, "Tomorrow you will hear him."

Paul in Front of Agrippa

[23]The next day Agrippa and Bernice arrived. They were treated like very important people. They entered the courtroom. The most important military officers and the leading men of the city came with them. When Festus gave the command, Paul was brought in. [24]Festus said, "King Agrippa, and everyone else here, take a good look at this man! A large number of Jews have come to me about him. They came to me in Jerusalem and also here in Caesarea. They keep shouting that he shouldn't live any longer. [25]I have found that he hasn't done anything worthy of death. But he made his appeal to the Emperor. So I decided to send him to Rome. [26]I don't have anything certain to write about him to His Majesty. So I have brought him here today. Now all of you will be able to hear him. King Agrippa, it will also be very good for you to hear him. As a result of this hearing, I will have something to write. [27]It doesn't make sense to send a prisoner on to Rome without listing the charges against him."

26 Agrippa said to Paul, "You may now present your case."

So Paul motioned with his hand. Then he began to present his case. [2]"King Agrippa," he said, "I am happy to be able to stand here today. I will answer all the charges brought against me by the Jews. [3]I am very pleased that you are familiar with Jewish ways. You know the kinds of things they argue about. So I beg you to be patient as you listen to me.

[4]"The Jewish people all know how I have lived ever since I was a child. They know all about me from the beginning of my life. They know how I lived in my own country and in Jerusalem. [5]They have known me for a long time. So if they wanted to, they could tell you how I have lived. I have lived by the rules of the Pharisees. Those rules are harder to obey than those of any other Jewish group. [6]Today I am on trial because of the hope I have. I believe in what God promised our people of long ago. [7]It is the promise that our 12 tribes are hoping to see come true. Because of this hope they serve God with faithful and honest hearts day and night. King Agrippa, it is also because of this hope that these Jews are bringing charges against me. [8]Why should any of you think it is impossible for God to raise the dead?

[9]"I believed that I should oppose the name of Jesus of Nazareth. So I did everything I could to oppose his name. [10]That's just what I was doing in Jerusalem. On the authority of the chief priests, I put many of the Lord's people in prison. I agreed

that they should die. 11 I often went from
one synagogue to another to have them
punished. I tried to force them to speak
evil things against Jesus. All I wanted to
do was hurt them. I even went looking for
them in the cities of other lands.
12 "On one of these journeys I was on
my way to Damascus. I had the authority and commission of the chief priests.
13 About noon, King Agrippa, I was on the
road. I saw a light coming from heaven. It
was brighter than the sun. It was shining
around me and my companions. 14 We all
fell to the ground. I heard a voice speak to
me in the Aramaic language. 'Saul! Saul!'
it said. 'Why are you opposing me? It is
hard for you to go against what you know
is right.'
15 "Then I asked, 'Who are you, Lord?'
" 'I am Jesus,' the Lord replied. 'I am
the one you are opposing. 16 Now get up.
Stand on your feet. I have appeared to you
to appoint you to serve me. And you must
tell other people about me. You must tell
others that you have seen me today. You
must also tell them that I will show myself
to you again. 17 I will save you from your
own people and from the Gentiles. I am
sending you to them 18 to open their eyes.
I want you to turn them from darkness to
light. I want you to turn them from Satan's
power to God. I want their sins to be forgiven. They will be forgiven when they
believe in me. They will have their place
among God's people.'
19 "So then, King Agrippa, I obeyed the
vision that appeared from heaven. 20 First
I preached to people in Damascus. Then
I preached in Jerusalem and in all Judea.
And then I preached to the Gentiles. I told
them to turn away from their sins to God.
The way they live must show that they
have turned away from their sins. 21 That's
why some Jews grabbed me in the temple
courtyard and tried to kill me. 22 But God
has helped me to this day. So I stand here
and tell you what is true. I tell it to everyone, both small and great. I have been
saying nothing different from what the
prophets and Moses said would happen.
23 They said the Messiah would suffer. He
would be the first to rise from the dead.
He would bring the message of God's
light. He would bring it to his own people
and to the Gentiles."
24 While Paul was still presenting his
case, Festus interrupted. "You are out of
your mind, Paul!" he shouted. "Your great
learning is driving you crazy!"
25 "I am not crazy, most excellent Festus," Paul replied. "What I am saying is
true and reasonable. 26 The king is familiar
with these things. So I can speak openly
to him. I am certain he knows everything
that has been going on. After all, it was not
done in secret. 27 King Agrippa, do you believe the prophets? I know you do."
28 Then Agrippa spoke to Paul. "Are you
trying to talk me into becoming a Christian?" he said. "Do you think you can do
that in such a short time?"
29 Paul replied, "I don't care if it takes a
short time or a long time. I pray to God for
you and all who are listening to me today.
I pray that you may become like me, except for these chains."
30 The king stood up. The governor and
Bernice and those sitting with them stood
up too. 31 They left the room and began to
talk with one another. "Why should this
man die or be put in prison?" they said.
"He has done nothing worthy of that!"
32 Agrippa said to Festus, "This man
could have been set free. But he has made
an appeal to Caesar."

Paul Sails for Rome

27 It was decided that we would sail
for Italy. Paul and some other prisoners were handed over to a Roman commander named Julius. He belonged to the
Imperial Guard. 2 We boarded a ship from
Adramyttium. It was about to sail for ports
along the coast of Asia Minor. We headed
out to sea. Aristarchus was with us. He
was a Macedonian from Thessalonica.
3 The next day we landed at Sidon.
There Julius was kind to Paul. He let Paul
visit his friends so they could give him
what he needed. 4 From there we headed
out to sea again. We passed the calmer
side of Cyprus because the winds were
against us. 5 We sailed across the open
sea off the coast of Cilicia and Pamphylia.
Then we landed at Myra in Lycia. 6 There
the commander found a ship from Alexandria sailing for Italy. He put us on
board. 7 We moved along slowly for many
days. We had trouble getting to Cnidus.
The wind did not let us stay on course. So
we passed the calmer side of Crete, opposite Salmone. 8 It was not easy to sail along

the coast. Then we came to a place called
Fair Havens. It was near the town of La-
sea.
9 A lot of time had passed. Sailing had
already become dangerous. By now it
was after the Day of Atonement, a day
of fasting. So Paul gave them a warning.
10 "Men," he said, "I can see that our trip is
going to be dangerous. The ship and everything in it will be lost. Our own lives
will be in danger also." 11 But the commander didn't listen to what Paul said.
Instead, he followed the advice of the
pilot and the ship's owner. 12 The harbor
wasn't a good place for ships to stay during winter. So most of the people decided
we should sail on. They hoped we would
reach Phoenix. They wanted to spend
the winter there. Phoenix was a harbor in
Crete. It faced both southwest and north-
west.

The Storm

13 A gentle south wind began to blow.
The ship's crew thought they saw their
chance to leave safely. So they pulled up
the anchor and sailed along the shore of
Crete. 14 Before very long, a wind blew
down from the island. It had the force of
a hurricane. It was called the Northeaster.
15 The ship was caught by the storm. We
could not keep it sailing into the wind.
So we gave up and were driven along by
the wind. 16 We passed the calmer side of
a small island called Cauda. We almost
lost the lifeboat that was tied to the side of
the ship. 17 So the men lifted the lifeboat
on board. Then they tied ropes under the
ship itself to hold it together. They were
afraid it would get stuck on the sandbars
of Syrtis. So they lowered the sea anchor
and let the ship be driven along. 18 We
took a very bad beating from the storm.
The next day the crew began to throw the
ship's contents overboard. 19 On the third
day, they even threw the ship's tools and
supplies overboard with their own hands.
20 The sun and stars didn't appear for
many days. The storm was terrible. So we
gave up all hope of being saved.
21 The men had not eaten for a long time.
Paul stood up in front of them. "Men," he
said, "you should have taken my advice
not to sail from Crete. Then you would
have avoided this harm and loss. 22 Now I
beg you to be brave. Not one of you will
die. Only the ship will be destroyed. 23 I
belong to God and serve him. Last night
his angel stood beside me. 24 The angel
said, 'Do not be afraid, Paul. You must go
on trial in front of Caesar. God has shown
his grace by sparing the lives of all those
sailing with you.' 25 Men, continue to be
brave. I have faith in God. It will happen
just as he told me. 26 But we must run the
ship onto the beach of some island."

The Ship Is Destroyed

27 On the 14th night the wind was
still pushing us across the Adriatic Sea.
About midnight the sailors had a feeling
that they were approaching land. 28 They
measured how deep the water was. They
found that it was 120 feet deep. A short
time later they measured the water again.
This time it was 90 feet deep. 29 They were
afraid we would crash against the rocks.
So they dropped four anchors from the
back of the ship. They prayed that daylight
would come. 30 The sailors wanted to escape from the ship. So they let the lifeboat
down into the sea. They pretended they
were going to lower some anchors from
the front of the ship. 31 But Paul spoke to
the commander and the soldiers. "These
men must stay with the ship," he said. "If
they don't, you can't be saved." 32 So the
soldiers cut the ropes that held the lifeboat. They let it drift away.
33 Just before dawn Paul tried to get
them all to eat. "For the last 14 days," he
said, "you have wondered what would
happen. You have gone without food. You
haven't eaten anything. 34 Now I am asking you to eat some food. You need it to
live. Not one of you will lose a single hair
from your head." 35 After Paul said this,
he took some bread and gave thanks to
God. He did this where they all could see
him. Then he broke it and began to eat.
36 All of them were filled with hope. So
they ate some food. 37 There were 276 of
us on board. 38 They ate as much as they
wanted. They needed to make the ship
lighter. So they threw the rest of the grain
into the sea.
39 When daylight came, they saw a bay
with a sandy beach. They didn't recognize the place. But they decided to run
the ship onto the beach if they could. 40 So
they cut the anchors loose and left them
in the sea. At the same time, they untied

the ropes that held the rudders. They
lifted the sail at the front of the ship to the
wind. Then they headed for the beach.
41 But the ship hit a sandbar. So the front
of it got stuck and wouldn't move. The
back of the ship was broken to pieces by
the pounding of the waves.

42 The soldiers planned to kill the prisoners. They wanted to keep them from
swimming away and escaping. 43 But the
commander wanted to save Paul's life.
So he kept the soldiers from carrying out
their plan. He ordered those who could
swim to jump overboard first and swim
to land. 44 The rest were supposed to get
there on boards or other pieces of the
ship. That is how everyone reached land
safely.

On Shore at Malta

28 When we were safe on shore, we
found out that the island was called
Malta. 2 The people of the island were un-
usually kind. It was raining and cold. So
they built a fire and welcomed all of us.
3 Paul gathered some sticks and put them
on the fire. A poisonous snake was driven
out by the heat. It fastened itself on Paul's
hand. 4 The people of the island saw the
snake hanging from his hand. They said
to one another, "This man must be a murderer. He escaped from the sea. But the
female god Justice won't let him live."
5 Paul shook the snake off into the fire. He
was not harmed. 6 The people expected
him to swell up. They thought he would
suddenly fall dead. They waited for a long
time. But they didn't see anything unusual happen to him. So they changed
their minds. They said he was a god.

7 Publius owned property nearby. He
was the chief official on the island. He
welcomed us to his home. For three days
he took care of us. He treated us with
kindness. 8 His father was sick in bed.
The man suffered from fever and dys-
entery. So Paul went in to see him. Paul
prayed for him. He placed his hands on
him and healed him. 9 Then the rest of the
sick people on the island came. They too
were healed. 10 The people of the island
honored us in many ways. When we were
ready to sail, they gave us the supplies we
needed.

Paul Arrives in Rome

11 After three months we headed out to
sea. We sailed in a ship from Alexandria
that had stayed at the island during the
winter. On the front of the ship the figures
of twin gods were carved. Their names
were Castor and Pollux. 12 We landed at
Syracuse and stayed there for three days.
13 From there we sailed to Rhegium. The
next day the south wind came up. The day
after that, we reached Puteoli. 14 There we
found some believers. They invited us to
spend a week with them. At last we came
to Rome. 15 The believers there had heard
we were coming. They traveled as far as
the Forum of Appius and the Three Tav-
erns to meet us. When Paul saw these
people, he thanked God for them and was
encouraged by them. 16 When we got to
Rome, Paul was allowed to live by himself. But a soldier guarded him.

Paul Preaches in Rome

17 Three days later Paul called a meeting of the local Jewish leaders. When they
came, Paul spoke to them. He said, "My
brothers, I have done nothing against our
people. I have also done nothing against
what our people of long ago practiced. But
I was arrested in Jerusalem. I was handed
over to the Romans. 18 They questioned
me. And they wanted to let me go. They
saw I wasn't guilty of any crime worthy of
death. 19 But the Jews objected, so I had to
make an appeal to Caesar. I certainly did
not mean to bring any charge against my
own people. 20 I share Israel's hope. That
is why I am held with this chain. So I have
asked to see you and talk with you."

21 They replied, "We have not received
any letters from Judea about you. None of
our people here from Judea has reported
or said anything bad about you. 22 But
we want to hear what your ideas are. We
know that people everywhere are talking
against those who believe as you do."

23 They decided to meet Paul on a certain day. At that time even more people
came to the place where he was staying.
From morning until evening, he told
them about God's kingdom. Using the
Law of Moses and the Prophets, he tried
to get them to believe in Jesus. 24 Some believed what he said, and others did not.
25 They didn't agree with one another.
They began to leave after Paul had made a

final statement. He said, "The Holy Spirit
was right when he spoke to your people
long ago. Through Isaiah the prophet the
Spirit said,

26 " 'Go to your people. Say to them,
"You will hear but never understand.
You will see but never know what
you are seeing."
27 These people's hearts have become
stubborn.
They can barely hear with their
ears.
They have closed their eyes.
Otherwise they might see with their
eyes.
They might hear with their ears.
They might understand with their
hearts.
They might turn, and then I would
heal them.' (Isaiah 6:9,10)

28-29 "Here is what I want you to know.
God has sent his salvation to the Gentiles.
And they will listen!"
30 For two whole years Paul stayed there
in a house he rented. He welcomed all
who came to see him. 31 He preached
boldly about God's kingdom. He taught
people about the Lord Jesus Christ. And
no one could keep him from teaching and
preaching about these things.

ROMANS

Paul wrote this letter to the believers who lived in Rome. He wrote them to ask for support. Paul wanted to bring the message about King Jesus to the western part of the Roman Empire. Paul's job was to tell all people that Jesus is the world's true ruler. In his message Paul shows that Jesus came from the family line of Israel's King David. Paul's message shows that God is faithful to his promise to Israel. Jesus the Messiah, or King, has come.

Paul's letter to the Romans tells how Jesus' death and resurrection saves the world. Paul presents this idea following the pattern of Israel's story. It is the pattern of being in slavery and then being brought to freedom. All humans are being held as prisoners or slaves. That's because sin and death came into the world. But Jesus came to set people free. He came to save both Jews and Gentiles from sin and death. He makes them into one new family of God. Jesus died and rose again. He broke the power of evil. Because of this the entire creation will be set free and made new.

In the second part of his letter Paul tells how many people in Israel did not believe in Jesus. But God used this to help bring life to the rest of the world. Now both Jews and Gentiles can find true life through Jesus. It is the Holy Spirit that leads the way into this new way of living. The new family that follows Jesus can live in joy and peace because of what Jesus did.

---

1 I, Paul, am writing this letter. I serve Christ Jesus. I have been appointed to be an apostle. God set me apart to tell others his good news. 2 He promised the good news long ago. He announced it through his prophets in the Holy Scriptures. 3 The good news is about God's Son. He was born into the family line of King David. 4 By the Holy Spirit, he was appointed to be the mighty Son of God. God did this by raising him from the dead. He is Jesus Christ our Lord. 5 We received grace because of what Jesus did. He made us apostles to the Gentiles. We must invite all of them to obey God by trusting in Jesus. We do this to bring glory to him. 6 You also are among those Gentiles who are appointed to belong to Jesus Christ.

7 I am sending this letter to all of you in Rome. You are loved by God and appointed to be his holy people.

May God our Father and the Lord Jesus Christ give you grace and peace.

Paul Longs to Visit Rome

8 First, I thank my God through Jesus Christ for all of you. People all over the world are talking about your faith. 9 I serve God with my whole heart. I preach the good news about his Son. God knows that I always remember you 10 in my prayers. I pray that now at last it may be God's plan to open the way for me to visit you.

11 I long to see you. I want to make you strong by giving you a gift from the Holy Spirit. 12 I want us to encourage one another in the faith we share. 13 Brothers and sisters, I want you to know that I planned many times to visit you. But until now I have been kept from coming. My work has produced results among the other Gentiles. In the same way, I want to see results among you.

14 I have a duty both to Greeks and to non-Greeks. I have a duty both to wise people and to foolish people. 15 So I really want to preach the good news also to you who live in Rome.

16 I want to preach it because I'm not ashamed of the good news. It is God's power to save everyone who believes. It is meant first for the Jews. It is meant also for the Gentiles. 17 The good news shows God's power to make people right with himself. God's power to be made right with him is given to the person who has faith. It happens by faith from beginning to end. It is written, "The one who is right with God will live by faith." (Habakkuk 2:4)

God's Anger Against Sinners

18 God shows his anger from heaven. It is against all the godless and evil things people do. They are so evil that they say no to the truth. 19 The truth about God is plain to them. God has made it plain. 20 Ever since the world was created it has been possible to see the qualities of God that are not seen. I'm talking about his

eternal power and about the fact that he is God. Those things can be seen in what he has made. So people have no excuse for what they do.

21 They knew God. But they didn't honor him as God. They didn't thank him. Their thinking became worthless. Their foolish hearts became dark. 22 They claimed to be wise. But they made fools of themselves. 23 They would rather have statues of gods than the glorious God who lives forever. Their statues of gods are made to look like people, birds, animals and reptiles.

24 So God let them go. He allowed them to do what their sinful hearts wanted to. He let them commit sexual sins. They made one another's bodies impure by what they did. 25 They chose a lie instead of the truth about God. They worshiped and served created things. They didn't worship the Creator. But he is praised forever. Amen.

26 So God let them continue to have their shameful desires. Their women committed sexual acts that were not natural. 27 In the same way, the men turned away from their natural love for women. They burned with sexual desire for each other. Men did shameful things with other men. They suffered in their bodies for all the wrong things they did.

28 They didn't think it was important to know God. So God let them continue to have evil thoughts. They did things they shouldn't do. 29 They are full of every kind of sin, evil and ungodliness. They want more than they need. They commit murder. They want what belongs to other people. They fight and cheat. They hate others. They say mean things about other people. 30 They tell lies about them. They hate God. They are rude and proud. They brag. They think of new ways to do evil. They don't obey their parents. 31 They do not understand. They can't be trusted. They are not loving and kind. 32 They know that God's commands are right. They know that those who do evil things should die. But they continue to do those very things. They also approve of others who do them.

God Judges Fairly

2 If you judge someone else, you have no excuse for it. When you judge another person, you are judging yourself. You do the same things you blame others for doing. 2 We know that when God judges those who do evil things, he judges fairly. 3 Though you are only a human being, you judge others. But you yourself do the same things. So how do you think you will escape when God judges you? 4 Do you disrespect God's great kindness and favor? Do you disrespect God when he is patient with you? Don't you realize that God's kindness is meant to turn you away from your sins?

5 But you are stubborn. In your heart you are not sorry for your sins. You are storing up anger against yourself. The day of God's anger is coming. Then his way of judging fairly will be shown. 6 God "will pay back each person in keeping with what they have done." (Psalm 62:12; Proverbs 24:12) 7 God will give eternal life to those who keep on doing good. They want glory, honor, and life that never ends. 8 But there are others who only look out for themselves. They don't accept the truth. They go astray. God will pour out his great anger on them. 9 There will be trouble and suffering for everyone who does evil. That is meant first for the Jews. It is also meant for the Gentiles. 10 But there will be glory, honor and peace for everyone who does good. That is meant first for the Jews. It is also meant for the Gentiles. 11 God treats everyone the same.

12 Some people do not know God's law when they sin. They will not be judged by the law when they die. Others do know God's law when they sin. They will be judged by the law. 13 Hearing the law does not make a person right with God. People are considered to be right with God only when they obey the law. 14 Gentiles do not have the law. Sometimes they just naturally do what the law requires. They are a law for themselves. This is true even though they don't have the law. 15 They show that what the law requires is written on their hearts. The way their minds judge them proves this fact. Sometimes their thoughts find them guilty. At other times their thoughts find them not guilty. 16 This will happen on the day God appoints Jesus Christ to judge people's secret thoughts. That's part of my good news.

The Jews and the Law

17 Suppose you call yourself a Jew. You
trust in the law. You brag that you know
God. 18 You know what God wants. You
agree with what is best because the law
teaches you. 19 You think you know so
much more than the people you teach.
You think you're helping blind people.
You think you are a light for those in the
dark. 20 You think you can make foolish
people wise. You act like you're teaching
little children. You think that the law gives
you all knowledge and truth. 21 You claim
to teach others, but you don't even teach
yourself! You preach against stealing. But
you steal! 22 You say that people should
not commit adultery. But you commit
adultery! You hate statues of gods. But
you rob temples! 23 You brag about the
law. But when you break it, you rob God
of his honor! 24 It is written, "The Gentiles
say evil things against God's name because of you." (Isaiah 52:5; Ezekiel 36:22)

25 Circumcision has value if you obey
the law. But if you break the law, it is just
as if you hadn't been circumcised. 26 And
sometimes those who aren't circumcised do what the law requires. Won't
God accept them as if they had been circumcised? 27 Many are not circumcised
physically, but they obey the law. They
will prove that you are guilty. You are
breaking the law, even though you have
the written law and are circumcised.

28 A person is not a Jew if they are a Jew
only on the outside. And circumcision
is more than just something done to the
outside of a man's body. 29 No, a person is
a Jew only if they are a Jew on the inside.
And true circumcision means that the
heart has been circumcised by the Holy
Spirit. The person whose heart has been
circumcised does more than obey the
written law. The praise that matters for
that kind of person does not come from
other people. It comes from God.

God Is Faithful

3 Is there any advantage in being a Jew?
Is there any value in being circumcised? 2 There is great value in every way!
First of all, the Jews have been given the
very words of God.

3 What if some Jews were not faithful?
Will the fact that they weren't faithful
keep God from being faithful? 4 Not at all!
God is true, even if every human being is
a liar. It is written,

"You are right when you sentence
me.
You are fair when you judge me."
(Psalm 51:4)

5 Doesn't the fact that we are wrong
prove more clearly that God is right? Then
what can we say? Can we say that God is
not fair when he brings his anger down
on us? As you can tell, I am just using human ways of thinking. 6 God is certainly
fair! If he weren't, how could he judge the
world? 7 Someone might argue, "When I
lie, it becomes clearer that God is truthful. It makes his glory shine more brightly.
Why then does he find me guilty of sin?"
8 Why not say, "Let's do evil things so that
good things will happen"? Some people
actually lie by reporting that this is what
we say. They are the ones who will rightly
be found guilty.

No One Is Right With God

9 What should we say then? Do we Jews
have any advantage? Not at all! We have
already claimed that Jews and Gentiles
are sinners. Everyone is under the power
of sin. 10 It is written,

"No one is right with God, no one at
all.
11 No one understands.
No one trusts in God.
12 All of them have turned away.
They have all become worthless.
No one does anything good,
no one at all." (Psalms 14:1–3; 53:1–3;
Ecclesiastes 7:20)
13 "Their throats are like open graves.
With their tongues they tell lies."
(Psalm 5:9)
"The words from their lips are
like the poison of a snake."
(Psalm 140:3)
14 "Their mouths are full of curses
and bitterness." (Psalm 10:7)
15 "They run quickly to commit
murder.
16 They leave a trail of harmful
actions.
17 They do not know how to live in
peace." (Isaiah 59:7,8)
18 "They don't have any respect for
God." (Psalm 36:1)

19 What the law says, it says to those who are ruled by the law. Its purpose is to shut every mouth and make the whole world accountable to God. 20 So no one will be considered right with God by obeying the law. Instead, the law makes us more aware of our sin.

Becoming Right With God by Faith

21 But now God has shown us his saving power without the help of the law. But the Law and the Prophets tell us about this. 22 We are made right with God by putting our faith in Jesus Christ. This happens to all who believe. It is no different for the Jews than for the Gentiles. 23 Everyone has sinned. No one measures up to God's glory. 24 The free gift of God's grace makes us right with him. Christ Jesus paid the price to set us free. 25 God gave Christ as a sacrifice to pay for sins through the spilling of his blood. So God forgives the sins of those who have faith. God did all this to prove that he does what is right. He is a God of mercy. So he did not punish for their sins the people who lived before Jesus lived. 26 God did all this to prove in our own time that he does what is right. He also makes right with himself those who believe in Jesus.

27 So who can brag? No one! Are people saved by the law that requires them to obey? Not at all! They are saved because of the law that requires faith. 28 We firmly believe that a person is made right with God because of their faith. They are not saved by obeying the law. 29 Or is God the God of Jews only? Isn't he also the God of Gentiles? Yes, he is their God too. 30 There is only one God. When those who are circumcised believe in him, he makes them right with himself. Suppose those who are not circumcised believe in him. Then God also will make them right with himself. 31 Does faith make the law useless? Not at all! We agree with the law.

Abraham's Faith Made Him Right With God

4 What should we say about these things? What did Abraham, the father of our people, discover about being right with God? 2 Did he become right with God because of something he did? If so, he could brag about it. But he couldn't brag to God. 3 What do we find in Scripture? It says, "Abraham believed God. God accepted Abraham's faith, and so his faith made him right with God." (Genesis 15:6)

4 When a person works, their pay is not considered a gift. It is owed to them. 5 But things are different with God. He makes ungodly people right with himself. If people trust in him, their faith is accepted even though they do not work. Their faith makes them right with God. 6 King David says the same thing. He tells us how blessed people are when God makes them right with himself. They are blessed because they don't have to do anything in return. David says,

7 "Blessed are those
  whose lawless acts are forgiven.
Blessed are those
  whose sins are taken away.
8 Blessed is the person
  whose sin the Lord never counts
    against them." (Psalm 32:1,2)

9 Is that blessing only for those who are circumcised? Or is it also for those who are not circumcised? We have been saying that God accepted Abraham's faith. So his faith made him right with God. 10 When did it happen? Was it after Abraham was circumcised, or before? It was before he was circumcised, not after! 11 He was circumcised as a sign of the covenant God had made with him. It showed that his faith had made him right with God before he was circumcised. So Abraham is the father of all believers who have not been circumcised. God accepts their faith. So their faith makes them right with him. 12 And Abraham is also the father of those who are circumcised and believe. So just being circumcised is not enough. Those who are circumcised must also follow the steps of our father Abraham. He had faith before he was circumcised.

13 Abraham and his family received a promise. God promised that Abraham would receive the world. It would not come to him because he obeyed the law. It would come because of his faith, which made him right with God. 14 Do those who depend on the law receive the promise? If they do, faith would mean nothing. God's promise would be worthless. 15 The law brings God's anger. Where there is no law, the law can't be broken.

16 The promise is based on God's grace.

The promise comes by faith. All of Abraham's children will certainly receive the promise. And it is not only for those who are ruled by the law. Those who have the same faith that Abraham had are also included. He is the father of us all. 17 It is written, "I have made you a father of many nations." (Genesis 17:5) God considers Abraham to be our father. The God that Abraham believed in gives life to the dead. Abraham's God also creates things that did not exist before.

18 When there was no reason for hope, Abraham believed because he had hope. He became the father of many nations, exactly as God had promised. God said, "That is how many children you will have." (Genesis 15:5) 19 Abraham did not become weak in his faith. He accepted the fact that he was past the time when he could have children. At that time Abraham was about 100 years old. He also realized that Sarah was too old to have children. 20 But Abraham kept believing in God's promise. He became strong in his faith. He gave glory to God. 21 He was absolutely sure that God had the power to do what he had promised. 22 That's why "God accepted Abraham because he believed. So his faith made him right with God." (Genesis 15:6) 23 The words "God accepted Abraham's faith" were written not only for Abraham. 24 They were written also for us. We believe in the God who raised Jesus our Lord from the dead. So God will accept our faith and make us right with himself. 25 Jesus was handed over to die for our sins. He was raised to life in order to make us right with God.

Peace and Hope

5 We have been made right with God because of our faith. Now we have peace with him because of our Lord Jesus Christ. 2 Through faith in Jesus we have received God's grace. In that grace we stand. We are full of joy because we expect to share in God's glory. 3 And that's not all. We are full of joy even when we suffer. We know that our suffering gives us the strength to go on. 4 The strength to go on produces character. Character produces hope. 5 And hope will never bring us shame. That's because God's love has been poured into our hearts. This happened through the Holy Spirit, who has been given to us.

6 At just the right time Christ died for ungodly people. He died for us when we had no power of our own. 7 It is unusual for anyone to die for a godly person. Maybe someone would be willing to die for a good person. 8 But here is how God has shown his love for us. While we were still sinners, Christ died for us.

9 The blood of Christ has made us right with God. So we are even more sure that Jesus will save us from God's anger. 10 Once we were God's enemies. But we have been brought back to him because his Son has died for us. Now that God has brought us back, we are even more secure. We know that we will be saved because Christ lives. 11 And that is not all. We are full of joy in God because of our Lord Jesus Christ. Because of him, God has brought us back to himself.

Death Through Adam, Life Through Christ

12 Sin entered the world because one man sinned. And death came because of sin. Everyone sinned, so death came to all people.

13 Before the law was given, sin was in the world. This is certainly true. But people are not judged for sin when there is no law. 14 Death ruled from the time of Adam to the time of Moses. Death ruled even over those who did not sin as Adam did. He broke God's command. But Adam also became a pattern of the Messiah. The Messiah was the one who was going to come.

15 God's gift can't be compared with Adam's sin. Many people died because of the sin of that one man. But it was even more sure that God's grace would also come through one man. That man is Jesus Christ. God's gift of grace was more than enough for the whole world. 16 The result of God's gift is different from the result of Adam's sin. That one sin brought God's judgment. But after many sins, God's gift made people right with him. 17 One man sinned, and death ruled over all people because of his sin. What will happen is even more sure than this. Those who receive the rich supply of God's grace will rule with Christ. They will rule in his kingdom. They have received God's gift and

have been made right with him. This will happen because of what the one man, Jesus Christ, has done.

18 So one man's sin brought guilt to all people. In the same way, one right act made people right with God. That one right act gave life to all people. 19 Many people were made sinners because one man did not obey. But one man did obey. That is why many people will be made right with God.

20 The law was given so that sin would increase. But where sin increased, God's grace increased even more. 21 Sin ruled and brought death. But grace rules in the lives of those who are right with God. The grace of God brings eternal life. That's because of what Jesus Christ our Lord has done.

Living a New Life in Christ

6 What should we say then? Should we keep on sinning so that God's grace can increase? 2 Not at all! As far as sin is concerned, we are dead. So how can we keep on sinning? 3 All of us were baptized into Christ Jesus. Don't you know that we were baptized into his death? 4 By being baptized, we were buried with Christ into his death. Christ has been raised from the dead by the Father's glory. And like Christ we also can live a new life.

5 By being baptized, we have been joined with him in a death like his. So we will certainly also be joined with him in a resurrection like his. 6 We know that what we used to be was nailed to the cross with him. That happened so our bodies that were ruled by sin would lose their power. So we are no longer slaves of sin. 7 That's because those who have died have been set free from sin.

8 We died with Christ. So we believe that we will also live with him. 9 We know that Christ was raised from the dead and will never die again. Death doesn't control him anymore. 10 When he died, he died once and for all time. He did this to break the power of sin. Now that he lives, he lives in the power of God.

11 In the same way, consider yourselves to be dead as far as sin is concerned. Now you believe in Christ Jesus. So consider yourselves to be alive as far as God is concerned. 12 So don't let sin rule your body, which is going to die. Don't obey its evil desires. 13 Don't give any part of yourself to serve sin. Don't let any part of yourself be used to do evil. Instead, give yourselves to God. You have been brought from death to life. So give every part of yourself to God to do what is right. 14 Sin will no longer control you like a master. That's because the law does not rule you. God's grace has set you free.

Slaves to Right Living

15 What should we say then? Should we sin because we are not ruled by the law but by God's grace? Not at all! 16 Don't you know that when you give yourselves to obey someone you become that person's slave? If you are slaves of sin, then you will die. But if you are slaves who obey God, then you will live a godly life. 17 You used to be slaves of sin. But thank God that with your whole heart you obeyed the teachings you were given! 18 You have been set free from sin. You have become slaves to right living.

19 Because you are human, you find this hard to understand. So I am using an everyday example to help you understand. You used to give yourselves to be slaves to unclean living. You were becoming more and more evil. Now give yourselves to be slaves to right living. Then you will become holy. 20 Once you were slaves of sin. At that time right living did not control you. 21 What benefit did you gain from doing the things you are now ashamed of? Those things lead to death! 22 You have been set free from sin. God has made you his slaves. The benefit you gain leads to holy living. And the end result is eternal life. 23 When you sin, the pay you get is death. But God gives you the gift of eternal life. That's because of what Christ Jesus our Lord has done.

An Example From Marriage

7 Brothers and sisters, I am speaking to you who know the law. Don't you know that the law has authority over someone only as long as they live? 2 For example, by law a married woman remains married as long as her husband lives. But suppose her husband dies. Then the law that joins her to him no longer applies. 3 But suppose that married woman sleeps with another man while her husband is still alive. Then she is called a woman who commits

adultery. But suppose her husband dies.
Then she is free from that law. She is not
guilty of adultery if she marries another
man.
4 My brothers and sisters, when Christ
died you also died as far as the law is concerned. Then it became possible for you
to belong to him. He was raised from the
dead. Now our lives can be useful to God.
5 The power of sin used to control us. The
law stirred up sinful desires in us. So the
things we did resulted in death. 6 But now
we have died to what used to control us.
We have been set free from the law. Now
we serve in the new way of the Holy Spirit.
We no longer serve in the old way of the
written law.

The Law and Sin

7 What should we say then? That the
law is sinful? Not at all! Yet I wouldn't
have known what sin was unless the law
had told me. The law says, "Do not want
what belongs to other people." (Exodus
20:17; Deuteronomy 5:21) If the law hadn't
said that, I would not have known what
it was like to want what belongs to others. 8 But the commandment gave sin an
opportunity. Sin caused me to want all
kinds of things that belong to others. A
person can't sin by breaking a law if that
law doesn't exist. 9 Before I knew about
the law, I was alive. But then the commandment came. Sin came to life, and I
died. 10 I found that the commandment
that was supposed to bring life actually
brought death. 11 When the commandment gave sin the opportunity, sin tricked
me. It used the commandment to put me
to death. 12 So the law is holy. The commandment also is holy and right and
good.
13 Did what is good cause me to die? Not
at all! Sin had to be recognized for what it
really is. So it used what is good to bring
about my death. Because of the commandment, sin became totally sinful.
14 We know that the law is holy. But I am
not. I have been sold to be a slave of sin.
15 I don't understand what I do. I don't do
what I want to do. Instead, I do what I hate
to do. 16 I do what I don't want to do. So I
agree that the law is good. 17 As it is, I am
no longer the one who does these things.
It is sin living in me that does them. 18 I
know there is nothing good in my desires controlled by sin. I want to do what
is good, but I can't. 19 I don't do the good
things I want to do. I keep on doing the
evil things I don't want to do. 20 I do what
I don't want to do. But I am not really the
one who is doing it. It is sin living in me
that does it.
21 Here is the law I find working in me.
When I want to do good, evil is right there
with me. 22 Deep inside me I find joy in
God's law. 23 But I see another law working in me. It fights against the law of my
mind. It makes me a prisoner of the law
of sin. That law controls me. 24 What a terrible failure I am! Who will save me from
this sin that brings death to my body?
25 I give thanks to God who saves me. He
saves me through Jesus Christ our Lord.
So in my mind I am a slave to God's
law. But sin controls my desires. So I am
a slave to the law of sin.

The Holy Spirit Gives Life

8 Those who belong to Christ Jesus are
no longer under God's judgment. 2 Because of what Christ Jesus has done, you
are free. You are now controlled by the
law of the Holy Spirit who gives you life.
The law of the Spirit frees you from the
law of sin that brings death. 3 The written
law was made weak by the power of sin.
But God did what the written law could
not do. He made his Son to be like those
who live under the power of sin. God
sent him to be an offering for sin. Jesus
suffered God's judgment against our sin.
4 Jesus does for us everything the holy
law requires. The power of sin should no
longer control the way we live. The Holy
Spirit should control the way we live.
5 So don't live under the control of sin.
If you do, you will think about what sin
wants. Live under the control of the Holy
Spirit. If you do, you will think about what
the Spirit wants. 6 The thoughts of a person ruled by sin bring death. But the mind
ruled by the Spirit brings life and peace.
7 The mind ruled by the power of sin is at
war with God. It does not obey God's law.
It can't. 8 Those who are under the power
of sin can't please God.
9 But you are not ruled by the power
of sin. Instead, the Holy Spirit rules over
you. This is true if the Spirit of God lives in
you. Anyone who does not have the Spirit
of Christ does not belong to Christ. 10 If

Christ lives in you, you will live. Though your body will die because of sin, the Spirit gives you life. The Spirit does this because you have been made right with God. [11]The Spirit of the God who raised Jesus from the dead is living in you. So the God who raised Christ from the dead will also give life to your bodies. He will do this because of his Spirit who lives in you.

[12]Brothers and sisters, we have a duty. Our duty is not to live under the power of sin. [13]If you live under the power of sin, you will die. But by the Spirit's power you can put to death the sins you commit. Then you will live.

[14]Those who are led by the Spirit of God are children of God. [15]The Spirit you received doesn't make you slaves. Otherwise you would live in fear again. Instead, the Holy Spirit you received made you God's adopted child. By the Spirit's power we call God Abba. Abba means Father. [16]The Spirit himself joins with our spirits. Together they tell us that we are God's children. [17]As his children, we will receive all that he has for us. We will share what Christ receives. But we must share in his sufferings if we want to share in his glory.

Suffering Now and Glory in the Future

[18]What we are suffering now is nothing compared with our future glory. [19]Everything God created looks forward to the future. That will be the time when his children appear in their full and final glory. [20]The created world was held back from fulfilling its purpose. But this was not the result of its own choice. It was planned that way by the one who held it back. God planned [21]to set the created world free. He didn't want it to rot away. Instead, God wanted it to have the same freedom and glory that his children have.

[22]We know that all that God created has been groaning. It is in pain as if it were giving birth to a child. The created world continues to groan even now. [23]And that's not all. We have the Holy Spirit as the promise of future blessing. But we also groan inside ourselves. We do this as we look forward to the time when God adopts as full members of his family. Then he will give us everything he has for us. He will raise our bodies and give glory to them. [24]That's the hope we had when we were saved. But hope that can be seen is no hope at all. Who hopes for what they already have? [25]We hope for what we don't have yet. So we are patient as we wait for it.

[26]In the same way, the Holy Spirit helps us when we are weak. We don't know what we should pray for. But the Spirit himself prays for us. He prays through groans too deep for words. [27]God, who looks into our hearts, knows the mind of the Spirit. And the Spirit prays for God's people just as God wants him to pray.

[28]We know that in all things God works for the good of those who love him. He appointed them to be saved in keeping with his purpose. [29]God planned that those he had chosen would become like his Son. In that way, Christ will be the first and most honored among many brothers and sisters. [30]And those God has planned for, he has also appointed to be saved. Those he has appointed, he has made right with himself. To those he has made right with himself, he has given his glory.

We Are More Than Winners

[31]What should we say then? Since God is on our side, who can be against us? [32]God did not spare his own Son. He gave him up for us all. Then won't he also freely give us everything else? [33]Who can bring any charge against God's chosen ones? God makes us right with himself. [34]Then who can sentence us to death? No one. Christ Jesus is at the right hand of God and is also praying for us. He died. More than that, he was raised to life. [35]Who can separate us from Christ's love? Can trouble or hard times or harm or hunger? Can nakedness or danger or war? [36]It is written,

> "Because of you, we face death all
> day long.
> We are considered as sheep to be
> killed." (Psalm 44:22)

[37]No! In all these things we are more than winners! We owe it all to Christ, who has loved us. [38]I am absolutely sure that not even death or life can separate us from God's love. Not even angels or demons, the present or the future, or any powers can separate us. [39]Not even the highest places or the lowest, or anything else in all creation can separate us. Nothing at all can ever separate us from God's love.

That's because of what Christ Jesus our
Lord has done.

Paul Mourns for Israel

9 I speak the truth in Christ. I am not lying. My mind tells me that what I say
is true. It is guided by the Holy Spirit. 2 My
heart is full of sorrow. My sadness never
ends. 3 I am so concerned about my people, who are members of my own race. I
am ready to be cursed, if that would help
them. I am even willing to be separated
from Christ. 4 They are the people of Israel. They have been adopted as God's
children. God's glory belongs to them. So
do the covenants. They received the law.
They were taught to worship in the temple. They were given the promises. 5 The
founders of our nation belong to them.
The Messiah comes from their family
line. He is God over all. May he always be
praised! Amen.

God's Free Choice

6 I do not mean that God's word has
failed. Not everyone in the family line of
Israel really belongs to Israel. 7 Not everyone in Abraham's family line is really his
child. Not at all! Scripture says, "Your family line will continue through Isaac." (Genesis 21:12) 8 In other words, God's children
are not just in the family line of Abraham.
Instead, they are the children God promised to him. They are the ones considered
to be Abraham's children. 9 God promised, "I will return at the appointed time.
Sarah will have a son." (Genesis 18:10,14)

10 And that's not all. Rebekah's children
were born at the same time by the same
father. He was our father Isaac. 11 Here is
what happened. Rebekah's twins had not
even been born. They hadn't done anything good or bad yet. So they show that
God's purpose is based firmly on his free
choice. 12 It was not because of anything
they did but because of God's choice. So
Rebekah was told, "The older son will
serve the younger one." (Genesis 25:23) 13 It
is written, "I chose Jacob instead of Esau."
(Malachi 1:2,3)

14 What should we say then? Is God unfair? Not at all! 15 He said to Moses,

"I will have mercy on whom I have
mercy.
I will show love to those I love."
(Exodus 33:19)

16 So it doesn't depend on what people
want or what they do. It depends on God's
mercy. 17 In Scripture, God says to Pharaoh, "I had a special reason for making
you king. I decided to use you to show
my power. I wanted my name to become
known everywhere on earth." (Exodus 9:16)
18 So God does what he wants to do. He
shows mercy to one person and makes
another stubborn.

19 One of you will say to me, "Then why
does God still blame us? Who can oppose
what he wants to do?" 20 But you are a
mere human being. So who are you to talk
back to God? Scripture says, "Can what is
made say to the one who made it, 'Why
did you make me like this?'" (Isaiah 29:16;
45:9) 21 Isn't the potter free to make different kinds of pots out of the same lump of
clay? Some are for special purposes. Others are for ordinary use.

22 What if God chose to show his great
anger? What if he chose to make his power
known? But he put up with the people he
was angry with. They were made to be destroyed. 23 What if he put up with them to
show the riches of his glory to other people? Those other people are the ones he
shows his mercy to. He made them to receive his glory. 24 We are those people. He
has chosen us. We do not come only from
the Jewish race. Many of us are not Jews.
25 God says in Hosea,

"I will call those who are not my
people 'my people.'
I will call the one who is not my
loved one 'my loved one.'"
(Hosea 2:23)

26 He also says,

"Once it was said to them,
'You are not my people.'
In that very place they will be
called 'children of the living
God.'" (Hosea 1:10)

27 Isaiah cries out concerning Israel. He
says,

"The number of people from Israel
may be like the sand by the
sea.
But only a few of them will be
saved.

28 The Lord will carry out his sentence.
He will be quick to carry it out
on earth, once and for all."
(Isaiah 10:22,23)

29 Earlier Isaiah had said,

"The Lord who rules over all
left us children and
grandchildren.
If he hadn't, we would have become
like Sodom.
We would have been like
Gomorrah." (Isaiah 1:9)

Israel Does Not Believe

30 What should we say then? Gentiles
did not look for a way to be right with
God. But they found it by having faith.
31 The people of Israel tried to obey the
law to make themselves right with God.
But they didn't reach their goal of being
right with God. 32 Why not? Because they
tried to do it without faith. They tried to
be right with God by what they did. They
tripped over the stone that causes people
to trip and fall. 33 It is written,

"Look! In Zion I am laying a stone
that causes people to trip.
It is a rock that makes them fall.
The one who believes in him
will never be put to shame."
(Isaiah 8:14; 28:16)

10 Brothers and sisters, with all my
heart I long for the people of Israel
to be saved. I pray to God for them. 2 I can
tell you for certain that they really want to
serve God. But how they are trying to do it
is not based on knowledge. 3 They didn't
know that God's power makes people
right with himself. They tried to get right
with God in their own way. They didn't
do it in God's way. 4 Christ has fulfilled everything the law was meant to do. So now
everyone who believes can be right with
God.

5 Moses writes about how the law could
help a person do what God requires.
He writes, "The person who does these
things will live by them." (Leviticus 18:5)
6 But the way to do what God requires
must begin by having faith in him. Scripture says, "Do not say in your heart, 'Who
will go up into heaven?'" (Deuteronomy
30:12) That means to go up into heaven
and bring Christ down. 7 "And do not
say, 'Who will go down into the grave?'"
(Deuteronomy 30:13) That means to bring
Christ up from the dead. 8 But what does
it say? "The message is near you. It's in
your mouth and in your heart." (Deuteronomy 30:14) This means the message about
faith that we are preaching. 9 Say with
your mouth, "Jesus is Lord." Believe in
your heart that God raised him from the
dead. Then you will be saved. 10 With your
heart you believe and are made right with
God. With your mouth you say what you
believe. And so you are saved. 11 Scripture says, "The one who believes in him
will never be put to shame." (Isaiah 28:16)
12 There is no difference between those
who are Jews and those who are not. The
same Lord is Lord of all. He richly blesses
everyone who calls on him. 13 Scripture
says, "Everyone who calls on the name of
the Lord will be saved." (Joel 2:32)

14 How can they call on him unless they
believe in him? How can they believe in
him unless they hear about him? How
can they hear about him unless someone
preaches to them? 15 And how can anyone
preach without being sent? It is written,
"How beautiful are the feet of those who
bring good news!" (Isaiah 52:7)

16 But not all the people of Israel accepted the good news. Isaiah says, "Lord,
who has believed our message?" (Isaiah
53:1) 17 So faith comes from hearing the
message. And the message that is heard
is the message about Christ. 18 But I ask,
"Didn't the people of Israel hear?" Of
course they did. It is written,

"Their voice has gone out into the
whole earth.
Their words have gone out from
one end of the world to the
other." (Psalm 19:4)

19 Again I ask, "Didn't Israel understand?"
First, Moses says,

"I will use people who are not a
nation to make you jealous.
I will use a nation that has no
understanding to make you
angry." (Deuteronomy 32:21)

20 Then Isaiah boldly speaks about what
God says. God said,

"I was found by those who were not
trying to find me.

I made myself known to those
who were not asking for me."
(Isaiah 65:1)

21 But Isaiah also speaks about what God
says concerning Israel. God said,

"All day long I have held out my
hands.
I have held them out to a stubborn
people who do not obey me."
(Isaiah 65:2)

The Israelites Who Are Faithful

11 So here is what I ask. Did God turn
his back on his people? Not at all! I
myself belong to Israel. I am one of Abraham's children. I am from the tribe of
Benjamin. 2 God didn't turn his back on
his people. After all, he chose them. Don't
you know what Scripture says about Elijah? He complained to God about Israel.
3 He said, "Lord, they have killed your
prophets. They have torn down your al-
tars. I'm the only one left. And they are
trying to kill me." (1 Kings 19:10,14) 4 How
did God answer him? God said, "I have
kept 7,000 people for myself. They have
not bowed down to Baal." (1 Kings 19:18)
5 Some are also faithful today. They have
been chosen by God's grace. 6 And if they
are chosen by grace, then they can't work
for it. If that were true, grace wouldn't be
grace anymore.
7 What should we say then? The people
of Israel did not receive what they wanted
so badly. Those Israelites who were chosen did receive it. But the rest of the people were made stubborn. 8 It is written,

"God made it hard for them to
understand.
He gave them eyes that could not
see.
He gave them ears that could not
hear.
And they are still like that today."
(Deuteronomy 29:4; Isaiah 29:10)

9 David says,

"Let their feast be a trap and a snare.
Let them trip and fall. Let them
get what's coming to them.
10 Let their eyes grow dark so they
can't see.
Let their backs be bent forever."
(Psalm 69:22,23)

Two Kinds of Olive Branches

11 Again, here is what I ask. The Israelites didn't trip and fall once and for all
time, did they? Not at all! Because Israel
sinned, the Gentiles can be saved. That
will make Israel jealous of them. 12 Israel's sin brought riches to the world. Their
loss brings riches to the Gentiles. So then
what greater riches will come when all Israel turns to God!
13 I am talking to you who are not Jews.
I am the apostle to the Gentiles. So I take
pride in the work I do for God and others. 14 I hope somehow to stir up my own
people to want what you have. Perhaps I
can save some of them. 15 When they were
not accepted, it became possible for the
whole world to be brought back to God.
So what will happen when they are accepted? It will be like life from the dead.
16 The first handful of dough that is offered
is holy. This makes all of the dough holy.
If the root is holy, so are the branches.
17 Some of the natural branches have
been broken off. You are a wild olive
branch. But you have been joined to the
tree with the other branches. Now you
enjoy the life-giving sap of the olive tree
root. 18 So don't think you are better than
the other branches. Remember, you don't
give life to the root. The root gives life to
you. 19 You will say, "Some branches were
broken off so that I could be joined to the
tree." 20 That's true. But they were broken
off because they didn't believe. You stand
only because you do believe. So don't be
proud, but tremble. 21 God didn't spare
the natural branches. He won't spare you
either.
22 Think about how kind God is! Also
think about how firm he is! He was hard
on those who stopped following him. But
he is kind to you. So you must continue to
live in his kindness. If you don't, you also
will be cut off. 23 If the people of Israel do
not continue in their unbelief, they will
again be joined to the tree. God is able
to join them to the tree again. 24 After all,
weren't you cut from a wild olive tree?
Weren't you joined to an olive tree that
was taken care of? And wasn't that the
opposite of how things should be done?
How much more easily will the natural
branches be joined to their own olive tree!

All Israel Will Be Saved

25 Brothers and sisters, here is a mystery
I want you to understand. It will keep you
from being proud. Part of Israel has refused to obey God. That will continue until the full number of Gentiles has entered
God's kingdom. 26 In this way all Israel will
be saved. It is written,

"The God who saves will come from
Mount Zion.
He will remove sin from Jacob's
family.
27 Here is my covenant with them.
I will take away their sins."
(Isaiah 59:20,21; 27:9;
Jeremiah 31:33,34)

28 As far as the good news is concerned,
the people of Israel are enemies. This is
for your good. But as far as God's choice is
concerned, the people of Israel are loved.
This is because of God's promises to the
founders of our nation. 29 God does not
take back his gifts. He does not change his
mind about those he has chosen. 30 At one
time you did not obey God. But now you
have received mercy because Israel did
not obey. 31 In the same way, Israel has not
been obeying God. But now they receive
mercy because of God's mercy to you.
32 God has found everyone guilty of not
obeying him. So now he can have mercy
on everyone.

Praise to God

33 How very rich are God's wisdom and
knowledge!
How he judges is more than we
can understand!
The way he deals with people is
more than we can know!
34 "Who can ever know what the Lord
is thinking?
Or who can ever give him advice?"
(Isaiah 40:13)
35 "Has anyone ever given anything to
God,
so that God has to pay them
back?" (Job 41:11)
36 All things come from him.
All things are directed by him.
All things are for his praise.
May God be given the glory
forever! Amen.

Living as a Holy Sacrifice to God

12
Brothers and sisters, God has shown
you his mercy. So I am asking you to
offer up your bodies to him while you are
still alive. Your bodies are a holy sacrifice
that is pleasing to God. When you offer
your bodies to God, you are worshiping
him in the right way. 2 Don't live the way
this world lives. Let your way of thinking
be completely changed. Then you will be
able to test what God wants for you. And
you will agree that what he wants is right.
His plan is good and pleasing and perfect.

Serving One Another in the Body of Christ

3 God's grace has been given to me. So
here is what I say to every one of you.
Don't think of yourself more highly than
you should. Be reasonable when you
think about yourself. Keep in mind the
faith God has given to each of you. 4 Each
of us has one body with many parts. And
the parts do not all have the same purpose. 5 So also we are many persons. But
in Christ we are one body. And each part
of the body belongs to all the other parts.
6 We all have gifts. They differ according to
the grace God has given to each of us. Do
you have the gift of prophecy? Then use
it according to the faith you have. 7 If your
gift is serving, then serve. If it is teaching, then teach. 8 Is it encouraging others?
Then encourage them. Is it giving to others? Then give freely. Is it being a leader?
Then work hard at it. Is it showing mercy?
Then do it cheerfully.

Love in Action

9 Love must be honest and true. Hate
what is evil. Hold on to what is good.
10 Love one another deeply. Honor others more than yourselves. 11 Stay excited
about your faith as you serve the Lord.
12 When you hope, be joyful. When you
suffer, be patient. When you pray, be
faithful. 13 Share with the Lord's people
who are in need. Welcome others into
your homes.

14 Bless those who hurt you. Bless them,
and do not curse them. 15 Be joyful with
those who are joyful. Be sad with those
who are sad. 16 Agree with one another.
Don't be proud. Be willing to be a friend
of people who aren't considered important. Don't think that you are better than
others.

17 Don't pay back evil with evil. Be careful to do what everyone thinks is right.
18 If possible, live in peace with everyone.
Do that as much as you can. 19 My dear
friends, don't try to get even. Leave room
for God to show his anger. It is written, "I
am the God who judges people. I will pay
them back," (Deuteronomy 32:35) says the
Lord. 20 Do just the opposite. Scripture
says,

"If your enemies are hungry, give
them food to eat.
If they are thirsty, give them
something to drink.
By doing those things, you will pile
up burning coals on their
heads." (Proverbs 25:21,22)

21 Don't let evil overcome you. Overcome
evil by doing good.

Obey Those in Authority

13 All of you must obey those who rule
over you. There are no authorities
except the ones God has chosen. Those
who now rule have been chosen by God.
2 So whoever opposes the authorities opposes leaders whom God has appointed.
Those who do that will be judged. 3 If you
do what is right, you won't need to be
afraid of your rulers. But watch out if you
do what is wrong! You don't want to be
afraid of those in authority, do you? Then
do what is right, and you will be praised.
4 The one in authority serves God for your
good. But if you do wrong, watch out!
Rulers don't carry a sword for no reason
at all. They serve God. And God is carrying out his anger through them. The
ruler punishes anyone who does wrong.
5 You must obey the authorities. Then you
will not be punished. You must also obey
them because you know it is right.

6 That's also why you pay taxes. The authorities serve God. Ruling takes up all
their time. 7 Give to everyone what you
owe them. Do you owe taxes? Then pay
them. Do you owe anything else to the
government? Then pay it. Do you owe respect? Then give it. Do you owe honor?
Then show it.

Love Fulfills the Law

8 Pay everything you owe. But you can
never pay back all the love you owe one
another. Whoever loves other people has
done everything the law requires. 9 Here
are some commandments to think about.
"Do not commit adultery." "Do not commit murder." "Do not steal." "Do not want
what belongs to others." (Exodus 20:13-
15,17; Deuteronomy 5:17-19,21) These and
all other commands are included in one
command. Here's what it is. "Love your
neighbor as you love yourself." (Leviticus
19:18) 10 Love does not harm its neighbor.
So love does everything the law requires.

The Day Is Near

11 When you do these things, keep in
mind the times we are living in. The hour
has already come for you to wake up from
your sleep. The full effects of our salvation
are closer now than when we first believed
in Christ. 12 The dark night of evil is nearly
over. The day of Christ's return is almost
here. So let us get rid of the works of darkness that harm us. Let us do the works
of light that protect us. 13 Let us act as we
should, like people living in the daytime.
Have nothing to do with wild parties, and
don't get drunk. Don't take part in sexual
sins or evil conduct. Don't fight with each
other or be jealous of anyone. 14 Instead,
put on the Lord Jesus Christ as if he were
your clothing. Don't think about how to
satisfy sinful desires.

The Weak and the Strong

14 Accept the person whose faith is
weak. Don't argue with them where
you have differences of opinion. 2 One
person's faith allows them to eat anything. But another person eats only veg-
etables because their faith is weak. 3 The
person who eats everything must not
look down on the one who does not. And
the one who doesn't eat everything must
not judge the person who does. That's
because God has accepted them. 4 Who
are you to judge someone else's servant?
Whether they are faithful or not is their
own master's concern. And they will be
faithful, because the Lord has the power
to make them faithful.

5 One person considers one day to be
more holy than another. Another person thinks all days are the same. Each of
them should be absolutely sure in their
own mind. 6 Whoever thinks that one
day is special does so to honor the Lord.
Whoever eats meat does so to honor the

Lord. They give thanks to God. And whoever doesn't eat meat does so to honor
the Lord. They also give thanks to God.
[7]We don't live for ourselves only. And we
don't die for ourselves only. [8]If we live, we
live to honor the Lord. If we die, we die to
honor the Lord. So whether we live or die,
we belong to the Lord. [9]Christ died and
came back to life. He did this to become
the Lord of both the dead and the living.

[10]Now then, who are you to judge your
brother or sister? Why do you act like
you're better than they are? We will all
stand in God's courtroom to be judged.
[11]It is written,

> " 'You can be sure that I live,' says the
> Lord.
> 'And you can be just as sure that
> everyone will kneel down in
> front of me.
> Every tongue will have to tell
> the truth about God.' "
> (Isaiah 45:23)

[12]So we will all have to explain to God the
things we have done.

[13]Let us stop judging one another. Instead, decide not to put anything in the
way of a brother or sister. Don't put anything in their way that would make them
trip and fall. [14]I am absolutely sure that
nothing is "unclean" in itself. The Lord
Jesus has convinced me of this. But someone may consider a thing to be "unclean."
If they do, it is "unclean" for them. [15]Your
brother or sister may be upset by what
you eat. If they are, you are no longer acting as though you love them. So don't destroy them by what you eat. Remember
that Christ died for them. [16]So suppose
you know something is good. Then don't
let it be spoken of as if it were evil. [17]God's
kingdom is not about eating or drinking.
It is about doing what is right and having peace and joy. All this comes through
the Holy Spirit. [18]Those who serve Christ
in this way are pleasing to God. They are
pleasing to people too.

[19]So let us do all we can to live in
peace. And let us work hard to build up
one another. [20]Don't destroy the work of
God because of food. All food is "clean."
But it's wrong to eat anything that might
cause problems for someone else's faith.
[21]Don't eat meat if it causes your brother or sister to sin. Don't drink wine or do
anything else that will make them sin.

[22]Whatever you believe about these
things, keep between yourself and God.
Blessed is the person who doesn't feel
guilty for what they do. [23]But whoever
has doubts about what they eat is guilty
if they eat. That's because their eating is
not based on faith. Everything that is not
based on faith is sin.

15 We who have strong faith should
help the weak with their problems.
We should not please only ourselves.
[2]Each of us should please our neighbors. Let us do what is good for them in
order to build them up. [3]Even Christ did
not please himself. It is written, "The bad
things people have said about you have
been aimed at me also." (Psalm 69:9) [4]Ev-
erything written in the past was written to
teach us. The Scriptures give us strength
to go on. They encourage us and give us
hope.

[5]Our God is a God who strengthens
and encourages you. May he give you the
same attitude toward one another that
Christ Jesus had. [6]Then you can give glory
to God with one mind and voice. He is the
God and Father of our Lord Jesus Christ.

[7]Christ has accepted you. So accept
one another in order to bring praise to
God. [8]I tell you that Christ has become
a servant of the Jews. He teaches us that
God is true. He shows us that God will
keep the promises he made to the founders of our nation. [9]Jesus became a servant
of the Jews. He did this so that the Gentiles might give glory to God for his mercy.
It is written,

> "I will praise you among the
> Gentiles.
> I will sing the praises of your
> name." (2 Samuel 22:50;
> Psalm 18:49)

[10]Again it says,

> "You Gentiles, be full of joy.
> Be joyful together with God's
> people." (Deuteronomy 32:43)

[11]And again it says,

> "All you Gentiles, praise the Lord.
> Let all the nations sing praises to
> him." (Psalm 117:1)

[12]And Isaiah says,

"The Root of Jesse will grow up
quickly.
He will rule over the nations.
The Gentiles will put their hope in
him." (Isaiah 11:10)

13 May the God who gives hope fill
you with great joy. May you have perfect
peace as you trust in him. May the power
of the Holy Spirit fill you with hope.

Paul Serves the Gentiles

14 My brothers and sisters, I am sure
that you are full of goodness. You are filled
with knowledge and able to teach one
another. 15 But I have written to you very
boldly about some things. I wanted to remind you of them again. The grace of God
has allowed me 16 to serve Christ Jesus
among the Gentiles. I have the duty of a
priest to preach God's good news. Then
the Gentiles will become an offering that
pleases God. The Holy Spirit will make
the offering holy.

17 Because I belong to Christ Jesus, I
can take pride in my work for God. 18 I will
speak about what Christ has done through
me. I won't try to speak about anything
else. He has been leading the Gentiles to
obey God. He has been doing this by what
I have said and done. 19 He has given me
power to do signs and wonders. I can do
these things by the power of the Spirit of
God. From Jerusalem all the way around
to Illyricum I have finished preaching. In
those places, I preached the good news
about Christ. 20 I have always wanted to
preach the good news where Christ was
not known. I don't want to build on what
someone else has started. 21 It is written,

"Those who were not told about him
will understand.
Those who have not heard will
know what it all means."
(Isaiah 52:15)

22 That's why I have often been kept from
coming to you.

Paul Plans to Visit Rome

23 Now there is no more place for me
to work in those areas. For many years
I have wanted to visit you. 24 So I plan to
see you when I go to Spain. I hope to visit
you while I am passing through. And I
hope you will help me on my journey
there. But first I want to enjoy being with
you for a while. 25 Now I am on my way
to Jerusalem to serve the Lord's people
there. 26 The believers in Macedonia and
Achaia were pleased to take an offering.
It was for those who were poor among the
Lord's people in Jerusalem. 27 They were
happy to do it. And of course they owe it
to them. The Gentiles have shared in the
Jews' spiritual blessings. So the Gentiles
should share their earthly blessings with
the Jews. 28 I want to finish my task. I want
to make sure that the poor in Jerusalem
have received this offering. Then I will go
to Spain. On my way I will visit you. 29 I
know that when I come to you, I will come
with the full blessing of Christ.

30 Brothers and sisters, I ask you to join
me in my struggle. Join me by praying
to God for me. I ask this through the authority of our Lord Jesus Christ. Pray for
me with the love the Holy Spirit provides.
31 Pray that I will be kept safe from those
in Judea who do not believe. I am taking
the offering to Jerusalem. Pray that it will
be welcomed by the Lord's people there.
32 Then I will come to you with joy just as
God has planned. We will be renewed by
being together. 33 May the God who gives
peace be with you all. Amen.

Personal Greetings

16 I would like you to welcome our sister Phoebe. She is a deacon of the
church in Cenchreae. 2 I ask you to receive
her as one who belongs to the Lord. Receive her in the way God's people should.
Give her any help she may need from you.
She has been a great help to many people,
including me.

3 Greet Priscilla and Aquila. They work
together with me in serving Christ Jesus.
4 They have put their lives in danger for
me. I am thankful for them. So are all the
Gentile churches.

5 Greet also the church that meets in the
house of Priscilla and Aquila.

Greet my dear friend Epenetus. He was
the first person in Asia Minor to become a
believer in Christ.

6 Greet Mary. She worked very hard for
you.

7 Greet Andronicus and Junia, my fellow Jews. They have been in prison with
me. They are leaders among the apostles.
They became believers in Christ before I
did.

8 Greet Ampliatus, my dear friend in the Lord.

9 Greet Urbanus. He works together with me in serving Christ. And greet my dear friend Stachys.

10 Greet Apelles. He remained faithful to Christ even when he was tested.

Greet those who live in the house of Aristobulus.

11 Greet Herodion, my fellow Jew.

Greet the believers who live in the house of Narcissus.

12 Greet Tryphena and Tryphosa. Those women work hard for the Lord.

Greet my dear friend Persis. She is another woman who has worked very hard for the Lord.

13 Greet Rufus. He is a chosen believer in the Lord. And greet his mother. She has been like a mother to me too.

14 Greet Asyncritus, Phlegon and Hermes. Greet Patrobas, Hermas and the other brothers and sisters with them.

15 Greet Philologus, Julia, Nereus and his sister. Greet Olympas and all of the Lord's people who are with them.

16 Greet one another with a holy kiss.

All the churches of Christ send their greetings.

17 I am warning you, brothers and sisters, to watch out for those who try to keep you from staying together. They want to trip you up. They teach you things opposite to what you have learned. Stay away from them. 18 People like that are not serving Christ our Lord. They are serving only themselves. With smooth talk and with words they don't mean they fool people who don't know any better. 19 Everyone has heard that you obey God. So you have filled me with joy. I want you to be wise about what is good. And I want you to have nothing to do with what is evil. 20 The God who gives peace will soon crush Satan under your feet.

May the grace of our Lord Jesus be with you.

21 Timothy works together with me. He sends his greetings to you. So do Lucius, Jason and Sosipater, my fellow Jews.

22 I, Tertius, wrote down this letter. I greet you as a believer in the Lord.

23-24 Gaius sends you his greetings. He has welcomed me and the whole church here into his house.

Erastus is the director of public works here in the city. He sends you his greetings. Our brother Quartus also greets you.

25 May God receive glory. He is able to strengthen your faith. He does this in keeping with the good news and the message I preach. It is the message about Jesus Christ. This message is in keeping with the mystery hidden for a very long time. 26 The mystery has now been made known through the writings of the prophets. The eternal God commanded that it be made known. God wanted all the Gentiles to obey him by trusting in him. 27 May the only wise God receive glory forever through Jesus Christ. Amen.

1 CORINTHIANS

The book of Acts tells us how Paul preached the good news about Jesus the Messiah in northern Greece. But Paul had to leave that area quickly because it wasn't safe. So he went to Achaia which is an area in southern Greece. Paul went to the city of Corinth where he would be safe. Corinth was a center for trade and business. It was a very wealthy city. While he was there, Paul began preaching the good news about Jesus. Many people became believers. So Paul stayed for one and a half years to teach them.

After he left, the people of Corinth wrote Paul a letter. We do not have that letter now. But we do know some of the questions that were in it. The people of Corinth had accepted a common Greek idea that physical things are bad. They thought that only things of the spirit or soul were good. They wanted to free the human spirit from the body. This idea affected the way the people of Corinth thought and behaved. It affected the way they thought about marriage. It affected how they thought about taking part in special meals offered to false gods. It even affected the way they thought about the resurrection of Jesus. Paul speaks about all of these things in his first letter to the Corinthians. Paul also answers questions about the true worship of God.

Paul tells the people of Corinth that this form of the world is passing away. He tells them to spend their time working for the Lord. Paul tells them that a new world is coming. They will rise from the dead. All this will make their work for the Lord worthwhile.

Paul's advice to the people of Corinth is also helpful for us. Paul's words can be used to guide us. They are useful as we daily seek to follow Jesus today.

---

1 I, Paul, am writing this letter. I have
been chosen to be an apostle of Christ
Jesus just as God planned. Our brother
Sosthenes joins me in writing.

2 We are sending this letter to you, the
members of God's church in Corinth. You
have been made holy because you belong
to Christ Jesus. God has chosen you to be
his holy people. He has done the same for
all people everywhere who pray to our Lord
Jesus Christ. Jesus is their Lord and ours.

3 May God our Father and the Lord
Jesus Christ give you grace and peace.

Paul Gives Thanks

4 I always thank my God for you. I thank
him because of the grace he has given
to you who belong to Christ Jesus. 5 You
have been blessed in every way because
of him. You have been blessed in all your
speech and knowledge. 6 God has shown
that what we have spoken to you about
Christ is true. 7 There is no gift of the Holy
Spirit that you don't have. You are full of
hope as you wait for our Lord Jesus Christ
to come again. 8 God will also keep you
strong in faith to the very end. Then you
will be without blame on the day our Lord
Jesus Christ returns. 9 God is faithful. He
has chosen you to share life with his Son,
Jesus Christ our Lord.

Taking Sides in the Church

10 Brothers and sisters, I make my appeal
to you. I do this in the name of our Lord
Jesus Christ. I ask that all of you agree with
one another in what you say. I ask that you
don't take sides. I ask that you are in complete agreement in all that you think. 11 My
brothers and sisters, I have been told you
are arguing with one another. Some people from Chloe's house have told me this.
12 Here is what I mean. One of you says, "I
follow Paul." Another says, "I follow Apollos." Another says, "I follow Peter." And still
another says, "I follow Christ."

13 Does Christ take sides? Did Paul die
on the cross for you? Were you baptized
in the name of Paul? 14 I thank God that I
didn't baptize any of you except Crispus
and Gaius. 15 No one can say that you were
baptized in my name. 16 It's true that I also
baptized those who live in the house of
Stephanas. Besides that, I don't remember if I baptized anyone else. 17 Christ did
not send me to baptize. He sent me to
preach the good news. He commanded
me not to preach with wisdom and fancy
words. That would take all the power
away from the cross of Christ.

Christ Is God's Power and Wisdom

18 The message of the cross seems foolish to those who are lost and dying. But it
is God's power to us who are being saved.
19 It is written,

"I will destroy the wisdom of those
who are wise.
I will do away with the cleverness
of those who think they are so
smart." (Isaiah 29:14)

20 Where is the wise person? Where is
the teacher of the law? Where are the great
thinkers of our time? Hasn't God made
the wisdom of the world foolish? 21 God
wisely planned that the world would not
know him through its own wisdom. It
pleased God to use the foolish things we
preach to save those who believe. 22 Jews
require signs. Greeks look for wisdom.
23 But we preach about Christ and his
death on the cross. That is very hard for
Jews to accept. And everyone else thinks
it's foolish. 24 But there are those God has
chosen, both Jews and Greeks. To them
Christ is God's power and God's wisdom.
25 The foolish things of God are wiser than
human wisdom. The weakness of God is
stronger than human strength.

26 Brothers and sisters, think of what
you were when God chose you. Not many
of you were considered wise by human
standards. Not many of you were powerful. Not many of you belonged to important families. 27 But God chose the foolish
things of the world to shame the wise.
God chose the weak things of the world to
shame the strong. 28 God chose the things
of this world that are common and looked
down on. God chose things considered
unimportant to do away with things considered important. 29 So no one can boast
to God. 30 Because of what God has done,
you belong to Christ Jesus. He has become God's wisdom for us. He makes us
right with God. He makes us holy and
sets us free. 31 It is written, "The one who
boasts should boast about what the Lord
has done." (Jeremiah 9:24)

2 And this was the way it was with me,
brothers and sisters. When I came to
you, I didn't come with fancy words or
human wisdom. I preached to you the
truth about God's love. 2 My goal while I
was with you was to talk about only one
thing. And that was Jesus Christ and his
death on the cross. 3 When I came to you,
I was weak and very afraid and trembling
all over. 4 I didn't preach my message with
clever and compelling words. Instead,
my preaching showed the Holy Spirit's
power. 5 This was so that your faith would
be based on God's power. Your faith
would not be based on human wisdom.

God's Wisdom Through the Holy Spirit

6 The words we speak to those who have
grown in the faith are wise. Our words are
different from the wisdom of this world.
Our words are different from those of the
rulers of this world. These rulers are becoming less and less powerful. 7 No, we
announce God's wisdom. His wisdom is a
mystery that has been hidden. But before
time began, God planned that his wisdom
would bring us heavenly glory. 8 None of
the rulers of this world understood God's
wisdom. If they had, they would not have
nailed the Lord of glory to the cross. 9 It is
written that

"no eye has seen,
no ear has heard,
and no human mind has known."
(Isaiah 64:4)
God has prepared these things for
those who love him.

10 God has shown these things to us
through his Spirit.

The Spirit understands all things. He
understands even the deep things of
God. 11 Who can know the thoughts of another person? Only a person's own spirit
can know them. In the same way, only
the Spirit of God knows God's thoughts.
12 What we have received is not the spirit
of the world. We have received the Spirit
who is from God. The Spirit helps us understand what God has freely given us.
13 That is what we speak about. We don't
use words taught to us by people. We use
words taught to us by the Holy Spirit. We
use the words taught by the Spirit to explain spiritual truths. 14 The person without the Spirit doesn't accept the things
that come from the Spirit of God. These
things are foolish to them. They can't understand them. In fact, such things can't
be understood without the Spirit's help.
15 The person who has the Spirit can judge
all things. But no human being can judge
those who have the Spirit. It is written,

16 "Who can ever know what is in the
Lord's mind?
Can anyone ever teach him?"
(Isaiah 40:13)

But we have the mind of Christ.

The Church and Its Leaders

3 Brothers and sisters, I couldn't speak
to you as people who live by the Holy
Spirit. I had to speak to you as people who
were still following the ways of the world.
You aren't growing as Christ wants you
to. You are still like babies. 2 The words I
spoke to you were like milk, not like solid
food. You weren't ready for solid food
yet. And you still aren't ready for it. 3 You
are still following the ways of the world.
Some of you are jealous. Some of you argue. So aren't you following the ways of
the world? Aren't you acting like ordinary
human beings? 4 One of you says, "I follow
Paul." Another says, "I follow Apollos."
Aren't you acting like ordinary human
beings?

5 After all, what is Apollos? And what is
Paul? We are only people who serve. We
helped you to believe. The Lord has given
each of us our own work to do. 6 I planted
the seed. Apollos watered it. But God has
been making it grow. 7 So the one who
plants is not important. The one who waters is not important. It is God who makes
things grow. He is the important one.
8 The one who plants and the one who waters have the same purpose. The Lord will
give each of them a reward for their work.
9 We work together to serve God. You are
like God's field. You are like his building.

10 God has given me the grace to lay a
foundation as a wise builder. Now someone else is building on it. But each one
should build carefully. 11 No one can lay
any other foundation than what has already been laid. That foundation is Jesus
Christ. 12 A person may build on it using
gold, silver, jewels, wood, hay or straw.
13 But each person's work will be shown
for what it is. On judgment day it will be
brought to light. It will be put through fire.
The fire will test how good each person's
work is. 14 If the building doesn't burn
up, God will give the builder a reward for
the work. 15 If the building burns up, the
builder will lose everything. The builder
will be saved, but only like one escaping
through the flames.

16 Don't you know that you yourselves
are God's temple? Don't you know that
God's Spirit lives among you? 17 If anyone
destroys God's temple, God will destroy
that person. God's temple is holy. And
you all together are that temple.

18 Don't fool yourselves. Suppose some
of you think you are wise by the standards
of the world. Then you should become
"fools" so that you can become wise.
19 The wisdom of this world is foolish in
God's eyes. It is written, "God catches
wise people in their own evil plans." (Job
5:13) 20 It is also written, "The Lord knows
that the thoughts of wise people don't
amount to anything." (Psalm 94:11) 21 So
no more bragging about human leaders!
All things are yours. 22 That means Paul
or Apollos or Peter or the world or life or
death or the present or the future. All are
yours. 23 You are joined to Christ and belong to him. And Christ is joined to God.

True Apostles of Christ

4 So here is how you should think of us.
We serve Christ. We are trusted with
the mysteries God has shown us. 2 Those
who have been given a trust must prove
that they are faithful. 3 I care very little
if I am judged by you or by any human
court. I don't even judge myself. 4 I don't
feel I have done anything wrong. But that
doesn't mean I'm not guilty. The Lord
judges me. 5 So don't judge anything before the appointed time. Wait until the
Lord returns. He will bring to light what is
hidden in the dark. He will show the real
reasons why people do what they do. At
that time each person will receive their
praise from God.

6 Brothers and sisters, I have used myself and Apollos as examples to help
you. You can learn from us the meaning
of the saying, "Don't go beyond what is
written." Then you won't be proud that
you follow one of us instead of the other.
7 Who makes you different from anyone
else? What do you have that you did not
receive? And if you did receive it, why do
you brag as though you did not?

8 You already have everything you want,
don't you? Have you already become
rich? Have you already begun to rule?
And did you do that without us? I wish
that you really had begun to rule. Then we
could also rule with you! 9 It seems to me
that God has put us apostles on display
at the end of a parade. We are like people sentenced to die in front of a crowd.
We have been made a show for the whole
creation to see. Angels and people are
staring at us. 10 We are fools for Christ. But

you are so wise in Christ! We are weak. But you are so strong! You are honored. But we are looked down on! [11]Up to this very hour we are hungry and thirsty. We are dressed in rags. We are being treated badly. We have no homes. [12]We work hard with our own hands. When others curse us, we bless them. When we are attacked, we put up with it. [13]When others say bad things about us, we answer with kind words. We have become the world's garbage. We are everybody's trash, right up to this moment.

Paul Warns Against Pride

[14]I am not writing this to shame you. You are my dear children, and I want to warn you. [15]Suppose you had 10,000 believers in Christ watching over you. You still wouldn't have many fathers. I became your father by serving Christ Jesus and telling you the good news. [16]So I'm asking you to follow my example. [17]That's the reason I have sent Timothy to you. He is like a son to me, and I love him. He is faithful in serving the Lord. He will remind you of my way of life in serving Christ Jesus. And that agrees with what I teach everywhere in every church.

[18]Some of you have become proud. You act as if I weren't coming to you. [19]But I will come very soon, if that's what the Lord wants. Then I will find out how those proud people are talking. I will also find out what power they have. [20]The kingdom of God is not a matter of talk. It is a matter of power. [21]Which do you want? Should I come to you to correct and punish you? Or should I come in love and with a gentle spirit?

Throw Out the Evil Person!

5 It is actually reported that there is sexual sin among you. I'm told that a man is sleeping with his father's wife. Even people who don't know God don't let that kind of sin continue. [2]And you are proud! Shouldn't you be very sad instead? Shouldn't you have thrown out of your church the man doing this? [3]Even though I am not right there with you, I am with you in spirit. And because I am with you in spirit, I have already judged the man doing this. I have judged him in the name of our Lord Jesus. [4]So when you come together, I will be with you in spirit. The power of our Lord Jesus will also be with you. [5]When you come together like this, hand this man over to Satan. Then the power of sin in his life will be destroyed. His spirit will be saved on the day the Lord returns.

[6]Your bragging is not good. It is like yeast. Don't you know that just a little yeast makes the whole batch of dough rise? [7]Get rid of the old yeast. Then you can be like a new batch of dough without yeast. That is what you really are. That's because Christ, our Passover Lamb, has been offered up for us. [8]So let us keep the Feast, but not with the old bread made with yeast. The yeast I'm talking about is hatred and evil. Let us keep the Feast with bread made without yeast. Let us keep it with bread that is honesty and truth.

[9]I wrote a letter to you to tell you to stay away from people who commit sexual sins. [10]I didn't mean the people of this world who sin in this way. I didn't mean those who always want more and more. I didn't mean those who cheat or who worship statues of gods. In that case you would have to leave this world! [11]But here is what I am writing to you now. You must stay away from anyone who claims to be a believer but does evil things. Stay away from anyone who commits sexual sins. Stay away from anyone who always wants more and more things. Stay away from anyone who worships statues of gods. Stay away from anyone who tells lies about others. Stay away from anyone who gets drunk or who cheats. Don't even eat with people like these.

[12]Is it my business to judge those outside the church? Aren't you supposed to judge those inside the church? [13]God will judge those outside. Scripture says, "Get rid of that evil person!" (Deuteronomy 17:7; 19:19; 21:21; 22:21,24; 24:7)

Do Not Take Believers to Court

6 Suppose one of you wants to bring a charge against another believer. Should you take it to ungodly people to be judged? Why not take it to the Lord's people? [2]Or don't you know that the Lord's people will judge the world? Since this is true, aren't you able to judge small cases? [3]Don't you know that we will judge angels? Then we should be able to judge the things of this life even more! [4]So suppose

you disagree with one another in matters like this. Who do you ask to decide which of you is right? Do you ask people who live in a way the church disapproves of? Of course not! [5]I say this to shame you. Is it possible that no one among you is wise enough to judge matters between believers? [6]Instead, one believer goes to court against another. And this happens in front of unbelievers!

[7]When you take another believer to court, you have lost the battle already. Why not be treated wrongly? Why not be cheated? [8]Instead, you yourselves cheat and do wrong. And you do it to your brothers and sisters. [9]Don't you know that people who do wrong will not receive God's kingdom? Don't be fooled. Those who commit sexual sins will not receive the kingdom. Neither will those who worship statues of gods or commit adultery. Neither will men who sleep with other men. [10]Neither will thieves or those who always want more and more. Neither will those who are often drunk or tell lies or cheat. People who live like that will not receive God's kingdom. [11]Some of you used to do those things. But your sins were washed away. You were made holy. You were made right with God. All of this was done in the name of the Lord Jesus Christ. It was also done by the Spirit of our God.

Sexual Sins

[12]Some of you say, "I have the right to do anything." But not everything is helpful. Again some of you say, "I have the right to do anything." But I will not be controlled by anything. [13]Some of you say, "Food is for the stomach, and the stomach is for food. And God will destroy both of them." But the body is not meant for sexual sins. The body is meant for the Lord. And the Lord is meant for the body. [14]By his power God raised the Lord from the dead. He will also raise us up. [15]Don't you know that your bodies belong to the body of Christ? Should I take what belongs to Christ and join it to a prostitute? Never! [16]When you join yourself to a prostitute, you become one with her in body. Don't you know this? Scripture says, "The two will become one." (Genesis 2:24) [17]But whoever is joined to the Lord becomes one with him in spirit.

[18]Keep far away from sexual sins. All the other sins a person commits are outside the body. But sexual sins are sins against their own body. [19]Don't you know that your bodies are temples of the Holy Spirit? The Spirit is in you, and you have received the Spirit from God. You do not belong to yourselves. [20]Christ has paid the price for you. So use your bodies in a way that honors God.

Advice for Those Who Are Married

7 Now I want to deal with the things you wrote me about. Some of you say, "It is good for a man not to sleep with a woman." [2]But since sexual sin is happening, each man should sleep with his own wife. And each woman should sleep with her own husband. [3]A husband should satisfy his wife's needs. And a wife should satisfy her husband's needs. [4]The wife's body does not belong only to her. It also belongs to her husband. In the same way, the husband's body does not belong only to him. It also belongs to his wife. [5]You shouldn't stop giving yourselves to each other. You might possibly do this when you both agree to it. And you should only agree to it to give yourselves time to pray. Then you should come together again. In that way, Satan will not tempt you when you can't control yourselves. [6]I say those things to you as my advice, not as a command. [7]I wish all of you were single like me. But you each have your own gift from God. One has this gift, and another has that one.

[8]I speak now to those who are not married. I also speak to widows. It is good for you to stay single like me. [9]But if you can't control yourselves, you should get married. It is better to get married than to burn with desire.

[10]I give a command to those who are married. It is a direct command from the Lord, not from me. A wife must not leave her husband. [11]But if she does, she must not get married again. Or she can go back to her husband. And a husband must not divorce his wife.

[12]I also have something to say to everyone else. It is from me, not a direct command from the Lord. Suppose a brother has a wife who is not a believer. If she is willing to live with him, he must not divorce her. [13]And suppose a woman has

a husband who is not a believer. If he is willing to live with her, she must not divorce him. [14]The unbelieving husband has been made holy through his wife. The unbelieving wife has been made holy through her believing husband. If that were not the case, your children would not be pure and "clean." But as it is, they are holy.

[15]But if the unbeliever leaves, let that person go. In that case, the believer does not have to stay married to the unbeliever. God wants us to live in peace. [16]Wife, how do you know if you will save your husband? Husband, how do you know if you will save your wife?

Stay as You Were When God Chose You

[17]But each believer should live in whatever situation the Lord has given them. Stay as you were when God chose you. That's the rule all the churches must follow. [18]Was a man already circumcised when God chose him? Then he should not become uncircumcised. Was he uncircumcised when God chose him? Then he should not be circumcised. [19]Being circumcised means nothing. Being uncircumcised means nothing. Doing what God commands is what counts. [20]Each of you should stay as you were when God chose you.

[21]Were you a slave when God chose you? Don't let it trouble you. But if you can get your master to set you free, do it. [22]The person who was a slave when the Lord chose them is now the Lord's free person. The one who was free when God chose them is now a slave of Christ. [23]Christ has paid the price for you. Don't become slaves of human beings. [24]Brothers and sisters, each person is accountable to God. So each person should stay as they were when God chose them.

Advice for Those Who Are Not Married

[25]Now I want to say something about virgins. I have no direct command from the Lord. But I give my opinion. Because of the Lord's mercy, I give it as one who can be trusted. [26]Times are hard for you right now. So I think it's good for a man to stay as he is. [27]Are you engaged to a woman? Then don't try to get out of it. Are you free from such a promise? Then don't look for a wife. [28]But if you do marry someone, you have not sinned. And if a virgin marries someone, she has not sinned. But those who marry someone will have many troubles in this life. I want to save you from this.

[29]Brothers and sisters, what I mean is that the time is short. From now on, those who have a husband or wife should live as if they did not. [30]Those who mourn should live as if they did not. Those who are happy should live as if they were not. Those who buy something should live as if it were not theirs to keep. [31]Those who use the things of the world should not become all wrapped up in them. The world as it now exists is passing away.

[32]I don't want you to have anything to worry about. A single man is concerned about the Lord's matters. He wants to know how he can please the Lord. [33]But a married man is concerned about the matters of this world. He wants to know how he can please his wife. [34]His concerns pull him in two directions. A single woman or a virgin is concerned about the Lord's matters. She wants to serve the Lord with both body and spirit. But a married woman is concerned about the matters of this world. She wants to know how she can please her husband. [35]I'm saying those things for your own good. I'm not trying to hold you back. I want you to be free to live in a way that is right. I want you to give yourselves completely to the Lord.

[36]Suppose someone is worried that he is not acting with honor toward the virgin he has promised to marry. Suppose his desires are too strong, and he feels that he should marry her. He should do as he wants. He is not sinning. They should get married. [37]But suppose the man has decided not to marry the virgin. And suppose he has no compelling need to get married and can control himself. If he has made up his mind not to get married, he also does the right thing. [38]So then, the man who marries the virgin does the right thing. But the man who doesn't marry her does a better thing.

[39]A woman has to stay married to her husband as long as he lives. If he dies, she is free to marry anyone she wants to. But the one she marries must belong to the Lord. [40]In my opinion, she is happier if she stays single. And I also think that I am led by the Spirit of God in saying this.

Food Sacrificed to Statues of Gods

8 Now I want to deal with food sacrificed to statues of gods. We know that "We all have knowledge." But knowledge makes people proud, while love builds them up. 2 Those who think they know something still don't know as they should. 3 But whoever loves God is known by God.

4 So then, here is what I say about eating food sacrificed to statues of gods. We know that "a god made by human hands is really nothing at all in the world." We know that "there is only one God." 5 There may be so-called gods either in heaven or on earth. In fact, there are many "gods" and many "lords." 6 But for us there is only one God. He is the Father. All things came from him, and we live for him. And there is only one Lord. He is Jesus Christ. All things came because of him, and we live because of him.

7 But not everyone knows this. Some people still think that statues of gods are real gods. They might eat food sacrificed to statues of gods. When they do, they think of it as food sacrificed to real gods. And because those people have a weak sense of what is right and wrong, they feel guilty. 8 But food doesn't bring us close to God. We are no worse if we don't eat. We are no better if we do eat.

9 But be careful how you use your rights. Be sure you don't cause someone weaker than you to fall into sin. 10 Suppose you, with all your knowledge, are eating in a temple of one of those gods. And suppose someone who has a weak sense of what is right and wrong sees you. Won't that person become bold and eat what is sacrificed to statues of gods? 11 If so, then your knowledge destroys that weak brother or sister for whom Christ died. 12 Suppose you sin against them in this way. Then you harm their weak sense of what is right and wrong. By doing this, you sin against Christ. 13 So suppose what I eat causes my brother or sister to fall into sin. Then what should I do? I will never eat meat again. In that way, I will not cause them to fall.

Paul's Rights as an Apostle

9 Am I not free? Am I not an apostle? Haven't I seen Jesus our Lord? Aren't you the result of my work for the Lord? 2 Others may not think of me as an apostle. But I am certainly one to you! You are the proof that I am the Lord's apostle.

3 That is what I say to stand up for myself when people judge me. 4 Don't we have the right to eat and drink? 5 Don't we have the right to take a believing wife with us when we travel? The other apostles do. The Lord's brothers do. Peter does. 6 Or are Barnabas and I the only ones who have to do other work for a living? Are we the only ones who can't just do the work of apostles all the time?

7 Who serves as a soldier but doesn't get paid? Who plants a vineyard but doesn't eat any of its grapes? Who takes care of a flock but doesn't drink any of the milk? 8 Do I say this only on human authority? The Law says the same thing. 9 Here is what is written in the Law of Moses. "Do not stop an ox from eating while it helps separate the grain from the straw." (Deuteronomy 25:4) Is it oxen that God is concerned about? 10 Doesn't he say that for us? Yes, it was written for us. Whoever plows and separates the grain hopes to share the harvest. And it is right for them to hope for this. 11 We have planted spiritual seed among you. Is it too much to ask that we receive from you some things we need? 12 Others have the right to receive help from you. Don't we have even more right to do so?

But we didn't use that right. No, we have put up with everything. We didn't want to keep the good news of Christ from spreading.

13 People who serve in the temple get their food from the temple. Don't you know this? People who serve at the altar eat from what is offered on the altar. Don't you know this? 14 So those who preach the good news should also receive their living from their work. That is what the Lord has commanded.

15 But I haven't used any of those rights. And I'm not writing because I hope you will do things like that for me. I would rather die than allow anyone to take away my pride in my work. 16 But when I preach the good news, I can't brag. I have to preach it. How terrible it will be for me if I do not preach the good news! 17 If I preach because I want to, I get a reward. If I preach because I have to, I'm only doing my duty. 18 Then what reward do I get? Here is what it is. I am able to preach the

good news free of charge. And I can do this without using all my rights as a person who preaches the good news.

Paul Uses His Freedom to Share the Good News

[19] I am free and don't belong to anyone. But I have made myself a slave to everyone. I do it to win as many as I can to Christ. [20] To the Jews I became like a Jew. That was to win the Jews. To those under the law I became like one who was under the law. I did this even though I myself am not under the law. That was to win those under the law. [21] To those who don't have the law I became like one who doesn't have the law. I did this even though I am not free from God's law. I am under Christ's law. Now I can win those who don't have the law. [22] To those who are weak I became weak. That was to win the weak. I have become all things to all people. I have done this so that in all possible ways I might save some. [23] I do all this because of the good news. And I want to share in its blessings.

Training to Win the Prize

[24] In a race all the runners run. But only one gets the prize. You know that, don't you? So run in a way that will get you the prize. [25] All who take part in the games train hard. They do it to get a crown that will not last. But we do it to get a crown that will last forever. [26] So I do not run like someone who doesn't run toward the finish line. I do not fight like a boxer who hits nothing but air. [27] No, I train my body and bring it under control. Then after I have preached to others, I myself will not break the rules. If I did break them, I would fail to win the prize.

Warnings From Israel's History

10 Brothers and sisters, I want you to know something about our people who lived long ago. They were all led by the cloud. They all walked through the Red Sea. [2] They were all baptized into Moses in the cloud and in the sea. [3] They all ate the same spiritual food. [4] They all drank the same spiritual water. They drank from the spiritual rock that went with them. That rock was Christ. [5] But God was not pleased with most of them. Their bodies were scattered in the desert.

[6] Now those things happened as examples for us. They are supposed to keep us from wanting evil things. The people of Israel wanted these evil things. [7] So don't worship statues of gods, as some of them did. It is written, "The people sat down to eat and drink. Then they got up to dance wildly in front of their god." (Exodus 32:6) [8] We should not commit sexual sins, as some of them did. In one day 23,000 of them died. [9] We should not test the Messiah, as some of them did. They were killed by snakes. [10] Don't speak against God. That's what some of the people of Israel did. And they were killed by the destroying angel.

[11] Those things happened to them as examples for us. They were written down to warn us. That's because we are living at the time when God's work is being completed. [12] So be careful. When you think you are standing firm, you might fall. [13] You are tempted in the same way all other human beings are. God is faithful. He will not let you be tempted any more than you can take. But when you are tempted, God will give you a way out. Then you will be able to deal with it.

Sharing in the Lord's Supper

[14] My dear friends, run away from statues of gods. Don't worship them. [15] I'm talking to people who are reasonable. Judge for yourselves what I say. [16] We give thanks for the cup at the Lord's Supper. When we do, aren't we sharing in the blood of Christ? When we break the bread, aren't we sharing in the body of Christ? [17] Just as there is one loaf, so we who are many are one body. We all share the one loaf.

[18] Think about the people of Israel. Don't those who eat the offerings share in the altar? [19] Do I mean that food sacrificed to a statue of a god is anything? Do I mean that a statue of a god is anything? [20] No! But what is sacrificed by those who worship statues of gods is really sacrificed to demons. It is not sacrificed to God. I don't want you to be sharing with demons. [21] You can't drink the cup of the Lord and the cup of demons too. You can't have a part in both the Lord's table and the table of demons. [22] Are we trying to make the Lord jealous? Are we stronger than he is?

The Believer's Freedom

23 You say, "I have the right to do anything." But not everything is helpful.
Again you say, "I have the right to do anything." But not everything builds us up.
24 No one should look out for their own interests. Instead, they should look out for
the interests of others.

25 Eat anything sold in the meat market.
Don't ask if it's right or wrong. 26 Scripture
says, "The earth belongs to the Lord. And
so does everything in it." (Psalm 24:1)

27 Suppose an unbeliever invites you to
a meal and you want to go. Then eat anything that is put in front of you. Don't ask
if it's right or wrong. 28 But suppose someone says to you, "This food has been sacrificed to a statue of a god." Then don't eat
it. Keep in mind the good of the person
who told you. And don't eat because of
a sense of what is right and wrong. 29 I'm
talking about the other person's sense of
what is right and wrong, not yours. Why is
my freedom being judged by what someone else thinks? 30 Suppose I give thanks
when I eat. Then why should I be blamed
for eating food I thank God for?

31 So eat and drink and do everything
else for the glory of God. 32 Don't do anything that causes another person to trip
and fall. It doesn't matter if that person
is a Jew or a Greek or a member of God's
church. 33 Follow my example. I try to
please everyone in every way. I'm not
looking out for what is good for me. I'm
looking out for the interests of others. I do
11 it so that they might be saved. 1 Follow my example, just as I follow the
example of Christ.

Proper Worship

2 I praise you for being faithful in remembering me. I also praise you for staying true to the teachings of the past. You
have stayed true to them, just as I gave
them to you. 3 But I want you to know
that the head of every man is Christ. The
head of the woman is the man. And the
head of Christ is God. 4 Every man who
prays or prophesies with his head covered brings shame on his head. 5 But every woman who prays or prophesies with
her head uncovered brings shame on her
head. It is the same as having her head
shaved. 6 What if a woman does not cover
her head? She might as well have her hair
cut off. But it is shameful for her to cut
her hair or shave her head. So she should
cover her head.

7 A man should not cover his head. He
is the likeness and glory of God. But woman is the glory of man. 8 Man did not come
from woman. Woman came from man.
9 Also, man was not created for woman.
Woman was created for man. 10 That's why
a woman should have authority over her
own head. She should have this because
of the angels. 11 But here is how things are
for those who belong to the Lord. Woman is not independent of man. And man
is not independent of woman. 12 Woman
came from man, and man is born from
woman. But everything comes from God.

13 You be the judge. Is it proper for a
woman to pray to God without covering
her head? 14 Suppose a man has long hair.
Doesn't the very nature of things teach
you that it is shameful? 15 And suppose
a woman has long hair. Doesn't the very
nature of things teach you that it is her
glory? Long hair is given to her as a covering. 16 If anyone wants to argue about this,
we don't have any other practice. And
God's churches don't either.

Celebrating the Lord's Supper in the Right Way

17 In the following matters, I don't
praise you. Your meetings do more harm
than good. 18 First, here is what people are
telling me. When you come together as a
church, you take sides. And in some ways
I believe it. 19 Do you really think you need
to take sides? You probably think God fa-
vors one side over the other! 20 So when
you come together, it is not the Lord's
Supper you eat. 21 As you eat, some of you
go ahead and eat your own private meals.
Because of this, one person stays hungry
and another gets drunk. 22 Don't you have
homes to eat and drink in? You are sham-
ing those in the church who have nothing.
Do you think so little of God's church that
you do this? What should I say to you?
Should I praise you? Certainly not about
the Lord's Supper!

23 I passed on to you what I received
from the Lord. On the night the Lord Jesus
was handed over to his enemies, he took
bread. 24 When he had given thanks, he
broke it. He said, "This is my body. It is
given for you. Every time you eat it, do it

in memory of me." [25]In the same way, after supper he took the cup. He said, "This cup is the new covenant in my blood. Every time you drink it, do it in memory of me." [26]You eat the bread and drink the cup. When you do this, you are announcing the Lord's death until he comes again.

[27]Eat the bread or drink the cup of the Lord in the right way. Don't do it in a way that isn't worthy of him. If you do, you will be guilty. You'll be guilty of sinning against the body and blood of the Lord. [28]Everyone should take a careful look at themselves before they eat the bread and drink from the cup. [29]Whoever eats and drinks must recognize the body of Christ. If they don't, judgment will come upon them. [30]That is why many of you are weak and sick. That is why a number of you have died. [31]We should think more carefully about what we are doing. Then we would not be found guilty for this. [32]When the Lord judges us in this way, he corrects us. Then in the end we will not be judged along with the rest of the world.

[33]My brothers and sisters, when you come together to eat, you should all eat together. [34]Anyone who is hungry should eat something at home. Then when you come together, you will not be judged.

When I come, I will give you more directions.

Gifts of the Holy Spirit

12 Brothers and sisters, I want you to know about the gifts of the Holy Spirit. [2]You know that at one time you were unbelievers. You were somehow drawn away to worship statues of gods that couldn't even speak. [3]So I want you to know that no one who is speaking with the help of God's Spirit says, "May Jesus be cursed." And without the help of the Holy Spirit no one can say, "Jesus is Lord."

[4]There are different kinds of gifts. But they are all given to believers by the same Spirit. [5]There are different ways to serve. But they all come from the same Lord. [6]There are different ways the Spirit works. But the same God is working in all these ways and in all people.

[7]The Holy Spirit is given to each of us in a special way. That is for the good of all. [8]To some people the Spirit gives a message of wisdom. To others the same Spirit gives a message of knowledge. [9]To others the same Spirit gives faith. To others that one Spirit gives gifts of healing. [10]To others he gives the power to do miracles. To others he gives the ability to prophesy. To others he gives the ability to tell the spirits apart. To others he gives the ability to speak in different kinds of languages they had not known before. And to still others he gives the ability to explain what was said in those languages. [11]All the gifts are produced by one and the same Spirit. He gives gifts to each person, just as he decides.

One Body but Many Parts

[12]There is one body, but it has many parts. But all its many parts make up one body. It is the same with Christ. [13]We were all baptized by one Holy Spirit. And so we are formed into one body. It didn't matter whether we were Jews or Gentiles, slaves or free people. We were all given the same Spirit to drink. [14]So the body is not made up of just one part. It has many parts.

[15]Suppose the foot says, "I am not a hand. So I don't belong to the body." By saying this, it cannot stop being part of the body. [16]And suppose the ear says, "I am not an eye. So I don't belong to the body." By saying this, it cannot stop being part of the body. [17]If the whole body were an eye, how could it hear? If the whole body were an ear, how could it smell? [18]God has placed each part in the body just as he wanted it to be. [19]If all the parts were the same, how could there be a body? [20]As it is, there are many parts. But there is only one body.

[21]The eye can't say to the hand, "I don't need you!" The head can't say to the feet, "I don't need you!" [22]In fact, it is just the opposite. The parts of the body that seem to be weaker are the ones we can't do without. [23]The parts that we think are less important we treat with special honor. The private parts aren't shown. But they are treated with special care. [24]The parts that can be shown don't need special care. But God has put together all the parts of the body. And he has given more honor to the parts that didn't have any. [25]In that way, the parts of the body will not take sides. All of them will take care of one another. [26]If one part suffers, every part suffers with it. If one part is honored, every part shares in its joy.

[27]You are the body of Christ. Each one of you is a part of it. [28]First, God has placed apostles in the church. Second, he has placed prophets in the church. Third, he has placed teachers in the church. Then he has given to the church miracles and gifts of healing. He also has given the gift of helping others and the gift of guiding the church. God also has given the gift of speaking in different kinds of languages. [29]Is everyone an apostle? Is everyone a prophet? Is everyone a teacher? Do all work miracles? [30]Do all have gifts of healing? Do all speak in languages they had not known before? Do all explain what is said in those languages? [31]But above all, you should want the more important gifts.

Love Is Necessary

But now I will show you the best way of all.

13 Suppose I speak in the languages of human beings or of angels. If I don't have love, I am only a loud gong or a noisy cymbal. [2]Suppose I have the gift of prophecy. Suppose I can understand all the secret things of God and know everything about him. And suppose I have enough faith to move mountains. If I don't have love, I am nothing at all. [3]Suppose I give everything I have to poor people. And suppose I give myself over to a difficult life so I can brag. If I don't have love, I get nothing at all.

[4]Love is patient. Love is kind. It does not want what belongs to others. It does not brag. It is not proud. [5]It does not dishonor other people. It does not look out for its own interests. It does not easily become angry. It does not keep track of other people's wrongs. [6]Love is not happy with evil. But it is full of joy when the truth is spoken. [7]It always protects. It always trusts. It always hopes. It never gives up.

[8]Love never fails. But prophecy will pass away. Speaking in languages that had not been known before will end. And knowledge will pass away. [9]What we know now is not complete. What we prophesy now is not perfect. [10]But when what is complete comes, the things that are not complete will pass away. [11]When I was a child, I talked like a child. I thought like a child. I had the understanding of a child. When I became a man, I put the ways of childhood behind me. [12]Now we see only a dim likeness of things. It is as if we were seeing them in a foggy mirror. But someday we will see clearly. We will see face to face. What I know now is not complete. But someday I will know completely, just as God knows me completely.

[13]The three most important things to have are faith, hope and love. But the greatest of them is love.

Worship in a Way That Helps People Understand

14 Follow the way of love. You should also want the gifts the Holy Spirit gives. Most of all, you should want the gift of prophecy. [2]Anyone who speaks in a language they had not known before doesn't speak to people. They speak only to God. In fact, no one understands them. What they say by the Spirit remains a mystery. [3]But the person who prophesies speaks to people. That person prophesies to make people stronger, to give them hope, and to comfort them. [4]Anyone who speaks in other languages builds up only themselves. But the person who prophesies builds up the church. [5]I would like all of you to speak in other languages. But I would rather have you prophesy. The person who prophesies is more helpful than those who speak in other languages. But that is not the case if someone explains what was said in the other languages. Then the whole church can be built up.

[6]Brothers and sisters, suppose I were to come to you and speak in other languages. What good would I be to you? None! I would need to come with new truth or knowledge. Or I would need to come with a prophecy or a teaching. [7]Here are some examples. Certain objects make sounds. Take a flute or a harp. No one will know what the tune is unless different notes are played. [8]Also, if the trumpet call isn't clear, who will get ready for battle? [9]It's the same with you. You must speak words that people understand. If you don't, no one will know what you are saying. You will just be speaking into the air. [10]It is true that there are all kinds of languages in the world. And they all have meaning. [11]But if I don't understand what someone is saying, I am a stranger to the person speaking. And that person is a stranger to me. [12]It's the same with you. You want the gifts of the Spirit. So try to

do your best in using gifts that build up
the church.
13 So here is what the person who
speaks in languages they had not known
before should do. They should pray that
they can explain what they say. 14 If I pray
in another language, my spirit prays. But
my mind does not pray. 15 So what should
I do? I will pray with my spirit. But I will
also pray with my understanding. I will
sing with my spirit. But I will also sing
with my understanding. 16 Suppose you
are praising God in the Spirit. And suppose there are visitors among you who
want to know what's going on. How can
they say "Amen" when you give thanks?
They don't know what you are saying.
17 You are certainly giving thanks. But no
one else is being built up.
18 I thank God that I speak in other languages more than all of you do. 19 In the
church, I wouldn't want to speak 10,000
words in an unfamiliar language. I'd
rather speak five words in a language
people could understand. Then I would
be teaching others.
20 Brothers and sisters, stop thinking
like children. Be like babies as far as evil
is concerned. But be grown up in your
thinking. 21 In the law it is written,

"With unfamiliar languages
and through the lips of outsiders
I will speak to these people.
But even then they will not listen
to me." (Isaiah 28:11,12)
That is what the Lord says.

22 So speaking in other languages is a
sign for those who don't believe. It is not a
sign for those who do believe. But prophecy is not for those who don't believe. It
is for those who believe. 23 Suppose the
whole church comes together and everyone speaks in other languages. And
suppose visitors or unbelievers come in.
Won't they say you are out of your minds?
24 But suppose unbelievers or visitors
come in while everyone is prophesying.
Then they will feel guilty about their sin.
They will be judged by all. 25 The secrets
of their hearts will be brought out into the
open. They will fall down and worship
God. They will exclaim, "God is really
here among you!"

Proper Worship

26 Brothers and sisters, what should
we say then? When you come together,
each of you brings something. You bring
a hymn or a teaching or a message from
God. You bring a message in another language or explain what was said in that
language. Everything must be done to
build up the church. 27 No more than two
or three people should speak in another
language. And they should speak one at
a time. Then someone must explain what
was said. 28 If there is no one to explain,
the person speaking should keep quiet in
the church. They can speak to themselves
and to God.
29 Only two or three prophets are supposed to speak. Others should decide
if what is being said is true. 30 What if a
message from God comes to someone
else who is sitting there? Then the one
who is speaking should stop. 31 Those
who prophesy can all take turns. In that
way, everyone can be taught and be given
hope. 32 Those who prophesy should control their speaking. 33 God is not a God of
disorder. He is a God of peace, just as in
all the churches of the Lord's people.
34 Women should remain silent in
church meetings. They are not allowed to
speak. They must follow the lead of those
who are in authority, as the law says. 35 If
they have a question about something,
they should ask their own husbands at
home. It is shameful for women to speak
in church meetings.
36 Or did the word of God begin with
you? Or are you the only people it has
reached? 37 Suppose anyone thinks they
are a prophet. Or suppose they think they
have other gifts given by the Holy Spirit.
They should agree that what I am writing
to you is the Lord's command. 38 But anyone who does not recognize this will not
be recognized.
39 Brothers and sisters, you should
want to prophesy. And don't stop people
from speaking in languages they had not
known before. 40 But everything should be
done in a proper and orderly way.

Christ Rose From the Dead

15 Brothers and sisters, I want to remind you of the good news I
preached to you. You received it and
have put your faith in it. 2 Because you

believed the good news, you are saved.
But you must hold firmly to the message
I preached to you. If you don't, you have
believed it for nothing.
3 What I received I passed on to you.
And it is the most important of all. Here
is what it is. Christ died for our sins, just
as Scripture said he would. 4 He was buried. He was raised from the dead on the
third day, just as Scripture said he would
be. 5 He appeared to Peter. Then he appeared to the 12 apostles. 6 After that, he
appeared to more than 500 brothers and
sisters at the same time. Most of them are
still living. But some have died. 7 He appeared to James. Then he appeared to all
the apostles. 8 Last of all, he also appeared
to me. I was like someone who wasn't
born at the right time.
9 I am the least important of the apostles. I'm not even fit to be called an apostle. I tried to destroy God's church. 10 But
because of God's grace I am what I am.
And his grace was not wasted on me. No,
I have worked harder than all the other
apostles. But I didn't do the work. God's
grace was with me. 11 So this is what we
preach, whether I or the other apostles
who preached to you. And that is what
you believed.

Believers Will Rise From the Dead

12 We have preached that Christ has
been raised from the dead. So how can
some of you say that no one rises from the
dead? 13 If no one rises from the dead, then
not even Christ has been raised. 14 And
if Christ has not been raised, what we
preach doesn't mean anything. Your faith
doesn't mean anything either. 15 More
than that, we would be lying about God.
We are witnesses that God raised Christ
from the dead. But he did not raise him
if the dead are not raised. 16 If the dead
are not raised, then Christ has not been
raised either. 17 And if Christ has not been
raised, your faith doesn't mean anything.
Your sins have not been forgiven. 18 Those
who have died believing in Christ are also
lost. 19 Do we have hope in Christ only for
this life? Then people should pity us more
than anyone else.
20 But Christ really has been raised from
the dead. He is the first of all those who
will rise from the dead. 21 Death came because of what a man did. Rising from the
dead also comes because of what a man
did. 22 Because of Adam, all people die. So
because of Christ, all will be made alive.
23 But here is the order of events. Christ is
the first of those who rise from the dead.
When he comes back, those who belong
to him will be raised. 24 Then the end will
come after Christ destroys all rule, authority and power. Then he will hand over
the kingdom to God the Father. 25 Christ
must rule until he has put all his enemies
under his control. 26 The last enemy that
will be destroyed is death. 27 Scripture
says that God "has put everything under
his control." (Psalm 8:6) It says that "everything" has been put under him. But it is
clear that this does not include God himself. That's because God put everything
under Christ. 28 When he has done that,
the Son also will be under God's rule. God
put everything under the Son. In that way,
God will be all in all.
29 Suppose no one rises from the dead.
Then what will people do who are baptized for the dead? Suppose the dead are
not raised at all. Then why are people
baptized for them? 30 And why would we
put ourselves in danger every hour? 31 I
face death every day. That's the truth. And
here is something you can be just as sure
of. I take pride in what Christ Jesus our
Lord has done for you through my work.
32 Did I fight wild animals in Ephesus with
nothing more than human hopes? Then
what have I gotten for it? If the dead are
not raised,

> "Let us eat and drink,
> because tomorrow we will die."
> (Isaiah 22:13)

33 Don't let anyone fool you. "Bad companions make a good person bad." 34 You
should come back to your senses and
stop sinning. Some of you don't know
anything about God. I say this to make
you ashamed.

The Body That Rises From the Dead

35 But someone will ask, "How are the
dead raised? What kind of body will they
have?" 36 How foolish! What you plant
doesn't come to life unless it dies. 37 When
you plant something, it isn't a completely
grown plant that you put in the ground.
You only plant a seed. Maybe it's wheat or
something else. 38 But God gives the seed

a body just as he has planned. And to each kind of seed he gives its own body. [39]Not all earthly creatures are the same. People have one kind of body. Animals have another. Birds have another kind. Fish have still another. [40]There are also heavenly bodies as well as earthly bodies. Heavenly bodies have one kind of glory. Earthly bodies have another. [41]The sun has one kind of glory. The moon has another kind. The stars have still another. And one star's glory is different from that of another star.

[42]It will be like that with bodies that are raised from the dead. The body that is planted does not last forever. The body that is raised from the dead lasts forever. [43]It is planted without honor. But it is raised in glory. It is planted in weakness. But it is raised in power. [44]It is planted as an earthly body. But it is raised as a spiritual body.

Just as there is an earthly body, there is also a spiritual body. [45]It is written, "The first man Adam became a living person." (Genesis 2:7) The last Adam became a spirit that gives life. [46]What is spiritual did not come first. What is earthly came first. What is spiritual came after that. [47]The first man came from the dust of the earth. The second man came from heaven. [48]Those who belong to the earth are like the one who came from the earth. And those who are spiritual are like the heavenly man. [49]We are like the earthly man. And we will be like the heavenly man.

[50]Brothers and sisters, here is what I'm telling you. Bodies made of flesh and blood can't share in the kingdom of God. And what dies can't share in what never dies. [51]Listen! I am telling you a mystery. We will not all die. But we will all be changed. [52]That will happen in a flash, as quickly as you can wink an eye. It will happen at the blast of the last trumpet. Then the dead will be raised to live forever. And we will be changed. [53]Our natural bodies don't last forever. They must be dressed with what does last forever. What dies must be dressed with what does not die. [54]In fact, that is going to happen. What does not last will be dressed with what lasts forever. What dies will be dressed with what does not die. Then what is written will come true. It says, "Death has been swallowed up. It has lost the battle." (Isaiah 25:8)

[55]"Death, where is the victory you
thought you had?
Death, where is your sting?"
(Hosea 13:14)

[56]The sting of death is sin. And the power of sin is the law. [57]But let us give thanks to God! He gives us the victory because of what our Lord Jesus Christ has done.

[58]My dear brothers and sisters, remain strong in the faith. Don't let anything move you. Always give yourselves completely to the work of the Lord. Because you belong to the Lord, you know that your work is not worthless.

The Offering for the Lord's People

16 Now I want to deal with the offering of money for the Lord's people. Do what I told the churches in Galatia to do. [2]On the first day of every week, each of you should put some money away. The amount should be in keeping with how much money you make. Save the money so that you won't have to take up an offering when I come. [3]When I arrive, I will send some people with your gift to Jerusalem. They will be people you consider to be good. And I will give them letters that explain who they are. [4]If it seems good for me to go also, they will go with me.

What Paul Asks for Himself

[5]After I go through Macedonia, I will come to you. I will only be passing through Macedonia. [6]But I might stay with you for a while. I might even spend the winter. Then you can help me on my journey everywhere I go. [7]I don't want to see you now while I am just passing through. Instead, I hope to spend some time with you, if the Lord allows it. [8]But I will stay at Ephesus until the day of Pentecost. [9]A door has opened wide for me to do some good work here. There are many people who oppose me.

[10]Timothy will visit you. Make sure he has nothing to worry about while he is with you. He is doing the work of the Lord, just as I am. [11]No one should treat him badly. Send him safely on his way so he can return to me. I'm expecting him to come back along with the others.

[12]I want to say something about our brother Apollos. I tried my best to get him to go to you with the others. But he didn't

want to go right now. He will go when he
can.
13 Be on your guard. Remain strong in
the faith. Be brave. 14 Be loving in everything you do.
15 You know that the first believers in
Achaia were from the family of Stephanas. They have spent all their time serving
the Lord's people. Brothers and sisters, I
am asking you 16 to follow the lead of people like them. Follow everyone who joins
in the task and works hard at it. 17 I was
glad when Stephanas, Fortunatus and
Achaicus arrived. They have supplied me
with what you couldn't give me. 18 They
renewed my spirit, and yours also. People
like them are worthy of honor.

Final Greetings

19 The churches in Asia Minor send you
greetings. Aquila and Priscilla greet you
warmly because of the Lord's love. So
does the church that meets in their house.
20 All the brothers and sisters here send
you greetings. Greet one another with a
holy kiss.
21 I, Paul, am writing this greeting with
my own hand.
22 If anyone does not love the Lord, let a
curse be on that person! Come, Lord!
23 May the grace of the Lord Jesus be
with you.
24 I give my love to all of you who belong
to Christ Jesus. Amen.

2 CORINTHIANS

In 1 Corinthians Paul writes about his personal struggles with the believers in Corinth. That relationship was not easy and sometimes unpleasant. In 2 Corinthians Paul continues to speak to these believers about their problems and struggles.

In this letter Paul tells them they are part of God's new world. But they live in the old world that is still fighting against God. So they will have problems as followers of Jesus. Paul writes about many practical issues. Paul tells them why he must change his plans to visit them. He tells them how to collect money as a gift for the very poor people in Jerusalem. Finally, Paul tells them to not believe false teachers. He tells these believers that he has been true to them. And that he brought the true message of good news to them.

As Paul writes this book, he sees himself in different places. In each setting Paul thinks about his relationship with the people in Corinth. Paul either recalls or looks forward to something in his relationship with them. There is a main theme connecting all the parts of the book. The theme is that God will bring comfort in the time of trouble. So believers everywhere must also offer this comfort to each other. Jesus' life was an example of this. Jesus suffered first and then was comforted. And so his life is an example for us. We are weak and suffer. But we live in the power of God through Jesus Christ. And that is our comfort.

In the final section of the book, Paul challenges the people in Corinth. They must not believe the false teachers who have come there. Then Paul ends the letter with hope. He asks the people to rejoice in God's grace, love and fellowship.

---

1 I, Paul, am writing this letter. I am an
apostle of Christ Jesus just as God
planned. Timothy our brother joins me in
writing.

We are sending this letter to you, the
members of God's church in Corinth. It is
also for all God's holy people everywhere
in Achaia.

2 May God our Father and the Lord
Jesus Christ give you grace and peace.

Praise to the God Who Gives Comfort

3 Give praise to the God and Father of
our Lord Jesus Christ! He is the Father who
gives tender love. All comfort comes from
him. 4 He comforts us in all our troubles.
Now we can comfort others when they are
in trouble. We ourselves receive comfort
from God. 5 We share very much in the
sufferings of Christ. So we also share very
much in his comfort. 6 If we are having
trouble, it is so that you will be comforted
and renewed. If we are comforted, it is so
that you will be comforted. Then you will
be able to put up with the same suffering
we have gone through. 7 Our hope for you
remains firm. We know that you suffer
just as we do. In the same way, God comforts you just as he comforts us.
8 Brothers and sisters, we want you to
know about the hard times we had in Asia
Minor. We were having a lot of trouble.
It was far more than we could stand. We
even thought we were going to die. 9 In
fact, we felt as if we were under the sentence of death. But that happened so that
we would not depend on ourselves but on
God. He raises the dead to life. 10 God has
saved us from deadly dangers. And he will
continue to do it. We have put our hope
in him. He will continue to save us. 11 You
must help us by praying for us. Then
many people will give thanks because of
what will happen to us. They will thank
God for his kindness to us in answer to
the prayers of many.

Paul Changes His Plans

12 Here is what we take pride in. Our
sense of what is right and wrong tells us
how we have acted. We have lived with
honor and godly honesty. We have depended on God's grace and not on the
world's wisdom. We lived that way most of
all when we were dealing with you. 13 We
are writing only what you can read and understand. And here is what I hope. 14 Up to
this point you have understood some of the
things we have said. But now here is what
I hope for when the Lord Jesus returns. I
hope that your pride in us will be the same
as our pride in you. When this happens,
you will understand us completely.
15 Because I was sure of this, I wanted
to visit you first. Here is how I thought

you would be helped twice. 16 I planned to
visit you on my way to Macedonia. I would
have come back to you from there. Then
you would have sent me on my way to Judea. 17 When I planned all this, was I ready
to change my mind for no good reason?
No. I don't make my plans the way the
world makes theirs. In the same breath the
world says both, "Yes! Yes!" and "No! No!"

18 But just as sure as God is faithful, our
message to you is not "Yes" and "No." 19 Silas, Timothy and I preached to you about
the Son of God, Jesus Christ. Our message
did not say "Yes" and "No" at the same
time. The message of Christ has always
been "Yes." 20 God has made a great many
promises. They are all "Yes" because of
what Christ has done. So through Christ
we say "Amen." We want God to receive
glory. 21 He makes both us and you remain
strong in the faith because we belong to
Christ. He anointed us. 22 He put his Spirit
in our hearts and marked us as his own.
We can now be sure that he will give us
everything he promised us.

23 I call God to be my witness. May he
take my life if I'm lying. I wanted to spare
you, so I didn't return to Corinth. 24 Your
faith is not under our control. You remain
strong in your own faith. But we work
2 together with you for your joy. 1 So
I made up my mind that I would not
make another painful visit to you. 2 If I
make you sad, who is going to make me
glad? Only you, the people I made sad.
3 What I wrote to you I wrote for a special
reason. When I came, I didn't want to be
troubled by those who should make me
glad. I was sure that all of you would share
my joy. 4 I was very troubled when I wrote
to you. My heart was sad. My eyes were
full of tears. I didn't want to make you sad.
I wanted to let you know that I love you
very deeply.

Forgive Those Who Make You Sad

5 Suppose someone has made us sad.
In some ways, he hasn't made me sad so
much as he has made all of you sad. But
I don't want to put this too strongly. 6 He
has been punished because most of you
decided he should be. This punishment
is enough. 7 Now you should forgive him
and comfort him. Then he won't be sad
more than he can stand. 8 So I'm asking
you to tell him again that you still love
him. 9 I wrote to you for another special
reason. I wanted to see if you could stand
the test. I wanted to see if you could obey
everything asked of you. 10 Anyone you
forgive I also forgive. Was there anything
to forgive? If so, I have forgiven it for your
benefit, knowing that Christ is watching.
11 We don't want Satan to outsmart us. We
know how he does his evil work.

Serving Under the New Covenant

12 I went to Troas to preach the good
news about Christ. There I found that the
Lord had opened a door of opportunity
for me. 13 But I still had no peace of mind.
I couldn't find my brother Titus there. So I
said goodbye to the believers at Troas and
went on to Macedonia.

14 Give thanks to God! He always leads
us as if we were prisoners in Christ's victory parade. Through us, God spreads the
knowledge of Christ everywhere like perfume. 15 God considers us to be the pleasing smell that Christ is spreading. He is
spreading it among people who are being saved and people who are dying. 16 To
those who are dying, we are the smell of
death. To those who are being saved, we
are the perfume of life. Who is able to
do this work? 17 Unlike many people, we
aren't selling God's word to make money.
In fact, it is just the opposite. Because of
Christ we speak honestly before God. We
speak like people God has sent.

3 Are we beginning to praise ourselves
again? Some people need letters that
speak well of them. Do we need those
kinds of letters, either to you or from you?
2 You yourselves are our letter. You are written on our hearts. Everyone knows you
and reads you. 3 You make it clear that you
are a letter from Christ. You are the result
of our work for God. You are a letter written
not with ink but with the Spirit of the living
God. You are a letter written not on tablets
made out of stone but on human hearts.

4 Through Christ, we can be sure of
this before God. 5 In ourselves we are not
able to claim anything for ourselves. The
power to do what we do comes from God.
6 He has given us the power to serve under a new covenant. The covenant is not
based on the written Law of Moses. It
comes from the Holy Spirit. The written
Law kills, but the Spirit gives life.

The Greater Glory of the New Covenant

7The Law was written in letters on stone. Even though it was a way of serving God, it led to death. But even that way of serving God came with glory. The glory lasted for only a short time. Even so, the people of Israel couldn't look at Moses' face very long. 8Since all this is true, won't the work of the Holy Spirit be even more glorious? 9The law that condemns people to death had glory. How much more glory does the work of the Spirit have! His work makes people right with God. 10The glory of the old covenant is nothing compared with the far greater glory of the new. 11The glory of the old lasts for only a short time. How much greater is the glory of the new! It will last forever.

12Since we have that kind of hope, we are very bold. 13We are not like Moses. He used to cover his face with a veil. That was to keep the people of Israel from seeing the end of what was passing away. 14But their minds were made stubborn. To this day, the same veil remains when the old covenant is read. The veil has not been removed. Only faith in Christ can take it away. 15To this day, when the Law of Moses is read, a veil covers the minds of those who hear it. 16But when anyone turns to the Lord, the veil is taken away. 17Now the Lord is the Holy Spirit. And where the Spirit of the Lord is, freedom is also there. 18None of our faces are covered with a veil. All of us can see the Lord's glory and think deeply about it. So we are being changed to become more like him so that we have more and more glory. And this glory comes from the Lord, who is the Holy Spirit.

A Treasure in Clay Jars

4 So because of God's mercy, we have work to do. He has given it to us. And we don't give up. 2Instead, we have given up doing secret and shameful things. We don't twist God's word. In fact, we do just the opposite. We present the truth plainly. In the sight of God, we make our appeal to everyone's sense of what is right and wrong. 3Suppose our good news is covered with a veil. Then it is veiled to those who are dying. 4The god of this world has blinded the minds of those who don't believe. They can't see the light of the good news that makes Christ's glory clear. Christ is the likeness of God. 5The message we preach is not about ourselves. Our message is about Jesus Christ. We say that he is Lord. And we say that we serve you because of Jesus. 6God said, "Let light shine out of darkness." (Genesis 1:3) He made his light shine in our hearts. His light gives us the light to know God's glory. His glory is shown in the face of Christ.

7Treasure is kept in clay jars. In the same way, we have the treasure of the good news in these earthly bodies of ours. That shows that the mighty power of the good news comes from God. It doesn't come from us. 8We are pushed hard from all sides. But we are not beaten down. We are bewildered. But that doesn't make us lose hope. 9Others make us suffer. But God does not desert us. We are knocked down. But we are not knocked out. 10We always carry around the death of Jesus in our bodies. In that way, the life of Jesus can be shown in our bodies. 11We who are alive are always in danger of death because we are serving Jesus. This happens so that his life can also be shown in our earthly bodies. 12Death is at work in us. But life is at work in you.

13It is written, "I believed, and so I have spoken." (Psalm 116:10) We have that same spirit of faith. So we also believe and speak. 14We know that God raised the Lord Jesus from the dead. And he will also raise us up with Jesus. And he will present both you and us to himself. 15All this is for your benefit. God's grace is reaching more and more people. So they will become more and more thankful. They will give glory to God.

16We don't give up. Our bodies are becoming weaker and weaker. But our spirits are being renewed day by day. 17Our troubles are small. They last only for a short time. But they are earning for us a glory that will last forever. It is greater than all our troubles. 18So we don't spend all our time looking at what we can see. Instead, we look at what we can't see. That's because what can be seen lasts only a short time. But what can't be seen will last forever.

Waiting for Our New Bodies

5 We know that the earthly tent we live in will be destroyed. But we have a building made by God. It is a house in heaven that lasts forever. Human hands did not build it. 2During our time on earth we groan. We long to put on our house in

heaven as if it were clothing. [3]Then we
will not be naked. [4]While we live in this
tent of ours, we groan under our heavy
load. We don't want to be naked. Instead,
we want to be fully dressed with our
house in heaven. What must die will be
swallowed up by life. [5]God has formed us
for that very purpose. He has given us the
Holy Spirit as a down payment. The Spirit
makes us sure of what is still to come.

[6]So here is what we can always be certain about. As long as we are at home in
our bodies, we are away from the Lord.
[7]We live by believing, not by seeing. [8]We
are certain about that. We would rather be
away from our bodies and at home with
the Lord. [9]So we try our best to please
him. We want to please him whether we
are at home in our bodies or away from
them. [10]We must all stand in front of
Christ to be judged. Each one of us will be
judged for what we do while in our bodies. We'll be judged for the good things
and the bad things. Then each of us will
receive what we are supposed to get.

Christ Brings Us Back to God

[11]We know what it means to have respect for the Lord. So we try to help other people to understand it. What we are
is plain to God. I hope it is also plain to
your way of thinking. [12]We are not trying
to make an appeal to you again. But we
are giving you a chance to take pride in
us. Some people take pride in their looks
rather than what's in their hearts. If you
take pride in us, you will be able to answer them. [13]Are we "out of our minds,"
as some people say? If so, it is because
we want to serve God. Does what we say
make sense? If so, it is because we want to
serve you. [14]Christ's love controls us. We
are sure that one person died for everyone. And so everyone died. [15]Christ died
for everyone. He died so that those who
live should not live for themselves anymore. They should live for Christ. He died
for them and was raised again.

[16]So from now on we don't look at anyone the way the world does. At one time
we looked at Christ in that way. But we
don't anymore. [17]When anyone lives in
Christ, the new creation has come. The
old is gone! The new is here! [18]All this is
from God. He brought us back to himself through Christ's death on the cross.
And he has given us the task of bringing
others back to him through Christ. [19]God
was bringing the world back to himself
through Christ. He did not hold people's
sins against them. God has trusted us with
the message that people may be brought
back to him. [20]So we are Christ's official
messengers. It is as if God were making
his appeal through us. Here is what Christ
wants us to beg you to do. Come back to
God! [21]Christ didn't have any sin. But God
made him become sin for us. So we can
be made right with God because of what
Christ has done for us.

6 We work together with God. So we are
asking you not to receive God's grace
and then do nothing with it. [2]He says,

"When I had mercy on you, I heard
you.
On the day I saved you, I helped
you." (Isaiah 49:8)

I tell you, now is the time God has mercy.
Now is the day he saves.

Paul's Sufferings

[3]We don't put anything in anyone's way.
So no one can find fault with our work for
God. [4]Instead, we make it clear that we
serve God in every way. We serve him by
standing firm in troubles, hard times and
suffering. [5]We don't give up when we are
beaten or put in prison. When people stir
up trouble in the streets, we continue to
serve God. We work hard for him. We go
without sleep and food. [6]We remain pure.
We understand completely what it means
to serve God. We are patient and kind. We
serve him in the power of the Holy Spirit.
We serve him with true love. [7]We speak the
truth. We serve in the power of God. We
hold the weapons of godliness in the right
hand and in the left. [8]We serve God in times
of glory and shame. We serve him whether
the news about us is bad or good. We are
true to our calling. But people treat us as
if we were pretenders. [9]We are known, but
people treat us as if we were unknown. We
are dying, but we continue to live. We are
beaten, but we are not killed. [10]We are sad,
but we are always full of joy. We are poor,
but we make many people rich. We have
nothing, but we own everything.

[11]Believers at Corinth, we have spoken
freely to you. We have opened our hearts
wide to you. [12]We are not holding back

our love from you. But you are holding
back your love from us. 13 I speak to you
as if you were my children. It is only fair
that you open your hearts wide to us also.

Paul Warns Against Worshiping False Gods

14 Do not be joined to unbelievers. What
do right and wrong have in common? Can
light and darkness be friends? 15 How can
Christ and Satan agree? Or what does a
believer have in common with an unbeliever? 16 How can the temple of the true
God and the statues of other gods agree?
We are the temple of the living God. God
has said,

"I will live with them.
I will walk among them.
I will be their God.
And they will be my people."
(Leviticus 26:12; Jeremiah 32:38;
Ezekiel 37:27)

17 So,

"Come out from among them
and be separate,
says the Lord.
Do not touch anything that is not
pure and 'clean.'
Then I will receive you."
(Isaiah 52:11; Ezekiel 20:34,41)

18 And,

"I will be your Father.
You will be my sons and
daughters,
says the Lord who rules over all."
(2 Samuel 7:14; 7:8)

7 Dear friends, we have these promises
from God. So let us make ourselves
pure from everything that makes our
bodies and spirits impure. Let us be completely holy. We want to honor God.

Paul Has Joy When the Church Turns Away From Sin

2 Make room for us in your hearts. We
haven't done anything wrong to anyone.
We haven't caused anyone to sin. We
haven't taken advantage of anyone. 3 I
don't say this to judge you. I have told you
before that you have an important place
in our hearts. We would live or die with
you. 4 I have spoken to you very honestly.
I am very proud of you. I am very happy.
Even with all our troubles, my joy has no
limit.

5 When we came to Macedonia, we
weren't able to rest. We were attacked no
matter where we went. We had battles
on the outside and fears on the inside.
6 But God comforts those who are sad. He
comforted us when Titus came. 7 We were
comforted not only when he came but
also by the comfort you had given him.
He told us how much you longed for me.
He told us about your deep sadness and
concern for me. That made my joy greater
than ever.

8 Even if my letter made you sad, I'm
not sorry I sent it. At first I was sorry. I
see that my letter hurt you, but only for
a little while. 9 Now I am happy. I'm not
happy because you were made sad. I'm
happy because your sadness led you to
turn away from your sins. You became
sad just as God wanted you to. So you
were not hurt in any way by us. 10 Godly
sadness causes us to turn away from our
sins and be saved. And we are certainly
not sorry about that! But worldly sadness
brings death. 11 Look at what that godly
sadness has produced in you. You are
working hard to clear yourselves. You are
angry and alarmed. You are longing to see
me. You are concerned. You are ready to
make sure that the right thing is done. In
every way you have proved that you are
not guilty in that matter. 12 So even though
I wrote to you, it wasn't because of the
one who did the wrong. It wasn't because
of the one who was hurt either. Instead, I
wrote you so that in the sight of God you
could see for yourselves how faithful you
are to us. 13 All this encourages us.

We were also very glad to see how
happy Titus was. You have all renewed his
spirit. 14 I had bragged about you to him.
And you have not let me down. Everything we said to you was true. In the same
way, our bragging about you to Titus has
also turned out to be true. 15 His love for
you is even greater when he remembers
that you all obeyed his teaching. You received him with fear and trembling. 16 I
am glad I can have complete faith in you.

Giving Freely to the Lord's People

8 Brothers and sisters, we want you to
know about the grace that God has
given to the churches in Macedonia.

[2]They have suffered a great deal. But in their suffering, their joy was more than full. Even though they were very poor, they gave very freely. [3]I tell you that they gave as much as they could. In fact, they gave even more than they could. Completely on their own, [4]they begged us for the chance to share in serving the Lord's people in that way. [5]They did more than we expected. First they gave themselves to the Lord. Then they gave themselves to us because that was what God wanted. [6]Titus had already started collecting money from you. So we asked him to help you finish making your kind gift. [7]You do well in everything else. You do well in faith and in speaking. You do well in knowledge and in complete commitment. And you do well in the love we have helped to start in you. So make sure that you also do well in the grace of giving to others.

[8]I am not commanding you to do it. But I want to test you. I want to find out if you really love God. I want to compare your love with that of others. [9]You know the grace shown by our Lord Jesus Christ. Even though he was rich, he became poor to help you. Because he became poor, you can become rich.

[10]Here is my opinion about what is best for you in that matter. Last year you were the first to give. You were also the first to want to give. [11]So finish the work. Then your desire to do it will be matched by your finishing it. Give on the basis of what you have. [12]Do you really want to give? Then the gift is measured by what someone has. It is not measured by what they don't have.

[13]We don't want others to have it easy at your expense. We want things to be equal. [14]Right now you have plenty in order to take care of what they need. Then they will have plenty to take care of what you need. The goal is to even things out. [15]It is written, "The one who gathered a lot didn't have too much. And the one who gathered a little had enough." (Exodus 16:18)

Paul Sends Titus to Corinth to Receive the Offering

[16]God put into the heart of Titus the same concern I have for you. Thanks should be given to God for this. [17]Titus welcomed our appeal. He is also excited about coming to you. It was his own idea. [18]Along with Titus, we are sending another brother. All the churches praise him for his service in telling the good news. [19]He was also chosen by the churches to go with us as we bring the offering. We are in charge of it. We want to honor the Lord himself. We want to show how ready we are to help. [20]We want to keep anyone from blaming us for how we take care of that large gift. [21]We are trying hard to do what both the Lord and people think is right.

[22]We are also sending another one of our brothers with them. He has often proved to us in many ways that he is very committed. He is now even more committed because he has great faith in you. [23]Titus is my helper. He and I work together among you. Our brothers are messengers from the churches. They honor Christ. [24]So show them that you really love them. Show them why we are proud of you. Then the churches can see it.

9 I don't need to write to you about giving to the Lord's people. [2]I know how much you want to help. I have been bragging about it to the people in Macedonia. I have been telling them that since last year you who live in Achaia were ready to give. You are so excited that it has stirred up most of them to take action. [3]But I am sending the brothers. Then our bragging about you in this matter will have a good reason. You will be ready, just as I said you would be. [4]Suppose people from Macedonia come with me and find out that you are not prepared. Then we, as well as you, would be ashamed of being so certain. [5]So I thought I should try to get the brothers to visit you ahead of time. They will finish the plans for the large gift you had promised. Then it will be ready as a gift freely given. It will not be given by force.

Paul's Advice to Give Freely

[6]Here is something to remember. The one who plants only a little will gather only a little. And the one who plants a lot will gather a lot. [7]Each of you should give what you have decided in your heart to give. You shouldn't give if you don't want to. You shouldn't give because you are forced to. God loves a cheerful giver. [8]And God is able to shower all kinds of

blessings on you. So in all things and at all times you will have everything you need. You will do more and more good works. [9]It is written,

> "They have spread their gifts around
> to poor people.
> Their good works continue
> forever." (Psalm 112:9)

[10]God supplies seed for the person who plants. He supplies bread for food. God will also supply and increase the amount of your seed. He will increase the results of your good works. [11]You will be made rich in every way. Then you can always give freely. We will take your many gifts to the people who need them. And they will give thanks to God.

[12]Your gifts meet the needs of the Lord's people. And that's not all. Your gifts also cause many people to thank God. [13]You have shown yourselves to be worthy by what you have given. So other people will praise God because you obey him. That proves that you really believe the good news about Christ. They will also praise God because you share freely with them and with everyone else. [14]Their hearts will be filled with love for you when they pray for you. God has given you grace that is better than anything. [15]Let us give thanks to God for his gift. It is so great that no one can tell how wonderful it really is!

Paul Speaks Up for His Service to the Church

10 Christ is humble and free of pride. Because of this, I make my appeal to you. I, Paul, am the one you call "shy" when I am face to face with you. But when I am away from you, you think I am "bold" toward you. [2]I am coming to see you. Please don't make me be as bold as I expect to be toward some people. They think that I live the way the people of this world live. [3]I do live in the world. But I don't fight my battles the way the people of the world do. [4]The weapons I fight with are not the weapons the world uses. In fact, it is just the opposite. My weapons have the power of God to destroy the camps of the enemy. [5]I destroy every claim and every reason that keeps people from knowing God. I keep every thought under control in order to make it obey Christ. [6]Until you have obeyed completely, I will be ready to punish you every time you don't obey.

[7]You are judging only by how things look on the surface. Suppose someone is sure they belong to Christ. Then they should consider again that we belong to Christ just as much as they do. [8]Do I brag too much about the authority the Lord gave me? If I do, it's because I want to build you up, not tear you down. And I'm not ashamed of that kind of bragging. [9]Don't think that I'm trying to scare you with my letters. [10]Some say, "His letters sound important. They are powerful. But in person he doesn't seem like much. And what he says doesn't amount to anything." [11]People like that have a lot to learn. What I say in my letters when I'm away from you, I will do in my actions when I'm with you.

[12]I don't dare to compare myself with those who praise themselves. I'm not that kind of person. They measure themselves by themselves. They compare themselves with themselves. When they do that, they are not wise. [13]But I won't brag more than I should. God himself has given me an opportunity for serving. I will only brag about what I have done with that opportunity. This opportunity for serving also includes you. [14]I am not going too far in my bragging. I would be going too far if I hadn't come to where you live. But I did get there with the good news about Christ. [15]And I won't brag about work done by others. If I did, I would be bragging more than I should. As your faith continues to grow, I hope that my work among you will greatly increase. [16]Then I will be able to preach the good news in the areas beyond you. I don't want to brag about work already done in someone else's territory. [17]But, "The one who brags should brag about what the Lord has done." (Jeremiah 9:24) [18]Those who praise themselves are not accepted. Those the Lord praises are accepted.

Paul and Those Who Pretend to Be Apostles

11 I hope you will put up with me in a little foolish bragging. Yes, please put up with me! [2]My jealousy for you comes from God himself. I promised to give you to only one husband. That husband is Christ. I wanted to be able to give you to him as if you were a pure virgin.

3 But Eve's mind was tricked by the snake's
clever lies. And here's what I'm afraid of.
Your minds will also somehow be led
astray. They will be led away from your
true and pure love for Christ. 4 Suppose
someone comes to you and preaches
about a Jesus different from the Jesus we
preached about. Or suppose you receive
a spirit different from the Spirit you received before. Or suppose you receive a
different message of good news. Suppose
it was different from the one you accepted
earlier. You put up with those kinds of
things easily enough.

5 I don't think I'm in any way less important than those "super-apostles."
6 It's true that I haven't been trained as
a speaker. But I do have knowledge. I've
made that very clear to you in every way.
7 I preached God's good news to you free
of charge. When I did that, I was putting
myself down in order to lift you up. Was
this a sin? 8 I received help from other
churches so I could serve you. This was
almost like robbing them. 9 When I was
with you and needed something, I didn't
cause you any expense. The believers
who came from Macedonia gave me what
I needed. I haven't caused you any expense at all. And I won't ever do it. 10 I'm
sure that the truth of Christ is in me. And
I'm just as sure that nobody in Achaia will
keep me from bragging. 11 Why? Because I
don't love you? No! God knows I do!

12 And I will keep on doing what I'm doing. That will stop those who claim they
have things to brag about. They think they
have a chance to be considered equal with
us. 13 People like that are false apostles.
They are workers who tell lies. They only
pretend to be apostles of Christ. 14 That
comes as no surprise. Even Satan himself pretends to be an angel of light. 15 So
it doesn't surprise us that Satan's servants
also pretend to be serving God. They will
finally get exactly what they deserve.

Paul Brags About His Sufferings

16 I will say it again. Don't let anyone
think I'm a fool. But if you do, put up with
me just as you would put up with a fool.
Then I can do a little bragging. 17 When I
brag about myself like this, I'm not talking the way the Lord would. I'm talking
like a fool. 18 Many are bragging the way
the people of the world do. So I will brag
like that too. 19 You are so wise! You gladly
put up with fools! 20 In fact, you even put
up with anyone who makes you a slave or
uses you. You put up with those who take
advantage of you. You put up with those
who claim to be better than you. You put
up with those who slap you in the face.
21 I'm ashamed to have to say that I was
too weak for that!

Whatever anyone else dares to brag
about, I also dare to brag about. I'm
speaking like a fool! 22 Are they Hebrews?
So am I. Do they belong to the people of
Israel? So do I. Are they Abraham's children? So am I. 23 Are they serving Christ? I
am serving him even more. I'm out of my
mind to talk like this! I have worked much
harder. I have been in prison more often. I
have suffered terrible beatings. Again and
again I almost died. 24 Five times the Jews
gave me 39 strokes with a whip. 25 Three
times I was beaten with sticks. Once they
tried to kill me by throwing stones at me.
Three times I was shipwrecked. I spent a
night and a day in the open sea. 26 I have
had to keep on the move. I have been in
danger from rivers. I have been in danger from robbers. I have been in danger
from my fellow Jews and in danger from
Gentiles. I have been in danger in the city,
in the country, and at sea. I have been
in danger from people who pretended
they were believers. 27 I have worked very
hard. Often I have gone without sleep.
I have been hungry and thirsty. Often I
have gone without food. I have been cold
and naked. 28 Besides everything else,
every day I am concerned about all the
churches. It is a very heavy load. 29 If anyone is weak, I feel weak. If anyone is led
into sin, I burn on the inside.

30 If I have to brag, I will brag about the
things that show how weak I am. 31 I am
not lying. The God and Father of the Lord
Jesus knows this. May God be praised forever. 32 In Damascus the governor who
served under King Aretas had their city
guarded. He wanted to arrest me. 33 But I
was lowered in a basket from a window in
the wall. So I escaped from the governor.

Paul's Vision and His Painful Problem

12 We can't gain anything by bragging.
But I have to do it anyway. I am going to tell you what I've seen. I want to
talk about what the Lord has shown me.

2 I know a believer in Christ who was taken up to the third heaven 14 years ago. I don't know if his body was taken up or not. Only God knows. 3 I don't know if that man was in his body or out of it. Only God knows. But I do know that 4 he was taken up to paradise. He heard things there that couldn't be put into words. They were things that no one is allowed to talk about. 5 I will brag about a man like that. But I won't brag about myself. I will brag only about how weak I am. 6 Suppose I decide to brag. That would not make me a fool, because I would be telling the truth. But I don't brag, so that no one will think more of me than they should. People should judge me by what I do and say. 7 God has shown me amazing and wonderful things. People should not think more of me because of it. So I wouldn't become proud of myself, I was given a problem. This problem caused pain in my body. It is a messenger from Satan to make me suffer. 8 Three times I begged the Lord to take it away from me. 9 But he said to me, "My grace is all you need. My power is strongest when you are weak." So I am very happy to brag about how weak I am. Then Christ's power can rest on me. 10 Because of how I suffered for Christ, I'm glad that I am weak. I am glad in hard times. I am glad when people say mean things about me. I am glad when things are difficult. And I am glad when people make me suffer. When I am weak, I am strong.

Paul's Concern for the People of Corinth

11 I have made a fool of myself. But you made me do it. You should have praised me. Even though I am nothing, I am in no way less important than the "super-apostles." 12 While I was with you, I kept on showing you the actions of a true apostle. These actions include signs, wonders and miracles. 13 How were you less important than the other churches? The only difference was that I didn't cause you any expense. Forgive me for that wrong!

14 Now I am ready to visit you for the third time. I won't cause you any expense. I don't want what you have. What I really want is you. After all, children shouldn't have to save up for their parents. Parents should save up for their children. 15 So I will be very happy to spend everything I have for you. I will even spend myself. If I love you more, will you love me less? 16 In any case, I haven't caused you any expense. But I'm so tricky! I have caught you by tricking you! Or so you think! 17 Did I take advantage of you through any of the men I sent to you? 18 I asked Titus to go to you. And I sent our brother with him. Titus didn't take advantage of you, did he? Didn't we walk in the same footsteps by the same Spirit?

19 All this time, have you been thinking that I've been speaking up for myself? No, I've been speaking with God as my witness. I've been speaking like a believer in Christ. Dear friends, everything I do is to help you become stronger. 20 I'm afraid that when I come I won't find you as I want you to be. I'm afraid that you won't find me as you want me to be. I'm afraid there will be arguing, jealousy and fits of anger. I'm afraid each of you will focus only on getting ahead. Then you will tell lies about each other. You will talk about each other. I'm afraid you will be proud and cause trouble. 21 I'm afraid that when I come again my God will put me to shame in front of you. Then I will be sad about many who sinned earlier and have not turned away from it. They have not turned away from uncleanness, sexual sins and wild living. They have done all those things.

Final Warnings

13 This will be my third visit to you. Scripture says, "Every matter must be proved by the words of two or three witnesses." (Deuteronomy 19:15) 2 I already warned you during my second visit. I now say it again while I'm away. When I return, I won't spare those who sinned earlier. I won't spare any of the others either. 3 You are asking me to prove that Christ is speaking through me. He is not weak in dealing with you. He is powerful among you. 4 It is true that Christ was nailed to the cross because he was weak. But Christ lives by God's power. In the same way, we share his weakness. But by God's power we will live with Christ as we serve you.

5 Take a good look at yourselves to see if you are really believers. Test yourselves. Don't you realize that Christ Jesus is in you? Unless, of course, you fail the test! 6 I hope you will discover that I haven't failed

the test. 7 I pray to God that you won't do
anything wrong. I don't pray so that people will see that I have passed the test. Instead, I pray this so that you will do what
is right, even if it seems I have failed. 8 I
can't do anything to stop the truth. I can
only work for the truth. 9 I'm glad when
I am weak but you are strong. I pray that
there will be no more problems among
you. 10 That's why I write these things before I come to you. Then when I do come,
I won't have to be hard on you when I use
my authority. The Lord gave me the authority to build you up. He didn't give it to
me to tear you down.

Final Greetings

11 Finally, brothers and sisters, be joyful! Work to make things right with one
another. Help one another and agree with
one another. Live in peace. And the God
who gives love and peace will be with you.

12 Greet one another with a holy kiss.
13 All God's people here send their greetings.

14 May the grace shown by the Lord
Jesus Christ be with you all. May the love
that God has given us be with you. And
may the sharing of life brought about by
the Holy Spirit be with you all.

GALATIANS

Galatia was a region located in Asia Minor. It was part of the Roman Empire. Paul visited Galatia three different times when he traveled. When he was there, Paul spoke to the people about the good news of Jesus the Messiah. The people of Galatia gladly received Paul and his message of the good news. But later other leaders and teachers came to Galatia. They challenged Paul's leadership. And they challenged the authority of Paul's teaching. So, Paul wrote this letter to believers in Galatia. In this letter Paul shows he has the right to teach the good news. He also shows that he is teaching the true good news. He states that faith in Jesus Christ is all that is needed. Membership in God's new community is by faith alone.

Paul begins his letter by stating that he has the right to preach the good news. He says that he did not receive the good news from human beings. He says he received that good news from Jesus himself. Paul also states that other apostles support him in his work.

Paul then moves to the main point of the letter. Paul states that Gentile believers don't have to follow all the laws of the Jews. They are members of the new community of believers because they believe in Jesus. This community fulfills God's promise that Abraham would have a worldwide family. The Bible's story has been pointing to this all along.

Paul ends the letter by reminding the Galatians that they live by the power of the Holy Spirit. Following Jewish laws is not what matters. "What really counts is that the new creation has come."

---

1 I, Paul, am writing this letter. I am an
apostle. People have not sent me. No
human authority has sent me. I have been
sent by Jesus Christ and by God the Father. God raised Jesus from the dead. 2 All
the brothers and sisters who are with me
join me in writing.

We are sending this letter to you, the
members of the churches in Galatia.

3 May God our Father and the Lord
Jesus Christ give you grace and peace.
4 Jesus gave his life for our sins. He set us
free from this evil world. That was what
our God and Father wanted. 5 Give glory
to God for ever and ever. Amen.

There Is No Other Good News

6 I am amazed. You are so quickly de-
serting the one who chose you. He chose
you to live in the grace that Christ has
provided. You are turning to a different "good news." 7 What you are accepting is really not the good news at all. It
seems that some people have gotten
you all mixed up. They are trying to twist
the good news about Christ. 8 But suppose even we should preach a different
"good news." Suppose even an angel from
heaven should preach it. Suppose it is different from the good news we gave you.
Then let anyone who does that be cursed
by God. 9 I have already said it. Now I will
say it again. Suppose someone preaches
a "good news" that is different from what
you accepted. That person should be
cursed by God.

10 Am I now trying to get people to think
well of me? Or do I want God to think well
of me? Am I trying to please people? If I
were, I would not be serving Christ.

Paul Was Appointed by God

11 Brothers and sisters, here is what
I want you to know. The good news I
preached does not come from human
beings. 12 No one gave it to me. No one
taught it to me. Instead, I received it from
Jesus Christ. He showed it to me.

13 You have heard how I lived earlier in
my Jewish way of life. With all my strength
I attacked the church of God. I tried to
destroy it. 14 I was moving ahead in my
Jewish way of life. I went beyond many of
my people who were my own age. I held
firmly to the teachings passed down by
my people. 15 But God set me apart from
before the time I was born. He showed
me his grace by appointing me. He was
pleased 16 to show his Son in my life. He
wanted me to preach about Jesus among
the Gentiles. When God appointed me, I
decided right away not to ask anyone for
advice. 17 I didn't go up to Jerusalem to see
those who were apostles before I was. Instead, I went into Arabia. Later I returned
to Damascus.

18 Then after three years I went up to Je-

rusalem. I went there to get to know Peter.
I stayed with him for 15 days. 19 I didn't
see any of the other apostles. I only saw
James, the Lord's brother. 20 Here is what
you can be sure of. And God is even a witness to it. What I am writing you is not a
lie.
21 Then I went to Syria and Cilicia.
22 The members of Christ's churches in Judea did not know me in a personal way.
23 They only heard others say, "The man
who used to attack us has changed. He is
now preaching the faith he once tried to
destroy." 24 And they praised God because
of me.

Paul Is Accepted by the Apostles

2 Then after fourteen years, I went up
again to Jerusalem. This time I went
with Barnabas. I took Titus along also. 2 I
went because God showed me what he
wanted me to do. I spoke in private to
those who are respected as leaders. I told
them the good news that I preach among
the Gentiles. I wanted to be sure I wasn't
running my race for no purpose. And I
wanted to know that I had not been running my race for no purpose. 3 Titus was
with me. He was a Greek. But even he was
not forced to be circumcised. 4 This matter came up because some people had
slipped in among us. They had pretended
to be believers. They wanted to find out
about the freedom we have because we
belong to Christ Jesus. They wanted to
make us slaves again. 5 We didn't give in
to them for a moment. We did this so that
the truth of the good news would be kept
safe for you.
6 Some people in Jerusalem were
thought to be important. But it makes
no difference to me what they were. God
does not treat people differently. Those
people added nothing to my message. 7 In
fact, it was just the opposite. They recognized the task I had been trusted with. It
was the task of preaching the good news
to the Gentiles. My task was like Peter's
task. He had been trusted with the task
of preaching to the Jews. 8 God was working in Peter as an apostle to the Jews. God
was also working in me as an apostle to
the Gentiles. 9 James, Peter and John are
respected as pillars in the church. They
recognized the special grace given to me.
So they shook my hand and the hand of
Barnabas. They wanted to show they accepted us. They agreed that we should
go to the Gentiles. They would go to the
Jews. 10 They asked only one thing. They
wanted us to continue to remember poor
people. That was what I had wanted to do
all along.

Paul Opposes Peter

11 When Peter came to Antioch, I told
him to his face that I was against what he
was doing. He was clearly wrong. 12 He
used to eat with the Gentiles. But certain
men came from a group sent by James.
When they arrived, Peter began to draw
back. He separated himself from the Gentiles. That's because he was afraid of the
circumcision group sent by James. 13 Peter's actions were not honest, and other
Jews in Antioch joined him. Even Barnabas was led astray.
14 I saw what they were doing. It was not
in line with the truth of the good news. So
I spoke to Peter in front of them all. "You
are a Jew," I said. "But you live like one
who is not. So why do you force Gentiles
to follow Jewish ways?"
15 We are Jews by birth. We are not sinful
Gentiles. 16 Here is what we know. No one
is made right with God by obeying the
law. It is by believing in Jesus Christ. So
we too have put our faith in Christ Jesus.
This is so we can be made right with God
by believing in Christ. We are not made
right by obeying the law. That's because
no one can be made right with God by
obeying the law.
17 We are seeking to be made right with
God through Christ. As we do, what if we
find that we who are Jews are also sinners? Does that mean that Christ causes
us to sin? Certainly not! 18 Suppose I build
again what I had destroyed. Then I would
really be breaking the law.
19 By the law, I died as far as the law is
concerned. I died so that I might live for
God. 20 I have been crucified with Christ.
I don't live any longer, but Christ lives in
me. Now I live my life in my body by faith
in the Son of God. He loved me and gave
himself for me. 21 I do not get rid of the
grace of God. What if a person could become right with God by obeying the law?
Then Christ died for nothing!

Faith or Obeying the Law

3 You foolish people of Galatia! Who has put you under an evil spell? When I preached, I clearly showed you that Jesus Christ had been nailed to the cross. 2 I would like to learn just one thing from you. Did you receive the Holy Spirit by obeying the law? Or did you receive the Spirit by believing what you heard? 3 Are you so foolish? You began by the Holy Spirit. Are you now trying to finish God's work in you by your own strength? 4 Have you experienced so much for nothing? And was it really for nothing? 5 So I ask you again, how does God give you his Spirit? How does he work miracles among you? Is it by doing what the law says? Or is it by believing what you have heard? 6 In the same way, Abraham "believed God. God was pleased with Abraham because he believed. So his faith made him right with God." (Genesis 15:6)

7 So you see, those who have faith are children of Abraham. 8 Long ago, Scripture knew that God would make the Gentiles right with himself. He would do this by their faith in him. He announced the good news ahead of time to Abraham. God said, "All nations will be blessed because of you." (Genesis 12:3; 18:18; 22:18) 9 So those who depend on faith are blessed along with Abraham. He was the man of faith.

10 All who depend on obeying the law are under a curse. It is written, "May everyone who doesn't continue to do everything written in the Book of the Law be under God's curse." (Deuteronomy 27:26) 11 We know that no one who depends on the law is made right with God. This is because "the one who is right with God will live by faith." (Habakkuk 2:4) 12 The law is not based on faith. In fact, it is just the opposite. It teaches that "the person who does these things will live by them." (Leviticus 18:5) 13 Christ set us free from the curse of the law. He did it by becoming a curse for us. It is written, "Everyone who is hung on a pole is under God's curse." (Deuteronomy 21:23) 14 Christ Jesus set us free so that the blessing given to Abraham would come to the Gentiles through Christ. He did it so that we might receive the promise of the Holy Spirit. The promised Spirit comes by believing in Christ.

The Law and the Promise

15 Brothers and sisters, let me give you an example from everyday life. No one can get rid of an official agreement between people. No one can add to it. It can't be changed after it has been made. It is the same with God's covenant agreement. 16 The promises were given to Abraham. They were also given to his seed. Scripture does not say, "and to seeds." That means many people. It says, "and to your seed." (Genesis 12:7; 13:15; 24:7) That means one person. And that one person is Christ. 17 Here is what I mean. The law came 430 years after the promise. But the law does not get rid of God's covenant and promise. The covenant had already been made by God. So the law does not do away with the promise. 18 The great gift that God has for us does not depend on the law. If it did, it would no longer depend on the promise. But God gave it to Abraham as a free gift through a promise.

19 Then why was the law given at all? It was added because of human sin. And it was supposed to control us until the promised Seed had come. The law was given through angels, and a go-between was put in charge of it. 20 A go-between means that there is more than one side to an agreement. But God didn't use a go-between when he made his promise to Abraham.

21 So is the law opposed to God's promises? Certainly not! What if a law had been given that could give life? Then people could become right with God by obeying the law. 22 But Scripture has locked up everything under the control of sin. It does so in order that what was promised might be given to those who believe. The promise comes through faith in Jesus Christ.

Children of God

23 Before faith in Christ came, we were guarded by the law. We were locked up until this faith was made known. 24 So the law was put in charge of us until Christ came. He came so that we might be made right with God by believing in Christ. 25 But now faith in Christ has come. So the law is no longer in charge of us.

26 So in Christ Jesus you are all children of God by believing in Christ. 27 This is because all of you who were baptized into Christ have put on Christ. You have put

him on as if he were your clothes. 28 There is no Jew or Gentile. There is no slave or free person. There is no male or female. That's because you are all one in Christ Jesus. 29 You who belong to Christ are Abraham's seed. So you will receive what God has promised.

4 Here is what I have been saying. As long as your own children are young, they are no different from slaves in your house. They are no different, even though they will own all the property. 2 People are in charge of the property. And other people are in charge of the children. The children remain under their care until they become adults. At that time their fathers give them the property. 3 It is the same with us. When we were children, we were slaves to the basic spiritual powers of the world. 4 But then the chosen time came. God sent his Son. A woman gave birth to him. He was born under the authority of the law. 5 He came to set free those who were under the authority of the law. He wanted us to be adopted as children with all the rights children have. 6 Because you are his children, God sent the Spirit of his Son into our hearts. He is the Holy Spirit. By his power we call God Abba. Abba means Father. 7 So you aren't a slave any longer. You are God's child. Because you are his child, God gives you the rights of those who are his children.

Paul's Concern for the Believers in Galatia

8 At one time you didn't know God. You were slaves to gods that are really not gods at all. 9 But now you know God. Even better, God knows you. So why are you turning back to those weak and worthless powers? Do you want to be slaves to them all over again? 10 You are observing special days and months and seasons and years! 11 I am afraid for you. I am afraid that somehow I have wasted my efforts on you.

12 I make my appeal to you, brothers and sisters. I'm asking you to become like me. After all, I became like you. You didn't do anything wrong to me. 13 Remember when I first preached the good news to you? Remember I did that because I was sick. 14 And my sickness was hard on you. But you weren't mean to me. You didn't make fun of me. Instead, you welcomed me as if I were an angel of God. You welcomed me as if I were Christ Jesus himself. 15 So why aren't you treating me the same way now? Suppose you could have torn out your own eyes and given them to me. Then you would have done it. I am a witness to this. 16 Have I become your enemy now by telling you the truth?

17 Those people are trying hard to win you over. But it is not for your good. They want to take you away from us. They want you to commit yourselves to them. 18 It is fine to be committed to something, if the purpose is good. And you shouldn't be committed only when I am with you. You should always be committed. 19 My dear children, I am in pain for you like I was when we first met. I have pain like a woman giving birth. And my pain will continue until Christ makes you like himself. 20 I wish I could be with you now. I wish I could change my tone of voice. As it is, I don't understand you.

Hagar and Sarah

21 You who want to be under the authority of the law, tell me something. Don't you know what the law says? 22 It is written that Abraham had two sons. The slave woman gave birth to one of them. The free woman gave birth to the other one. 23 Abraham's son by the slave woman was born in the usual way. But his son by the free woman was born because of God's promise.

24 These things are examples. The two women stand for two covenants. One covenant comes from Mount Sinai. It gives birth to children who are going to be slaves. It is Hagar. 25 Hagar stands for Mount Sinai in Arabia. She stands for the present city of Jerusalem. That's because she and her children are slaves. 26 But the Jerusalem that is above is free. She is our mother. 27 It is written,

"Be glad, woman,
  you who have never had children.
Shout for joy and cry out loud,
  you who have never had labor
    pains.
The woman who is all alone has
    more children
  than the woman who has a
    husband." (Isaiah 54:1)

28 Brothers and sisters, you are children because of God's promise just as

Isaac was. [29]At that time, the son born in
the usual way tried to hurt the other son.
The other son was born by the power of
the Holy Spirit. It is the same now. [30]But
what does Scripture say? "Get rid of the
slave woman. Get rid of her son. The slave
woman's son will never have a share of
the family's property. He'll never share it
with the free woman's son." (Genesis 21:10)
[31]Brothers and sisters, we are not the
slave woman's children. We are the free
woman's children.

Christ Sets Us Free

5 Christ has set us free to enjoy our freedom. So remain strong in the faith.
Don't let the chains of slavery hold you
again.

[2]Here is what I, Paul, say to you. Don't
let yourselves be circumcised. If you do,
Christ won't be of any value to you. [3]I say
it again. Every man who lets himself be
circumcised must obey the whole law.
[4]Some of you are trying to be made right
with God by obeying the law. You have
been separated from Christ. You have
fallen away from God's grace. [5]But we
long to be made completely holy because
of our faith in Christ. Through the Holy
Spirit we wait for this in hope. [6]Circum-
cision and uncircumcision aren't worth
anything to those who believe in Christ
Jesus. The only thing that really counts is
faith that shows itself through love.

[7]You were running a good race. Who
has kept you from obeying the truth?
[8]The God who chooses you does not keep
you from obeying the truth. [9]You should
know that "just a little yeast works its way
through the whole batch of dough." [10]The
Lord makes me certain that you will see
the truth of this. The one who has gotten you all mixed up will have to pay the
price. This will happen no matter who has
done it. [11]Brothers and sisters, I no longer
preach that people must be circumcised.
If I did, why am I still being opposed? If
I preached that, then the cross wouldn't
upset anyone. [12]So then, what about trou-
blemakers who try to get others to be circumcised? I wish they would go the whole
way! I wish they would cut off everything
that marks them as men!

Living by the Holy Spirit's Power

[13]My brothers and sisters, you were
chosen to be free. But don't use your freedom as an excuse to live under the power
of sin. Instead, serve one another in love.
[14]The whole law is fulfilled by obeying
this one command. "Love your neighbor
as you love yourself." (Leviticus 19:18) [15]If
you say or do things that harm one another, watch out! You could end up destroying one another.

[16]So I say, live by the Holy Spirit's
power. Then you will not do what your
desires controlled by sin want you to do.
[17]The desires controlled by sin do not
want what the Spirit delights in. And the
Spirit does not want what the desires controlled by sin delight in. The two are at
war with each other. That's why you are
not supposed to do whatever you want.
[18]But if you are led by the Spirit, you are
not under the authority of the law.

[19]The result of sin's control in our lives
is clear. It includes sexual sins, impure
acts and wild living. [20]It includes worshiping statues of gods and worshiping
evil powers. It also includes hatred and
fighting, jealousy and fits of anger. Sinful
desire is interested only in getting ahead.
It stirs up trouble. It separates people into
their own little groups. [21]It wants what
others have. It gets drunk and takes part
in wild parties. It does many things of that
kind. I warn you now as I did before. People who live like this will not receive God's
kingdom.

[22]But the fruit the Holy Spirit produces
is love, joy and peace. It is being patient,
kind and good. It is being faithful [23]and
gentle and having control of oneself.
There is no law against things of that kind.
[24]Those who belong to Christ Jesus have
nailed their sinful desires to his cross.
They don't want these things anymore.
[25]Since we live by the Spirit, let us keep in
step with the Spirit. [26]Let us not become
proud. Let us not make each other angry.
Let us not want what belongs to others.

Do Good to Everyone

6 Brothers and sisters, what if someone
is caught in a sin? Then you who live
by the Spirit should correct that person.
Do it in a gentle way. But be careful. You
could be tempted too. [2]Carry one another's heavy loads. If you do, you will fulfill
the law of Christ. [3]If anyone thinks they
are somebody when they are nobody,

they are fooling themselves. [4]Each person should test their own actions. Then
they can take pride in themselves. They
won't be comparing themselves to someone else. [5]Each person should carry their
own load. [6]But those who are taught the
word should share all good things with
their teacher.

[7]Don't be fooled. You can't outsmart
God. A man gathers a crop from what he
plants. [8]Some people plant to please their
desires controlled by sin. From these desires they will harvest death. Others plant
to please the Holy Spirit. From the Spirit
they will harvest eternal life. [9]Let us not
become tired of doing good. At the right
time we will gather a crop if we don't give
up. [10]So when we can do good to everyone, let us do it. Let's try even harder to do
good to the family of believers.

Not Circumcision but the New Creation

[11]Look at the big letters I'm using as I
write to you with my own hand!

[12]Some people are worried about how
things look on the outside. They are trying
to force you to be circumcised. They do it
for only one reason. They don't want to
suffer by being connected with the cross
of Christ. [13]Even those who are circumcised don't obey the law. But they want
you to be circumcised. Then they can
brag about what has been done to your
body. [14]I never want to brag about anything except the cross of our Lord Jesus
Christ. Through that cross the ways of the
world have been crucified as far as I am
concerned. And I have been crucified as
far as the ways of the world are concerned.
[15]Circumcision and uncircumcision don't
mean anything. What really counts is that
the new creation has come. [16]May peace
and mercy be given to all who follow this
rule. May peace and mercy be given to the
Israel that belongs to God.

[17]From now on, let no one cause trouble for me. My body has marks that show
I belong to Jesus.

[18]Brothers and sisters, may the grace of
our Lord Jesus Christ be with your spirit.
Amen.

EPHESIANS

Paul wrote the letter that we call Ephesians. Paul spent at least two years in Ephesus, but this letter seems to be written to people he doesn't know. Paul uses a pattern in writing this book. First, he explains the new identity believers have in Jesus the Messiah. After that, Paul explains what this new way of life means in practice.

Paul begins by explaining that God has brought everything together under the rule of Jesus the Messiah. Jesus is above all things. Paul quotes from Psalm 8, which talks about the job that humans have. That task was to properly rule over all creation. Jesus has fulfilled the original task given to human beings. Paul also writes that Jews and Gentiles have been brought together into one family. Jesus is the head of this family. Through the renewing work of Jesus, God is making one new people. He is gathering people together from all over the world.

Paul then tells these believers how to live. They must give up their old way of living. They are to live a way of life that is truly good and holy. They are to live a life of love and peace with their neighbors. God expects all the believers to serve each other. They are to respect each other just as they have respect for the Lord.

Paul reminds these believers that they must remain strong against evil things. They must use everything God has provided to remain strong. And they must do that until the Lord returns. Then God will "bring together all things in heaven and on earth under Christ."

---

1 I, Paul, am writing this letter. I am an
apostle of Christ Jesus just as God
planned.

I am sending this letter to you, God's
holy people in Ephesus. Because you belong to Christ Jesus, you are faithful.

2 May God our Father and the Lord
Jesus Christ give you grace and peace.

Praise God for His Spiritual Blessings in Christ

3 Give praise to the God and Father of
our Lord Jesus Christ. He has blessed us
with every spiritual blessing. Those blessings come from the heavenly world. They
belong to us because we belong to Christ.
4 God chose us to belong to Christ before
the world was created. He chose us to be
holy and without blame in his eyes. He
loved us. 5 So he decided long ago to adopt
us. He adopted us as his children with all
the rights children have. He did it because
of what Jesus Christ has done. It pleased
God to do it. 6 All those things bring praise
to his glorious grace. God freely gave us
his grace because of the One he loves.
7 We have been set free because of what
Christ has done. Because he bled and
died our sins have been forgiven. We have
been set free because God's grace is so
rich. 8 He poured his grace on us. By giving us great wisdom and understanding,
9 he showed us the mystery of his plan. It
was in keeping with what he wanted to
do. It was what he had planned through
Christ. 10 It will all come about when history has been completed. God will then
bring together all things in heaven and on
earth under Christ.

11 We were also chosen to belong to
him. God decided to choose us long ago
in keeping with his plan. He works out
everything to fit his plan and purpose.
12 We were the first to put our hope in
Christ. We were chosen to bring praise to
his glory. 13 You also became believers in
Christ. That happened when you heard
the message of truth. It was the good news
about how you could be saved. When you
believed, he stamped you with an official
mark. That official mark is the Holy Spirit
that he promised. 14 The Spirit marks us
as God's own. We can now be sure that
someday we will receive all that God has
promised. That will happen after God sets
all his people completely free. All these
things will bring praise to his glory.

Paul Prays and Gives Thanks

15 I have heard about your faith in the
Lord Jesus. I have also heard about your
love for all God's people. That is why 16 I
have not stopped thanking God for you.
I always remember you in my prayers. 17 I
pray to the God of our Lord Jesus Christ.
God is the glorious Father. I keep asking
him to give you the wisdom and understanding that come from the Holy Spirit. I
want you to know God better. 18 I pray that

you may understand more clearly. Then
you will know the hope God has chosen
you to receive. You will know that what
God will give his holy people is rich and
glorious. 19 And you will know God's great
power. It can't be compared with anything else. His power works for us who believe. It is the same mighty strength 20 God
showed. He showed this when he raised
Christ from the dead. God seated him at
his right hand in his heavenly kingdom.
21 There Christ sits far above all who rule
and have authority. He also sits far above
all powers and kings. He is above every
name that is appealed to in this world and
in the world to come. 22 God placed all
things under Christ's rule. He appointed
him to be ruler over everything for the
church. 23 The church is Christ's body and
is filled by Christ. He fills everything in every way.

God Has Given Us New Life Through Christ

2 You were living in your sins and lawless ways. But in fact you were dead.
2 You used to live as sinners when you
followed the ways of this world. You
served the one who rules over the spiritual forces of evil. He is the spirit who
is now at work in those who don't obey
God. 3 At one time we all lived among
them. Our desires were controlled by
sin. We tried to satisfy what they wanted
us to do. We followed our desires and
thoughts. God was angry with us like he
was with everyone else. That's because
of the kind of people we all were. 4 But
God loves us deeply. He is full of mercy.
5 So he gave us new life because of what
Christ has done. He gave us life even
when we were dead in sin. God's grace
has saved you. 6 God raised us up with
Christ. He has seated us with him in his
heavenly kingdom. That's because we
belong to Christ Jesus. 7 He has done it to
show the riches of his grace for all time to
come. His grace can't be compared with
anything else. He has shown it by being
kind to us. He was kind to us because of
what Christ Jesus has done. 8 God's grace
has saved you because of your faith in
Christ. Your salvation doesn't come from
anything you do. It is God's gift. 9 It is
not based on anything you have done.
No one can brag about earning it. 10 We
are God's creation. He created us to belong to Christ Jesus. Now we can do good
works. Long ago God prepared these
works for us to do.

God's New Family of Jews and Gentiles

11 You who are not Jews by birth, here
is what I want you to remember. You are
called "uncircumcised" by those who call
themselves "circumcised." But they have
only been circumcised in their bodies by
human hands. 12 Before you believed in
Christ, you were separated from him. You
were not considered to be citizens of Israel. You were not included in what the
covenants promised. You were without
hope and without God in the world. 13 At
one time you were far away from God. But
now you belong to Christ Jesus. He spilled
his blood for you. This has brought you
near to God.

14 Christ himself is our peace. He has
made Jews and Gentiles into one group of
people. He has destroyed the hatred that
was like a wall between us. 15 Through his
body on the cross, Christ set aside the
law with all its commands and rules. He
planned to create one new people out of
Jews and Gentiles. He wanted to make
peace between them. 16 He planned to
bring both Jews and Gentiles back to
God as one body. He planned to do this
through the cross. On that cross, Christ
put to death their hatred toward one another. 17 He came and preached peace to
you who were far away. He also preached
peace to those who were near. 18 Through
Christ we both come to the Father by the
power of one Holy Spirit.

19 So you are no longer outsiders and
strangers. You are citizens together with
God's people. You are also members of
God's family. 20 You are a building that is
built on the apostles and prophets. They
are the foundation. Christ Jesus himself
is the most important stone in the building. 21 The whole building is held together
by him. It rises to become a holy temple
because it belongs to the Lord. 22 And because you belong to him, you too are being
built together. You are being made into a
house where God lives through his Spirit.

God's Wonderful Plan for the Gentiles

3 I, Paul, am a prisoner because of Christ Jesus. I am in prison because of my work among you who are Gentiles.

2 I am sure you have heard that God appointed me to share his grace with you. 3 I'm talking about the mystery God showed me. I have already written a little about it. 4 By reading about this mystery, you will be able to understand what I know. You will know about the mystery of Christ. 5 The mystery was not made known to people of other times. But now the Holy Spirit has made this mystery known to God's holy apostles and prophets. 6 Here is the mystery. Because of the good news, God's promises are for Gentiles as well as for Jews. Both groups are parts of one body. They share in the promise. It belongs to them because they belong to Christ Jesus.

7 I now serve the good news because God gave me his grace. His power is at work in me. 8 I am by far the least important of all the Lord's holy people. But he gave me the grace to preach to the Gentiles about the unlimited riches that Christ gives. 9 God told me to make clear to everyone how the mystery came about. In times past it was kept hidden in the mind of God, who created all things. 10 He wanted the rulers and authorities in the heavenly world to come to know his great wisdom. The church would make it known to them. 11 That was God's plan from the beginning. He has fulfilled his plan through Christ Jesus our Lord. 12 Through him and through faith in him we can approach God. We can come to him freely. We can come without fear. 13 So here is what I'm asking you to do. Don't lose hope because I am suffering for you. It will lead to the time when God will give you his glory.

Paul Prays for the Ephesians

14 I bow in prayer to the Father because of my work among you. 15 From the Father every family in heaven and on earth gets its name. 16 I pray that he will use his glorious riches to make you strong. May his Holy Spirit give you his power deep down inside you. 17 Then Christ will live in your hearts because you believe in him. And I pray that your love will have deep roots. I pray that it will have a strong foundation. 18 May you have power together with all the Lord's holy people to understand Christ's love. May you know how wide and long and high and deep it is. 19 And may you know his love, even though it can't be known completely. Then you will be filled with everything God has for you.

20 God is able to do far more than we could ever ask for or imagine. He does everything by his power that is working in us. 21 Give him glory in the church and in Christ Jesus. Give him glory through all time and for ever and ever. Amen.

Growing Up Together in the Body of Christ

4 I am a prisoner because of the Lord. So I am asking you to live a life worthy of what God chose you for. 2 Don't be proud at all. Be completely gentle. Be patient. Put up with one another in love. 3 The Holy Spirit makes you one in every way. So try your best to remain as one. Let peace keep you together. 4 There is one body and one Spirit. You were appointed to one hope when you were chosen. 5 There is one Lord, one faith and one baptism. 6 There is one God and Father of all. He is over everything. He is through everything. He is in everything.

7 But each one of us has received a gift of grace. These gifts are given to us by Christ. 8 That is why Scripture says,

> "When he went up to his place on
> high,
> he took many prisoners.
> He gave gifts to his people."
> (Psalm 68:18)

9 What does "he went up" mean? It can only mean that he also came down to the lower, earthly places. 10 The one who came down is the same one who went up. He went up higher than all the heavens. He did it in order to fill all creation. 11 So Christ himself gave the gift of the apostles to the church. He gave the prophets and those who preach the good news. And he also gave the pastors and teachers as a gift to the church. 12 He gave all these people so that they might prepare God's people to serve. Then the body of Christ will be built up. 13 That will continue until we all become one in the faith. We will also become one in the knowledge of God's Son. Then we will be grown up in the faith. We

will receive everything that Christ has for
us.
14 We will no longer be babies in the
faith. We won't be like ships tossed
around by the waves. We won't be blown
here and there by every new teaching. We
won't be blown around by cleverness and
tricks. Certain people use them to hide
their evil plans. 15 Instead, we will speak
the truth in love. So we will grow up in
every way to become the body of Christ.
Christ is the head of the body. 16 He makes
the whole body grow and build itself up
in love. Under the control of Christ, each
part of the body does its work. It supports
the other parts. In that way, the body is
joined and held together.

Teachings for Living as Christians

17 Here is what I'm telling you. I am
speaking for the Lord as I warn you. You
must no longer live as the Gentiles do.
Their thoughts don't have any purpose.
18 They can't understand the truth. They
are separated from the life of God. That's
because they don't know him. And they
don't know him because their hearts are
stubborn. 19 They have lost all feeling for
what is right. So they have given themselves over to all kinds of evil pleasures.
They take part in every kind of unclean
act. And they are full of greed.
20 But that is not the way of life in Christ
that you learned about. 21 You heard about
Christ and were taught about life in him.
What you learned was the truth about
Jesus. 22 You were taught not to live the
way you used to. You must get rid of your
old way of life. That's because it has been
made impure by the desire for things that
lead you astray. 23 You were taught to be
made new in your thinking. 24 You were
taught to start living a new life. It is created to be truly good and holy, just as
God is.
25 So each of you must get rid of your lying. Speak the truth to your neighbor. We
are all parts of one body. 26 Scripture says,
"When you are angry, do not sin." (Psalm
4:4) Do not let the sun go down while
you are still angry. 27 Don't give the devil
a chance. 28 Anyone who has been stealing must never steal again. Instead, they
must work. They must do something useful with their own hands. Then they will
have something to give to people in need.
29 Don't let any evil talk come out of
your mouths. Say only what will help to
build others up and meet their needs.
Then what you say will help those who
listen. 30 Do not make God's Holy Spirit
mourn. The Holy Spirit is the proof that
you belong to God. And the Spirit is the
proof that God will set you completely
free. 31 Get rid of all hard feelings, anger
and rage. Stop all fighting and lying. Don't
have anything to do with any kind of hatred. 32 Be kind and tender to one another.
Forgive one another, just as God forgave
you because of what Christ has done.
5 1 You are the children that God dearly
loves. So follow his example. 2 Lead
a life of love, just as Christ did. He loved
us. He gave himself up for us. He was a
sweet-smelling offering and sacrifice to
God.
3 There should not be even a hint of sexual sin among you. Don't do anything impure. And do not always want more and
more. These are not the things God's holy
people should do. 4 There must not be
any bad language or foolish talk or dirty
jokes. They are out of place. Instead, you
should give thanks. 5 Here is what you can
be sure of. Those who give themselves
over to sexual sins are lost. So are people
whose lives are impure. The same is true
of those who always want more and more.
People who do these things might as well
worship statues of gods. No one who does
them will receive a share in the kingdom
of Christ and of God. 6 Don't let anyone
fool you with worthless words. People
who say things like that aren't obeying
God. He is angry with them. 7 So don't go
along with people like that.
8 At one time you were in the dark. But
now you are in the light because of what
the Lord has done. Live like children of
the light. 9 The light produces what is
completely good, right and true. 10 Find
out what pleases the Lord. 11 Have nothing to do with the acts of darkness. They
don't produce anything good. Show what
they are really like. 12 It is shameful even to
talk about what people who don't obey do
in secret. 13 But everything the light shines
on can be seen. And everything that the
light shines on becomes a light. 14 That is
why it is said,

"Wake up, sleeper.
Rise from the dead.

Then Christ will shine on you."

15 So be very careful how you live. Do not live like people who aren't wise. Live like people who are wise. 16 Make the most of every opportunity. The days are evil. 17 So don't be foolish. Instead, understand what the Lord wants. 18 Don't fill yourself up with wine. Getting drunk will lead to wild living. Instead, be filled with the Holy Spirit. 19 Speak to one another with psalms, hymns and songs from the Spirit. Sing and make music from your heart to the Lord. 20 Always give thanks to God the Father for everything. Give thanks to him in the name of our Lord Jesus Christ.

Teachings for Christian Families

21 Follow the lead of one another because of your respect for Christ.

22 Wives, follow the lead of your own husbands as you follow the Lord. 23 The husband is the head of the wife, just as Christ is the head of the church. The church is Christ's body. He is its Savior. 24 The church follows the lead of Christ. In the same way, wives should follow the lead of their husbands in everything.

25 Husbands, love your wives. Love them just as Christ loved the church. He gave himself up for her. 26 He did it to make her holy. He made her clean by washing her with water and the word. 27 He did it to bring her to himself as a brightly shining church. He wants a church that has no stain or wrinkle or any other flaw. He wants a church that is holy and without blame. 28 In the same way, husbands should love their wives. They should love them as they love their own bodies. Any man who loves his wife loves himself. 29 After all, no one ever hated their own body. Instead, they feed and care for their body. And this is what Christ does for the church. 30 We are parts of his body. 31 Scripture says, "That's why a man will leave his father and mother and be joined to his wife. The two will become one." (Genesis 2:24) 32 That is a deep mystery. But I'm talking about Christ and the church. 33 A husband also must love his wife. He must love her just as he loves himself. And a wife must respect her husband.

6 Children, obey your parents as believers in the Lord. Obey them because it's the right thing to do. 2 Scripture says, "Honor your father and mother." That is the first commandment that has a promise. 3 "Then things will go well with you. You will live a long time on the earth." (Deuteronomy 5:16)

4 Fathers, don't make your children angry. Instead, instruct them and teach them the ways of the Lord as you raise them.

5 Slaves, obey your masters here on earth. Respect them and honor them with a heart that is true. Obey them just as you would obey Christ. 6 Don't obey them only to please them when they are watching. Do it because you are slaves of Christ. Be sure your heart does what God wants. 7 Serve your masters with all your heart. Work as serving the Lord and not as serving people. 8 You know that the Lord will give each person a reward. He will give to them in keeping with the good they do. It doesn't matter whether they are a slave or not.

9 Masters, treat your slaves in the same way. When you warn them, don't be too hard on them. You know that the God who is their Master and yours is in heaven. And he treats everyone the same.

God's Armor for Believers

10 Finally, let the Lord make you strong. Depend on his mighty power. 11 Put on all of God's armor. Then you can remain strong against the devil's evil plans. 12 Our fight is not against human beings. It is against the rulers, the authorities and the powers of this dark world. It is against the spiritual forces of evil in the heavenly world. 13 So put on all of God's armor. Evil days will come. But you will be able to stand up to anything. And after you have done everything you can, you will still be standing. 14 So remain strong in the faith. Put the belt of truth around your waist. Put the armor of godliness on your chest. 15 Wear on your feet what will prepare you to tell the good news of peace. 16 Also, pick up the shield of faith. With it you can put out all the flaming arrows of the evil one. 17 Put on the helmet of salvation. And take the sword of the Holy Spirit. The sword is God's word.

18 At all times, pray by the power of the Spirit. Pray all kinds of prayers. Be watchful, so that you can pray. Always keep on praying for all the Lord's people. 19 Pray also for me. Pray that whenever I speak,

the right words will be given to me. Then I can be bold as I tell the mystery of the good news. [20] Because of the good news, I am being held by chains as the Lord's messenger. So pray that I will be bold as I preach the good news. That's what I should do.

Final Greetings

[21] Tychicus is a dear brother. He is faithful in serving the Lord. He will tell you everything about me. Then you will know how I am and what I am doing. [22] That's why I am sending him to you. I want you to know how we are. And I want him to encourage you.

[23] May God the Father and the Lord Jesus Christ give peace to the brothers and sisters. May they also give the believers love and faith. [24] May grace be given to everyone who loves our Lord Jesus Christ with a love that will never die.

PHILIPPIANS

Paul wrote this letter to the people in Philippi who believed in Jesus. Philippi was an important city in the Roman Empire. Many retired Roman soldiers lived there. Paul visited this city on one of his trips bringing the good news about Jesus to the Gentile world. Paul started a church in Philippi. The Philippians became Paul's friends and gave him support for the rest of his life.

The Philippians heard that Paul was a prisoner in Rome. They collected money to assist him. They sent it to Paul with one of their members. He was a man named Epaphroditus. Later Paul sent Epaphroditus back to the Philippians with a letter. In that letter he thanked them for their friendship and support.

Paul knew that the faith of the Philippians was being challenged. So Paul uses his own life as an example. Paul is a prisoner of the Roman emperor. But Paul openly preaches that Jesus is the true ruler of the world. His life is an example of how to respond to hardship with joy and courage. Paul shows the strength of his faith. He hopes that the believers in Philippi will also be bold. And he hopes they will dare to preach the good news about Jesus without fear.

Paul also writes a beautiful hymn about Jesus. The hymn describes how humble Jesus was. He gave up his high position to become a servant. Jesus even gave up his life for the sake of others. Paul asks the people of Philippi to think and act like Jesus. Paul says this is the new way of living as members of God's kingdom.

God's kingdom is not completed yet. So Paul encourages the Philippians to live with hope. He tells them that Jesus will return. When that happens, believers will get new resurrection bodies just like Jesus.

---

1 We, Paul and Timothy, are writing this letter. We serve Christ Jesus.

We are sending this letter to you, all God's holy people in Philippi. You belong to Christ Jesus. We are also sending this letter to your leaders and deacons.

2 May God our Father and the Lord Jesus Christ give you grace and peace.

Paul Prays and Gives Thanks

3 I thank my God every time I remember you. 4 In all my prayers for all of you, I
always pray with joy. 5 I am happy because
you have joined me in spreading the good
news. You have done so from the first day
until now. 6 God began a good work in
you. And I am sure that he will carry it on
until it is completed. That will be on the
day Christ Jesus returns.
7 It is right for me to feel this way about
all of you. I love you with all my heart. I
may be held by chains, or I may be standing up for the truth of the good news. Either way, all of you share in God's grace
together with me. 8 God is my witness that
I long for all of you. I love you with the
love that Christ Jesus gives.
9 I pray that your love will grow more
and more. And let it be based on knowledge and understanding. 10 Then you will
be able to know what is best. Then you
will be pure and without blame for the
day that Christ returns. 11 You will be filled
with the fruit of right living produced by
Jesus Christ. All these things bring glory
and praise to God.

Paul Spreads the Good News While in Prison

12 Brothers and sisters, here is what I want
you to know. What has happened to me has
actually helped to spread the good news.
13 One thing has become clear. I am being
held by chains because I am a witness for
Christ. All the palace guards and everyone
else know it. 14 And because I am a prisoner,
most of the believers have become bolder
in the Lord. They now dare even more to
preach the good news without fear.
15 It's true that some preach about
Christ because they are jealous. But others preach about Christ to help me in my
work. 16 The last group acts out of love.
They know I have been put here to be a
witness for the good news. 17 But the others preach about Christ only to get ahead.
They preach Christ for the wrong reasons. They think they can stir up trouble
for me while I am being held by chains.
18 But what does it matter? Here is the important thing. Whether for right or wrong
reasons, Christ is being preached about.
That makes me very glad.

And I will continue to be glad. 19 I know
that you are praying for me. I also know

that God will give me the Spirit of Jesus
Christ to help me. So no matter what happens, I'm sure I will still be set free. 20 I
completely expect and hope that I won't
be ashamed in any way. I'm sure I will be
brave enough. Now as always Christ will
receive glory because of what happens to
me. He will receive glory whether I live or
die. 21 For me, life finds all its meaning in
Christ. Death also has its benefits. 22 Suppose I go on living in my body. Then I will
be able to carry on my work. It will bear
a lot of fruit. But what should I choose? I
don't know! 23 I can't decide between the
two. I long to leave this world and be with
Christ. That is better by far. 24 But it is more
important for you that I stay alive. 25 I'm
sure of this. So I know I will remain with
you. And I will continue with all of you
to help you grow in your faith. I will also
continue to help you be joyful in what you
have been taught. 26 I'm sure I will be with
you again. Then you will be able to boast
in Christ Jesus even more because of me.

Living to Honor the Good News

27 No matter what happens, live in a
way that brings honor to the good news
about Christ. Then I will know that you
remain strong together in the one Spirit.
I will know this if I come and see you or
only hear about you. I will know that you
work together as one person. I will know
that you work to spread the teachings
about the good news. 28 So don't be afraid
in any way of those who oppose you.
This will show them that they will be destroyed and that you will be saved. That's
what God will do. 29 Here is what he has
given you to do for Christ. You must not
only believe in him. You must also suffer
for him. 30 You are going through the same
struggle you saw me go through. As you
have heard, I am still struggling.

Being Humble Like Christ

2 So does belonging to Christ help you
in any way? Does his love comfort you
at all? Do you share anything in common
because of the Holy Spirit? Has Christ
ever been gentle and loving toward you?
2 If any of these things has happened to
you, then agree with one another. Have
the same love. Be one in spirit and in the
way you think and act. By doing this, you
will make my joy complete. 3 Don't do
anything only to get ahead. Don't do it
because you are proud. Instead, be humble. Value others more than yourselves.
4 None of you should look out just for your
own good. Each of you should also look
out for the good of others.

5 As you deal with one another, you
should think and act as Jesus did.

6 In his very nature he was God.
Jesus was equal with God. But
Jesus didn't take advantage of
that fact.
7 Instead, he made himself nothing.
He did this by taking on the nature
of a servant.
He was made just like human
beings.
8 He appeared as a man.
He was humble and obeyed God
completely.
He did this even though it led to
his death.
Even worse, he died on a cross!
9 So God lifted him up to the highest
place.
God gave him the name that is
above every name.
10 When the name of Jesus is spoken,
everyone will kneel down to
worship him.
Everyone in heaven and on earth
and under the earth will
kneel down to worship him.
11 Everyone's mouth will say that Jesus
Christ is Lord.
And God the Father will receive
the glory.

Live Without Complaining

12 My dear friends, you have always
obeyed God. You obeyed while I was with
you. And you have obeyed even more
while I am not with you. So continue to
work out your own salvation. Do it with
fear and trembling. 13 God is working in
you. He wants your plans and your acts to
fulfill his good purpose.

14 Do everything without complaining or
arguing. 15 Then you will be pure and without blame. You will be children of God
without fault among sinful and evil people.
Then you will shine among them like stars
in the sky. 16 You will shine as you hold on
tight to the word of life. Then I will be able
to boast about you on the day Christ re-

turns. I can be happy that I didn't run or
work for nothing. [17]But my life might even
be poured out like a drink offering on your
sacrifices. I'm talking about the way you
serve because you believe. Even so, I am
glad. I am joyful with all of you. [18]So you
too should be glad and joyful with me.

Timothy and Epaphroditus

[19]I hope to send Timothy to you soon if
the Lord Jesus allows it. Then I will be encouraged when I receive news about you.
[20]I have no one else like Timothy. He will
truly care about how you are doing. [21]All
the others are looking out for their own
interests. They are not looking out for the
interests of Jesus Christ. [22]But you know
that Timothy has proved himself. He has
served with me like a son with his father
in spreading the good news. [23]So I hope
to send him as soon as I see how things
go with me. [24]And I'm sure I myself will
come soon if the Lord allows it.

[25]But I think it's necessary to send
Epaphroditus back to you. He is my
brother in the Lord. He is a worker and a
soldier of Christ together with me. He is
also your messenger. You sent him to take
care of my needs. [26]He longs for all of you.
He is troubled because you heard he was
sick. [27]He was very sick. In fact, he almost
died. But God had mercy on him. He also
had mercy on me. God spared me sadness after sadness. [28]So I want even more
to send him to you. Then when you see
him again, you will be glad. And I won't
worry so much. [29]So then, welcome him
as a brother in the Lord with great joy.
Honor people like him. [30]He almost died
for the work of Christ. He put his life in
danger to make up for the help you yourselves couldn't give me.

Do Not Trust in Who You Are or What You Can Do

3 Further, my brothers and sisters, be
joyful because you belong to the Lord!
It is no trouble for me to write about some
important matters to you again. If you
know about them, you will have a safe
path to follow. [2]Watch out for those dogs.
They are people who do evil things. When
they circumcise, it is nothing more than a
useless cutting of the body. [3]But we have
been truly circumcised. We serve God by
the power of his Spirit. We boast about
what Christ Jesus has done. We don't put
our trust in who we are or what we can do.
[4]I have many reasons to trust in who I am
and what I have done. Someone else may
think they have reasons to trust in these
things. But I have even more.

[5]I was circumcised on the eighth day. I
am part of the people of Israel. I am from
the tribe of Benjamin. I am a pure Hebrew. As far as the law is concerned, I am
a Pharisee. [6]As far as being committed is
concerned, I opposed and attacked the
church. As far as keeping the law is concerned, I kept it perfectly.

[7]I thought things like that were really
something great. But now I consider them
to be nothing because of Christ. [8]Even
more, I consider everything to be nothing compared to knowing Christ Jesus my
Lord. To know him is worth much more
than anything else. Because of him I have
lost everything. But I consider all of it to
be garbage so I can know Christ better. [9]I
want to be joined to him. Being right with
God does not come from my obeying the
law. It comes because I believe in Christ.
It comes from God because of faith. [10]I
want to know Christ better. Yes, I want to
know the power that raised him from the
dead. I want to join him in his sufferings.
I want to become like him by sharing in
his death. [11]Then by God's grace I will rise
from the dead.

[12]I have not yet received all these
things. I have not yet reached my goal.
Christ Jesus took hold of me so that I
could reach that goal. So I keep pushing
myself forward to reach it. [13]Brothers and
sisters, I don't consider that I have taken
hold of it yet. But here is the one thing I
do. I forget what is behind me. I push hard
toward what is ahead of me. [14]I push myself forward toward the goal to win the
prize. God has appointed me to win it.
The heavenly prize is Christ Jesus himself.

Following Paul's Example

[15]So all of us who are grown up in the
faith should see things this way. Maybe
you think differently about something. But
God will make it clear to you. [16]Only let us
live up to what we have already reached.

[17]Brothers and sisters, join together
in following my example. You have us as
a model. So pay close attention to those
who live as we do. [18]I have told you these

things many times before. Now I tell you again with tears in my eyes. Many people live like enemies of the cross of Christ. 19 The only thing they have coming to them is death. Their stomach is their god. They brag about what they should be ashamed of. They think only about earthly things. 20 But we are citizens of heaven. And we can hardly wait for a Savior from there. He is the Lord Jesus Christ. 21 He has the power to bring everything under his control. By his power he will change our earthly bodies. They will become like his glorious body.

Remain Strong in the Lord

4 My brothers and sisters, in this way remain strong in the Lord. I love you and long for you. Dear friends, you are my joy and my crown.

2 Here is what I'm asking Euodia and Syntyche to do. I'm asking them to work together in the Lord. That's because they both belong to the Lord. 3 My true companion, here is what I ask you to do. Help these women, because they have served at my side. They have worked with me to spread the good news. So have Clement and the rest of those who have worked together with me. Their names are all written in the book of life.

Final Commands

4 Always be joyful because you belong to the Lord. I will say it again. Be joyful! 5 Let everyone know how gentle you are. The Lord is coming soon. 6 Don't worry about anything. No matter what happens, tell God about everything. Ask and pray, and give thanks to him. 7 Then God's peace will watch over your hearts and your minds. He will do this because you belong to Christ Jesus. God's peace can never be completely understood.

8 Finally, my brothers and sisters, always think about what is true. Think about what is noble, right and pure. Think about what is lovely and worthy of respect. If anything is excellent or worthy of praise, think about those kinds of things. 9 Do what you have learned or received or heard from me. Follow my example. The God who gives peace will be with you.

Paul Gives Thanks for the Philippians' Gifts

10 At last you are concerned about me again. That makes me very happy. We belong to the Lord. I know that you were concerned. But you had no chance to show it. 11 I'm not saying this because I need anything. I have learned to be content no matter what happens to me. 12 I know what it's like not to have what I need. I also know what it's like to have more than I need. I have learned the secret of being content no matter what happens. I am content whether I am well fed or hungry. I am content whether I have more than enough or not enough. 13 I can do all this by the power of Christ. He gives me strength.

14 But it was good of you to share in my troubles. 15 And you believers at Philippi know what happened when I left Macedonia. Not one church helped me in the matter of giving and receiving. You were the only one that did. That was in the early days when you first heard the good news. 16 Even when I was in Thessalonica, you sent me help when I needed it. And you did it more than once. 17 It is not that I want your gifts. What I really want is what is best for you. 18 I have received my full pay and have more than enough. I have everything I need. That's because Epaphroditus brought me the gifts you sent. They are a sweet-smelling offering. They are a gift that God accepts. He is pleased with it. 19 My God will meet all your needs. He will meet them in keeping with his wonderful riches. These riches come to you because you belong to Christ Jesus.

20 Give glory to our God and Father for ever and ever. Amen.

Final Greetings

21 Greet all God's people. They belong to Christ Jesus. The brothers and sisters who are with me send greetings. 22 All God's people here send you greetings. Most of all, those who live in the palace of Caesar send you greetings.

23 May the grace of the Lord Jesus Christ be with your spirit. Amen.

COLOSSIANS

Paul was in prison in Rome. He was waiting for his trial before the Emperor Caesar. It was during this time Paul wrote to the believers in the city of Colossae. Paul had never met this group of believers. But they knew who he was. And they respected Paul's leadership and teaching. When Paul was in Ephesus, he had worked with a man named Epaphras. Epaphras was from the city of Colossae. So Paul sent Epaphras back to Colossae to bring the good new about Jesus. Epaphras shared the good news about Jesus in Colossae. He also brought the good news to the cities of Laodicea and Hierapolis. Epaphras was later arrested and brought to Rome as a prisoner. Paul learned what was happening in these cities from Epaphras.

The people in Colossae were mostly Gentiles. But like the believers in Galatia they were being pushed to follow the Jewish laws. They were being asked to add extra rules and false teachings to their faith. Some of this group of believers thought they were better than the others. That's because they had visions and believed they received secret spiritual knowledge. So Paul wrote this letter to all of them. Paul told them that nothing needs to be added to their faith. Faith in Jesus the Messiah is all they need to be saved.

Paul states clearly that all things in heaven and earth were created through Jesus. All things were brought back to God by Jesus' death on the cross. Jesus Christ is the fullness of God's being. Paul tells the Colossians that belief in Jesus Christ is all they need to be saved. God has made them into new people. So now they can live their faith to the fullest. Nothing needs to be added to it. Paul ends his letter with practical advice on how to live the new life of following Jesus.

---

1 I, Paul, am writing this letter. I am an apostle of Christ Jesus just as God planned. Our brother Timothy joins me in writing.

2 We are sending this letter to you, our brothers and sisters in Colossae. You belong to Christ. You are holy and faithful.

May God our Father give you grace and peace.

Paul Prays and Gives Thanks

3 We always thank God, the Father of our Lord Jesus Christ, when we pray for
you. 4 We thank him because we have heard about your faith in Christ Jesus. We have also heard that you love all God's
people. 5 Your faith and love are based on the hope you have. What you hope for is stored up for you in heaven. You have already heard about it. You were told about it when the true message was given to you. I'm talking about the good news
6 that has come to you. In the same way, the good news is bearing fruit. It is bearing fruit and growing all over the world. It has been doing that among you since the day you heard it. That is when you really
understood God's grace. 7 You learned the good news from Epaphras. He is dear to us. He serves Christ together with us. He faithfully works for Christ and for us
among you. 8 He also told us about your love that comes from the Holy Spirit.

9 That's why we have not stopped praying for you. We have been praying for you since the day we heard about you. We keep asking God to fill you with the knowledge of what he wants. We pray he will give you the wisdom and understanding that the Spirit gives.
10 Then you will be able to lead a life that is worthy of the Lord. We pray that you will please him in every way. So we want you to bear fruit in every good thing you do. We pray that you will grow to know God better.
11 We want you to be very strong, in keeping with his glorious power. We want you to be patient. We pray that you will never
give up. 12 We want you to give thanks with joy to the Father. He has made you fit to have what he will give to all his holy people. You will all receive a share in the
kingdom of light. 13 He has saved us from the kingdom of darkness. He has brought us into the kingdom of the Son he loves.
14 Because of what the Son has done, we have been set free. Because of him, all our sins have been forgiven.

The Son of God Is Better Than Everything Else

15 The Son is the exact likeness of God, who can't be seen. The Son is first, and
he is over all creation. 16 All things were

created in him. He created everything in heaven and on earth. He created everything that can be seen and everything that can't be seen. He created kings, powers, rulers and authorities. All things have been created by him and for him. 17 Before anything was created, he was already there. He holds everything together. 18 And he is the head of the body, which is the church. He is the beginning. He is the first to be raised from the dead. That happened so that he would be far above everything. 19 God was pleased to have his whole nature living in Christ. 20 God was pleased to bring all things back to himself. That's because of what Christ has done. These things include everything on earth and in heaven. God made peace through Christ's blood, by his death on the cross.

21 At one time you were separated from God. You were enemies in your minds because of your evil ways. 22 But because Christ died, God has brought you back to himself. Christ's death has made you holy in God's sight. So now you don't have any flaw. You are free from blame. 23 But you must keep your faith steady and firm. You must not move away from the hope the good news holds out to you. This is the good news that you heard. It has been preached to every creature under heaven. I, Paul, now serve the good news.

Paul's Work for the Church

24 I am happy because of what I am suffering for you. My suffering joins with and continues the sufferings of Christ. I suffer for his body, which is the church. 25 I serve the church. God appointed me to bring the complete word of God to you. 26 That word contains the mystery that has been hidden for many ages. But now it has been made known to the Lord's people. 27 God has chosen to make known to them the glorious riches of that mystery. He has made it known among the Gentiles. And here is what it is. Christ is in you. He is your hope of glory.

28 Christ is the one we preach about. With all the wisdom we have, we warn and teach everyone. When we bring them to God, we want them to be like Christ. We want them to be grown up as people who belong to Christ. 29 That's what I'm working for. I work hard with all the strength of Christ. His strength works powerfully in me.

2 I want you to know how hard I am working for you. I'm concerned for those who are in Laodicea. I'm also concerned for everyone who has not met me in person. 2 My goal is that their hearts may be encouraged and strengthened. I want them to be joined together in love. Then their understanding will be rich and complete. They will know the mystery of God. That mystery is Christ. 3 All the treasures of wisdom and knowledge are hidden in him. 4 But I don't want anyone to fool you with words that only sound good. 5 So even though I am away from you in body, I am with you in spirit. And I am glad to see that you are controlling yourselves. I am happy that your faith in Christ is so strong.

Having All Things in Christ

6 You received Christ Jesus as Lord. So keep on living your lives in him. 7 Have your roots in him. Build yourselves up in him. Grow strong in what you believe, just as you were taught. Be more thankful than ever before.

8 Make sure no one controls you. They will try to control you by using false reasoning that has no meaning. Their ideas depend on human teachings. They also depend on the basic spiritual powers of this world. They don't depend on Christ.

9 God's whole nature is living in Christ in human form. 10 Because you belong to Christ, you have been made complete. He is the ruler over every power and authority. 11 When you received Christ, your circumcision was not done by human hands. Instead, your circumcision was done by Christ. He put away the person you used to be. At that time, sin's power ruled over you. 12 When you were baptized, you were buried together with Christ. And you were raised to life together with him when you were baptized. You were raised to life by believing in God's work. God himself raised Jesus from the dead.

13 At one time you were dead in your sins. Your desires controlled by sin were not circumcised. But God gave you new life together with Christ. He forgave us all our sins. 14 He wiped out what the law said that we owed. The law stood against us. It judged us. But he has taken it away and nailed it to the cross. 15 He took away the weapons of the powers and authorities. He made a public show of them. He won the battle over them by dying on the cross.

Freedom From Human Rules

16 So don't let anyone judge you because of what you eat or drink. Don't let anyone judge you about holy days. I'm talking about special feasts and New Moons and Sabbath days. 17 They are only a shadow of the things to come. But what is real is found in Christ. 18 Some people enjoy pretending they aren't proud. They worship angels. But don't let people like that judge you. These people tell you every little thing about what they have seen. They are proud of their useless ideas. That's because their minds are not guided by the Holy Spirit. 19 They aren't connected anymore to the head, who is Christ. But the whole body grows from the head. The muscles and tendons hold the body together. And God causes it to grow.

20 Some people still follow the basic spiritual powers of the world. But you died with Christ as far as these powers are concerned. So why do you act as if you still belong to the world? Here are the rules you follow. 21 "Do not handle! Do not taste! Do not touch!" 22 Rules like these are about things that will pass away soon. They are based on merely human rules and teachings. 23 It is true that these rules seem wise. Because of them, people give themselves over to their own kind of worship. They pretend they are humble. They treat their bodies very badly. But rules like these don't help. They don't stop people from chasing after sinful pleasures.

Teachings About Holy Living

3 You have been raised up with Christ. So think about things that are in heaven. That is where Christ is. He is sitting at God's right hand. 2 Think about things that are in heaven. Don't think about things that are only on earth. 3 You died. Now your life is hidden with Christ in God. 4 Christ is your life. When he appears again, you also will appear with him in heaven's glory.

5 So put to death anything that comes from sinful desires. Get rid of sexual sins and impure acts. Don't let your feelings get out of control. Remove from your life all evil desires. Stop always wanting more and more. You might as well be worshiping statues of gods. 6 God's anger is going to come because of these things. 7 That's the way you lived at one time in your life. 8 But now here are the kinds of things you must also get rid of. You must get rid of anger, rage, hate and lies. Let no dirty words come out of your mouths. 9 Don't lie to one another. You have gotten rid of your old way of life and its habits. 10 You have started living a new life. Your knowledge of how that life should have the Creator's likeness is being made new. 11 Here there is no Gentile or Jew. There is no difference between those who are circumcised and those who are not. There is no rude outsider, or even a Scythian. There is no slave or free person. But Christ is everything. And he is in everything.

12 You are God's chosen people. You are holy and dearly loved. So put on tender mercy and kindness as if they were your clothes. Don't be proud. Be gentle and patient. 13 Put up with one another. Forgive one another if you are holding something against someone. Forgive, just as the Lord forgave you. 14 And over all these good things put on love. Love holds them all together perfectly as if they were one.

15 Let the peace that Christ gives rule in your hearts. As parts of one body, you were appointed to live in peace. And be thankful. 16 Let the message about Christ live among you like a rich treasure. Teach and correct one another wisely. Teach one another by singing psalms and hymns and songs from the Spirit. Sing to God with thanks in your hearts. 17 Do everything you say or do in the name of the Lord Jesus. Always give thanks to God the Father through Christ.

Teachings About Christian Families

18 Wives, follow the lead of your husbands. That's what the Lord wants you to do.

19 Husbands, love your wives. Don't be mean to them.

20 Children, obey your parents in everything. That pleases the Lord.

21 Fathers, don't make your children bitter. If you do, they will lose hope.

22 Slaves, obey your earthly masters in everything. Don't do it just to please them when they are watching you. Obey them with an honest heart. Do it out of respect for the Lord. 23 Work at everything you do with all your heart. Work as if you were working for the Lord, not for human masters. 24 Work because you know that you

will finally receive as a reward what the
Lord wants you to have. You are slaves
of the Lord Christ. 25 Anyone who does
wrong will be paid back for what they do.
God treats everyone the same.

4 Masters, give your slaves what is right
and fair. Do it because you know that
you also have a Master in heaven.

More Teachings

2 Give a lot of time and effort to prayer.
Always be watchful and thankful. 3 Pray
for us too. Pray that God will give us an
opportunity to preach our message. Then
we can preach the mystery of Christ. Because I preached it, I am being held by
chains. 4 Pray that I will preach it clearly,
as I should. 5 Be wise in the way you act
toward outsiders. Make the most of every
opportunity. 6 Let the words you speak always be full of grace. Learn how to make
your words what people want to hear.
Then you will know how to answer everyone.

Final Greetings

7 Tychicus will tell you all the news
about me. He is a dear brother. He is a
faithful worker. He serves the Lord together with us. 8 I am sending him to you
for one reason. I want you to know what is
happening here. I want him to encourage
you and make your hearts strong. 9 He is
coming with Onesimus, our faithful and
dear brother. He is one of you. They will
tell you everything that is happening here.

10 Aristarchus is in prison with me. He
sends you his greetings. So does Mark, the
cousin of Barnabas. You have been given
directions about him. If he comes to you,
welcome him. 11 Jesus, who is called Justus, also sends greetings. They are the
only Jews who have worked together with
me for God's kingdom. They have been a
comfort to me. 12 Epaphras sends greetings. He is one of you. He serves Christ
Jesus. He is always praying hard for you.
He prays that you will hold on tightly to
all that God has in mind for us. He prays
that you will keep growing in your knowledge of what God wants. He also prays
that you will be completely sure about it.
13 I am happy to tell you that he is working
very hard for you. He is also working hard
for everyone in Laodicea and Hierapolis.
14 Our dear friend Luke, the doctor, sends
greetings. So does Demas. 15 Give my
greetings to the brothers and sisters in Laodicea. Also give my greetings to Nympha
and the church that meets in her house.

16 After this letter has been read to you,
send it on. Be sure that it is also read to
the church in Laodicea. And be sure that
you read the letter from Laodicea.

17 Tell Archippus, "Be sure that you
complete the work the Lord gave you to
do."

18 I, Paul, am writing this greeting with
my own hand. Remember that I am being
held by chains. May grace be with you.

1 THESSALONIANS

Paul, Silas and Timothy went to the city of Thessalonica. There they preached the good news about Jesus the Messiah. Many people became believers. But that caused disorder in the city. Paul and Silas were accused of disobeying the Roman emperor's laws. That's because they preached that there was another king. And that king was Jesus. Paul and Silas narrowly escaped and had to run away from the city.

Later Paul became concerned about the believers in Thessalonica. These believers were suffering because of their faith. Because of this, Paul was afraid they would lose their faith. So Paul sent Timothy to encourage them. It was safe for Timothy to go there because he was Greek. When Timothy returned to Achaia where Paul was staying, he had good news. The believers in Thessalonica had remained faithful. So Paul wrote this letter to tell them how happy he was.

In this short letter, Paul begins by remembering his time in Thessalonica. He gives thanks for the believers' faith even though they have struggles and challenges. Paul then teaches them how to live lives that are pleasing to God. They are to avoid sexual immorality. They are to love one another. And they are to work hard to earn their own living.

Paul then writes about a very important question. The believers in Thessalonica were asking what happens to believers who die before Jesus returns. Paul explains that believers who die are not lost. They will be raised from the dead when Jesus returns as the world's king. Paul reminds the Thessalonians that Jesus will appear suddenly when no one expects it. So they must live lives that are pleasing to God. Then they will not be ashamed when he comes again. Throughout the letter Paul tells them to keep up their good work.

---

1 I, Paul, am writing this letter. Silas and
Timothy join me in writing.

We are sending this letter to you, the members of the church in Thessalonica. You belong to God the Father and the Lord Jesus Christ.

May grace and peace be given to you.

Paul Gives Thanks for the Thessalonians' Faith

2 We always thank God for all of you. We
keep on praying for you. 3 We remember
you when we pray to our God and Father.
Your work is produced by your faith. Your
service is the result of your love. Your
strength to continue comes from your
hope in our Lord Jesus Christ.
4 Brothers and sisters, you are loved by
God. We know that he has chosen you.
5 Our good news didn't come to you only
in words. It came with power. It came with
the Holy Spirit's help. He gave us complete faith in what we were preaching. You
know how we lived among you for your
good. 6 We and the Lord were your examples. You followed us. You welcomed
our message even when you were suffering terribly. You welcomed it with the joy
the Holy Spirit gives. 7 So you became a
model to all the believers in the lands of
Macedonia and Achaia. 8 The Lord's message rang out from you. That was true not
only in Macedonia and Achaia. Your faith
in God has also become known everywhere. So we don't have to say anything
about it. 9 The believers themselves report
the kind of welcome you gave us. They tell
about how you turned away from statues
of gods. And you turned to serve the living and true God. 10 They tell about how
you are waiting for his Son to come from
heaven. God raised him from the dead.
He is Jesus. He saves us from God's anger,
and his anger is sure to come.

Paul's Work for God in Thessalonica

2 Brothers and sisters, you know that
our visit to you produced results.
2 You know what happened earlier in the
city of Philippi. We suffered, and people treated us very badly there. But God
gave us the boldness to tell you his good
news. We preached to you even when
people strongly opposed us. 3 The appeal we make is based on truth. It comes
from a pure heart. We are not trying to
trick you. 4 In fact, it is just the opposite.
God has approved us to preach. He has
trusted us with the good news. We aren't
trying to please people. We want to please
God. He tests our hearts. 5 As you know,
we never praised you if we didn't mean it.
We didn't put on a mask to cover up any
sinful desire. God is our witness that this
is true. 6 We were not expecting people to

praise us. We were not looking for praise from you or anyone else. Yet as Christ's apostles, we could have used our authority over you. 7 Instead, we were like young children when we were with you.

As a mother feeds and cares for her little children, 8 we cared for you. We loved you so much. So we were happy to share with you God's good news. We were also happy to share our lives with you. 9 Brothers and sisters, I am sure you remember how hard we worked. We labored night and day while we preached to you God's good news. We didn't want to cause you any expense. 10 You are witnesses of how we lived among you believers. God is also a witness that we were holy and godly and without blame. 11 You know that we treated each of you as a father treats his own children. 12 We gave you hope and strength. We comforted you. We really wanted you to live in a way that is worthy of God. He chooses you to enter his glorious kingdom.

13 We never stop thanking God for the way you received his word. You heard it from us. But you didn't accept it as a human word. You accepted it for what it really is. It is God's word. It is really at work in you who believe. 14 Brothers and sisters, you became like the members of God's churches in Judea. They are believers in Christ Jesus, just as you are. Your own people made you suffer. You went through the same things the church members in Judea suffered from the Jews. 15 The Jews who killed the Lord Jesus and the prophets also forced us to leave. They do not please God. They are enemies of everyone. 16 They try to keep us from speaking to the Gentiles. These Jews don't want the Gentiles to be saved. In this way, these Jews always increase their sins to the limit. God's anger has come on them at last.

Paul Wants to See the Believers in Thessalonica

17 Brothers and sisters, we were separated from you for a short time. Apart from you, we were like children without parents. We were no longer with you in person. But we kept you in our thoughts. We really wanted to see you. So we tried very hard to do so. 18 We wanted to come to you. Again and again I, Paul, wanted to come. But Satan blocked our way. 19 What is our hope? What is our joy? When our Lord Jesus returns, what is the crown we will delight in? Isn't it you? 20 Yes, you are our glory and our joy.

3 We couldn't wait any longer. So we thought it was best to be left by ourselves in Athens. 2 We sent our brother Timothy to give you strength and hope in your faith. He works together with us in God's service to spread the good news about Christ. 3 We sent him so that no one would be upset by times of testing. You know very well that we have to go through times of testing. 4 In fact, when we were with you, here is what we kept telling you. We were telling you that our enemies would make us suffer. As you know very well, it has turned out that way. 5 That's the reason I sent someone to find out about your faith. I couldn't wait any longer. I was afraid that Satan had tempted you in some way. Then our work among you would have been useless.

Timothy Brings a Good Report

6 But Timothy has come to us from you just now. He has brought good news about your faith and love. He has told us that you always have happy memories of us. He has also said that you desire to see us, just as we desire to see you. 7 Brothers and sisters, in all our trouble and suffering your faith encouraged us. 8 Now we really live, because you are standing firm in the Lord. 9 How can we thank God enough for you? We thank God because of all the joy we have in his presence. We have this joy because of you. 10 Night and day we pray very hard that we will see you again. We want to give you what is missing in your faith.

11 Now may a way be opened up for us to come to you. May our God and Father himself and our Lord Jesus do this. 12 May the Lord make your love grow. May it be like a rising flood. May your love for one another increase. May it also increase for everyone else. May it be just like our love for you. 13 May the Lord give you strength in your hearts. Then you will be holy and without blame in the sight of our God and Father. May that be true when our Lord Jesus comes with all his holy ones.

Living in a Way That Pleases God

4 Now I want to talk about some other matters, brothers and sisters. We

taught you how to live in a way that
pleases God. In fact, that is how you are
living. In the name of the Lord Jesus we
ask and beg you to do it more and more.
2 You know the directions we gave you.
They were given by the authority of the
Lord Jesus.

3 God wants you to be made holy. He
wants you to stay away from sexual sins.
4 He wants all of you to learn to control
your own bodies. You must live in a way
that is holy. You must live with honor.
5 Don't desire to commit sexual sins like
people who don't know God. 6 None of
you should sin against your brother or
sister by doing that. You should not take
advantage of your brother or sister. The
Lord will punish everyone who commits
these kinds of sins. We have already told
you and warned you about this. 7 That's
because God chose us to live pure lives.
He wants us to be holy. 8 Suppose someone refuses to accept our teaching. They
are not turning their back on us. They are
turning their back on God. This same God
gives you his Holy Spirit.

9 We don't need to write to you about
your love for one another. God himself has taught you to love one another.
10 In fact, you do love all God's family all
around Macedonia. Brothers and sisters,
we are asking you to love one another
more and more. 11 And do everything you
can to live a quiet life. You should mind
your own business. And work with your
hands, just as we told you to. 12 Then unbelievers will have respect for your everyday life. And you won't have to depend on
anyone.

What Happens to Believers Who Have Died

13 Brothers and sisters, we want you to
know what happens to those who die. We
don't want you to mourn, as other people do. They mourn because they don't
have any hope. 14 We believe that Jesus
died and rose again. When he returns,
many who believe in him will have died
already. We believe that God will bring
them back with Jesus. 15 This agrees with
what the Lord has said. When the Lord
comes, many of us will still be alive. We
tell you that we will certainly not go up
before those who have died. 16 The Lord
himself will come down from heaven.
We will hear a loud command. We will
hear the voice of the leader of the angels.
We will hear a blast from God's trumpet.
Many who believe in Christ will have died
already. They will rise first. 17 After that,
we who are still alive and are left will be
caught up together with them. We will be
taken up in the clouds. We will meet the
Lord in the air. And we will be with him
forever. 18 So encourage one another with
these words of comfort.

The Day of the Lord Is Coming

5 Brothers and sisters, we don't have to
write to you about times and dates.
2 You know very well how the day of the
Lord will come. It will come like a thief
in the night. 3 People will be saying that
everything is peaceful and safe. Then
suddenly they will be destroyed. It will
happen like birth pains coming on a pregnant woman. None of the people will escape.

4 Brothers and sisters, you are not in
darkness. So that day should not surprise
you as a thief would. 5 All of you are children of the light. You are children of the
day. We don't belong to the night. We
don't belong to the darkness. 6 So let us
not be like the others. They are asleep.
Instead, let us be wide awake and in full
control of ourselves. 7 Those who sleep,
sleep at night. Those who get drunk, get
drunk at night. 8 But we belong to the day.
So let us control ourselves. Let us put on
our chest the armor of faith and love. Let
us put on the hope of salvation like a helmet. 9 God didn't choose us to receive his
anger. He chose us to receive salvation
because of what our Lord Jesus Christ has
done. 10 Jesus died for us. Some will be
alive when he comes. Others will be dead.
Either way, we will live together with him.
11 So encourage one another with the
hope you have. Build each other up. In
fact, that's what you are doing.

Final Teachings

12 Brothers and sisters, we ask you to
accept the godly leaders who work hard
among you. They care for you in the Lord.
They correct you. 13 Have a lot of respect
for them. Love them because of what
they do. Live in peace with one another.
14 Brothers and sisters, we are asking you
to warn certain people. These people

don't want to work. Instead, they make
trouble. We are also asking you to encourage those who have lost hope. Help those
who are weak. Be patient with everyone.
15 Make sure that no one pays back one
wrong act with another. Instead, always
try to do what is good for each other and
for everyone else.

16 Always be joyful. 17 Never stop praying. 18 Give thanks no matter what happens. God wants you to thank him
because you believe in Christ Jesus.

19 Don't try to stop what the Holy
Spirit is doing. 20 Don't treat prophecies
as if they weren't important. 21 But test
all prophecies. Hold on to what is good.
22 Say no to every kind of evil.

23 God is the God who gives peace. May
he make you holy through and through.
May your whole spirit, soul and body be
kept free from blame. May you be without blame from now until our Lord Jesus
Christ comes. 24 The God who has chosen
you is faithful. He will do all these things.

25 Brothers and sisters, pray for us.

26 Greet all God's people with a holy
kiss.

27 While the Lord is watching, here is
what I command you. Have this letter
read to all the brothers and sisters.

28 May the grace of our Lord Jesus Christ
be with you.

2 THESSALONIANS

Paul wrote a second letter to the Thessalonians shortly after the first letter. Paul had to write to correct a false report about something he had said. Some believers thought Paul had said the day of the Lord had already come. The words "day of the Lord" are from the Old Testament prophets. These words are used to describe God's victory over all of his enemies. And these words tell when his faithful followers will receive their reward. The Thessalonians were concerned about this. If that was so, they thought they could not expect anything better from God. Nothing more would be made right. And that was discouraging because they were suffering for their faith.

Paul begins by encouraging these believers in Thessalonica. He assures them God will pay back those who were giving them trouble. He goes on to remind them of details he had given them before. He had told them how the day of the Lord would arrive. Paul then repeats some instructions about how to live lives that please God. He tells them not to be lazy but to work hard. They are to earn their own living.

The letter was most likely written by a scribe. The scribe would write as Paul spoke to him. But at the end of the letter, Paul adds a greeting in his own handwriting. He does this so the Thessalonians will know for sure these teachings come from him.

---

1 I, Paul, am writing this letter. Silas and
Timothy join me in writing.

We are sending this letter to you, the members of the church in Thessalonica. You belong to God our Father and the Lord Jesus Christ.

2 May God the Father and the Lord Jesus
Christ give you grace and peace.

Paul Prays and Gives Thanks

3 Brothers and sisters, we should always
thank God for you. That is only right, because your faith is growing more and
more. We also thank God that the love
you all have for one another is increasing.
4 So among God's churches we brag about
the fact that you don't give up easily. We
brag about your faith in all the suffering
and testing you are going through.
5 All of this proves that when God
judges, he is fair. So you will be considered worthy to enter God's kingdom.
You are suffering for his kingdom. 6 God
is fair. He will pay back trouble to those
who give you trouble. 7 He will help you
who are troubled. And he will also help
us. All these things will happen when
the Lord Jesus appears from heaven. He
will come in blazing fire. He will come
with his powerful angels. 8 He will punish
those who don't know God. He will punish those who don't obey the good news
about our Lord Jesus. 9 They will be destroyed forever. They will be shut out of
heaven. They will never see the glory of
the Lord's strength. 10 All these things will
happen when he comes. On that day his
glory will be seen in his holy people. Everyone who has believed will be amazed
when they see him. This includes you,
because you believed the witness we
gave you.
11 Keeping this in mind, we never stop
praying for you. Our God has chosen you.
We pray that he will make you worthy of
his choice. We pray he will make every
good thing you want to do come true.
We pray that he will do this by his power.
We pray that he will make perfect all that
you have done by faith. 12 We pray this so
that the name of our Lord Jesus will receive glory through what you have done.
We also pray that you will receive glory
through what he has done. We pray all
these things in keeping with the grace of
our God and the Lord Jesus Christ.

The Man of Sin

2 Brothers and sisters, we want to ask
you something. It has to do with the
coming of our Lord Jesus Christ. It concerns the time when we will go to be with
him. 2 What if you receive a message that
is supposed to have come from us? What
if it says that the day of the Lord has already come? If it does, we ask you not to
become easily upset or alarmed. Don't
be upset whether that message is spoken
or written or prophesied. 3 Don't let anyone trick you in any way. That day will not
come until people rise up against God.
It will not come until the man of sin appears. He is a marked man. He is headed
for ruin. 4 He will oppose everything that

is called God. He will oppose everything that is worshiped. He will give himself power over everything. He will set himself up in God's temple. He will announce that he himself is God.

5 Don't you remember? When I was with you, I used to tell you these things. 6 Now you know what is holding back the man of sin. He is held back so that he can make his appearance at the right time. 7 The secret power of sin is already at work. But the one who now holds back that power will keep doing it until he is taken out of the way. 8 Then the man of sin will appear. The Lord Jesus will overthrow him with the breath of his mouth. The glorious brightness of Jesus' coming will destroy the man of sin. 9 The coming of the man of sin will fit how Satan works. The man of sin will show his power through all kinds of signs and wonders. These signs and wonders will lead people astray. 10 So people who are dying will be fooled by this evil. These people are dying because they refuse to love the truth. The truth would save them. 11 So God will fool them completely. Then they will believe the lie. 12 Many will not believe the truth. They will take pleasure in evil. They will be judged.

Remain Strong in the Faith

13 Brothers and sisters, we should always thank God for you. The Lord loves you. That's because God chose you as the first to be saved. Salvation comes through the Holy Spirit's work. He makes people holy. It also comes through believing the truth. 14 He chose you to be saved by accepting the good news that we preach. And you will share in the glory of our Lord Jesus Christ.

15 Brothers and sisters, remain strong in the faith. Hold on to what we taught you. We passed our teachings on to you by what we preached and wrote.

16 Our Lord Jesus Christ and God our Father loved us. By his grace God gave us comfort that will last forever. The hope he gave us is good. May our Lord Jesus Christ and God our Father 17 comfort your hearts. May they make you strong in every good thing you do and say.

Paul Asks for Prayer

3 Now I want to talk about some other matters. Brothers and sisters, pray for us. Pray that the Lord's message will spread quickly. Pray that others will honor it just as you did. 2 And pray that we will be saved from sinful and evil people. Not everyone is a believer. 3 But the Lord is faithful. He will strengthen you. He will guard you from the evil one. 4 We trust in the Lord. So we are sure that you are doing the things we tell you to do. And we are sure that you will keep on doing them. 5 May the Lord fill your hearts with God's love. May Christ give you the strength to go on.

Paul Warns Those Who Do Not Want to Work

6 Brothers and sisters, here is a command we give you. We give it in the name of the Lord Jesus Christ. Keep away from every believer who doesn't want to work and makes trouble. Keep away from any believer who doesn't live up to the teaching you received from us. 7 You know how you should follow our example. We worked when we were with you. 8 We didn't eat anyone's food without paying for it. In fact, it was just the opposite. We worked night and day. We worked very hard so that we wouldn't cause any expense to any of you. 9 We worked, even though we have the right to receive help from you. We did it in order to be a model for you to follow. 10 Even when we were with you, we gave you a rule. We said, "Anyone who won't work shouldn't be allowed to eat."

11 We hear that some people among you don't want to work and are making trouble. They aren't really busy. Instead, they are bothering others. 12 We belong to the Lord Jesus Christ. So we strongly command people like that to settle down. They have to earn the food they eat. 13 Brothers and sisters, don't ever get tired of doing what is good.

14 Keep an eye on anyone who doesn't obey the teachings in our letter. Don't have anything to do with that person. Then they will feel ashamed. 15 But don't think of them as an enemy. Instead, warn them as you would warn another believer.

Final Greetings

[16]May the Lord who gives peace give
you peace at all times and in every way.
May the Lord be with all of you.

[17]I, Paul, write this greeting in my own
handwriting. That's how I prove that I am
the author of all my letters. I always do it
that way.

[18]May the grace of our Lord Jesus Christ
be with you all.

1 TIMOTHY

After Paul had been freed from prison in Rome he heard there were problems in the church at Ephesus. Some leaders in Ephesus had changed the message of the good news. They changed the message Paul had preached to them. These leaders misused the Jewish law by limiting the foods people could eat. These leaders also taught wrong ideas about how to grow spiritually. And they used some practices from the worldly beliefs of that day. These false leaders even allowed immoral behavior.

So Paul sent Timothy to Ephesus and wrote him a letter. Paul wanted Timothy to share the letter with the believers there. Paul hoped the letter would give Timothy the power and authority to set things right. Timothy would have to be in charge until Paul could come himself.

Paul writes in this letter about leadership in the church. He describes what true leadership looks like. This would help the Ephesians say no to those who weren't qualified to lead. And they would know how to choose those who were. Paul includes a special warning near the end of the letter. He warns about the dangers of being greedy. Paul wants them to know it is important to not trust money. God is the one we can trust.

Throughout the letter Paul uses the phrase "Christ Jesus" meaning "Jesus the Messiah." Paul wants to point out that Jesus rules as King. This would help remind the church that Jesus was their real leader. And Jesus the Messiah was and is the best example of true leadership.

---

1 I, Paul, am writing this letter. I am an
apostle of Christ Jesus, just as God our
Savior commanded. Christ Jesus also commanded it. We have put our hope in him.

2 Timothy, I am sending you this letter.
You are my true son in the faith.

May God the Father and Christ Jesus
our Lord give you grace, mercy and peace.

Paul Warns Timothy to Oppose False Teachers

3 Timothy, stay there in Ephesus. That
is what I told you to do when I went into
Macedonia. I want you to command certain people not to teach things that aren't
true. 4 And command them not to spend
their time on stories that are made up.
They must not waste time on family his-
tories that never end. These things only
lead to fights about ideas. They don't help
God's work move forward. His work is
done by faith. 5 Love is the purpose of my
command. Love comes from a pure heart.
It comes from a good sense of what is
right and wrong. It comes from faith that
is honest and true. 6 Some have turned
from these teachings. They would rather
talk about things that have no meaning.
7 They want to be teachers of the law. And
they are very sure about that law. But they
don't know what they are talking about.

8 We know that the law is good if it is
used properly. 9 We also know that the law
isn't made for godly people. It is made for
those who break the law. It is for those who
refuse to obey. It is for ungodly and sinful
people. It is for those who aren't holy and
who don't believe. It is for those who kill
their fathers or mothers. It is for murderers. 10 It is for those who commit sexual
sins. It is for those who commit homosex-
ual acts. It is for people who buy and sell
slaves. It is for liars. It is for people who tell
lies in court. It is for those who are a witness to things that aren't true. And it is for
anything else that is the opposite of true
teaching. 11 True teaching agrees with the
good news about the glory of the blessed
God. He trusted me with that good news.

The Lord Pours Out His Grace on Paul

12 I am thankful to Christ Jesus our Lord.
He has given me strength. I thank him
that he considered me faithful. I thank
him for appointing me to serve him. 13 I
used to speak evil things against Jesus. I
tried to hurt his followers. I really pushed
them around. But God showed me mercy
anyway. I did those things without knowing any better. I wasn't a believer. 14 Our
Lord poured out more and more of his
grace on me. Along with it came faith and
love from Christ Jesus.

15 Here is a saying that you can trust. It
should be accepted completely. Christ
Jesus came into the world to save sinners.
And I am the worst sinner of all. 16 But for
that very reason, God showed me mercy.
And I am the worst of sinners. He showed

me mercy so that Christ Jesus could show that he is very patient. I was an example for those who would come to believe in him. Then they would receive eternal life. 17 The eternal King will never die. He can't be seen. He is the only God. Give him honor and glory for ever and ever. Amen.

Paul Commands Timothy

18 My son Timothy, I am giving you this command. It is in keeping with the prophecies once made about you. By remembering them, you can fight the battle well. 19 Then you will hold on to faith. You will hold on to a good sense of what is right and wrong. Some have not accepted this knowledge of right and wrong. So they have destroyed their faith. They are like a ship that has sunk. 20 Hymenaeus and Alexander are among them. I have handed them over to Satan. That will teach them not to speak evil things against God.

Teachings About Worship

2 First, I want you to pray for all people. Ask God to help and bless them. Give thanks for them. 2 Pray for kings. Pray for everyone who is in authority. Pray that we can live peaceful and quiet lives. And pray that we will be godly and holy. 3 This is good, and it pleases God our Savior. 4 He wants all people to be saved. He wants them to come to know the truth. 5 There is only one God. And there is only one go-between for God and human beings. He is the man Christ Jesus. 6 He gave himself to pay for the sins of all people. We have been told this message at just the right time. 7 I was appointed to be a messenger and an apostle to preach the good news. I am telling the truth. I'm not lying. God appointed me to be a true and faithful teacher of the Gentiles.

8 So I want the men in every place to pray. I want them to lift up holy hands. I don't want them to be angry when they pray. I don't want them to argue. 9 In the same way, I want the women to be careful how they dress. They should wear clothes that are right and proper. They shouldn't wear their hair in very fancy styles. They shouldn't wear gold or pearls. They shouldn't wear clothes that cost a lot of money. 10 Instead, they should put on good works as if good works were their clothes. This is proper for women who claim to worship God.

11 When a woman is learning, she should be quiet. She should follow her leaders in every way. 12 I do not let women teach or take authority over a man. They must be quiet. 13 That's because Adam was made first. Then Eve was made. 14 Adam was not the one who was tricked. The woman was tricked and became a sinner. 15 Will women be saved by having children? Only if they keep on believing, loving, and leading a holy life in a proper way.

Rules for Choosing Leaders and Deacons

3 Here is a saying you can trust. If anyone wants to be a leader in the church, they want to do a good work for God and people. 2 A leader must be free from blame. He must be faithful to his wife. In anything he does, he must not go too far. He must control himself. He must be worthy of respect. He must welcome people into his home. He must be able to teach. 3 He must not get drunk. He must not push people around. He must be gentle. He must not be a person who likes to argue. He must not love money. 4 He must manage his own family well. He must make sure that his children obey him. And he must do this in a way that gains him respect. 5 Suppose someone doesn't know how to manage his own family. Then how can he take care of God's church? 6 The leader must not be a new believer. If he is, he might become proud. Then he would be judged just like the devil. 7 The leader must also be respected by those who are outside the church. Then he will not be put to shame. He will not fall into the devil's trap.

8 In the same way, deacons must be worthy of respect. They must be honest and true. They must not drink too much wine. They must not try to get money by cheating people. 9 They must hold on to the deep truths of the faith. Even their own minds tell them to do that. 10 First they must be tested. Then let them serve as deacons if there is nothing against them.

11 In the same way, the women must be worthy of respect. They must not say things that harm others. In anything they do, they must not go too far. They must be worthy of trust in everything.

12 A deacon must be faithful to his wife. He must manage his children and family

well. [13]Those who have served well earn the full respect of others. They also become more sure of their faith in Christ Jesus.

Paul's Reasons for Giving Instructions to Timothy

[14]I hope I can come to you soon. But now I am writing these instructions to you. [15]Then if I have to put off my visit, you will know how people should act in God's family. The family of God is the church of the living God. It is the pillar and foundation of the truth. [16]There is no doubt that true godliness comes from this great mystery.

Jesus came as a human being.
  The Holy Spirit proved that he was the Son of God.
He was seen by angels.
  He was preached among the nations.
People in the world believed in him.
  He was taken up to heaven in glory.

4 The Holy Spirit clearly says that in the last days some people will leave the faith. They will follow spirits that will fool them. They will believe things that demons will teach them. [2]Teachings like those come from liars who pretend to be what they are not. Their sense of what is right and wrong has been destroyed. It's as though it has been burned with a hot iron. [3]They do not allow people to get married. They order them not to eat certain foods. But God created those foods. So people who believe and know the truth should receive them and give thanks for them. [4]Everything God created is good. You shouldn't turn anything down. Instead, you should thank God for it. [5]The word of God and prayer make it holy.

[6]Point out these things to the brothers and sisters. Then you will serve Christ Jesus well. You will show that you've grown in the truths of the faith. You will show that you've been trained by the good teaching you've obeyed. [7]Don't have anything to do with godless stories and silly tales. Instead, train yourself to be godly. [8]Training the body has some value. But being godly has value in every way. It promises help for the life you are now living and the life to come. [9]This is the truth you can trust and accept completely. [10]This is why we work and try so hard. It's because we have put our hope in the living God. He is the Savior of all people. Most of all, he is the Savior of those who believe.

[11]Command and teach these things. [12]Don't let anyone look down on you because you are young. Set an example for the believers in what you say and in how you live. Also set an example in how you love and in what you believe. Show the believers how to be pure. [13]Until I come, spend your time reading Scripture out loud to one another. Spend your time preaching and teaching. [14]Don't fail to use the gift the Holy Spirit gave you. He gave it to you through a prophecy from God. It was given when the elders placed their hands on you.

[15]Keep on doing these things. Give them your complete attention. Then everyone will see how you are coming along. [16]Be careful of how you live and what you believe. Never give up. Then you will save yourself and those who hear you.

Instructions About Widows, Elders and Slaves

5 Correct an older man in a way that shows respect. Make an appeal to him as if he were your father. Treat younger men as if they were your brothers. [2]Treat older women as if they were your mothers. Treat younger women as if they were your sisters. Be completely pure in the way you treat them.

[3]Take care of the widows who really need help. [4]But suppose a widow has children or grandchildren. They should first learn to put their faith into practice. They should care for their own family. In that way they will pay back their parents and grandparents. That pleases God. [5]A widow who really needs help and is left all alone puts her hope in God. Night and day she keeps on praying. Night and day she asks God for help. [6]But a widow who lives for pleasure is dead even while she is still living. [7]Give these instructions to the people. Then no one can be blamed. [8]Everyone should provide for their own relatives. Most of all, everyone should take care of their own family. If they don't, they have left the faith. They are worse than someone who doesn't believe.

9 No widow should be put on the list of
widows unless she is more than 60 years
old. She must also have been faithful to
her husband. 10 She must be well known
for the good things she does. That includes bringing up children. It includes
inviting guests into her home. It includes
washing the feet of the Lord's people. It
includes helping those who are in trouble. A widow should spend her time doing all kinds of good things.

11 Don't put younger widows on that
kind of list. They might want pleasure
more than they want Christ. Then they
would want to get married again. 12 If they
do that, they will be judged. They have
broken their first promise. 13 Besides, they
get into the habit of having nothing to
do. They go around from house to house.
They waste their time. They also bother
other people and say things that make no
sense. They shouldn't say those things.
14 So here is the advice I give to younger
widows. Get married. Have children. Take
care of your own homes. Don't give the
enemy the chance to tell lies about you.
15 In fact, some have already turned away
to follow Satan.

16 Suppose a woman is a believer and
takes care of widows. She should continue
to help them. She shouldn't let the church
pay the expenses. Then the church can
help the widows who really need it.

17 The elders who do the church's work
well are worth twice as much honor. That
is true in a special way of elders who
preach and teach. 18 Scripture says, "Do
not stop an ox from eating while it helps
separate the grain from the straw." (Deuteronomy 25:4) Scripture also says, "Workers are worthy of their pay." (Luke 10:7)
19 Don't believe a charge against an elder
unless two or three witnesses bring it.
20 But those elders who are sinning should
be corrected in front of everyone. This
will be a warning to the others. 21 I command you to follow these instructions.
I command you in the sight of God and
Christ Jesus and the chosen angels. Treat
everyone the same. Don't favor one person over another.

22 Don't be too quick to place your
hands on others to set them apart to serve
God. Don't take part in the sins of others.
Keep yourself pure.

23 Stop drinking only water. If your
stomach is upset, drink a little wine. It can
also help the other sicknesses you often
have.

24 The sins of some people are easy to
see. They are already being judged. Others will be judged later. 25 In the same way,
good works are easy to see. But even good
works that are hard to see can't stay hidden forever.

6 All who are forced to serve as slaves
should consider their masters worthy of full respect. Then people will not
speak evil things against God's name
and against what we teach. 2 Some slaves
have masters who are believers. They
shouldn't show their masters disrespect
just because they are also believers. Instead, they should serve them even better. That's because their masters are loved
by them as believers. These masters are
committed to caring for their slaves.

People Who Teach Lies or Love Money

These are the things you are to teach.
Try hard to get the believers to do them.
3 Suppose someone teaches something
different than I have taught. Suppose that
person doesn't agree with the true teaching of our Lord Jesus Christ. Suppose they
don't agree with godly teaching. 4 Then
that person is proud and doesn't understand anything. They like to argue more
than they should. They can't agree about
what words mean. All of this results in
wanting what others have. It causes fighting, harmful talk, and evil distrust. 5 It stirs
up trouble all the time among people
whose minds are twisted by sin. The truth
they once had has been taken away from
them. They think they can get rich by being godly.

6 You gain a lot when you live a godly
life. But you must be happy with what
you have. 7 We didn't bring anything into
the world. We can't take anything out of
it. 8 If we have food and clothing, we will
be happy with that. 9 People who want
to get rich are tempted. They fall into
a trap. They are tripped up by wanting
many foolish and harmful things. Those
who live like that are dragged down by
what they do. They are destroyed and die.
10 Love for money causes all kinds of evil.
Some people want to get rich. They have
wandered away from the faith. They have
wounded themselves with many sorrows.

Paul Gives a Final Command to Timothy

11 But you are a man of God. Run away
from all these things. Try hard to do what
is right and godly. Have faith, love and
gentleness. Hold on to what you believe.
12 Fight the good fight along with all other believers. Take hold of eternal life.
You were chosen for it when you openly
told others what you believe. Many witnesses heard you. 13 God gives life to everything. Christ Jesus told the truth when
he was a witness in front of Pontius Pilate. In the sight of God and Christ, I give
you a command. 14 Obey it until our Lord
Jesus Christ appears. Obey it completely.
Then no one can find fault with it or you.
15 God will bring Jesus back at a time that
pleases him. God is the blessed and only
Ruler. He is the greatest King of all. He is
the most powerful Lord of all. 16 God is the
only one who can't die. He lives in light
that no one can get close to. No one has
seen him. No one can see him. Honor and
power belong to him forever. Amen.
17 Command people who are rich in this
world not to be proud. Tell them not to
put their hope in riches. Wealth is so un-
certain. Command those who are rich to
put their hope in God. He richly provides
us with everything to enjoy. 18 Command
the rich to do what is good. Tell them to
be rich in doing good things. They must
give freely. They must be willing to share.
19 In this way, they will store up true riches
for themselves. It will provide a firm basis
for the next life. Then they will take hold
of the life that really is life.
20 Timothy, guard what God has trusted
you with. Turn away from godless chat-
ter. Stay away from opposing ideas that
are falsely called knowledge. 21 Some people believe them. By doing that they have
turned away from the faith.

May God's grace be with you all.

2 TIMOTHY

Paul's helper Timothy was in the church at Ephesus. Timothy had to deal with some of the church's leaders. These leaders were teaching things that were not true. When Timothy struggled with this problem, Paul came back to Ephesus. Paul suffered a great deal of harm there. This was from Alexander who was one of these false leaders. Because of what Alexander did, Paul was once again taken as a prisoner. Paul was sent to Rome. And this time Paul expected there would be a trial and he would be killed. So Paul wrote to Timothy asking him to come quickly to Rome.

The two leaders who opposed Paul were named Alexander and Hymenaeus. These men were leading the believers into a false understanding of the faith. Their teaching encouraged arguing rather than faithful living. Paul ordered both Alexander and Hymenaeus to not be leaders any more. But they continued to oppose Paul. Then other people joined with them to oppose Paul.

Timothy was discouraged by what had happened. So Paul wrote this letter to encourage Timothy to be faithful to the true message. Paul told Timothy to be faithful even if it means suffering or death. He reminds Timothy there will trouble and suffering before Jesus comes again as king. Paul states that there will be false teachers. They will challenge the faithfulness of God's people.

Paul encourages Timothy to remember the good news. The message is that Jesus Christ died and rose again from the dead. Jesus is the promised Messiah from the family line of David. Paul reminds Timothy that the sacred writings come from God. Timothy has known those writings since he was a child. Knowing this will help Timothy continue doing the good work he was called to do.

---

1 I, Paul, am writing this letter. I am an
apostle of Christ Jesus just as God
planned. He sent me to tell about the
promise of life found in Christ Jesus.

2Timothy, I am sending you this letter.
You are my dear son.

May God the Father and Christ Jesus
our Lord give you grace, mercy and peace.

Paul Gives Thanks

3I thank God, whom I serve as did our
people of long ago. I serve God, knowing
that what I have done is right. Night and
day I thank God for you. Night and day I
always remember you in my prayers. 4I
remember your tears. I long to see you so
that I can be filled with joy. 5I remember
your honest and true faith. It was alive
first in your grandmother Lois and in your
mother Eunice. And I am certain that it is
now alive in you also.

Paul Encourages Timothy to Be Faithful

6This is why I remind you to help God's
gift grow, just as a small spark grows into a
fire. God put his gift in you when I placed
my hands on you. 7God gave us his Spirit.
And the Spirit doesn't make us weak and
fearful. Instead, the Spirit gives us power
and love. He helps us control ourselves.
8So don't be ashamed of the message
about our Lord. And don't be ashamed
of me, his prisoner. Instead, join with me
as I suffer for the good news. God's power
will help us do that. 9God has saved us. He
has chosen us to live a holy life. It wasn't
because of anything we have done. It was
because of his own purpose and grace.
Through Christ Jesus, God gave us this
grace even before time began. 10It has now
been made known through the coming of
our Savior, Christ Jesus. He has broken the
power of death. Because of the good news,
he has brought life out into the light. That
life never dies. 11I was appointed to announce the good news. I was appointed to
be an apostle and a teacher. 12That's why
I'm suffering the way I am. But this gives
me no reason to be ashamed. That's because I know who I have believed in. I am
sure he is able to take care of what I have
given him. I can trust him with it until the
day he returns as judge.

13Follow what you heard from me as
the pattern of true teaching. Follow it with
faith and love because you belong to Christ
Jesus. 14Guard the truth of the good news
that you were trusted with. Guard it with
the help of the Holy Spirit who lives in us.

Examples of Faithful and Unfaithful People

15You know that all the believers in Asia
Minor have deserted me. They include
Phygelus and Hermogenes.

16 May the Lord show mercy to all who
live in the house of Onesiphorus. He often
encouraged me. He was not ashamed that
I was being held by chains. 17 In fact, it was
just the opposite. When he was in Rome,
he looked everywhere for me. At last he
found me. 18 May Onesiphorus find mercy
from the Lord on the day Jesus returns
as judge! You know very well how many
ways Onesiphorus helped me in Ephesus.

Paul Again Encourages Timothy to Be Faithful

2 My son, be strong in the grace that is
yours in Christ Jesus. 2 You have heard
me teach in front of many witnesses. Pass
on to people you can trust the things
you've heard me say. Then they will be
able to teach others also. 3 Like a good soldier of Christ Jesus, join with me in suffering. 4 A soldier does not take part in things
that don't have anything to do with the
army. Instead, he tries to please his commanding officer. 5 It is the same for anyone who takes part in a sport. They don't
receive the winner's crown unless they
play by the rules. 6 The farmer who works
hard should be the first to receive a share
of the crops. 7 Think about what I'm saying. The Lord will help you understand
what all of it means.

8 Remember Jesus Christ. He came
from David's family line. He was raised
from the dead. That is my good news. 9 I
am suffering for it. I have even been put in
chains like someone who has committed
a crime. But God's word is not held back
by chains. 10 So I put up with everything
for the good of God's chosen people.
Then they also can be saved. Christ Jesus
saves them. He gives them glory that will
last forever.

11 Here is a saying you can trust.

If we died with him,
    we will also live with him.
12 If we don't give up,
    we will also rule with him.
If we say we don't know him,
    he will also say he doesn't
        know us.
13 Even if we are not faithful,
    he remains faithful.
    He must be true to himself.

What to Do About False Teachers

14 Keep reminding God's people of
these things. While God is watching,
warn them not to argue about words. That
doesn't have any value. It only destroys
those who listen. 15 Do your best to please
God. Be a worker who doesn't need to
be ashamed. Teach the message of truth
correctly. 16 Stay away from godless chat-
ter. Those who take part in it will become
more and more ungodly. 17 Their teaching will spread like a deadly sickness. Hymenaeus and Philetus are two of those
teachers. 18 They have turned away from
the truth. They say that the time when
people will rise from the dead has already
come. They destroy the faith of some people. 19 But God's solid foundation stands
firm. Here is the message written on it.
"The Lord knows who his own people
are." (Numbers 16:5) Also, "All who say they
believe in the Lord must turn away from
evil."

20 In a large house there are things made
out of gold and silver. But there are also
things made out of wood and clay. Some
have special purposes. Others have common purposes. 21 Suppose someone stays
away from what is common. Then the
Master will be able to use them for special
purposes. They will be made holy. They
will be ready to do any good work.

22 Run away from the evil things that
young people long for. Try hard to do
what is right. Have faith, love and peace.
Do these things together with those
who call on the Lord from a pure heart.
23 Don't have anything to do with arguing.
It is dumb and foolish. You know it only
leads to fights. 24 Anyone who serves the
Lord must not be hard to get along with.
Instead, they must be kind to everyone.
They must be able to teach. The one who
serves must not hold anything against
anyone. 25 They must gently teach those
who are against them. Maybe God will
give a change of heart to those who are
against you. That will lead them to know
the truth. 26 Maybe they will come to their
senses. Maybe they will escape the devil's
trap. He has taken them as prisoners to do
what he wanted.

3 Here is what I want you to know.
There will be terrible times in the last
days. 2 People will love themselves. They
will love money. They will brag and be

proud. They will tear others down. They will not obey their parents. They won't be thankful or holy. 3 They won't love others. They won't forgive others. They will tell lies about people. They will be out of control. They will be wild. They will hate what is good. 4 They will turn against their friends. They will act without thinking. They will think they are better than others. They will love what pleases them instead of loving God. 5 They will act as if they were serving God. But what they do will show that they have turned their backs on God's power. Have nothing to do with these people.

6 They are the kind who trick their way into the homes of some women. These women are ready to believe anything. And they take control over these women. These women are loaded down with sins. They give in to all kinds of evil desires. 7 They are always learning. But they are never able to come to know the truth. 8 Jannes and Jambres opposed Moses. In the same way, the teachers I'm talking about oppose the truth. Their minds are twisted. As far as the faith is concerned, God doesn't accept them. 9 They won't get very far. Just like Jannes and Jambres, their foolish ways will be clear to everyone.

Paul Gives a Final Command to Timothy

10 But you know all about my teaching. You know how I live and what I live for. You know about my faith and love. You know how patient I am. You know I haven't given up. 11 You know that I was treated badly. You know that I suffered greatly. You know what kinds of things happened to me in Antioch, Iconium and Lystra. You know how badly I have been treated. But the Lord saved me from all my troubles. 12 In fact, everyone who wants to live a godly life in Christ Jesus will be treated badly. 13 Evil people and pretenders will go from bad to worse. They will fool others, and others will fool them. 14 But I want you to continue to follow what you have learned and are sure about. You know the people you learned it from. 15 You have known the Holy Scriptures ever since you were a little child. They are able to teach you how to be saved by believing in Christ Jesus. 16 God has breathed life into all Scripture. It is useful for teaching us what is true. It is useful for correcting our mistakes. It is useful for making our lives whole again. It is useful for training us to do what is right. 17 By using Scripture, the servant of God can be completely prepared to do every good thing.

4 I give you a command in the sight of God and Christ Jesus. Christ will judge the living and the dead. Because he and his kingdom are coming, here is the command I give you. 2 Preach the word. Be ready to serve God in good times and bad. Correct people's mistakes. Warn them. Encourage them with words of hope. Be very patient as you do these things. Teach them carefully. 3 The time will come when people won't put up with true teaching. Instead, they will try to satisfy their own desires. They will gather a large number of teachers around them. The teachers will say what the people want to hear. 4 The people will turn their ears away from the truth. They will turn to stories that aren't true. 5 But I want you to keep your head no matter what happens. Don't give up when times are hard. Work to spread the good news. Do everything God has given you to do.

6 I am already being poured out like a drink offering. The time when I will leave is near. 7 I have fought the good fight. I have finished the race. I have kept the faith. 8 Now there is a crown waiting for me. It is given to those who are right with God. The Lord, who judges fairly, will give it to me on the day he returns. He will not give it only to me. He will also give it to all those who are longing for him to return.

Personal Words

9 Do your best to come to me quickly. 10 Demas has deserted me. He has gone to Thessalonica. He left me because he loved this world. Crescens has gone to Galatia. Titus has gone to Dalmatia. 11 Only Luke is with me. Get Mark and bring him with you. He helps me in my work for the Lord. 12 I sent Tychicus to Ephesus. 13 When you come, bring my coat. I left it with Carpus at Troas. Also bring my books. Most of all, bring the ones made out of animal skins.

14 Remember Alexander, the one who works with metal. He did me a great deal of harm. The Lord will pay him back for what he has done. 15 You too should watch out for him. He strongly opposed our message.

[16]The first time I was put on trial, no one came to help me. Everyone deserted me. I hope they will be forgiven for it. [17]The Lord stood at my side. He gave me the strength to preach the whole message. Then all the Gentiles heard it. I was saved from the lion's mouth. [18]The Lord will save me from every evil attack. He will bring me safely to his heavenly kingdom. Give him glory for ever and ever. Amen.

Final Greetings

[19]Greet Priscilla and Aquila. Greet those who live in the house of Onesiphorus. [20]Erastus stayed in Corinth. I left Trophimus sick in Miletus. [21]Do your best to get here before winter. Eubulus greets you. So do Pudens, Linus, Claudia and all the brothers and sisters.

[22]May the Lord be with your spirit. May God's grace be with you all.

TITUS

The church on the island of Crete was in trouble. Some false leaders there were hurting the community of believers. Paul had to give authority to Titus who was one of his important helpers. With that authority Titus could represent Paul in Crete.

This letter from Paul is addressed to Titus. But it is meant for the whole church on Crete. Paul gives his own authority to Titus so that he could teach and lead. Paul instructs Titus to appoint godly leaders. Paul describes the false teachings found in the church in Crete. The leaders are misusing Jewish laws. They told the people not to eat certain foods. They told the people they needed to be circumcised. And they taught ideas that made people argue. None of these teachings helped the people live lives that were pleasing to God. Paul tells the community of believers that the grace of God has come into the world. It is for all people. Through faith in Jesus the Messiah, people can live a new kind of life.

Then Paul tells of his plan to spend the winter in Nicopolis. It is a city on the west coast of Macedonia. From Nicopolis Paul could bring the good news to the western part of the Roman Empire. Paul trusts that Titus will help bring order to the church in Crete. Then Titus could go with Paul on this new adventure.

---

1 I, Paul, am writing this letter. I serve
God, and I am an apostle of Jesus
Christ. God sent me to help his chosen
people believe in Christ more and more.
God sent me to help them understand
even more the truth that leads to godly
living. [2]That belief and understanding
lead to the hope of eternal life. Before
time began, God promised to give that
life. And he does not lie. [3]Now, at just the
right time, he has made his promise clear.
He did this through the preaching that he
trusted me with. God our Savior has commanded all these things.

[4]Titus, I am sending you this letter. You
are my true son in the faith we share.

May God the Father and Christ Jesus our Savior give you grace and peace.

Choosing Elders Who Love What Is Good

[5]I left you on the island of Crete. I did
this because there were some things that
hadn't been finished. I wanted you to
put them in order. I also wanted you to
appoint elders in every town. I told you
how to do it. [6]An elder must be without
blame. He must be faithful to his wife.
His children must be believers. They
must not give anyone a reason to say that
they are wild and don't obey. [7]A church
leader takes care of God's family. That's
why he must be without blame. He must
not look after only his own interests. He
must not get angry easily. He must not
get drunk. He must not push people
around. He must not try to get money
by cheating people. [8]Instead, a church
leader must welcome people into his
home. He must love what is good. He
must control his mind and feelings. He
must do what is right. He must be holy.
He must control the desires of his body.
[9]The message as it has been taught can
be trusted. He must hold firmly to it.
Then he will be able to use true teaching to comfort others and build them up.
He will be able to prove that people who
oppose it are wrong.

Warning People Who Fail to Do Good

[10]Many people refuse to obey God. All
they do is talk about things that mean
nothing. They try to fool others. No one
does these things more than the circumcision group. [11]They must be stopped.
They are making trouble for entire families. They do this by teaching things they
shouldn't. They do these things to cheat
people. [12]One of Crete's own prophets
has a saying. He says, "People from Crete
are always liars. They are evil beasts. They
don't want to work. They live only to eat."
[13]This saying is true. So give a strong warning to people who refuse to obey God.
Then they will understand the faith correctly. [14]Then they will pay no attention to
Jewish stories that aren't true. They won't
listen to the mere human commands of
people who turn away from the truth. [15]To
people who are pure, all things are pure.
But to those who have twisted minds and
don't believe, nothing is pure. In fact,
their minds and their sense of what is

right and wrong are twisted. 16 They claim
to know God. But their actions show they
don't know him. They are hated by God.
They refuse to obey him. They aren't fit to
do anything good.

Doing Good Because of the Good News

2 But what you teach must agree with
true teaching. 2 Tell the older men that
in anything they do, they must not go too
far. They must be worthy of respect. They
must control themselves. They must have
true faith. They must love others. They
must not give up.
3 In the same way, teach the older wom-
en to lead a holy life. They must not tell
lies about others. They must not let wine
control them. Instead, they must teach
what is good. 4 Then they can advise the
younger women to love their husbands
and children. 5 The younger women must
control themselves and be pure. They
must take good care of their homes. They
must be kind. They must follow the lead of
their husbands. Then no one will be able
to speak evil things against God's word.
6 In the same way, help the young men
to control themselves. 7 Do what is good.
Set an example for them in everything.
When you teach, be honest and serious.
8 No one can question the truth. So teach
what is true. Then those who oppose you
will be ashamed. That's because they will
have nothing bad to say about us.
9 Teach slaves to obey their masters in
everything they do. Tell them to try to
please their masters. They must not talk
back to them. 10 They must not steal from
them. Instead, they must show that they
can be trusted completely. Then they will
make the teaching about God our Savior
appealing in every way.
11 God's grace has now appeared. By his
grace, God offers to save all people. 12 His
grace teaches us to say no to godless ways
and sinful desires. We must control ourselves. We must do what is right. We must
lead godly lives in today's world. 13 That's
how we should live as we wait for the
blessed hope God has given us. We are
waiting for Jesus Christ to appear in his
glory. He is our great God and Savior. 14 He
gave himself for us. By doing that, he set
us free from all evil. He wanted to make
us pure. He wanted us to be his very own
people. He wanted us to desire to do what
is good.
15 These are the things you should
teach. Encourage people and give them
hope. Correct them with full authority.
Don't let anyone look down on you.

Do What Is Good Because You Are Saved

3 Remind God's people to obey rulers
and authorities. Remind them to be
ready to do what is good. 2 Tell them not to
speak evil things against anyone. Remind
them to live in peace. They must consider
the needs of others. They must always be
gentle toward everyone.
3 At one time we too acted like fools.
We didn't obey God. We were tricked.
We were controlled by all kinds of desires and pleasures. We were full of evil.
We wanted what belongs to others. People hated us, and we hated one another.
4 But the kindness and love of God our
Savior appeared. 5 He saved us. It wasn't
because of the good things we had done.
It was because of his mercy. He saved us
by washing away our sins. We were born
again. The Holy Spirit gave us new life.
6 God poured out the Spirit on us freely.
That's because of what Jesus Christ our
Savior has done. 7 His grace made us right
with God. So now we have received the
hope of eternal life as God's children.
8 You can trust this saying. These things
are important. Treat them that way. Then
those who trust in God will be careful to
commit themselves to doing good. These
things are excellent. They are for the
good of everyone.
9 But keep away from foolish disagree-
ments. Don't argue about family his-
tories. Don't make trouble. Don't fight
about what the law teaches. Don't argue
about things like that. It doesn't do any
good. It doesn't help anyone. 10 Warn anyone who tries to get believers to separate
from one another. Warn that person more
than once. After that, have nothing to do
with them. 11 You can be sure that people
like this are twisted and sinful. Their own
actions judge them.

Final Words

12 I will send Artemas or Tychicus to
you. Then do your best to come to me at
Nicopolis. I've decided to spend the win-

ter there. [13] Do everything you can to help Zenas the lawyer and Apollos. Send them on their way. See that they have everything they need. [14] Our people must learn to commit themselves to doing what is good. Then they can provide for people when they are in great need. If they do that, their lives won't turn out to be useless.

[15] Everyone who is with me sends you greetings. Greet those who love us in the faith.

May God's grace be with you all.

PHILEMON

Philemon was a wealthy man who lived in the city of Colossae. There was a church that met in his home. Paul writes this letter to Philemon about a problem. The problem has to do with a man named Onesimus. Onesimus was originally from Colossae. He was a slave who belonged to Philemon. It seems that Onesimus had taken some things from Philemon and run away. He had gone all the way to Rome. But while in Rome, Onesimus met Paul and became a believer in Jesus. Paul was in prison and Onesimus had been helping him. Now Paul needed him to return to Colossae. Paul hoped that when Onesimus returned, Philemon would forgive him. Paul hoped Philemon would welcome Onesimus as a brother and not as a slave.

Paul's letter to Philemon is brief. He tells Philemon about the important changes in Onesimus' life. The name Onesimus means "useful" in Greek. Paul tells Philemon that Onesimus was "useless." He was a slave who couldn't be trusted. But Onesimus began to follow Jesus. Now he has become useful to both of them. Paul does not force Philemon to do anything. Paul bases his appeal to him on love. Paul promises to pay anything that Onesimus owes Philemon.

Most likely Paul's appeal was successful. Otherwise, this letter would not have been saved. The life of Onesimus is a clear example of how the good news about Jesus can change a person. This is the message that spread throughout the Roman Empire. And thousands of lives were changed.

---

1 I, Paul, am writing this letter. I am a
prisoner because of Christ Jesus. Our
brother Timothy joins me in writing.

Philemon, we are sending you this letter. You are our dear friend. You work together with us. 2 We are also sending it to
our sister Apphia and to Archippus. He is
a soldier of Christ together with us. And
we are sending it to the church that meets
in your home.

3 May God our Father and the Lord
Jesus Christ give you grace and peace.

Paul Prays and Gives Thanks

4 I always thank my God when I remember you in my prayers. 5 That's because I
hear about your love for all God's people. I also hear about your faith in the
Lord Jesus. 6 I pray that what we share by
believing will help you understand even
more. Then you will completely understand every good thing we share by believing in Christ. 7 Your love has given
me great joy. It has encouraged me. My
brother, you have renewed the hearts of
the Lord's people.

Paul Makes an Appeal for Onesimus

8 Because of the authority Christ has
given me, I could be bold. I could order
you to do what you should do anyway.
9 But we love each other. And I would
rather appeal to you on the basis of that
love. I, Paul, am an old man. I am now
also a prisoner because of Christ Jesus.
10 I am an old man, and I'm in prison.
This is how I make my appeal to you
for my son Onesimus. He became a son
to me while I was being held in chains.
11 Before that, he was useless to you. But
now he has become useful to you and to
me.

12 I'm sending Onesimus back to you.
All my love for him goes with him. 13 I'm
being held in chains because of the good
news. So I would have liked to keep
Onesimus with me. And he could take
your place in helping me. 14 But I didn't
want to do anything unless you agreed.
Any favor you do must be done because
you want to do it, not because you have
to. 15 Onesimus was separated from you
for a little while. Maybe that was so you
could have him back forever. 16 You could
have him back not as a slave. Instead, he
would be better than a slave. He would
be a dear brother. He is very dear to me
but even more dear to you. He is dear to
you not only as another human being.
He is also dear to you as a brother in the
Lord.

17 Do you think of me as a believer who
works together with you? Then welcome
Onesimus as you would welcome me.
18 Has he done anything wrong to you?
Does he owe you anything? Then charge
it to me. 19 I'll pay it back. I, Paul, am writ-

ing this with my own hand. I won't even
mention that you owe me your life. 20 My
brother, we both belong to the Lord. So
I wish I could receive some benefit from
you. Renew my heart. We know that
Christ is the one who really renews it.
21 I'm sure you will obey. So I'm writing to
you. I know you will do even more than
I ask.

22 There is one more thing. Have a guest
room ready for me. I hope I can return to
all of you in answer to your prayers.

23 Epaphras sends you greetings. Together with me, he is a prisoner because
of Christ Jesus. 24 Mark, Aristarchus, Demas and Luke work together with me.
They also send you greetings.

25 May the grace of the Lord Jesus Christ
be with your spirit.

HEBREWS

Neither the author nor the specific audience for the book of Hebrews is known. It may be that the people who received the book were from Italy. The author does send greetings to them from those who are from Italy. But it is clear the book was written for Jews who believe in Jesus the Messiah. They were, however, in danger of leaving the faith. The book is clearly written to encourage them. It presents the truths God has revealed in his new covenant. It states that they are far better than the temporary ones of the first covenant. It encourages these new Jewish believers to remain strong in their faith in Jesus.

The book presents two types of teachings. And it goes back and forth between the two types. One type reviews Israel's history or tells about worship in the temple. The other type presents the challenges based on these teachings. The book presents four pairs of these sets of teachings.

First, the writer states that Jesus and the salvation he brings are the greatest. Jesus is higher and greater than the angels and the law given by Moses.

Second, the writer states that Jesus is our apostle. An apostle is one sent by God on a specific mission. Jesus brings us into a greater peace and a better, renewed land. These are far better than the land Moses and Joshua brought Israel to.

Third, the writer states that Jesus is a more effective high priest. He is better than the priests appointed by the law of Moses.

Fourth, believers are reminded to remain faithful as people have for many, many years. Believers must move forward in faith. They can do that because Jesus is bringing a kingdom that can't be shaken.

God Speaks His Final Word Through His Son

1 In the past, God spoke to our people through the prophets. He spoke at
many times. He spoke in different ways.
2 But in these last days, he has spoken to
us through his Son. He is the one whom
God appointed to receive all things. God
also made everything through him. 3 The
Son is the shining brightness of God's
glory. He is the exact likeness of God's being. He uses his powerful word to hold all
things together. He provided the way for
people to be made pure from sin. Then he
sat down at the right hand of the King, the
Majesty in heaven. 4 So he became higher
than the angels. The name he received is
more excellent than theirs.

The Son Is Greater Than the Angels

5 God never said to any of the angels,

"You are my Son.
Today I have become your Father."
(Psalm 2:7)

Or,

"I will be his Father.
And he will be my Son."
(2 Samuel 7:14; 1 Chronicles 17:13)

6 God's first and only Son is over all things.
When God brings him into the world, he
says,

"Let all God's angels worship him."
(Deuteronomy 32:43)

7 Here is something else God says about
the angels.

"God makes his angels to be like
spirits.
He makes those who serve him to
be like flashes of lightning."
(Psalm 104:4)

8 But here is what he says about the Son.

"You are God. Your throne will last
for ever and ever.
Your kingdom will be ruled by
justice.
9 You have loved what is right and
hated what is evil.
So your God has placed you above
your companions.
He has filled you with joy by
pouring the sacred oil on
your head." (Psalm 45:6,7)

10 He also says,

"Lord, in the beginning you made
the earth secure. You placed
it on its foundations.
The heavens are the work of your
hands.

[11] They will pass away. But you remain.
They will all wear out like a piece
of clothing.
[12] You will roll them up like a robe.
They will be changed as a person
changes clothes.
But you remain the same.
Your years will never end."
(Psalm 102:25–27)

[13] God never said to an angel,

"Sit at my right hand
until I put your enemies
under your control." (Psalm 110:1)

[14] All angels are spirits who serve. God sends them to serve those who will receive salvation.

A Warning to Pay Attention

2 So we must pay the most careful attention to what we have heard. Then we
will not drift away from it. [2] Even the mes-
sage God spoke through angels had to
be obeyed. Every time people broke the
Law, they were punished. Every time they
didn't obey, they were punished. [3] Then
how will we escape if we don't pay attention to God's great salvation? The Lord
first announced this salvation. Those who
heard him gave us the message about it.
[4] God showed that this message is true by
signs and wonders. He showed that it's
true by different kinds of miracles. God
also showed that this message is true by
the gifts of the Holy Spirit. God gave them
out as it pleased him.

Jesus Was Made Fully Human

[5] God has not put angels in charge of
the world that is going to come. We are
talking about that world. [6] There is a place
where someone has spoken about this.
He said,

"What are human beings that you
think about them?
What is a son of man that you take
care of him?
[7] You made them a little lower than
the angels.
You placed on them a crown of
glory and honor.
[8] You have put everything under
their control." (Psalm 8:4–6)

So God has put everything under his Son. Everything is under his control. We do
not now see everything under his con-
trol. [9] But we do see Jesus already given a
crown of glory and honor. He was made lower than the angels for a little while. He suffered death. By the grace of God, he tasted death for everyone. That is why he was given his crown.
[10] God has made everything. He is now
bringing his many sons and daughters to
share in his glory. It is only right that Jesus
is the one to lead them into their salvation. That's because God made him perfect by his sufferings. [11] And Jesus, who
makes people holy, and the people he
makes holy belong to the same family.
So Jesus is not ashamed to call them his
brothers and sisters. [12] He says,

"I will announce your name to my
brothers and sisters.
I will sing your praises among
those who worship you."
(Psalm 22:22)

[13] Again he says,

"I will put my trust in him."
(Isaiah 8:17)

And again he says,

"Here I am. Here are the children
God has given me."
(Isaiah 8:18)

[14] Those children have bodies made out
of flesh and blood. So Jesus became human like them in order to die for them.
By doing this, he could break the power
of the devil. The devil is the one who
rules over the kingdom of death. [15] Jesus
could set people free who were afraid of
death. All their lives they were held as
slaves by that fear. [16] It is certainly Abraham's children that he helps. He doesn't
help angels. [17] So he had to be made like
people, fully human in every way. Then
he could serve God as a kind and faithful
high priest. And then he could pay for the
sins of the people by dying for them. [18] He
himself suffered when he was tempted.
Now he is able to help others who are being tempted.

Jesus Is Greater Than Moses

3 Holy brothers and sisters, God chose you to be his people. So keep thinking about Jesus. We embrace him as our
apostle and our high priest. [2] Moses was

faithful in everything he did in the house
of God. In the same way, Jesus was faithful
to the God who appointed him. 3The person who builds a house has greater honor
than the house itself. In the same way,
Jesus has been found worthy of greater
honor than Moses. 4Every house is built
by someone. But God is the builder of everything. 5"Moses was faithful as one who
serves in the house of God." (Numbers 12:7)
He was a witness to what God would say
in days to come. 6But Christ is faithful as
the Son over the house of God. And we
are his house if we hold tightly to what
we are certain about. We must also hold
tightly to the hope we boast in.

A Warning Against Unbelief

7The Holy Spirit says,

"Listen to his voice today.
8 If you hear it, don't be stubborn.
You were stubborn when you
opposed me.
You did that when you were tested
in the desert.
9There your people of long ago tested
me.
Yet for 40 years they saw what I did.
10That is why I was angry with them.
I said, 'Their hearts are always
going astray.
They have not known my ways.'
11So when I was angry, I made a
promise.
I said, 'They will never enjoy the
rest I planned for them.' "
(Psalm 95:7–11)

12Brothers and sisters, make sure that
none of you has a sinful heart. Do not let
an unbelieving heart turn you away from
the living God. 13But build one another
up every day. Do it as long as there is still
time. Then none of you will become stubborn. You won't be fooled by sin's tricks.
14We belong to Christ if we hold tightly to
the faith we had at first. But we must hold it
tightly until the end. 15It has just been said,

"Listen to his voice today.
If you hear it, don't be stubborn.
You were stubborn when you
opposed me." (Psalm 95:7,8)

16Who were those who heard and refused to obey? Weren't they all the people Moses led out of Egypt? 17Who was
God angry with for 40 years? Wasn't it
with those who sinned? They died in the
desert. 18God promised that those people
would never enjoy the rest he planned for
them. God gave his word when he made
that promise. Didn't he make that promise to those who didn't obey? 19So we see
that they weren't able to enter. That's because they didn't believe.

God's People Enter His Sabbath Rest

4 God's promise of enjoying his rest still
stands. So be careful that none of you
fails to receive it. 2The good news was announced to our people of long ago. It has
also been preached to us. The message
they heard didn't have any value for them.
That's because they didn't share the faith
of those who obeyed. 3Now we who have
believed enjoy that rest. God said,

"When I was angry, I made a
promise.
I said, 'They will never enjoy the
rest I planned for them.' "
(Psalm 95:11)

Ever since God created the world, his
works have been finished. 4Somewhere
he spoke about the seventh day. He said,
"On the seventh day God rested from
all his works." (Genesis 2:2) 5In the part
of Scripture I talked about earlier God
spoke. He said, "They will never enjoy the
rest I planned for them." (Psalm 95:11)
6It is still true that some people will
enjoy this rest. But those who had the
good news announced to them earlier
didn't go in. That's because they didn't
obey. 7So God again chose a certain day.
He named it Today. He did this when he
spoke through David a long time later.
Here is what was written in the Scripture
already given.

"Listen to his voice today.
If you hear it, don't be stubborn."
(Psalm 95:7,8)

8Suppose Joshua had given them rest. If
he had, God would not have spoken later
about another day. 9So there is still a Sabbath rest for God's people. 10God rested
from his work. Those who enjoy God's
rest also rest from their works. 11So let us
make every effort to enjoy that rest. Then
no one will die by disobeying as they did.
12The word of God is alive and active.

It is sharper than any sword that has two edges. It cuts deep enough to separate soul from spirit. It can separate bones from joints. It judges the thoughts and purposes of the heart. [13]Nothing God created is hidden from him. His eyes see everything. He will hold us responsible for everything we do.

Jesus Is the Great High Priest

[14]We have a great high priest. He has gone up into heaven. He is Jesus the Son of God. So let us hold firmly to what we say we believe. [15]We have a high priest who can feel it when we are weak and hurting. We have a high priest who has been tempted in every way, just as we are. But he did not sin. [16]So let us boldly approach God's throne of grace. Then we will receive mercy. We will find grace to help us when we need it.

5 Every high priest is chosen from among the people. He is appointed to act for the people. He acts for them in whatever has to do with God. He offers gifts and sacrifices for their sins. [2]Some people have gone astray without knowing it. He is able to deal gently with them. He can do that because he himself is weak. [3]That's why he has to offer sacrifices for his own sins. He must also do it for the sins of the people. [4]And no one can take this honor for himself. Instead, he receives it when he is appointed by God. That is just how it was for Aaron.

[5]It was the same for Christ. He did not take for himself the glory of becoming a high priest. But God said to him,

"You are my Son.
Today I have become your Father."
(Psalm 2:7)

[6]In another place God said,

"You are a priest forever,
just like Melchizedek." (Psalm 110:4)

[7]Jesus prayed while he lived on earth. He made his appeal with sincere cries and tears. He prayed to the God who could save him from death. God answered Jesus because he truly honored God. [8]Jesus was God's Son. But by suffering he learned what it means to obey. [9]In this way he was made perfect. Eternal salvation comes from him. He saves all those who obey him. [10]God appointed him to be the high priest, just like Melchizedek.

A Warning Against Falling Away

[11]We have a lot to say about this. But it is hard to make it clear to you. That's because you are no longer trying to understand. [12]By this time you should be teachers. But in fact, you need someone to teach you all over again. You need even the simple truths of God's word. You need milk, not solid food. [13]Anyone who lives on milk is still a baby. That person does not want to learn about living a godly life. [14]Solid food is for those who are grown up. They have trained themselves to tell the difference between good and evil. That shows they have grown up.

6 So let us move beyond the simple teachings about Christ. Let us grow up as believers. Let us not start all over again with the basic teachings. They taught us that we need to turn away from doing things that lead to death. They taught us that we must have faith in God. [2]These basic teachings taught us about different ways of becoming "clean." They taught us about placing hands of blessing on people. They taught us that people will rise from the dead. They taught us that God will judge everyone. And they taught us that what he decides will last forever. [3]If God permits, we will go beyond those teachings and grow up.

[4]What if some people fall away from the faith? It won't be possible to bring them back. It is true that they have seen the light. They have tasted the heavenly gift. They have shared in the Holy Spirit. [5]They have tasted the good things of God's word. They have tasted the powers of the age to come. [6]But they have fallen away from the faith. So it won't be possible to bring them back. They won't be able to turn away from their sins. They are losing everything. That's because they are nailing the Son of God to the cross all over again. They are bringing shame on him in front of everyone. [7]Some land drinks the rain that falls on it. It produces a crop that is useful to those who farm the land. That land receives God's blessing. [8]But other land produces only thorns and weeds. That land isn't worth anything. It is in danger of coming under God's curse. In the end, it will be burned.

9 Dear friends, we have to say these
things. But we are sure of better things
in your case. We are talking about the
things that have to do with being saved.
10 God is fair. He will not forget what you
have done. He will remember the love
you have shown him. You showed it when
you helped his people. And you show it
when you keep on helping them. 11 We
want each of you to be faithful to the very
end. If you are, then what you hope for
will fully happen. 12 We don't want you
to slow down. Instead, be like those who
have faith and are patient. They will receive what God promised.

God Keeps His Promise

13 When God made his promise to Abraham, God gave his word. There was no
one greater than himself to promise by.
So he promised by making an appeal to
himself. 14 He said, "I will certainly bless
you. I will give you many children." (Genesis 22:17) 15 Abraham was patient while
he waited. Then he received what God
promised him.

16 People promise things by someone
greater than themselves. Giving your
word makes a promise certain. It puts an
end to all arguing. 17 So God gave his word
when he made his promise. He wanted to
make it very clear that his purpose does
not change. He wanted those who would
receive what was promised to know this.
18 When God made his promise, he gave
his word. He did this so we would have
good reason not to give up. Instead, we
have run to take hold of the hope set
before us. This hope is set before us in
God's promise. So God made his promise and gave his word. These two things
can't change. He couldn't lie about them.
19 Our hope is certain. It is something for
the soul to hold on to. It is strong and secure. It goes all the way into the Most Holy
Room behind the curtain. 20 That is where
Jesus has gone. He went there to open the
way ahead of us. He has become a high
priest forever, just like Melchizedek.

Melchizedek the Priest

7 Melchizedek was the king of Salem. He
was the priest of God Most High. He
met Abraham, who was returning from
winning a battle over some kings. Melchizedek blessed him. 2 Abraham gave
him a tenth of everything. First, the name
Melchizedek means "king of what is
right." Also, "king of Salem" means "king
of peace." 3 Melchizedek has no father or
mother. He has no family line. His days
have no beginning. His life has no end. He
remains a priest forever. In this way, he is
like the Son of God.

4 Think how great Melchizedek was!
Even our father Abraham gave him a
tenth of what he had captured. 5 Now the
law lays down a rule for the sons of Levi
who become priests. They must collect a
tenth from the people. They must collect
it from the other Israelites. They must do
this, even though all of them belong to the
family line of Abraham. 6 Melchizedek did
not trace his family line from Levi. But he
collected a tenth from Abraham. Melchizedek blessed the one who had received
the promises. 7 Without a doubt, the more
important person blesses the less important one. 8 In the one case, the tenth is collected by people who die. But in the other
case, it is collected by the one who is said
to be living. 9 Levi collects the tenth. But
we might say that Levi paid the tenth
through Abraham. 10 That's because when
Melchizedek met Abraham, Levi was still
in Abraham's body.

Jesus Is Like Melchizedek

11 The law that was given to the people called for the priestly system. That
system began with Levi. Suppose the
priestly system could have made people
perfect. Then why was there still a need
for another priest to come? And why did
he need to be like Melchizedek? Why
wasn't he from Aaron's family line? 12 A
change of the priestly system requires
a change of law. 13 We are talking about
a priest who is from a different tribe. No
one from that tribe has ever served at the
altar. 14 It is clear that our Lord came from
the family line of Judah. Moses said nothing about priests who were from the tribe
of Judah. 15 But suppose another priest
like Melchizedek appears. Then what we
have said is even more clear. 16 He has not
become a priest because of a rule about
his family line. He has become a priest
because of his powerful life. His life can
never be destroyed. 17 Scripture says,

"You are a priest forever,
just like Melchizedek." (Psalm 110:4)

18 The old rule is set aside. It was weak and useless. 19 The law didn't make anything perfect. Now a better hope has been given to us. That hope brings us near to God.

20 The change of priestly system was made with a promise. Others became priests without any promise. 21 But Jesus became a priest with a promise. God said to him,

"The Lord has given his word and
made a promise.
He will not change his mind. He
has said,
'You are a priest forever.' "
(Psalm 110:4)

22 Because God gave his word, Jesus makes certain the promise of a better covenant.

23 There were many priests in Levi's family line. Death kept them from continuing in office. 24 But Jesus lives forever. So he always holds the office of priest. 25 People now come to God through him. And he is able to save them completely and for all time. Jesus lives forever. He prays for them.

26 A high priest like that really meets our need. He is holy, pure and without blame. He isn't like other people. He does not sin. He is lifted high above the heavens. 27 He isn't like the other high priests. They need to offer sacrifices day after day. First they bring offerings for their own sins. Then they do it for the sins of the people. But Jesus gave one sacrifice for the sins of the people. He gave it once and for all time. He did it by offering himself. 28 The law appoints as high priests men who are weak. But God's promise came after the law. By his promise the Son was appointed. The Son has been made perfect forever.

The High Priest of a New Covenant

8 Here is the main point of what we are saying. We have a high priest like that. He sat down at the right hand of the throne of the King, the Majesty in heaven. 2 He serves in the sacred tent. The Lord set up the true holy tent. A mere human being did not set it up.

3 Every high priest is appointed to offer gifts and sacrifices. So this priest also had to have something to offer. 4 What if he were on earth? Then he would not be a priest. There are already priests who offer the gifts required by the law. 5 They serve at a sacred tent. But it is only a copy and shadow of what is in heaven. That's why God warned Moses when he was about to build the holy tent. God said, "Be sure to make everything just like the pattern I showed you on the mountain." (Exodus 25:40) 6 But Jesus has been given a greater work to do for God. He is the go-between for the new covenant. This covenant is better than the old one. The new covenant is based on better promises.

7 Suppose nothing had been wrong with that first covenant. Then no one would have looked for another covenant. 8 But God found fault with the people. He said,

"The days are coming, announces
the Lord.
I will make a new covenant
with the people of Israel.
I will also make it with the people
of Judah.
9 It will not be like the covenant
I made with their people of long
ago.
That was when I took them by the
hand.
I led them out of Egypt.
My new covenant will be different
because they didn't remain
faithful to my old covenant.
So I turned away from them,
announces the Lord.
10 This is the covenant I will establish
with the people of Israel
after that time, says the Lord.
I will put my laws in their minds.
I will write them on their hearts.
I will be their God.
And they will be my people.
11 People will not teach their neighbor
anymore.
They will not say to one another,
'Know the Lord.'
That's because everyone will know
me.
From the least important to the
most important,
all of them will know me.
12 I will forgive their evil ways.
I will not remember their sins
anymore." (Jeremiah 31:31–34)

13 God called this covenant "new." So he has done away with the first one. And

what is out of date and has been done away with will soon disappear.

Worship in the Holy Tent on Earth

9 The first covenant had rules for worship. It also had a sacred tent on earth. [2]A holy tent was set up. The lampstand was in the first room. So was the table with its holy bread. That was called the Holy Room. [3]Behind the second curtain was a room called the Most Holy Room. [4]It had the golden altar for incense. It also had the wooden chest called the ark of the covenant. The ark was covered with gold. It held the gold jar of manna. It held Aaron's walking stick that had budded. It also held the stone tablets. The words of the covenant were written on them. [5]The cherubim were above the ark. God showed his glory there. The cherubim spread their wings over the place where sin was paid for. But we can't say everything about these things now.

[6]That's how everything was arranged in the holy tent. The priests entered it at regular times. They went into the outer room to do their work for God and others. [7]But only the high priest went into the inner room. He went in only once a year. He never entered without taking blood with him. He offered the blood for himself. He also offered it for the sins the people had committed because they didn't know any better. [8]Here is what the Holy Spirit was showing us. He was telling us that God had not yet clearly shown the way into the Most Holy Room. It would not be clearly shown as long as the first holy tent was still being used. [9]That's an example for the present time. It shows us that the gifts and sacrifices people offered were not enough. They were not able to remove the worshiper's feelings of guilt. [10]They deal only with food and drink and different kinds of special washings. They are rules people had to obey only until the new covenant came.

The Blood of Christ

[11]But Christ came to be the high priest of the good things already here now. When he came, he went through the greater and more perfect holy tent. This tent was not made with human hands. In other words, it is not a part of this creation. [12]He did not enter by spilling the blood of goats and calves. He entered the Most Holy Room by spilling his own blood. He did it once and for all time. In this way, he paid the price to set us free from sin forever. [13]The blood of goats and bulls is sprinkled on people. So are the ashes of a young cow. They are sprinkled on people the law called "unclean." The people are sprinkled to make them holy. That makes them "clean" on the outside. [14]But Christ offered himself to God without any flaw. He did this through the power of the eternal Holy Spirit. So how much cleaner will the blood of Christ make us! It washes away our feelings of guilt for committing sin. Sin always leads to death. But now we can serve the living God.

[15]That's why Christ is the go-between of a new covenant. Now those God calls to himself will receive the eternal gift he promised. They will receive it now that Christ has died to save them. He died to set them free from the sins they committed under the first covenant.

[16]What happens when someone leaves a will? It is necessary to prove that the person who made the will has died. [17]A will is in effect only when somebody has died. It never takes effect while the one who made it is still living. [18]That's why even the first covenant was not put into effect without the spilling of blood. [19]Moses first announced every command of the law to all the people. Then he took the blood of calves. He also took water, bright red wool and branches of a hyssop plant. He sprinkled the Book of the Covenant. He also sprinkled all the people. [20]He said, "This is the blood of the covenant God has commanded you to keep." (Exodus 24:8) [21]In the same way, he sprinkled the holy tent with blood. He also sprinkled everything that was used in worship there. [22]In fact, the law requires that nearly everything be made "clean" with blood. Without the spilling of blood, no one can be forgiven.

[23]So the copies of the heavenly things had to be made pure with these sacrifices. But the heavenly things themselves had to be made pure with better sacrifices. [24]Christ did not enter a sacred tent made with human hands. That tent was only a copy of the true one. He entered heaven itself. He did it to stand in front of God for us. He is there right now. [25]The high priest enters the Most Holy Room every year. He

enters with blood that is not his own. But
Christ did not enter heaven to offer himself again and again. 26 If he had, he would
have had to suffer many times since the
world was created. But he has appeared
once and for all time. He has come at
the time when God's work is being completed. He has come to do away with sin
by offering himself. 27 People have to die
once. After that, God will judge them. 28 In
the same way, Christ was offered up once.
He took away the sins of many people. He
will also come a second time. At that time
he will not suffer for sin. Instead, he will
come to bring salvation to those who are
waiting for him.

Christ's Sacrifice Is Once and for All Time

10 The law is only a shadow of the good
things that are coming. It is not the
real things themselves. The same sacrifices have to be offered over and over
again. They must be offered year after
year. That's why the law can never make
perfect those who come near to worship.
2 If the law could, wouldn't the sacrifices
have stopped being offered? The worshipers would have been made "clean" once
and for all time. They would not have felt
guilty for their sins anymore. 3 But those
offerings remind people of their sins every year. 4 It isn't possible for the blood of
bulls and goats to take away sins.

5 So when Christ came into the world,
he said,

"You didn't want sacrifices and
offerings.
Instead, you prepared a body for
me.
6 You weren't pleased
with burnt offerings and sin
offerings.
7 Then I said, 'Here I am. It is written
about me in the book.
I have come to do what you want,
my God.' " (Psalm 40:6–8)

8 First Christ said, "You didn't want sacrifices and offerings. You didn't want burnt
offerings and sin offerings. You weren't
pleased with them." He said this even
though they were offered in keeping with
the law. 9 Then he said, "Here I am. I have
come to do what you want." He did away
with the shadow of the good things that
were coming. He did it to put in place the
good things themselves. 10 We have been
made holy by what God wanted. We have
been made holy because Jesus Christ offered his body once and for all time.

11 Day after day every priest stands and
does his special duties. He offers the same
sacrifices again and again. But they can
never take away sins. 12 Jesus our priest
offered one sacrifice for sins for all time.
Then he sat down at the right hand of God.
13 And since that time, he waits for his enemies to be put under his control. 14 By that
one sacrifice he has made perfect forever
those who are being made holy.

15 The Holy Spirit also speaks to us
about this. First he says,

16 "This is the covenant I will make
with them
after that time, says the Lord.
I will put my laws in their hearts.
I will write my laws on their
minds." (Jeremiah 31:33)

17 Then he adds,

"I will not remember their sins
anymore.
I will not remember the evil
things they have done."
(Jeremiah 31:34)

18 Where these sins have been forgiven, an
offering for sin is no longer necessary.

An Appeal and Warning to Remain Faithful

19 Brothers and sisters, we are not afraid
to enter the Most Holy Room. We enter
boldly because of the blood of Jesus. 20 His
way is new because he lives. It has been
opened for us through the curtain. I'm
talking about his body. 21 We also have a
great priest over the house of God. 22 So let
us come near to God with a sincere heart.
Let us come near boldly because of our
faith. Our hearts have been sprinkled. Our
minds have been cleansed from a sense
of guilt. Our bodies have been washed
with pure water. 23 Let us hold firmly to
the hope we claim to have. The God who
promised is faithful. 24 Let us consider how
we can stir up one another to love. Let us
help one another to do good works. 25 And
let us not give up meeting together. Some
are in the habit of doing this. Instead, let
us encourage one another with words of

hope. Let us do this even more as you see
Christ's return approaching.
26 What if we keep sinning on purpose?
What if we do it even after we know the
truth? Then there is no offering for our
sins. 27 All we can do is to wait in fear for
God to judge. His blazing fire will burn up
his enemies. 28 Suppose someone did not
obey the law of Moses. And suppose two
or three witnesses made charges against
them. That person would die without
mercy. 29 People who deserve even more
punishment include those who have
hated the Son of God. They include people who have said no to him. They include
people who have treated as unholy the
blood of the covenant that makes them
holy. They also include people who have
disrespected the Holy Spirit who brings
God's grace. Don't you think people like
this should be punished more than anyone else? 30 We know the God who said, "I
am the God who judges people. I will pay
them back." (Deuteronomy 32:35) Scripture
also says, "The Lord will judge his people." (Deuteronomy 32:36; Psalm 135:14) 31 It is
a terrible thing to fall into the hands of the
living God.
32 Remember those earlier days after you
received the light. You remained strong
in a great battle that was full of suffering.
33 Sometimes people spoke badly about
you in front of others. Sometimes you were
treated badly. At other times you stood side
by side with people being treated like this.
34 You suffered along with people in prison.
When your property was taken from you,
you accepted it with joy. You knew that
God had given you better and more lasting
things. 35 So don't throw away your bold
faith. It will bring you rich rewards.
36 You need to be faithful. Then you will
do what God wants. You will receive what
he has promised.

37 "In just a little while,
he who is coming will come.
He will not wait any longer."

38 And,

"The one who is right with God will
live by faith.
And I am not pleased with
the one who pulls back."
(Habakkuk 2:3,4)

39 But we don't belong to the people who
pull back and are destroyed. We belong to
the people who believe and are saved.

Faith That Produces Action

11 Faith is being sure of what we hope
for. It is being sure of what we do not
see. 2 That is what the people of long ago
were praised for.
3 We have faith. So we understand that
everything was made when God commanded it. That's why we believe that
what we see was not made out of what
could be seen.
4 Abel had faith. So he brought to God a
better offering than Cain did. Because of
his faith Abel was praised as a godly man.
God said good things about his offerings.
Because of his faith Abel still speaks. He
speaks even though he is dead.
5 Enoch had faith. So he was taken from
this life. He didn't die. "He couldn't be
found, because God had taken him away."
(Genesis 5:24) Before God took him, Enoch
was praised as one who pleased God.
6 Without faith it is impossible to please
God. Those who come to God must believe that he exists. And they must believe
that he rewards those who look to him.
7 Noah had faith. So he built an ark to
save his family. He built it because of his
great respect for God. God had warned
him about things that could not yet be
seen. Because of his faith Noah showed
the world that it was guilty. Because of his
faith he was considered right with God.
8 Abraham had faith. So he obeyed God.
God called him to go to a place he would
later receive as his own. So he went. He
did it even though he didn't know where
he was going. 9 Because of his faith he
made his home in the land God had
promised him. Abraham was like an outsider in a strange country. He lived there
in tents. So did Isaac and Jacob. They received the same promise he did. 10 Abraham was looking forward to the city that
has foundations. He was waiting for the
city that God planned and built. 11 And
Sarah had faith. So God made it possible
for her to become a mother. She became
a mother even though she was too old to
have children. But Sarah believed that the
God who made the promise was faithful.
12 Abraham was past the time when he
could have children. But many children
came from that one man. They were as

many as the stars in the sky. They were
as many as the grains of sand on the seashore. No one could count them.

13 All these people were still living by
faith when they died. They didn't receive
the things God had promised. They only
saw them and welcomed them from a
long way off. They openly said that they
were outsiders and strangers on earth.
14 People who say things like that show
that they are looking for a country of their
own. 15 What if they had been thinking
of the country they had left? Then they
could have returned to it. 16 Instead, they
longed for a better country. They wanted
a heavenly one. So God is pleased when
they call him their God. In fact, he has
prepared a city for them.

17 Abraham had faith. So when God
tested him, Abraham offered Isaac as a
sacrifice. Abraham had held on tightly to
the promises. But he was about to offer his
one and only son. 18 God had said to him,
"Your family line will continue through
Isaac." (Genesis 21:12) Even so, Abraham
was going to offer him up. 19 Abraham did
this, because he believed that God could
even raise the dead. In a way, he did receive Isaac back from death.

20 Isaac had faith. So he blessed Jacob
and Esau. He told them what was ahead
for them.

21 Jacob had faith. So he blessed each
of Joseph's sons. He blessed them when
he was dying. Because of his faith he
worshiped God. Jacob worshiped as he
leaned on the top of his walking stick.

22 Joseph had faith. So he spoke to the
people of Israel about how they would
leave Egypt someday. When his death
was near, he spoke about where to bury
his bones.

23 Moses' parents had faith. So they hid
him for three months after he was born.
They saw he was a special child. They
were not afraid of the king's command.

24 Moses had faith. So he refused to
be called the son of Pharaoh's daughter.
That happened after he had grown up.
25 He chose to be treated badly together
with the people of God. He chose not to
enjoy sin's pleasures. They only last for
a short time. 26 He suffered shame because of Christ. He thought it had great
value. Moses considered it better than the
riches of Egypt. He was looking ahead to
his reward. 27 Because of his faith, Moses
left Egypt. It wasn't because he was afraid
of the king's anger. He didn't let anything
stop him. That's because he saw the God
who can't be seen. 28 Because of his faith,
Moses was the first to keep the Passover
Feast. He commanded the people of Israel to sprinkle blood on their doorways.
He did it so that the destroying angel
would not touch their oldest sons.

29 The people of Israel had faith. So they
passed through the Red Sea. They went
through it as if it were dry land. The Egyp-
tians tried to do it also. But they drowned.

30 Israel's army had faith. So the walls of
Jericho fell down. It happened after they
had marched around the city for seven
days.

31 Rahab, the prostitute, had faith. So she
welcomed the spies. That's why she wasn't
killed with those who didn't obey God.

32 What more can I say? I don't have time
to tell about all the others. I don't have time
to talk about Gideon, Barak, Samson and
Jephthah. I don't have time to tell about
David and Samuel and the prophets. 33 Because of their faith they took over kingdoms. They ruled fairly. They received the
blessings God had promised. They shut
the mouths of lions. 34 They put out great
fires. They escaped being killed by swords.
Their weakness was turned to strength.
They became powerful in battle. They beat
back armies from other countries. 35 Wom-
en received back their dead. The dead
were raised to life again. There were others who were made to suffer greatly. But
they refused to be set free. They did this
so that after death they would be raised to
an even better life. 36 Some were made fun
of and even whipped. Some were held by
chains. Some were put in prison. 37 Some
were killed with stones. Some were sawed
in two. Some were killed by swords. They
went around wearing the skins of sheep
and goats. They were poor. They were attacked. They were treated badly. 38 The
world was not worthy of them. They wandered in deserts and mountains. They
lived in caves. They lived in holes in the
ground.

39 All these people were praised because they had faith. But none of them received what God had promised. 40 That's
because God had planned something

better for us. So they would only be made
perfect together with us.

12 A huge cloud of witnesses is all
around us. So let us throw off everything that stands in our way. Let us
throw off any sin that holds on to us so
tightly. And let us keep on running the
race marked out for us. 2 Let us keep looking to Jesus. He is the one who started this
journey of faith. And he is the one who
completes the journey of faith. He paid
no attention to the shame of the cross. He
suffered there because of the joy he was
looking forward to. Then he sat down at
the right hand of the throne of God. 3 He
made it through these attacks by sinners.
So think about him. Then you won't get
tired. You won't lose hope.

God Trains His Children

4 You struggle against sin. But you have
not yet fought to the point of spilling your
blood. 5 Have you completely forgotten
this word of hope? It speaks to you as a father to his children. It says,

"My son, think of the Lord's training
as important.
Do not lose hope when he
corrects you.
6 The Lord trains the one he loves.
He corrects everyone he accepts
as his son." (Proverbs 3:11,12)

7 Put up with hard times. God uses
them to train you. He is treating you as his
children. What children are not trained by
their parents? 8 God trains all his children.
But what if he doesn't train you? Then
you are not really his children. You are
not God's true sons and daughters at all.
9 Besides, we have all had human fathers
who trained us. We respected them for
it. How much more should we be trained
by the Father of spirits and live! 10 Our
parents trained us for a little while. They
did what they thought was best. But God
trains us for our good. He does this so
we may share in his holiness. 11 No training seems pleasant at the time. In fact, it
seems painful. But later on it produces a
harvest of godliness and peace. It does
this for those who have been trained by it.
12 So put your hands to work. Strengthen
your legs for the journey. 13 "Make level
paths for your feet to walk on." (Proverbs
4:26) Then those who have trouble walking won't be disabled. Instead, they will
be healed.

A Warning and an Appeal

14 Try your best to live in peace with everyone. Try hard to be holy. Without holiness no one will see the Lord. 15 Be sure
that no one misses out on God's grace. See
to it that a bitter plant doesn't grow up. If it
does, it will cause trouble. And it will make
many people impure. 16 See to it that no
one commits sexual sins. See to it that no
one is godless like Esau. He sold the rights
to what he would receive as the oldest son.
He sold them for a single meal. 17 As you
know, after that he wanted to receive his
father's blessing. But he was turned away.
With tears he tried to get the blessing. But
he couldn't change what he had done.

The Mountain of Fear and the Mountain of Joy

18 You haven't come to a mountain that
can be touched. You haven't come to a
mountain burning with fire. You haven't
come to darkness, gloom and storm. 19 You
haven't come to a blast from God's trumpet. You haven't come to a voice speaking
to you. When people heard that voice long
ago, they begged it not to say anything
more to them. 20 What God commanded
was too much for them. He said, "If even
an animal touches the mountain, it must
be killed with stones." (Exodus 19:12,13)
21 The sight was terrifying. Moses said, "I
am trembling with fear." (Deuteronomy 9:19)
22 But you have come to Mount Zion.
You have come to the city of the living
God. This is the heavenly Jerusalem. You
have come to a joyful gathering of angels. There are thousands and thousands
of them. 23 You have come to the church
of God's people. God's first and only Son
is over all things. God's people share in
what belongs to his Son. Their names are
written in heaven. You have come to God,
who is the Judge of all people. You have
come to the spirits of godly people who
have been made perfect. 24 You have come
to Jesus. He is the go-between of a new
covenant. You have come to the sprinkled
blood. It promises better things than the
blood of Abel.
25 Be sure that you don't say no to the
one who speaks. People did not escape
when they said no to the one who warned

them on earth. And what if we turn away from the one who warns us from heaven? How much less will we escape! 26 At that time his voice shook the earth. But now he has promised, "Once more I will shake the earth. I will also shake the heavens." (Haggai 2:6) 27 The words "once more" point out that what can be shaken can be taken away. I'm talking about created things. Then what can't be shaken will remain.

28 We are receiving a kingdom that can't be shaken. So let us be thankful. Then we can worship God in a way that pleases him. Let us worship him with deep respect and wonder. 29 Our "God is like a fire that burns everything up." (Deuteronomy 4:24)

Final Appeals

13 Keep on loving one another as brothers and sisters. 2 Don't forget to welcome outsiders. By doing that, some people have welcomed angels without knowing it. 3 Keep on remembering those in prison. Do this as if you were together with them in prison. And remember those who are treated badly as if you yourselves were suffering.

4 All of you should honor marriage. You should keep the marriage bed pure. God will judge the person who commits adultery. He will judge everyone who commits sexual sins. 5 Don't be controlled by love for money. Be happy with what you have. God has said,

"I will never leave you.
I will never desert you."
(Deuteronomy 31:6)

6 So we can say boldly,

"The Lord helps me. I will not be afraid.
What can mere human beings do to me?" (Psalm 118:6,7)

7 Remember your leaders. They spoke God's word to you. Think about the results of their way of life. Copy their faith. 8 Jesus Christ is the same yesterday and today and forever.

9 Don't let all kinds of strange teachings lead you astray. It is good that God's grace makes our hearts strong. Don't try to grow strong by eating foods that the law requires. They have no value for the people who eat them. 10 The priests, who are Levites, worship at the holy tent. But we have an altar that they have no right to eat from.

11 The high priest carries the blood of animals into the Most Holy Room. He brings their blood as a sin offering. But the bodies are burned outside the camp. 12 Jesus also suffered outside the city gate. He suffered to make the people holy by spilling his own blood. 13 So let us go to him outside the camp. Let us be willing to suffer the shame he suffered. 14 Here we do not have a city that lasts. But we are looking for the city that is going to come.

15 So let us never stop offering to God our praise through Jesus. Let us talk openly about our faith in him. Then our words will be like an offering to God. 16 Don't forget to do good. Don't forget to share with others. God is pleased with those kinds of offerings.

17 Trust in your leaders. Put yourselves under their authority. Do this, because they keep watch over you. They know they are accountable to God for everything they do. Do this, so that their work will be a joy. If you make their work a heavy load, it won't do you any good.

18 Pray for us. We feel sure we have done what is right. We desire to live as we should in every way. 19 I beg you to pray that I may return to you soon.

Final Blessing and Greetings

20 Our Lord Jesus is the great Shepherd of the sheep. The God who gives peace brought him back from the dead. He did it because of the blood of the eternal covenant. Now may God 21 supply you with everything good. Then you can do what he wants. May he do in us what is pleasing to him. We can do it only with the help of Jesus Christ. Give him glory for ever and ever. Amen.

22 Brothers and sisters, I beg you to accept my word. It tells you to be faithful. Accept my word because I have written to you only a short letter.

23 I want you to know that our brother Timothy has been set free. If he arrives soon, I will come with him to see you.

24 Greet all your leaders. Greet all the Lord's people. The believers from Italy send you their greetings.

25 May grace be with you all.

JAMES

James was one of the brothers of Jesus. After Jesus' death and resurrection, James became a leader of the church in Jerusalem. James was respected for the good advice he gave. He was also respected for the wise decisions he helped the community of believers make. James decided to write down some of his best teachings and advice. He sent his writings to Jewish believers in Jesus. These believers were scattered throughout the Roman Empire. What he wrote to them has become known as the book of James.

This book begins like a letter because it's being sent to people far away. But it is not very much like other letters of that time. It is a collection of short sayings and slightly longer writings on practical topics. The style is like one person talking to another. The sayings are short and to the point. And the themes weave together. All of these make this book like the wisdom writings of Proverbs and Ecclesiastes.

Like those wisdom books, James gives attention to questions of daily living. He considers practical issues like helping the poor and using money wisely. He talks about controlling one's tongue and living a pure life. He encourages the community of believers to live in unity with each other. And above all he encourages believers to endure struggles with patience.

We have the same concerns in our world. So the godly wisdom of the book of James continues to be a valuable guide. James teaches us how to live well and please God.

---

1 I, James, am writing this letter. I serve
God and the Lord Jesus Christ.

I am sending this letter to you, the 12
tribes scattered among the nations.

Greetings.

Facing All Kinds of Trouble

2 My brothers and sisters, you will face
all kinds of trouble. When you do, think
of it as pure joy. 3 Your faith will be tested.
You know that when this happens it will
produce in you the strength to continue.
4 And you must allow this strength to finish
its work. Then you will be all you should
be. You will have everything you need. 5 If
any of you needs wisdom, you should ask
God for it. He will give it to you. God gives
freely to everyone and doesn't find fault.
6 But when you ask, you must believe. You
must not doubt. That's because a person who doubts is like a wave of the sea.
The wind blows and tosses them around.
7 They shouldn't expect to receive anything from the Lord. 8 This kind of person
can't make up their mind. They can never
decide what to do.

9 Here's what believers who are in low
positions in life should be proud of. They
should be proud that God has given them
a high position in the kingdom. 10 But rich
people should take pride in their low positions. That's because they will fade away
like wild flowers. 11 The sun rises. Its burning heat dries up the plants. Their blossoms
fall. Their beauty is destroyed. In the same
way, rich people will fade away. They fade
away even as they go about their business.

12 Blessed is the person who keeps on
going when times are hard. After they
have come through hard times, this person will receive a crown. The crown is life
itself. The Lord has promised it to those
who love him.

13 When a person is tempted, they
shouldn't say, "God is tempting me." God
can't be tempted by evil. And he doesn't
tempt anyone. 14 But each person is
tempted by their own evil desires. These
desires lead them on and drag them away.
15 When these desires are allowed to remain, they lead to sin. And when sin is allowed to remain and grow, it leads to death.

16 My dear brothers and sisters, don't let
anyone fool you. 17 Every good and perfect
gift is from God. This kind of gift comes
down from the Father who created the
heavenly lights. These lights create shadows that move. But the Father does not
change like these shadows. 18 God chose
to give us new birth through the message
of truth. He wanted us to be the first harvest of his new creation.

Listen to the Word and Do What It Says

19 My dear brothers and sisters, pay attention to what I say. Everyone should be quick
to listen. But they should be slow to speak.

They should be slow to get angry. 20 Human anger doesn't produce the holy life God wants. 21 So get rid of everything that is sinful. Get rid of the evil that is all around us. Don't be too proud to accept the word that is planted in you. It can save you.

22 Don't just listen to the word. You fool yourselves if you do that. You must do what it says. 23 Suppose someone listens to the word but doesn't do what it says. Then they are like a person who looks at their face in a mirror. 24 After looking at themselves, they leave. And right away they forget what they look like. 25 But suppose someone takes a good look at the perfect law that gives freedom. And they keep looking at it. Suppose they don't forget what they've heard, but they do what the law says. Then this person will be blessed in what they do.

26 Suppose people think their beliefs and how they live are both right. But they don't control what they say. Then they are fooling themselves. Their beliefs and way of life are not worth anything at all. 27 Here are the beliefs and way of life that God our Father accepts as pure and without fault. When widows are in trouble, take care of them. Do the same for children who have no parents. And don't let the world make you impure.

Treat Everyone the Same

2 My brothers and sisters, you are believers in our glorious Lord Jesus Christ. So treat everyone the same. 2 Suppose a man comes into your meeting wearing a gold ring and fine clothes. And suppose a poor man in dirty old clothes also comes in. 3 Would you show special attention to the man wearing fine clothes? Would you say, "Here's a good seat for you"? Would you say to the poor man, "You stand there"? Or "Sit on the floor by my feet"? 4 If you would, aren't you treating some people better than others? Aren't you like judges who have evil thoughts?

5 My dear brothers and sisters, listen to me. Hasn't God chosen those who are poor in the world's eyes to be rich in faith? Hasn't he chosen them to receive the kingdom? Hasn't he promised it to those who love him? 6 But you have disrespected poor people. Aren't rich people taking advantage of you? Aren't they dragging you into court? 7 Aren't they speaking evil things against the worthy name of Jesus? Remember, you belong to him.

8 The royal law is found in Scripture. It says, "Love your neighbor as you love yourself." (Leviticus 19:18) If you really keep this law, you are doing what is right. 9 But you sin if you don't treat everyone the same. The law judges you because you have broken it. 10 Suppose you keep the whole law but trip over just one part of it. Then you are guilty of breaking all of it. 11 God said, "Do not commit adultery." (Exodus 20:14; Deuteronomy 5:18) He also said, "Do not commit murder." (Exodus 20:13; Deuteronomy 5:17) Suppose you don't commit adultery but do commit murder. Then you have broken the law.

12 Speak and act like people who are going to be judged by the law that gives freedom. 13 Those who have not shown mercy will not receive mercy when they are judged. To show mercy is better than to judge.

Show Your Faith by What You Do

14 Suppose a person claims to have faith but doesn't act on their faith. My brothers and sisters, can this kind of faith save them? 15 Suppose a brother or a sister has no clothes or food. 16 Suppose one of you says to them, "Go. I hope everything turns out fine for you. Keep warm. Eat well." And suppose you do nothing about what they really need. Then what good have you done? 17 It is the same with faith. If it doesn't cause us to do something, it's dead.

18 But someone will say, "You have faith. I do good deeds."

Show me your faith that doesn't cause you to do good deeds. And I will show you my faith by the goods deeds I do. 19 You believe there is one God. Good! Even the demons believe that. And they tremble!

20 You foolish person! Do you want proof that faith without good deeds is useless? 21 Our father Abraham offered his son Isaac on the altar. Wasn't he considered to be right with God because of what he did? 22 So you see that what he believed and what he did were working together. What he did made his faith complete. 23 That is what Scripture means where it says, "Abraham believed God. God accepted Abraham because he believed. So his faith made him right with God." (Genesis 15:6) And that's not all. God called

Abraham his friend. 24 So you see that a person is considered right with God by what they do. It doesn't happen only because they believe.

25 Didn't God consider even Rahab the prostitute to be right with him? That's because of what she did for the spies. She gave them a place to stay. Then she sent them off in a different direction. 26 A person's body without their spirit is dead. In the same way, faith without good deeds is dead.

Control What You Say

3 My brothers and sisters, most of you shouldn't become teachers. That's because you know that those of us who teach will be held more accountable. 2 All of us get tripped up in many ways. Suppose someone is never wrong in what they say. Then they are perfect. They are able to keep their whole body under control.

3 We put a small piece of metal in the mouth of a horse to make it obey us. We can control the whole animal with it. 4 And how about ships? They are very big. They are driven along by strong winds. But they are steered by a very small rudder. It makes them go where the captain wants to go. 5 In the same way, the tongue is a small part of a person's body. But it talks big. Think about how a small spark can set a big forest on fire. 6 The tongue is also a fire. The tongue is the most evil part of the body. It makes the whole body impure. It sets a person's whole way of life on fire. And the tongue itself is set on fire by hell.

7 People have tamed all kinds of wild animals, birds, reptiles and sea creatures. And they still tame them. 8 But no one can tame the tongue. It is an evil thing that never rests. It is full of deadly poison.

9 With our tongues we praise our Lord and Father. With our tongues we curse people. We do it even though people have been created to be like God. 10 Praise and cursing come out of the same mouth. My brothers and sisters, it shouldn't be this way. 11 Can fresh water and salt water flow out of the same spring? 12 My brothers and sisters, can a fig tree produce olives? Can a grapevine produce figs? Of course not. And a saltwater spring can't produce fresh water either.

Two Kinds of Wisdom

13 Is anyone among you wise and understanding? That person should show it by living a good life. A wise person isn't proud when they do good deeds. 14 But suppose your hearts are jealous and bitter. Suppose you are concerned only about getting ahead. Then don't brag about it. And don't say no to the truth. 15 Wisdom like this doesn't come down from heaven. It belongs to the earth. It doesn't come from the Holy Spirit. It comes from the devil. 16 Are you jealous? Are you concerned only about getting ahead? Then your life will be a mess. You will be doing all kinds of evil things.

17 But the wisdom that comes from heaven is pure. That's the most important thing about it. And that's not all. It also loves peace. It thinks about others. It obeys. It is full of mercy and good fruit. It is fair. It doesn't pretend to be what it is not. 18 Those who make peace plant it like a seed. They will harvest a crop of right living.

Obey God

4 Why do you fight and argue among yourselves? Isn't it because of your sinful desires? They fight within you. 2 You want something, but you don't have it. So you kill. You want what others have, but you can't get what you want. So you argue and fight. You don't have what you want, because you don't ask God. 3 When you do ask for something, you don't receive it. That's because you ask for the wrong reason. You want to spend your money on your sinful pleasures.

4 You are not faithful to God. Don't you know that to be a friend of the world is to hate God? So anyone who chooses to be the world's friend becomes God's enemy. 5 Don't you know what Scripture says? God wants the spirit in us to belong only to him. God caused this spirit to live in us. Don't you think Scripture has a reason for saying this? 6 But God continues to give us more grace. That's why Scripture says,

> "God opposes those who are proud.
> But he gives grace to those who
> are humble." (Proverbs 3:34)

7 So obey God. Stand up to the devil. He will run away from you. 8 Come near to God, and he will come near to you. Wash your hands, you sinners. Make your hearts pure, you who can't make up your minds.

9 Be full of sorrow. Cry and weep. Change
your laughter to mourning. Change your
joy to sadness. 10 Be humble in front of the
Lord. And he will lift you up.

11 My brothers and sisters, don't speak
against one another. Anyone who speaks
against a brother or sister speaks against
the law. And anyone who judges another
believer judges the law. When you judge
the law, you are not keeping it. Instead, you
are acting as if you were its judge. 12 There
is only one Lawgiver and Judge. He is the
God who is able to save life or destroy it.
But who are you to judge your neighbor?

Bragging About Tomorrow

13 Now listen, you who say, "Today or tomorrow we will go to this or that city. We
will spend a year there. We will buy and
sell and make money." 14 You don't even
know what will happen tomorrow. What
is your life? It is a mist that appears for a
little while. Then it disappears. 15 Instead,
you should say, "If it pleases the Lord, we
will live and do this or that." 16 As it is, you
brag. You brag about the evil plans your
pride produces. This kind of bragging is
evil. 17 So suppose someone knows the
good deeds they should do. But suppose
they don't do them. By not doing these
good deeds, they sin.

A Warning to Rich People

5 You rich people, listen to me. Cry and
weep, because you will soon be suffering. 2 Your riches have rotted. Moths have
eaten your clothes. 3 Your gold and silver
have lost their brightness. Their dullness
will be a witness against you. Your wanting more and more will eat your body like
fire. You have stored up riches in these
last days. 4 You have even failed to pay the
workers who mowed your fields. Their
pay is crying out against you. The cries
of those who gathered the harvest have
reached the ears of the Lord. He rules over
all. 5 You have lived an easy life on earth.
You have given yourselves everything
you wanted. You have made yourselves
fat like cattle that will soon be butchered.
6 You have judged and murdered people
who aren't guilty. And they weren't even
opposing you.

Be Patient When You Suffer

7 Brothers and sisters, be patient until
the Lord comes. See how the farmer waits
for the land to produce its rich crop. See
how patient the farmer is for the fall and
spring rains. 8 You too must be patient.
You must remain strong. The Lord will
soon come back. 9 Brothers and sisters,
don't find fault with one another. If you
do, you will be judged. And the Judge is
standing at the door!

10 Brothers and sisters, think about the
prophets who spoke in the name of the
Lord. They are an example of how to be
patient when you suffer. 11 As you know,
we think that people who don't give up
are blessed. You have heard that Job was
patient. And you have seen what the Lord
finally did for him. The Lord is full of tender mercy and loving concern.

12 My brothers and sisters, here is what
is most important. Don't make a promise by giving your word. Don't promise
by heaven or earth. And don't promise by
anything else to back up what you say. All
you need to say is a simple "Yes" or "No." If
you do more than this, you will be judged.

The Prayer of Faith

13 Is anyone among you in trouble?
Then that person should pray. Is anyone among you happy? Then that person
should sing songs of praise. 14 Is anyone
among you sick? Then that person should
send for the elders of the church to pray
over them. They should ask the elders to
anoint them with olive oil in the name of
the Lord. 15 The prayer offered by those
who have faith will make the sick person well. The Lord will heal them. If they
have sinned, they will be forgiven. 16 So
confess your sins to one another. Pray for
one another so that you might be healed.
The prayer of a godly person is powerful.
Things happen because of it.

17 Elijah was a human being, just as we
are. He prayed hard that it wouldn't rain.
And it didn't rain on the land for three
and a half years. 18 Then he prayed again.
That time it rained. And the earth produced its crops.

19 My brothers and sisters, suppose one
of you wanders away from the truth. And
suppose someone brings that person back.
20 Then here is what I want you to remember. Anyone who keeps a sinner from going astray will save them from death. God
will erase many sins by forgiving them.

1 PETER

The apostle Peter was one of Jesus' twelve disciples. Later, Peter traveled to Rome. Peter spent the final years of his life and ministry in Rome. And he became a leader of the church there.

Peter learned that churches in other parts of the Roman Empire were experiencing hard times. So he wrote to encourage these believers to remain faithful to Jesus. Peter's letter was brought to these churches by Silas. Silas was a man who also worked with the apostle Paul. In this letter Peter introduces Silas and explains that Silas helped write the letter.

After the opening part, the letter has three main sections. First, Peter tells his readers to be holy in everything they do. As Gentiles they once lived not knowing the ways of God. But now they are a holy nation. They are part of God's own people. So they are called to a new way of life.

Second, Peter explains how this new way of life may affect those who see it. Some people who don't believe in Jesus may attack believers. But these attackers will see the good lives of the believers.

Finally, Peter states that he knows his readers are suffering for their faith. He explains that this is to be expected. Jesus Christ himself experienced suffering. And believers all over the world face suffering. But even in their suffering believers can show they belong to God. Their strength is found in the grace and strength of God through faith in Jesus the Messiah.

---

1 I, Peter, am writing this letter. I am an apostle of Jesus Christ.

I am sending this letter to you, God's chosen people. You are people who have had to wander in the world. You are scattered all over the areas of Pontus, Galatia, Cappadocia, Asia and Bithynia. [2] You have been chosen in keeping with what God the Father had planned. That happened through the Spirit's work to make you pure and holy. God chose you so that you might obey Jesus Christ. God wanted you to be in a covenant relationship with him. He established this relationship by the blood of Christ.

May more and more grace and peace be given to you.

Peter Praises God for a Living Hope

[3] Give praise to the God and Father of our Lord Jesus Christ. In his great mercy he has given us a new birth and a living hope. This hope is living because Jesus Christ rose from the dead. [4] He has given us new birth so that we might share in what belongs to him. This is a gift that can never be destroyed. It can never spoil or even fade away. It is kept in heaven for you. [5] Through faith you are kept safe by God's power. Your salvation is going to be completed. It is ready to be shown to you in the last days. [6] Because you know all this, you have great joy. You have joy even though you may have had to suffer for a little while. You may have had to suffer sadness in all kinds of trouble. [7] Your troubles have come in order to prove that your faith is real. Your faith is worth more than gold. That's because gold can pass away even when fire has made it pure. Your faith is meant to bring praise, honor and glory to God. This will happen when Jesus Christ returns. [8] Even though you have not seen him, you love him. Though you do not see him now, you believe in him. You are filled with a glorious joy that can't be put into words. [9] You are receiving the salvation of your souls. This salvation is the final result of your faith.

[10] The prophets searched very hard and with great care to find out about this salvation. They spoke about the grace that was going to come to you. [11] They wanted to find out when and how this salvation would come. The Spirit of Christ in them was telling them about the sufferings of the Messiah. These were his sufferings that were going to come. The Spirit of Christ was also telling them about the glory that would follow. [12] It was made known to the prophets that they were not serving themselves. Instead, they were serving you when they spoke about the things that you have now heard. Those who have preached the good news to you have told you these things. They have done it with the help of the Holy Spirit sent from heaven. Even angels long to look into these things.

Be Holy

[13]So be watchful, and control yourselves completely. In this way, put your hope in the grace that lies ahead. This grace will be brought to you when Jesus Christ returns. [14]You should obey your Father. You shouldn't give in to evil desires. They controlled your life when you didn't know any better. [15]The God who chose you is holy. So you should be holy in all that you do. [16]It is written, "Be holy, because I am holy." (Leviticus 11:44,45; 19:2)

[17]You call on a Father who judges each person's work without favoring one over another. So live as outsiders during your time here. Live with the highest respect for God. [18]You were set free from an empty way of life. This way of life was handed down to you by your own people of long ago. You know that you were not bought with things that can pass away, like silver or gold. [19]Instead, you were bought with the priceless blood of Christ. He is a perfect lamb. He doesn't have any flaws at all. [20]He was chosen before God created the world. But he came into the world for your sake in these last days. [21]Because of what Christ has done, you believe in God. It was God who raised him from the dead. And it was God who gave him glory. So your faith and hope are in God.

[22]You have made yourselves pure by obeying the truth. So you have an honest and true love for each other. So love one another deeply, from your hearts. [23]You have been born again by means of the living word of God. His word lasts forever. You were not born again from a seed that will die. You were born from a seed that can't die. [24]It is written,

"All people are like grass.
All their glory is like the flowers in the field.
The grass dries up. The flowers fall to the ground.
25 But the word of the Lord lasts forever." (Isaiah 40:6–8)

And this is the word that was preached to you.

2 So get rid of every kind of evil, and stop telling lies. Don't pretend to be something you are not. Stop wanting what others have, and don't speak against one another. [2]Like newborn babies, you should long for the pure milk of God's word. It will help you grow up as believers. [3]You can do this now that you have tasted how good the Lord is.

The Living Stone and a Chosen People

[4]Christ is the living Stone. People did not accept him, but God chose him. God places the highest value on him. [5]You also are like living stones. As you come to Christ, you are being built into a house for worship. There you will be holy priests. You will offer spiritual sacrifices. God will accept them because of what Jesus Christ has done. [6]In Scripture it says,

"Look! I am placing a stone in Zion.
It is a chosen and very valuable stone.
It is the most important stone in the building.
The one who trusts in him
will never be put to shame."
(Isaiah 28:16)

[7]This stone is very valuable to you who believe. But to people who do not believe,

"The stone the builders did not accept
has become the most important stone of all." (Psalm 118:22)

[8]And,

"It is a stone that causes people to trip.
It is a rock that makes them fall."
(Isaiah 8:14)

They trip and fall because they do not obey the message. That is also what God planned for them.

[9]But God chose you to be his people. You are royal priests. You are a holy nation. You are God's special treasure. You are all these things so that you can give him praise. God brought you out of darkness into his wonderful light. [10]Once you were not a people. But now you are the people of God. Once you had not received mercy. But now you have received mercy.

Living Godly Lives Among People Who Don't Believe

[11]Dear friends, you are outsiders and those who wander in this world. So I'm asking you not to give in to your sinful desires. They fight against your soul. [12]People who don't believe might say you are

doing wrong. But lead good lives among them. Then they will see your good deeds. And they will give glory to God on the day he comes to judge.

13 Follow the lead of every human authority. Do this for the Lord's sake. Obey the emperor. He is the highest authority. 14 Obey the governors. The emperor sends them to punish those who do wrong. He also sends them to praise those who do right. 15 By doing good you will put a stop to the talk of foolish people. They don't know what they are saying. 16 Live as free people. But don't use your freedom to cover up evil. Live as people who are God's slaves. 17 Show proper respect to everyone. Love the family of believers. Have respect for God. Honor the emperor.

18 Slaves, obey your masters out of deep respect for God. Obey not only those who are good and kind. Obey also those who are not kind. 19 Suppose a person suffers pain unfairly because they want to obey God. This is worthy of praise. 20 But suppose you receive a beating for doing wrong, and you put up with it. Will anyone honor you for this? Of course not. But suppose you suffer for doing good, and you put up with it. God will praise you for this. 21 You were chosen to do good even if you suffer. That's because Christ suffered for you. He left you an example that he expects you to follow. 22 Scripture says,

"He didn't commit any sin.
No lies ever came out of his
mouth." (Isaiah 53:9)

23 People shouted at him and made fun of him. But he didn't do the same thing back to them. When he suffered, he didn't say he would make them suffer. Instead, he trusted in the God who judges fairly. 24 "He himself carried our sins" in his body on the cross. (Isaiah 53:5) He did it so that we would die as far as sins are concerned. Then we would lead godly lives. "His wounds have healed you." (Isaiah 53:5) 25 "You were like sheep wandering away." (Isaiah 53:6) But now you have returned to the Shepherd. He is the one who watches over your souls.

3 Wives, follow the lead of your own husbands. Suppose some of them don't believe God's word. Then let them be won to Christ without words by seeing how their wives behave. 2 Let them see how pure you are. Let them see that your lives are full of respect for God. 3 Fancy hairstyles don't make you beautiful. Wearing gold jewelry or fine clothes doesn't make you beautiful. 4 Instead, your beauty comes from inside you. It is the beauty of a gentle and quiet spirit. Beauty like this doesn't fade away. God places great value on it. 5 This is how the holy women of the past used to make themselves beautiful. They put their hope in God. And they followed the lead of their own husbands. 6 Sarah was like that. She obeyed Abraham. She called him her master. Do you want to be like her? Then do what is right. And don't give in to fear.

7 Husbands, consider the needs of your wives. They are weaker than you. So treat them with respect. Honor them as those who will share with you the gracious gift of life. Then nothing will stand in the way of your prayers.

Suffering for Doing Good

8 Finally, I want all of you to agree with one another. Be understanding. Love one another. Be kind and tender. Be humble. 9 Don't pay back evil with evil. Don't pay back unkind words with unkind words. Instead, pay back evil with kind words. This is what you have been chosen to do. You will receive a blessing by doing this. 10 Scripture says,

"Suppose someone wants to love life
and see good days.
Then they must keep their tongues
from speaking evil.
They must keep their lips from
telling lies.
11 They must turn away from evil and
do good.
They must look for peace and go
after it.
12 The Lord's eyes look on godly
people, and he blesses them.
His ears are open to their prayers.
But the Lord doesn't bless those who
do evil." (Psalm 34:12–16)

13 Who is going to hurt you if you really want to do good? 14 But suppose you do suffer for doing what is right. Even then you will be blessed. Scripture says, "Don't fear what others say they will do to hurt you. Don't be afraid." (Isaiah 8:12) 15 But make sure that in your hearts you honor

Christ as Lord. Always be ready to give an answer to anyone who asks you about the hope you have. Be ready to give the reason for it. But do it gently and with respect. [16] Live so that you don't have to feel you've done anything wrong. Some people may say evil things about your good conduct as believers in Christ. If they do, they will be put to shame for speaking like this about you. [17] God may want you to suffer for doing good. That's better than suffering for doing evil. [18] Christ also suffered once for sins. The one who did what is right suffered for those who don't do right. He suffered to bring you to God. His body was put to death. But the Holy Spirit brought him back to life. [19] After that, Christ went and made an announcement to the spirits in prison. [20] Long ago these spirits did not obey. That was when God was patient while Noah was building the ark. And only a few people went into the ark. In fact, there were only eight. Those eight people were saved through water. [21] The water of the flood is a picture. It is a picture of the baptism that now saves you too. This baptism has nothing to do with removing dirt from your body. Instead, it promises God that you will keep a clear sense of right and wrong. This baptism saves you by the same power that raised Jesus Christ from the dead. [22] He has gone into heaven. He is at God's right hand. Angels, authorities and powers are under his control.

Living for God

4 Christ suffered in his body. So prepare yourselves to think in the same way Christ did. Do this because whoever suffers in their body is finished with sin. [2] As a result, they don't live the rest of their earthly life for evil human desires. Instead, they live to do what God wants. [3] You have spent enough time in the past doing what ungodly people choose to do. You lived a wild life. You longed for evil things. You got drunk. You went to wild parties. You worshiped statues of gods, which the Lord hates. [4] Ungodly people are surprised that you no longer join them in what they do. They want you to join them in their wild and wasteful living. So they say bad things about you. [5] But they will have to explain their actions to God. He is ready to judge those who are alive and those who are dead. [6] That's why the good news was preached even to people who are now dead. It was preached to them for two reasons. It was preached so that their bodies might be judged. This judgment is made by human standards. But the good news was also preached so that their spirits might live. This life comes by means of God's power.

[7] The end of all things is near. So be watchful and control yourselves. Then you may pray. [8] Most of all, love one another deeply. Love erases many sins by forgiving them. [9] Welcome others into your homes without complaining. [10] God's gifts of grace come in many forms. Each of you has received a gift in order to serve others. You should use it faithfully. [11] If anyone speaks, they should do it as one speaking God's words. If anyone serves, they should do it with the strength God provides. Then in all things God will be praised through Jesus Christ. Glory and power belong to him for ever and ever. Amen.

Suffering for Being a Christian

[12] Dear friends, don't be surprised by the terrible things happening to you. The trouble you are having has come to test you. So don't feel as if something strange were happening to you. [13] Instead, be joyful that you are taking part in Christ's sufferings. Then you will have even more joy when Christ returns in glory. [14] Suppose people say bad things about you because you believe in Christ. Then you are blessed, because God's Spirit rests on you. He is the Spirit of glory. [15] If you suffer, it shouldn't be because you are a murderer. It shouldn't be because you are a thief or someone who does evil things. It shouldn't be because you interfere with other people's business. [16] But suppose you suffer for being a Christian. Then don't be ashamed. Instead, praise God because you are known by the name of Christ. [17] It is time for judgment to begin with the household of God. And since it begins with us, what will happen to people who don't obey God's good news? [18] Scripture says,

> "Suppose it is hard for godly people
>   to be saved.
> Then what will happen to ungodly
>   people and sinners?"
> (Proverbs 11:31)

[19]Here is what people who suffer because of God's plan should do. They
should commit themselves to their faithful Creator. And they should continue to
do good.

To Older and Younger Believers

5 I'm speaking to the elders among you.
I was a witness of Christ's sufferings.
And I will also share in the glory that is
going to come. I'm making my appeal to
you as one who is an elder together with
you. [2]Be shepherds of God's flock, the believers under your care. Watch over them,
though not because you have to. Instead,
do it because you want to. That's what
God wants you to do. Don't do it because
you want to get money in dishonest ways.
Do it because you really want to serve.
[3]Don't act as if you were a ruler over those
under your care. Instead, be examples to
the flock. [4]The Chief Shepherd will come
again. Then you will receive the crown
of glory. It is a crown that will never fade
away.
[5]In the same way, I'm speaking to you
who are younger. Follow the lead of those
who are older. All of you, put on a spirit
free of pride toward one another. Put it on
as if it were your clothes. Do this because
Scripture says,

"God opposes those who are proud.
But he gives grace to those who
are humble." (Proverbs 3:34)

[6]So make yourselves humble. Put yourselves under God's mighty hand. Then he
will honor you at the right time. [7]Turn all
your worries over to him. He cares about
you.
[8]Be watchful and control yourselves.
Your enemy the devil is like a roaring lion.
He prowls around looking for someone
to swallow up. [9]Stand up to him. Remain
strong in what you believe. You know that
you are not alone in your suffering. The
family of believers throughout the world
is going through the same thing.
[10]God always gives you all the grace you
need. So you will only have to suffer for a
little while. Then God himself will build
you up again. He will make you strong
and steady. And he has chosen you to
share in his eternal glory because you belong to Christ. [11]Give him the power for
ever and ever. Amen.

Final Greetings

[12]I consider Silas to be a faithful brother. With his help I have written you this
short letter. I have written it to encourage you. And I have written to speak the
truth about the true grace of God. Remain
strong in it.

[13]The members of the church in Babylon send you their greetings. They were
chosen together with you. Mark, my son
in the faith, also sends you his greetings.
[14]Greet each other with a kiss of friendship.

May God give peace to all of you who
believe in Christ.

2 PETER

The Roman emperor Nero put the apostle Peter in prison. And Peter realized he would soon be put to death. So Peter decided to write another letter to the believers he had written to before. Peter wanted these believers to be certain of the truth about Jesus. Peter wrote this letter with authority because he had been with Jesus during his entire ministry.

False teachers had come into the churches. They were saying that Jesus really wasn't going to come back. Some believers had accepted this false teaching. They didn't expect Jesus to return or to bring justice. So, they started living very ungodly lives.

Peter shows that the false teachers are wrong. He points out that he personally saw the glory and majesty of Jesus. He saw it when he was with Jesus on the sacred mountain. Peter states that everyone will see this glory when Jesus comes again. Peter states that the false teachers will lead some people astray. And then he provides a powerful example of the judgment waiting for them.

In the final section of the letter, Peter states specifically that Jesus is coming again. But God has delayed when Jesus is coming so people will turn away from their sin. God wants people to live in a way that pleases him. And we are to wait with hope since we all look forward to a new heaven and a new earth.

---

1 I, Simon Peter, am writing this letter. I serve Jesus Christ. I am his apostle.

I am sending this letter to you. You are those who have received a faith as valuable as ours. You received it because our God and Savior Jesus Christ does what is right.

2 May more and more grace and peace be given to you. May they come to you as you learn more about God and about Jesus our Lord.

Showing That God Has Chosen You

3 God's power has given us everything we need to lead a godly life. All of this has come to us because we know the God who chose us. He chose us because of his own glory and goodness.
4 He has also given us his very great and valuable promises. He did it so you could share in his nature. You can share in it because you've escaped from the evil in the world. This evil is caused by sinful desires.

5 So you should try very hard to add goodness to your faith. To goodness, add knowledge.
6 To knowledge, add the ability to control yourselves. To the ability to control yourselves, add the strength to keep going. To the strength to keep going, add godliness.
7 To godliness, add kindness for one another. And to kindness for one another, add love.
8 All these things should describe you more and more. They will make you useful and fruitful as you know our Lord Jesus Christ better.
9 But what if these things don't describe someone at all? Then that person can't see very well. In fact, they are blind. They have forgotten that their past sins have been washed away.

10 My brothers and sisters, try very hard to show that God has appointed you to be saved. Try hard to show that he has chosen you. If you do everything I have just said, you will never trip and fall.
11 You will receive a rich welcome into the kingdom that lasts forever. It is the kingdom of our Lord and Savior Jesus Christ.

Prophecy of Scripture Comes From God

12 So I will always remind you of these things. I'll do it even though you know them. I'll do it even though you now have deep roots in the truth.
13 I think it is right for me to remind you. It is right as long as I live in this tent. I'm talking about my body.
14 I know my tent will soon be removed. Our Lord Jesus Christ has made that clear to me.
15 I hope that you will always be able to remember these things after I'm gone. I will try very hard to see that you do.

16 We told you about the time our Lord Jesus Christ came with power. But we didn't make up clever stories when we told you about it. With our own eyes we saw him in all his majesty.
17 God the Father gave him honor and glory. The voice of the Majestic Glory came to him. It said, "This is my Son, and I love him. I am very pleased with him." (Matthew 17:5; Mark 9:7;

Luke 9:35) 18 We ourselves heard this voice
that came from heaven. We were with
him on the sacred mountain.
19 We also have the message of the
prophets. This message can be trusted
completely. You must pay attention to it.
The message is like a light shining in a
dark place. It will shine until the day Jesus
comes. Then the Morning Star will rise in
your hearts. 20 Above all, here is what you
must understand. No prophecy in Scripture ever came from a prophet's own understanding of things. 21 Prophecy never
came simply because a prophet wanted
it to. Instead, the Holy Spirit guided the
prophets as they spoke. So, although
prophets are human, prophecy comes
from God.

False Teachers Will Be Destroyed

2 But there were also false prophets
among the people. In the same way
there will be false teachers among you. In
secret they will bring in teachings that will
destroy you. They will even turn against
the Lord and Master who died to pay for
their sins. So they will quickly destroy
themselves. 2 Many people will follow
their lead. These people will do the same
evil things the false teachers do. They will
cause people to think badly about the way
of truth. 3 These teachers are never satisfied. They want to get something out of
you. So they make up stories to take advantage of you. They have been under
a sentence of death for a long time. The
God who will destroy them has not been
sleeping.
4 God did not spare angels when they
sinned. Instead, he sent them to hell. He
chained them up in dark prisons. He will
keep them there until he judges them.
5 God did not spare the world's ungodly
people long ago. He brought the flood on
them. But Noah preached about the right
way to live. God kept him safe. He also
saved seven others. 6 God judged the cities of Sodom and Gomorrah. He burned
them to ashes. He made them an example of what is going to happen to ungodly
people. 7 God saved Lot, a man who did
what was right. Lot was shocked by the
evil conduct of people who didn't obey
God's laws. 8 That good man lived among
them day after day. He saw and heard the
evil things they were doing. They were
breaking God's laws. And the godly spirit
of Lot was deeply troubled. 9 Since all
this is true, then the Lord knows how to
save godly people. He knows how to keep
them safe in times of testing. The Lord
also knows how to keep ungodly people
under guard. He will do so until the day
they will be judged and punished. 10 Most
of all, this is true of people who follow desires that come from sin's power. These
people hate to be under authority.
They are bold and proud. So they aren't
even afraid to speak evil things against
heavenly beings. 11 Now angels are stronger and more powerful than these people.
But even angels don't speak evil things
against heavenly beings. They don't do
this when they bring judgment on them
from the Lord. 12 These people speak evil
about things they don't understand. They
are like wild animals who can't think. Instead, they do what comes naturally to
them. They are born only to be caught
and destroyed. Just like animals, these
people too will die.
13 They will be paid back with harm
for the harm they have done. Their idea
of pleasure is to have wild parties in the
middle of the day. They are like dirty
spots and stains. They enjoy their sinful
pleasures while they eat with you. 14 They
stare at women who are not their wives.
They want to sleep with them. They never
stop sinning. They trap those who are not
firm in their faith. They have mastered
the art of getting what they want. God has
placed them under his judgment. 15 They
have left God's way. They have wandered
off. They follow the way of Balaam, son
of Beor. He loved to get paid for doing
his evil work. 16 But a donkey corrected
him for the wrong he did. Animals don't
speak. But the donkey spoke with a human voice. It tried to stop the prophet
from doing a very dumb thing.
17 These people are like springs without water. They are like mists driven by a
storm. The blackest darkness is reserved
for them. 18 They speak empty, bragging
words. They make their appeal to the evil
desires that come from sin's power. They
tempt new believers who are just escaping from the company of sinful people.
19 They promise to give freedom to these
new believers. But they themselves are
slaves to sinful living. That's because

"people are slaves to anything that controls them." [20]They may have escaped the
sin of the world. They may have come to
know our Lord and Savior Jesus Christ.
But what if they are once again caught
up in sin? And what if it has become their
master? Then they are worse off at the end
than they were at the beginning. [21]Sup-
pose they had not known the way of godliness. This would have been better than
to know godliness and then turn away
from it. The way of godliness is the sacred
command passed on to them. [22]What the
proverbs say about them is true. "A dog
returns to where it has thrown up." (Proverbs 26:11) And, "A pig that is washed goes
back to rolling in the mud."

The Day of the Lord

3 Dear friends, this is now my second
letter to you. I have written both of
them as reminders. I want to encourage you to think in a way that is pure. [2]I
want you to remember the words the holy
prophets spoke in the past. Remember
the command our Lord and Savior gave
through your apostles.

[3]Most of all, here is what you must
understand. In the last days people will
make fun of the truth. They will laugh at
it. They will follow their own evil desires.
[4]They will say, "Where is this 'return'
he promised? Everything goes on in the
same way it has since our people of long
ago died. In fact, it has continued this way
since God first created everything." [5]Long
ago, God's word brought the heavens into
being. His word separated the earth from
the waters. And the waters surrounded
it. But these people forget things like that
on purpose. [6]The waters also flooded the
world of that time. And so they destroyed
the world. [7]By God's word the heavens
and earth of today are being reserved for
fire. They are being kept for the day when
God will judge. Then ungodly people will
be destroyed.

[8]Dear friends, here is one thing you
must not forget. With the Lord a day is
like a thousand years. And a thousand
years are like a day. [9]The Lord is not slow
to keep his promise. He is not slow in the
way some people understand it. Instead,
he is patient with you. He doesn't want
anyone to be destroyed. Instead, he wants
all people to turn away from their sins.

[10]But the day of the Lord will come like
a thief. The heavens will disappear with a
roar. Fire will destroy everything in them.
God will judge the earth and everything
done in it.

[11]So everything will be destroyed in this
way. And what kind of people should you
be? You should lead holy and godly lives.
[12]Live like this as you look forward to the
day of God. Living like this will make the
day come more quickly. On that day fire
will destroy the heavens. Its heat will melt
everything in them. [13]But we are looking forward to a new heaven and a new
earth. Godliness will live there. All this is
in keeping with God's promise.

[14]Dear friends, I know you are looking forward to this. So try your best to
be found pure and without blame. Be at
peace with God. [15]Remember that while
our Lord is waiting patiently to return,
people are being saved. Our dear brother Paul also wrote to you about this. God
made him wise to write as he did. [16]Paul
writes the same way in all his letters. He
speaks about what I have just told you.
His letters include some things that are
hard to understand. People who don't
know better and aren't firm in the faith
twist what he says. They twist the other
Scriptures too. So they will be destroyed.

[17]Dear friends, you have already been
warned about this. So be on your guard.
Then you won't be led astray by people who don't obey the law. Instead, you
will remain safe. [18]Grow in the grace and
knowledge of our Lord and Savior Jesus
Christ.

Glory belongs to him both now and forever. Amen.

1 JOHN

The apostle John who was also a disciple of Jesus wrote this book. It is a caring letter sent to believers that he calls his "dear children."

These believers were in the middle of an unsettling situation. Some of them had left the faith in Jesus that they had been taught. They couldn't believe that God had come to earth in a human body. There was a common Greek idea that the physical body was evil. The Greek thinkers said that only the spirit was good. So they thought if Jesus became human then he couldn't be God. Soon these people denied that Jesus was the Messiah. They lived lives that were immoral. And they did not take care of each other. Yet, they still said they knew God and belonged to him. They even said that their spiritual understanding was better than the rest of the group. And so they left that group of believers.

The believers who were left behind were hurt and upset. They even wondered if what they had been taught about Jesus was true. So John wrote this letter to encourage all these believers. He states that everything they learned from the very beginning is true. It is true that Jesus came as a human being. And it is true that Jesus is the Messiah. He shows that the Greek thinkers are wrong. John then encourages them to show their true love for God. They are to show it by living good lives and by caring for each other.

The Word of Life Became a Human Being

1 Here is what we announce to everyone about the Word of life. The Word
was already here from the beginning. We
have heard him. We have seen him with
our eyes. We have looked at him. Our
hands have touched him. 2 This life has
appeared. We have seen him. We are witnesses about him. And we announce to
you this same eternal life. He was already
with the Father. He has appeared to us.
3 We announce to you what we have seen
and heard. We do it so you can share life
together with us. And we share life with
the Father and with his Son, Jesus Christ.
4 We are writing this to make our joy complete.

Walking in the Light

5 Here is the message we have heard
from him and announce to you. God is
light. There is no darkness in him at all.
6 Suppose we say that we share life with
God but still walk in the darkness. Then
we are lying. We are not living out the
truth. 7 But suppose we walk in the light,
just as he is in the light. Then we share life
with one another. And the blood of Jesus,
his Son, makes us pure from all sin.

8 Suppose we claim we are without sin.
Then we are fooling ourselves. The truth
is not in us. 9 But God is faithful and fair.
If we confess our sins, he will forgive our
sins. He will forgive every wrong thing we
have done. He will make us pure. 10 If we
claim we have not sinned, we are calling
God a liar. His word is not in us.

2 My dear children, I'm writing this to
you so that you will not sin. But suppose someone does sin. Then we have a
friend who speaks to the Father for us. He
is Jesus Christ, the Blameless One. 2 He
gave his life to pay for our sins. But he not
only paid for our sins. He also paid for the
sins of the whole world.

Instructions About Loving and Hating Other Believers

3 We know that we have come to know
God if we obey his commands. 4 Suppose
someone says, "I know him." But suppose
this person does not do what God commands. Then this person is a liar and is
not telling the truth. 5 But if anyone obeys
God's word, then that person truly loves
God. Here is how we know we belong to
him. 6 Those who claim to belong to him
must live just as Jesus did.

7 Dear friends, I'm not writing you a
new command. Instead, I'm writing one
you have heard before. You have had it
since the beginning. 8 But I am writing
what amounts to a new command. Its
truth was shown in how Jesus lived. It is
also shown in how you live. That's because the darkness is passing away. And
the true light is already shining.

9 Suppose someone claims to be in the
light but hates a brother or sister. Then
they are still in the darkness. 10 Anyone
who loves their brother and sister lives
in the light. There is nothing in them to
make them fall into sin. 11 But anyone who
hates a brother or sister is in the darkness.

They walk around in the darkness. They don't know where they are going. The darkness has made them blind.

Reasons for Writing

12 Dear children, I'm writing to you
because your sins have been
forgiven.
They have been forgiven because
of what Jesus has done.
13 Fathers, I'm writing to you
because you know the one who is
from the beginning.
Young men, I'm writing to you
because you have won the battle
over the evil one.

14 Dear children, I'm writing to you
because you know the Father.
Fathers, I'm writing to you
because you know the one who is
from the beginning.
Young men, I'm writing to you
because you are strong.
God's word lives in you.
You have won the battle over the
evil one.

Do Not Love the World

15 Do not love the world or anything in it. If anyone loves the world, love for the Father is not in them. 16 Here is what people who belong to this world do. They try to satisfy what their sinful desires want to do. They long for what their sinful eyes look at. They take pride in what they have and what they do. All of this comes from the world. None of it comes from the Father. 17 The world and its evil desires are passing away. But whoever does what God wants them to do lives forever.

Warnings About Saying No to the Son

18 Dear children, we are living in the last days. You have heard that the great enemy of Christ is coming. But even now many enemies of Christ have already come. That's how we know that these are the last days. 19 These enemies left our community of believers. They didn't really belong to us. If they had belonged to us, they would have remained with us. But by leaving they showed that none of them belonged to us.

20 You have received the Spirit from the Holy One. And all of you know the truth. 21 I'm not writing to you because you don't know the truth. I'm writing because you do know it. I'm writing to you because no lie comes from the truth. 22 Who is the liar? It is anyone who says that Jesus is not the Christ. The person who says this is the great enemy of Christ. They say no to the Father and the Son. 23 The person who says no to the Son doesn't belong to the Father. But anyone who says yes to the Son belongs to the Father also.

24 Make sure that you don't forget what you have heard from the beginning. Then you will remain joined to the Son and to the Father. 25 And here is what God has promised us. He has promised us eternal life.

26 I'm writing these things to warn you. I am warning you about people trying to lead you astray. 27 But you have received the Holy Spirit from God. He continues to live in you. So you don't need anyone to teach you. God's Spirit teaches you about everything. What he says is true. He doesn't lie. Remain joined to Christ, just as you have been taught by the Spirit.

God's Children and Sin

28 Dear children, remain joined to Christ. Then when he comes, we can be bold. We will not be ashamed to meet him when he comes.

29 You know that God is right and always does what is right. And you know that everyone who does what is right is God's child.

3 See what amazing love the Father has given us! Because of it, we are called children of God. And that's what we really are! The world doesn't know us because it didn't know him. 2 Dear friends, now we are children of God. He still hasn't let us know what we will be. But we know that when Christ appears, we will be like him. That's because we will see him as he really is. 3 Christ is pure. All who hope to be like him make themselves pure.

4 Everyone who sins breaks the law. In fact, breaking the law is sin. 5 But you know that Christ came to take our sins away. And there is no sin in him. 6 No one who remains joined to him keeps on sinning. No one who keeps on sinning has seen him or known him.

7 Dear children, don't let anyone lead you astray. The person who does what is

right is holy, just as Christ is holy. 8 The
person who does what is sinful belongs
to the devil. That's because the devil has
been sinning from the beginning. But the
Son of God came to destroy the devil's
work. 9 Those who are God's children will
not keep on sinning. God's very nature remains in them. They can't go on sinning.
That's because they are God's children.
10 Here is how you can tell the difference
between God's children and the devil's
children. Anyone who doesn't do what is
right isn't God's child. And anyone who
doesn't love their brother or sister isn't
God's child either.

More Instructions About Loving and Hating One Another

11 From the beginning we have heard
that we should love one another. 12 Don't
be like Cain. He belonged to the evil one.
He murdered his brother. And why did
he murder him? Because the things Cain
had done were wrong. But the things his
brother had done were right. 13 My brothers and sisters, don't be surprised if the
world hates you. 14 We know that we have
left our old dead way of life. And we have
entered into new life. We know this because we love one another. Anyone who
doesn't love still lives in their old condition. 15 Anyone who hates their brother or
sister is a murderer. And you know that no
murderer has eternal life.

16 We know what love is because Jesus
Christ gave his life for us. So we should
give our lives for our brothers and sisters.
17 Suppose someone sees a brother or sister in need and is able to help them. And
suppose that person doesn't take pity on
these needy people. Then how can the
love of God be in that person? 18 Dear children, don't just talk about love. Put your
love into action. Then it will truly be love.

19 Here's how we know that we hold
to the truth. And here's how we put our
hearts at rest, knowing that God is watching. 20 If our hearts judge us, we know
that God is greater than our hearts. And
he knows everything. 21 Dear friends,
if our hearts do not judge us, we can be
bold with God. 22 And he will give us anything we ask. That's because we obey his
commands. We do what pleases him.
23 God has commanded us to believe in
the name of his Son, Jesus Christ. He has
also commanded us to love one another.
24 The one who obeys God's commands
remains joined to him. And he remains
joined to them. Here is how we know that
God lives in us. We know it because of the
Holy Spirit he gave us.

Jesus Came as a Human Being

4 Dear friends, do not believe every
spirit. Test the spirits to see if they belong to God. Many false prophets have
gone out into the world. 2 Here is how you
can recognize the Spirit of God. Every
spirit agreeing that Jesus Christ came in a
human body belongs to God. 3 But every
spirit that doesn't agree with this does not
belong to God. You have heard that the
spirit of the great enemy of Christ is coming. Even now it is already in the world.

4 Dear children, you belong to God.
You have not accepted the teachings of
the false prophets. That's because the
one who is in you is powerful. He is more
powerful than the one who is in the world.
5 False prophets belong to the world. So
they speak from the world's point of view.
And the world listens to them. 6 We belong to God. And those who know God
listen to us. But those who don't belong
to God don't listen to us. That's how we
can tell the difference between the Spirit
of truth and the spirit of lies.

We Love Because God Loved Us

7 Dear friends, let us love one another,
because love comes from God. Everyone
who loves has become a child of God and
knows God. 8 Anyone who does not love
does not know God, because God is love.
9 Here is how God showed his love among
us. He sent his one and only Son into the
world. He sent him so we could receive
life through him. 10 Here is what love is.
It is not that we loved God. It is that he
loved us and sent his Son to give his life to
pay for our sins. 11 Dear friends, since God
loved us this much, we should also love
one another. 12 No one has ever seen God.
But if we love one another, God lives in us.
His love is made complete in us.

13 Here's how we know that we are
joined to him and he to us. He has given
us his Holy Spirit. 14 The Father has sent
his Son to be the Savior of the world. We
have seen it and are witnesses to it. 15 God
lives in anyone who agrees that Jesus is

the Son of God. This kind of person remains joined to God. [16]So we know that
God loves us. We depend on it.

God is love. Anyone who leads a life of
love is joined to God. And God is joined
to them. [17]Suppose love is fulfilled among
us. Then we can be without fear on the
day God judges the world. Love is fulfilled
among us when in this world we are like
Jesus. [18]There is no fear in love. Instead,
perfect love drives away fear. That's because fear has to do with being punished.
The one who fears does not have perfect
love.

[19]We love because he loved us first.
[20]Suppose someone claims to love God
but hates a brother or sister. Then they
are a liar. They don't love their brother
or sister, whom they have seen. So they
can't love God, whom they haven't seen.
[21]Here is the command God has given
us. Anyone who loves God must also love
their brother and sister.

Faith in God's Son Who Became a Human Being

5 Everyone who believes that Jesus is the
Christ is a child of God. And everyone
who loves the Father loves his children as
well. [2]Here is how we know that we love
God's children. We know it when we love
God and obey his commands. [3]In fact,
here is what it means to love God. We love
him by obeying his commands. And his
commands are not hard to obey. [4]That's
because everyone who is a child of God
has won the battle over the world. Our
faith has won the battle for us. [5]Who is
it that has won the battle over the world?
Only the person who believes that Jesus is
the Son of God.

[6]Jesus Christ was born as we are, and
he died on the cross. He wasn't just born
as we are. He also died on the cross. The
Holy Spirit is a truthful witness about
him. That's because the Spirit is the truth.
[7]There are three that are witnesses about
Jesus. [8]They are the Holy Spirit, the birth
of Jesus, and the death of Jesus. And the
three of them agree. [9]We accept what
people say when they are witnesses. But
it's more important when God is a witness. That's because it is what God says
about his Son. [10]Whoever believes in the
Son of God accepts what God says about
him. Whoever does not believe God is
calling him a liar. That's because they
have not believed what God said about
his Son. [11]Here is what God says about
the Son. God has given us eternal life. And
this life is found in his Son. [12]Whoever belongs to the Son has life. Whoever doesn't
belong to the Son of God doesn't have life.

Final Words

[13]I'm writing these things to you who
believe in the name of the Son of God.
I'm writing so you will know that you
have eternal life. [14]Here is what we can be
sure of when we come to God in prayer.
If we ask anything in keeping with what
he wants, he hears us. [15]If we know that
God hears what we ask for, we know that
we have it.

[16]Suppose you see any brother or sister
commit a sin. But this sin is not the kind
that leads to death. Then you should pray,
and God will give them life. I'm talking
about someone whose sin does not lead
to death. But there is a sin that does lead
to death. I'm not saying you should pray
about that sin. [17]Every wrong thing we do
is sin. But there are sins that do not lead
to death.

[18]We know that those who are children of God do not keep on sinning. The
Son of God keeps them safe. The evil one
can't harm them. [19]We know that we are
children of God. We know that the whole
world is under the control of the evil one.
[20]We also know that the Son of God has
come. He has given us understanding. So
we can know the God who is true. And we
belong to the true God by belonging to his
Son, Jesus Christ. He is the true God and
eternal life.

[21]Dear children, keep away from statues of gods.

2 JOHN

The apostle John wrote a second letter. He identifies himself in the letter as a church leader. He does this by using the title of elder. In this letter John refers to the church as a lady. And he refers to the members of the church as her children. This is typical of the greetings used by early followers of Jesus. The same type of greeting is used at the end of Peter's first letter.

Some people from this church had just come to visit John. He was pleased to learn that they continued to believe the truth. But John wrote this letter to warn them about false teachers. He was concerned that the false teachers would spread their false ideas and practices. He warns the church not to support the false teachers in anyway.

This brief letter presents all of the themes stated in 1 John. In 1 John, however, the themes are developed more completely.

---

1 I, the elder, am writing this letter.

I am sending it to the lady chosen by God and to her children. I love all of you because of the truth. I'm not the only one who loves you. So does everyone who knows the truth. 2 I love you because of the truth that is alive in us. This truth will be with us forever.

3 God the Father and Jesus Christ his Son will give you grace, mercy and peace. These blessings will be with us because we love the truth.

4 It has given me great joy to find some of your children living by the truth. That's just what the Father commanded us to do. 5 Dear lady, I'm not writing you a new command. I'm writing a command we've had from the beginning. I'm asking that we love one another. 6 The way we show our love is to obey God's commands. He commands you to lead a life of love. That's what you have heard from the beginning.

7 I say this because many people have tried to fool others. These people have gone out into the world. They don't agree that Jesus Christ came in a human body. People like this try to trick others. These people are like the great enemy of Christ. 8 Watch out that you don't lose what we have worked for. Make sure that you get your full reward. 9 Suppose someone thinks they know more than we do. So they don't follow Christ's teaching. Then that person doesn't belong to God. But whoever follows Christ's teaching belongs to the Father and the Son. 10 Suppose someone comes to you and doesn't teach these truths. Then don't take them into your house or welcome them. 11 Anyone who welcomes them shares in their evil work.

12 I have a lot to write to you. But I don't want to use paper and ink. I hope I can visit you instead. Then I can talk with you face to face. That will make our joy complete.

13 The children of your sister, who is chosen by God, send their greetings.

3 JOHN

This letter was written for a person named Gaius. It is a note of thanks and encouragement. John had sent a separate letter to the church of which Gaius was a member. That letter introduced and approved certain individuals. But in that church there was a leader named Diotrephes. Diotrephes opposed John's authority. Diotrephes refused to accept that letter and the individuals John had sent. Diotrephes would not provide food for them nor a place to stay. He even sent away any church member who supported the people John had sent.

Gaius, however, did just the opposite. Gaius took these teachers into his own home. He supported them in their work. John is so thankful for what Gaius has done. He makes it clear in this letter that what Gaius is doing is right. The church must support these traveling preachers. That's because these preachers bring the true good news. At the end of the letter John promises to visit soon.

---

1 I, the elder, am writing this letter.

I am sending it to you, my dear friend Gaius. I love you because of the truth.

2 Dear friend, I know that your spiritual life is going well. I pray that you also may enjoy good health. And I pray that everything else may go well with you. 3 Some believers came to me and told me that you are faithful to the truth. They told me that you continue to live by it. This news gave me great joy. 4 I have no greater joy than to hear that my children are living by the truth.

5 Dear friend, you are faithful in what you are doing for the brothers and sisters. You are faithful even though they are strangers to you. 6 They have told the church about your love. Please help them by sending them on their way in a manner that honors God. 7 They started on their journey to serve Jesus Christ. They didn't receive any help from those who aren't believers. 8 So we should welcome people like them. We should work together with them for the truth.

9 I wrote to the church. But Diotrephes will not welcome us. He loves to be the first in everything. 10 So when I come, I will point out what he is doing. He is saying evil things that aren't true about us. Even this doesn't satisfy him. So he refuses to welcome other believers. He also keeps others from welcoming them. In fact, he throws them out of the church.

11 Dear friend, don't be like those who do evil. Be like those who do good. Anyone who does what is good belongs to God. Anyone who does what is evil hasn't really seen or known God. 12 Everyone says good things about Demetrius. He lives in keeping with the truth. We also say good things about him. And you know that what we say is true.

13 I have a lot to write to you. But I don't want to write with pen and ink. 14 I hope I can see you soon. Then we can talk face to face.

May you have peace. The friends here send their greetings. Greet each one of the friends there.

JUDE

Jude and James were brothers of Jesus. James was a leader in the church in Jerusalem. He was the writer of the book of James. Jude also had authority as a leader in the church. Jude most likely wrote this letter to Jewish believers. This letter would have special meaning for these believers. That's because it talks about Israel's history and about angels. And it talks about other writings that would have meaning for them.

Jude speaks about the problem of false teachers in the church. They are teaching against the true faith. These false teachers claim they have had inspired dreams. They reject the authority of the church leaders. And they use their bodies in unholy ways. These false teachers claim that they are bringing God's message. But they don't show that they have the spirit of God in them. They live following their own ungodly desires. Jude warns the believers to actively resist these false teachers. He tells them to clean out their community by saying no to these false teachings.

It seems that the apostle Peter received a copy of Jude's letter. Peter then wrote a letter of his own. Peter's letter supported what Jude had said. It stated that Jude had faithfully presented the teachings of Jesus' own apostles.

---

1 I, Jude, am writing this letter. I serve Jesus Christ. I am a brother of James.

I am sending this letter to you who have been chosen by God. You are loved by God the Father. You are kept safe for Jesus Christ.

2 May more and more mercy, peace and love be given to you.

A Warning Against the Sin of Ungodly People

3 Dear friends, I really wanted to write to you about the salvation we share. But now I feel I should write and ask you to stand up for the faith. God's holy people were trusted with it once and for all time.
4 Certain people have secretly slipped in among you. Long ago it was written that they would be judged. They are ungodly people. They misuse the grace of our God as an excuse for sexual sins. They say no to Jesus Christ, our only Lord and King.

5 I want to remind you about some things you already know. The Lord saved his people. At one time he brought them out of Egypt. But later he destroyed those who did not believe.
6 Some of the angels didn't stay where they belonged. They didn't keep their positions of authority. The Lord has kept those angels in darkness. They are held by chains that last forever. On judgment day, God will judge them.
7 The people of Sodom and Gomorrah and the towns around them also did evil things. They freely committed sexual sins. They committed sins of the worst possible kind. There is a fire that never goes out. Those people are an example of those who are punished with it.

8 In the very same way, these ungodly people act on their evil dreams. So they make their own bodies impure. They don't accept authority. And they say evil things against heavenly beings.
9 But even Michael, the leader of the angels, didn't dare to say these things. He didn't even say these things when he argued with the devil about the body of Moses. Michael didn't dare to judge the devil. He didn't say the devil was guilty of saying evil things. Instead, Michael said, "May the Lord judge you!"
10 But these people say evil things against whatever they don't understand. And the very things they do understand will destroy them. That's because they are like wild animals that can't think for themselves. Instead, they do what comes naturally to them.

11 How terrible it will be for them! They have followed the way of Cain. They have rushed into the same mistake Balaam made. They did it because they loved money. They are like Korah. He turned against his leaders. These people will certainly be destroyed, just as Korah was.

12 These ungodly people are like stains at the meals you share. They have no shame. They are shepherds who feed only themselves. They are like clouds without rain. They are blown along by the wind. They are like trees in the fall. Since they have no fruit, they are pulled out of the ground. So they die twice.
13 They are like wild waves of the sea. Their shame rises up like foam. They are like falling stars.

God has reserved a place of very black
darkness for them forever.
14 Enoch was the seventh man in the
family line of Adam. He gave a prophecy
about these people. He said, "Look! The
Lord is coming with thousands and thousands of his holy ones. 15 He is coming to
judge everyone. He is coming to sentence
all of them. He will judge them for all the
ungodly acts they have done. They have
done them in ungodly ways. He will sentence ungodly sinners for all the things
they have said to oppose him." 16 These
people complain and find fault with others. They follow their own evil desires.
They brag about themselves. They praise
others to get what they want.

Remain in God's Love

17 Dear friends, remember what the
apostles of our Lord Jesus Christ said
would happen. 18 They told you, "In the
last days, some people will make fun of
the truth. They will follow their own ungodly desires." 19 They are the people who
separate you from one another. They do
only what comes naturally. They are not
led by the Holy Spirit.
20 But you, dear friends, build yourselves up in your most holy faith. Let the
Holy Spirit guide and help you when you
pray. 21 And by doing these things, remain
in God's love as you wait. You are waiting
for the mercy of our Lord Jesus Christ to
bring you eternal life.
22 Show mercy to those who doubt.
23 Save others by pulling them out of the
fire. To others, show mercy mixed with
fear of sin. Hate even the clothes that are
stained by the sins of those who wear
them.

Praise to God

24 Give praise to the God who is able
to keep you from falling into sin. He will
bring you into his heavenly glory without any fault. He will bring you there with
great joy. 25 Give praise to the only God
our Savior. Glory, majesty, power and authority belong to him. Give praise to him
through Jesus Christ our Lord. His praise
was before all time, continues now, and
will last forever. Amen.

REVELATION

The Roman Empire protected its economic and political control in spiritual terms. They called their gospel the Roman Peace. And the emperor became their god. During this time a Jewish-Christian prophet named John was living on the island of Patmos. He had been sent there as a prisoner. While he was there, John received a vision. John was told to write what he saw and experienced in that vision. What he wrote is called the book of Revelation. That book was sent to the seven cities in the Roman province of Asia Minor. The main point of the book is to warn believers not to give up their true faith. It is a warning about evil practices and false teachings of the Romans. And the book is written to encourage them in their difficult struggles.

The book of Revelation is in a style of writing called apocalyptic. That means it has many symbols or word pictures. It was a style of writing that was common when John lived. These symbols or word pictures tell about the secrets of unseen things in heaven. And they tell about what is coming in the future. These symbols or word pictures may seem strange at first. But thinking about the time in which the book was written helps in understanding them. It also helps to think about other word pictures used in the Bible.

John's vision has four main parts. It begins with words of warning and encouragement for each of the seven churches. Next are visions that center on Jesus. They show how Jesus has saved the world and how he will bring justice. All the people and forces that rebel against God will be destroyed. Then it shows that Jesus is the true Messiah. Jesus will have the final victory over death and all his enemies. The vision ends with the promise that the faithful followers of Jesus will rule over the new creation.

The book of Revelation also functions as the conclusion to the entire story of the Bible. John concludes his writing with word pictures from the Garden of Eden. That was the first story in the Bible. Now John says there will be a new beginning. "He who was sitting on the throne said, 'I am making everything new!' "

The Revelation Is Given

1 This is the revelation from Jesus Christ.
God gave it to him to show those who
serve God what will happen soon. God
made it known by sending his angel to his
servant John. 2 John is a witness to everything he saw. What he saw is God's word
and what Jesus Christ has said. 3 Blessed
is the one who reads out loud the words
of this prophecy. Blessed are those who
hear it and think everything it says is important. The time when these things will
come true is near.

Greetings and Praise to God

4 I, John, am writing this letter.

I am sending it to the seven churches in
Asia Minor.

May grace and peace come to you from
God. He is the one who is, and who was,
and who will come. May grace and peace
come to you from the seven spirits. These
spirits are in front of God's throne. 5 May
grace and peace come to you from Jesus
Christ. He is the faithful witness, so what
he has shown can be trusted. He was the
first to rise from the dead. He rules over
the kings of the earth.

Glory and power belong to Jesus Christ
who loves us! He has set us free from our
sins by pouring out his blood for us. 6 He
has made us members of his royal family.
He has made us priests who serve his God
and Father. Glory and power belong to
Jesus Christ for ever and ever! Amen.

7 "Look! He is coming with the
clouds!" (Daniel 7:13)
"Every eye will see him.
Even those who pierced him will see
him."
All the nations of the earth "will
mourn because of him."
(Zechariah 12:10)
This will really happen! Amen.

8 "I am the Alpha and the Omega, the
Beginning and the End," says the Lord
God. "I am the God who is, and who was,
and who will come. I am the Mighty One."

John's Vision of Christ

9 I, John, am a believer like you. I am
a friend who suffers like you. As members of Jesus' royal family, we can put up

with anything that happens to us. I was on the island of Patmos because I taught God's word and what Jesus said. 10 The Holy Spirit gave me a vision on the Lord's Day. I heard a loud voice behind me that sounded like a trumpet. 11 The voice said, "Write on a scroll what you see. Send it to the seven churches in Asia Minor. They are Ephesus, Smyrna, Pergamum, Thyatira, Sardis, Philadelphia and Laodicea."

12 I turned around to see who was speaking to me. When I turned, I saw seven golden lampstands. 13 In the middle of them was someone who looked "like a son of man." (Daniel 7:13) He was dressed in a long robe with a gold strip of cloth around his chest. 14 The hair on his head was white like wool, as white as snow. His eyes were like a blazing fire. 15 His feet were like bronze metal glowing in a furnace. His voice sounded like rushing waters. 16 He held seven stars in his right hand. Coming out of his mouth was a sharp sword with two edges. His face was like the sun shining in all its brightness.

17 When I saw him, I fell at his feet as if I were dead. Then he put his right hand on me and said, "Do not be afraid. I am the First and the Last. 18 I am the Living One. I was dead. But now look! I am alive for ever and ever! And I hold the keys to Death and Hell.

19 "So write down what you have seen. Write about what is happening now and what will happen later. 20 Here is the meaning of the mystery of the seven stars you saw in my right hand. They are the angels of the seven churches. And the seven golden lampstands you saw stand for the seven churches.

The Letter to the Church in Ephesus

2 "Here is what I command you to write to the church in Ephesus.

Here are the words of Jesus, who holds the seven stars in his right hand. He also walks among the seven golden lampstands. He says, 2 'I know what you are doing. You work long and hard. I know you can't put up with evil people. You have tested those who claim to be apostles but are not. You have found out that they are liars. 3 You have been faithful and have put up with a lot of trouble because of me. You have not given up.

4 'But here is something I hold against you. You have turned away from the love you had at first. 5 Think about how far you have fallen! Turn away from your sins. Do the things you did at first. If you don't, I will come to you and remove your lampstand from its place. 6 But you do have this in your favor. You hate the way the Nicolaitans act. I hate it too.

7 'Whoever has ears should listen to what the Holy Spirit says to the churches. Here is what I will do for anyone who has victory over sin. I will let that person eat from the tree of life in God's paradise.'

The Letter to the Church in Smyrna

8 "Here is what I command you to write to the church in Smyrna.

Here are the words of Jesus, who is the First and the Last. He is the one who died and came to life again. He says, 9 'I know that you suffer and are poor. But you are rich! Some people say they are Jews but are not. I know that their words are evil. Their worship comes from Satan. 10 Don't be afraid of what you are going to suffer. I tell you, the devil will put some of you in prison to test you. You will be treated badly for ten days. Be faithful, even if it means you must die. Then I will give you life as your crown of victory.

11 'Whoever has ears should listen to what the Holy Spirit says to the churches. Here is what I will do for anyone who has victory over sin. I will not let that person be hurt at all by the second death.'

The Letter to the Church in Pergamum

12 "Here is what I command you to write to the church in Pergamum.

Here are the words of Jesus, who has the sharp sword with two edges. He says, 13 'I know that you live where Satan has his throne. But you remain faithful to me. You did not give up your faith in me. You didn't give it up even in the days of Antipas. Antipas, my faithful witness, was put to death in your city, where Satan lives.

14 'But I have a few things against you. Some of your people follow the

teaching of Balaam. He taught Balak
to lead the people of Israel into sin. So
they ate food that had been offered to
statues of gods. And they committed
sexual sins. 15 You also have people
who follow the teaching of the Nicolaitans. 16 So turn away from your
sins! If you don't, I will come to you
soon. I will fight against those people
with the sword that comes out of my
mouth.
17 'Whoever has ears should listen
to what the Holy Spirit says to the
churches. Here is what I will do for
anyone who has victory over sin. I
will give that person hidden manna
to eat. I will also give each of them a
white stone with a new name written
on it. Only the one who receives this
name will know what it is.'

The Letter to the Church in Thyatira

18 "Here is what I command you to write
to the church in Thyatira.

Here are the words of the Son of
God. He is Jesus, whose eyes are
like blazing fire. His feet are like pol-
ished bronze. He says, 19 'I know what
you are doing. I know your love and
your faith. I know how well you have
served. I know you don't give up easily. In fact, you are doing more now
than you did at first.
20 'But here is what I have against
you. You put up with that woman
Jezebel. She calls herself a prophet.
With her teaching, she has led my
servants into sexual sin. She has
tricked them into eating food offered to statues of gods. 21 I've given
her time to turn away from her sinful ways. But she doesn't want to.
22 She lay down to commit her sin so
I will make her lie down in suffering.
Those who commit adultery with her
will suffer greatly too. Their only way
out is to turn away from what she
taught them to do. 23 I will strike her
children dead. Then all the churches
will know that I search hearts and
minds. I will pay each of you back for
what you have done.
24 'I won't ask the rest of you in Thyatira to do anything else. You don't
follow the teaching of Jezebel. You
haven't learned what some people
call Satan's deep secrets. 25 Just hold
on to what you have until I come.
26 'Here is what I will do for anyone who has victory over sin. I will
do it for anyone who carries out my
plans to the end. I will give that person authority over the nations. 27 It is
written,

"They will rule them with an iron
scepter.
They will break them to pieces like
clay pots." (Psalm 2:9)

Their authority is like the authority
I've received from my Father. 28 I will
also give the morning star to all who
have victory. 29 Whoever has ears
should listen to what the Holy Spirit
says to the churches.'

The Letter to the Church in Sardis

3 "Here is what I command you to write
to the church in Sardis.

Here are the words of Jesus, who
holds the seven spirits of God. He has
the seven stars in his hand. He says,
'I know what you are doing. People
think you are alive, but you are dead.
2 Wake up! Strengthen what is left, or
it will die. You have not done all that
my God wants you to do. 3 So remember what you have been taught and
have heard. Hold firmly to it. Turn
away from your sins. If you don't
wake up, I will come like a thief. You
won't know when I will come to you.
4 'But you have a few people in Sardis who are pure. They aren't covered
with evil like dirty clothes. They will
walk with me, dressed in white, because they are worthy. 5 Here is what
I will do for anyone who has victory
over sin. I will dress that person in
white like those worthy people. I will
never erase their names from the book
of life. I will speak of them by name to
my Father and his angels. 6 Whoever
has ears should listen to what the
Holy Spirit says to the churches.'

The Letter to the Church in Philadelphia

7 "Here is what I command you to write
to the church in Philadelphia.

Here are the words of Jesus, who
is holy and true. He holds the key
of David. No one can shut what he

opens. And no one can open what he shuts. He says, [8]'I know what you are doing. Look! I have put an open door in front of you. No one can shut it. I know that you don't have much strength. But you have obeyed my word. You have not said no to me. [9]Some people claim they are Jews but are not. They are liars. Their worship comes from Satan. I will make them come and fall down at your feet. I will make them say in public that I have loved you. [10]You have kept my command to remain strong in the faith no matter what happens. So I will keep you from the time of suffering. That time is going to come to the whole world. It will test those who live on the earth.

[11]'I am coming soon. Hold on to what you have. Then no one will take away your crown. [12]Here is what I will do for anyone who has victory over sin. I will make that person a pillar in the temple of my God. They will never leave it again. I will write the name of my God on them. I will write the name of the city of my God on them. This is the new Jerusalem, which is coming down out of heaven from my God. I will also write my new name on them. [13]Whoever has ears should listen to what the Holy Spirit says to the churches.'

The Letter to the Church in Laodicea

[14]"Here is what I command you to write to the church in Laodicea.

Here are the words of Jesus, who is the Amen. What he speaks is faithful and true. He rules over what God has created. He says, [15]'I know what you are doing. I know you aren't cold or hot. I wish you were either one or the other! [16]But you are lukewarm. You aren't hot or cold. So I am going to spit you out of my mouth. [17]You say, "I am rich. I've become wealthy and don't need anything." But you don't realize how pitiful and miserable you have become. You are poor, blind and naked. [18]So here's my advice. Buy from me gold made pure by fire. Then you will become rich. Buy from me white clothes to wear. Then you will be able to cover the shame of your naked bodies. And buy from me healing lotion to put on your eyes. Then you will be able to see.

[19]'I warn and correct those I love. So be sincere, and turn away from your sins. [20]Here I am! I stand at the door and knock. If anyone hears my voice and opens the door, I will come in. I will eat with that person, and they will eat with me.

[21]'Here is what I will do for anyone who has victory over sin. I will give that person the right to sit with me on my throne. In the same way, I had victory. Then I sat down with my Father on his throne. [22]Whoever has ears should listen to what the Holy Spirit says to the churches.'"

The Throne in Heaven

4 After this I looked, and there in front of me was a door standing open in heaven. I heard the voice I had heard before. It sounded like a trumpet. The voice said, "Come up here. I will show you what must happen after this." [2]At once the Holy Spirit gave me a vision. There in front of me was a throne in heaven with someone sitting on it. [3]The one who sat there shone like jasper and ruby. Around the throne was a rainbow shining like an emerald. [4]Twenty-four other thrones surrounded that throne. Twenty-four elders were sitting on them. The elders were dressed in white. They had gold crowns on their heads. [5]From the throne came flashes of lightning, rumblings and thunder. Seven lamps were blazing in front of the throne. These stand for the seven spirits of God. [6]There was something that looked like a sea of glass in front of the throne. It was as clear as crystal.

In the inner circle, around the throne, were four living creatures. They were covered with eyes, in front and in back. [7]The first creature looked like a lion. The second looked like an ox. The third had a man's face. The fourth looked like a flying eagle. [8]Each of the four living creatures had six wings. Each creature was covered all over with eyes. It had eyes even under its wings. Day and night, they never stop saying,

"'Holy, holy, holy
is the Lord God who rules over all.'
(Isaiah 6:3)
He was, and he is, and he will come."

9 The living creatures give glory, honor and thanks to the one who sits on the throne. He lives for ever and ever. 10 At the same time, the 24 elders fall down and worship the one who sits on the throne. He lives for ever and ever. They lay their crowns in front of the throne. They say,

11 "You are worthy, our Lord and God!
You are worthy to receive glory
and honor and power.
You are worthy because you created
all things.
They were created and they exist.
This is the way you planned it."

The Scroll and the Lamb

5 Then I saw a scroll in the right hand of the one sitting on the throne. The scroll had writing on both sides. It was sealed with seven seals. 2 I saw a mighty angel calling out in a loud voice. He said, "Who is worthy to break the seals and open the scroll?" 3 But no one in heaven or on earth or under the earth could open the scroll. No one could even look inside it. 4 I cried and cried. That's because no one was found who was worthy to open the scroll or look inside. 5 Then one of the elders said to me, "Do not cry! The Lion of the tribe of Judah has won the battle. He is the Root of David. He is able to break the seven seals and open the scroll."

6 Then I saw a Lamb that looked as if he had been put to death. He stood at the center of the area around the throne. The Lamb was surrounded by the four living creatures and the elders. He had seven horns and seven eyes. The eyes stand for the seven spirits of God, which are sent out into all the earth. 7 The Lamb went and took the scroll. He took it from the right hand of the one sitting on the throne. 8 Then the four living creatures and the 24 elders fell down in front of the Lamb. Each one had a harp. They were holding golden bowls full of incense. They stand for the prayers of God's people. 9 Here is the new song they sang.

"You are worthy to take the scroll
and break open its seals.
You are worthy because you were
put to death.
With your blood you bought
people for God.
They come from every tribe,
people and nation,
no matter what language they
speak.
10 You have made them members of a
royal family.
You have made them priests to
serve our God.
They will rule on the earth."

11 Then I looked and heard the voice of millions and millions of angels. They surrounded the throne. They surrounded the living creatures and the elders. 12 In a loud voice they were saying,

"The Lamb, who was put to death, is
worthy!
He is worthy to receive power
and wealth and wisdom and
strength!
He is worthy to receive honor and
glory and praise!"

13 All creatures in heaven, on earth, under the earth, and on the sea were speaking. The whole creation was speaking. I heard all of them say,

"Praise and honor belong
to the one who sits on the throne
and to the Lamb!
Glory and power belong to God for
ever and ever!"

14 The four living creatures said, "Amen." And the elders fell down and worshiped.

The Seals of the Scroll Are Broken

6 I watched as the Lamb broke open the first of the seven seals. Then I heard one of the four living creatures say in a voice that sounded like thunder, "Come!" 2 I looked, and there in front of me was a white horse! Its rider held a bow in his hands. He was given a crown. He rode out like a hero on his way to victory.

3 The Lamb broke open the second seal. Then I heard the second living creature say, "Come!" 4 Another horse came out. It was red like fire. Its rider was given power to take peace from the earth. He was given power to make people kill each other. He was given a large sword.

5 The Lamb broke open the third seal. Then I heard the third living creature say, "Come!" I looked, and there in front of me was a black horse! Its rider was holding a pair of scales in his hand. 6 Next, I heard what sounded like a voice coming from among the four living creatures. It said,

"Two pounds of wheat for a day's pay. And
six pounds of barley for a day's pay. And
leave the olive oil and the wine alone!"
7 The Lamb broke open the fourth seal.
Then I heard the voice of the fourth living
creature say, "Come!" 8 I looked, and there
in front of me was a pale horse! Its rider's
name was Death. Following close behind
him was Hell. They were given power
over a fourth of the earth. They were given
power to kill people by swords. They
could also use hunger, sickness and the
earth's wild animals to kill.
9 The Lamb broke open the fifth seal. I
saw souls under the altar. They were the
souls of people who had been killed. They
had been killed because of God's word
and their faithful witness. 10 They called
out in a loud voice. "How long, Lord and
King, holy and true?" they asked. "How
long will you wait to judge those who live
on the earth? How long will it be until you
pay them back for killing us?" 11 Then each
of them was given a white robe. "Wait a
little longer," they were told. "There are
still more of your believing brothers and
sisters who will be killed. They will be
killed just as you were."
12 I watched as the Lamb broke open
the sixth seal. There was a powerful
earthquake. The sun turned black like the
clothes people wear when they're sad.
Those clothes are made out of goat's hair.
The whole moon turned as red as blood.
13 The stars in the sky fell to earth. They
dropped like figs from a tree shaken by
a strong wind. 14 The sky rolled back like
a scroll. Every mountain and island was
moved out of its place.
15 Everyone hid in caves and among the
rocks of the mountains. This included
the kings of the earth, the princes and
the generals. It included rich people and
powerful people. It also included everyone else, both slaves and people who
were free. 16 They called out to the mountains and rocks, "Fall on us! Hide us from
the face of the one who sits on the throne!
Hide us from the anger of the Lamb! 17 The
great day of their anger has come. Who
can live through it?"

144,000 People Are Marked With the Seal of the Living God

7 After this I saw four angels. They were
standing at the four corners of the
earth. They were holding back the four
winds of the earth. This kept the winds
from blowing on the land or the sea or on
any tree. 2 Then I saw another angel coming up from the east. He brought the official seal of the living God. He called out
in a loud voice to the four angels. They
had been allowed to harm the land and
the sea. 3 "Do not harm the land or the sea
or the trees," he said. "Wait until we mark
with this seal the foreheads of those who
serve our God." 4 Then I heard how many
people were marked with the seal. There
were 144,000 from all the tribes of Israel.

5 From the tribe of Judah, 12,000 were
marked with the seal.
From the tribe of Reuben, 12,000.
From the tribe of Gad, 12,000.
6 From the tribe of Asher, 12,000.
From the tribe of Naphtali, 12,000.
From the tribe of Manasseh, 12,000.
7 From the tribe of Simeon, 12,000.
From the tribe of Levi, 12,000.
From the tribe of Issachar, 12,000.
8 From the tribe of Zebulun, 12,000.
From the tribe of Joseph, 12,000.
From the tribe of Benjamin, 12,000.

The Huge Crowd Wearing White Robes

9 After this I looked, and there in front
of me was a huge crowd of people. They
stood in front of the throne and in front
of the Lamb. There were so many that no
one could count them. They came from
every nation, tribe and people. That's
true no matter what language they spoke.
They were wearing white robes. In their
hands they were holding palm branches.
10 They cried out in a loud voice,

"Salvation belongs to our God,
who sits on the throne.
Salvation also belongs to the Lamb."

11 All the angels were standing around the
throne. They were standing around the
elders and the four living creatures. They
fell down on their faces in front of the
throne and worshiped God. 12 They said,

"Amen!
May praise and glory
and wisdom be given to our God for
ever and ever.
Give him thanks and honor and
power and strength.
Amen!"

13 Then one of the elders spoke to me.

"Who are these people dressed in white
robes?" he asked. "Where did they come
from?"

14 I answered, "Sir, you know."

He said, "They are the ones who have
come out of the time of terrible suffering.
They have washed their robes and made
them white in the blood of the Lamb. 15 So

"they are in front of the throne of
God.
They serve him day and night in
his temple.
The one who sits on the throne
will be with them to keep them
safe.
16 'Never again will they be hungry.
Never again will they be thirsty.
The sun will not beat down on
them.' (Isaiah 49:10)
The heat of the desert will not
harm them.
17 The Lamb, who is at the center of the
area around the throne,
will be their shepherd.
'He will lead them to springs of
living water.' (Isaiah 49:10)
'And God will wipe away every
tear from their eyes.' "
(Isaiah 25:8)

The Seventh Seal and the Gold Cup

8 The Lamb opened the seventh seal.
Then there was silence in heaven for
about half an hour.

2 I saw the seven angels who stand in
front of God. Seven trumpets were given
to them.

3 Another angel came and stood at the
altar. He had a shallow gold cup for burning incense. He was given a lot of incense
to offer on the golden altar. The altar was
in front of the throne. With the incense
he offered the prayers of all God's people. 4 The smoke of the incense rose up
from the angel's hand. The prayers of
God's people rose up together with it. The
smoke and the prayers went up in front of
God. 5 Then the angel took the gold cup
and filled it with fire from the altar. He
threw it down on the earth. There were
rumblings and thunder, flashes of lightning, and an earthquake.

The Trumpets

6 Then the seven angels who had the
seven trumpets got ready to blow them.

7 The first angel blew his trumpet. Hail
and fire mixed with blood were thrown
down on the earth. A third of the earth was
burned up. A third of the trees were burned
up. All the green grass was burned up.

8 The second angel blew his trumpet.
Something that looked like a huge mountain on fire was thrown into the sea. A
third of the sea turned into blood. 9 A third
of the living creatures in the sea died. A
third of the ships were destroyed.

10 The third angel blew his trumpet. Then a great star fell from the sky.
It looked like a blazing torch. It fell on a
third of the rivers and on the springs of
water. 11 The name of the star is Worm-
wood. A third of the water turned bitter.
Many people died from it.

12 The fourth angel blew his trumpet.
Then a third of the sun was struck. A
third of the moon was struck. A third of
the stars were struck. So a third of each of
them turned dark. Then a third of the day
had no light. The same thing happened to
a third of the night.

13 As I watched, I heard an eagle that
was flying high in the air. It called out in a
loud voice, "How terrible! How terrible it
will be for those living on the earth! How
terrible! They will suffer as soon as the
next three angels blow their trumpets!"

9 The fifth angel blew his trumpet. Then
I saw a star that had fallen from the sky
to the earth. The star was given the key
to the tunnel leading down into a bot-
tomless pit. The pit was called the Abyss.
2 The star opened the Abyss. Then smoke
rose up from it like the smoke from a huge
furnace. The sun and sky were darkened
by the smoke from the Abyss. 3 Out of the
smoke came locusts. They came down
on the earth. They were given power
like the power of scorpions of the earth.
4 They were told not to harm the grass of
the earth or any plant or tree. They were
supposed to harm only the people without God's official seal on their foreheads.
5 The locusts were not allowed to kill these
people. But the locusts could hurt them
over and over for five months. The pain
the people suffered was like the sting of
a scorpion when it strikes. 6 In those days,
people will look for a way to die but won't
find it. They will want to die, but death
will escape them.

7 The locusts looked like horses ready for
battle. On their heads they wore something

like crowns of gold. Their faces looked like human faces. [8]Their hair was like women's hair. Their teeth were like lions' teeth. [9]Their chests were covered with something that looked like armor made out of iron. The sound of their wings was like the thundering of many horses and chariots rushing into battle. [10]They had tails that could sting people like scorpions do. And in their tails they had power to hurt people over and over for five months. [11]Their king was the angel of the Abyss. In the Hebrew language his name is Abaddon. In Greek it is Apollyon. His name means Destroyer.

[12]The first terrible judgment is past. Two others are still coming.

[13]The sixth angel blew his trumpet. Then I heard a voice coming from the four corners of the golden altar. The altar stands in front of God. [14]The voice spoke to the sixth angel who had the trumpet. The voice said, "Set the four angels free who are held at the great river Euphrates." [15]The four angels had been ready for this very hour and day and month and year. They were set free to kill a third of all people. [16]The number of troops on horseback was 200,000,000. I heard how many there were.

[17]The horses and riders I saw in my vision had armor on their chests. It was red like fire, dark blue, and yellow like sulfur. The heads of the horses looked like lions' heads. Out of their mouths came fire, smoke and sulfur. [18]A third of all people were killed by the three plagues of fire, smoke and sulfur that came out of the horses' mouths. [19]The power of the horses was in their mouths and in their tails. The tails were like snakes whose heads could bite.

[20]There were people who were not killed by these plagues. But they still didn't turn away from what they had been doing. They did not stop worshiping demons. They kept worshiping statues of gods made out of gold, silver, bronze, stone and wood. These statues can't see or hear or walk. [21]The people also did not turn away from their murders, witchcraft, sexual sins and stealing.

The Angel and the Little Scroll

10 Then I saw another mighty angel coming down from heaven. He was wearing a cloud like a robe. There was a rainbow above his head. His face was like the sun. His legs were like pillars of fire. [2]He was holding a little scroll. It was lying open in his hand. The angel put his right foot on the sea and his left foot on the land. [3]Then he gave a loud shout like the roar of a lion. When he shouted, the voices of the seven thunders spoke. [4]When they had spoken, I was getting ready to write. But I heard a voice from heaven say, "Seal up what the seven thunders have said. Do not write it down."

[5]I had seen an angel standing on the sea and on the land. This angel raised his right hand to heaven. [6]He made a promise in the name of the God who lives for ever and ever. This is the God who created the sky, earth and sea and all that is in them. The angel said, "There will be no more waiting! [7]God's plan will be carried out. This will happen when the seventh angel is ready to blow his trumpet. God told all this to the prophets who served him long ago."

[8]Then the voice I had heard from heaven spoke to me again. It said, "The angel is standing on the sea and on the land. Go and take the scroll from him. It is lying open in his hand."

[9]So I went to the angel and asked him to give me the little scroll. He said to me, "Take it and eat it. It will become sour in your stomach. But 'in your mouth it will taste as sweet as honey.'" (Ezekiel 3:3) [10]I took the little scroll from the angel's hand and ate it. In my mouth it tasted as sweet as honey. But when I had eaten it, it became sour in my stomach. [11]Then I was told, "You must prophesy again about many peoples, nations, languages and kings."

The Two Witnesses

11 I was given a long stick that looked like a measuring rod. I was told, "Go and measure the temple of God. And measure the altar where the people are worshiping. [2]But do not measure the outer courtyard. That's because it has been given to the Gentiles. They will take over the holy city for 42 months. [3]I will appoint my two witnesses. And they will prophesy for 1,260 days. They will be dressed in the rough clothes people wear when they're sad." [4]The witnesses are "the two olive trees" and the two lampstands. And "they stand in front of the Lord of the earth." (Zechariah 4:3,11,14) [5]If anyone tries to harm them, fire comes from their mouths and eats up their enemies. This is how

anyone who wants to harm them must
die. 6These witnesses have power to close
up the sky. Then it will not rain while they
are prophesying. They also have power to
turn the waters into blood. And they can
strike the earth with every kind of plague.
They can do this as often as they want to.
7When they have finished speaking, the
beast that comes up from the Abyss will
attack them. He will overpower them and
kill them. 8Their bodies will lie in the main
street of the great city. It is also the city
where their Lord was nailed to a cross. The
city is sometimes compared to Sodom or
Egypt. 9For three and a half days, people
will stare at their bodies. These people will
be from every tribe and nation, no matter
what language they speak. They will refuse to bury them. 10Those who live on the
earth will be happy about this. That's because those two prophets had made them
suffer. The people will celebrate by sending one another gifts.
11But after the three and a half days, the
breath of life from God entered the witnesses. They both stood up. Terror struck
those who saw them. 12Then the two witnesses heard a loud voice from heaven. It
said to them, "Come up here." They went
up to heaven in a cloud. Their enemies
watched it happen.
13At that same time there was a powerful earthquake. A tenth of the city crumbled and fell. In the earthquake, 7,000
people were killed. Those who lived
through it were terrified. They gave glory
to the God of heaven.
14The second terrible judgment has
passed. The third is coming soon.

The Seventh Trumpet

15The seventh angel blew his trumpet.
There were loud voices in heaven. They
said,

"The kingdom of the world has
become
the kingdom of our Lord and of
his Messiah.
He will rule for ever and ever."

16The 24 elders were sitting on their
thrones in front of God. They fell on their
faces and worshiped God. 17They said,

"Lord God who rules over all, we
give thanks to you.
You are the God who is and who
was.
We give you thanks.
That's because you have begun to
rule with your great power.
18The nations were angry,
and the time for your anger has
come.
The time has come to judge the
dead.
It is time to reward your servants the
prophets
and your people who honor you.
There is a reward for all your people,
both great and small.
It is time to destroy those who
destroy the earth."

19Then God's temple in heaven was
opened. Inside it the wooden chest called
the ark of his covenant could be seen.
There were flashes of lightning, rumblings and thunder, an earthquake and a
severe hailstorm.

The Woman and the Dragon

12 A great sign appeared in heaven. It
was a woman wearing the sun like
clothes. The moon was under her feet.
On her head she wore a crown of 12 stars.
2She was pregnant. She cried out in pain
because she was about to have a baby.
3Then another sign appeared in heaven. It
was a huge red dragon. It had seven heads
and ten horns. On its seven heads it wore
seven crowns. 4The dragon's tail swept a
third of the stars out of the sky. It threw
the stars down to earth. The dragon stood
in front of the woman who was about to
have a baby. The dragon wanted to eat
her child the moment he was born. 5She
gave birth to a son. He "will rule all the
nations with an iron scepter." (Psalm 2:9)
And her child was taken up to God and to
his throne. 6The woman escaped into the
desert where God had a place prepared
for her. There she would be taken care of
for 1,260 days.
7Then a war began in heaven. Michael
and his angels fought against the dragon.
And the dragon and his angels fought
back. 8But the dragon wasn't strong
enough. Both he and his angels lost their
place in heaven. 9The great dragon was
thrown down to the earth, and his angels
with him. The dragon is that old serpent

called the devil, or Satan. He leads the
whole world astray.
10 Then I heard a loud voice in heaven.
It said,

"Now the salvation and the power
and the kingdom of our God
have come.
The authority of his Messiah has
come.
Satan, who brings charges against
our brothers and sisters,
has been thrown down.
He brings charges against them
in front of our God day and
night.
11 They had victory over him
by the blood the Lamb spilled for
them.
They had victory over him
by speaking the truth about Jesus
to others.
They were willing to risk their lives,
even if it led to death.
12 So be joyful, you heavens!
Be glad, all you who live there!
But how terrible it will be for the
earth and the sea!
The devil has come down to you.
He is very angry.
He knows his time is short."

13 The dragon saw that he had been
thrown down to the earth. So he chased
the woman who had given birth to the boy.
14 The woman was given the two wings of
a great eagle. She was given these wings
so that she could fly away. She could fly to
the place prepared for her in the desert.
There she would be taken care of for three
and a half years. She would be out of the
serpent's reach. 15 Then out of his mouth
the serpent spit water like a river. He
wanted to catch the woman and sweep
her away in the flood. 16 But the earth
helped the woman. It opened its mouth
and swallowed the river that the dragon
had spit out. 17 The dragon was very angry
with the woman. He went off to make war
against the rest of her children. They obey
God's commands. And they hold firmly to
the truth they have said about Jesus.

The Beast Who Comes Out of the Sea

13 The dragon stood on the seashore.
I saw a beast coming out of the
sea. It had ten horns and seven heads.
There were ten crowns on its horns. On
each head was an evil name that brought
shame to God. 2 The beast I saw looked
like a leopard. But it had feet like a bear
and a mouth like a lion. The dragon
gave the beast his power, his throne, and
great authority. 3 One of the beast's heads
seemed to have had a deadly wound. But
the wound had been healed. The whole
world was amazed and followed the
beast. 4 People worshiped the dragon, because he had given authority to the beast.
They also worshiped the beast. They
asked, "Who is like the beast? Who can
make war against it?"
5 The beast was given a mouth to brag
and speak evil things against God. The
beast was allowed to use its authority for
42 months. 6 The beast opened its mouth
to speak evil things against God. It told
lies about God and about the place where
God lives. And it told lies about those
who live in heaven with him. 7 The beast
was allowed to make war against God's
holy people and to overcome them. It
was given authority over every tribe, people and nation, no matter what language
they spoke. 8 Many people who live on
the earth will worship the beast. They are
the ones whose names are not written in
the Lamb's book of life. The Lamb is the
one whose death was planned before the
world was created.
9 Whoever has ears should listen.

10 "Everyone who is supposed to be
captured
will be captured.
Everyone who is supposed to be
killed by a sword
will be killed by a sword."
(Jeremiah 15:2)

So God's people must be patient and
faithful.

The Beast Who Comes Out of the Earth

11 Then I saw a second beast. This one
came out of the earth. It had two horns
like a lamb. But it spoke like a dragon.
12 This beast had all the authority of the
first beast. It did what the first beast
wanted. It made the earth and all who
live on it worship the first beast. The first
beast was the one whose deadly wound
had been healed. 13 The second beast performed great signs. It even made fire come
from heaven to the earth. And the fire was
seen by everyone. 14 The first beast had

given the second beast the power to perform these signs. By these signs, the second beast tricked those who live on the
earth. The second beast ordered people
to set up a statue to honor the first beast.
The first beast was the one who had been
wounded by a sword and still lived. [15]The
second beast was allowed to give breath
to this statue so it could speak. The statue
could kill all who refused to worship it.
[16]It also forced everyone to receive a mark
on their right hand or on their forehead.
People great or small, rich or poor, free
or slave had to receive the mark. [17]They
could not buy or sell anything unless they
had the mark. The mark is the name of the
beast or the number of its name.
[18]This problem requires wisdom. Anyone who is wise should figure out what
the beast's number means. It is the number of a man. And that number is 666.

The Lamb and the 144,000

14 I looked, and there in front of me
was the Lamb. He was standing on
Mount Zion. With him were 144,000 people. Written on their foreheads were his
name and his Father's name. [2]I heard a
sound from heaven. It was like the roar
of rushing waters and loud thunder. The
sound I heard was like the music of harps
being played. [3]Then everyone sang a new
song in front of the throne. They sang it in
front of the four living creatures and the
elders. No one could learn the song except the 144,000. They had been set free
from the evil of the earth. [4]They had not
committed sexual sins with women. They
had kept themselves pure. They follow the
Lamb wherever he goes. They were purchased from among human beings as a
first offering to God and the Lamb. [5]They
told no lies. They are without blame.

The Three Angels

[6]I saw another angel. He was flying
high in the air. He came to tell everyone
on earth the good news that will always
be true. He told it to every nation, tribe
and people, no matter what language they
spoke. [7]In a loud voice he said, "Have respect for God. Give him glory. The hour
has come for God to judge. Worship him
who made the heavens and the earth.
Worship him who made the sea and the
springs of water."
[8]A second angel followed him. He said,
"'Fallen! Babylon the Great has fallen!'
(Isaiah 21:9) The city of Babylon made all
the nations drink the strong wine of her
terrible sins."
[9]A third angel followed them. He said
in a loud voice, "There will be trouble
for anyone who worships the beast and
its statue! There will be trouble for anyone who has its mark on their forehead
or their hand! [10]They, too, will drink the
wine of God's great anger. His wine has
been poured full strength into the cup of
his anger. They will be burned with flaming sulfur. The holy angels and the Lamb
will see it happen. [11]The smoke of their
terrible suffering will rise for ever and
ever. Day and night, there will be no rest
for anyone who worships the beast and
its statue. There will be no rest for anyone who receives the mark of its name."
[12]God's people need to be very patient.
They are the ones who obey God's commands. And they remain faithful to Jesus.
[13]Then I heard a voice from heaven.
"Write this," it said. "Blessed are the dead
who die as believers in the Lord from now
on."

"Yes," says the Holy Spirit. "They will
rest from their labor. What they have done
will not be forgotten."

The Harvest of the Earth

[14]I looked, and there in front of me was
a white cloud. Sitting on the cloud was
one who looked "like a son of man." (Daniel 7:13) He wore a gold crown on his head.
In his hand was a sharp, curved blade
for cutting grain. [15]Then another angel
came out of the temple. He called in a
loud voice to the one sitting on the cloud.
"Take your blade," he said. "Cut the grain.
The time has come. The earth is ready to
be harvested." [16]So the one sitting on the
cloud swung his blade over the earth. And
the earth was harvested.
[17]Another angel came out of the temple in heaven. He too had a sharp, curved
blade. [18]Still another angel came from
the altar. He was in charge of the fire on
the altar. He called out in a loud voice
to the angel who had the sharp blade.
"Take your blade," he said, "and gather
the bunches of grapes from the earth's
vine. Its grapes are ripe." [19]So the angel
swung his blade over the earth. He gathered its grapes. Then he threw them into

a huge winepress. The winepress stands
for God's anger. 20 In the winepress outside the city, the grapes were stomped
on. Blood flowed out of the winepress. It
spread over the land for about 180 miles.
It rose as high as the horses' heads.

Seven Angels With Seven Plagues

15 I saw in heaven another great and
wonderful sign. Seven angels were
about to bring the seven last plagues. The
plagues would complete God's anger.
2 Then I saw something that looked like
a sea of glass glowing with fire. Standing
beside the sea were those who had won
the battle over the beast. They had also
overcome its statue and the number of
its name. They held harps given to them
by God. 3 They sang the song of God's servant Moses and of the Lamb. They sang,

"Lord God who rules over all,
everything you do is great and
wonderful.
King of the nations,
your ways are true and fair.
4 Lord, who will not have respect for
you?
Who will not bring glory to your
name?
You alone are holy.
All nations will come
and worship you.
They see that the things you do are
right."

5 After this I looked, and I saw the temple in heaven. And it was opened. The
temple is the holy tent where the tablets
of the covenant law were kept. 6 Out of the
temple came the seven angels who were
bringing the seven plagues. They were
dressed in clean, shining linen. They wore
gold strips of cloth around their chests.
7 Then one of the four living creatures
gave seven golden bowls to the seven angels. The bowls were filled with the anger
of God, who lives for ever and ever. 8 The
temple was filled with smoke that came
from the glory and power of God. No one
could enter the temple at that time. They
had to wait until the seven plagues of the
seven angels were completed.

The Seven Bowls of God's Great Anger

16 Then I heard a loud voice from the
temple speaking to the seven angels.
"Go," it said. "Pour out the seven bowls of
God's great anger on the earth."

2 The first angel went and poured out
his bowl on the land. Ugly and painful
sores broke out on people. Those people
had the mark of the beast and worshiped
its statue.

3 The second angel poured out his bowl
on the sea. It turned into blood like the
blood of a dead person. Every living thing
in the sea died.

4 The third angel poured out his bowl
on the rivers and springs of water. They
became blood. 5 Then I heard the angel
who was in charge of the waters. He said,

"Holy One, the way you judge is fair.
You are the God who is and who
was.
6 Those who worship the beast have
poured out blood.
They have poured out the life's
blood of your holy people
and your prophets.
So you have given blood to drink to
those who worship the beast.
That's exactly what they should
get."

7 Then I heard the altar reply. It said,

"Lord God who rules over all,
the way you judge is true and fair."

8 The fourth angel poured out his bowl
on the sun. The sun was allowed to burn
people with fire. 9 They were burned by
the blazing heat. So they spoke evil things
against the name of God, who controlled
these plagues. But they refused to turn
away from their sins. They did not give
glory to God.

10 The fifth angel poured out his bowl
on the throne of the beast. The kingdom
of the beast became very dark. People
chewed on their tongues because they
were suffering so much. 11 They spoke evil
things against the God of heaven. They
did this because of their pains and their
sores. But they refused to turn away from
the sins they had committed.

12 The sixth angel poured out his bowl
on the great river Euphrates. Its water
dried up to prepare the way for the kings
from the East. 13 Then I saw three evil spirits that looked like frogs. They came out of
the mouths of the dragon, the beast and
the false prophet. 14 They are spirits of demons that perform signs. They go out to

gather the kings of the whole world for
battle. This battle will take place on the
great day of the God who rules over all.

15 "Look! I am coming like a thief!
Blessed is anyone who stays awake
and keeps their clothes on. Then they
will be ready. They will not be caught
naked and so be put to shame."

16 Then the evil spirits gathered the kings
together. In the Hebrew language, the
place where the kings met is called Arma-
geddon.
17 The seventh angel poured out his
bowl into the air. Out of the temple came
a loud voice from the throne. It said, "It is
done!" 18 Then there came flashes of lightning, rumblings, thunder and a powerful earthquake. There has never been an
earthquake as terrible as this. One like
this hasn't happened while human beings
have lived on earth. 19 The great city split
into three parts. The cities of the nations
crumbled and fell. God remembered Babylon the Great. He gave Babylon the cup
filled with the wine of his terrible anger.
20 Every island ran away. The mountains
could not be found. 21 Huge hailstones
weighing about 100 pounds each fell
from the sky. The hail crushed people.
And they spoke evil things against God
because of the plague. That's because the
plague of hail was so terrible.

Babylon the Great Prostitute Sits on the Beast

17 One of the seven angels who had the
seven bowls came to me. He said,
"Come. I will show you how the great
prostitute will be punished. She is the one
who sits by many waters. 2 The kings of the
earth took part in her evil ways. The people living on earth were drunk with the
wine of her terrible sins."
3 Then in a vision the angel carried me
away to a desert. There the Holy Spirit
showed me a woman sitting on a bright
red beast. It was covered with names that
say evil things about God. It had seven
heads and ten horns. 4 The woman was
dressed in purple and bright red. She was
gleaming with gold, jewels and pearls. In
her hand she held a golden cup filled with
things that God hates. It was filled with
her terrible, dirty sins. 5 The name written on her forehead was a mystery. Here
is what it said.

THE GREAT CITY OF BABYLON
THE MOTHER OF PROSTITUTES
THE MOTHER OF EVERYTHING ON EARTH
THAT GOD HATES

6 I saw that the woman was drunk with the
blood of God's holy people. They are the
ones who are witnesses about Jesus.
When I saw her, I was very amazed.
7 Then the angel said to me, "Why are you
amazed? I will explain to you the mystery
of the woman. And I will explain the mystery of the beast she rides on. The beast is
the one who has the seven heads and ten
horns. 8 The beast that you saw used to exist and now does not. Yet it will come up
out of the Abyss and be destroyed. Some
people on the earth will be amazed when
they see the beast. Their names have not
been written in the book of life from the
time the world was created. They will be
amazed at the beast. That's because it will
come again even though it used to exist
and now does not.
9 "Here is a problem that you have to be
wise to understand. The seven heads are
seven hills that the woman sits on. 10 They
are also seven kings. Five have fallen, one
is ruling, and the other has still not come.
When he does come, he must remain for
only a little while. 11 The beast who used
to exist, and now does not, is an eighth
king. He belongs to the other seven. He
will be destroyed.
12 "The ten horns you saw are ten kings.
They have not yet received a kingdom.
But for one hour they will receive authority to rule together with the beast. 13 They
have only one purpose. So they will give
their power and authority to the beast.
14 They will make war against the Lamb.
But the Lamb will have victory over them.
That's because he is the most powerful
Lord of all and the greatest King of all. His
appointed, chosen and faithful followers
will be with him."
15 Then the angel spoke to me. "You
saw the waters the prostitute sits on," he
said. "They stand for all the nations of the
world, no matter what their race or language is. 16 The beast and the ten horns
you saw will hate the prostitute. They will
destroy her and leave her naked. They will
eat her flesh and burn her with fire. 17 God
has put it into their hearts to carry out his
purpose. So they agreed to give the beast
their royal authority. They will give him

this authority until God's words come
true. [18] The woman you saw stands for the
great city of Babylon. That city rules over
the kings of the earth."

Weeping When Babylon Falls

18 After these things I saw another angel coming down from heaven. He
had great authority. His glory filled the
earth with light. [2] With a mighty voice he
shouted,

"'Fallen! Babylon the Great has
fallen!' (Isaiah 21:9)
She has become a place where
demons live.
She has become a den for every evil
spirit.
She has become a place where
every 'unclean' bird is found.
She has become a place where
every 'unclean' and hated
animal is found.
[3] All the nations have drunk
the strong wine of her terrible
sins.
The kings of the earth took part in
her evil ways.
The traders of the world grew rich
from her great wealth."

Warning to Run from Babylon's Judgment

[4] Then I heard another voice from
heaven. It said,

"'Come out of her, my people.'
(Jeremiah 51:45)
Then you will not take part in her
sins.
You will not suffer from any of her
plagues.
[5] Her sins are piled up to heaven.
God has remembered her crimes.
[6] Do to her as she has done to others.
Pay her back double for what she
has done.
Pour her a double dose of what
she has poured for others.
[7] Give her as much pain and suffering
as the glory and wealth she gave
herself.
She brags to herself,
'I rule on a throne like a queen.
I am not a widow.
I will never mourn.' (Isaiah 47:7,8)
[8] But she will be plagued by death,
sadness and hunger.
In a single day she will suffer all
these plagues.
She will be burned up by fire.
That's because the Lord God who
judges her is mighty.

How Terrible When Babylon Falls!

[9] "The kings of the earth who committed terrible sins with her will weep. They
will mourn because they used to share
her riches. They will see the smoke rising as she burns. [10] They will be terrified
by her suffering. They will stand far away
from her. And they will cry out,

"'How terrible! How terrible it is for
you, great city!
How terrible for you, mighty city
of Babylon!
In just one hour you have been
destroyed!'

[11] "The traders of the world will weep
and mourn over her. No one buys what
they sell anymore. [12] Here is what they had
for sale.

Gold, silver, jewels, pearls.
Fine linen, purple, silk, bright red
cloth.
Every kind of citron wood.
All sorts of things made out of ivory,
valuable wood, bronze, iron, marble.
[13] Cinnamon, spice, incense, myrrh,
frankincense.
Wine, olive oil, fine flour, wheat.
Cattle, sheep, horses, carriages, and
human beings sold as slaves.

[14] "The merchants will say, 'The pleasure you longed for has left you. All your
riches and glory have disappeared forever.' [15] The traders who sold these things
became rich because of Babylon. When
she suffers, they will stand far away. Her
suffering will terrify them. They will weep
and mourn. [16] They will cry out,

"'How terrible! How terrible it is for
you, great city,
dressed in fine linen, purple and
bright red!
How terrible for you, great city,
gleaming with gold, jewels
and pearls!
[17] In just one hour your great wealth
has been destroyed!'

"Every sea captain and all who travel by

ship will stand far away. So will the sailors and all who earn their living from the
sea. [18] They will see the smoke rising as Babylon burns. They will ask, 'Was there
ever a city like this great city?' [19] They will
throw dust on their heads. They will weep and mourn. They will cry out,

" 'How terrible! How terrible it is for
you, great city!
All who had ships on the sea
became rich because of her
wealth!
In just one hour she has been
destroyed!'
[20] "You heavens, be glad for this!
You people of God, be glad!
You apostles and prophets, be
glad!
God has judged her
with the judgment she gave to
you."

Babylon's Judgment Is Final

[21] Then a mighty angel picked up a huge rock. It was the size of a large millstone. He threw it into the sea. Then he said,

"That is how
the great city of Babylon will be
thrown down.
Never again will it be found.
[22] The songs of musicians will never be
heard in you again.
Gone will be the music of harps,
flutes and trumpets.
No worker of any kind
will ever be found in you again.
The sound of a millstone
will never be heard in you again.
[23] The light of a lamp
will never shine in you again.
The voices of brides and grooms
will never be heard in you again.
Your traders were among the world's
most important people.
By your magic spell all the nations
were led astray.
[24] You were guilty of the murder of
prophets and God's holy
people.
You were guilty of the blood of all
who have been killed on the
earth."

Three Hallelujahs for the Fall of Babylon!

19 After these things I heard a roar in heaven. It sounded like a huge crowd shouting,

"Hallelujah!
Salvation and glory and power
belong to our God.
[2] The way he judges is true and fair.
He has judged the great prostitute.
She made the earth impure with
her terrible sins.
God has paid her back for killing
those who served him."

[3] Again they shouted,

"Hallelujah!
The smoke from her fire goes up for
ever and ever."

[4] The 24 elders and the four living creatures bowed down. They worshiped God, who was sitting on the throne. They cried out,

"Amen! Hallelujah!"

[5] Then a voice came from the throne. It said,

"Praise our God,
all you who serve him!
Praise God, all you who have respect
for him,
both great and small!"

[6] Then I heard the noise of a huge crowd. It sounded like the roar of rushing waters and like loud thunder. The people were shouting,

"Hallelujah!
Our Lord God is the King who
rules over all.
[7] Let us be joyful and glad!
Let us give him glory!
It is time for the Lamb's wedding.
His bride has made herself ready.
[8] Fine linen, bright and clean,
was given to her to wear."

Fine linen stands for the right things that God's holy people do.

[9] Here is what the angel told me to write. "Blessed are those invited to the wedding supper of the Lamb!" Then he added, "These are the true words of God."

[10] When I heard this, I fell at his feet to worship him. But he said to me, "Don't do that! I serve God, just as you do. I am God's servant, just like believers who hold

firmly to what Jesus has taught. Worship
God! The Spirit of prophecy tells the truth
about Jesus."

The Heavenly Warrior Has Victory Over the Beast

11 I saw heaven standing open. There in
front of me was a white horse. Its rider is
called Faithful and True. When he judges
or makes war, he is always fair. 12 His eyes
are like blazing fire. On his head are many
crowns. A name is written on him that
only he knows. 13 He is dressed in a robe
dipped in blood. His name is the Word
of God. 14 The armies of heaven were following him, riding on white horses. They
were dressed in fine linen, white and
clean. 15 Coming out of the rider's mouth
is a sharp sword. He will strike down the
nations with the sword. Scripture says,
"He will rule them with an iron scepter."
(Psalm 2:9) He stomps on the grapes of
God's winepress. The winepress stands
for the terrible anger of the God who rules
over all. 16 Here is the name that is written
on the rider's robe and on his thigh.

THE GREATEST KING OF ALL AND THE
MOST POWERFUL LORD OF ALL

17 I saw an angel standing in the sun.
He shouted to all the birds flying high in
the air, "Come! Gather together for the
great supper of God. 18 Come and eat the
dead bodies of kings, generals, and other
mighty people. Eat the bodies of horses
and their riders. Eat the bodies of all people, free and slave, great and small."
19 Then I saw the beast and the kings
of the earth with their armies. They had
gathered together to make war against the
rider on the horse and his army. 20 But the
beast and the false prophet were captured.
The false prophet had done signs for the
beast. In this way the false prophet had
tricked some people. Those people had
received the mark of the beast and had
worshiped its statue. The beast and the
false prophet were thrown alive into the
lake of fire. The lake of fire burns with sulfur. 21 The rest were killed by the sword that
came out of the rider's mouth. All the birds
stuffed themselves with the dead bodies.

The Thousand Years

20 I saw an angel coming down out
of heaven. He had the key to the
Abyss. In his hand he held a heavy chain.
2 He grabbed the dragon, that old serpent.
The serpent is also called the devil, or Satan. The angel put him in chains for 1,000
years. 3 Then he threw him into the Abyss.
He locked it and sealed him in. This was
to keep Satan from causing the nations
to believe his lies anymore. Satan will
be locked away until the 1,000 years are
ended. After that, he must be set free for
a short time.
4 I saw thrones. Those who had been
given authority to judge were sitting on
them. I also saw the souls of those whose
heads had been cut off. They had been
killed because they had spoken what
was true about Jesus. They had also been
killed because of the word of God. They
had not worshiped the beast or its statue.
They had not received its mark on their
foreheads or hands. They came to life and
ruled with Christ for 1,000 years. 5 This is
the first resurrection. The rest of the dead
did not come to life until the 1,000 years
were ended. 6 Blessed and holy are those
who share in the first resurrection. The
second death has no power over them.
They will be priests of God and of Christ.
They will rule with him for 1,000 years.

Satan Is Judged

7 When the 1,000 years are over, Satan
will be set free from his prison. 8 He will
go out to cause the nations to believe lies.
He will gather them from the four corners of the earth. He will bring Gog and
Magog together for battle. Their troops
are as many as the grains of sand on the
seashore. 9 They marched across the
whole earth. They surrounded the place
where God's holy people were camped. It
was the city he loves. But fire came down
from heaven and burned them up. 10 The
devil had caused them to believe lies. He
was thrown into the lake of burning sulfur. That is where the beast and the false
prophet had been thrown. They will all
suffer day and night for ever and ever.

The Dead Are Judged

11 I saw a great white throne. And I saw
God sitting on it. When the earth and sky
saw his face, they ran away. There was
no place for them. 12 I saw the dead, great
and small, standing in front of the throne.
Books were opened. Then another book
was opened. It was the book of life. The

dead were judged by what they had done. The things they had done were written in the books. 13 The sea gave up the dead that were in it. And Death and Hell gave up their dead. Each person was judged by what they had done. 14 Then Death and Hell were thrown into the lake of fire. The lake of fire is the second death. 15 Anyone whose name was not written in the book of life was thrown into the lake of fire.

A New Heaven and a New Earth

21 I saw "a new heaven and a new earth." (Isaiah 65:17) The first heaven and the first earth were completely gone. There was no longer any sea. 2 I saw the Holy City, the new Jerusalem. It was coming down out of heaven from God. It was prepared like a bride beautifully dressed for her husband. 3 I heard a loud voice from the throne. It said, "Look! God now makes his home with the people. He will live with them. They will be his people. And God himself will be with them and be their God. 4 'He will wipe away every tear from their eyes. There will be no more death.' (Isaiah 25:8) And there will be no more sadness. There will be no more crying or pain. Things are no longer the way they used to be."

5 He who was sitting on the throne said, "I am making everything new!" Then he said, "Write this down. You can trust these words. They are true."

6 He said to me, "It is done. I am the Alpha and the Omega, the Beginning and the End. I will give water to anyone who is thirsty. The water will come from the spring of the water of life. It doesn't cost anything! 7 Those who have victory will receive all this from me. I will be their God, and they will be my children. 8 But others will be thrown into the lake of fire that burns with sulfur. Those who are afraid and those who do not believe will be there. Murderers and those who make themselves impure will join them. Those who commit sexual sins and those who practice witchcraft will go there. Those who worship statues of gods and all who tell lies will be there too. The lake of fire is the second death."

The New Jerusalem is the Bride of the Lamb

9 One of the seven angels who had the seven bowls came and spoke to me. The bowls were filled with the seven last plagues. The angel said, "Come. I will show you the bride, the wife of the Lamb." 10 Then he carried me away in a vision. The Spirit took me to a huge, high mountain. He showed me Jerusalem, the Holy City. It was coming down out of heaven from God. 11 It shone with the glory of God. It gleamed like a very valuable jewel. It was like a jasper, as clear as crystal. 12 The city had a huge, high wall with 12 gates. Twelve angels were at the gates, one at each of them. On the gates were written the names of the 12 tribes of Israel. 13 There were three gates on the east and three on the north. There were three gates on the south and three on the west. 14 The wall of the city had 12 foundations. Written on them were the names of the 12 apostles of the Lamb.

15 The angel who talked with me had a gold measuring rod. He used it to measure the city, its gates and its walls. 16 The city was laid out like a square. It was as long as it was wide. The angel measured the city with the rod. It was 1,400 miles long. It was as wide and high as it was long. 17 The angel measured the wall as human beings measure things. It was 200 feet thick. 18 The wall was made out of jasper. The city was made out of pure gold, as pure as glass. 19 The foundations of the city walls were decorated with every kind of jewel. The first foundation was made out of jasper. The second was made out of sapphire. The third was made out of agate. The fourth was made out of emerald. 20 The fifth was made out of onyx. The sixth was made out of ruby. The seventh was made out of chrysolite. The eighth was made out of beryl. The ninth was made out of topaz. The tenth was made out of turquoise. The eleventh was made out of jacinth. The twelfth was made out of amethyst. 21 The 12 gates were made from 12 pearls. Each gate was made out of a single pearl. The main street of the city was made out of gold. It was gold as pure as glass that people can see through clearly.

22 I didn't see a temple in the city. That's because the Lamb and the Lord God who rules over all are its temple. 23 The city does not need the sun or moon to shine on it. God's glory is its light, and the Lamb is its lamp. 24 The nations will walk by the

light of the city. The kings of the world
will bring their glory into it. 25 Its gates
will never be shut, because there will be
no night there. 26 The glory and honor of
the nations will be brought into it. 27 Only
what is pure will enter the city. No one
who causes people to believe lies will enter it. No one who does shameful things
will enter it either. Only those whose
names are written in the Lamb's book of
life will enter the city.

The Earth Is Made Like New Again

22 Then the angel showed me the river
of the water of life. It was as clear
as crystal. It flowed from the throne of
God and of the Lamb. 2 It flowed down
the middle of the city's main street. On
each side of the river stood the tree of life,
bearing 12 crops of fruit. Its fruit was ripe
every month. The leaves of the tree bring
healing to the nations. 3 There will no longer be any curse. The throne of God and
of the Lamb will be in the city. God's servants will serve him. 4 They will see his
face. His name will be on their foreheads.
5 There will be no more night. They will
not need the light of a lamp or the light
of the sun. The Lord God will give them
light. They will rule for ever and ever.

John and the Angel

6 The angel said to me, "You can trust
these words. They are true. The Lord is the
God who gives messages to the prophets.
He sent his angel to show his servants the
things that must soon take place."

7 "Look! I am coming soon! Words of
prophecy are written in this book. Blessed
is the person who obeys them."

8 I, John, am the one who heard and saw
these things. After that, I fell down to worship at the feet of the angel. He is the one
who had been showing me these things.
9 But he said to me, "Don't do that! I serve
God, just as you do. I am God's servant,
just like the other prophets. And I serve
God along with all who obey the words of
this book. Worship God!"

10 Then he told me, "Do not seal up the
words of the prophecy in this book. These
things are about to happen. 11 Let the
person who does wrong keep on doing
wrong. Let the evil person continue to be
evil. Let the person who does right keep
on doing what is right. And let the holy
person continue to be holy."

The Revelation Ends With Warnings and Blessings

12 "Look! I am coming soon! I bring my
rewards with me. I will reward each person for what they have done. 13 I am the
Alpha and the Omega. I am the First and
the Last. I am the Beginning and the End.

14 "Blessed are those who wash their
robes. They will have the right to come to
the tree of life. They will be allowed to go
through the gates into the city. 15 Outside
the city are those who are impure. These
people include those who practice witchcraft. Outside are also those who commit
sexual sins and murder. Outside are those
who worship statues of gods. And outside
is everyone who loves and does what is
false.

16 "I, Jesus, have sent my angel to give
you this witness for the churches. I am the
Root and the Son of David. I am the bright
Morning Star."

17 The Holy Spirit and the bride say,
"Come!" And the person who hears
should say, "Come!" Anyone who is
thirsty should come. Anyone who wants
to take the free gift of the water of life
should do so.

18 I am warning everyone who hears the
words of the prophecy of this book. Suppose someone adds anything to them.
Then God will add to that person the
plagues told about in this book. 19 Suppose someone takes away any words from
this book of prophecy. Then God will take
away from that person the blessings told
about in this book. God will take away
their share in the tree of life. God will also
take away their place in the Holy City.

20 Jesus is a witness about these things.
He says, "Yes. I am coming soon." Amen.
Come, Lord Jesus!

21 May the grace of the Lord Jesus be
with God's people. Amen.

A WORD ABOUT THE NIrV

Have You Ever Heard of the New International Version?

We call it the NIV. Many people read the NIV. In fact, more people read the NIV than any other English Bible. They like it because it's easy to read and understand.

And now we are happy to give you another Bible that's easy to read and understand. It's the New International Reader's Version. We call it the NIrV.

Who Will Enjoy Reading the New International Reader's Version?

People who are just starting to read will understand and enjoy the NIrV. Children will be able to read it and understand it. So will older people who are learning how to read. People who are reading the Bible for the first time will be able to enjoy reading the NIrV. So will people who have a hard time understanding what they read. And so will people who use English as their second language. We hope this Bible will be just right for you.

How Is the NIrV Different From the NIV?

The NIrV is based on the NIV. The NIV Committee on Bible Translation (CBT) didn't produce the NIrV. But a few of us who worked on the NIrV are members of CBT. We worked hard to make the NIrV possible. We used the words of the NIV when we could. When the words of the NIV were too long, we used shorter words. We tried to use words that are easy to understand. We also made the sentences of the NIV much shorter.

Why did we do all these things? Because we wanted to make the NIrV very easy to read and understand.

What Other Helps Does the NIrV Have?

We decided to give you a lot of other help too. For example, sometimes a verse is quoted from another place in the Bible. When it is, we tell you the Bible book, chapter and verse it comes from. We put that information right after the verse that quotes from another place.

We separated each chapter into shorter sections. We gave a title to almost every chapter. Sometimes we even gave a title to a section. We did these things to help you understand what the chapter or section is all about.

Another example of a helpful change has to do with the word "Selah" in the Psalms. What this Hebrew word means is still not clear. So, for now, this word is not helpful for readers. The NIV has moved the word to the bottom of the page. We have followed the NIV and removed this Hebrew word from the NIrV. Perhaps one day we will learn what this word means. But until then, the Psalms are easier to read and understand without it.

Sometimes the writers of the Bible used more than one name for the same person or place. For example, in the New Testament the Sea of Galilee is also called the Sea of Gennesaret. Sometimes it is also called the Sea of Tiberias. But in the NIrV we decided to call it the Sea of Galilee everywhere it appears. We called it that because that is its most familiar name.

We also wanted to help you learn the names of people and places in the Bible. So sometimes we provided names even in verses where those names don't actually appear. For example, sometimes the Bible says "the River" where it means "the Euphrates River." In those places, we used the full name "the Euphrates River." Sometimes the word "Pharaoh" in the Bible means "Pharaoh Hophra." In those places, we used his full name "Pharaoh Hophra." We did all these things in order to make the NIrV as clear as possible.

Does the NIrV Say What the First Writers of the Bible Said?

We wanted the NIrV to say just what the first writers of the Bible said. So we kept checking the Greek New Testament as we did our work. That's because the New Testament's first writers used Greek. We also kept checking the Hebrew Old Testament as we did our work. That's because the Old Testament's first writers used Hebrew.

We used the best copies of the Greek New Testament. We also used the best copies of the Hebrew Old Testament. Older English Bibles couldn't use those copies because they had not yet been found. The oldest copies are best because they are closer in time to the ones the first Bible writers wrote. That's why we kept checking the older copies instead of the newer ones.

Some newer copies of the Greek New Testament added several verses that the older ones don't have. Sometimes it's several verses in a row. This occurs at Mark 16:9 - 20 and John 7:53 — 8:11. We have included these verses in the NIrV. Sometimes the newer copies added only a single verse. An example is Mark 9:44. That verse is not in the oldest Greek New Testaments. So we put the verse number 43/44 right before Mark 9:43. You can look on the list below for Mark 9:44 and locate the verse that was added.

Verses That Were Not Found in Oldest Greek New Testaments

Matthew 17:21	But that kind does not go out except by prayer and fasting.
Matthew 18:11	The Son of Man came to save what was lost.
Matthew 23:14	How terrible for you, teachers of the law and Pharisees! You pretenders! You take over the houses of widows. You say long prayers to show off. So God will punish you much more.
Mark 7:16	Everyone who has ears to hear should listen.
Mark 9:44	In hell, / " 'the worms don't die, / and the fire doesn't go out.'
Mark 9:46	In hell, / " 'the worms don't die, / and the fire doesn't go out.'
Mark 11:26	But if you do not forgive, your Father who is in heaven will not forgive your sins either.
Mark 15:28	Scripture came true. It says, "And he was counted among those who disobey the law."
Luke 17:36	Two men will be in the field. One will be taken and the other left.

Luke 23:17	It was Pilate's duty to let one prisoner go free for them at the Feast.
John 5:4	From time to time an angel of the Lord would come down. The angel would stir up the waters. The first disabled person to go into the pool after it was stirred would be healed.
Acts 8:37	Philip said, "If you believe with all your heart, you can." The official answered, "I believe that Jesus Christ is the Son of God."
Acts 15:34	But Silas decided to remain there.
Acts 24:7	But Lysias, the commander, came. By using a lot of force, he took Paul from our hands.
Acts 28:29	After he said that, the Jews left. They were arguing strongly among themselves.
Romans 16:24	May the grace of our Lord Jesus Christ be with all of you. Amen.

What Is Our Prayer for You?

The Lord has blessed the New International Version in a wonderful way. He has used it to help millions of Bible readers. Many people have put their faith in Jesus after reading it. Many others have become stronger believers because they have read it.

We hope and pray that the New International Reader's Version will help you in the same way. If that happens, we will give God all the glory.

A Word About This Edition

This edition of the New International Reader's Version has been revised to include the changes of the New International Version. Over the years, many helpful changes have been made to the New International Version. Those changes were made because our understanding of the original writings is better. Those changes also include changes that have taken place in the English language. We wanted the New International Reader's Version to include those helpful changes as well. We wanted the New International Reader's Version to be as clear and correct as possible.

We want to thank the people who helped us prepare this new edition. They are Jeannine Brown from Bethel Seminary St. Paul, Yvonne Van Ee from Calvin College, Michael Williams from Calvin Theological Seminary, and Ron Youngblood from Bethel Seminary San Diego. We also want to thank the people at Biblica who encouraged and supported this work.